CONNECTED MATHEMATICS® 3

CMP3

Grade 8 Algebra 1

Glenda Lappan, Elizabeth Difanis Phillips,
James T. Fey, Susan N. Friel

PEARSON

Boston, Massachusetts • Chandler, Arizona • Glenview, Illinois • Upper Saddle River, New Jersey

Connected Mathematics® was developed at Michigan State University with financial support from the Michigan State University Office of the Provost, Computing and Technology, and the College of Natural Science.

This material is based upon work supported by the National Science Foundation under Grant No. MDR 9150217 and Grant No. ESI 9986372. Opinions expressed are those of the authors and not necessarily those of the Foundation.

As with prior editions of this work, the authors and administration of Michigan State University preserve a tradition of devoting royalties from this publication to support activities sponsored by the MSU Mathematics Education Enrichment Fund.

PEARSON

Authors

A Team of Experts

Glenda Lappan is a University Distinguished Professor in the Program in Mathematics Education (PRIME) and the Department of Mathematics at Michigan State University. Her research and development interests are in the connected areas of students' learning of mathematics and mathematics teachers' professional growth and change related to the development and enactment of K–12 curriculum materials.

Elizabeth Difanis Phillips is a Senior Academic Specialist in the Program in Mathematics Education (PRIME) and the Department of Mathematics at Michigan State University. She is interested in teaching and learning mathematics for both teachers and students. These interests have led to curriculum and professional development projects at the middle school and high school levels, as well as projects related to the teaching and learning of algebra across the grades.

James T. Fey is a Professor Emeritus at the University of Maryland. His consistent professional interest has been development and research focused on curriculum materials that engage middle and high school students in problem-based collaborative investigations of mathematical ideas and their applications.

Susan N. Friel is a Professor of Mathematics Education in the School of Education at the University of North Carolina at Chapel Hill. Her research interests focus on statistics education for middle-grade students and, more broadly, on teachers' professional development and growth in teaching mathematics K–8.

With... Yvonne Grant and Jacqueline Stewart

Yvonne Grant teaches mathematics at Portland Middle School in Portland, Michigan. Jacqueline Stewart is a recently retired high school teacher of mathematics at Okemos High School in Okemos, Michigan. Both Yvonne and Jacqueline have worked on a variety of activities related to the development, implementation, and professional development of the CMP curriculum since its beginning in 1991.

Development Team

CMP3 Authors

Glenda Lappan, University Distinguished Professor, Michigan State University

Elizabeth Difanis Phillips, Senior Academic Specialist, Michigan State University

James T. Fey, Professor Emeritus, University of Maryland

Susan N. Friel, Professor, University of North Carolina – Chapel Hill

With...

Yvonne Grant, Portland Middle School, Michigan

Jacqueline Stewart, Mathematics Consultant, Mason, Michigan

In Memory of... William M. Fitzgerald, Professor (Deceased), Michigan State University, who made substantial contributions to conceptualizing and creating CMP1.

Administrative Assistant

Michigan State University
Judith Martus Miller

Support Staff

Michigan State University
Undergraduate Assistants:
Bradley Robert Corlett, Carly Fleming, Erin Lucian, Scooter Nowak

Development Assistants

Michigan State University
Graduate Research Assistants:
Richard "Abe" Edwards, Nic Gilbertson, Funda Gonulates, Aladar Horvath, Eun Mi Kim, Kevin Lawrence, Jennifer Nimtz, Joanne Philhower, Sasha Wang

Assessment Team

Maine
Falmouth Public Schools
Falmouth Middle School: Shawn Towle

Michigan
Ann Arbor Public Schools
Tappan Middle School
Anne Marie Nicoll-Turner

Portland Public Schools
Portland Middle School
Holly DeRosia, Yvonne Grant

Traverse City Area Public Schools
Traverse City East Middle School
Jane Porath, Mary Beth Schmitt

Traverse City West Middle School
Jennifer Rundio, Karrie Tufts

Ohio
Clark-Shawnee Local Schools
Rockway Middle School: Jim Mamer

Content Consultants

Michigan State University
Peter Lappan, Professor Emeritus, Department of Mathematics

Normandale Community College
Christopher Danielson, Instructor, Department of Mathematics & Statistics

University of North Carolina – Wilmington
Dargan Frierson, Jr., Professor, Department of Mathematics & Statistics

Student Activities
Michigan State University
Brin Keller, Associate Professor, Department of Mathematics

Consultants

Indiana
Purdue University
Mary Bouck, Mathematics Consultant

Michigan
Oakland Schools
Valerie Mills, Mathematics Education Supervisor
Mathematics Education Consultants:
Geraldine Devine, Dana Gosen

Ellen Bacon, Independent Mathematics Consultant

New York
University of Rochester
Jeffrey Choppin, Associate Professor

Ohio
University of Toledo
Debra Johanning, Associate Professor

Pennsylvania
University of Pittsburgh
Margaret Smith, Professor

Texas
University of Texas at Austin
Emma Trevino, Supervisor of Mathematics Programs, The Dana Center

Mathematics for All Consulting
Carmen Whitman, Mathematics Consultant

···

Reviewers

Michigan
Ionia Public Schools
Kathy Dole, Director of Curriculum and Instruction

Grand Valley State University
Lisa Kasmer, Assistant Professor

Portland Public Schools
Teri Keusch, Classroom Teacher

Minnesota
Hopkins School District 270
Michele Luke, Mathematics Coordinator

···

Field Test Sites for CMP3

Michigan
Ann Arbor Public Schools
Tappan Middle School
Anne Marie Nicoll-Turner*

Portland Public Schools
Portland Middle School: Mark Braun, Angela Buckland, Holly DeRosia, Holly Feldpausch, Angela Foote, Yvonne Grant*, Kristin Roberts, Angie Stump, Tammi Wardwell

Traverse City Area Public Schools
Traverse City East Middle School
Ivanka Baic Berkshire, Brenda Dunscombe, Tracie Herzberg, Deb Larimer, Jan Palkowski, Rebecca Perreault, Jane Porath*, Robert Sagan, Mary Beth Schmitt*

Traverse City West Middle School
Pamela Alfieri, Jennifer Rundio, Maria Taplin, Karrie Tufts*

Maine
Falmouth Public Schools
Falmouth Middle School: Sally Bennett, Chris Driscoll, Sara Jones, Shawn Towle*

Minnesota
Minneapolis Public Schools
Jefferson Community School
Leif Carlson*,
Katrina Hayek Munsisoumang*

Ohio
Clark-Shawnee Local Schools
Reid School: Joanne Gilley
Rockway Middle School: Jim Mamer*
Possum School: Tami Thomas

*Indicates a Field Test Site Coordinator

CONNECTED MATHEMATICS 3

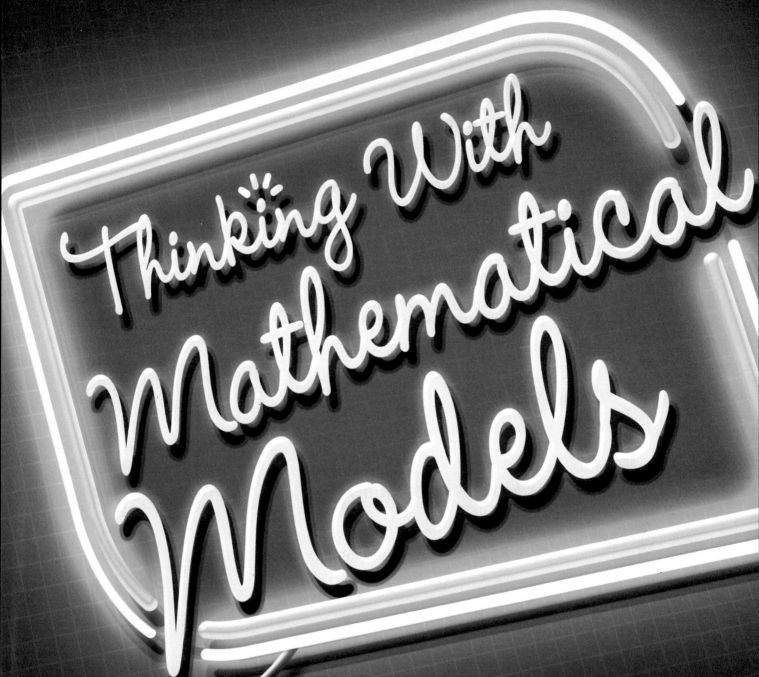

Thinking With Mathematical Models

Linear and Inverse Variation

Lappan, Phillips, Fey, Friel

Thinking With Mathematical Models

Linear and Inverse Variation

Looking Ahead 2

Mathematical Highlights 4

Standards for Mathematical Practice 5

1

Exploring Data Patterns   7

1.1 Bridge Thickness and Strength 7

1.2 Bridge Length and Strength 10

1.3 Custom Construction Parts Finding Patterns 12

Ⓐ ⒸⒺ Homework 15

Mathematical Reflections 28

2

Linear Models and Equations   30

2.1 Modeling Linear Data Patterns 31

2.2 Up and Down the Staircase Exploring Slope 34

2.3 Tree Top Fun Equations for Linear Functions 38

2.4 Boat Rental Business Solving Linear Equations 40

2.5 Amusement Park or Movies Intersecting Linear Models 43

Ⓐ ⒸⒺ Homework 45

Mathematical Reflections 59

3 Inverse Variation — 61

3.1 Rectangles With Fixed Area — 61

3.2 Distance, Speed, and Time — 63

3.3 Planning a Field Trip Finding Individual Cost — 66

3.4 Modeling Data Patterns — 68

ⒶⒸⒺ Homework — 69

Mathematical Reflections — 79

4 Variability and Associations in Numerical Data — 81

4.1 Vitruvian Man Relating Body Measurements — 82

4.2 Older and Faster Negative Correlations — 84

4.3 Correlation Coefficients and Outliers — 87

4.4 Measuring Variability Standard Deviation — 93

ⒶⒸⒺ Homework — 96

Mathematical Reflections — 111

5 Variability and Associations in Categorical Data — 113

5.1 Wood or Steel? That's the Question — 114

5.2 Politics of Girls and Boys Analyzing Data in Two-Way Tables — 115

5.3 After-School Jobs and Homework Working Backward: Setting up a Two-Way Table — 117

ⒶⒸⒺ Homework — 119

Mathematical Reflections — 127

Looking Back — 129

English/Spanish Glossary — 132

Index — 140

Acknowledgments — 142

Looking Ahead

How is the thickness of a steel beam or bridge related to its strength? How is the length of a beam or bridge related to its strength?

The equation $c = 0.15t + 2.50$ gives the charge c in dollars for renting a paddle boat for t minutes. How much time can you buy on a paddle boat if you have $12?

An all-star basketball player in the National Basketball Association (NBA) is 6 feet 9 inches (206 cm) tall. How can you use this measurement to estimate his shoe size, his weight, or his arm span?

In earlier *Connected Mathematics* units, you explored relationships between two variables. You learned how to find linear relationships from tables and graphs and to write their equations. Using the equations, you solved problems. In this unit, you will develop your skills for recognizing and analyzing linear relationships. You will compare linear and nonlinear patterns and learn about inverse variation, a specific nonlinear pattern.

You will conduct experiments, analyze data, and write equations to summarize, or model, the data patterns. You will use your equations to estimate, or predict, values not found in the data set.

The skills you develop in this unit will help you answer questions such as those on the facing page.

Mathematical Highlights

Thinking With Mathematical Models

In *Thinking With Mathematical Models*, you will model relationships with graphs and equations. You will use your models to analyze situations and solve problems.

The Investigations in this Unit will help you understand the following ideas.

- Represent data using graphs, tables, word descriptions and algebraic expressions.

- Recognize linear and nonlinear relationships in tables and graphs.

- Use linear and inverse variation equations to model bivariate data.

- Use residual analysis to measure the fit of linear and inverse variation models.

- Analyze, approximate, and solve linear equations.

- Use linear and inverse variation equations to solve problems and to make predictions and decisions

- Use scatter plots, two-way tables, and correlation coefficients to describe patterns of association in pairs of variables.

- Use standard deviation to measure variability in data distributions.

When you encounter a new problem, it is a good idea to ask yourself questions. In this Unit, you might ask questions such as:

What are the key variables in this situation?

If there is a pattern relating the variables, is it strong enough to allow me to make predictions?

What is the pattern relating the variables?

What kind of equation will express the relationship?

How can I use the equation to answer questions about the relationship?

Mathematical Practices and Habits of Mind

In the *Connected Mathematics* curriculum you will develop an understanding of important mathematical ideas by solving problems and reflecting on the mathematics involved. Every day, you will use "habits of mind" to make sense of problems and apply what you learn to new situations. Some of these habits are described by the *Common Core State Standards for Mathematical Practices* (MP).

MP1 Make sense of problems and persevere in solving them.

When using mathematics to solve a problem, it helps to think carefully about

- data and other facts you are given and what additional information you need to solve the problem;
- strategies you have used to solve similar problems and whether you could solve a related simpler problem first;
- how you could express the problem with equations, diagrams, or graphs;
- whether your answer makes sense.

MP2 Reason abstractly and quantitatively.

When you are asked to solve a problem, it often helps to

- focus first on the key mathematical ideas;
- check that your answer makes sense in the problem setting;
- use what you know about the problem setting to guide your mathematical reasoning.

MP3 Construct viable arguments and critique the reasoning of others.

When you are asked to explain why a conjecture is correct, you can

- show some examples that fit the claim and explain why they fit;
- show how a new result follows logically from known facts and principles.

When you believe a mathematical claim is incorrect, you can

- show one or more counterexamples—cases that don't fit the claim;
- find steps in the argument that do not follow logically from prior claims.

MP4 Model with mathematics.

When you are asked to solve problems, it often helps to

- think carefully about the numbers or geometric shapes that are the most important factors in the problem, then ask yourself how those factors are related to each other;
- express data and relationships in the problem with tables, graphs, diagrams, or equations, and check your result to see if it makes sense.

MP5 Use appropriate tools strategically.

When working on mathematical questions, you should always

- decide which tools are most helpful for solving the problem and why;
- try a different tool when you get stuck.

MP6 Attend to precision.

In every mathematical exploration or problem-solving task, it is important to

- think carefully about the required accuracy of results: is a number estimate or geometric sketch good enough, or is a precise value or drawing needed?
- report your discoveries with clear and correct mathematical language that can be understood by those to whom you are speaking or writing.

MP7 Look for and make use of structure.

In mathematical explorations and problem solving, it is often helpful to

- look for patterns that show how data points, numbers, or geometric shapes are related to each other;
- use patterns to make predictions.

MP8 Look for and express regularity in repeated reasoning.

When results of a repeated calculation show a pattern, it helps to

- express that pattern as a general rule that can be used in similar cases;
- look for shortcuts that will make the calculation simpler in other cases.

You will use all of the Mathematical Practices in this Unit. Sometimes, when you look at a Problem, it is obvious which practice is most helpful. At other times, you will decide on a practice to use during class explorations and discussions. After completing each Problem, ask yourself:

- What mathematics have I learned by solving this Problem?
- What Mathematical Practices were helpful in learning this mathematics?

Investigation 1

Exploring Data Patterns

People in many professions use data and mathematical reasoning to solve problems and make decisions. For example, engineers analyze data from lab tests to determine how much weight a bridge can hold. Market researchers use survey data to predict demand for new products. Stockbrokers use formulas to forecast growth of investments over time.

In several previous *Connected Mathematics* units, you used tables, graphs, and equations to explore and describe relationships between variables. In this Investigation, you will develop your skill in using these tools to organize data from experiments, find patterns, and make predictions.

1.1 Bridge Thickness and Strength

Many bridges are built with frames of steel beams. Steel is very strong, but any beam will bend or break if you put too much weight on it.

Common Core State Standards

8.F.A.3 Interpret the equation $y = mx + b$ as defining a linear function whose graph is a straight line; give examples of functions that are not linear.

8.F.B.5 Describe qualitatively the functional relationship between two quantities by analyzing a graph (e.g., where the function is increasing or decreasing, linear or nonlinear) . . .

Also 8.F.A.2, 8.SP.A.1, F-IF.B.4, F-IF.B.6, F-IF.C.7a, F-BF.A.1a

- How do you think the strength of a beam is related to its thickness?

- What other variables might affect the strength of a bridge?

Problem 1.1

Engineers often use scale models to test their designs. You can do your own experiments to discover mathematical patterns involved in building bridges.

Instructions for a Bridge-Thickness Experiment

Materials:

- Two books of the same thickness

- A small paper cup

- About 50 pennies

- Several 11 inch-by-$4\frac{1}{4}$ inch strips of paper

Instructions:

- Start with one of the paper strips. Make a "bridge" by folding up 1 inch on each long side.

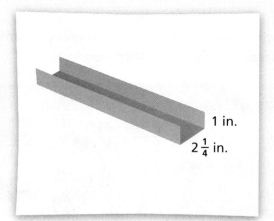

1 in.

$2\frac{1}{4}$ in.

continued on the next page >

Problem **1.1** *continued*

- Suspend the bridge between the books. The bridge should overlap each book by 1 inch. Place the cup in the center of the bridge.

- Put pennies into the cup, one at a time, until the bridge collapses. Record the number of pennies you added to the cup. This number is the *breaking weight* of the bridge.

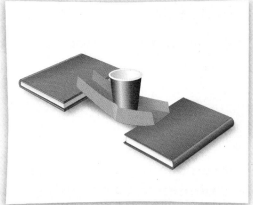

- Put two *new* strips of paper together to make a bridge with twice as many layers. Find the breaking weight for this bridge.

- Repeat this experiment to find the breaking weights of bridges made from three, four, and five strips of paper.

A Make a table and a graph of your (bridge layers, breaking weight) data.

B Does the relationship between the number of layers and the breaking weight seem to be linear or nonlinear? How do the graph and the table show this relationship?

C Suppose you could split layers of paper in half. What breaking weight would you predict for a bridge 2.5 layers thick? Explain.

D Predict the breaking weight for a bridge 6 layers thick. Explain your reasoning.

E Test your prediction of strength for the 6-layer bridge. Explain why results from such a test might not exactly match predictions.

A C E Homework starts on page 15.

1.2 Bridge Length and Strength

In the last problem you tested the strength of some paper bridges. You found that bridges with more layers are stronger than bridges with fewer layers.

- How do you think the length and strength of a bridge are related?

- Are longer bridges stronger or weaker than shorter bridges?

Problem 1.2

You can do an experiment to find out how the length and strength of a bridge are related.

Instructions for a Bridge-Length Experiment

Materials:

- Two books of the same thickness

- A small paper cup

- About 50 pennies

- $4\frac{1}{4}$-inch-wide paper strips with lengths 4, 6, 8, 9, and 11 inches

continued on the next page >

Problem 1.2 continued

Instructions:

- Fold the paper strips to make bridges as shown below.

- Start with the 4-inch bridge. Suspend the bridge between the two books as you did before. The bridge should overlap each book by 1 inch. Place the paper cup in the center of the bridge.

- Put pennies into the cup, one at a time, until the bridge collapses. Record the number of pennies you added to the cup. As in the first experiment, this number is the breaking weight of the bridge.

- Repeat the experiment to find breaking weights for the other bridges.

A Make a graph of your data.

B Describe the relationship between bridge length and breaking weight. How is that relationship shown by patterns in your table and graph?

C Use your data to predict the breaking weights for bridges of lengths 3, 5, 10, and 12 inches. Explain how you made your predictions.

D Compare your data from this experiment to the data from the experiment on bridges with different numbers of layers. How is the relationship between the number of layers in a bridge and its breaking weight similar to the relationship between bridge length and breaking weight? How is it different?

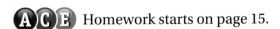 **A C E** Homework starts on page 15.

1.3 Custom Construction Parts
Finding Patterns

Suppose a company called Custom Steel Products (CSP for short) supplies materials to builders. One common structure that CSP makes is called a *truss*, as shown in the figure below. (You might see a truss holding up the roof of a building.) It is made by fastening together steel rods 1 foot long.

1-foot steel rod   7-foot truss made from 27 rods

This truss has an overall length of 7 feet. The manager at CSP needs to know the number of rods in any length of truss a customer might order.

Problem 1.3

Study the drawing above to see if you can figure out what the manager needs to know. It might help to work out several cases and look for a pattern.

A Copy and complete the table below to show the number of rods in trusses of different overall lengths.

Length of Truss (ft)	2	3	4	5	6	7	8
Number of Rods	7	11	▪	▪	▪	27	▪

1. Make a graph of the data in your table.

2. Describe the pattern of change in the number of rods used as the truss length increases.

continued on the next page >

Problem 1.3 *continued*

3. How is the pattern you described shown in the table? How is it shown in the graph?

4. How many steel rods are in a truss 50 feet long overall? Explain how to find this number without drawing the truss.

5. By counting the triangles she could see for any length, Jenna says she figured out a pattern for the number of rods. For overall length 7, she sees 7 triangles and 6 rods connecting these triangles, so she writes $7 \times 3 + 6 = 27$. For length L, she writes $N = 3L + L - 1$. Explain where she gets the $3L$ and the $L - 1$ in her expression.

B Custom Steel Products also makes staircase frames like those shown here.

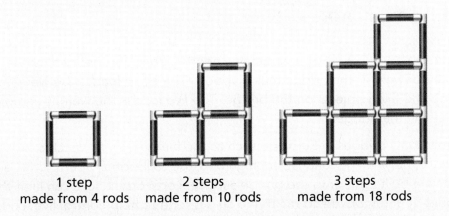

1 step	2 steps	3 steps
made from 4 rods	made from 10 rods	made from 18 rods

1. Copy and complete the table below to show the number of rods in staircase frames with different numbers of steps.

CSP Staircase Frames

Number of Steps	1	2	3	4	5	6	7	8
Number of Rods	4	10	18	▪	▪	▪	▪	▪

2. Make a graph of the data in your table.

3. Describe the pattern of change in the number of rods as the number of steps increases.

4. How is the pattern you described shown in the table? How is it shown in the graph?

5. How many steel rods are in a staircase frame with 12 steps? Explain how you could find this number without drawing the staircase frame.

continued on the next page >

Problem **1.3** *continued*

C How is the pattern in Question A similar to the pattern in Question B? How is it different? Explain how the similarities and differences are shown in the tables and graphs.

D Compare the patterns of change in this problem with the patterns of change in Problems 1.1 and 1.2. Describe any similarities and differences you find.

ACE Homework starts on page 15.

Did You Know?

When designing a bridge, engineers need to consider the *load*, or the amount of weight, the bridge must support. The *dead load* is the weight of the bridge and fixed objects on the bridge. The *live load* is the weight of moving objects on the bridge.

On many city bridges in Europe—such as the famous Ponte Vecchio in Florence, Italy—dead load is very high because tollbooths, apartments, and shops are built right onto the bridge surface. Local ordinances can limit the amount of automobile and rail traffic on a bridge to help control live load.

Applications

1. The table shows the maximum weight a crane arm can lift at various distances from its cab.

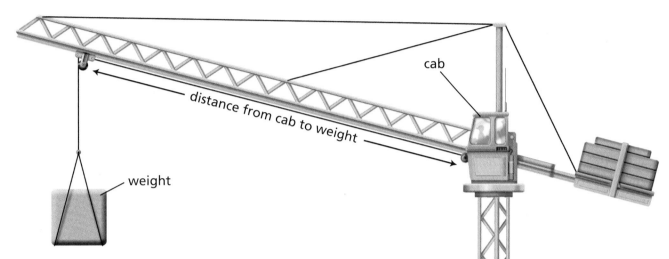

distance from cab to weight

cab

weight

Construction-Crane Data

Distance from Cab to Weight (ft)	12	24	36	48	60
Weight (lb)	7,500	3,750	2,500	1,875	1,500

a. Describe the relationship between distance and weight for the crane.

b. Make a graph of the (distance, weight) data. Explain how the graph's shape shows the relationship you described in part (a).

c. Estimate the weight the crane can lift at distances of 18 feet, 30 feet, and 72 feet from the cab.

d. How, if at all, are the data for the crane similar to the data from the bridge experiments in Problems 1.1 and 1.2?

2. A group of students conducted the bridge-thickness experiment with construction paper. The table below contains their results.

Bridge-Thickness Experiment

Number of Layers	1	2	3	4	5	6
Breaking Weight (pennies)	12	20	29	42	52	61

a. Make a graph of the (number of layers, breaking weight) data. Describe the relationship between breaking weight and number of layers.

b. Suppose it is possible to use half-layers of construction paper. What breaking weight would you predict for a bridge 3.5 layers thick? Explain.

c. Predict the breaking weight for a construction-paper bridge of 8 layers. Explain how you made your prediction.

3. A truss or staircase frame from Custom Steel Products costs $2.25 for each rod, plus $50 for shipping and handling.

a. Refer to your data from Question A of Problem 1.3. Copy and complete the table below to show the costs of trusses of different lengths.

Cost of CSP Truss

Truss Length (ft)	1	2	3	4	5	6	7	8
Number of Rods	3	7	■	■	■	■	27	■
Cost of Truss	■	■	■	■	■	■	■	■

b. Make a graph of the (truss length, cost) data.

c. Describe the relationship between truss length and cost.

d. Refer to your data from Question B of Problem 1.3. Copy and complete the table below to show the costs of staircase frames with different numbers of steps.

Cost of CSP Staircase Frames

Number of Steps	1	2	3	4	5	6	7	8
Number of Rods	4	10	18	■	■	■	■	■
Cost of Frame	■	■	■	■	■	■	■	■

e. Make a graph of the (number of steps, cost) data.

f. Describe the relationship between number of steps and cost.

4. During the medal ceremonies at a track meet, the top athletes stand on platforms made from stacked wooden boxes. The number of boxes depends on the number of medal winners.

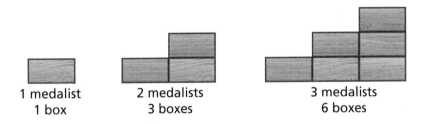

1 medalist
1 box

2 medalists
3 boxes

3 medalists
6 boxes

a. Copy and complete the table below.

Medal Platforms

Number of Medalists	1	2	3	4	5	6	7	8
Number of Boxes	1	3	6	■	■	■	■	■

b. Make a graph of the (number of medalists, number of boxes) data.

c. Describe the pattern of change shown in the table and graph.

d. Each box is 1 foot high and 2 feet wide. A red carpet starts 10 feet from the base of the platform and covers all the risers and steps.

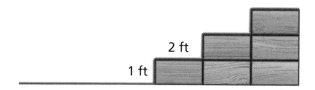

2 ft

1 ft

Copy and complete the table below.

Carpet for Platforms

Number of Steps	1	2	3	4	5	6	7	8
Carpet Length (ft)	■	■	■	■	■	■	■	■

e. Make a graph of the (number of steps, carpet length) data.

f. Describe the pattern of change in the carpet length as the number of steps increases. Compare this pattern to the pattern in the (number of medalists, number of boxes) data.

5. Parts (a)–(f) refer to relationships between variables you have studied in this Investigation. Tell whether each is *linear* or *nonlinear*.

a. Cost depends on truss length (ACE Exercise 3).

b. Cost depends on the number of rods in a staircase frame (ACE Exercise 3).

c. Bridge strength depends on bridge thickness (Problem 1.1).

d. Bridge strength depends on bridge length (Problem 1.2).

e. Number of rods depends on truss length (Problem 1.3).

f. Number of rods depends on the number of steps in a staircase frame (Problem 1.3).

g. Compare the patterns of change for all the nonlinear relationships in parts (a)–(f).

6. CSP also sells ladder bridges made from 1-foot steel rods arranged to form a row of squares. Below is a sketch of a 6-foot ladder bridge.

6-foot ladder bridge made from 19 rods

a. Make a table and a graph showing how the number of rods in a ladder bridge is related to the length of the bridge.

b. Compare the pattern of change for the ladder bridges with those for the trusses and staircase frames in Problem 1.3.

Connections

A survey of one class at Pioneer Middle School found that 20 out of 30 students would spend $12 for a school T-shirt. Use this information for Exercises 7 and 8.

7. **Multiple Choice** Suppose there are 600 students in the school. Based on the survey, how many students do you predict would spend $12 for a school T-shirt?

   A. 20   B. 200

   C. 300   D. 400

8. **Multiple Choice** Suppose there are 450 students in the school. Based on the survey, how many students do you predict would spend $12 for a school T-shirt?

   F. 20   G. 200

   H. 300   J. 400

9. At the right is a drawing of a rectangle with an area of 300 square feet.

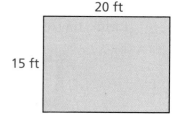

20 ft

15 ft

a. Make drawings of at least three other rectangles with an area of 300 square feet.

b. What is the width of a rectangle with an area of 300 square feet if its length is 1 foot? If its length is 2 feet? If its length is 3 feet?

c. What is the width of a rectangle with an area of 300 square feet and a length of ℓ feet?

d. How does the width of a rectangle change if the length increases, but the area remains 300 square feet?

e. Make a graph of (width, length) pairs for rectangles with an area of 300 square feet. Explain how your graph illustrates your answer for part (d).

10. The rectangle pictured in Exercise 9 has a perimeter of 70 feet.

a. Make drawings of at least three other rectangles with a perimeter of 70 feet.

b. What is the width of a rectangle with a perimeter of 70 feet if its length is 1 foot? 2 feet? ℓ feet?

c. What is the width of a rectangle with a perimeter of 70 feet if its length is $\frac{1}{2}$ foot? $\frac{3}{2}$ feet?

d. Give the dimensions of rectangles with a perimeter of 70 feet and length-to-width ratios of 3 to 4, 4 to 5, and 1 to 1.

e. Suppose the length of a rectangle increases, but the perimeter remains 70 feet. How does the width change?

f. Make a graph of (length, width) pairs that give a perimeter of 70 feet. How does your graph illustrate your answer for part (e)?

11. The 24 students in Ms. Cleary's homeroom are surveyed. They are asked which of several prices they would pay for a ticket to the school fashion show. The table shows the results.

Ticket-Price Survey

Ticket Price	$1.00	$1.50	$2.00	$2.50	$3.00	$3.50	$4.00	$4.50
Probable Sales	20	20	18	15	12	10	8	7

a. There are 480 students in the school. Use the data from Ms. Cleary's class to predict ticket sales for the entire school for each price.

b. Use your results from part (a). For each price, find the school's projected income from ticket sales.

c. Which price should the school charge if it wants to earn the maximum possible income?

12. At the right is a graph of the amount of money Jake earned while babysitting for several hours.

a. Put scales on the axes that make sense. Explain why you chose your scales.

b. What would the equation of the graph be, based on the scale you chose in part (a)?

c. If the line on this graph were steeper, what would it tell about the money Jake is making? Write an equation for such a line.

13. In each pair of equations below, solve the first and graph the second.

a. $0 = 3x + 6$ $y = 3x + 6$

b. $0 = x - 2$ $y = x - 2$

c. $0 = 3x + 10$ $y = 3x + 10$

d. In each pair, how is the solution related to the graph?

For Exercises 14–17, tell which graph matches the equation or the set of criteria.

14. $y = 3x + 1$

15. $y = -2x + 2$

16. $y = x - 3$

17. y-intercept $= 1$; slope $= \frac{1}{2}$

Graph A

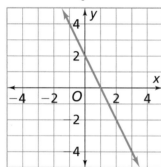

Graph B

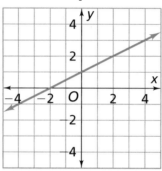

Graph C

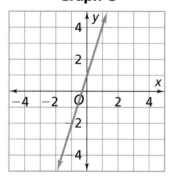

Graph D

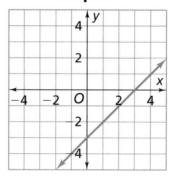

In Exercises 18 and 19, each pouch holds the same number of coins. The coins all have the same value. Find the number of coins in each pouch. Explain your method.

18.

19.

20. Refer to Exercises 18 and 19.

   a. For each exercise, write an equation to represent the situation. Let x represent the number of coins in a pouch.

   b. Solve each equation. Explain the steps in your solutions.

   c. Compare your strategies with those you used in Exercises 18 and 19.

In Exercises 21–28, solve each equation for x.

   21. $3x + 4 = 10$

   22. $6x + 3 = 4x + 11$

   23. $6x - 3 = 11$

   24. $-3x + 5 = 7$

   25. $4x - \frac{1}{2} = 8$

   26. $\frac{x}{2} - 4 = -5$

   27. $3x + 3 = -2x - 12$

   28. $\frac{x}{4} - 4 = \frac{3x}{4} - 6$

For Exercises 29–31, tell whether the statement is *true* or *false*. Explain your reasoning.

29. $6(12 - 5) > 50$ **30.** $3 \cdot 5 - 4 > 6$ **31.** $10 - 5 \cdot 4 > 0$

32. For this exercise, you will need two 8.5-inch by 11-inch sheets of paper and some scrap paper.

  a. Roll one sheet of paper to make a cylinder 11 inches high. Overlap the edges very slightly and tape them together. Make bases for the cylinder by tracing the circles on the ends of the cylinder, cutting out the tracings, and taping them in place.

  b. Roll the other sheet of paper to make a cylinder 8.5 inches high. Make bases as you did in part (a).

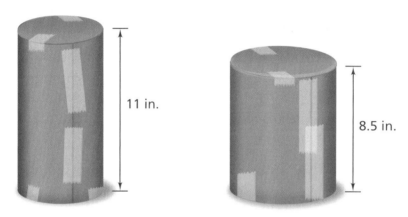

11 in.

8.5 in.

  c. Do the cylinders appear to have the same surface area (including the bases)? If not, which has the greater surface area?

  d. Suppose you start with two identical rectangular sheets of paper that are *not* 8.5 by 11 inches. You make two cylinders as you did before. Which cylinder will have the greater surface area, the taller cylinder or the shorter one? How do you know?

33. The volume of the cone in the drawing below is $\frac{1}{3}(28\pi)$ cm^3. Recall that the formula for the volume of a cone is $\frac{1}{3}\pi r^2 h$. What are some possible values of radius and height for the cone?

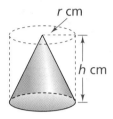

Extensions

34. Study the patterns in this table. Note that the numbers in the x column may not be consecutive after $x = 6$.

x	p	q	y	z
1	1	1	2	1
2	4	8	4	$\frac{1}{2}$
3	9	27	8	$\frac{1}{3}$
4	16	64	16	$\frac{1}{4}$
5	25	125	32	$\frac{1}{5}$
6	▨	▨	▨	▨
▨	▨	▨	1,024	▨
▨	▨	▨	2,048	▨
▨	▨	1,728	▨	▨
n	▨	▨	▨	▨

a. Use the patterns in the first several rows to find the missing values.

b. Are any of the patterns linear? Explain.

35. The table below gives data for a group of middle school students.

Data for Some Middle School Students

Student	Name Length	Height (cm)	Foot Length (cm)
Thomas Petes	11	126	23
Michelle Hughes	14	117	21
Shoshana White	13	112	17
Deborah Locke	12	127	21
Tonya Stewart	12	172	32
Richard Mudd	11	135	22
Tony Tung	8	130	20
Janice Vick	10	134	21
Bobby King	9	156	29
Kathleen Boylan	14	164	28

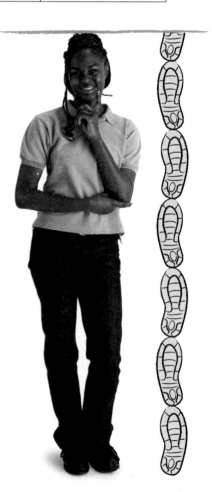

a. Make graphs of the (name length, height) data, the (name length, foot length) data, and the (height, foot length) data.

b. Look at the graphs you made in part (a). Which seem to show linear relationships? Explain.

c. Estimate the average height-to-foot-length ratio. How many foot-lengths tall is the typical student in the table?

d. Which student has the greatest height-to-foot-length ratio? Which student has the least height-to-foot-length ratio?

36. A staircase is a type of prism. This is easier to see if the staircase is viewed from a different perspective. In the prism shown here, each of the small squares on the top has an area of 1 square unit.

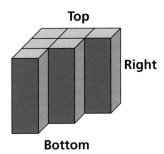

Top

Right

Bottom

a. Sketch the base of the prism. What is the area of the base?

b. Rashid tries to draw a flat pattern that will fold up to form the staircase prism. Below is the start of his drawing. Finish Rashid's drawing and give the surface area of the entire staircase.

Hint: You may want to draw your pattern on grid paper and then cut it out and fold it to check.

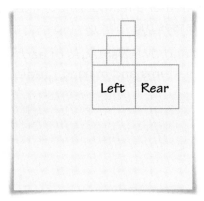

Left   Rear

c. Suppose the prism has six stairs instead of three. Assume each stair is the same width as those in the prism above. Is the surface area of this six-stair prism twice that of the three-stair prism? Explain.

Mathematical Reflections 1

In this Investigation, you used tables and graphs to represent relationships between variables and to make predictions. The following questions will help you summarize what you have learned.

Think about these questions. Discuss your ideas with other students and your teacher. Then write a summary of your findings in your notebook.

1. **You** can represent a relationship between variables with a table, a graph, a description in words, or an equation.

   a. **How** can you decide whether a relationship is linear by studying the pattern in a data table?

   b. **How** can you decide whether a relationship is linear by studying the pattern in a graph?

   c. **How** can you decide whether a relationship is linear by studying the words used to describe the variables?

   d. **How** can you decide whether a relationship is linear by studying the equation that expresses the relationship in symbolic form?

2. **What** are the advantages and disadvantages of each representation in finding patterns and making predictions?

Common Core Mathematical Practices

As you worked on the problems in this Investigation, you used prior knowledge to make sense of them. You also applied Mathematical Practices to solve the Problems. Think back over your work, the ways you thought about the Problems, and how you used Mathematical Practices.

Jayden described his thoughts in the following way:

For Problem 1.1, we noticed from our table and graph that the data look linear. The graph shows this the best. The data points are in a nearly straight line.

In the table, the rate of change for different thicknesses varies from 7 pennies (change from 1 to 2 layers) to 10 pennies (change from 3 to 4 layers), with the average rate of change being about 8 pennies for each additional layer.

Some variability occurs because this is an experiment. We predict that 6 layers would hold about 50 pennies if we use the rate of change of 8 pennies to predict the increase.

Common Core Standards for Mathematical Practice
MP4 Model with mathematics

- What other Mathematical Practices can you identify in Jayden's reasoning?

- Describe a Mathematical Practice that you and your classmates used to solve a different Problem in this Investigation.

Linear Models and Equations

In Investigation 1, you used tables, graphs, and equations to study relationships between variables. You found that the strength of a paper bridge depends on both its number of layers and its length. You found that the number of steel pieces needed to build a truss depends on the length of the truss. The number of pieces in a staircase frame depends on the number of steps.

If there is exactly one value of the dependent variable related to each value of the independent variable, mathematicians call the relationship a **function.** For example, the relationship between bridge breaking weight and length is a function. The relationship between the number of steel pieces used and the length of a truss is a function.

Common Core State Standards

8.EE.B.5 Graph proportional relationships, interpreting the unit rate as the slope of the graph. Compare two different proportional relationships represented in different ways.

8.EE.C.7b Solve linear equations with rational number coefficients, including equations whose solutions require expanding expressions using the distributive property and collecting like terms.

8.EE.C.8a Understand that solutions to a system of two linear equations in two variables corresponds to points of intersection of their graphs, because points of intersection satisfy both equations simultaneously.

8.F.A.1 Understand that a function is a rule that assigns to each input exactly one output. The graph of a function is the set of ordered pairs consisting of an input and the corresponding output.

8.F.A.2 Compare properties of two functions each represented in a different way (algebraically, graphically, numerically in tables, or with verbal descriptions).

Also **8.EE.C.8c, 8.F.A.3, 8.F.B.4, 8.F.B.5, 8.SP.A.1, 8.SP.A.2, 8.SP.A.3, A-SSE.A.1a, A-CED.A.1, A-REI.C.6, F-IF.A.1, F-IF.C.7a, F-BF.A.1a, F-LE.A.2, F-LE.B.5, S-ID.B.6, S-ID.B.6a, S-ID.B.6b, S-ID.B.6c**

It is often helpful to express functions with equations or formulas. The functions and their equations are called **mathematical models** of the relationships between variables. Equations tell you how to calculate the value of the dependent variable when you know the value of the independent variable. In this Investigation, you will develop skills in writing and using linear equations to model relationships between variables.

2.1 Modeling Linear Data Patterns

Organizing and displaying the data from experiments such as the tests of bridge strength helps you see patterns and make predictions. For linear data, you can usually find a graph and an equation to express the approximate relationship between the variables.

The table and graph below show sample data from Investigation 1.

Bridge Thickness (layers)	Breaking Weight (pennies)
1	12
2	18
3	32
4	40
5	48
6	64

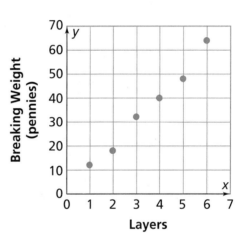

You can see that the points do not lie exactly on a line, but you can draw a line that is a good match for the data pattern. Drawing such a line gives you a model for the data.

 • What line would you draw as a model for the data pattern?

• How would you find an equation for this linear function?

Problem 2.1

A The lines in Figure 1 and Figure 2 below represent two different equations or models for the data. The line in Figure 1 connects the points at the left and right ends of the plot. The line in Figure 2 passes among the points but hits none exactly.

    1. Which of the two lines seems to fit the data better? Explain your choice.

    2. Can you sketch a line that is a better fit than these two?

Figure 1

Figure 2

B To find out how accurate each model is, you can calculate errors in the predictions made by the model. Those errors are the differences between the actual data and what each model predicts. Each such error is called a **residual**. Copy and complete the table below for Figure 1 and Figure 2.

Number of Layers	1	2	3	4	5	6
Breaking Weight (pennies)						
Actual	12	18	32	40	48	64
Predicted by Model	▪	▪	▪	▪	▪	▪
Residual (actual − predicted)	▪	▪	▪	▪	▪	▪

    1. The first line goes through points (1, 12) and (6, 64). The equation for this line is $y = 10.4x + 1.6$. How would you describe the errors of prediction, or residuals, for this linear model?

continued on the next page >

Problem 2.1 continued

2. Sally thinks the equation of the second modeling line is $y = 10x$. Do you agree with Sally? Explain.

3. How would you describe the errors of prediction, or residuals, for Sally's linear model?

4. Do the residuals suggest that one of the models is better than the other? Explain.

C You can find linear models for many situations.

The Student Paint Crew gives weekend and vacation jobs painting houses and apartments to high school and college students. The time a job takes depends on the area to be painted.

Prior jobs give some data relating job area (in units of 1,000 square feet) and time to paint (in hours). The table below shows some of the data.

Area (1,000 sq ft)	1	3	5	8	10
Time (hours)	3	8	12	20	25

1. Plot the given (area, time) data on a graph.

2. Draw a line to match the data pattern.

3. Find the equation of your modeling line.

4. Find the residuals for the model you develop. Explain what they tell you about the accuracy of the linear model.

A C E Homework starts on page 45.

2.2 Up and Down the Staircase
Exploring Slope

Linear functions are often used as models for patterns in data plots. In *Moving Straight Ahead*, you learned several facts about equations representing linear functions.

- Any linear function can be expressed by an equation in the form $y = mx + b$.

- The value of the coefficient m tells the rate at which the values of y increase (or decrease) as the values of x increase by 1. Since m tells you the change in y for every one-unit change in x, it can also be called the *unit rate*. A unit rate is a rate in which the second number is 1, or 1 of a quantity.

- The value of m also tells the steepness and direction (upward or downward) of the graph of the function.

- The value of b tells the point at which the graph of the function crosses the y-axis. That point has coordinates $(0, b)$ and is called the **y-intercept.**

In any problem that calls for a linear model, the goal is to find the values of m and b for an equation with a graph that fits the data pattern well. To measure the steepness of a linear equation graph, it helps to imagine a staircase that lies underneath the line.

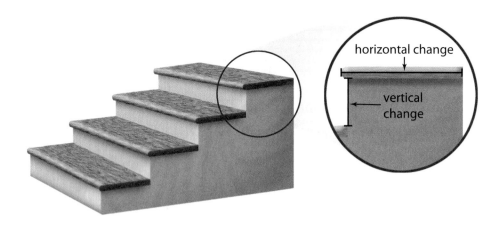

The steepness of a staircase is commonly measured by comparing two numbers, the *rise* and the *run*. The rise is the vertical change from one step to the next, and the run is the horizontal change from one step to the next.

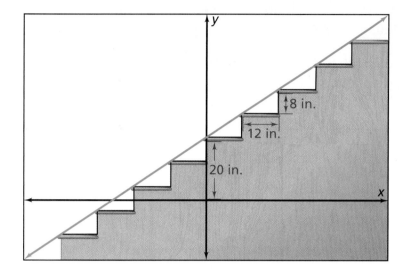

The steepness of the line is the ratio of rise to run. This ratio is the **slope** of the line.

$$\text{slope} = \frac{\text{vertical change}}{\text{horizontal change}} = \frac{\text{rise}}{\text{run}}$$

In the diagram of the staircase, the slope of the line is $\frac{2}{3}$. The y-intercept is $(0, 20)$. So the equation for the linear function is $y = \frac{2}{3}x + 20$.

Problem 2.2

Use the data given in each question to find the equation of the
linear function relating y and x.

Ⓐ For the functions with the graphs below, find the slope and y-intercept.
Then write the equations for the lines in the form $y = mx + b$.

1.
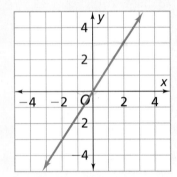

2.
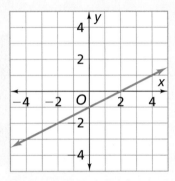

3.
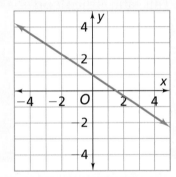

4.
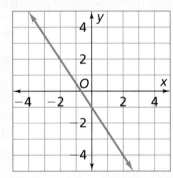

continued on the next page >

Problem **2.2** continued

B 1. Find equations for the linear functions that give these tables. Write them in the form $y = mx + b$.

a.

x	−2	−1	0	1	2
y	−1	1	3	5	7

b.

x	−6	−2	2	6	10
y	−4	−2	0	2	4

2. For each table, find the unit rate of change of y compared to x.

3. Does the line represented by this table have a slope that is greater than or less than the equations you found in part 1(a) and part 1(b)?

x	−1	0	1	2	3
y	4	1	−2	−5	−8

C The points $(4, 2)$ and $(−1, 7)$ lie on a line.

1. What is the slope of the line?

2. Find two more points that lie on this line. Describe your method.

3. Yvonne and Jackie observed that any two points on a line can be used to find the slope. Are they correct? Explain why or why not.

D Kevin said that the line with equation $y = 2x$ passes through the points $(0, 0)$ and $(1, 2)$. He also said the line with equation $y = −3x$ passes through the points $(0, 0)$ and $(1, −3)$. In general, lines with equations of the form $y = mx$ always pass through the points $(0, 0)$ and $(1, m)$. Is he correct? Explain.

E What is the slope of a horizontal line? Of a vertical line?

A C E Homework starts on page 45.

2.3 Tree Top Fun
Equations for Linear Functions

 Tree Top Fun (TTF, for short) runs adventure sites with zip lines, swings, rope ladders, bridges, and trapezes. The company uses mathematical models to relate the number of customers, prices, costs, income, and profit at its many locations.

Problem 2.3

When finding an equation, it may help to calculate values of the dependent variable for some specific values of the independent variable. Then you can look for a pattern in those calculations. You can use the information given in words, tables of data, and graphs.

A Use what you know about linear equations to work out models for the Tree Top Fun business. Find an equation for each of the linear functions described below.

1. The standard charge per customer at TTF is $25. Write an equation that relates the daily income I to the number n of customers.

2. Each TTF site has operating costs of $500 per day. Write an equation that relates daily profit P to the number n of customers.

3. One TTF site bought a new rope bridge for $4,500. TTF will make monthly payments of $350 until the bill is paid. Write an equation for the unpaid balance B after m monthly payments.

continued on the next page >

Problem **2.3** *continued*

B One operator of a Tree Top Fun franchise suggested the group admission fees in the table below.

Number in Group	1	2	3	4	5	10	15	20
Admission (dollars)	75	90	105	120	135	210	285	360

1. Explain how you know the relationship between the admission fee for a group and the number of people in the group is linear.

2. What are the slope and *y*-intercept of the graph of the data?

3. What equation relates admission fee *A* to the number *n* in the group?

C The owners of Tree Top Adventures opened a snack bar at one site. The graph below shows the income from snack sales for six different days. What is the equation of the linear model on the graph?

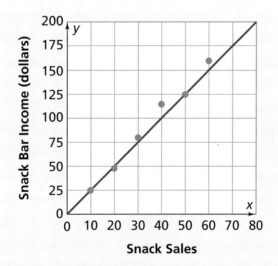

D Suppose you are asked to write an equation of the form $y = mx + b$ to represent a linear function. What is your strategy for each situation?

1. You are given a description of the function in words.

2. You are given two or more (x, y) values or a table of (x, y) values.

3. You are given a graph showing points with coordinates.

continued on the next page >

Problem 2.3 continued

E A state mathematics test asked students to find equations for linear functions. Two students, Dana and Chris, gave the answers below.

1. To find an equation for the line with slope -3 that passes through the point $(4, 3)$, Dana wrote the following steps. Is he correct? Explain.

$$y = -3x + b, \text{ so } 3 = -3(4) + b$$
$$\text{This means } b = 15 \text{ and } y = -3x + 15.$$

2. To find an equation for the line that passes through points $(4, 5)$ and $(6, 9)$, Chris wrote the following steps. Is she correct? Explain.

$$m = \frac{6-4}{9-5}, \text{ so } y = \frac{1}{2}x + b$$
$$\text{This means } 5 = \frac{1}{2}(4) + b, b = 3, \text{ and } y = \frac{1}{2}x + 3.$$

A C E Homework starts on page 45.

2.4 Boat Rental Business
Solving Linear Equations

Sandy's Boat House rents canoes at a cost advertised as $9 per hour for trips on the Red Cedar River. The owner actually gives customers a better deal. She was once a mathematics teacher, and she uses the equation $c = 0.15t + 2.50$ to find the charge c in dollars for renting a canoe for t minutes.

Problem 2.4

When Rashida and Serena applied for jobs at Sandy's, the owner gave them the following test questions to see if they could calculate charges correctly.

(A) **1.** Explain what the numbers in the equation $c = 0.15t + 2.50$ tell you about the situation.

2. How much does it cost to rent a canoe for 25 minutes?

3. A customer is charged $9.25. How long did he use the canoe?

4. A customer has $6 to spend. How long can she use a canoe?

(B) The owner gave Rashida a graph of $c = 0.15t + 2.50$ and asked her how it could be used to estimate answers to Question A. How could Rashida respond?

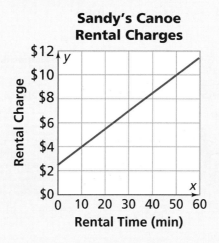

Sandy's Canoe Rental Charges

(C) The owner asked Serena to explain how she could use the table below to estimate answers to Question A. How could Serena respond?

Canoe Rental Time (min)	10	20	30	40	50	60
Rental Charge (dollars)	4.00	5.50	7.00	8.50	10.00	11.50

continued on the next page >

Problem **2.4** *continued*

D The owner next asked Serena and Rashida to work together to find exact answers, not estimates, for Question A, parts (3) and (4).

1. For part (3) of Question A, the girls solved the linear equation $0.15t + 2.50 = 9.25$. They reasoned as follows:

- If $0.15t + 2.50 = 9.25$, then $0.15t = 6.75$.
- If $0.15t = 6.75$, then $t = 45$.
- To check the answer, substitute 45 for t: $0.15(45) + 2.50 = 9.25$.

Are Serena and Rashida correct? How do you know?

2. For Question A, part (4), Rashida said, "The customer can use the canoe for 23.3 minutes if she has \$6." Serena said there are other possibilities—for example, 20 minutes or 15 minutes. Rashida said you can find the answer by solving the **inequality** $0.15t + 2.50 \le 6$. This inequality represents the times for which the rental costs at most \$6.

Use the table, graph, and the equation $0.15t + 2.50 = 6$ to find all times for which the inequality is true. Express the solution as an inequality.

E River Fun Boats rents paddle boats. The equation $c = 4 + 0.10t$ gives the charge in dollars c for renting a paddle boat for t minutes.

1. What is the charge to rent a paddle boat for 20 minutes?

2. A customer at River Fun is charged \$9. How long did the customer use a paddle boat?

3. Suppose you want to spend at most \$12. How long could you use a paddle boat?

A C E Homework starts on page 45.

2.5 Amusement Park or Movies
Intersecting Linear Models

A company owns two attractions in a resort area—the Big Fun amusement park and the Get Reel movie multiplex. At each attraction, the number of visitors on a given day is related to the probability of rain. The company wants to be able to predict Saturday attendance at each attraction in order to assign its workers efficiently.

This table gives attendance and rain-forecast data for several recent Saturdays.

Saturday Resort Attendance

Probability of Rain (%)	0	20	40	60	80	100
Big Fun Attendance	1,000	850	700	550	400	250
Get Reel Attendance	300	340	380	420	460	500

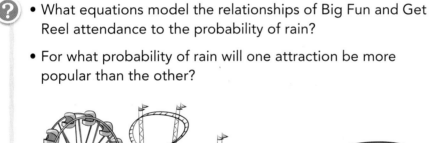

• What equations model the relationships of Big Fun and Get Reel attendance to the probability of rain?

• For what probability of rain will one attraction be more popular than the other?

Problem **2.5**

A Use the table to find linear functions relating the probability of rain *p* to the following quantities.

1. Saturday attendance *F* at Big Fun

2. Saturday attendance *R* at Get Reel

Saturday Resort Attendance

Probability of Rain (%)	0	20	40	60	80	100
Big Fun Attendance	1,000	850	700	550	400	250
Get Reel Attendance	300	340	380	420	460	500

B Use your functions from Question A to answer these questions. Show your calculations and explain your reasoning.

1. Suppose there is a 50% probability of rain this Saturday. What is the expected attendance at each attraction?

2. Suppose 475 people visited Big Fun one Saturday. Estimate the probability of rain on that day.

3. What probability of rain gives a predicted Saturday attendance of at least 360 people at Get Reel?

4. Is there a probability of rain for which the predicted attendance is the same at both attractions?

5. For what probability of rain is attendance at Big Fun likely to be greater than at Get Reel?

6. For what probability of rain is attendance at Big Fun likely to be less than at Get Reel?

 Homework starts on page 45.

Applications

1. Below are some results from the bridge experiment in a CMP class.

Bridge-Thickness Experiment

Number of Layers	2	4	6	8
Breaking Weight (pennies)	15	30	50	65

   a. Plot the (number of layers, breaking weight) data. Draw a line that models the data.

   b. Find an equation for the line you drew.

   c. Use your equation to predict the breaking weights of paper bridges 3, 5, and 7 layers thick.

2. The two graphs below show the same data points. Which line models the data better? Explain.

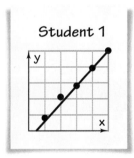
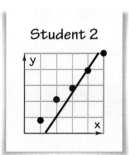

3. Copy each graph onto grid paper. Draw a line that fits each set of data as closely as possible. Describe the strategies you used.

Graph A   **Graph B**   **Graph C**

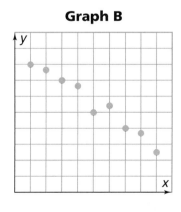
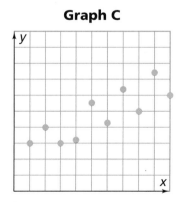

4. This table gives the average weights of Chihuahuas from birth to 16 weeks.

Average Weights for Chihuahuas

Age (wk)	0	2	4	6	8	10	12	14	16
Weight (oz)	4	9	13	17.5	21.5	25	30	34	39

SOURCE: *The Complete Chihuahua Encyclopedia*

a. Graph the (age, weight) data. Draw a line that models the data pattern.

b. Write an equation of the form $y = mx + b$ for your line. Explain what the values of m and b tell you about this situation.

c. Use your equation to predict the average weight of Chihuahuas for odd-numbered ages from 1 to 15 weeks.

d. What average weight does your linear model predict for a Chihuahua that is 72 weeks old? Explain why this prediction is likely to be inaccurate.

5. The U-Wash-It car wash did market research to determine how much to charge for a car wash. The company made this table based on its findings.

U-Wash-It Projections

Price per Wash ($)	0	5	10	15	20
Customers Expected per Day	100	80	65	45	20

a. Graph the (price, expected customers) data. Draw a line that models the data pattern.

b. Write an equation in the form $y = mx + b$ for your graph. Explain what the values of m and b tell you about this situation.

c. Use your equation to find the number of customers expected for prices of $2.50, $7.50, and $12.50.

6. Here is a graph of three lines.

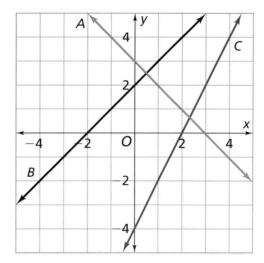

a. Complete the table.

Line	Constant Rate of Change	y-intercept	x-intercept
A	▦	▦	▦
B	▦	▦	▦
C	▦	▦	▦

b. Here are the equations of the three lines. Match each line with its equation.

equation D: $y = 2 + x$ equation E: $y = -4 + 2x$ equation F: $y = 3 - x$

line A   line B   line C

7. Two points determine a line.

a. Which of these points are on the line that passes through $(0, 3)$ and $(2, 5)$?

$(4, 7)$ $(4, 8)$ $(4, 10)$

b. Which of these points are on the line that passes through $(-2, 10)$ and $(1, 4)$?

$(2, 0)$ $(2, 2)$ $(2, 10)$

8. Find the slope, y-intercept, and equation of each line.

a.
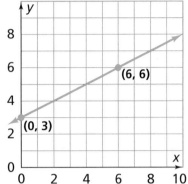
(6, 6)
(0, 3)

b.
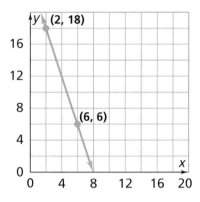
(2, 18)
(6, 6)

c.
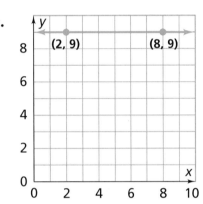
(2, 9)   (8, 9)

d.
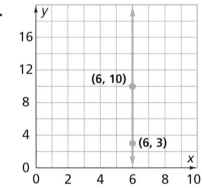
(6, 10)
(6, 3)

Assume that the relationships in Exercises 9–12 are linear.

9. Kaya buys a $20 phone card. She is charged $.15 per minute for calls. What equation gives the value v left on her card after she makes t minutes of calls?

10. A typical American baby weighs about 8 pounds at birth and gains about 1.5 pounds per month for the first year of life. What equation relates weight w in pounds to age a in months?

1 month   **6 months**   **1 year**

11. Dakota lives 1,500 meters from school. She leaves for school, walking at a speed of 60 meters per minute. Write an equation for her distance d in meters from school after she walks for t minutes.

12. A car can average 140 miles on 5 gallons of gasoline. Write an equation for the distance d in miles the car can travel on g gallons of gas.

13. Write a linear equation relating x and y for each table.

a.

x	0	3	6	10
y	2	8	14	22

b.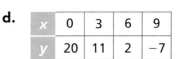

x	0	3	6	10
y	20	8	−4	−20

c.

x	2	4	6	8
y	5	8	11	14

d.

x	0	3	6	9
y	20	11	2	−7

For Exercises 14–19, find an equation for the line that satisfies the conditions.

14. slope 4.2; y-intercept $(0, 3.4)$

15. slope $\frac{2}{3}$; y-intercept $(0, 5)$

16. slope 2; passing through $(4, 12)$

17. passing through $(0, 15)$ and $(5, 3)$

18. passing through $(-2, 2)$ and $(5, -4)$

19. parallel to the line with equation $y = 15 - 2x$ and passing through $(3, 0)$

20. Write an equation for each line in the graph below.

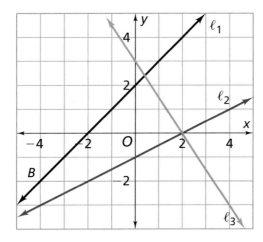

21. Anchee and Jonah earn weekly allowances for doing chores over the summer.

- Anchee's father pays her $5 each week.

- Jonah's mother paid him $20 at the beginning of the summer and now pays him $3 each week.

The relationships between number of weeks and dollars earned are shown in this graph.

Earnings From Chores

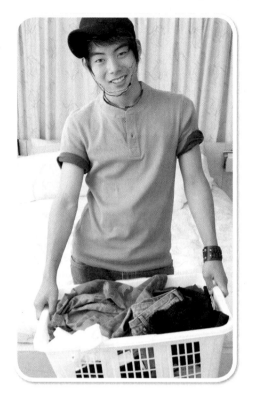

a. Which line represents Jonah's earnings? Which line represents Anchee's earnings? Explain.

b. Write two linear equations in the form $y = mx + b$ to show the relationships between Anchee's earnings and the number of weeks she works and between Jonah's earnings and the number of weeks he works.

c. In each equation, what do the values of m and b tell you about the relationship between the number of weeks and the dollars earned?

d. What do the values of m and b tell you about each line?

For Exercises 22–25, do the following.
 (a) Solve the equation and show your steps.
 (b) Graph the related linear function. (For example, for
   $5.5x + 32 = 57$, graph $y = 5.5x + 32$.)
 (c) Label the point on the graph that gives the solution.

22. $5.5x + 32 = 57$

23. $-24 = 4x - 12$

24. $5x - 51 = 24$

25. $74 = 53 - 7x$

26. At Water Works Amusement Park, the daily profit from the concession stands depends on the number of park visitors. The equation $P = 2.50v - 500$ gives the estimated profit P in dollars if v people visit the park. In parts (a)-(c), use a graph to estimate the answer. Then find the answer by writing and solving an equation or inequality.

    a. For what number of visitors will the profit be about $2,000?

    b. One day 200 people visit the park. What is the approximate concession-stand profit for that day?

    c. For what number of visitors will the profit be at least $500?

27. The following formulas give the fare f, in dollars, charged by two bus companies for trips of d miles.

    • Transcontinental: $f = 0.15d + 12$

    • Intercity Express: $f = 5 + 0.20d$

    In parts (a)-(c), use a graph to estimate the answer. Then find the answer by writing and solving an equation or inequality.

    a. For Transcontinental, how many miles is a trip that costs $100?

    b. For Intercity Express, how far can a person travel for a fare that is at most $100?

    c. Is there a distance for which the fare for the two bus lines is the same? If so, give the distance and the fare.

In Exercises 28–30, solve each equation. Show the steps in your solutions.

    28. $5x + 7 = 3x - 5$ **29.** $7 + 3x = 5x - 5$ **30.** $2.5x - 8 = 5x + 12$

In Exercises 31–34, find at least three values of x for which the inequality is true.

    31. $4x \leq 12$ **32.** $3x < 18$

    33. $4x + 5 \leq 13$ **34.** $3x - 9 \leq 18$

35. Every Friday, the mechanic for Columbus Public Schools records the miles driven and gallons of gas used by each school bus. One week, the mechanic records the data below.

Data for Columbus Bus Fleet

Bus Number	1	2	3	4	5	6	7	8
Gas Used (gal)	5	8	12	15	18	20	22	25
Miles Driven	80	100	180	225	280	290	320	375

a. Write a linear equation that models the relationship between miles driven d and gallons of gas used g.

b. Use your equation to predict the number of miles a school bus could travel on 10 gallons of gas.

c. Use your equation to predict the number of gallons of gas required to drive a school bus 250 miles.

d. What do the values of m and b in your equation $d = mg + b$ tell about the fuel efficiency of the school bus fleet?

36. One of the most popular items at a farmers' market is sweet corn. This table shows relationships among the price of the corn, the supply of corn (how much corn the market has), and the demand for the corn (how much corn people want to buy).

Sweet Corn Supply and Demand

Price per Dozen ($)	1.00	1.50	2.00	2.50	3.00	3.50
Demand (dozens)	200	175	140	120	80	60
Supply (dozens)	40	75	125	175	210	260

a. Why do you think the demand for corn decreases as the price goes up?

b. Why do you think the supply of corn increases as the price goes up?

c. Write a linear equation that models the relationship between demand d and price p.

d. Write a linear equation that models the relationship between supply s and price p.

e. Use graphs to estimate the price for which the supply equals the demand. Then find the price by solving symbolically.

Connections

37. Tell whether each table represents a linear relationship. Explain your reasoning.

a.

x	2	4	6	8	10	12	14
y	0	1	2	3	4	5	6

b.

x	1	2	3	4	5	6	7
y	0	3	8	15	24	35	48

c.

x	1	4	6	7	10	12	16
y	2	−1	−3	−4	−7	−9	−13

38. For parts (a)–(d), copy the table. Then use the equation to complete the table. Tell whether the relationship is linear. Explain your reasoning.

a. $y = -3x - 8$

x	−5	−2	1	4
y	▨	▨	▨	▨

b. $y = 4(x - 7) + 6$

x	−3	0	3	6
y	▨	▨	▨	▨

c. $y = x(3x + 2)$

x	−3	0	3	6
y	▨	▨	▨	▨

d. $y = 4 - 3x$

x	−3	0	3	10
y	▨	▨	▨	▨

Copy each pair of numbers in Exercises 39–44. Insert $<$, $>$, or $=$ to make a true statement.

39. $-5 \; ▨ \; 3$

40. $\frac{2}{3} \; ▨ \; \frac{1}{2}$

41. $\frac{9}{12} \; ▨ \; \frac{3}{4}$

42. $3.009 \; ▨ \; 3.1$

43. $-\frac{2}{3} \; ▨ \; -\frac{1}{2}$

44. $-4.25 \; ▨ \; -2.45$

45. Madeline sets the scale factor on a copy machine at 150%. She then uses the machine to copy a polygon. Write an equation that relates the perimeter of the polygon after the enlargement, a, to the perimeter before the enlargement, b.

For Exercises 46–54, evaluate the expression without using a calculator.

46. $-15 + (-7)$

47. $-7 - 15$

48. $-7 - (-15)$

49. $-15 + 7$

50. $-20 \div 5$

51. $-20 \div (-5)$

52. $20 \div (-4)$

53. $-20 \div (-2.5)$

54. $-20 \cdot (-2.5)$

55. You can express the slope of a line in different ways. The slope of the line below is $\frac{6}{10}$, or 0.6. You can also say the slope is 60% because the rise is 60% of the run.

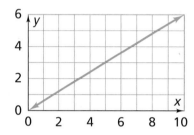

These numbers represent slopes of lines.

$\frac{-4}{-2}$ 60% $\frac{4}{4}$ 1.5   150%   200%

a. Which numbers represent the same slope?

b. Which number represents the greatest slope?

c. Which number represents the least slope?

56. The figures below are *similar*. (They have the same shape but are different sizes.)

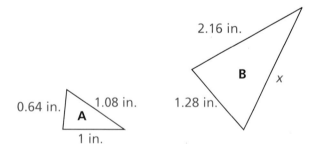

a. Find the value of x.

b. What is the scale factor from Triangle A to Triangle B?

c. What is the scale factor from Triangle B to Triangle A?

d. How are the scale factors in parts (b) and (c) related?

57. Read the following stories and look at the graphs.

   a. Match each story with a graph. Tell how you would label the axes of the graph. Explain how each part of the story is represented in the graph.

- **Story 1** A parachutist is taken up in a plane. After she jumps, the wind blows her off course. She ends up tangled in the branches of a tree.

- **Story 2** Ella puts some money in the bank. She leaves it there to earn interest for several years. Then one day, she withdraws half the money in the account.

- **Story 3** Gerry has a big pile of gravel to spread on his driveway. On the first day, he moves half the gravel from the pile to his driveway. The next day he is tired and moves only half of what is left. The third day he again moves half of what is left in the pile. He continues in this way until the pile has almost disappeared.

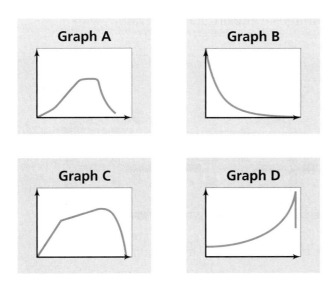

   b. One of the graphs does not match a story. Make up your own story for that graph.

Extensions

58. Recall that Custom Steel Products builds trusses from steel pieces. Here is a 7-foot truss.

7-foot truss made from 27 rods

a. Which of these formulas represents the relationship between truss length L and number of pieces r?

$r = 3L$ $r = L + (L - 1) + 2L$ $r = 4(L - 1) + 3$ $r = 4L - 1$

b. How might you have reasoned to come up with each formula?

59. Multiple Choice Recall that Custom Steel Products uses steel pieces to make staircase frames. Here are staircase frames with 1, 2, and 3 steps.

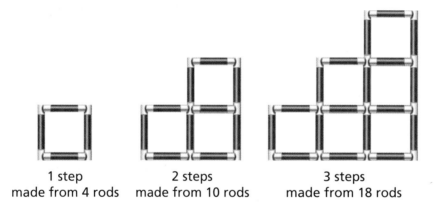

| 1 step | 2 steps | 3 steps |
| made from 4 rods | made from 10 rods | made from 18 rods |

Which of these formulas represents the relationship between the number of steps n and number of pieces r?

A. $r = n^2 + 3n$ **B.** $r = n(n + 3)$ **C.** $r = n^2 + 3$ **D.** $r = (n + 3)n$

Custom Steel Products builds cubes out of square steel plates
measuring 1 foot on a side. Below is a 1-foot cube. Use this information
for Exercises 61–63.

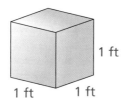

1 ft

1 ft   1 ft

60. How many square plates are needed to make a 1-foot cube?

61. Multiple Choice Suppose CSP wants to triple the dimensions of the
cube. How many times greater than the original area will the surface
area of this larger cube be?

    A. 2   **B.** 3   **C.** 4   **D.** 9

62. Multiple Choice Suppose CSP triples the dimensions of the original
cube. How many times the volume of the original cube is the volume
of the new cube?

    F. 8   **G.** 9   **H.** 27   **J.** 81

63. A bridge-painting company uses the formula $C = 5{,}000 + 150L$ to
estimate painting costs. C is the cost in dollars, and L is the length
of the bridge in feet. To make a profit, the company increases a cost
estimate by 20% to arrive at a bid price. For example, if the cost
estimate is $10,000, the bid price will be $12,000.

   a. Find bid prices for bridges 100 feet, 200 feet, and 400 feet long.

   b. Write a formula relating the final bid price to bridge length.

   c. Use your formula to find bid prices for bridges 150 feet, 300 feet,
and 450 feet long.

   d. How would your formula change if the markup for profit was 15%
instead of 20%?

64. At Yvonne's Auto Detailing, car washes cost $5 for any time up to 10 minutes, plus $.40 per minute after that. The managers at Yvonne's are trying to agree on a formula for calculating the cost c for a t-minute car wash.

   a. Sid thinks $c = 0.4t + 5$ is correct. Is he right?

   b. Tina proposes the formula $c = 0.4(t - 10) + 5$. Is she right?

   c. Jamal says Tina's formula can be simplified to $c = 0.4t + 1$. Is he right?

Write an equation for each relationship.

65. The Bluebird Taxi Company charges $3.00 for the first 2 miles of any trip and $2.40 for each mile after that. How is the taxi fare related to the distance of a trip?

66. An airport offers free parking for 30 minutes and then charges $2.00 for each hour after that. How is the price for parking related to the total time a car is parked?

67. The Regal Cinema makes $6.50 on each ticket sold. The cinema has operating expenses of $750 per day, as well. How is daily profit related to number of tickets sold?

68. Rush Computer Repair sends technicians to businesses to fix computers. Technicians charge a fixed fee of $50, plus $50 per hour. How is total cost for a repair related to the time the repair takes?

Mathematical Reflections 2

In this Investigation, you learned how to find linear models for data patterns. You also developed skill in writing linear equations, practiced translating verbal descriptions into linear equations, and extended your knowledge of solving linear equations. The following questions will help you summarize what you have learned.

Think about these questions. Discuss your ideas with other students and your teacher. Then write a summary of your findings in your notebook.

1. **Why** is it helpful to use a linear model for a set of data?

2. **When** does it make sense to choose a linear function to model a set of data?

3. **How** would you find the equation for a linear function in the following situations?

   a. **You** are given a description of the variables in words.

   b. **You** are given a table of values for the variables.

   c. **You** are given a graph of sample data points.

4. **What** strategies can you use to solve a linear equation such as $500 = 245 + 5x$?

5. **What** kind of mathematical sentences express "at least" and "at most" questions about linear functions?

Common Core Mathematical Practices

As you worked on the Problems in this Investigation, you used prior knowledge to make sense of them. You also applied Mathematical Practices to solve the Problems. Think back over your work, the ways you thought about the Problems, and how you used Mathematical Practices.

Elena described her thoughts in the following way:

In Problem 2.1, we learned about computing residuals as a way to evaluate different models (lines) for a set of data. I was confused by this idea. Jamie and I added rows to the table that was included with the problem. Tables can really help organize ideas. When we used one model, we computed the differences of the actual values and the values predicted by the model line.

For Model 1, we got residuals 0, −4, −1, −3, −6, and 0, or a total of −14. For Model 2, the total of the residuals was 4. We think Model 2 might be a better model to use.

Common Core Standards for Mathematical Practice
MP7 Look for and make use of structure.

- What other Mathematical Practices can you identify in Elena's reasoning?

- Describe a Mathematical Practice that you and your classmates used to solve a different Problem in this Investigation.

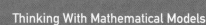

Investigation 3

Inverse Variation

In Investigation 1, you explored the relationship of strength, number of layers, and length of a bridge. You found that the relationship between strength and number of layers was approximately linear. You also found that the relationship between strength and length was not linear. In this investigation, you will explore other nonlinear functions.

3.1 Rectangles With Fixed Area

In recent years, the populations of many small towns have declined as residents move to large cities for jobs. The town of Roseville has a plan to attract new residents.

Roseville offers free land to "homesteaders" who are willing to build houses. Each lot is rectangular and has an area of 21,780 square feet. The lengths and widths of the lots vary.

The town planners want a quick way to check lot sizes for the new homesteaders.

Common Core State Standards

8.F.A.3 Interpret the equation $y = mx + b$ as defining a linear function whose graph is a straight line; give examples of functions that are not linear.

Also 8.F.A.1, 8.F.B.5, 8.SP.A.1, A-CED.A.2, A-CED.A.4, F-IF.C.8, F-BF.A.1a, S-ID.B.6a

• What function relates the length and width of rectangles with area 21,780 square feet?

• What patterns appear in tables and graphs of that function?

 Problem 3.1

In Problem 3.1, you will look at patterns in length and width values for rectangles with fixed area.

A 1. Copy and complete this table.

Rectangles With Area 24 in.²

Length (in.)	1	2	3	4	5	6	7	8
Width (in.)								

 2. Plot your (length, width) data from part (1) on a graph like the one below. Then draw a line or curve that models the pattern in the data.

Rectangles With Area 24 in.²

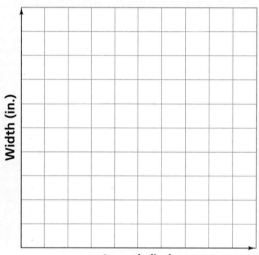

Length (in.)

3. Describe the pattern of change in the width of a rectangle as the length increases. Is the relationship between length and width linear?

4. Write an equation relating width w to length ℓ for rectangles with an area of 24 square inches.

continued on the next page >

Problem **3.1** *continued*

B Now consider rectangles with area of 32 square inches.

1. Write an equation for the relationship between the width w and the length ℓ.

2. Make a table and a graph of values for w and ℓ. Show lengths from 1 to 10 inches.

C Compare tables, graphs, and rules for the functions relating width and length of rectangles with area 24 square inches and area 32 square inches. Then use your results to answer the Roseville planners' questions about lots with area 21,780 square feet.

A C E Homework starts on page 69.

3.2 Distance, Speed, and Time

The relationship between length and width for rectangles with a fixed area is not linear. As ℓ increases, w decreases, but not at a constant rate. The graph is a curve showing how ℓ and w relate to each other.

The relationship between ℓ and w is an example of an important relationship called an inverse variation. Two nonzero variables x and y are related by an **inverse variation** if

$$y = \frac{k}{x} \quad \text{or} \quad xy = k$$

where k is a constant other than 0.

Here are some questions about inverse variation that you can keep in mind as you work on the following problems about distance, speed, and time of travel.

- How does the value of one variable change as the value of the other changes?

- How is that pattern of change shown in a table of data and on a graph?

- What equation shows how the two variables are related?

Problem **3.2**

Inverse variation occurs in many situations. You have probably thought about how the length of a trip depends on speed.

A Mr. Cordova lives in Detroit, Michigan. He often travels to Baltimore, Maryland, to visit his grandfather. The trip is about 500 miles each way. Here are Mr. Cordova's notes for his trips to Baltimore last year.

Date	Notes	Travel Time
February 15	Traveled by plane.	1.5 hours
May 22	Drove.	10 hours
July 3	Drove. Stopped for repairs.	14 hours
November 23	Flew. Flight delayed.	4 hours
December 23	Took overnight train.	18 hours

1. Calculate the average speed in miles per hour for each trip. Record your results in a table like this.

Mr. Cordova's Baltimore Trips

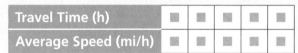

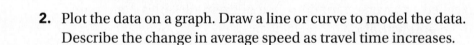

Travel Time (h)	▪	▪	▪	▪	▪
Average Speed (mi/h)	▪	▪	▪	▪	▪

2. Plot the data on a graph. Draw a line or curve to model the data. Describe the change in average speed as travel time increases.

3. Write an equation for the relationship between time *t* and speed *s*.

4. Is the relationship between distance and time an inverse variation? Explain why or why not.

continued on the next page >

Problem 3.2 continued

B The Cordova family is planning a trip of 300 miles to Mackinac Island, near the upper peninsula of Michigan. Mr. Cordova does some calculations to see how the travel time will change if the family drives at different average speeds.

Travel Times for Different Speeds

Average Speed (mi/h)	30	40	50	60	70
Travel Time (h)	10	7.5	6	5	4.3

1. Describe the change in travel time as the average speed increases.

2. What equation relates travel time t to average speed s?

3. How is the pattern relating travel time to average speed shown in a graph of (s, t) data?

4. Is the relationship between travel time and average speed an inverse variation? Explain why or why not.

C Suppose Mr. Cordova decides to aim for an average speed of 50 miles per hour for the trip to Mackinac Island.

1. Make a table and a graph to show how the distance traveled will increase as time passes. Show times from when the family leaves home to when they reach their destination.

2. Describe the pattern of change in distance as time passes. Explain how that pattern is shown by values in your table and points on your graph.

3. Mr. Cordova's sister plans to go to Mackinac Island, also. She can drive from Detroit to the island in 5 hours. Use your table and graph from part (1) to compare Mr. Cordova's average speed to his sister's average speed. Who drives faster?

4. Write equations relating distance traveled d to time t for Mr. Cordova and his sister. How do these equations support your answer to part (3)?

5. Is the equation relating distance and time an inverse variation? Explain why or why not.

 Homework starts on page 69.

3.3 Planning a Field Trip
Finding Individual Cost

The science teachers at Everett Middle School want to take their eighth-graders on a field trip to a nature center. It costs $750 to rent the center facilities.

The school budget does not provide funds to rent the nature center, so students must pay a fee. The trip will cost $3 per student if all 250 go. The teachers know, however, that it is unlikely that all students will go. They want a way to find the cost per student for any number of students.

- What kind of relationship between number of students and cost should the teachers expect?

- How can that relationship be expressed with an equation and a graph?

Problem 3.3

To identify the relationship between the number of students and the cost, begin with sample calculations. Then look for a pattern in your results.

A 1. Copy and complete the table below.

Number of Students	25	50	75	100	125	150	175	200	250
Cost per Student (dollars)	▪	▪	▪	▪	▪	▪	▪	▪	▪

2. Describe the pattern relating the cost per student to the number of students who visit the nature center.

3. Write an equation relating cost per student c to number of students n.

4. Sketch a graph showing how the cost per student changes as the number of students increases.

continued on the next page >

Problem **3.3** | continued

B **1.** Find the change in the cost per student as the number of students increases in the following ways.

   a. from 10 to 20   **b.** from 100 to 110   **c.** from 200 to 210

2. Is the function relating number of students and cost linear? Explain.

3. Do equal increases in numbers of students cause equal decreases in cost per student? Explain.

C How will doubling the number of students change the cost per student? To test your ideas about that question, find answers to these related questions.

1. Find the change in per-student cost as the number of students increases in the following ways.

   a. from 20 to 40   **b.** from 40 to 80   **c.** from 80 to 160

2. Describe any patterns you see in your answers to part (1).

3. How does your equation from Question A help to explain the effect of doubling the number of students?

D The science teachers decide to charge $5 per student for the field trip. They will use any extra money to buy science equipment for the school.

1. Write an equation for the amount *A* the teachers will collect if *n* students go on the trip.

2. Sketch a graph of the relationship.

3. Does the graph show a linear relationship or an inverse variation? Explain.

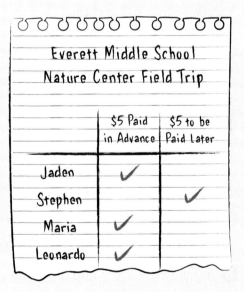

Everett Middle School
Nature Center Field Trip

	$5 Paid in Advance	$5 to be Paid Later
Jaden	✔	
Stephen		✔
Maria	✔	
Leonardo	✔	

A C E Homework starts on page 69.

3.4 Modeling Data Patterns

In many real-world problems it is impossible to find an equation that fits given data exactly. For example, consider the table and graph below. They show the bridge experiment data collected by a group of students.

Bridge Experiment Data

Length (in.)	Breaking Weight (pennies)
4	41
6	26
8	19
9	17
10	15

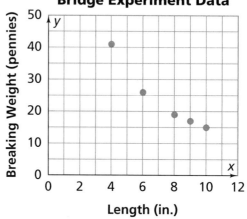

Bridge Experiment Data

- Do the data suggest the relationship between length and breaking weight is linear or an inverse variation?

- What equation would model the relationship well?

Problem **3.4**

Use the data from the table and the graph.

A What do you see in the table and the graph that suggests an inverse variation relationship between breaking weight w and bridge length ℓ?

B What value of k would make the equation $k = w\ell$ true for a length of 4 inches? For a length of 6 inches?

C What equation is a good model for the function relating weight w to length ℓ?

D What breaking weights does your model predict for bridges of length 3, 5, 7, and 11 inches?

 Homework starts on page 69.

 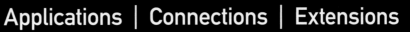

Applications

1. Consider rectangles with an area of 16 square inches.

   a. Copy and complete the table.

   Rectangles With Area 16 in.²

Length (in.)	1	2	3	4	5	6	7	8
Width (in.)	▦	▦	▦	▦	▦	▦	▦	▦

   b. Make a graph of the data.

   c. Describe the pattern of change in width as length increases.

   d. Write an equation that shows how the width w depends on the length ℓ. Is the relationship linear?

2. Consider rectangles with an area of 20 square inches.

   a. Make a table of length and width data for at least five rectangles.

   b. Make a graph of your data.

   c. Write an equation that shows how the width w depends on the length ℓ. Is the relationship linear?

   d. Compare and contrast the graphs in this exercise and those in Exercise 1.

   e. Compare and contrast the equations in this exercise and those in Exercise 1.

3. A student collected these data from the bridge-length experiment.

   Bridge-Length Experiment

Length (in.)	4	6	8	9	10
Breaking Weight (pennies)	24	16	13	11	9

   a. Find an inverse variation equation that models the data.

   b. Explain how your equation shows that breaking weight decreases as length increases. Is this decrease reasonable for the situation? Explain.

For Exercises 4–7, tell whether the relation between x and y is an inverse variation. If it is, write an equation for the relationship.

4.

x	1	2	3	4	5	6	7	8	9	10
y	10	9	8	7	6	5	4	3	2	1

5.

x	1	2	3	4	5	6	7	8	9	10
y	48	24	16	12	9.6	8	6.8	6	5.3	4.8

6.

x	2	3	5	8	10	15	20	25	30	40
y	50	33	20	12.5	10	6.7	5	4	3.3	2.5

7.

x	0	1	2	3	4	5	6	7	8	9
y	100	81	64	49	36	25	16	9	4	1

8. The marathon is a 26.2-mile race. The best marathon runners can complete the race in a bit more than 2 hours.

   a. Make a table and graph that show how the average running speed for a marathon changes as the time to complete the race increases. Show times from 2 to 8 hours in one-hour intervals.

   b. Write an equation for the relationship between time t and average running speed s for a marathon.

   c. Tell how the average running speed changes as the time increases from 2 hours to 3 hours, from 3 hours to 4 hours, and from 4 hours to 5 hours.

   d. How do the answers for part (c) show that the relationship between average running speed and time is not linear?

9. Testers drove eight vehicles 200 miles on a track at the same speed. The table below shows the amount of fuel each car used.

Fuel-Efficiency Test

Vehicle Type	Fuel Used (gal)
Large Truck	20
Large SUV	18
Limousine	16
Large Sedan	12
Small Truck	10
Sports Car	12
Compact Car	7
Sub-Compact Car	5

a. Find the fuel efficiency in miles per gallon for each vehicle.

b. Make a graph of the (fuel used, miles per gallon) data. Describe the pattern of change shown in the graph.

c. Write a formula for calculating the fuel efficiency based on the fuel used for a 200-mile test drive.

d. Use your formula to find how fuel efficiency changes as the number of gallons of fuel increases from 5 to 10, from 10 to 15, and from 15 to 20.

e. How do the answers for part (d) show that the relationship between fuel used and fuel efficiency is not linear?

10. The route for one day of a charity bike ride covers 50 miles. Individual participants ride this distance at different average speeds.

a. Make a table and a graph that show how the riding time changes as the average speed increases. Show speeds from 4 to 20 miles per hour in intervals of 4 miles per hour.

b. Write an equation for the relationship between the riding time t and average speed s.

c. Tell how the riding time changes as the average speed increases from 4 to 8 miles per hour, from 8 to 12 miles per hours, and from 12 to 16 miles per hour.

d. How do the answers for part (c) show that the relationship between average speed and time is not linear?

11. Students in Mr. Einstein's science class complain about the length of his tests. He argues that a test with more questions is better for students because each question is worth fewer points. All of Mr. Einstein's tests are worth 100 points. Each question is worth the same number of points.

   a. Make a table and a graph that show how the number of points per question changes as the number of questions increases. Show point values for 2 to 20 questions in intervals of 2.

   b. Write an equation for the relationship between the number of questions n and points per question p.

   c. What is the change in points per question if the number of questions increases from 2 to 4? From 4 to 6? From 6 to 8? From 8 to 10?

   d. How do the answers for part (c) show that the relationship between the number of questions and points per question is not linear?

Connections

12. Here are some possible descriptions of a line.

> Descriptions of a Line
> • slope positive, 0, or negative
> • y-intercept positive, 0, or negative
> • crossing the x-axis to the right of the origin
> • passing through the origin at (0, 0)
> • crossing the x-axis to the left of the origin
> • never crossing the x-axis

For each equation below, list all of the properties that describe the graph of that equation.

   a. $y = x$

   b. $y = 2x + 1$

   c. $y = -5$

   d. $y = 4 - 3x$

   e. $y = -3 - x$

13. Write equations and sketch the graphs of lines with the following properties.

    a. slope of 3.5, y-intercept at $(0, 4)$

    b. slope $\frac{3}{2}$, passing through $(-2, 0)$

    c. passing through the points $(2, 7)$ and $(6, 15)$

    d. slope $-\frac{15}{5}$, passing through the point $(-2.5, 4.5)$

14. Suppose the town of Roseville is giving away lots with a perimeter of 500 feet, rather than with an area of 21,780 square feet.

    a. Copy and complete this table.

Rectangles With a Perimeter of 500 ft

Length (ft)	50	100	150	200	225
Width (ft)	▢	▢	▢	▢	▢

    b. Make a graph of the (length, width) data. Draw a line or curve that models the data pattern.

    c. Describe the pattern of change in width as length increases.

    d. Write an equation for the relationship between length and width. Explain why it is or is not a linear function.

A number b is the **additive inverse** of the number a if $a + b = 0$.
For example, -5 is the additive inverse of 5 because $5 + (-5) = 0$.
For Exercises 15–20, find the additive inverse of each number.

15. 2   **16.** $-\frac{6}{2}$ **17.** 2.5

18. -2.11 **19.** $\frac{7}{3}$ **20.** $\frac{3}{7}$

21. On a number line, graph each number from Exercises 15–20 and its additive inverse. Describe any patterns you see.

A number b is the **multiplicative inverse** of the number a if $ab = 1$. For example, $\frac{3}{2}$ is the multiplicative inverse of $\frac{2}{3}$ because $\left(\frac{3}{2} \cdot \frac{2}{3}\right) = 1$. For Exercises 22–27, find the multiplicative inverse of each number.

22. 2

23. −2

24. 0.5

25. 4

26. $\frac{3}{4}$

27. $\frac{5}{3}$

28. On a number line, graph each number in Exercises 22–27 and its multiplicative inverse. Describe any patterns you see.

Jamar takes a 10-point history quiz each week. Here are his scores on the first five quizzes: 8, 9, 6, 7, 10. Use this information for Exercises 29–30.

29. Multiple Choice What is Jamar's average quiz score?

A. 6   **B.** 7   **C.** 8   **D.** 9

30. Jamar misses the next quiz and gets a 0.

    a. What is his average after six quizzes?

    b. After 20 quizzes, Jamar's average is 8. He gets a 0 on the 21st quiz. What is his average after 21 quizzes?

    c. Why did a score of 0 have a different effect on the average when it was the sixth score than it did when it was the 21st score?

In Exercises 31 and 32, solve each equation using a symbolic method. Then describe how the solution can be found using a graph and a table.

31. $5x - 28 = -3$

32. $10 - 3x = 7x - 10$

For Exercises 33–35, find the equation of the line with the given properties.

33. slope $\frac{1}{2}$, y-intercept $(0, 5)$

34. slope 3, passing through the point $(2, 2)$

35. passing through the points $(5, 2)$ and $(1, 10)$

36. Find the equation for the line shown below.

Al Jabr's Self-Serve Wash

37. Suppose a car travels at a speed of 60 miles per hour. The function $d = 60t$ relates time t in hours and distance d in miles. This function is an example of *direct variation*. A relationship between variables x and y is a direct variation if it can be expressed as $y = kx$, where k is a constant.

a. Describe two functions in this unit that are direct variations. Give the rule for each function as an equation.

b. For each function from part (a), find the ratio of the dependent variable to the independent variable. How is the ratio related to k in the general function?

c. Suppose the relationship between x and y is a direct variation. How do the y-values change as the x-values increase? How does this pattern of change appear in a graph of the relationship?

d. Compare direct variation and inverse variation. Be sure to discuss the graphs and equations of each.

For Exercises 38–40, tell which store offers the better buy. Explain your choice.

Gus's Groceries   The Super Market

38. 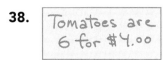 Tomatoes are 6 for $4.00   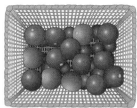   TOMATOES ARE 8 FOR $4.60

39. 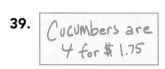 Cucumbers are 4 for $1.75   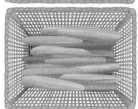   CUCUMBERS ARE 5 FOR $2.00

40. 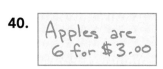 Apples are 6 for $3.00   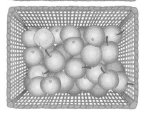   APPLES ARE 5 FOR $2.89

41. Suppose 6 cans of tomato juice cost $3.20. Find the cost of the following numbers of cans.

   a. 1 can   **b.** 10 cans   **c.** n cans

Extensions

42. The drama club members at Henson Middle School are planning their spring show. They decide to charge $4.50 per ticket. They estimate their expenses for the show at $150.

    a. Write a function for the relationship between the number of tickets sold and the club's total profit.

    b. Make a table to show how the profit changes as the ticket sales increase from 0 to 500 in intervals of 50.

    c. Make a graph of the (tickets sold, total profit) data.

    d. Add a column (or row) to your table to show the per-ticket profit for each number of tickets sold. For example, for 200 tickets, the total profit is $750, so the per-ticket profit is $750 ÷ 200, or $3.75.

    e. Make a graph of the (tickets sold, per-ticket profit) data.

    f. How are the patterns of change for the (tickets sold, total profit) data and (tickets sold, per-ticket profit) data similar? How are they different? How are the similarities and differences shown in the tables and graphs of each function?

43. The net below folds to make a rectangular prism.

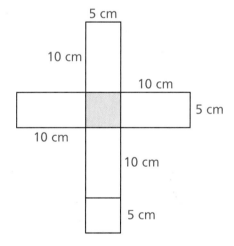

    a. What is the volume of the prism?

    b. Suppose the dimensions of the shaded face of the prism are doubled. The other dimensions are adjusted so the volume remains the same. What are the new dimensions of the prism?

    c. Which prism has the smaller surface area, the original prism or the prism from part (b)? Explain.

44. Ms. Singh drives 40 miles to her sister's house. Her average speed is 20 miles per hour. On her way home, her average speed is 40 miles per hour. What is her average speed for the round trip?

For Exercises 45–47, find the value of c for which both ordered pairs satisfy the same inverse variation. Then write an equation for the relationship.

45. $(3, 16)$, $(12, c)$ **46.** $(3, 9)$, $(4, c)$ **47.** $(3, 4)$, $(4, c)$

48. Multiple Choice The acceleration of a falling object is related to the object's mass and the force of gravity acting on it. For a fixed force F, the relationship between mass m and acceleration a is an inverse variation. Which equation describes the relationship of F, m, and a?

A. $F = ma$ **B.** $m = Fa$

C. $\frac{m}{F} = a$ **D.** $\frac{m}{a} = F$

49. Multiple Choice Suppose the time t in the equation $d = rt$ is held constant. What happens to the distance d as the rate r increases?

F. d decreases.   **G.** d increases.

H. d stays constant.   **J.** There is not enough information.

50. Multiple Choice Suppose the distance d in the equation $d = rt$ is held constant. What happens to the time t as the rate r increases?

A. t decreases.   **B.** t increases.

C. t stays constant.   **D.** There is not enough information.

Mathematical Reflections 3

In this Investigation, you explored several examples of inverse variation and looked for patterns in the tables, graphs, and equations of these relationships. These questions will help you summarize what you have learned.

Think about these questions. Discuss your ideas with other students and your teacher. Then write a summary of your findings in your notebook.

1. **Suppose** the relationship between variables x and y is an inverse variation.

   a. **How** do the values of y change as the values of x increase?

   b. **Describe** the trend in a graph of (x, y) values.

   c. **Describe** the equation that relates the values of x and y.

2. **How** is an inverse variation similar to a linear relationship? How is it different?

Common Core Mathematical Practices

As you worked on the Problems in this Investigation, you used prior knowledge to make sense of them. You also applied Mathematical Practices to solve the Problems. Think back over your work, the ways you thought about the Problems, and how you used Mathematical Practices.

Nick described his thoughts in the following way:

In Question C of Problem 3.3, we looked at what happens to the cost per student when we double the number of students. Bill said that the per-student cost is cut in half. The cost per student when 20 students go is $37.50. If 40 students go, the cost per student would be $18.75.

When the number of students doubles from 40 to 80, the cost is cut in half again. This makes sense because you spread the cost among twice as many people, so each person pays half as much.

Then Jen asked, "What would happen if we tripled the number of students?" Bill explained that the cost per student would be one third as much. The cost per student when 20 students go is $37.50, so the cost per student if 60 students go is one third of $37.50, which is $12.50.

Common Core Standards for Mathematical Practice

MP3 Construct viable arguments and critique the reasoning of others.

- What other Mathematical Practices can you identify in Nick's reasoning?

- Describe a Mathematical Practice that you and your classmates used to solve a different Problem in this Investigation.

Investigation 4

Variability and Associations in Numerical Data

When playing basketball, it helps to be tall and to have long arms. The average player in the National Basketball Association is more than 6 feet 7 inches tall.

- How rare do you think it is for a man to be as tall as those average NBA players?
- Do you think height and arm span are closely related variables for NBA players?
- Do you think height and arm span are closely related variables for students in your class?

Working on the Problems in this Investigation will help you understand how to measure variability and associations of data values.

....

Common Core State Standards

8.SP.A.1 Construct and interpret scatter plots for bivariate measurement data to investigate patterns of association between two quantities. Describe patterns such as clustering, outliers, positive or negative association, linear association, and nonlinear association.

8.SP.A.2 . . . For scatter plots that suggest a linear association, informally fit a straight line, and informally assess the model fit by judging the closeness of the data points to the line.

8.SP.A.3 Use the equation of a linear model to solve problems in the context of bivariate measurement data, interpreting the slope and intercept.

Also 8.EE.B.5, 8.EE.C.7, 8.F.A.1, 8.F.A.3, 8.F.B.4, 8.F.B.5, S-ID.A.2, S-ID.B.6, S-ID.B.6b, S-ID.C.7, S-ID.C.8, and S-ID.C.9

4.1 Vitruvian Man
Relating Body Measurements

More than 2,000 years ago, a Roman architect and writer named Vitruvius found patterns by relating two body measurements. He claimed a person's arm span is equal to his or her height.

- Do you think the relationship between arm span and height applies to the students in your class?

- How would you display and analyze data collected to test the claim made by Vitruvius?

Problem 4.1

The table shows the height and arm span of students in a CMP class.

Height (in.)	56	57	57	58	59	60	60	60	62	64	64	66	67	67	67	68
Arm span (in.)	54	57	54	61	56	58	59	60	62	63	62	62	65	67	69	67

Do you think the data support the claim that arm span and height are about equal?

A Analyze the data to test your ideas.

1. Plot the (height, arm span) data on a coordinate graph. The resulting graph is called a **scatter plot**.

2. Do you think the scatter plot supports the claim that arm span and height are about equal for most people?

continued on the next page >

Problem 4.1 *continued*

3. If each student in the class had arm span *s* equal to height *h*, what equation would relate the two variables?

   a. Graph the equation on your scatter plot.

   b. Which data points (if any) does your line pass through? Explain how arm span and height are related in those points.

   c. Choose several data points that are not on your line. Explain how arm span and height are related in each case. How do you describe the relationship shown on the graph?

B The tallest person in recorded history was Robert Pershing Wadlow. At age 22, he was 8 feet 11.1 inches (272 cm) tall. His arm span was 9 feet 5.75 inches (289 cm).

   1. Where would you plot the point (height, arm span) for Robert Wadlow? Would the point be *on*, *above*, or *below* the line you drew in Question A, part (3)?

   2. Does the data point for Robert Wadlow support the claim that arm span and height are roughly equal?

C The accuracy of fit for a linear model is measured by calculating errors from the model. These errors, called **residuals,** are the differences between the actual data and what the model predicts.

   1. Find the arm span residuals (actual arm span − predicted arm span) using the model $s = h$ for the CMP class data.

Height (inches)	56	57	57	58	59	60	60	60	62	64	64	66	67	67	67	68
Arm span (inches)																
Actual	54	57	54	61	56	58	59	60	62	63	62	62	65	67	69	67
Predicted by Model	56	57	57	58	59	60	60	60	62	64	64	66	67	67	67	68
Residual	−2	0	−3	▪	▪	▪	▪	▪	▪	▪	▪	▪	▪	▪	▪	▪

   2. To see if there is any pattern in the residuals it helps to plot the (height, residual) data. Use such a plot and data in the table to describe the pattern (if any) in the residuals. Then explain why you think the equation $s = h$ is or is not an accurate model for predicting arm span from height.

continued on the next page >

Problem 4.1 *continued*

D The dinosaur *Tyrannosaurus rex* grew to 20 feet in height with an arm span of about 10 feet.

    1. Do you think the *T. rex* data point fits the pattern that arm span and height are roughly equal? Explain.

    2. If you plot the data point, would it be *on*, *above*, or *below* the line you drew in Question A, part (3)?

A C E Homework starts on page 96.

4.2 Older and Faster
Negative Correlation

Magnolia Elementary is a school with students who are 5 to 14 years old. One field day, all students were timed in a 100-meter race. The table shows data for some of the students.

Student Age (years)	5	5	6	8	8	8	9	9	10	10	10	11	11	12	13	13	14
Race Time (seconds)	25	22	23	18	16	17	15	16	17	20	14	15	13	14	17	12	13

The graph below shows the data from the table and a line that models the data.

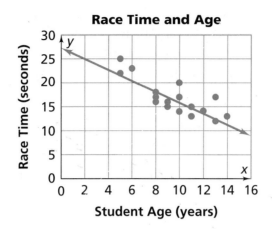

Race Time and Age

• How would you describe the relationship between age and race time?

• Would you say the relationship is *strong* or *weak*?

• Are the data points close to the line or spread out?

Problem 4.2

Use the Race Time and Age graph.

A The line drawn on the graph models the relationship between age and race time.

1. What is the approximate slope of the line?

2. How does the slope help you understand the relationship between age and race time?

3. Do you think it makes sense to predict a race time for a 7-year-old student using the line? If so, what do you predict for a 7-year-old? How confident are you in your prediction?

4. Do you think it makes sense to predict a race time for a 21-year-old person using the line? If so, what do you predict for a 21-year-old? How confident are you in your prediction?

continued on the next page >

Problem 4.2 *continued*

B Some data points are very close to the line while others are far from it. The points far from the line don't seem to fit the model.

1. Find two points that don't seem to fit the model. What are their coordinates (age, race time)?

2. Why do you think the points don't match the overall pattern? Explain. Think about the relationship between race time and age.

3. In Problem 4.1, you used a line to model (height, arm span).

   a. If a 6-foot-9-inch NBA basketball player has a 7-foot-5-inch arm span, would that data point fit the model?

   b. Would you plot the data point, *on*, *above*, or *below* the $s = h$ line? Explain.

C The table and graph show age and grade point average (GPA) for 14 students at Magnolia High School.

Student Age (years)	14	14	14	15	15	15	15	16	16	17	17	17	18	18
GPA	2.5	3.2	3.8	1.8	2.6	3.7	1.2	1.6	3.9	2.0	3.4	3.5	1.9	3.0

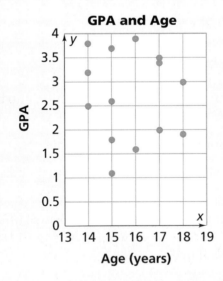

GPA and Age

1. Are age and GPA strongly related for these students? Explain.

2. How is your answer to part (1) supported by the table?

3. How is your answer to part (1) supported by the scatter plot?

A C E Homework starts on page 96.

4.3 Correlation Coefficients and Outliers

Roller coasters are popular rides at amusement parks. A recent survey counted 1,797 roller coaster rides in the world. 734 of them are in North America. Roller coasters differ in maximum drop, maximum height, track length, ride time, and coaster type (wood or steel).

• Which roller coaster variables do you think are strongly related to the top speed on the ride?

Problem 4.3

Statisticians measure the strength of a linear relationship between two variables using a number called the **correlation coefficient.** This number is a decimal between −1 and 1. When the points lie close to a straight line, the correlation coefficient is close to −1 or 1.

continued on the next page >

Problem 4.3 *continued*

- When points cluster close to a line with positive slope, the correlation coefficient is almost 1, and with negative slope, the correlation coefficient is almost −1.

- Points that do not cluster close to any line have a correlation coefficient of almost 0.

- Positive association has correlation coefficients greater than 0 while negative association has correlation coefficients less than 0.

A   **1.** The graph below has a correlation coefficient of 1.0. What do you think a correlation coefficient of 1.0 means?

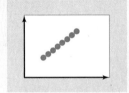

2. Which of the six scatter plots below (a)–(f) has a correlation coefficient of −1.0? What do you think a correlation coefficient of −1.0 means?

a.
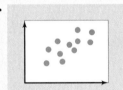

b.
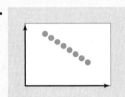

c.
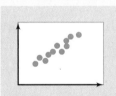

d.
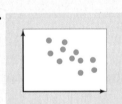

e.
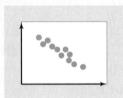

f.
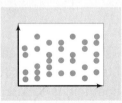

3. Match correlation coefficients −0.8, −0.4, 0.0, 0.4, and 0.8 with the other five scatter plots. Explain your reasoning.

continued on the next page >

Problem 4.3 continued

When you inspect a scatter plot, often you are looking for a strong association between the variables.

B The scatter plot below shows the relationship between the top speed of a roller coaster and its maximum drop. The pink dots represent wood-frame roller coasters. The blue dots represent steel-frame coasters.

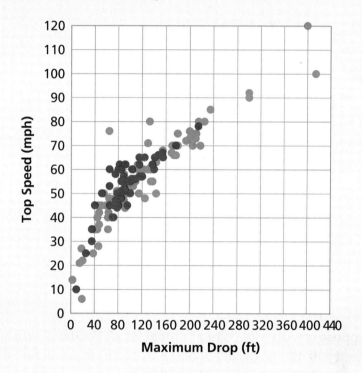

1. Suppose you drew one linear model for all the data in the graph. Could you use the model to make an accurate prediction about the top speed of the roller coaster with a given maximum drop? Explain.

2. Estimate the correlation coefficient for the top speed and the maximum drop. Is the correlation coefficient closest to −1, −0.5, 0, 0.5, or 1?

3. Is the maximum drop of a roller coaster likely to be one of the causes of the top speed of the coaster? Why or why not?

continued on the next page >

Problem **4.3**   *continued*

C The scatter plot below shows the relationship between the top speed of a roller coaster and its track length. The pink dots represent wood-frame roller coasters. The blue dots represent steel-frame coasters.

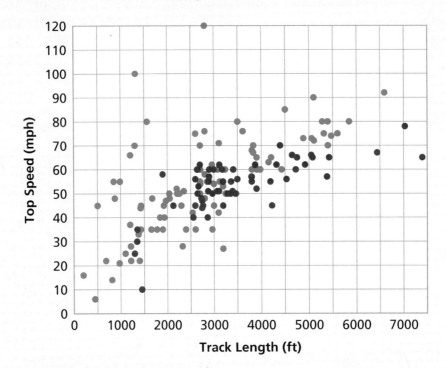

1. Suppose you drew one linear model for all the data in the graph. Could you use the model to make an accurate prediction about the top speed of the roller coaster with a given track length? Explain.

2. Estimate the correlation coefficient for the top speed and track length. Is the correlation coefficient closest to −1, −0.5, 0, 0.5, or 1?

3. Is the track length of a roller coaster likely to be one of the causes of the top speed of the coaster? Why or why not?

4. Computer and calculator data analysis tools can take data pairs like those plotted above and calculate exact correlation coefficients. Use the tool that you have available to find the correlation coefficient for the sample of (track length, top speed) data in the table.

Track Length (ft)	500	1,000	1,500	2,000	2,500	3,000	3,500	4,000	4,500	5,000
Top Speed (mph)	5	20	45	50	40	50	55	60	85	65

continued on the next page >

Problem 4.3 continued

D The scatter plot below shows the relationship between the top speed of a roller coaster and the ride time. The pink dots represent wood-frame roller coasters. The blue dots represent steel-frame coasters.

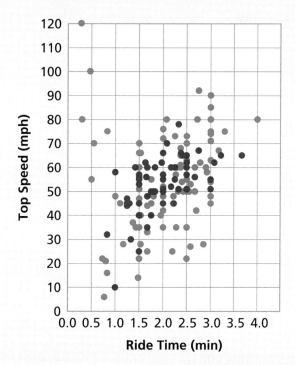

1. Suppose you drew one linear model for all the data in the graph. Could you use the model to make an accurate prediction about the top speed of the roller coaster with a given ride time? Explain.

2. Estimate the correlation coefficient for the top speed and ride time. Is the correlation coefficient closest to −1, −0.5, 0, 0.5, or 1?

3. Suppose most of the points on a scatter plot cluster near a line, with only a few that don't fit the pattern. The points that lie outside a cluster are called **outliers.** Use the graph above. Find each point. Then decide whether the point is an outlier. If it is, explain why you think it is an outlier.

   a. (1.75, 50)   **b.** (0.30, 80)   **c.** (3.35, 75)

   d. (0.28, 120)   **e.** (0.80, 21)   **f.** (1.0, 10)

   g. Use the scatter plot in Question C. Find two outliers on that graph and estimate their coordinates (track length, top speed).

continued on the next page >

Problem **4.3** *continued*

E The scatter plot shows the number of roller coaster riders and their ages on a given day. The pink dots represent wood-frame roller coasters. The blue dots represent steel-frame coasters.

On that day, forty-four 15-year-olds rode one of the roller coasters. The data point is (15, 44).

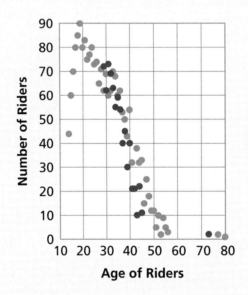

1. Suppose you drew one linear model for all the data in the graph. Could you use the model to make an accurate prediction about the number of riders on the roller coaster with a given age? Explain.

2. Is the age of riders on a roller coaster likely to be one of the causes of the number of riders on the coaster? Why or why not?

3. Estimate the correlation coefficient for the number of riders and age of riders. Is the correlation coefficient closest to −1, −0.5, 0, 0.5, or 1?

4. Are any of the data points outliers? If so, estimate the coordinates of those points.

F Is it possible to have a correlation coefficient close to −1 or 1 with only a few outliers? Explain your thinking.

A **C** **E** Homework starts on page 96.

4.4 Measuring Variability
Standard Deviation

A height of 6 feet 7 inches is unusual for an adult man.

- What height would make an eighth-grade boy or girl above average?

You can use range and interquartile range to describe how data values in a sample vary. You can also use the mean absolute deviation (MAD) to measure the spread of data values. This problem reviews those measures and introduces a measure of spread called *standard deviation*.

Problem 4.4

The table shows the heights of several CMP students. You used this information in Problem 4.1.

Height (in.)	56	57	57	58	59	60	60	60	62	64	64	66	67	67	67	68

A Make a line plot to show the distribution of the data.

B Calculate the summary statistics below, and explain what each number says about the distribution of heights.

   1. Range

   2. Mean

   3. Mean Absolute Deviation (MAD)

continued on the next page >

Problem **4.4** *continued*

C Like the MAD, you calculate the **standard deviation** of a data set from the differences between data values and the mean. To calculate the standard deviation for the height data, complete each part below.

1. Find the difference of each data value and the mean. In the table below, for example, Jayne's height is 56 inches and the mean is 62 inches. The difference is $(56 - 62) = -6$. Copy the table and complete the middle row with the differences.

2. Square each difference. For example, for Jayne's height, $(-6)^2 = 36$. Complete the third row with the squares of the differences.

Jayne's height

Height (inches)	56	57	57	58	59	60	60	60	62	64	64	66	67	67	67	68
Height − Mean	−6	−5	−5	−4												
Squares of differences	36	25														

Square the difference.

3. Next, sum the squared differences and divide by $(n - 1)$, the number of data values minus 1. This number is called the **variance** of the distribution.

   a. Add the squared differences: $36 + 25 + \ldots + 36 = $ ▪

   b. Divide by $(n - 1)$, the number of students minus one: $16 - 1 = 15$

   c. The variance is ▪.

4. The square root of a number n is written in symbols as $\sqrt{n}$. It is the positive number you multiply by itself to equal n. For example, $\sqrt{25} = 5$ and $\sqrt{6.25} = 2.5$.

   Take the square root of the variance. This number is the standard deviation of the distribution of heights.

continued on the next page >

Problem 4.4 *continued*

D Each dot plot shows the distribution, mean, and standard deviation of heights of 20 athletes. The 20 athletes are a random sample.

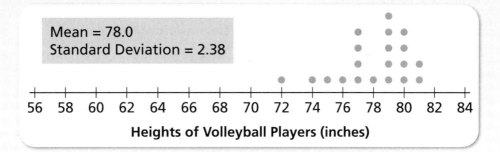

Mean = 78.0
Standard Deviation = 2.38

Heights of Volleyball Players (inches)

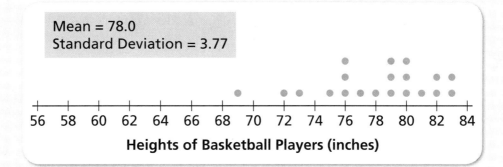

Mean = 78.0
Standard Deviation = 3.77

Heights of Basketball Players (inches)

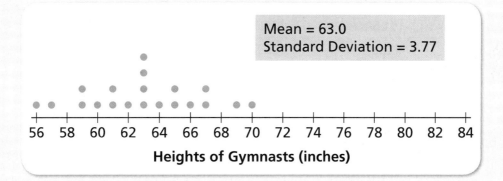

Mean = 63.0
Standard Deviation = 3.77

Heights of Gymnasts (inches)

1. Compare the heights of volleyball players with the heights of basketball players. What can you say about the similarities and differences using the dot plots?

2. Compare the gymnasts with the basketball players. What can you say about the similarities and differences using the dot plots?

A C E Homework starts on page 96.

Applications

For Exercises 1 and 2, use the table below. It shows the height and stride distance for 10 students.

For humans, walking is the most basic form of transportation. An average person is able to walk at a pace of about 3 miles per hour.

The distance a person covers in one step depends on his or her stride. To measure stride distance, measure from the heel of the first foot to the heel of that same foot on the next step.

Height (cm)	Stride Distance (cm)
150.8	125.2
149.5	124.2
151.2	125.2
153.1	126.8
150.6	124.4
149.9	123.8
146.5	121.8
146.5	120.8
151.5	125.6
153.5	126.8

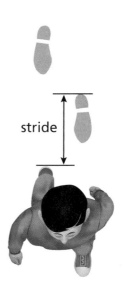

stride

1. **a.** What is the median height of these students? Explain how you found the median.

   b. What is the median stride distance of these students? Explain how you found the median.

   c. What is the ratio of median height to median stride distance? Explain.

2. a. Draw a coordinate graph with height (in centimeters) on the horizontal axis and stride distance (in centimeters) on the vertical axis. To choose a scale for each axis, look at the greatest and least values of each measure.

   b. Explain how you can use your graph to determine whether the shortest student also has the shortest stride distance.

   c. Describe how to estimate the heights of people with each stride distance.

   i. 1.50 meters   **ii.** 0.90 meters   **iii.** 1.10 meters

3. In Problem 4.1 you explored the relationship between arm span and height. The scatter plot below shows data for another group of middle school students.

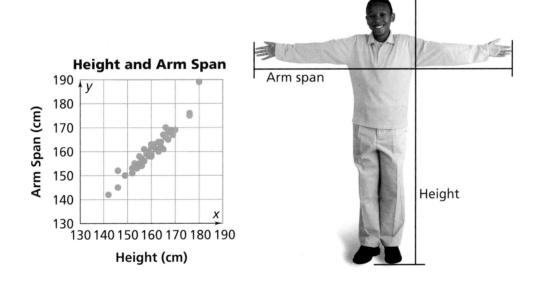

a. Draw a model line from (130, 130) to (190, 190) on your scatter plot.

b. Use the line to describe the relationship between height and arm span.

c. Write an equation for the line using *h* for height and *a* for arm span.

d. What is true about the relationship between height and arm span for points in each part of the graph?

   i. points on the model line

   ii. points above the model line

   iii. points below the model line

4. a. Make a scatter plot from the table. To keep track of engine type, use two different colors as you plot the points. Use one color for jet engines and one color for propeller engines.

Airplane Comparisons

Plane	Engine type	Body length (m)	Wingspan (m)
Boeing 707	jet	47	44
Boeing 747	jet	71	60
Ilyushin IL-86	jet	60	48
McDonnell Douglas DC-8	jet	57	45
Antonov An-124	jet	69	73
British Aerospace 146	jet	29	26
Lockheed C-5 Galaxy	jet	76	68
Antonov An-225	jet	84	88
Airbus A300	jet	54	45
Airbus A310	jet	46	44
Airbus A320	jet	38	34
Boeing 737	jet	33	29
Boeing 757	jet	47	38
Boeing 767	jet	49	48
Lockheed Tristar L-1011	jet	54	47
McDonnell Douglas DC-10	jet	56	50
Douglas DC-4 C-54 Skymaster	propeller	29	36
Douglas DC-6	propeller	32	36
Lockheed L-188 Electra	propeller	32	30
Vickers Viscount	propeller	26	29
Antonov An-12	propeller	33	38
de Havilland DHC Dash-7	propeller	25	28
Lockheed C-130 Hercules/L-100	propeller	34	40
British Aerospace 748/ATP	propeller	26	31
Convair 240	propeller	24	32
Curtiss C-46 Commando	propeller	23	33
Douglas DC-3	propeller	20	29
Grumman Gulfstream I/I-C	propeller	19	24
Ilyushin IL-14	propeller	22	32
Martin 4-0-4	propeller	23	28
Saab 340	propeller	20	21

SOURCE: Airport Airplanes

b. Use your results from Exercise 3. Does your equation for the relationship between height and arm span also describe the relationship between body length and wingspan for airplanes? Explain.

c. Predict the wingspan of an airplane with a body length of 40 meters.

d. Predict the body length of an airplane with a wingspan of 60 meters.

5. The scatter plot below shows the relationship between body length and wingspan for different birds.

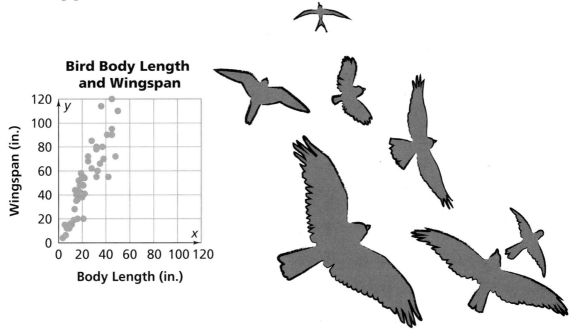

a. Use your results from Exercise 3. Does your equation for the relationship between height and arm span also describe the relationship between body length and wingspan for birds? Explain.

b. Find a line that fits the overall pattern of points in the scatter plot. What is the equation of your line?

c. Predict the wingspan of a bird with a body length of 60 inches. Explain your reasoning.

6. a. The table shows math and science test scores for 10 students. Make a scatter plot of the data.

Student	1	2	3	4	5	6	7	8	9	10
Math	67	51	87	36	56	44	72	63	45	93
Science	71	69	85	35	60	47	74	63	46	96

b. Describe the relationship between the math and science scores.

c. If the data are linear, sketch a line that fits the data.

d. Identify any data values that you think are outliers. Explain why they are outliers.

e. Estimate a correlation coefficient for the data. Is it closest to −1, −0.5, 0, 0.5, or 1? Explain your choice.

7. a. The table shows math scores and distances from home to school for 10 students. Make a scatter plot of the data.

Student	1	2	3	4	5	6	7	8	9	10
Math Score	67	51	87	36	56	44	72	63	45	93
Distance from home to school (miles)	0.6	1.7	0.3	2.2	3.1	0.25	2.6	1.5	0.75	2.1

b. Describe the relationship between the math score and distance from home to school.

c. Estimate a correlation coefficient for the data. Is it closest to −1, −0.5, 0, 0.5, or 1? Explain your choice.

8. a. The table shows the number of servers and average time to fill an order at fast-food restaurants. Make a scatter plot of the data.

Number of Servers	3	4	5	6	7
Average Time to Fill an Order (min)	0.6	1.7	0.3	2.2	3.1

   b. Describe the relationship between the number of servers and average time to fill an order.

   c. Identify any data values that you think are outliers. Explain why they are outliers.

   d. Estimate a correlation coefficient for the data. Is it closest to -1, -0.5, 0, 0.5, or 1? Explain your choice.

9. a. The table shows the number of absences from school and math scores. Make a scatter plot of the data.

   b. Describe the relationship between the number of absences and math scores.

   c. If the data are linear, write an equation for a line that models the data.

   d. Estimate a correlation coefficient for the data. Is it closest to -1, -0.5, 0, 0.5, or 1? Explain your choice.

Absences	Math Scores
3	67
5	49
1	96
1	82
3	79
7	37
5	71
3	55
0	100
8	34
7	46
2	69
10	32
0	94
6	53
6	41
2	90
0	92
5	60
7	50
11	10
1	80

Students collected height measurements from two eighth-grade classes. The measurements are in centimeters.

10. Use the dot plot, data, and summary statistics of height measurements from Class 2 below. Describe the distribution of heights in this class.

Class 2: 130, 132, 132, 137, 137, 138, 138, 138, 139, 139, 139, 145, 146, 147, 147, 147, 147, 150, 152, 153, 155, 156, 163

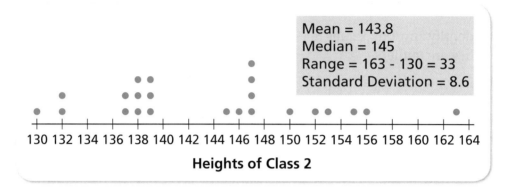

Mean = 143.8
Median = 145
Range = 163 - 130 = 33
Standard Deviation = 8.6

130 132 134 136 138 140 142 144 146 148 150 152 154 156 158 160 162 164

Heights of Class 2

11. a. The data below show heights from another class of eighth graders. Make a dot plot of the data below.

Class 1: 130, 132, 134, 135, 136, 136, 137, 138, 138, 138, 139, 139, 139, 140, 140, 141, 142, 142, 142, 142, 143, 147, 148

b. Calculate the mean, median, range, and standard deviation of the distribution.

c. Use information from parts (a) and (b) to describe the distribution of heights.

d. Compare the distribution of heights in this class to that of the class in Exercise 10.

e. Could you use either distribution to predict the typical height for eighth-graders? Explain your thinking.

12. Use data sets A, B, and C.

$$Set\ A = \{9, 10, 11, 7, 13\}$$
$$Set\ B = \{10, 10, 10, 10, 10\}$$
$$Set\ C = \{1, 1, 10, 19, 19\}$$

a. Calculate the mean of each data set.

b. Calculate the standard deviation of each data set.

c. Explain how you could identify the data set with the greatest standard deviation before doing any calculations.

13. The table shows the monthly salaries of 20 people.

Number of People	5	8	5	2
Salary (dollars)	3,500	4,000	4,200	4,300

   a. Calculate the mean of the salaries.

   b. Calculate the standard deviation of the salaries.

Connections

14. The table shows height, arm span, and the ratio of arm span to height.

   a. Recall Problem 4.1 and the line $s = h$. Where would you find a point with a ratio greater than 1 (*on*, *above*, or *below* the line)? What does it mean when the ratio is greater than 1?

   b. For the line $s = h$, where would you find a point with a ratio equal to 1 (*on*, *above*, or *below* the line)? What does it mean when the ratio equals 1?

   c. For the line $s = h$, where would you find a point with a ratio less than 1 (*on*, *above*, or *below* the line)? What does it mean when the ratio is less than 1?

Height (inches)	Arm Span (inches)	Ratio of Arm Span to Height
172	169	0.98
167	163	0.98
163	164	1.01
162	164	1.01
163	159	0.97
164	158	0.96
161	159	0.99
161	155	0.96
159	161	1.01
156	156	1.00
154	162	1.05
154	157	1.02
154	156	1.01
155	150	0.97
155	154	0.99
177	174	0.98
171	172	1.01
149	144	0.97
143	148	1.03
142	142	1.00

15. Multiple Choice In testing two new sneakers, the shoe designers judged performance by measuring the heights of jumps. Now a shoe designer needs to choose the better sneaker. Which measure is best for deciding between the two sneakers? Use the graph for each sneaker.

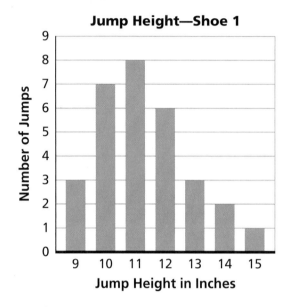

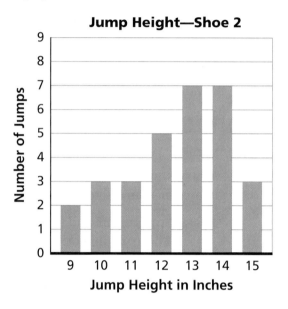

A. Use the mode. The most frequent height jumped for Shoe 1 was 11 inches, and the most frequent height jumped for Shoe 2 was 13 or 14 inches.

B. Use the mean. The average jump height for Shoe 1 was 11 inches. For Shoe 2, it was 12.5 inches.

C. Use clusters. Overall, 70% of the students jumped 10 inches to 12 inches in Shoe 1, and the data vary from 9 inches to 15 inches. About 63% of the students jumped 12 inches to 14 inches in Shoe 2, and the data vary from 9 inches to 15 inches.

D. None of the above.

16. a. What is the shape of a distribution when the mean is greater than the median?

b. What is the shape of a distribution when the mean is less than the median?

c. What is the shape of a distribution when the mean and the median are about the same value?

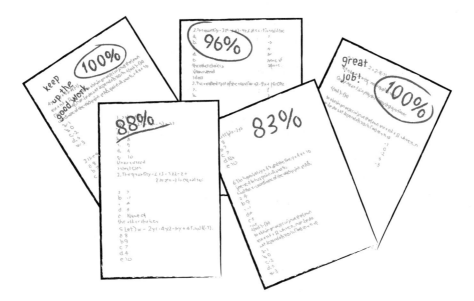

17. **Multiple Choice** Del Kenya's test scores are 100, 83, 88, 96, and 100. His teacher told the class that they could choose whichever measure of center they wanted her to use to determine final grades. Which measure do you think Del Kenya should choose?

    F. Mean   **G.** Median   **H.** Mode   **J.** Range

18. **Multiple Choice** Five packages with a mean weight of 6.7 pounds were shipped by the Send-It-Quick Mail House. If the mean weight for four of these packages is 7.2 pounds, what is the weight of the fifth package?

    A. 3.35 lb   **B.** 4.7 lb   **C.** 6.95 lb   **D.** 8.7 lb

19. **Multiple Choice** In Mr. Mamer's math class, there are three times as many girls as boys. The girls' mean grade on a recent quiz was 90, and the boys' mean grade was 86. What was the mean grade for the entire class?

    F. 88   **G.** 44   **H.** 89   **J.** 95

20. Some numbered cards are put in a hat, and one is drawn at random. There is an even number of cards, no two of which are alike. How many cards might be in the hat to give the probability equal to the following values of choosing a number greater than the median?

    a. $\frac{1}{2}$ **b.** $\frac{1}{3}$ **c.** 0

Extensions

21. If you know the number of chirps a cricket makes in a certain period of time, you can estimate the temperature in degrees Fahrenheit or Celsius.

   a. Count the number of chirps in one minute, divide by 4, and add 40 to get the temperature in degrees Fahrenheit. Write a formula using F for temperature and s for chirps per minute.

   b. Graph your formula. Use a temperature scale from 0 to 212° F.

   c. Use your graph to estimate the number of chirps at each temperature.

     i. 0° F   **ii.** 50° F   **iii.** 100° F   **iv.** 212° F

22. **a.** The chirp frequency of a different kind of cricket allows you to estimate temperatures in degrees Celsius rather than in degrees Fahrenheit. Graph the data in the table.

Frequency	195	123	212	176	162	140	119	161	118	175	161	171	164	174	144
Temperature (°C)	31.4	22	34.1	29.1	27	24	20.9	27.8	20.8	28.5	26.4	28.1	27	28.6	24.6

   b. Find a formula that lets you predict the temperature in degrees Celsius from the number of chirps.

   c. Use your formula from part (b) to draw a line on the graph using the points plotted in part (a). How well does the line fit the data?

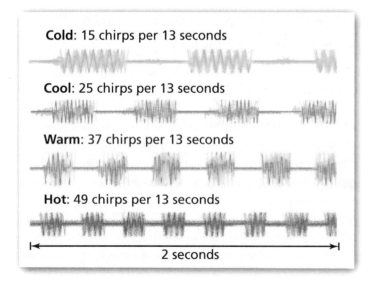

Cold: 15 chirps per 13 seconds

Cool: 25 chirps per 13 seconds

Warm: 37 chirps per 13 seconds

Hot: 49 chirps per 13 seconds

2 seconds

23. A newspaper article said students carry heavy backpacks. One middle school class decided to check whether the claim was true. Each student estimated the weight of his or her backpack and then weighed it. The scatter plot shows the estimated and actual backpack weights for each student. The dot plots show the distributions for each variable with their mean.

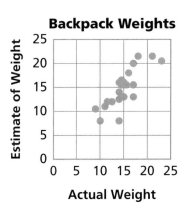

Backpack Weights

a. Use the statistics in the box to describe the spread of the estimated backpack weights.

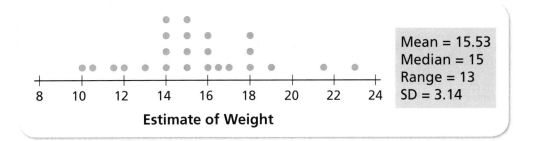

Mean = 15.53
Median = 15
Range = 13
SD = 3.14

Estimate of Weight

b. Use the statistics in the box to describe the spread of the actual backpack weights.

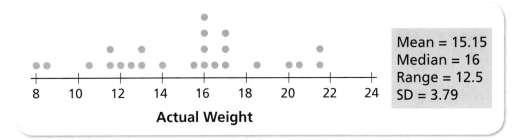

Mean = 15.15
Median = 16
Range = 12.5
SD = 3.79

Actual Weight

c. Estimate a correlation coefficient for the scatter plot. Is it closest to −1, −0.5, 0, 0.5, or 1? Explain your choice.

24. A group of students estimated, and then counted, the number of seeds in several pumpkins. The two tables show the same data sorted differently: One shows the data sorted by actual count and the other by estimate.

Number of Pumpkin Seeds Sorted by Actual Count

Actual	Estimate
309	630
325	621
336	1,423
354	1,200
365	1,200
367	621
381	801
384	604
387	1,900
387	1,100
408	605
410	622
423	759
441	655
442	300
446	621
455	722
462	556
467	621
479	900
486	680
492	1,000
494	564
498	1,458
505	720
506	624
507	200
512	500
523	350
545	2,000
553	202
568	766
606	521
607	1,200

Number of Pumpkin Seeds Sorted by Estimate

Actual	Estimate
507	200
553	202
442	300
523	350
512	500
606	521
462	556
494	564
384	604
408	605
325	621
367	621
446	621
467	621
410	622
506	624
309	630
441	655
486	680
505	720
455	722
423	759
568	766
381	801
479	900
492	1,000
387	1,100
354	1,200
365	1,200
607	1,200
336	1,423
498	1,458
387	1,900
545	2,000

a. How do the actual counts vary? Find the median, the least, and the greatest counts.

b. How do the estimates vary? Find the median, the least, and the greatest estimates.

c. Make a scatter plot of the data. Draw a line on the graph to connect the points (0, 0), (250, 250), (500, 500), and (2250, 2250). What is true about the estimates and actual counts for points near the line?

d. What is true about the estimates and actual counts for points *above* the line you graphed in part (c)?

e. What is true about the estimates and actual counts for points *below* the line you graphed in part (c)?

f. In general, did the students make good estimates? Use the median and the range of the data to explain your reasoning.

g. Would a correlation coefficient be closest to −1, −0.5, 0, 0.5, or 1? Explain your choice.

h. One student graphed the data on the scatter plot below. It shows the data bunched together. How could you change the scale(s) on the graph to show the data points better?

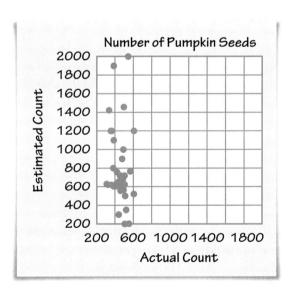

25. **Multiple Choice** Janelle made a scatter plot that shows the relationship between her MP3 music downloads and the unused space on her music player. Which statement would you expect to be true?

A. As the number of MP3s downloaded increases, the amount of unused space increases.

B. As the number of MP3s downloaded increases, the amount of unused space stays the same.

C. As the number of MP3s downloaded increases, the amount of unused space decreases.

D. As the number of MP3s downloaded decreases, the amount of space used decreases.

26. **a.** The graph shows a model of the relationship between pumpkin circumference and pumpkin weight. How does the graph suggest that the linear equation $w = c$ would not be a very accurate model for the relationship of weight and circumference?

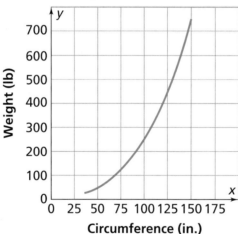

Pumpkin Measurements

Weight (lb) vs. Circumference (in.)

b. Which of the following functions would you expect to express the relationship between pumpkin circumference and pumpkin weight? Explain your choice.

$$w = kc \qquad w = kc^2 \qquad w = kc^3 \qquad w = \frac{k}{c}$$

Mathematical Reflections 4

In this Investigation, you studied data tables and graphs to discover and test the relationship between variables. These questions will help you summarize what you have learned.

Think about these questions. Discuss your ideas with other students and your teacher. Then write a summary of your findings in your notebook.

1. **Think** about the pattern of points you see in a scatter plot.

   a. **What** pattern would you expect when two variables are related by a linear model with positive slope?

   b. **What** pattern would you expect when two variables are related by a linear model with negative slope?

   c. **What** would you expect to see in a scatter plot when two variables are unrelated?

2. **You** assessed the accuracy of linear models.

   a. **What** do outliers on a scatter plot indicate?

   b. **What** can you learn from the errors of prediction or residuals?

   c. **What** do you know about a linear model from the correlation coefficient?

3. **What** does the standard deviation tell you about a set of data?

Common Core Mathematical Practices

As you worked on the Problems in this Investigation, you used prior knowledge to make sense of them. You also applied Mathematical Practices to solve the Problems. Think back over your work, the ways you thought about the Problems, and how you used Mathematical Practices.

Sophie described her thoughts in the following way:

In Problem 4.1A, we had fun experimenting with the graph and looking for patterns. When we plotted the points on the scatter plot, we saw a linear pattern that looks like height and arm span are definitely related.

We know that data vary, but we think we can say that the equation $s = h$ is a good way to model this graph. Then we sketched in the line $s = h$.

We saw that some data points are on the line and then others are above or below. If they are above, it means the arm span is greater than the height. If they are below, it means the height is greater than the arm span.

Common Core Standards for Mathematical Practice
MP4 Model with mathematics

- What other Mathematical Practices can you identify in Sophie's reasoning?

- Describe a Mathematical Practice that you and your classmates used to solve a different Problem in this Investigation.

Investigation 5

Variability and Associations in Categorical Data

Early roller coasters had wooden frames. Now, most roller coasters have steel frames, even though wood is still popular. A recent roller coaster census counted 174 wood-frame coasters, with 129 in North America.

How can people compare wood- and steel-frame roller coasters? Wood and steel are types of frames, not numbers. *Type of roller coaster* is what statisticians call a **categorical variable** that has values *wood* and *steel*.

A study comparing popularity of dogs would investigate the categorical variable *breed of dog* with values *standard poodle, Irish setter, German pointer, Chihuahua, whippet,* and so on.

....

Common Core State Standards

8.SP.A.4 Understand that patterns of association can also be seen in bivariate categorical data by displaying frequencies and relative frequencies in a two-way table. Construct and interpret a two-way table summarizing data on two categorical variables collected from the same subjects. Use relative frequencies calculated for rows or columns to describe possible association between the two variables.

Also 8.EE.B.5, 8.EE.C.7, S.ID.B.5 and S.ID.C.9

5.1 Wood or Steel? That's the Question
Relationships in Categorical Data

 To plan a new amusement park, a team of coaster designers asked customers, "Do you prefer wood or steel frames in roller coasters?" The table shows the preferences by age group.

	Prefer Wood	Prefer Steel
Age ≤ 40 years	45	60
Age > 40 years	15	20

less (handwritten, beside Age ≤ 40 years)
more (handwritten, beside Age > 40 years)

? Does it look like younger and older riders have the same preferences in roller coaster type?

Problem 5.1

Study the roller coaster survey data by age of rider. Make a recommendation about the type of coaster that should be installed in the new park.

A Use the survey data. Is each statement *true* or *false*? Explain.

1. Younger riders are three times as likely as older riders to prefer wood-frame coasters.

2. Younger riders are three times as likely as older riders to prefer steel-frame coasters.

3. The number of riders who prefer wood-frame coasters is about three quarters of the number who prefer steel-frame coasters.

4. Younger riders are more likely than older riders to prefer steel-frame coasters.

5. Older riders are more likely than younger riders to prefer wood-frame coasters.

continued on the next page >

Problem 5.1 continued

B Suppose that a park installed one of each type of roller coaster. One day there were 210 riders over the age of 40 and 420 riders under the age of 40. Use the survey data from Question A.

1. How many riders would you expect on the wood-frame coaster and how many on the steel-frame coaster?

2. How would you expect those riders to be distributed by age and coaster type in the following table?

	Prefer Wood	Prefer Steel	Total
Age ≤ 40 years	▪	▪	420
Age > 40 years	▪	▪	210
Total	▪	▪	▪

C If only one roller coaster type could be installed in the park, which would you recommend? Explain your choice.

A C E Homework starts on page 119.

5.2 Politics of Girls and Boys
Analyzing Data in Two-Way Tables

Every four years social studies teachers at the middle school hold a mock election. Each student registers as a Democrat, Independent, or Republican, all of which are categorical data values. Then the classes hold primary and final elections for President.

The table shows the student registrations in one class.

	Democrat	Independent	Republican
Boys	8	4	12
Girls	8	2	6

- Do you think boys and girls have different party preferences?

- What evidence could you give as support?

Problem 5.2

There are different ways to answer the question about political preferences of girls and boys in the sampled class.

A Use the table on the previous page. Do you think each statement is *true* or *false*? Justify your answers.

1. Girls and boys are equally likely to be Democrats.

2. Boys are more likely than girls to be Independents.

3. Boys are more likely than girls to be Republicans.

4. Girls are only half as likely as boys to be Republicans.

B Study the table of party choices and claims about differences between boys and girls. Notice that there are 24 boys and 16 girls in the class.

1. Copy and complete this extended table.

	Democrat	Independent	Republican	Totals
Boys	8	4	12	■
Girls	8	2	6	■
Totals	■	■	■	■

2. Do the totals of political party choices change your answers to Question A? Explain your reasoning.

C One way to compare groups with unequal numbers of members is to compute percents.

1. Copy and complete the table below to show the fractions or percents of boys and girls with each preference.

	Democrat	Independent	Republican
Boys	$\frac{8}{24} = \frac{1}{3} = 33\frac{1}{3}\%$	■	■
Girls	■	■	■

2. Do the percent calculations change your answers to Question A? Explain your reasoning.

A C E Homework starts on page 119.

5.3 After-School Jobs and Homework
Working Backward: Setting up a Two-Way Table

The teachers at the high school did a study to see whether students who had jobs after school were more or less likely to turn in homework on time than students who did not have after-school jobs. Each student was categorized as *usually on time* or *often late* with homework and as *having a job* or *not having a job*. Here are the results.

on time homework and after-school job: ꟷꟷꟷ ꟷꟷꟷ ꟷꟷꟷ (8)

on time homework and no after-school job: ꟷꟷꟷ ꟷꟷꟷ ꟷꟷꟷ ꟷꟷꟷ ꟷꟷꟷ (25)

often late or missing homework and after school job: ꟷꟷꟷ ꟷꟷꟷ ꟷꟷ (12)

often late or missing homework and no after school job: ꟷꟷꟷ ꟷꟷꟷ ꟷꟷꟷ (15)

? Is there evidence that students with after-school jobs are more likely to have late or missing homework than students without after-school jobs?

Problem 5.3

Use the information about the students to answer these questions.

A Make a table to display the data on students and after-school jobs.

B Use your table from Question A. Do you think each statement is *true* or *false*? Justify your answers.

1. Students without after-school jobs are more likely to have late or missing homework than students with after-school jobs.

2. Students with after-school jobs are more likely to have late or missing homework than on-time homework.

3. Students without after-school jobs are three times as likely as students with after-school jobs to have on-time homework.

4. Students with after-school jobs are less likely to have on-time homework than students without after-school jobs.

C 1. The numbers of students with and without after-school jobs are not the same. Rewrite the data in your table as fractions and percents.

2. Do the fractions and percents in your table change your answers to Question B? Explain your reasoning.

D If someone claims that the data and analysis show that after-school jobs cause students to have late or unfinished homework, what alternate explanations would you offer? What do you think could be the cause of late or unfinished homework other than after-school jobs?

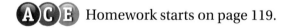 Homework starts on page 119.

Applications

Classify each variable as categorical (C) or numerical (N).

1. number of text messages you send in a day

2. brands of breakfast cereal

3. heights of students in your class

4. daily maximum temperature for your city

5. breeds of dogs

6. number of hours you sleep each night

7. types of flowers available from a florist

8. number of oranges in the 5-lb bags at a supermarket

9. heights of trees that were planted one year ago

10. number of students absent from school each day for one month

List possible categories for each categorical variable.

11. types of cars

12. methods of travel to school

13. types of instruments in an orchestra

14. sports played at school

15. You can analyze data in many ways, using graphs, tables, measures of center, and measures of spread.

Graphs	Tables	Measures of Center	Measures of Spread
bar graphs	frequency table	mean	range
circle graphs	two-way table	median	interquartile range
dot plots		mode	MAD
line plots			SD
histogram			
box plot			
scatter plot			
line graph			

Make a table similar to the one below. Enter the types of graphs, measures of center, and measures of spread you can use with each data type.

What can I use?

Categorical Data	Numerical Data
Graphs:	Graphs:
Measures of center:	Measures of center:
Measures of spread:	Measures of spread:

Exercises 16 and 17 use the survival rate data of men, women, and children on the *Titanic*.

Passenger Category	Saved	Lost
Men	338	1,352
Women	316	109
Children	56	53

16. Which of these claims about survival rates on the *Titanic* are true? Explain your reasoning.

   a. More men than women were saved.

   b. Women were more likely than children to be lost.

   c. Men were about six times as likely to be saved as children.

17. Another way to see whether men, women, and children were lost at the same rate is to find the overall survival rate for all *Titanic* passengers. Use the overall rate to find expected survival counts for each passenger category. Overall, 32% of passengers were saved and 68% lost their lives.

   a. Use the total numbers of men, women, and children on board the *Titanic* and use the overall survival rates. Copy and complete the table below.

Passenger Category	Expected Saved	Expected Lost
Men	▨	▨
Women	▨	▨
Children	▨	▨

   b. Compare the table in part (a) with the data table. Which passenger categories had greater numbers of survivors than you would expect if all categories had the same proportion? Explain.

18. Suppose you are interested in learning about the effects of parents' smoking habits on their adult children. Use the data from the table below.

	Adult children smoke	Adult children do not smoke	Total	Percent of adult children who smoke
Both parents smoke	400	1,380	▪	▪
One parent smokes	416	1,823	▪	▪
Neither parent smokes	188	1,168	▪	▪
Total	▪	▪	▪	▪
Percent of adults with at least one parent who smokes	▪	▪	▪	

a. Copy and complete the table.

b. Find the percent of adult children who smoke in each situation.

   i. both parents smoke

  ii. one parent smokes

 iii. neither parent smokes

c. Draw a bar graph to compare the three percents you found in part (b).

d. Does the table show evidence that if parents smoke, then their adult children are more likely to be smokers? Explain.

e. Does the table show evidence that if only one parent smokes, their adult children are more likely to be smokers? Explain.

f. Does the table show evidence that adult children of nonsmoking parents are smokers? Explain.

19. The table below compares a treatment for rheumatoid arthritis to a placebo. A *placebo* is a treatment that has no medicine. The outcome of the experiment reflects whether individuals showed *no improvement, some improvement,* or *marked improvement* taking either the placebo or the active medicine.

Does the table show evidence that a person given the active treatment is more likely to show at least some improvement than a person given the placebo? Explain.

Treatment	Improvement			
	None	Some	Marked	Total
Active	14 32.6%	7 16.3%	22 51.1%	43
Placebo	28 68.3%	6 14.6%	7 17.1%	41
Total	42	13	29	84

Connections

20. Fifty households on a street were asked which brand of television they owned. The table shows the results from the survey.

TV Brands	A	B	C	D	E	F
TV Owners	9	4	12	8	7	10

a. Draw a horizontal bar graph of the data.

b. Suppose you wanted to use the data to determine buying patterns of people living in the city. Is it possible that this sample is *biased* for particular TV brands? Explain your reasoning.

c. Which measures—mode, median, or mean—would you use to describe the typical television brand owned? Explain.

21. The circle graph shows the results of a survey in which people were asked, "What is your favorite fruit?" The angle of 68° represents 277 people who said their favorite fruit is oranges. Find the sample size used to the nearest 10 people.

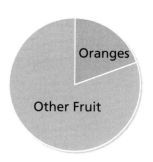

Find the measure of the angle of a circle graph for each frequency.

22. 23 in a sample of 180

23. 128 in a sample of 720

24. 238 in a sample of 1,250

25. A gymnast received scores from five judges in the state competition.

Parallel Bars: 7.6, 8.2, 8.5, 8.2, and 8.9

  a. What happens to the mean of scores when you multiply each data point by 2? By $\frac{2}{3}$? By 0.2?

  b. Why do you think the mean changes like that? Explain.

26. Multiple Choice A store owner keeps a tally of the sizes of shoes bought at her store. Which measure of central tendency best describes the average shoe size sold?

  A. mean   **B.** mode   **C.** median   **D.** range

27. Multiple Choice Suppose all the students who took a math test yesterday scored over 75. Three students missed the test. Their scores are listed as 0 until they take the test. Which measure best represents the data?

  F. mean   **G.** range   **H.** median   **J.** standard deviation

28. Multiple Choice A bag contains red and black chips. The probability of selecting a red chip from the bag is $\frac{1}{4}$. What is the probability of drawing a black chip?

  A. $\frac{1}{4}$ **B.** $\frac{1}{2}$ **C.** $\frac{3}{4}$ **D.** None of these

29. A student scored 40 out of 100 points on this week's test. Her teacher announced that this week's test will be averaged with next week's test. Can the student still get a C if she scores a 100 on next week's test? The lowest C is 70 points. She reasons, "My average will be 70, a C, because half of 40 is 20 and half of 100 is 50 and 20 plus 50 is 70." Does her method always work? Explain.

30. Multiple Choice Which situation can be represented using a scatter plot?

   F. Jennifer keeps a list of the amount of time she spends on her social studies homework each day.

   G. Mr. Jones wants to see if his students' shoe sizes are directly related to their heights.

   H. Mr. DiSanti records his customers' best video game scores during the summer.

   J. Sam keeps track of his algebra grades for the quarter.

31. a. Make a scatter plot of the data in the table below.

Hours at Mall	10	8	9	3	1	2	5	6	7	8	2	3
Dollars Spent	42	14	25	21	9	32	50	60	16	22	100	45

   b. What type of correlation (positive, negative, or zero) exists between the number of hours spent in the mall and the number of dollars spent?

Extensions

32. The triple box plot below shows the distribution of the lifetime (in hours) of three different batteries (low, medium, and high price).

Battery Lifetime by Price

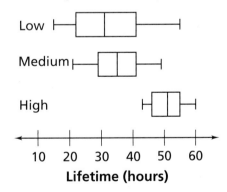

Lifetime (hours)

   a. The two variables in the box plot are *battery lifetime* and *battery price*. Which variable is numerical and which is categorical?

   b. Does the graph support the claim that battery life depends on price? Explain your thinking.

33. Students collected two sets of data, the weight of a student and the weight of the student's backpack, from Grades 1, 3, 5, and 7. Then they computed the ratio of backpack weight to student weight as a percent. The graph below shows the data.

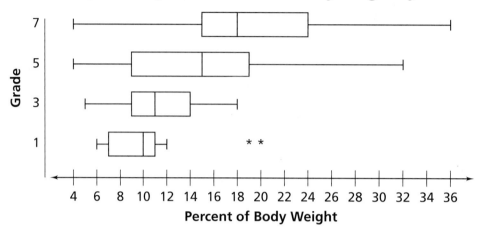

Backpack Weight as a Percent of Body Weight by Grade

a. Which box plot has the greatest interquartile range? What does this tell you about the middle 50% of the backpack weights for that grade compared to the other grades?

b. What is the median of the data for Grade 1? What does this tell you about the data for these students?

c. Suppose that some health officials claim that backpacks should be only 15% of a student's weight. From the graph, are there any grades for which this is *not* the case? If so, which grades? Explain.

d. Do the box plots support the claim that students at higher grades tend to carry heavier backpacks? Explain.

34. A survey of people's favorite colors reported the results below.

Red: 12% **Orange:** 14% **Purple:** 28% **Blue:** 30% **Green:** 16%

a. Make a circle graph and a bar graph to show the results.

b. How do you use percents to make the circle graph? The bar graph?

c. What is the least number of people who could have taken the survey? Explain.

Mathematical Reflections

In this Investigation you analyzed data in two-way tables to find similarities and differences in groups. You learned how to draw accurate conclusions from these data arrays. The following questions will help you summarize what you have learned.

Think about these questions. Discuss your ideas with other students and your teacher. Then write a summary of your findings in your notebook.

1. **What** are categorical variables and what do they measure?

2. **Suppose** a survey asked teenagers and adults whether or not they use text messaging.

   a. **How** could you arrange the data to compare the groups?

   b. **How** would you decide that the two groups—teenagers and adults—were different in their use of text messaging?

   c. **Suppose** that one analysis compared only the numbers in each group—teenage text messager, teenage non-text messager, adult text messager, and adult non-text messager. How might the analysis result in misleading conclusions?

Common Core Mathematical Practices

As you worked on the Problems in this Investigation, you used prior knowledge to make sense of them. You also applied Mathematical Practices to solve the Problems. Think back over your work, the ways you thought about the Problems, and how you used Mathematical Practices.

Tori described her thoughts in the following way:

In Problem 5.1, Question A, we were confused about how to make sense of the data presented in the table showing customers' preferences about which kind of roller coaster they like to ride. The data are grouped in two age categories.

Jen wondered how many customers were surveyed. So we decided to add up columns first. We saw that 60 customers prefer wood coasters and 80 customers prefer steel coasters. Then we added up rows. We saw that there were 105 customers surveyed who were 40 or younger; there were 35 customers who were older than that.

So when we find the total number of preferences separated by kind of coaster, does it equal the total number of customers separated by age? It does! We think 140 customers were surveyed.

Common Core Standards for Mathematical Practice
MP4 Model with mathematics.

- What other Mathematical Practices can you identify in Tori's reasoning?

- Describe a Mathematical Practice that you and your classmates used to solve a different Problem in this Investigation.

Looking Back

While working on the problems in this Unit, you extended your skills in writing equations to express linear relationships. You also learned about a type of nonlinear relationship called an inverse variation. You used inverse and linear relationships to solve problems and make predictions. You learned new ways to measure the spread of a data distribution and the strength of an association between two variables.

Use Your Understanding

Solve the following problems to test your understanding of linear relationships, inverse variation, the correlation coefficient, and standard deviation. These problems are about a park with a small farm, a train, and a snack bar.

1. This table shows the growth of one pig raised on the farm.

Average Growth of a Properly Fed Pig

Age (mo)	0	1	2	3	4	5	6
Weight (lb)	3	48	92	137	182	228	273

SOURCE: Your 4-H Market Hog Project, Iowa State University.

a. Make a graph of the (age, weight) data. Draw a line that fits the data.

b. Find a linear equation in the form $y = mx + b$ for the line in part (a).

c. What do the values of m and b in your equation tell you about the pig's growth?

d. Use your equation to estimate the pig's weight at 3.5 months and at 7 months.

2. A group of students suspect that farm animals eat less when the weather is warm. They asked the farm staff to record the food an adult goat ate on days with different average temperatures.

Food Consumption of a Goat

Average Daily Temperature (°F)	30	40	45	55	60	75	85	90
Food Eaten (kg)	3.9	3.6	3.4	3.0	2.7	2.5	2.2	1.9

a. Make a graph of the (temperature, food eaten) data. Draw a line that fits the data.

b. Find a linear equation in the form $y = mx + b$ for your line in part (a).

c. What do the values of m and b in your equation tell you about the relationship between average daily temperature and the goat's food consumption?

d. Use your equation to predict how much the goat would eat on a day with an average temperature of 50°F and on a day with an average temperature of 70°F.

3. A small train gives visitors rides around the park on a 5,000-meter track. The time the trip takes varies. When many people are waiting in line, the drivers go quickly. When there are fewer people waiting, they go more slowly.

a. Sketch a graph showing how average speed (in meters per minute) changes as the trip time (in minutes) increases from 1 to 10 minutes.

b. For what parts of your graph are the predicted speeds realistic? Explain.

c. Write an equation relating average speed s to trip time t.

d. Write several sentences explaining as accurately as possible how average speed changes as trip time changes. In particular, describe the type of variation in this relationship.

4. The table shows the number of train trips over 10 summer days. Find the standard deviation of the data.

Day	1	2	3	4	5	6	7	8	9	10
Trains	5	8	6	12	15	6	20	12	14	12

5. The next table shows the relationship between the number of train trips and profit at the train station snack bar over 10 summer days.

Day	1	2	3	4	5	6	7	8	9	10
Trains	5	8	6	12	15	6	20	12	14	12
Snack Bar Profit	$40	$85	$55	$110	$165	$65	$190	$125	$130	$125

a. Make a scatter plot of the (number of trains, snack bar profit) data.

b. Estimate the correlation coefficient for the scatter plot. Is the correlation coefficient closest to -1, -0.5, 0, 0.5, or 1? Explain how you chose your estimate.

6. Park operators asked visitors which parts of the park needed improvement. They recorded the suggestions in the table.

	Farm	Playground	Picnic Area
Kids	48	24	8
Adults	30	15	5

a. Do kids and adults have different opinions about what areas of the park need improvement? Use the data to support your answer.

b. Suppose someone claimed that kids value the farm more than adults do. What would you say about that claim?

c. Suppose someone claimed that kids value the playground more than adults do. What would you say about that claim?

English / Spanish Glossary

A additive inverses Two numbers, a and b, that satisfy the equation $a + b = 0$. For example, 3 and -3 are additive inverses, and $\frac{1}{2}$ and $-\frac{1}{2}$ are additive inverses.

inversos de suma Dos números, a y b, que cumplen con la ecuación $a + b = 0$. Por ejemplo, 3 y -3 son inversos de suma, y $\frac{1}{2}$ y $-\frac{1}{2}$ son inversos de suma.

C categorical variables Variables that measure characteristics using words that represent possible responses within a given category. Frequency counts can be made of the values for a given category. The table below shows examples of categories and their possible values.

Category	Possible Values
Month people are born	January, February, March
Favorite color to wear	magenta, blue, yellow
Kinds of pets people have	cats, dogs, fish, horses

variables por categorías Variables que miden características usando "palabras" que representan respuestas posibles en una categoría dada. Se pueden contar las frecuencias de los valores para una categoría dada. La siguiente tabla muestra ejemplos de categorías y sus posibles valores.

Categoría	Valores posibles
Mes de nacimiento de las personas	enero, febrero, marzo
Color preferido para vestir	magenta, azul, amarillo
Tipos de mascotas que tienen las personas	gatos, perros, peces, caballos

correlation coefficient A measure of the strength of a linear relationship between two variables using a decimal number between -1 and 1.

coeficiente de correlación Medida del grado de la relación lineal entre dos variables, usando un número decimal que esté entre -1 y 1.

D **describe** Academic Vocabulary To explain or tell in detail. A written description can contain facts and other information needed to communicate your answer. A diagram or a graph may also be included when you describe something.

related terms *express, explain*

Hours Worked	1	2	3
Total Pay	$5.50	$11.00	$16.50

sample Describe the relationship between hours worked and pay.

The relationship is linear. Total pay varies directly with the number of hours worked. That is, as the number of hours worked increases by one, the pay increases by $5.50. This means that the employee earns $5.50 for each hour worked. I can also draw a graph that shows this relationship.

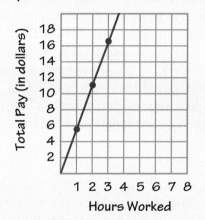

I plotted each point on the graph and I drew one line through all of the points. I can also write an equation, $P = 5.5t$, where P is the amount of money earned and t is the number of hours worked, to represent this relationship.

describir Vocabulario académico Explicar o decir con detalle. Una descripción escrita puede contener datos y otro tipo de información necesaria para comunicar tu respuesta. También puedes incluir un diagrama o una gráfica cuando describes algo.

términos relacionados *expresar, explicar*

Horas trabajadas	1	2	3
Pago total	$5.50	$11.00	$16.50

ejemplo Describe la relación entre las horas trabajadas y el pago recibido.

La relación es lineal. El pago total varía directamente con el número de horas trabajadas. Es decir, a medida que el número de horas trabajadas aumenta en uno, el pago aumenta en $5.50 dólares. Esto significa que el empleado gana $5.50 por cada hora trabajada. También puedo dibujar una gráfica que muestre esta relación.

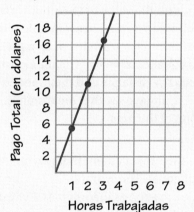

Marqué cada punto en la gráfica y tracé una línea a través de todos los puntos. Para representar estar elación, también puedo escribir una ecuación, $P = 5.5t$, donde P es la cantidad de dinero ganado y tes el número de horas trabajadas.

E **explain** Academic Vocabulary To give facts and details that make an idea easier to understand. Explaining can involve a written summary supported by a diagram, chart, table, or a combination of these.

related terms *analyze, clarify, describe, justify, tell*

sample The equation $c = 75d + 15$ gives the charge c in dollars for renting a car for d days. Explain what the numbers and variables in the equation represent.

> The variable c represents the total amount the customer is charged. The variable d is the number of days the car is rented. 75 is the cost per day of renting the car. 15 is an additional one-time fee for the customer.

explicar Vocabulario académico Dar datos y detalles que hacen que una idea sea más fácil de comprender. Explicar puede implicar hacer un resumen escrito apoyado por un diagrama, una gráfica, una tabla o una combinación de éstos.

términos relacionados *analizar, aclarar, describir, justificar, decir*

ejemplo La ecuación $c = 75d + 15$ da el cargo c en dólares para alquilar un carro por d días. Explica qué representan los números y las variables en la ecuación.

> La variable c representa la cantidad total que se le cobra al cliente. La variable d es el número de días que se alquiló el carro. 75 es el costo de alquilar el carro por día. 15 es un monto adicional que se le cobra al cliente sólo una vez.

F **function** A relationship between two variables in which the value of one variable depends on the value of the other variable. For example, the distance d in miles covered in t hours by a car traveling at 55 mph is given by the equation $d = 55t$. The relationship between the distance and the time is a function, and we say that the distance is a function of the time.

función Una relación entre dos variables en la que el valor de una variable depende del valor de la otra. Por ejemplo, la distancia d recorrida en t horas por un carro que viaja a 55 mph, está representada por la ecuación $d = 55t$. La relación entre la distancia y el tiempo es una función, y decimos que la distancia es una función del tiempo.

I **inequality** A statement that two quantities are not equal. The symbols $>$, $<$, $\geq$, and $\leq$ are used to express inequalities. For example, if a and b are two quantities, then "a is greater than b" is written as $a > b$, and "a is less than b" is written as $a < b$. The statement $a \geq b$ means "a is greater than or equal to b." The statement $a \leq b$ means "a is less than or equal to b."

desigualdad Enunciado que dice que dos cantidades no son iguales. Los símbolos $>$, $<$, $\geq$, y $\leq$ se usan para expresar desigualdades. Por ejemplo, si a y b son dos cantidades, entonces "a es mayor que b" se escribe $a > b$, y "a es menor que b" se escribe $a < b$. El enunciado $a \geq b$ quiere decir "a es mayor que o igual a b". El enunciado $a \leq b$ quiere decir "a es menor que o igual a b."

inverse variation A nonlinear relationship in which the product of two variables is constant. An inverse variation can be represented by an equation of the form $y = \frac{k}{x}$, or $xy = k$, where k is a constant (for $k > 0$). In an inverse variation, the values of one variable decrease as the values of the other variable increase.

variación inversa Una relación no lineal en la que el producto de dos variables es constante. Una variación inversa se puede representar por una ecuación de la forma $y = \frac{k}{x}$, ó $xy = k$, donde k es una constante (por $k > 0$). En una variación inversa, los valores de una variable disminuyen a medida que los valores de la otra variable aumentan.

linear relationship A relationship in which there is a constant rate of change between two variables. A linear relationship can be represented by a straight-line graph and by an equation of the form $y = mx + b$. In the equation, m is the slope of the line, and b is the y-intercept.

relación lineal Una relación en la que hay una tasa de cambio constante entre dos variables. Una relación lineal puede estar representada por una gráfica de línea recta y por una ecuación en la forma $y = mx + b$. En la ecuación, m es la pendiente de la recta y b es el intercepto en y.

M **mathematical model** An equation or a graph that describes, at least approximately, the relationship between two variables. To make a mathematical model, acquire data, plot the data points, and, when the points show a pattern, find the equation of a line or curve that fits the trend in the data. A mathematical model allows you to make reasonable guesses for values between and beyond the data points.

modelo matemático Una ecuación o gráfica que describe, al menos aproximadamente, la relación entre dos variables. Para hacer un modelo matemático es necesario reunir datos, marcar los puntos asociados con los datos y, cuando los puntos muestren un patrón, hallar la ecuación de la línea o curva que se corresponde con la tendencia de los datos. Un modelo matemático te permite hacer predicciones razonables para valores dentro y fuera de los datos obtenidos.

multiplicative inverses Two numbers, a and b, that satisfy the equation $ab = 1$. For example, 3 and $\frac{1}{3}$ are multiplicative inverses, and $-\frac{1}{2}$ and -2 are multiplicative inverses.

inversos multiplicativos Dos números, a y b, que cumplen con la ecuación $ab = 1$. Por ejemplo, 3 y $\frac{1}{3}$ son inversos multiplicativos, y $-\frac{1}{2}$ y -2 son inversos multiplicativos.

O **outlier** A value that lies far from the "center" of a distribution. *Outlier* is a relative term, but it indicates a data point that is much higher or much lower than the values that could be normally expected for the distribution.

valor extremo Valor que se sitúa lejos del "centro" de una distribución. *El valor extremo* es un término relativo, pero indica un dato que es mucho más alto o mucho más bajo que los valores que se podrían esperar normalmente de la distribución.

R **residual** The error calculated by finding the difference between an actual data point and the value that a model for the data predicts.

residuo El error que se calcula hallando la diferencia entre un punto real y el valor que predice el modelo de datos.

S **scatter plot** A graph used to explore the relationship between two variables. The graph below is a scatter plot of (height, arm span) for several people. Each point represents the height and arm span for each person.

diagrama de dispersión Una gráfica que se usa para explorar la relación entre dos variables. La siguiente gráfica muestra un diagrama de dispersión (estatura, envergadura de los brazos extendidos) de varias personas. Cada punto representa la estatura y el espacio entre los brazos extendidos de cada persona.

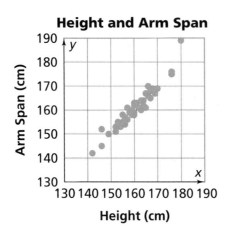

Height and Arm Span

Estatura y envergadura de los brazos extendidos

slope The number that expresses the steepness of a line. The slope is the ratio of the vertical change to the horizontal change between any two points on the line. Sometimes this ratio is referred to as *the rise over the run*. The slope of a horizontal line is 0. Slopes are positive if the y-values increase from left to right on a coordinate grid and negative if the y-values decrease from left to right. The slope of a vertical line is undefined. The slope of a line is the same as the constant rate of change between the two variables. For example, the points $(0, 0)$ and $(3, 6)$ lie on the graph of $y = 2x$. Between these points, the vertical change is 6 and the horizontal change is 3, so the slope is $\frac{6}{3} = 2$, which is the coefficient of x in the equation.

pendiente El número que expresa la inclinación de una recta. La pendiente es la razón entre la variación vertical y la horizontal entre dos puntos cualesquiera de la recta. A veces a esta razón se le denomina *distancia vertical sobre distancia horizontal*. La pendiente de una recta horizontal es 0. Las pendientes son positivas si los valores de y aumentan de izquierda a derecha en una gráfica de coordenadas, y negativas si los valores de y disminuyen de izquierda a derecha. La pendiente de una recta vertical es indefinida. La pendiente de una recta es igual a la tasa de cambio constante entre dos variables. Por ejemplo, los puntos $(0, 0)$ y $(3, 6)$ están representados en la gráfica de $y = 2x$. Entre estos puntos, el cambio vertical es 6 y el cambio horizontal es 3, de manera que la pendiente es $\frac{6}{3} = 2$, que es el coeficiente de x en la ecuación.

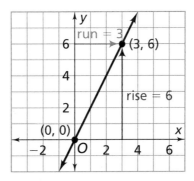

solve Academic Vocabulary To determine the value or values that make a given statement true. Several methods and strategies can be used to solve a problem, including estimating, isolating the variable, drawing a graph, or using a table of values.

related terms *calculate, find*

sample Solve the equation $8x - 16 = 12$ for x.

> I can solve the equation by isolating x on the left side of the equation.
> $8x - 16 = 12$
> $\qquad 8x = 28$
> $\quad x = \dfrac{28}{8} = \dfrac{7}{2} = 3.5$
>
> I can also sketch a graph of $y = 8x - 16$. When $y = 12$, x is between 3 and 4, so I know my solution is reasonable.

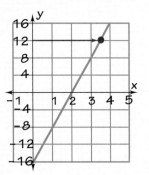

resolver Vocabulario académico Determinar el valor o los valores que hacen cierto un enunciado. Se pueden usar varios métodos y estrategias para resolver un problema incluyendo hacer una estimación, aislar la variable, dibujar una gráfica o usar una tabla de valores.

términos relacionados *calcular, hallar*

ejemplo Resuelve la ecuación $8x - 16 = 12$ para hallar el valor de x.

> Puedo resolver la ecuación aislando x en el lado izquierdo de la ecuación.
> $8x - 16 = 12$
> $\qquad 8x = 28$
> $\quad x = \dfrac{28}{8} = \dfrac{7}{2} = 3.5$
>
> También puedo hacer el bosquejo de una gráfica de $y = 8x - 16$. Cuando $y = 12$, x está entre 3 y 4, por lo tanto sé que mi solución es razonable.

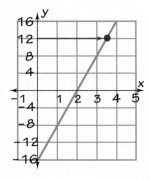

standard deviation Standard deviation measures the spread of a data set. The greater the standard deviation, the greater the spread of the data. To calculate the standard deviation, find the differences between the actual values and the mean. These differences are squared and averaged by dividing by $(n - 1)$. This average is the variance. Take the square root of the variance to get the standard deviation.

desviación estándar La desviación estándar mide la dispersión de un conjunto de datos. Mientras mayor sea la desviación estándar, mayor será la dispersión de los datos. Para calcular la desviación estándar, halla las diferencias entre los valores reales y la media. Estas diferencias se elevan al cuadrado y se promedian dividiendo por $(n - 1)$. Ese promedio es la varianza. Usa la raíz cuadrada de una varianza para obtener la desviación estándar.

U **unit rate** A unit rate is a rate in which the second number (usually written as the denominator) is 1, or 1 of a quantity. For example, 1.9 children per family, 32 miles per gallon, and $\frac{3 \text{ flavors of ice cream}}{1 \text{ banana split}}$ are unit rates. Unit rates are often found by scaling other rates.

tasa por unidad Tasa en la que el segundo número (normalmente escrito como el denominador) es 1, ó 1 de una cantidad. Por ejemplo, 1.9 niños por familia, 32 millas por galón, y $\frac{3 \text{ sabores de helado}}{1 \text{ banana split}}$ son tasas por unidad. Las tasas por unidad se calculan a menudo poniendo a escala otras tasas.

V **variance** Variance is calculated from the differences between the actual value and the mean. These differences are squared and averaged by dividing by $(n - 1)$.

varianza La varianza se calcula a partir de las diferencias entre el valor real y la media. Estas diferencias se elevan al cuadrado y se promedian dividiendo por $(n - 1)$.

Y **y-intercept** The point where the graph crosses the y-axis. In a linear equation of the form $y = mx + b$, the y-intercept is the constant, b. In the graph, the y-intercept is $(0, 2)$ or 2.

intercepto en y El punto en el que la gráfica cruza el eje de las y. En una ecuación lineal de la forma $y = mx + b$, el intercepto en y es la constante, b. En la gráfica, el intercepto en y es $(0, 2)$ ó 2.

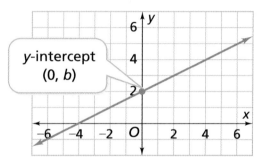

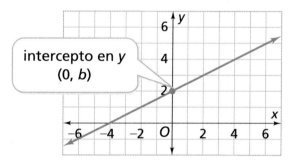

Index

Additive inverse
definition, 73, 132
ACE, 73

Area model
ACE, 20, 24, 27, 57, 77

Ask Yourself, 4, 8, 10, 31, 43, 62, 63, 66, 68, 81, 82, 85, 87, 88, 93, 114, 115, 116

Box plot
ACE, 125–126

Bridge model, 7–14, 68
length, 10, 68
thickness, 7–8
ACE, 15–16, 18–19, 45, 69

Correlation coefficient, 87–92
definition, 87
ACE, 100–101, 107, 109, 125

Cost model, 38–39, 40, 41–42, 66–67
ACE, 46, 48, 57–58, 76, 77

Diagram, 5–6, 35, 133–134

Did You Know?, 14

Direct variation
definition, 75
ACE, 75

Dot plot, 93–95
ACE, 102, 107, 120

Engineering model
bridge model, 7–14
medal platform, 17–18
rod model, 12

Equation, 4, 13, 32–33, 36–42, 62–68
formula for direct variation, 75
formula for inverse variation, 63
formula for linear, 34
as a mathematical model, 30

y-intercept, 34
ACE, 21–23, 45–54, 56–58, 69–78, 97, 99, 106

Equation model
bridge model, length, 10, 68
bridge model, thickness, 7–8

Folding paper model
ACE, 24, 27

Formula, 25
formula for direct variation, 75
formula for inverse variation, 63
formula for linear, 34

Function
definition, 30, 134

Glossary, 132–140

Graph, 9, 11–13, 31, 34, 32–33, 39, 64–68, 82–86, 129–131
as a mathematical model, 30
ACE, 15–22, 26, 45–52, 54–55, 69–75, 106, 122–126

Inequality
definition, 42, 135
problems, 42
ACE, 24, 51, 53

Interpreting data,
see Graph; Model; Table; Unit rate

Inverse, 64–65, 67–68
relationship, 41
variation, 4, 63, 135
ACE, 69, 75

Inverses
additive, 73, 132
multiplicative, 74, 136

Investigations
Exploring Data Patterns, 7–29
Inverse Variation, 61–80

Linear Models and
Equations, 30–60
Variability and Associations
in Categorical Data, 113–128
Variability and Associations
in Numerical Data, 81–112

Linear, 4, 9, 32–33, 36–37, 38–42, 44, 62–63, 67, 83–85, 87–92, 129–131
equation, 30, 34–35, 59
model, 31, 34–35, 43, 59
relationship, 28, 135
ACE, 18, 25–26, 45–54, 69–78, 97, 99–101, 110

Load, dead, live, 14

Looking Ahead, 3–4

Looking Back, 129–131

Manipulatives
bridge model, 7–14
folding paper model, 24, 27

Mathematical Highlights, 4

Mathematical Practices, 5–6, 29, 60, 80, 112, 128

Mathematical model
definition, 30, 136

Mathematical Reflections, 28, 59, 79, 111, 127

Medal platform model
ACE, 17–18

Model
area model, 20
bridge model, 7–14
folding paper model, 24
graph model, 30
net model, 77
rod model, 12
scale model, 54

Multiplicative inverse
definition, 74
ACE, 74

Net
ACE, 77

Nonlinear, 9, 62–68
relationship, 4, 61–62
ACE, 18, 25–26, 69–78, 110

Non-numerical graph
problems, 130
ACE, 55

Notebook, 28, 59, 79, 111, 127

Number line
ACE, 74, 125–126

Pattern, 12–14, 28, 31, 34, 82–85
ACE, 17–19, 25, 27, 62, 65–67, 77

Prediction, 9, 11, 43, 44, 68, 85, 99
ACE, 16, 19, 21, 45–46, 52, 106

Probability, 44
ACE, 105, 124

Relationship, 4, 9, 11, 30, 32–33, 36–37, 38–42, 44, 62–68, 83–85, 87–92, 129–131
linear, 28, 135
nonlinear, 4, 61–64
ACE, 15–19, 25–26, 45–54, 56, 69–78, 97, 99–101, 110

Rod model, 12–14
making, 12
ACE, 16–17, 19, 56

Scale model
ACE, 54

Scatter plot, 4, 82–84, 88–92
definition, 82
ACE, 97–101, 106–107, 109, 125

Slope, 36–37, 39, 85, 129–131
definition, 34–35, 138
ACE, 46, 48–50, 52, 54, 72

Statistics, 32–33, 83, 91–95, 130
outlier, 91
residual, 4, 83
standard deviation, 4, 93, 94
variance, 94
ACE, 96, 100–107, 120, 123–126

Table, 4, 9, 11–13, 31, 33, 39, 41, 62–68, 83, 94, 115–116, 118
ACE, 16–19, 25, 47, 52–53, 69–74, 77, 115–116, 120–122, 129–131

Tree Top Fun, 38–39

Unit rate, 37
definition, 34, 140

Variables, 30
categorical, 113
ACE, 119–120, 125

y-intercept, 36, 39
definition, 34, 140
ACE, 46, 48–50, 52, 72

Index

Acknowledgments

Cover Design

Three Communication Design, Chicago

Text

089–092 "Roller Coaster Census Report" by Duane Marden from
WWW.RCDB.COM/CENSUS.HTM

098 "Airplane Comparisons by Engine, Body Length, and Wingspan"
by William and Frank Berk from GUIDE TO AIRPORT AIRPLANES.
©1993 Plymouth Press, Ltd.

Photographs

Every effort has been made to secure permission and provide appropriate credit
for photographic material. The publisher deeply regrets any omission and pledges
to correct errors called to its attention in subsequent editions.

Unless otherwise acknowledged, all photographs are the property of Pearson
Education, Inc.

Photo locators denoted as follows: Top (T), Center (C), Bottom (B), Left (L),
Right (R), Background (Bkgd)

2TR Stockbyte/Getty images; **2CR** Jeff Greenberg/Alamy; **2BR** IS996/Image
Source/Alamy; **3T** Nomad/SuperStock; **7BC** James A. Harris/Shutterstock;
14BC Simon DesRochers/Masterfile Corporation; **16BC** Stockbyte/Getty
images; **26BR** Pearson Education, Inc.; **38TC** Audrey Snider-Bell/Shutterstock;
40BC Gunter Marx/RE/Alamy; **42BC** Jeff Greenberg/Alamy; **50TR** Radius Images/
Alamy; **81CR** Shannon Fagon/Image Source; **87C** Chad Slattery/Stone/Getty
Images; **97CR** Pearson Education, Inc.; **106BR** Tim Gainey/Alamy;
113CL Arinahabich/Fotolia; **113CR** Arno van Dulmen/Shutterstock;
117BR Antenna/Getty images; **117CR** Craftvision/Getty Images; **129BC** Nigel
Cattlin/Alamy.

Looking for Pythagoras

The Pythagorean Theorem

Lappan, Phillips, Fey, Friel

Looking for Pythagoras

The Pythagorean Theorem

Looking Ahead 2

Mathematical Highlights 4

Mathematical Practices and Habits of Mind 5

1 Coordinate Grids   7

1.1 **Driving Around Euclid** Locating Points and Finding Distances 10

1.2 **Planning Parks** Shapes on a Coordinate Grid 12

1.3 **Finding Areas** 13

Ⓐ Ⓒ Ⓔ Homework 14

Mathematical Reflections 20

2 Squaring Off   22

2.1 Looking for Squares 22

2.2 Square Roots 23

2.3 Using Squares to Find Lengths 25

2.4 Cube Roots 27

Ⓐ Ⓒ Ⓔ Homework 29

Mathematical Reflections 36

3 The Pythagorean Theorem   38

3.1 Discovering the Pythagorean Theorem 39

3.2 A Proof of the Pythagorean Theorem 41

3.3 Finding Distances 44

3.4 Measuring the Egyptian Way Lengths That Form a Right Triangle 46

Ⓐ Ⓒ Ⓔ Homework 49

Mathematical Reflections 58

4 Using the Pythagorean Theorem: Understanding Real Numbers   60

4.1 Analyzing the Wheel of Theodorus Square Roots on a Number Line 61

4.2 Representing Fractions as Decimals 63

4.3 Representing Decimals as Fractions 66

4.4 Getting Real Irrational Numbers 68

Ⓐ Ⓒ Ⓔ Homework 71

Mathematical Reflections 77

5 Using the Pythagorean Theorem: Analyzing Triangles and Circles 79

5.1 Stopping Sneaky Sally Finding Unknown Side Lengths 79

5.2 Analyzing Triangles 82

5.3 Analyzing Circles 85

Ⓐ Ⓒ Ⓔ Homework 88

Mathematical Reflections 103

Looking Back 105

English/Spanish Glossary 108

Index 115

Acknowledgments 118

Looking Ahead

Suppose you are flying by helicopter from Union Station to Dupont Circle. **What** types of information would you need to give the pilot so he would know where to go?

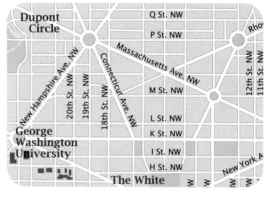

To mark the square corners of their property, ancient Egyptians used a rope divided with knots into 12 equal segments. **How** do you think they used this tool?

On a standard baseball diamond, the bases are 90 feet apart. **How** far must a catcher at home plate throw the ball to get a runner out at second base?

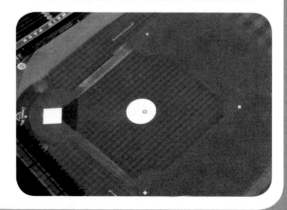

In this Unit, you will explore side lengths and areas of right triangles and squares. Your explorations will lead you to discover one of the most important relationships in all of mathematics: the *Pythagorean Theorem*. The Pythagorean Theorem is so important that much of geometry, trigonometry, and calculus would be impossible without it.

In earlier *Connected Mathematics* Units, you used whole numbers and fractions to describe lengths. In *Looking for Pythagoras,* you will work with lengths that are impossible to describe with whole numbers or fractions. To talk about such lengths, you need to use another type of number, called an *irrational number*.

The skills you develop in this Unit will help you answer questions like those on the facing page.

Mathematical Highlights

Looking for Pythagoras

In *Looking for Pythagoras,* you will explore an important relationship among the side lengths of a right triangle.

You will learn how to

- Develop strategies for finding the distance between two points on a coordinate grid

- Explain a proof of the Pythagorean Theorem

- Understand and use the Pythagorean Theorem to solve everyday problems

- Write fractions as repeating or terminating decimals

- Write decimals as fractions

- Recognize rational and irrational numbers

- Locate irrational numbers on a number line

- Relate the area of a square to its side length, and the volume of a cube to its side length

- Estimate square roots and cube roots

When you encounter a new problem, it is a good idea to ask yourself questions. In this Unit, you might ask questions such as:

What are the quantities in this problem?

Is the Pythagorean Theorem useful and appropriate in this situation?

How do I know?

Do I need to find the distance between two points?

How are the side length and the area of a square related?

How can I estimate the square root or cube root of a number?

Mathematical Practices and Habits of Mind

In the *Connected Mathematics* curriculum you will develop an understanding of important mathematical ideas by solving problems and reflecting on the mathematics involved. Every day, you will use "habits of mind" to make sense of problems and apply what you learn to new situations. Some of these habits are described by the *Common Core State Standards for Mathematical Practices* (MP).

MP1 Make sense of problems and persevere in solving them.

When using mathematics to solve a problem, it helps to think carefully about

- data and other facts you are given and what additional information you need to solve the problem;
- strategies you have used to solve similar problems and whether you could solve a related simpler problem first;
- how you could express the problem with equations, diagrams, or graphs;
- whether your answer makes sense.

MP2 Reason abstractly and quantitatively.

When you are asked to solve a problem, it often helps to

- focus first on the key mathematical ideas;
- check that your answer makes sense in the problem setting;
- use what you know about the problem setting to guide your mathematical reasoning.

MP3 Construct viable arguments and critique the reasoning of others.

When you are asked to explain why a conjecture is correct, you can

- show some examples that fit the claim and explain why they fit;
- show how a new result follows logically from known facts and principles.

When you believe a mathematical claim is incorrect, you can

- show one or more counterexamples—cases that don't fit the claim;
- find steps in the argument that do not follow logically from prior claims.

MP4 Model with mathematics.

When you are asked to solve problems, it often helps to

- think carefully about the numbers or geometric shapes that are the most important factors in the problem, then ask yourself how those factors are related to each other;
- express data and relationships in the problem with tables, graphs, diagrams, or equations, and check your result to see if it makes sense.

MP5 Use appropriate tools strategically.

When working on mathematical questions, you should always

- decide which tools are most helpful for solving the problem and why;
- try a different tool when you get stuck.

MP6 Attend to precision.

In every mathematical exploration or problem-solving task, it is important to

- think carefully about the required accuracy of results; is a number estimate or geometric sketch good enough, or is a precise value or drawing needed?
- report your discoveries with clear and correct mathematical language that can be understood by those to whom you are speaking or writing.

MP7 Look for and make use of structure.

In mathematical explorations and problem solving, it is often helpful to

- look for patterns that show how data points, numbers, or geometric shapes are related to each other;
- use patterns to make predictions.

MP8 Look for and express regularity in repeated reasoning.

When results of a repeated calculation show a pattern, it helps to

- express that pattern as a general rule that can be used in similar cases;
- look for shortcuts that will make the calculation simpler in other cases.

You will use all of the Mathematical Practices in this Unit. Sometimes, when you look at a Problem, it is obvious which practice is most helpful. At other times, you will decide on a practice to use during class explorations and discussions. After completing each Problem, ask yourself:

- What mathematics have I learned by solving this Problem?
- What Mathematical Practices were helpful in learning this mathematics?

Coordinate Grids

In this Investigation, you will use a coordinate grid to locate points on the plane. You will then explore how to find distances between points and areas of figures on a coordinate grid.

In the first two Problems of this Investigation, the coordinate grid is in the form of a street map of a fictional city called Euclid. The streets in most cities do not form perfect coordinate grids as they do in Euclid. However, many cities have streets that are loosely based on a coordinate system. One well-known example is Washington, D.C.

Common Core State Standards

Essential for 8.G.B.6 Explain a proof of the Pythagorean Theorem and its converse.

Essential for 8.G.B.8 Apply the Pythagorean Theorem to find the distance between two points in a coordinate system.

The map on the next page shows the central part of Washington, D.C. The city's street system was designed by Pierre L'Enfant in 1791.

L'Enfant's design is based on a coordinate system. Here are some key features of L'Enfant's system:

- The north-south and east-west streets form grid lines.

- The origin is at the Capitol.

- The vertical axis is formed by North and South Capitol Streets.

- The horizontal axis is the line stretching from the Lincoln Memorial, through the Mall, and down East Capitol Street.

- The axes divide the city into four quadrants known as Northeast (NE), Northwest (NW), Southwest (SW), and Southeast (SE).

- Describe the locations of these landmarks:

    George Washington University

    Dupont Circle

    Benjamin Banneker Park

    The White House

    Union Station

- How can you find the distance from Union Station to Dupont Circle?

- Find the intersection of G Street and 8th Street SE and the intersection of G Street and 8th Street NW. How are these locations related to the U.S. Capitol Building?

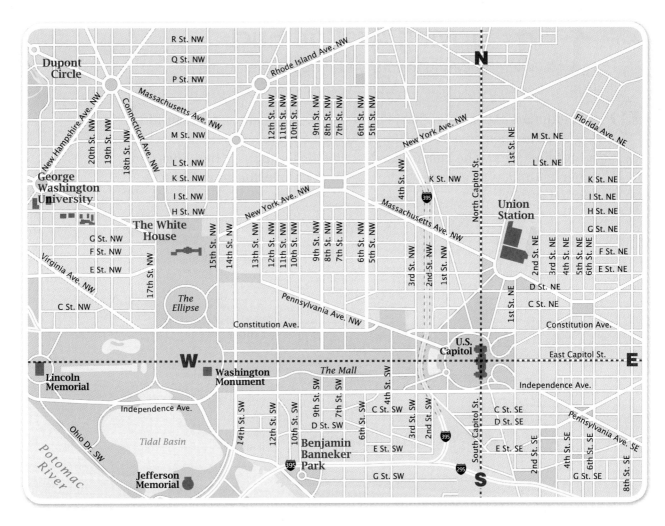

In mathematics, you use a coordinate system to describe the locations of points. Recall that horizontal and vertical number lines, called the *x*- and *y*-axes, divide the plane into four quadrants.

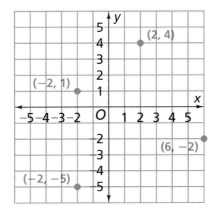

You describe the location of a point by giving its coordinates as an ordered pair of the form (*x*, *y*). The coordinate grid above shows four points labeled with their coordinates. For example, the point (−2, −5) is 2 units to the left and 5 units below the origin.

1.1 Driving Around Euclid
Locating Points and Finding Distances

The founders of the city of Euclid loved math. They named their city after a famous mathematician, and they designed the street system to look like a coordinate grid. The Euclideans describe the locations of buildings and other landmarks by giving coordinates. For example, the art museum is located at (6, 1).

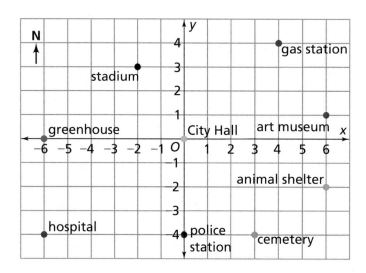

- In the city of Euclid, how does driving distance compare to flying distance?

Problem 1.1

A Give the coordinates of each landmark in the map above.

   1. gas station

   2. animal shelter

   3. stadium

Problem 1.1 *continued*

B Euclid's chief of police is planning emergency routes. She needs to find the shortest route between the following pairs of locations:

Pair 1: the police station to City Hall

Pair 2: the hospital to City Hall

Pair 3: the hospital to the art museum

    1. Give precise directions for an emergency car route for each pair.

    2. For each pair, find the total distance in blocks a police car following your route would travel.

C   **1.** The stadium is at $(-2, 3)$ and the high school is at $(1, 8)$. What is the shortest driving distance (in blocks) between these two locations? Can you figure this out without looking at the grid? Explain.

    2. Suppose you know the coordinates of two landmarks in Euclid. How can you determine the shortest driving distance (in blocks) between them?

D   **1.** A helicopter can travel directly from one point to another. For each pair in Question B, find the approximate distance (in blocks) a helicopter would have to travel to get from the starting location to the ending location. You may find it helpful to use a centimeter ruler.

    2. Will a direct helicopter route between two locations always be shorter than a car route? Explain your reasoning.

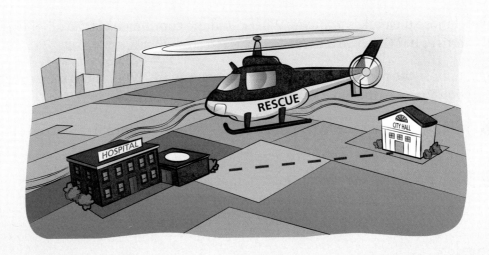

A C E Homework starts on page 14.

1.2 Planning Parks
Shapes on a Coordinate Grid

The Euclid City Council is developing parks with geometric shapes. For some of the parks, the council gives the park designers constraints. For example, Descartes Park must have corners at vertices (1, 1) and (4, 2).

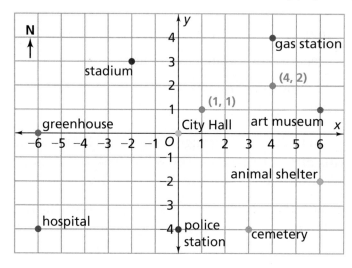

- What information do you need to show that the shape made by connecting four vertices is a square?

Problem 1.2

For each Question, explain how you know Descartes Park is the given shape.

A Suppose the park is a square. What could the coordinates of the other two vertices be? Give two answers.

B Suppose the park is a rectangle that is not a square. What could the coordinates of the other two vertices be?

C Suppose the park is a right triangle. What could the coordinates of the other vertex be?

D Suppose the park is a parallelogram that is not a rectangle. What could the coordinates of the other two vertices be?

A C E Homework starts on page 14.

1.3 Finding Areas

Below are some park designs submitted to the Euclid City Council. To determine costs, the council needs to know the area of each park.

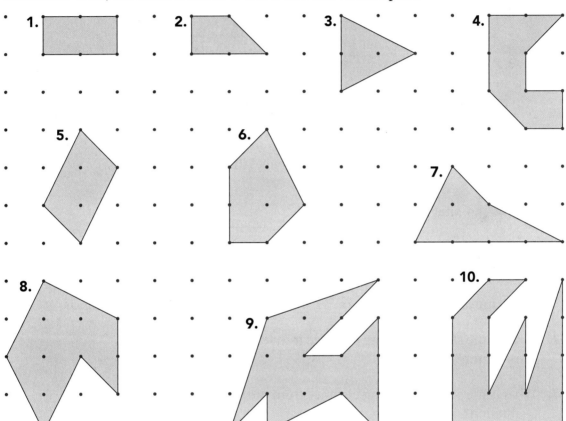

• How might you find the areas of irregular figures on dot paper?

Problem 1.3

Consider the horizontal or vertical distance between two adjacent dots to be 1 unit.

A Find the area of each figure.

B Find the area of one of the square parks you suggested in Problem 1.2.

C Describe the strategies you used in Questions A and B.

 Homework starts on page 14.

Applications

For Exercises 1–7, use the map of Euclid from Problem 1.1.

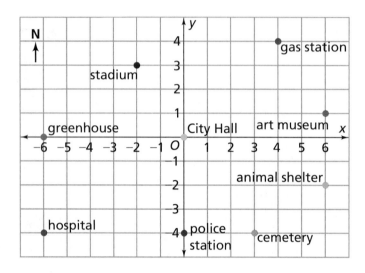

1. Give the coordinates of each landmark.

   a. art museum **b.** hospital **c.** greenhouse

2. What is the shortest driving distance from the animal shelter to the stadium?

3. What is the shortest driving distance from the hospital to the gas station?

4. Suppose you travel by taxi. What are the coordinates of a point halfway from City Hall to the hospital? Is there more than one possibility? Explain.

5. Suppose you traveled by helicopter. What are the coordinates of a point halfway from City Hall to the hospital? Is there more than one possibility? Explain.

6. **a.** Which landmarks are 7 blocks from City Hall by car?

   b. Give precise driving directions from City Hall to each landmark you listed in part (a).

7. Euclid Middle School is located at the intersection of two streets. The school is the same driving distance from the gas station as the hospital is from the greenhouse.

   a. List the coordinates of each place on the map where the school might be located.

   b. Find the flying distance (in blocks) from the gas station to each location you listed in part (a).

The points (0, 0) and (3, 2) are two vertices of a polygon with integer coordinates.

8. Suppose the polygon is a square. What could the other two vertices be?

9. Suppose the polygon is a nonrectangular parallelogram. What could the other two vertices be?

10. Suppose the polygon is a right triangle. What could the other vertex be?

The points (3, 3) and (2, 6) are two vertices of a right triangle. Use this information for Exercises 11–13.

11. Multiple Choice Which point could be the third vertex of the right triangle?

   A. (3, 2)   **B.** (−1, 5)   **C.** (7, 4)   **D.** (0, 3)

12. Give the coordinates of at least two other points that could be the third vertex.

13. How many right triangles with vertices (3, 3) and (2, 6) can you draw? Explain.

14. Can you connect the following points to form a parallelogram? Explain.

   (1, 1)   (2, −2)   (4, 2)   (3, 5)

Find the area of each triangle. If necessary, copy the triangles onto dot paper.

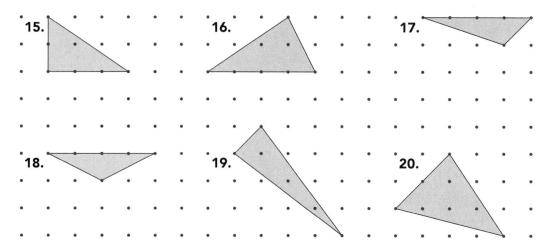

Find the area of each figure. Describe the method you use. If necessary, copy the figures onto dot paper.

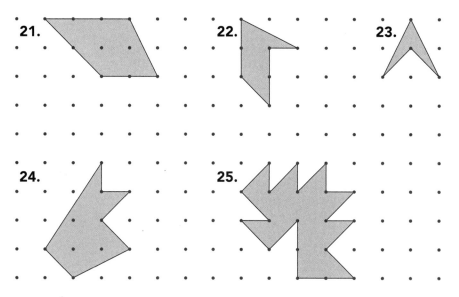

Connections

In the city of Euclid, the length of each block is 150 meters. Use this information and the map from Problem 1.1 for Exercises 26–28.

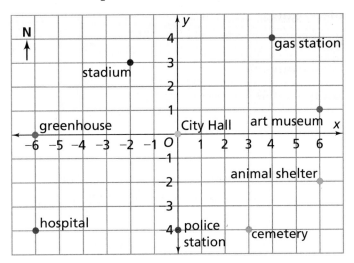

26. What is the shortest driving distance, in meters, from City Hall to the animal shelter?

27. What is the shortest driving distance, in meters, from the police station to the gas station?

28. Between which two landmarks is the shortest driving distance 750 meters?

For Exercises 29–33, use the map of Euclid from Problem 1.1.

29. Matsu walks 2 blocks west from the police station and then walks 3 blocks north. Give the coordinates of the place where he stops.

30. Amy is at City Hall. She wants to meet Matsu at his ending location from Exercise 29. What is the shortest route she can take if she walks along city streets? Is there more than one possible shortest route?

31. Simon leaves the stadium and walks 3 blocks east, then 3 blocks south, then 2 blocks west, and finally 4 blocks north. Give the coordinates of the place where he stops.

32. Aida wants to meet Simon at his ending location from Exercise 31. She is at City Hall. What is the shortest route she can take if she walks along city streets? Is there more than one possible shortest route?

33. In general, how can you use coordinates to find the shortest walking route from City Hall to any point in Euclid?

34. Refer to the ordered pairs below. Do *not* plot the points on a grid to answer the questions. Explain each answer.

$(2, -3)$ $(3, -4)$ $(-4, -5)$ $(4, 5)$

$(-4, 6)$ $(-5, -5)$ $(0, -6)$ $(6, 0)$

  a. Which point is farthest right?

  b. Which point is farthest left?

  c. Which point is above the others?

  d. Which point is below the others?

35. When Fabiola solved Problem 1.2, she used slopes to help explain her answers.

  a. In Question A, she used slopes to show that adjacent sides of the figure were **perpendicular** (form a right angle). How might she have done this?

  b. In Question D, she used slopes to show that the figure was a parallelogram. How might she have done this?

36. Below are equations for eight lines.

    line 1: $y = 3x + 5$ line 2: $y = 0.5x + 3$

    line 3: $y = 10 - 2x$ line 4: $y = 1 - \frac{1}{3}x$

    line 5: $y = 7 + 3x$ line 6: $y = -2x + 1$

    line 7: $y = 5 + 6x$ line 8: $y = 3x$

  a. Which of the lines are parallel to each other?

  b. Which of the lines are perpendicular to each other?

37. Marcia finds the area of a figure on dot paper by dividing it into smaller shapes. She finds the area of each smaller shape and writes the sum of the areas as $\frac{1}{2} \cdot 3 + \frac{1}{2} + \frac{1}{2} + 1$.

  a. What is the total area of the figure?

  b. On dot paper, draw a possible picture of the figure.

38. In the figure, a circle is inscribed in a square.

    a. Find the area of the circle.

    b. Find the area of the shaded region.

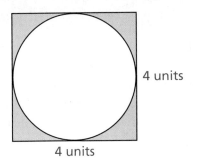

4 units

4 units

Extensions

39. Find a road map of your city or county. Figure out how to use the map's index to locate a city, street, or other landmark. How is finding a landmark by using an index description similar to and different from finding a landmark in Euclid by using its coordinates?

40. Use a map of your state to plan an airplane trip from your city or town to four other locations in your state. Write a set of directions for your trip that you could give to the pilot.

41. On grid paper, draw several parallelograms with diagonals that are perpendicular to each other. What do you observe about these parallelograms?

42. Find the areas of triangles *AST, BST, CST,* and *DST.* How do the areas compare? Why do you think this is true?

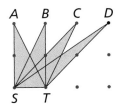

43. Find the areas of triangles *VMN, WMN, XMN, YMN,* and *ZMN.* How do the areas compare? Why do you think this is true?

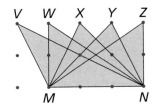

Mathematical Reflections

1

In this Investigation, you solved problems involving coordinate grids. You located points, calculated distances and areas, and found the vertices of polygons that satisfied given conditions. The following questions will help you summarize what you have learned.

Think about these questions. Discuss your ideas with other students and your teacher. Then write a summary of your findings in your notebook.

1. In the city of Euclid, **how** does the driving distance from one place to another compare to the flying distance?

2. Suppose you know the coordinates of two landmarks in Euclid. **How** can you find the distance between the landmarks?

3. **What** are some strategies for finding areas of figures drawn on a grid?

Common Core Mathematical Practices

As you worked on the Problems in this Investigation, you used prior knowledge to make sense of them. You also applied Mathematical Practices to solve the Problems. Think back over your work, the ways you thought about the Problems, and how you used Mathematical Practices.

Shawna described her thoughts in the following way:

> We noticed that we could use a ruler to find the horizontal, vertical, or helicopter distance on the grid in Problem 1.1. Since each block was 1 centimeter, a ruler gave us another way to measure distance instead of counting blocks.
>
> We also noticed that the diagonal of a square block is longer than each block, so counting blocks does not work for helicopter distances.

....

Common Core Standards for Mathematical Practice
MP5 Use appropriate tools strategically.

- What other Mathematical Practices can you identify in Shawna's reasoning?

- Describe a Mathematical Practice that you and your classmates used to solve a different Problem in this Investigation.

Squaring Off

In this Investigation, you will explore the relationship between the side lengths and areas of squares. You will then use that relationship to find the lengths of segments on dot grids.

2.1 Looking for Squares

You can draw squares with different areas by connecting the points on a 5 dot-by-5 dot grid. Two simple examples follow.

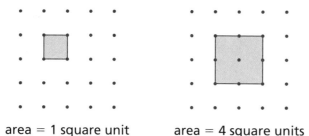

area = 1 square unit   area = 4 square units

- What is the area of the largest square on a 5 dot-by-5 dot grid? Smallest square?

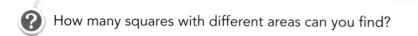

> **?** How many squares with different areas can you find?

Common Core State Standards

8.NS.A.2 Use rational approximations of irrational numbers to compare the size of irrational numbers, locate them approximately on a number line diagram . . .

8.EE.A.2 Use square root and cube root symbols to represent solutions to equations of the form $x^2 = p$ and $x^3 = p$, where p is a positive rational number. Evaluate square roots of small perfect squares and cube roots of small perfect cubes . . .

Also N-Q.A.3

Problem 2.1

Ⓐ On 5 dot-by-5 dot grids, draw squares of various sizes by connecting dots. Draw squares with as many different areas as possible. Label each square with its area. Include at least two squares whose sides are not horizontal and vertical.

Ⓑ Organize your set of squares by size. Then, describe the side lengths you found.

Ⓐ Ⓒ Ⓔ Homework starts on page 29.

2.2 Square Roots

The area of a square is the length of a side multiplied by itself. This can be expressed by the formula $A = s \cdot s$, or $A = s^2$.

If you know the area of a square, you can work backward to find the length of a side. For example, suppose a square has an area of 4 square units. To find the length of a side, you need to figure out what positive number multiplied by itself equals 4. Because $2 \cdot 2 = 4$, the side length is 2 units. The number 2 is called a **square root** of 4.

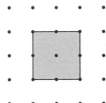

This square has an area of 4 square units. The length of each side is the square root of 4 units, which is equal to 2 units.

In general, if $A = s^2$, then s is a square root of A. Because $2 \cdot 2 = 4$ and $-2 \cdot (-2) = 4$, 2 and -2 are both square roots of 4. Every positive number has two square roots. The number 0 has only one square root, 0.

For any positive number N, $\sqrt{N}$ indicates the positive square root of N. For example, $\sqrt{4} = 2$. The negative square root of 4 is $-\sqrt{4} = -2$.

- What is the side length of a square with an area of 2 square units?

- Is this length greater than 1? Is it greater than 2?

- Is 1.5 a good estimate for $\sqrt{2}$?

- Can you find a better estimate for $\sqrt{2}$?

Problem 2.2

In this Problem, use your calculator only when instructed to do so.

A 1. Find the side lengths of squares with areas of 1, 9, 16, and 25 square units.

2. Find the values of $\sqrt{1}$, $\sqrt{9}$, $\sqrt{16}$, and $\sqrt{25}$.

B 1. What is the area of a square with a side length of 12 units? What is the area of a square with a side length of 2.5 units?

2. Find the missing numbers.

   a. $\sqrt{\square} = 12$ b. $\sqrt{\square} = 2.5$

3. Find x.

   a. $x^2 = 121$ b. $x^2 = 2.25$

   c. $\sqrt{x} = 121$ d. $\sqrt{2.25} = x$

4. Explain what each positive value of x in part (3) might represent in terms of area and length.

C Refer to the square with an area of 2 square units you drew in Problem 2.1. The exact side length of this square is $\sqrt{2}$ units.

1. Estimate $\sqrt{2}$ by measuring a side of the square with a centimeter ruler.

2. Calculate the area of the square, using your measurement from part (1). Is the result exactly equal to 2? Could you use your ruler to make a more accurate measurement for $\sqrt{2}$? Explain.

3. Use the square root key on your calculator to estimate $\sqrt{2}$.

4. How does your ruler estimate compare to your calculator estimate?

5. Suppose you are designing a square sand box that has an area of 2 square meters. What is a reasonable and accurate measure for the side length?

Problem 2.2 continued

D 1. Between which two consecutive whole numbers does $\sqrt{5}$ lie? Explain.

2. Which whole number from part (1) is closer to $\sqrt{5}$? Explain.

3. Without using your calculator, estimate the value of $\sqrt{5}$ to one decimal place.

4. Without using your calculator, can you get an even closer estimate than in part (3)?

E Give the exact side length of each square you drew in Problem 2.1.

A C E Homework starts on page 29.

2.3 Using Squares to Find Lengths

You can use a square to find the length of a segment connecting dots on a grid. For example, to find the length of the segment on the left, draw a square with the segment as a side. The square has an area of 5 square units, so the segment has an exact length of $\sqrt{5}$ units.

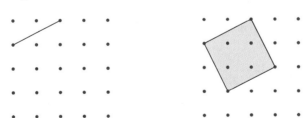

• How can you find the exact length of a line segment connecting any two dots on grid paper?

• How many different length segments can you draw on the 5 dot-by-5 dot grid?

Problem 2.3

A　**1.** On 5 dot-by-5 dot grids, draw line segments with as many different lengths as possible by connecting dots. Label each segment with its length. Use the $\sqrt{}$ symbol to express lengths that are not whole numbers. (**Hint:** You will need to draw squares that extend beyond the 5 dot-by-5 dot grids.)

　2. List the lengths in increasing order.

　3. Estimate each nonwhole number length to one decimal place. Then locate the lengths on a number line. How can you use the number line to decide which length is the greatest? Least?

　4. Describe a situation where measuring to one decimal place is not accurate enough.

B　**1.** Ella says the length of the segment in Figure 1 is $\sqrt{8}$ units. Oskar says it is $2\sqrt{2}$ units. Are both students correct? Explain.

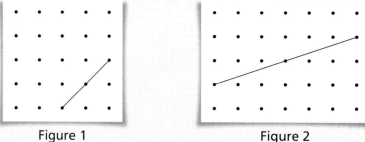

Figure 1　　　　　　　　　Figure 2

　2. Express the exact length of the segment in Figure 2 in two ways.

　3. Can you find a segment whose length cannot be expressed in two ways? Explain.

　4. Which of the following lengths can be expressed in two ways: $\sqrt{5}$, $\sqrt{10}$, $\sqrt{18}$? Check your answers on a grid.

A C E Homework starts on page 29.

2.4 Cube Roots

The volume of a cube is the length of an *edge* multiplied by itself three times. Multiplying two edges of the base of a cube gives the area of the base. The area of the base times an edge that is the height gives the volume. The volume can be expressed by the formula $V = e \cdot e \cdot e$, or $V = e^3$.

If you know the volume of a cube, you can work backward to find the length of an edge. For example, suppose a cube has a volume of 8 cubic units. To find the length of an edge, you need to figure out what number multiplied by itself three times equals 8. Because $2 \cdot 2 \cdot 2 = 8$, the edge length is 2 units. The number 2 is called the **cube root** of 8.

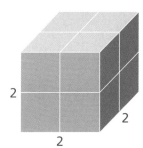

This cube has the volume of 8 cubic units. The length of each edge is the cube root of 8 units, which is equal to 2 units.

In general, if $V = e^3$, then e is the cube root of V. Because $2 \cdot 2 \cdot 2 = 8$, 2 is the cube root of 8. Because $-2 \cdot (-2) \cdot (-2) = -8$, -2 is the cube root of -8.

You can use the symbol, $\sqrt[3]{}$, to indicate cube root. For any number N, $\sqrt[3]{N}$ indicates the cube root of N. For example, $\sqrt[3]{8} = 2$ and $\sqrt[3]{-8} = -2$.

• How is finding the cube roots the same or different from finding square roots?

Problem **2.4**

In this Problem, use your calculator only when instructed to do so.

A **1.** Find the edge lengths of cubes with volumes of 1, 27, 64, and 125 cubic units.

    2. Find the values of $\sqrt[3]{1}$, $\sqrt[3]{27}$, $\sqrt[3]{64}$, and $\sqrt[3]{125}$.

B **1.** What is the volume of a cube with an edge length of 5 units? What is the volume of a cube with an edge length of 2.5 units?

    2. Find the missing numbers.

      a. $\sqrt[3]{\blacksquare} = 5$ **b.** $\sqrt[3]{\blacksquare} = 2.5$

    3. Find x.

      a. $x^3 = 27$ **b.** $x^3 = -27$ **c.** $x^3 = \frac{1}{8}$

      d. $\sqrt[3]{x} = 27$ **e.** $\sqrt[3]{x} = -27$ **f.** $\sqrt[3]{x} = -\frac{1}{8}$

    4. Explain what each positive value of x might represent in terms of volume and length.

C **1.** Between which two consecutive whole numbers does $\sqrt[3]{10}$ lie? Explain.

    2. Which whole number from part (1) is closer to $\sqrt[3]{10}$? Explain.

    3. Without using your calculator, estimate the value of $\sqrt[3]{10}$ to one decimal place.

    4. Without using your calculator, can you get an even closer estimate than in part (3)?

    5. Three students find the edge length for a cube with a volume of 10 cubic inches. How might have each student arrived at their answer?

        Nick: 2.15 feet   Josie: 2.1 feet   Kevin: 2.1544 feet

D **1.** Which is greater, $\sqrt{8}$ or $\sqrt[3]{8}$?

    2. Which is greater, $\sqrt{N}$ or $\sqrt[3]{N}$? Explain.

A C E Homework starts on page 29.

Applications

1. Find the area of every square that can be drawn by connecting dots on a 3 dot-by-3 dot grid.

2. On dot paper, draw a hexagon with an area of 16 square units.

3. On dot paper, draw a square with an area of 2 square units. Write an argument to convince a friend that the area is 2 square units.

For Exercises 4–37, do not use the $\sqrt{}$ key on your calculator.

4. Graph the following set of numbers in order on a number line.

2.3	$2\frac{1}{4}$	$\sqrt{5}$	$\sqrt{2}$	$\frac{5}{2}$	$\sqrt{4}$
4	-2.3	$-2\frac{1}{4}$	$\frac{4}{2}$	$-\frac{4}{2}$	2.09

For Exercises 5–7, estimate each square root to one decimal place.

5. $\sqrt{11}$ 6. $\sqrt{30}$ 7. $\sqrt{172}$

8. **Multiple Choice** Between which pair of numbers does $\sqrt{15}$ lie?

   A. 3.7 and 3.8   B. 3.8 and 3.9

   C. 3.9 and 4.0   D. 14 and 16

Find exact values for each square root.

9. $\sqrt{144}$ 10. $\sqrt{0.36}$ 11. $\sqrt{961}$

Find the two consecutive whole numbers between which each square lies. Explain.

12. $\sqrt{27}$ 13. $\sqrt{1,000}$

Tell whether each statement is true.

14. $6 = \sqrt{36}$

15. $1.5 = \sqrt{2.25}$

16. $11 = \sqrt{101}$

Find the missing number.

17. $\sqrt{\blacksquare} = 81$

18. $14 = \sqrt{\blacksquare}$

19. $\blacksquare = \sqrt{28.09}$

20. $\sqrt{\blacksquare} = 3.2$

21. $\sqrt{\blacksquare} = \frac{1}{4}$

22. $\sqrt{\frac{4}{9}} = \blacksquare$

Find each product.

23. $\sqrt{2} \cdot \sqrt{2}$

24. $\sqrt{3} \cdot \sqrt{3}$

25. $\sqrt{4} \cdot \sqrt{4}$

26. $\sqrt{5} \cdot \sqrt{5}$

Find the positive and negative square roots of each number.

27. 1

28. 4

29. 2

30. 16

31. 25

32. 5

Find x.

33. $x^2 = 144$ **34.** $x^2 = \frac{1}{4}$ **35.** $\sqrt{x} = \frac{1}{4}$ **36.** $\sqrt{\frac{1}{4}} = x$ **37.** $\sqrt{144} = x$

38. Consider segment AB at the right.

    a. On dot paper, draw a square with side AB. What is the area of the square?

    b. Use a calculator to estimate the length of segment AB.

39. Consider segment CD at the right.

    a. On dot paper, draw a square with side CD. What is the area of the square?

    b. Use a calculator to estimate the length of segment CD.

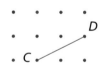

40. Find the area and the side length of this square.

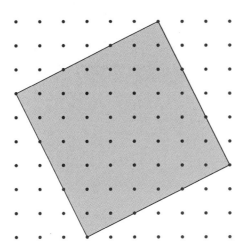

41. Find the length of every line segment that can be drawn by connecting dots on a 3 dot-by-3 dot grid.

42. Consider this segment.

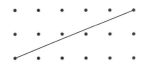

    a. Express the length of the segment, using the $\sqrt{}$ symbol.

    b. Between which two consecutive whole numbers does the length of the segment lie?

43. Show that $2\sqrt{5}$ is equal to $\sqrt{20}$ by finding the length of line segment *AC* in two ways.

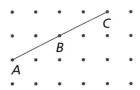

44. Multiple Choice Which line segment has a length of $\sqrt{17}$ units?

F.

G.

H.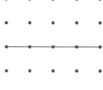

J.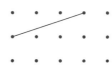

For Exercise 45 and 46, find the length of each side of the figure.

45.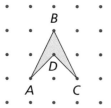

46.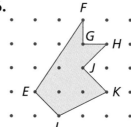

Find the edge length of a cube with the given volume.

47. 216 cube units

48. 512 cubic inches

49. 1,000 cubic feet

Find the value of each cube root.

50. $\sqrt[3]{216}$

51. $\sqrt[3]{512}$

52. $\sqrt[3]{1,000}$

Find the volume of a cube with the given edge length.

53. 6 yards

54. 8 inches

55. 10 feet

Find the missing number.

56. $\sqrt[3]{\blacksquare} = 6$

57. $\sqrt[3]{\blacksquare} = 8$

58. $\sqrt[3]{\blacksquare} = 10$

59. **a.** Between which two consecutive whole numbers does $\sqrt[3]{80}$ lie? Explain.

   b. Which whole number from part (a) is closer to $\sqrt[3]{80}$? Explain.

   c. Estimate the value of $\sqrt[3]{80}$ to one decimal place.

Find x.

60. $x^3 = 64$ **61.** $x^3 = -64$ **62.** $x^3 = \frac{27}{64}$ **63.** $\sqrt[3]{x} = -8$ **64.** $\sqrt[3]{-8} = x$

Connections

65. **a.** Which of the triangles below are right triangles? Explain.

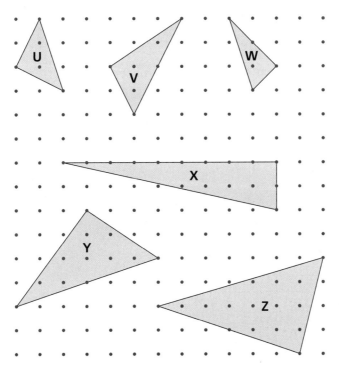

   b. Find the area of each right triangle.

66. Refer to the squares you drew in Problem 2.1.

   a. Find the perimeter of each square to the nearest hundredth of a unit.

   b. What rule can you use to calculate the perimeter of a square when you know the length of a side?

67. In Problem 2.1, it was easier to find the "upright" squares. Two of these squares are represented on the coordinate grid.

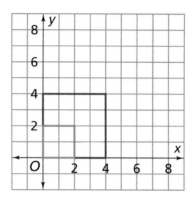

a. Are these squares similar? Explain.

b. How are the coordinates of the corresponding vertices related?

c. How are the areas of the squares related?

d. Copy the drawing. Add two more "upright" squares with a vertex at $(0, 0)$. How are the coordinates of the vertices of these new squares related to the 2×2 square? How are their areas related?

68. On grid paper, draw coordinate axes like the ones below. Plot point P at $(1, -2)$.

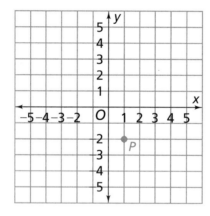

a. Draw a square $PQRS$ with an area of 10 square units.

b. Name a vertex of your square that is $\sqrt{10}$ units from point P.

c. Give the coordinates of at least two other points that are $\sqrt{10}$ units from point P.

69. In Problem 2.3, you drew segments of length 1 unit, $\sqrt{2}$ units, 4 units, and so on. On a copy of the number line below, locate and label each length you drew. On the number line, $\sqrt{1}$ and $\sqrt{2}$ have been marked as examples.

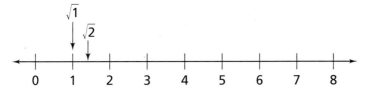

70. Sketch a cube with a volume of 64 cube units. Label the edge length of the cube on your drawing.

Extensions

71. On dot paper, draw a nonrectangular parallelogram with an area of 6 square units.

72. On dot paper, draw a triangle with an area of 5 square units.

73. Dalida claims that $\sqrt{8} + \sqrt{8}$ is equal to $\sqrt{16}$ because 8 plus 8 is 16. Is she right? Explain.

You know that $\sqrt{5} \cdot \sqrt{5} = \sqrt{5 \cdot 5} = \sqrt{25} = 5$. Tell whether each product is a whole number. Explain.

74. $\sqrt{2} \cdot \sqrt{50}$ **75.** $\sqrt{4} \cdot \sqrt{16}$ **76.** $\sqrt{4} \cdot \sqrt{6}$

77. The drawing shows three right triangles with a common side.

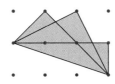

    a. Find the length of the common side.

    b. Do the three triangles have the same area? Explain.

You know that $\sqrt[3]{4} \cdot \sqrt[3]{4} \cdot \sqrt[3]{4} = \sqrt[3]{4 \cdot 4 \cdot 4} = \sqrt[3]{64} = 4$. Tell whether each product is a whole number. Explain.

78. $\sqrt[3]{5} \cdot \sqrt[3]{25}$ **79.** $\sqrt[3]{4} \cdot \sqrt[3]{16}$ **80.** $\sqrt[3]{5} \cdot \sqrt[3]{125}$

Mathematical Reflections

2

In this Investigation, you worked with square roots and cube roots, and explored squares and segments drawn on dot paper. You learned that the side length of a square is the positive square root of the square's area. You also discovered that, in many cases, a square root is not a whole number. The following questions will help you summarize what you have learned.

Think about these questions. Discuss your ideas with other students and your teacher. Then write a summary of your findings in your notebook.

1. **Describe** how you would find the length of a line segment connecting two dots on dot paper. Be sure to consider horizontal, vertical, and tilted segments.

2. a. **Explain** what it means to find the square root of a number.

   b. **Explain** whether or not a number can have more than one square root.

3. a. **Explain** what it means to find the cube root of a number.

   b. **Explain** whether or not a number can have more than one cube root.

Common Core Mathematical Practices

As you worked on the Problems in this Investigation, you used prior knowledge to make sense of them. You also applied Mathematical Practices to solve the Problems. Think back over your work, the ways you thought about the Problems, and how you used Mathematical Practices.

Ken described his thoughts in the following way:

In Problem 2.1, we showed that we had a square using the same reasoning we used in Problem 1.2 to show that the figures we drew on the coordinate grid were squares, rectangles, and right triangles. Then, to find the area of the square, we counted the number of square units inside the square.

Common Core Standards for Mathematical Practice

MP8 Look for and express regularity in repeated reasoning.

• What other Mathematical Practices can you identify in Ken's reasoning?

• Describe a Mathematical Practice that you and your classmates used to solve a different Problem in this Investigation.

The Pythagorean Theorem

In earlier grades, you learned about the properties of triangles. In this Investigation, you will learn about a special property of one type of triangle.

- What are characteristics that all triangles share?

- In what ways are the three triangles below different?

- How do the three side lengths of any triangle relate to each other?

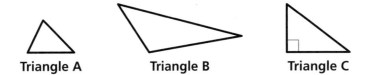

| Triangle A | Triangle B | Triangle C |

Triangle A is an acute triangle. An **acute triangle** has three acute angles.

Triangle B is an obtuse triangle. An **obtuse triangle** has one obtuse angle.

Triangle C is a right triangle. A **right triangle** has one angle with a measure of exactly 90°. A 90° angle is called a *right angle* and is often marked with a small square. The longest side of a right triangle is the side opposite the right angle. This side is called the **hypotenuse.** The other two sides are called the **legs.**

- Can a triangle have more than one angle that is 90°? Explain.

. . . .

Common Core State Standards

8.G.B.6 Explain a proof of the Pythagorean Theorem and its converse.

8.G.B.7 Apply the Pythagorean Theorem to determine unknown side lengths in right triangles in real-world and mathematical problems in two and three dimensions.

8.G.B.8 Apply the Pythagorean Theorem to find the distance between two points in a coordinate system.

3.1 Discovering the Pythagorean Theorem

In this Investigation, you will use squares to find the side lengths of the acute, right, and obtuse triangles shown below.

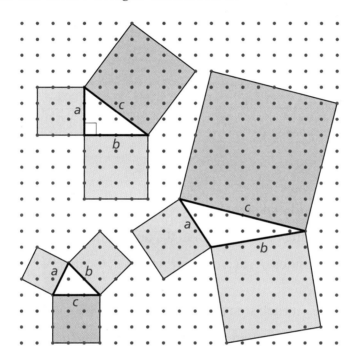

- Is there a relationship among the areas of squares drawn on the sides of a triangle?

- If so, what is the relationship?

- Is this relationship the same for all types of triangles?

Problem 3.1

A **1.** Make a copy of the table below. Record the areas and lengths for the three given triangles.

Type of Triangle	Area of Square on Side *a*	Area of Square on Side *b*	Area of Square on Side *c*	Length of Side *a*	Length of Side *b*	Length of Side *c*
Right	■	■	■	■	■	■
Right	■	■	■	■	■	■
Acute	■	■	■	■	■	■
Acute	■	■	■	■	■	■
Obtuse	■	■	■	■	■	■
Obtuse	■	■	■	■	■	■

2. On dot paper or grid paper, make three more drawings.

- Draw a right triangle, an acute triangle, and an obtuse triangle.
- Label the three sides of each of the triangles *a*, *b*, and *c*, where *c* the longest side.
- Draw a square on each side of the triangles.
- Find the areas of the squares and record the results in your table.
- Find the lengths of the sides and record the results in your table.

B **1.** For each triangle, look for a relationship among the areas of the three squares on the sides. Make a conjecture about the areas of the squares drawn on the sides of a triangle and the type of triangle.

2. Test your conjecture by drawing another triangle.

ACE Homework starts on page 49.

3.2 A Proof of the Pythagorean Theorem

The pattern you discovered in Problem 3.1 is a theorem in mathematics. A **theorem** is a general mathematical statement that has been proven true. This theorem is named after the Greek mathematician Pythagoras. The **Pythagorean Theorem** states a relationship among the lengths of the sides of a right triangle. It is one of the most famous theorems in mathematics.

More than 300 different proofs have been given for the Pythagorean Theorem. One of these proofs is based on the geometric argument you will explore in this Problem.

Did You Know?

Pythagoras lived in the 500s B.C. He had a devoted group of followers known as the Pythagoreans.

The Pythagoreans were a powerful group. Their influence became so strong that some people feared they threatened the local political structure. They were forced to disband. However, many Pythagoreans continued to meet in secret and to teach the ideas of Pythagoras.

I had help!

PYTHAGORAS

The Pythagoreans held Pythagoras in high regard—so high that they gave him credit for all of their discoveries. Much of what we now attribute to Pythagoras may actually be the work of one or several of his followers. That includes the Pythagorean Theorem.

You can use the puzzle pieces below to explore the Pythagorean Theorem.

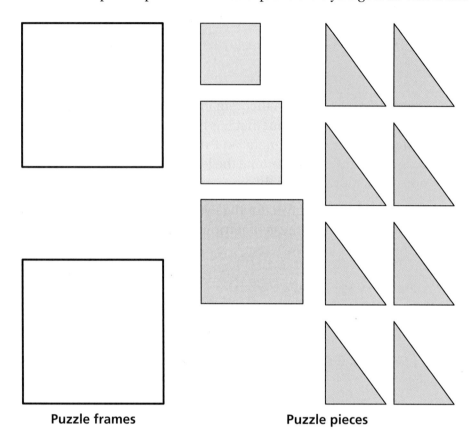

Puzzle frames   **Puzzle pieces**

? How can you use these puzzle pieces to prove the Pythagorean Theorem geometrically?

Problem 3.2

Copy the shapes on the previous page or use the puzzle pieces your teacher gives you.

A Study a triangle piece and the three square puzzle pieces. How do the side lengths of the squares compare to the side lengths of the triangle?

B **1.** Arrange the 11 puzzle pieces to fit exactly into the two puzzle frames.

2. What conclusion can you draw about the relationship among the areas of the three colored squares?

3. What does the conclusion you reached in part (2) mean in terms of the side lengths of the triangles?

4. Compare your results with those of another group. Did that group come to the same conclusion your group did? Is this conclusion true for all right triangles? Explain.

C Suppose a right triangle has legs of length 3 centimeters and 5 centimeters.

1. Use your conclusion from Question B to find the area of a square drawn on the hypotenuse of the triangle.

2. What is the length of the hypotenuse?

D In Problem 3.1 and Problem 3.2, you have explored the Pythagorean Theorem, a relationship among the side lengths of a right triangle. State this theorem as a rule for any right triangle with leg lengths a and b and hypotenuse length c.

 Homework starts on page 49.

3.3 Finding Distances

In Investigation 2, you found the lengths of tilted segments by drawing squares and finding their areas. You can also find these lengths using the Pythagorean Theorem.

- How can you use the Pythagorean Theorem to find the distance between any two points on a dot grid?
- How can you use it to find the end points of a line with length $\sqrt{13}$ units?

Problem 3.3

In Questions A–D, refer to the grid below.

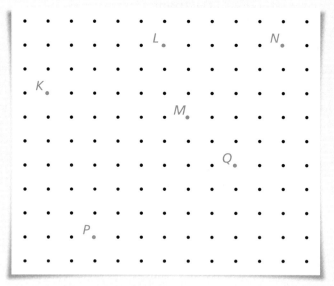

  A 1. Copy the points above onto dot paper. Then, draw a right triangle with segment *KL* as its hypotenuse.

2. Find the lengths of the legs of the triangle.

3. Use the Pythagorean Theorem to find the length of segment *KL*.

Problem **3.3** *continued*

B Find the distance between points *M* and *N* by connecting them with a segment and using the method in Question A.

C Find the distance between points *P* and *Q*.

D In Problem 1.1, Question C, you found the driving distance between the stadium at $(-2, 3)$ and the high school at $(1, 8)$. What is the helicopter distance between these two locations? Estimate the difference of the two distances.

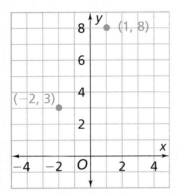

E Find the coordinates of two points that are $\sqrt{13}$ units apart. Label the points *R* and *S*. Explain how you know the distance between the points is $\sqrt{13}$ units.

A C E Homework starts on page 49.

3.4 Measuring the Egyptian Way
Lengths That Form a Right Triangle

In ancient Egypt, the Nile River overflowed every year. It flooded the surrounding lands and often removed markers for property boundaries. As a result, the Egyptians had to remeasure their land every year.

Because many plots of land were rectangular, the Egyptians needed a reliable way to mark right angles. They devised a clever method involving a rope with equally spaced knots that formed 12 equal intervals.

To understand the Egyptians' method, mark off 12 segments of the same length on a piece of rope or string. Tape the ends of the string together to form a closed loop. Form a right triangle with side lengths that are whole numbers of segments.

- What are the side lengths of the triangle you formed?

- What are some ways you could check that this is a right triangle?

- How do you think the Egyptians used the knotted rope?

In this Problem, you will explore these questions about the opposite, or *converse*, of the Pythagorean Theorem:

- Is any triangle whose side lengths a, b, and c satisfy the relationship $a^2 + b^2 = c^2$ a right triangle?

- Suppose the side lengths of a triangle do not satisfy the relationship $a^2 + b^2 = c^2$. Does this mean the triangle is *not* a right triangle?

Problem 3.4

A Copy the table below. Each row gives three side lengths. Use string, straws, or polystrips to build triangles with the given side lengths. Then, complete the second and third columns of the table.

Side Lengths (units)	Do the side lengths satisfy $a^2 + b^2 = c^2$?	Is the triangle a right triangle?
3, 4, 5	▦	▦
5, 12, 13	▦	▦
5, 6, 10	▦	▦
6, 8, 10	▦	▦
4, 4, 4	▦	▦
1, 2, 2	▦	▦

B **1.** Make a conjecture about triangles with side lengths that satisfy the relationship $a^2 + b^2 = c^2$.

2. Make a conjecture about triangles with side lengths that do *not* satisfy the relationship $a^2 + b^2 = c^2$.

3. Check your conjecture with two other triangles.

continued on the next page >

Problem **3.4** continued

C Determine whether a triangle with the given side lengths is a right triangle.

    1. 12 units, 16 units, 20 units

    2. 8 units, 15 units, 17 units

    3. 12 units, 9 units, 16 units

    4. Diego says he knew that one of the above triangles would be a right triangle. It is a scale copy of one of the right triangles in Question A. Do you agree with his thinking? Explain.

    5. Raeka claims that if the lengths of three sides of a triangle satisfy the relationship $a^2 + b^2 = c^2$, then the triangle is a right triangle. She reasons as follows:

- Take the two shorter side lengths a and b. Use these to form a right angle and then a right triangle. Call the length of the hypotenuse d.

- Since this triangle is a right triangle, then $a^2 + b^2 = d^2$.

- You also know that $a^2 + b^2 = c^2$. Therefore, $c^2 = d^2$, or $c = d$.

- Since three sides of one triangle are the same as the three sides of another triangle, then these two triangles are the same. This means that the original right triangle is unique.

    Does Raeka's reasoning prove the conjecture that if $a^2 + b^2 = c^2$, then the triangle with side lengths a, b, and c is a right triangle? Explain.

D The Egyptians' knotted rope had 12 segments. The rope could be used to make several triangles with whole-number side lengths. Only one of the combinations of side lengths gives a right triangle.

    1. What combination of whole-number side lengths makes a right triangle? How do you know this combination makes a right triangle?

    2. What combination of whole-number side lengths makes a nonright triangle? How do you know this combination is not a right triangle?

A C E Homework starts on page 49.

 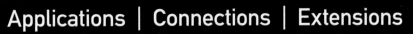

Applications

1. The diagram below shows a right triangle with a square on each side.

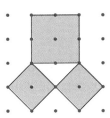

   a. Find the areas of the three squares.

   b. Use the areas from part (a) to show that the squares on the sides of this triangle satisfy the Pythagorean relationship, $a^2 + b^2 = c^2$.

2. The triangle below is a right triangle. Show that this triangle satisfies the Pythagorean Theorem.

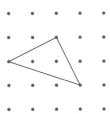

3. A right triangle has legs of length 5 inches and 12 inches.

   a. Find the area of a square drawn on the hypotenuse of the triangle.

   b. Find the length of the hypotenuse.

4. Use the Pythagorean Theorem to find the length of the hypotenuse of this triangle.

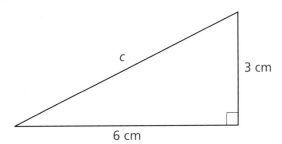

In Exercises 5 and 6, find each missing length.

5.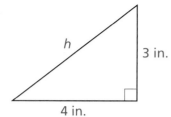

3 in.

4 in.

6.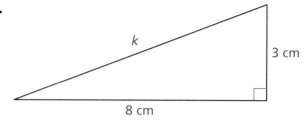

k

3 cm

8 cm

7. On dot paper, find two points that are $\sqrt{17}$ units apart. Label the points W and X. Explain how you know the distance between the points is $\sqrt{17}$ units.

8. On dot paper, find two points that are $\sqrt{20}$ units apart. Label the points Y and Z. Explain how you know the distance between the points is $\sqrt{20}$ units.

For Exercises 9–12, use the map of Euclid. Find the flying distance in blocks between each pair of landmarks without using a ruler. Explain.

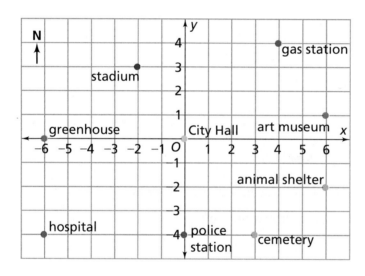

9. greenhouse and stadium

10. police station and art museum

11. greenhouse and hospital

12. City Hall and gas station

13. **Multiple Choice** Refer to the map of Euclid. Which landmarks are $\sqrt{40}$ blocks apart?

   A. greenhouse and stadium
   B. City Hall and gas station
   C. hospital and art museum
   D. animal shelter and police station

14. **Multiple Choice** Which set of side lengths makes a right triangle?

   F. 10 cm, 24 cm, 26 cm
   G. 4 cm, 6 cm, 10 cm
   H. 5 cm, 10 cm, $\sqrt{50}$ cm
   J. 8 cm, 9 cm, 15 cm

In Exercises 15 and 16, tell whether the triangle with the given side lengths is a right triangle.

15. 10 cm, 10 cm, $\sqrt{200}$ cm

16. 9 in., 16 in., 25 in.

Connections

17. The prism below has a base that is a right triangle.

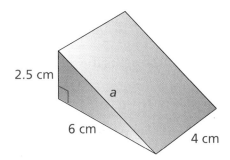

2.5 cm

a

6 cm

4 cm

   a. What is the value of a?

   b. Do you need to know the value of a to find the volume of the prism? Do you need to know the value of a to find the surface area? Explain.

   c. What is the volume?

   d. What is the surface area?

   e. Sketch a net for the prism.

For Exercises 18–21, refer to the figures below.

Cylinder

Cone

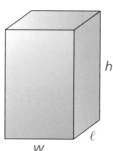

Prism

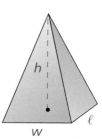

Pyramid

18. **Multiple Choice** Which expression represents the volume of the cylinder?

   A. $2\pi r^2 + 2\pi rh$ **B.** $\pi r^2 h$

   C. $\frac{1}{3}\pi r^2 h$ **D.** $\frac{1}{2}\pi r^2 h$

19. **Multiple Choice** Which expression represents the volume of the cone?

   F. $2\pi r^2 + 2\pi rh$ **G.** $\pi r^2 h$

   H. $\frac{1}{3}\pi r^2 h$ **J.** $\frac{1}{2}\pi r^2 h$

20. **Multiple Choice** Which expression represents the volume of the prism?

   A. $2(\ell w + \ell h + wh)$ **B.** ℓwh

   C. $\frac{1}{3}\ell wh$ **D.** $\frac{1}{2}\ell wh$

21. **Multiple Choice** Which expression represents the volume of the pyramid?

   F. $2(\ell w + \ell h + wh)$ **G.** ℓwh

   H. $\frac{1}{3}\ell wh$ **J.** $\frac{1}{2}\ell wh$

22. Nayo draws a quadrilateral. It has adjacent sides measuring 16 inches and 20 inches and a diagonal measuring 25 inches. Is her quadrilateral a rectangle? Explain.

23. Bo is building a tree house. He has marked locations for four holes that will hold his corner posts. They form a figure with a long side of 12 feet and a short side of 9 feet. What must the diagonal of the figure be to make sure the base of his tree house is a rectangle?

24. One method for checking whether a wall is perpendicular to the ground involves a 10-foot pole. A builder makes a mark exactly 6 feet high on the wall, and rests one end of the pole at that mark. The other end of the pole rests on the ground. A triangle is formed.

If the triangle is a right triangle, how far from the base of the wall is the bottom of the pole? Explain.

25. In the city of Euclid, Hilary's house is located at $(5, -3)$, and Jamilla's house is located at $(2, -4)$.

a. Without plotting points, find the shortest driving distance in blocks between the two houses.

b. What is the exact flying distance between the two houses?

26. Which labeled point is the same distance from point *A* as point *B* is from point *A*? Explain.

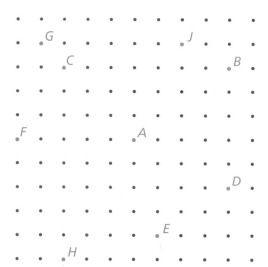

Extensions

27. Find the missing lengths.

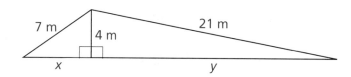

28. Jolon looks at the diagram below. He says, "If the center of this circle is at the origin, then I can figure out the radius."

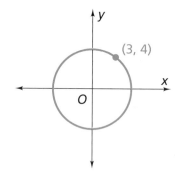

a. Explain how Jolon can find the radius.

b. What is the radius?

In Exercises 29–31, you will look for relationships among the areas of shapes other than squares drawn on the sides of a right triangle.

29. Half circles have been drawn on the sides of this right triangle.

  a. Find the area of each half circle.

  b. How are the areas of the half circles related?

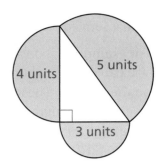

30. Equilateral triangles have been drawn on the sides of this right triangle.

  a. Find the area of each equilateral triangle.

  b. How are the areas of the equilateral triangles related?

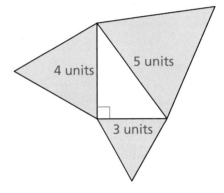

31. Regular hexagons have been drawn on the sides of this right triangle.

  a. Find the area of each hexagon.

  b. How are the areas of the hexagons related?

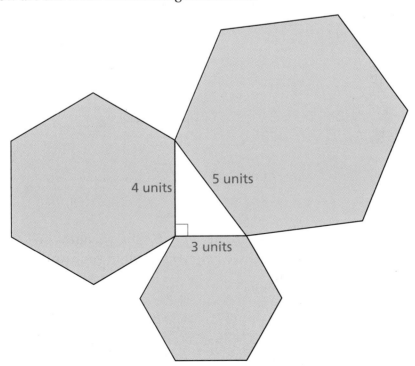

32. Any tilted segment that connects two dots on dot paper can be the hypotenuse of a right triangle. You can use this idea to draw segments of a given length. The key is finding two square numbers with a sum equal to the square of the length you want to draw.

For example, suppose you want to draw a segment with length $\sqrt{5}$ units. You can draw a right triangle in which the sum of the areas of the squares on the legs is 5. The area of the square on the hypotenuse will be 5 square units, so the length of the hypotenuse will be $\sqrt{5}$ units. Because 1 and 4 are square numbers, and $1 + 4 = 5$, a right triangle with legs of lengths 1 unit and 2 units has a hypotenuse of length $\sqrt{5}$ units.

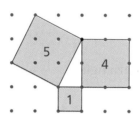

a. To use this method, it helps to be familiar with sums of square numbers. Copy and complete the addition table to show the sums of pairs of square numbers.

+	1	4	9	16	25	36	49	64
1	2	5						
4	5							
9								
16								
25								
36								
49								
64								

For parts (b)–(d), find two square numbers with the given sum.

b. 10   **c.** 25   **d.** 89

For parts (e)–(h), draw tilted segments with the given lengths on dot paper. Use the addition table to help you. Explain your work.

e. $\sqrt{26}$ units   **f.** 10 units   **g.** $\sqrt{10}$ units   **h.** $\sqrt{50}$ units

For Exercises 33–38, tell whether it is possible to draw a segment of the given length by connecting dots on dot paper. Explain.

33. $\sqrt{2}$ units

34. $\sqrt{3}$ units

35. $\sqrt{4}$ units

36. $\sqrt{5}$ units

37. $\sqrt{6}$ units

38. $\sqrt{7}$ units

39. Use the graph to answer parts (a)–(c).

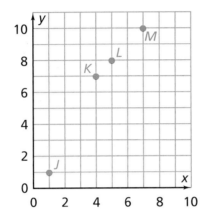

a. Find the coordinates of points *J* and *K*.

b. Use the coordinates to find the distance from point *J* to point *K*. Explain your method.

c. Use your method from part (b) to find the distance from point *L* to point *M*.

Mathematical Reflections 3

In this Investigation, you worked with a very important mathematical relationship called the Pythagorean Theorem. The following questions will help you summarize what you have learned.

Think about these questions. Discuss your ideas with other students and your teacher. Then write a summary of your findings in your notebook.

1. Suppose you are given the lengths of two sides of a right triangle. **Describe** how you can find the length of the third side.

2. Suppose two points on a grid are not on the same horizontal or vertical line. **Describe** how you can use the Pythagorean Theorem to find the distance between the points without measuring.

3. **How** can you determine whether a triangle is a right triangle if you know only the lengths of its sides?

Common Core Mathematical Practices

As you worked on the Problems in this Investigation, you used prior knowledge to make sense of them. You also applied Mathematical Practices to solve the Problems. Think back over your work, the ways you thought about the Problems, and how you used Mathematical Practices.

Hector described his thoughts in the following way:

In Problem 3.1, we found a rule about the areas of the squares on the sides of a right triangle. We noticed in Problem 3.4 that we could apply our rule to triangles with side lengths that were a multiple of the lengths of our original triangle.

We knew that a triangle with sides measuring 3, 4, and 5 was a right triangle. So a triangle with sides measuring 6, 8, and 10 would also be a right triangle because the triangles are similar. We did not have to check it with our theorem.

Common Core Standards for Mathematical Practice

MP8 Look for and express regularity in repeated reasoning.

- What other Mathematical Practices can you identify in Hector's reasoning?

- Describe a Mathematical Practice that you and your classmates used to solve a different Problem in this Investigation.

Using the Pythagorean Theorem: Understanding Real Numbers

In Investigation 3, you studied the Pythagorean Theorem.

The area of the square on the hypotenuse of a right triangle is equal to the sum of the areas of the squares on the legs.

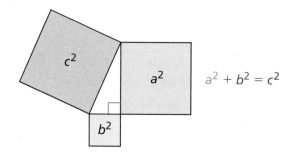

$$a^2 + b^2 = c^2$$

In this Investigation, you will explore some interesting applications of the Pythagorean Theorem.

Common Core State Standards

8.NS.A.1 Understand informally that every number has a decimal expansion; the rational numbers are those with decimal expansions that terminate in 0s or eventually repeat. Know that other numbers are called irrational.

8.NS.A.2 Use rational approximations of irrational numbers to compare the size of irrational numbers, locate them approximately on a number line diagram, and estimate the value of expressions (e.g., π^2).

8.G.B.7 Apply the Pythagorean Theorem to determine unknown side lengths in right triangles in real-world and mathematical problems in two and three dimensions.

Also 8.EE.A.2, 8.EE.C.7a, A-CED.A.1, N-Q.A.3

4.1 Analyzing the Wheel of Theodorus
Square Roots on a Number Line

The diagram below is named for its creator, Theodorus of Cyrene (sy ree nee), a former Greek colony. Theodorus was a Pythagorean.

The Wheel of Theodorus begins with a triangle with legs 1 unit long and winds around counterclockwise. Each triangle is drawn using the hypotenuse of the previous triangle as one leg and a segment of length 1 unit as the other leg. To make the Wheel of Theodorus, you need only know how to draw right angles and segments 1 unit long.

The Wheel of Theodorus

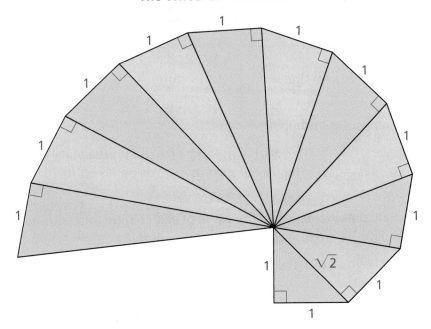

- What are the lengths of the spokes of the wheel?

Problem 4.1

A Use the Pythagorean Theorem to find the length of each hypotenuse in the Wheel of Theodorus. On a copy of the wheel, label each hypotenuse with its length. Use the $\sqrt{}$ symbol to express lengths that are not whole numbers.

B Use a cut-out copy of the ruler below to measure each hypotenuse on the wheel. Label the place on the ruler that represents the length of each hypotenuse. For example, the first hypotenuse length would be marked like this:

C For each hypotenuse length that is not a whole number:

1. Give the two consecutive whole numbers between which the length lies. For example, $\sqrt{2}$ is between 1 and 2.

2. Use your ruler to find two decimal numbers (to the tenths place) between which the length lies. For example, $\sqrt{2}$ is between 1.4 and 1.5.

3. Use your calculator to estimate the value of each length and compare the result to the approximations you found in part (2).

4. In Question B, you used a ruler to measure length. What is a reasonable level of accuracy for the lengths you found? Explain.

D Joey uses his calculator to find $\sqrt{3}$. He gets 1.732050808. Geeta says this must be wrong because when she multiplies 1.732050808 by 1.732050808, she gets 3.000000001. Why do these students disagree?

A C E Homework starts on page 71.

4.2 Representing Fractions as Decimals

Rational numbers are numbers that you can express as ratios of integers. For example, $\frac{3}{4}$, $\frac{-2}{5}$, $\frac{5}{7}$, $\frac{7}{3}$, $\frac{4}{1}$ (or 4), and $-2\frac{1}{2}$ $\left(\text{or } -\frac{5}{2}\right)$ are rational numbers.

You can also represent rational numbers as decimals. In your earlier math work, you learned that you can express as a decimal any fraction with a numerator and a denominator that are integers. You find the decimal by dividing the numerator by the denominator.

In the examples below, you can see that sometimes the decimal representation terminates after a limited number of digits. These decimals are **terminating decimals.** Sometimes the decimal representation has a repeating pattern of digits that never ends. These decimals are **repeating decimals.**

$$\frac{5}{16} = 0.3125$$
$$\frac{-7}{3} = -7 \div 3 = -2.333333\ldots$$
$$-1\frac{3}{7} = \frac{-10}{7} = -1.428571428571\ldots$$

You can write a repeating decimal with a bar over the repeating digits: $-1.\overline{428571}$.

However, there are other decimal numbers that neither terminate nor repeat. Here are two examples of decimal numbers that have a pattern, but do not terminate or repeat a set of digits.

$$1.0100100010000100000100000010000000\ldots$$

$$10.11121314151617181920212223242526272 8\ldots$$

- What would be the next four digits in each string of digits?

You have seen rational numbers, such as $\frac{1}{3}$, with decimal representations that are repeating decimals. You have also seen rational numbers, such as $\frac{5}{16}$, with decimal representations that are terminating decimals.

- Is the decimal representation for any rational number always a repeating or terminating decimal; or can you represent some rational numbers as nonterminating, nonrepeating decimals?

? How can you predict whether a fraction will have a repeating or terminating decimal representation?

Problem 4.2

Ⓐ Use a calculator to write each fraction as a decimal. Tell whether the decimal is *terminating* or *repeating*. If the decimal is repeating, tell which digits repeat.

1. $\frac{2}{5}$ 2. $\frac{1}{4}$ 3. $\frac{3}{8}$ 4. $\frac{1}{16}$

5. $\frac{35}{10}$ 6. $\frac{2}{3}$ 7. $\frac{8}{99}$ 8. $\frac{170}{999}$

Ⓑ 1. Jose says he knows that the decimal representation of a fraction, such as $\frac{3}{8}$, will be a terminating decimal if he can scale up the denominator to make a power of 10. What scale factor would Jose need to use to rewrite $\frac{3}{8}$ as $\frac{x}{1,000}$? What is the decimal representation?

2. Mei says she can scale up $\frac{2}{3}$ to $\frac{66\frac{2}{3}}{100}$, but the decimal representation of $\frac{2}{3}$ is a repeating decimal. Do Jose and Mei disagree? Explain.

3. Make a conjecture about how to predict when a fraction will have a terminating decimal representation. Test your conjecture on the following fractions:

$\frac{4}{7}$ $\frac{5}{6}$ $\frac{25}{12}$ $\frac{19}{20}$

Problem **4.2** *continued*

C For each decimal, find three equivalent fractions, if possible.

1. 0.3

2. 0.3333 . . .

3. 0.13133133313333 . . .

D **1.** Nic's calculator batteries are dead so he has to do the long division to find a decimal representation for $\frac{2}{7}$.

$$
\begin{array}{r}
0.285 \\
7\overline{)2.000} \\
-14 \\
\hline
60 \\
-56 \\
\hline
40 \\
-35 \\
\hline
5
\end{array}
$$

Continue the long division process until you are sure you can predict whether this decimal is terminating, repeating, or neither. Explain why you think your prediction is correct. Then, check your answer on a calculator.

2. Is it possible for a fraction to have a decimal equivalent that does *not* repeat and does *not* terminate? Explain.

A C E Homework starts on page 71.

4.3 Representing Decimals as Fractions

In Problem 4.2, you found that you can represent every rational number in fraction form as a terminating or repeating decimal. In this Problem, you will investigate how to do the reverse and represent decimals as fractions.

- Can you represent every repeating or terminating decimal as a fraction?

Problem 4.3

A **1.** On a copy of the table below, write each fraction as a decimal.

Fraction	Decimal	Fraction	Decimal
$\frac{1}{9}$	▨	$\frac{1}{11}$	▨
$\frac{2}{9}$	▨	$\frac{2}{11}$	▨
$\frac{3}{9}$	▨	$\frac{3}{11}$	▨
$\frac{4}{9}$	▨	$\frac{4}{11}$	▨
$\frac{5}{9}$	▨	$\frac{5}{11}$	▨
$\frac{6}{9}$	▨	$\frac{6}{11}$	▨
$\frac{7}{9}$	▨	$\frac{7}{11}$	▨

2. Describe any patterns you see in your table.

B Use the patterns you found in Question A to write a decimal representation for each rational number. Use your calculator to check your work.

1. $\frac{9}{9}$ **2.** $-\frac{10}{9}$ **3.** $\frac{10}{11}$ **4.** $\frac{^-12}{11}$

Problem 4.3 | *continued*

C Find a fraction equivalent to each decimal, if possible.

1. 1.222 . . .   **2.** 2.777 . . .   **3.** 0.818181 . . .

4. 0.27277277727777 . . .   **5.** 1.99999   **6.** 0.99999 . . .

D The patterns from Question A can help you represent some repeating decimals as fractions. What about other repeating decimals, such as 0.121212 . . . ? You need a method that will help you find an equivalent fraction for any repeating decimal.

1. Suppose $x = 0.121212$ . . . . What is $100x$? Is it still a repeating decimal?

2. Complete the subtraction.

$$100x = 12.121212\ldots$$
$$-\ \ x = 0.121212\ldots$$
$$\overline{99x = \blacksquare}$$

Is the answer for $99x$ still a repeating decimal?

3. Find a fraction form for 0.121212 . . . by solving for x.

4. Why do you think this method starts out by multiplying by 100? Explain.

5. Use this method to write each repeating decimal as a fraction.

a. 0.151515 . . .   **b.** 0.123123123 . . .   **c.** 1.354354354 . . .

E Tell whether each statement is *true* or *false*.

1. You can write any fraction as a terminating or repeating decimal.

2. You can write any terminating or repeating decimal as a fraction.

A C E Homework starts on page 71.

4.4 Getting Real
Irrational Numbers

In Problem 4.2, you saw that 10.111213141516 . . . is an example of a decimal that never repeats and never terminates. Here is another example:

$$0.12122122212222 \ldots$$

- Why does this pattern go on forever without repeating?

You can never represent a nonrepeating, nonterminating decimal as a fraction, or rational number. For example, $\frac{1}{10}$ is a close fraction representation of the decimal above, $\frac{12}{100}$ is closer, and $\frac{121}{1,000}$ is even closer. You cannot, however, get an exact fraction representation for this decimal.

- How is this kind of decimal the same as or different from the repeating decimal 0.6666 . . . ? The repeating decimal 0.121212 . . . ? The terminating decimal 1.414213562?

Numbers with decimal representations that are nonterminating and nonrepeating are called **irrational numbers.** Some irrational numbers have patterns, as above. Some have no patterns, but the decimals never terminate and never repeat. You cannot express these numbers as ratios of integers.

You have worked with irrational numbers before. For example, the decimal representation of the number π starts with the digits 3.14159265 . . . and goes forever without repeating any sequence of digits. The number π is irrational.

The number $\sqrt{2}$ is also irrational. You could not find an exact terminating or repeating decimal representation for $\sqrt{2}$ because such a representation does not exist! Other irrational numbers are $\sqrt{3}$, $\sqrt{5}$, and $\sqrt{11}$. In fact, $\sqrt{n}$ is an irrational number for any whole number value of n that is not a square number.

- Are the following numbers rational or irrational: $\sqrt{7}$, $\sqrt{9}$, $\sqrt{0.25}$? Why or why not?

- Can you give another number that has a rational square root?

- Can you give another number that does not have a rational square root?

The set of irrational and rational numbers is called the set of **real numbers.** An amazing fact is that there are an infinite number of irrational numbers between any two fractions! You will explore irrational and rational numbers in this Problem.

Problem 4.4

Ⓐ **1.** Write three or more nonterminating, nonrepeating decimals that are greater than 0.5 but less than 0.6.

2. Why is there no limit to the number of nonterminating, nonrepeating decimals that are between 0.5 and 0.6?

Ⓑ **1.** Write a rational-number estimate for $\sqrt{5}$ that is less than $\sqrt{5}$ and one that is greater than $\sqrt{5}$.

2. Write an irrational-number estimate for $\sqrt{5}$ that is less than $\sqrt{5}$ and one that is greater than $\sqrt{5}$.

Ⓒ **1.** The diagram shows a square drawn on the hypotenuse of a right triangle. Find the lengths of the sides of the square and the area of the square. If you use a ruler to measure the hypotenuse, how accurate can you be? Explain.

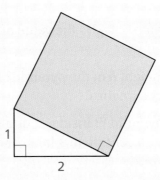

2. Ty says that this proves that $\sqrt{5} \cdot \sqrt{5} = 5$. Do you agree? Explain.

continued on the next page >

Problem 4.4 continued

D Tell whether each number is *rational* or *irrational*. Explain your reasoning.

1. $\sqrt{7}$ 2. $\sqrt{16}$ 3. $\sqrt{4} \cdot \sqrt{4}$

4. $\sqrt{7} \cdot \sqrt{7}$ 5. $2\sqrt{7}$ 6. $\sqrt{28}$

7. $\sqrt{14}$ 8. $\sqrt{\frac{1}{16}}$ 9. 2.45455

10. 2.45454545...   11. 2.454554555...   12. 2.455455545555...

E As part of her math project, Angela is making a pyramid. She starts with the net shown below, drawn on centimeter grid paper.

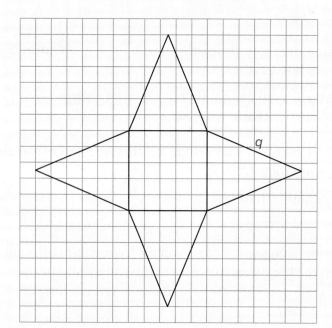
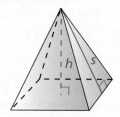

1. What is the exact value of *q*? Is the value of *q* a rational or irrational number? Explain.

2. What is the exact height *h* of the pyramid? Is the height a rational or irrational number? Explain.

3. Will the finished pyramid fit inside a cube-shaped box that is 6 centimeters wide, 6 centimeters long, and 6 centimeters high? Explain.

A C E Homework starts on page 71.

Applications

1. The hypotenuse of a right triangle is 15 centimeters long. One leg is 9 centimeters long. How long is the other leg?

2. The Wheel of Theodorus in Problem 4.1 includes only the first 11 triangles in the wheel. The wheel can go on forever.

   a. Find the side lengths of the next three triangles.

   b. Find the areas of the first five triangles in the wheel. Describe any patterns you observe.

   c. Suppose you continue adding triangles to the wheel. Which triangle will have a hypotenuse of length 5 units?

Write each fraction as a decimal. Tell whether the decimal is *terminating* or *repeating*. If the decimal is repeating, tell which digits repeat.

3. $\frac{5}{8}$ 4. $\frac{3}{5}$ 5. $\frac{1}{6}$ 6. $\frac{4}{99}$ 7. $\frac{43}{10}$

Find a fraction equivalent to each terminating decimal.

8. 0.1875   9. 5.125   10. 43.6

11. a. Explore decimal representations of fractions with a denominator of 99. Look at fractions less than 1: $\frac{1}{99}$, $\frac{2}{99}$, $\frac{3}{99}$, and so on. What pattern do you see?

    b. Write a decimal representation for the fraction $\frac{51}{99}$.

12. a. Explore decimal representations of fractions with a denominator of 999. Look at fractions less than 1: $\frac{1}{999}$, $\frac{2}{999}$, $\frac{3}{999}$, and so on. What pattern do you see?

    b. Write a decimal representation for the fraction $\frac{1,000}{999}$.

Use the patterns you discovered in Problem 4.3 and Exercises 11 and 12 to find a fraction or mixed number equivalent to each decimal.

13. 0.3333 . . .

14. 0.050505 . . .

15. 0.454545 . . .

16. 0.045045 . . .

17. 10.121212 . . .

18. 3.9999 . . .

19. The decimal below is close to, but between, which two fractions? (**Hint:** There is more than one answer to this question.)

0.101001000100001 . . .

20. Find an irrational number between 6.23 and 6.35.

21. Find an irrational number between $\frac{1}{7}$ and $\frac{1}{6}$.

Find the length of diagonal d in each rectangular prism.

22.

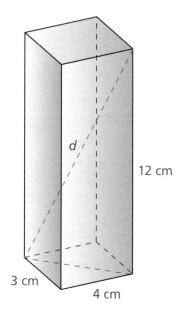

12 cm

3 cm

4 cm

23.

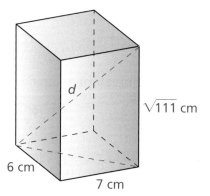

$\sqrt{111}$ cm

6 cm

7 cm

Connections

24. **Multiple Choice** Which set of irrational numbers is in order from least to greatest?

   A. $\sqrt{2}, \sqrt{5}, \sqrt{11}, \pi$

   B. $\sqrt{2}, \sqrt{5}, \pi, \sqrt{11}$

   C. $\sqrt{2}, \pi, \sqrt{5}, \sqrt{11}$

   D. $\pi, \sqrt{2}, \sqrt{5}, \sqrt{11}$

Find the two consecutive whole numbers the square root is between. Explain.

25. $\sqrt{39}$ 26. $\sqrt{600}$

Tell whether the statement is *true* or *false*. Explain.

27. $0.06 = \sqrt{0.36}$

28. $1.1 = \sqrt{1.21}$

29. $20 = \sqrt{40}$

Tell whether a triangle with the given side lengths is a right triangle. Explain how you know.

30. 5 cm, 7 cm, $\sqrt{74}$ cm

31. $\sqrt{2}$ ft, $\sqrt{3}$ ft, 3 ft

Estimate the square root to one decimal place *without* using the $\sqrt{}$ key on your calculator. Then, tell whether the number is *rational* or *irrational*.

32. $\sqrt{121}$ 33. $\sqrt{0.49}$

34. $\sqrt{15}$ 35. $\sqrt{1,000}$

36. In the drawing below, the cone and the cylinder have the same height and radius. Suppose the radius r of the cone is 2 units and the slant height s is $\sqrt{29}$ units.

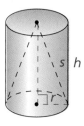

    a. What is the height of the cone?

    b. What is the volume of the cone?

37. In the drawing below, the pyramid and the cube have the same height and base.

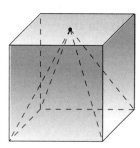

    a. Suppose the edge length of the cube is 6 units. What is the volume of the pyramid?

    b. Suppose the edge length of the cube is x units. What is the volume of the pyramid?

Extensions

Find the area of the shaded region.

38.

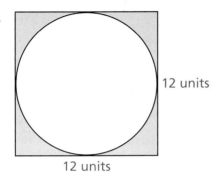

12 units

12 units

39.

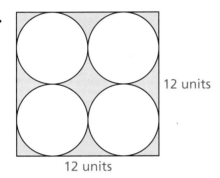

12 units

12 units

40.

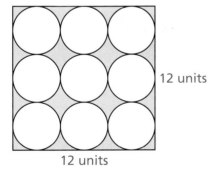

12 units

12 units

41. Simplify each expression. Leave your answer as either an integer or a square root.

    a. $\sqrt{2} \cdot 2\sqrt{2}$ **b.** $2 \div \sqrt{2}$ **c.** $\sqrt{2}(1 + \sqrt{2}) - \sqrt{2}$

42. Below are a square pyramid and its net.

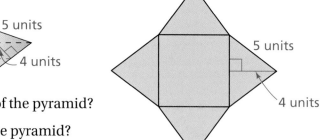

    a. What is the area of the base of the pyramid?

    b. What is the surface area of the pyramid?

    c. What is the height of the pyramid?

    d. What is the volume of the pyramid?

43. The managers of Izzie's Ice Cream Shop are trying to decide on the best size for their waffle cones.

    a. Izzie suggests that the cone should have a diameter of 4.5 inches and a height of 6 inches. What is the volume of the cone that Izzie suggests?

    b. Izzie's sister, Becky, suggests that the cone should have a height of 6 inches and a slant height of 7 inches. (The slant height is labeled *s* in the diagram.) What is the volume of the cone that Becky suggests?

Mathematical Reflections 4

In this Investigation, you looked at decimal representations of fractions and fraction representations of decimals. You discovered that some decimals do not terminate or repeat. You cannot represent these decimals as fractions with numerators and denominators that are integers. The following questions will help you summarize what you have learned.

Think about these questions. Discuss your ideas with other students and your teacher. Then write a summary of your findings in your notebook.

1. **Give** three examples of fractions with decimal representations that terminate.

2. **Give** three examples of fractions with decimal representations that repeat.

3. **Give** three examples of irrational numbers, including one irrational number greater than 5.

4. **How** can you determine whether you can write a given decimal as a fraction?

Common Core Mathematical Practices

As you worked on the Problems in this Investigation, you used prior knowledge to make sense of them. You also applied Mathematical Practices to solve the Problems. Think back over your work, the ways you thought about the Problems, and how you used Mathematical Practices.

Elena described her thoughts in the following way:

In Problem 4.3, we noticed a pattern among certain fractions that had 9's in the denominators. We found a specific group of fractions that we could represent as repeating decimals. We made a conjecture based on this pattern that we could represent fractions of the form $\frac{n}{9}$ by the decimal $0.nnnn\ldots$, where n is a positive whole number. Then we used our conjecture to find the decimal representations of other fractions that followed this same pattern.

Common Core Standards for Mathematical Practice

MP7 Look for and make use of structure.

- What other Mathematical Practices can you identify in Elena's reasoning?

- Describe a Mathematical Practice that you and your classmates used to solve a different Problem in this Investigation.

Investigation 5

Using the Pythagorean Theorem: Analyzing Triangles and Circles

In this Investigation, you will apply the Pythagorean Theorem in some very different situations. Whenever there is a right triangle in a figure, you can use the Pythagorean Theorem to deduce the side lengths of the triangle. Sometimes the triangle is not obvious.

5.1 Stopping Sneaky Sally
Finding Unknown Side Lengths

A baseball diamond is actually a square. If you can find right triangles in this shape, you can use the Pythagorean Theorem to solve problems about distances.

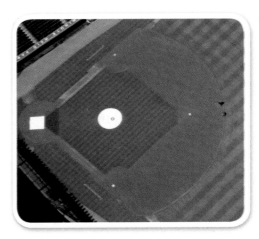

Common Core State Standards

8.G.A.4 Understand that a two-dimensional figure is similar to another if the second can be obtained from the first by a sequence of rotations, reflections, translations, and dilations; given two similar two-dimensional figures, describe a sequence that exhibits the similarity between them.

8.G.B.7 Apply the Pythagorean Theorem to determine unknown side lengths in right triangles in real-world and mathematical problems in two and three dimensions.

8.G.B.8 Apply the Pythagorean Theorem to find the distance between two points in a coordinate system.

Also A-CED.A.2, A-REI.D.10, N-Q.A.3

Problem 5.1

Horace Hanson is the catcher for the Humboldt Bees baseball team. Sneaky Sally Smith, the star of the Canfield Cats, is on first base. Sally is known for stealing bases, so Horace is keeping an eye on her.

The pitcher throws a fastball, and the batter swings and misses. Horace catches the pitch and, out of the corner of his eye, he sees Sally take off for second base.

Use the diagram to answer Questions A–C.

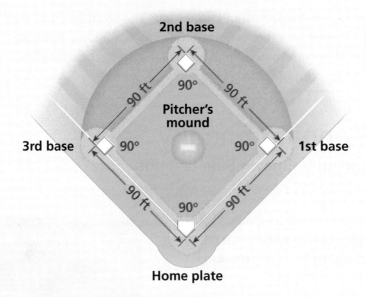

2nd base

90 ft   90°   90 ft

Pitcher's mound

3rd base   90°   90°   **1st base**

90 ft   90°   90 ft

Home plate

A **1.** How far must Horace throw the baseball to get Sally out at second base? Explain.

2. Jen says the distance that Horace throws the baseball is a rational number. Funda says that it is an irrational number. Explain each student's reasoning.

B The shortstop is standing on the baseline, halfway between second base and third base. How far is the shortstop from Horace?

C The pitcher's mound is 60 feet 6 inches from home plate. Use this information and your answer to Question A to find the distance from the pitcher's mound to each base.

ACE Homework starts on page 88.

Did You Know?

Most people consider baseball an American invention. A similar game called *rounders*, however, was played in England as early as the 1600s. Like baseball, rounders involved hitting a ball and running around bases. However, in rounders, the fielders actually threw the ball at the base runners. If a ball hit a runner while he was off base, he was out.

Alexander Cartwright was a founding member of the Knickerbockers Base Ball Club of New York City, baseball's first organized club. Cartwright played a key role in writing the first set of formal rules for baseball in 1845.

According to Cartwright's rules, a batter was out if a fielder caught the ball either on the fly or on the first bounce. Today, balls caught on the first bounce are not outs. Cartwright's rules also stated that the first team to have 21 runs at the end of an inning was the winner. Today, the team with the highest score after nine innings wins the game.

5.2 Analyzing Triangles

You can use the Pythagorean Theorem to investigate some interesting properties of an equilateral triangle. One property is that all equilateral triangles have reflection symmetries.

Triangle *ABC* is an equilateral triangle. Line *AP* is a reflection line for triangle *ABC*. If you fold an equilateral triangle along the line of reflection, you will find some properties of any equilateral triangle.

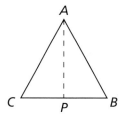

- What is true about the angle measures of an equilateral triangle?

- What is true about the side lengths of an equilateral triangle?

- What can you say about the measures of angle *CAP*, angle *BAP*, angle *CPA*, and angle *BPA*?

- What can you say about line segments *CP* and *BP*?

- What can you say about triangles *ACP* and *ABP*?

- Is there a relationship among the lengths of line segments *CP*, *AP*, and *AC*?

Problem 5.2

Ⓐ Suppose the lengths of the sides of equilateral triangle *ABC* above are 2 units. On a copy of triangle *ABC*, label the following measures:

1. angle *CAP* **2.** angle *BAP*

3. angle *CPA* **4.** angle *BPA*

5. length of *CP* **6.** length of *BP*

7. length of *AP*

Problem **5.2** *continued*

B Suppose the lengths of the sides of equilateral triangle *ABC* on the facing page are 4 units. On a copy of triangle *ABC*, label the following measures:

1. angle *CAP*   **2.** angle *BAP*

3. angle *CPA*   **4.** angle *BPA*

5. length of *CP*   **6.** length of *BP*

7. length of *AP*

C Thang thinks he has a way of predicting the length of the height *AP* for any equilateral triangle. He has drawn the results of Questions A and B in the diagram below.

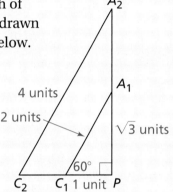

1. The triangles look similar. Are they? Explain.

2. What is the length of A_2P? What is the length of C_2P?

3. Is the length of A_2P the same as the length of *AP* you found in Question B? Explain.

D A right triangle with a 60° angle is called a 30-60-90 triangle. The 30-60-90 triangle at the right has a hypotenuse of length 10 units.

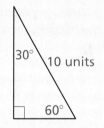

1. What are the lengths of the other two sides? Explain how you found your answers.

2. What relationships among the side lengths do you observe for this 30-60-90 triangle? Is this relationship true for all 30-60-90 triangles? Explain.

3. If the hypotenuse of a 30-60-90 triangle is *s* units long, what are the lengths of the other two sides?

continued on the next page >

Problem **5.2** | *continued*

E Use the figure below.

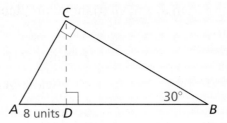

1. How many right triangles do you see in the figure?

2. Find the perimeter of triangle *ABC*. Explain your strategy.

3. Find the area of triangle *ABC*. Explain your strategy.

A C E Homework starts on page 88.

Did You Know?

In the movie *The Wizard of Oz*, the scarecrow celebrates his new brain by reciting the following:

"The sum of the square roots of any two sides of an isosceles triangle is equal to the square root of the remaining side."

Now you know what the scarecrow meant to say, even though his still imperfect brain got it wrong.

Given an isosceles triangle, suppose the sides with equal lengths are *s* units and the base is *b* units. Then one possible way to represent what the scarecrow said is:

$$\sqrt{s} + \sqrt{s} = \sqrt{b}$$

- Can you think of two numbers that would make this statement true?

- Could the numbers you thought of be the lengths of the sides of an isosceles triangle?

5.3 Analyzing Circles

A Cartesian coordinate plane can be helpful for the study of geometric figures because you can locate and label points on the figure using coordinates. A circle with its center at the origin is shown below. The **radius** of a circle is the distance from the center to any point on the circle.

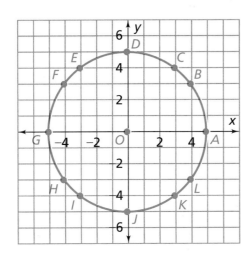

- How can you use the Pythagorean Theorem to find radius *OC*? Radius *OB*? Radius *OL*? Explain.

- What is the radius of the circle above?

 If the coordinates of a point on a circle centered at the origin is (*x*, *y*), what is the relationship between *x* and *y*?

Problem 5.3

A Dustin looks at the diagram below. He says, "If the center of this circle is at the origin, then I can find the length of the radius."

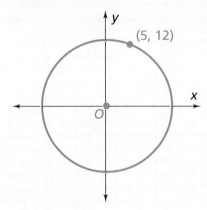

1. Explain how Dustin can find the length of the radius of this circle.

2. What is the length of the radius?

B The coordinates of a point on the circle below are (x, y).

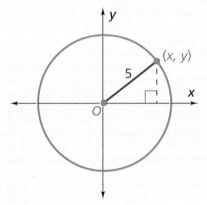

1. Use the Pythagorean Theorem to write an equation showing a relationship between x and y.

2. Would your equation describe the relationship between coordinates (x, y) for any point on any circle? Explain.

Problem **5.3** *continued*

C **1.** Use the Pythagorean Theorem to write the equation of any circle with a center at the origin and radius *r*.

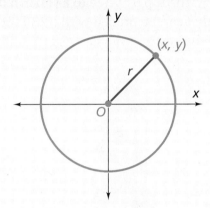

2. The hospital in a big city is located at $(0, 0)$ on a gridded map. The lines on the grid are 1 mile apart. The paramedics make a circle on a map, showing all the locations within a helicopter distance of 10 miles of the hospital. Which equation matches the circle they draw? Explain.

I. $x^2 + y^2 = 10$

II. $x^2 + y^2 = 20$

III. $x^2 + y^2 = 100$

3. A stadium is 5 miles east and 5 miles north of the hospital. It is located at $(5, 5)$ on the map. Is this inside, outside, or on the circle drawn by the paramedics?

ACE Homework starts on page 88.

Applications | **Connections** | **Extensions**

Applications

1. At an evergreen farm, the taller trees are braced by wires. A wire extends from 2 feet below the top of a tree to a stake in the ground. What is the tallest tree that can be braced with a 25-foot wire staked 15 feet from the base of the tree?

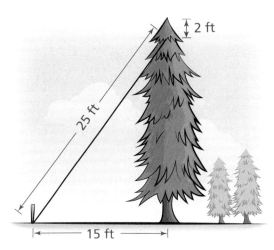

2. Scott, a college student, needs to walk from his dorm room in Wilson Hall to his math class in Wells Hall. Normally, he walks 500 meters east and 600 meters north along the sidewalks, but today he is running late. He decides to take the shortcut through the Quad.

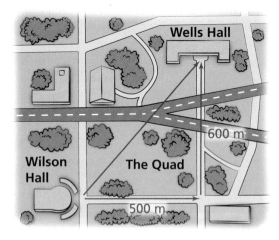

   a. How many meters long is Scott's shortcut?

   b. How much shorter is the shortcut than Scott's usual route?

3. Sierra wants to buy a new laptop computer. She likes two computers that look very similar. Sierra wants to figure out how they differ. Here are her two options:

Option 1: 13-inch screen with a 5.5-inch side length

Option 2: 13.3-inch screen with a 5.1-inch side length

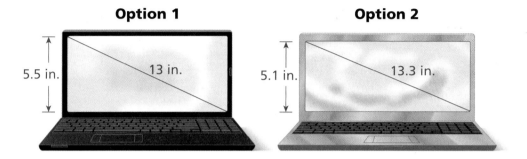

Option 1   **Option 2**

5.5 in.   13 in.   5.1 in.   13.3 in.

  a. What are the dimensions of the rectangular computer screen for each option?

  b. Which screen has the greater area?

4. Kala and Ali are making a kite. To make the frame, they place a 40-inch stick horizontally across a 60-inch stick so that both sides of the horizontal stick are equal in length. Then they tie the two sticks together with the string to form right angles. The longer part of the 60-inch stick measures 50 inches, as shown below.

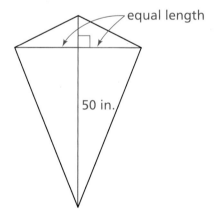

equal length

50 in.

Kala says that 130 inches of string will be enough to stretch all around the kite frame. Ali says that they will need at least 153 inches of string. Who is correct? Explain.

5. As part of his math assignment, Santos has to estimate the height of a lighthouse. He decides to use what he knows about 30-60-90 triangles. Santos makes the measurements shown below. About how tall is the tower? Explain.

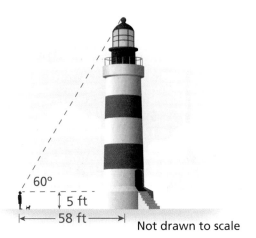

60°

5 ft

← 58 ft →

Not drawn to scale

6. Use the figure below.

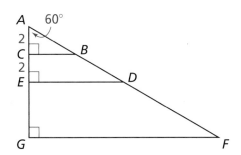

a. Name all the 30-60-90 triangles in the figure. Are all of these triangles similar to each other? Explain.

b. Find the ratio of the length of segment *BA* to the length of segment *AC*. What can you say about the corresponding ratio in the other 30-60-90 triangles?

c. Find the ratio of the length of segment *BC* to the length of segment *AC*. What can you say about the corresponding ratios in the other 30-60-90 triangles?

d. Find the ratio of the length of segment *BC* to the length of segment *AB*. What can you say about the corresponding ratios in the other 30-60-90 triangles?

e. Suppose segment *AG* is 8 units long. How long are segments *AF* and *GF*?

7. Use the figure below.

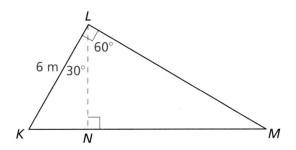

a. How many 30-60-90 triangles do you see in the figure?

b. What is the perimeter of triangle *KLM*?

8. In Problem 5.2, you found the side lengths of the triangle below left.

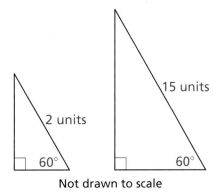

Not drawn to scale

a. Explain how you know that the triangle on the right is similar to the triangle on the left.

b. Use the side lengths of the smaller triangle to find the unknown side lengths of the larger triangle. Explain.

c. How are the areas of the two triangles related?

9. Use the circle below.

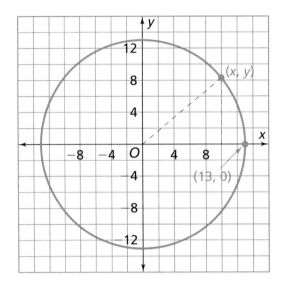

a. Write an equation that relates x and y for any point (x, y) on the circle.

b. Find the missing coordinates for each of these points on the circle. If there is more than one possible point, give the missing coordinate for each possibility. Show that each ordered pair satisfies the equation.

$(0, \blacksquare)$ $(5, \blacksquare)$ $(-4, \blacksquare)$ $(-8, \blacksquare)$

$(\blacksquare, 10)$ $(\blacksquare, -6)$ $(\blacksquare, 0)$ $(\blacksquare, -2)$

10. Use the circle below.

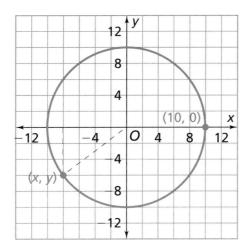

a. Write an equation that relates x and y for any point (x, y) on the circle.

b. Find the missing coordinates for each of these points on the circle. If there is more than one possible point, give the missing coordinate for each possibility. Show that each ordered pair satisfies the equation.

$(8, \blacksquare)$ $(3, \blacksquare)$ $(-4, \blacksquare)$ $(0, \blacksquare)$

$(\blacksquare, -4)$ $(\blacksquare, -6)$ $(\blacksquare, 0)$ $(\blacksquare, 2)$

11. Jada's parents get a new wireless router that has signal range up to 1,400 feet. Jada wants to know whether she will have Internet access in her tree house. She makes a coordinate map of their house with the router at the origin.

a. Jada's tree house is located at (600, 800) on her coordinate map. Will Jada have an Internet connection? Explain.

b. What is the equation of the circle representing Internet coverage?

Connections

12. For each type of quadrilateral in the first column, identify all the properties from the second column that apply to that type of quadrilateral.

Quadrilateral Types

a. square

b. rectangle

c. rhombus

d. parallelogram

Properties

i. Two pairs of parallel sides

ii. Four right angles

iii. Two pairs of congruent sides

iv. Interior angle measures with a sum of 360°

v. Opposite angle measures with a sum of 180°

vi. Perpendicular diagonals

13. A tangram is a puzzle that contains seven pieces: 5 isosceles right triangles, a parallelogram, and a square. You can form a big square by putting all seven pieces together. Suppose the length of the leg of the small isosceles right triangle is 1.7 centimeters. What is the side length of the big square? (**Hint**: Two small triangles can form the medium-sized right triangle and the parallelogram.)

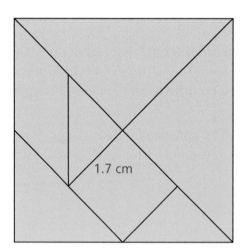

1.7 cm

Two cars leave a city at noon. One car travels north and the other travels east. Use this information for Exercises 14 and 15.

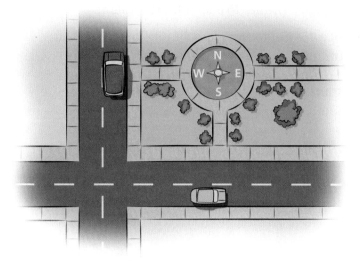

14. Suppose the northbound car is traveling at 60 miles per hour and the eastbound car is traveling at 50 miles per hour. Make a table that shows the distance each car has traveled and the distance between the two cars after 1 hour, 2 hours, 3 hours, and so on. Describe how the distances are changing.

15. Suppose the northbound car is traveling at 40 miles per hour. After 2 hours, the cars are 100 miles apart. How fast is the other car going? Explain.

16. Square *ABCD* has sides of length 1 unit. Copy the square. Draw diagonal *BD*, forming two triangles. Cut out the square and fold it along the diagonal.

    a. How do the two triangles compare?

    b. Find the angle measures for one of the triangles. Explain how you found each measure.

    c. What is the length of the diagonal? Explain.

    d. Suppose square *ABCD* had sides of length 5 units instead of 1 unit. How would this change your answers to parts (b) and (c)?

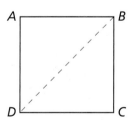

17. A right triangle with a 45° angle is called a 45-45-90 triangle, or an isosceles right triangle.

   a. Are all 45-45-90 triangles similar to each other? Explain.

   b. Suppose one leg of a 45-45-90 triangle is 5 units long. Find the perimeter of the triangle.

18. The diagram shows tram cars gliding along a cable. How long is the cable to the nearest tenth of a meter?

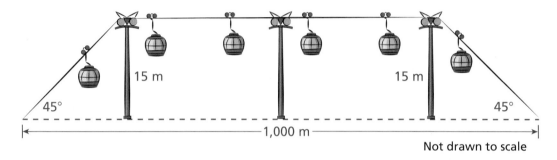

15 m   15 m

45°   45°

1,000 m

Not drawn to scale

19. Ming is building a large equilateral triangle using pattern blocks that are small equilateral triangles. Each side of the triangular pattern blocks measures $1\frac{1}{2}$ inches.

 a. Ming thinks that four pattern blocks will be enough to make the large equilateral triangle. Do you agree with him? Use a drawing to explain.

 b. What is the height of the large equilateral triangle?

 c. Pat claims that he can transform this large equilateral triangle into a rectangle if he can use pattern blocks that are cut in half. Is this possible? If so, what are the dimensions of this rectangle?

For Exercises 20–31, find the value of each expression.

20. $12 + (-18)$ **21.** $-9 + (-19)$ **22.** $-32 - 73$

23. $-23 - (-12)$ **24.** $90 - (-24)$ **25.** $34 - 76$

26. $-23 \cdot (-3)$ **27.** $5 \cdot (-13)$ **28.** $-12 \cdot 20$

29. $-24 \div 6$ **30.** $-42 \div (-2)$ **31.** $84 \div (-4)$

Write an equation for the line with the given slope and y-intercept.

32. slope $\frac{1}{2}$, y-intercept $(0, 3)$

33. slope $-\frac{1}{3}$, y-intercept $(0, 5)$

34. slope 6, y-intercept $(0, \frac{1}{2})$

Write an equation for the line with the given slope and that passes through the given point.

35. slope 2, point $(3, 1)$

36. slope -4, point $(-1, 7)$

37. slope $-\frac{5}{6}$, point $(0, 5)$

38. In the design below, the radius of the circle is 6 meters.

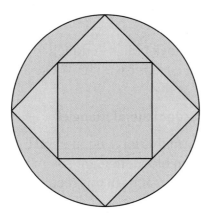

    a. What is the side length of the larger square? What is the area of the larger square?

    b. What is the area of the smaller square?

    c. What is the area of the region between the smaller and larger squares?

    d. What is the area of the region between the larger square and the circle?

39. Use the design below.

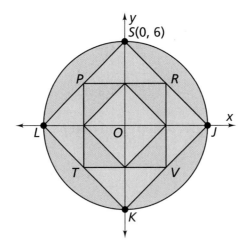

    a. Find the equation of the circle.

    b. Find the length of segment LS and the area of square $LSJK$.

    c. Find the length of segment PR and the area of square $PRVT$.

    d. What are the coordinates of points P and R? Explain.

Extensions

40. The roads connecting a store, a library, and a movie theater form a right triangle. It takes half an hour to go from the store to the library traveling at 50 miles per hour. It takes half an hour to go from the library to the movie theater traveling at 60 miles per hour.

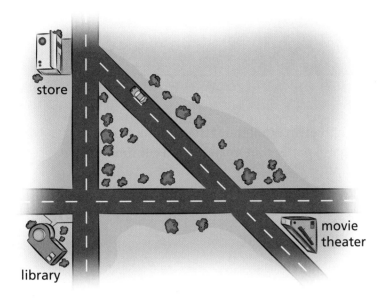

    a. How far is it from the store to the movie theater?

    b. How long will it take to travel from the store to the movie theater traveling at 55 miles per hour?

41. Segment *AB* below makes a 45° angle with the *x*-axis. The length of segment *AB* is 5 units.

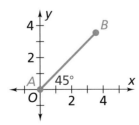

    a. Find the coordinates of point *B* to two decimal places.

    b. What is the slope of line *AB*?

42. In origami, you mostly use square paper. However, if you want to make a flower with three petals, you need to use paper in the shape of an equilateral triangle. You can make paper in the shape of an equilateral triangle from square paper.

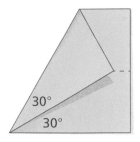
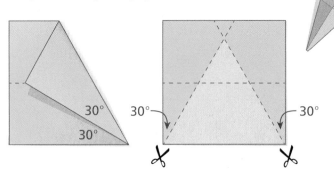

a. What is the side length of an equilateral triangle made out of a piece of square origami paper that measures 15 centimeters by 15 centimeters?

b. What is the height of the equilateral triangle?

43. Use the figure below.

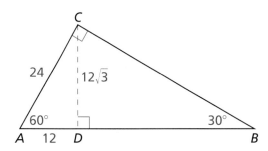

a. What is the length of segment *BD*? Segment *AB*?

b. What is the length of segment *BC*?

c. Ky figures the area of triangle *ABC* is $\frac{1}{2}(24)(24\sqrt{3})$ square units. Is he correct? Explain his reasoning.

d. Mario thinks the area of triangle *ABC* is $\frac{1}{2}(48)(12\sqrt{3})$ square units. Is he correct? Explain his reasoning.

e. Jen thinks the area of triangle *ABC* is $\frac{1}{2}(12)(12\sqrt{3}) + \frac{1}{2}(36)(12\sqrt{3})$ square units. Is she correct? Explain her reasoning.

f. Are the answers in parts (c)–(e) equivalent? Explain.

44. Use the design below.

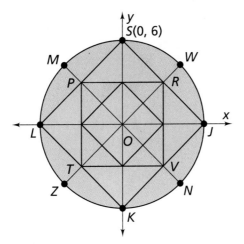

a. What are the coordinates of points *P*, *R*, *V*, and *T*?

b. What is the equation of the line through points *R* and *T*?

c. If you extend the line through points *R* and *T*, the line would meet the circle at two points, *W* and *Z*. What are the coordinates of points *W* and *Z*? Explain how you know these points are on the circle.

d. If you extend the line through points *P* and *V*, the line would meet the circle at two points, *M* and *N*. What are the coordinates of points *M* and *N*?

e. Is *WMZN* a square? Explain.

45. This circle has radius 5 and center (1, 2).

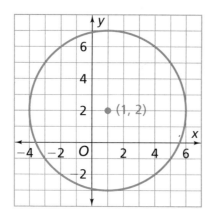

Find or estimate the missing coordinates for these points on the circle. In each case, use the Pythagorean Theorem to check that the point is 5 units from the center.

a. (■, 6)   **b.** (5, ■)   **c.** (−3, ■)

d. (1, ■)   **e.** (■, 2)   **f.** (4, ■)

46. This circle has radius 5 and center (1, 2). Segment *AC* is parallel to the *x*-axis. Segment *BC* is parallel to the *y*-axis.

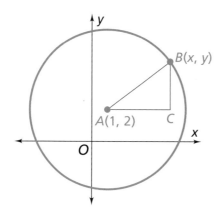

a. What are the lengths of segments *AC*, *BC*, and *AB* in terms of *x* and *y*?

b. What equation shows how these side lengths are related?

c. Suppose you redraw the figure with *B*(*x*, *y*) in a different position, but still on the circle. Would the coordinates of point *B* still fit the equation you wrote in part (b)?

d. Based on this Exercise, what do you think is the general equation for points on a circle with center (*m*, *n*) and radius *r*?

Mathematical Reflections 5

In this Investigation, you applied the ideas from the first three Investigations. The following questions will help you summarize what you have learned.

Think about these questions. Discuss your ideas with other students and your teacher. Then write a summary of your findings in your notebook.

1. **Give** at least two examples of ways in which the Pythagorean Theorem can be useful.

2. **Describe** the special properties of a 30-60-90 triangle.

3. **What** information do you need to write the equation of a circle with a center at the origin?

Common Core Mathematical Practices

As you worked on the Problems in this Investigation, you used prior knowledge to make sense of them. You also applied Mathematical Practices to solve the Problems. Think back over your work, the ways you thought about the Problems, and how you used Mathematical Practices.

Nick described his thoughts in the following way:

In Problem 5.2, we noticed that equilateral triangles have reflectional symmetry. So we could draw a vertical line from a vertex to the base opposite the vertex.

Once we divided the triangle into two separate triangles, we recognized which angles and sides were important and how they related to other parts of the triangle. We were then able to use this information and the Pythagorean Theorem to find the perimeter and area of the triangle.

Common Core Standards for Mathematical Practice
MP4 Model with mathematics.

- What other Mathematical Practices can you identify in Nick's reasoning?

- Describe a Mathematical Practice that you and your classmates used to solve a different Problem in this Investigation.

While working on the Problems in this Unit, you extended your skill in using coordinate systems to locate points and figures. Then, by studying patterns in the side lengths and areas of squares on coordinate grids, you learned the Pythagorean Theorem for right triangles. You used that property of right triangles to solve a variety of practical problems, some of which involved irrational numbers.

Use Your Understanding: The Pythagorean Theorem

Test your understanding of the Pythagorean Theorem by solving the following problems.

1. The diagram below shows a Chinese tangram puzzle on a 10-by-10 grid.

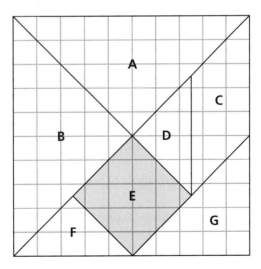

    a. What is the area of Shape E?

    b. What is the length of each side of Shape E?

    c. What are the lengths of the sides of Triangle A?

    d. Name all the triangles that are similar to Triangle A. In each case, give a scale factor for the similarity relationship.

2. A 60-foot piece of wire is strung between the top of a tower and the ground, making a 30-60-90 triangle.

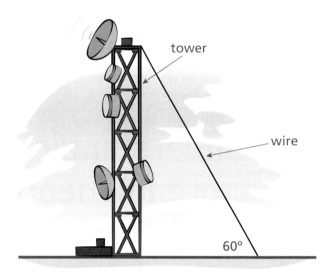

a. How far from the center of the base of the tower is the wire attached to the ground?

b. How high is the tower?

Explain Your Reasoning

When you present work based on the Pythagorean relationship, you should be able to justify your calculations and conclusions.

3. How can you find the side length of a square if you know its area?

4. How can you find the length of a segment joining two points on a coordinate grid?

5. The diagrams below show squares on the sides of triangles.

Figure 1   **Figure 2**

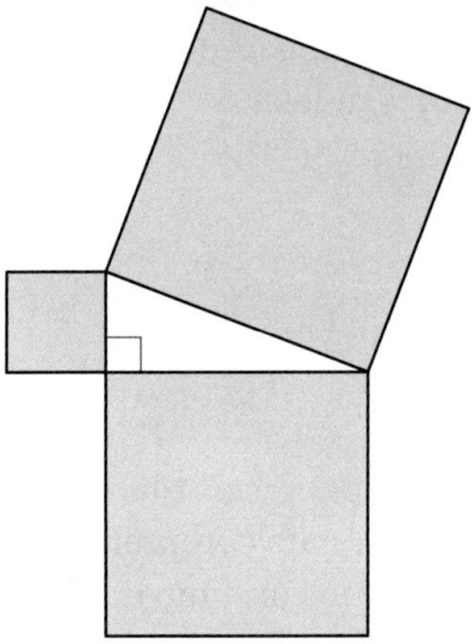

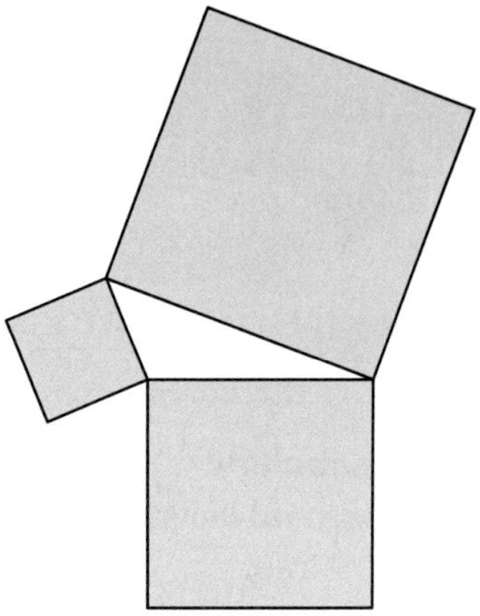

a. In Figure 1, what is the relationship among the areas of the squares?

b. Explain why the relationship you described in part (a) is not true for Figure 2.

6. Explain with words and symbols how to use the Pythagorean Theorem to find the following:

a. the length of a diagonal of a square with side length s.

b. the length of a diagonal of a rectangle with side lengths s and t.

c. the length of the hypotenuse of a right triangle with legs of lengths s and t.

d. the height of an equilateral triangle with side length s.

e. the length of one leg of a triangle when the lengths of the hypotenuse and the other leg are h and t, respectively.

English / Spanish Glossary

A **acute triangle** An acute triangle is a triangle with three acute angles.

triángulo acutángulo Un triángulo acutángulo es un triángulo cuyos tres ángulos son agudos.

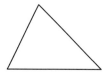

analyze Academic Vocabulary
To think about and understand facts and details about a given set of information. Analyzing can involve providing a written summary supported by factual information, a diagram, chart, table, or a combination of these.

related terms *explain, describe, justify*

sample Analyze the squares. How is the side length of a square related to the area?

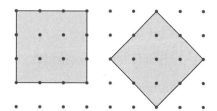

The first square has an area of 9 units² and a side length of 3 units. The side length is the square root of the area. The second square has an area of 4 full units² and 8 half-units² for a total of 8 units². The side length is the square root of the area or √8 units.

analizar Vocabulario académico
Pensar para comprender datos y detalles sobre un conjunto determinado de información dada. Analizar puede incluir un resumen escrito apoyado por información real, un diagrama, una gráfica, una tabla o una combinación de estos.

términos relacionados *explicar, describir, justificar*

ejemplo Analiza los cuadrados. ¿Cómo se relaciona la longitud del lado con el área?

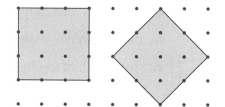

El primer cuadrado tiene un área de 9 unidades² y una longitud del lado de 3 unidades. La longitud del lado es la raíz cuadrada del área. El segundo cuadrado tiene un área de 4 unidades² completas y 8 unidades² medias que hacen un total de 8 unidades². La longitud del lado es la raíz cuadrada del área o √8 unidades.

C **cube root** If $A = s^3$, then s is the cube root of A. For example, 2 is the cube root of 8 because $2 \cdot 2 \cdot 2 = 8$. The $\sqrt[3]{}$ symbol is used to denote the cube root.

raíz cúbica Si $A = s^3$, entonces s es la raíz cúbica de A. Por ejemplo, 2 es la raíz cúbica de 8 porque $2 \cdot 2 \cdot 2 = 8$. El símbolo $\sqrt[3]{}$ se usa para indicar la raíz cúbica.

This cube has the volume of 8 cubic units. The length of each edge is the cube root of 8 units, which is equal to 2 units.

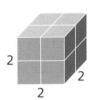

Este cubo tiene un volumen de 8 unidades cúbicas. La longitud de cada arista es la raíz cúbica de 8 unidades, que es igual a 2 unidades.

E **estimate** Academic Vocabulary
To find an approximate answer.

related terms *approximate, guess*

sample Estimate $\sqrt{10}$.

> I know that $\sqrt{9} = 3$ and $\sqrt{16} = 4$. Since $\sqrt{10}$ is much closer to $\sqrt{9}$ than it is to $\sqrt{16}$, my estimate will be closer to 3 than to 4. I tried 3.1, but $3.1^2 < 10$. I tried 3.2, but $3.2^2 > 10$. I estimate $\sqrt{10}$ as about 3.2.

hacer una estimación Vocabulario académico Hallar una respuesta aproximada.

términos relacionados *aproximar, suponer*

ejemplo Estima $\sqrt{10}$.

> Sé que $\sqrt{9} = 3$ y $\sqrt{16} = 4$. Puesto que $\sqrt{10}$ está mucho más cerca de $\sqrt{9}$ que de $\sqrt{16}$, mi estimación estaría más cercana a 3 que a 4. Intenté con 3.1, pero $3.1^2 < 10$. Intenté con 3.2, pero $3.2^2 > 10$. Estimo que $\sqrt{10}$ es aproximadamente 3.2.

F **find** Academic Vocabulary To use the given information and any related facts to determine or calculate a value. You may use mathematical algorithms, properties, formulas, or a combination of these, as well as other mathematical strategies, when finding a value.

related terms *calculate, discover, determine*

sample Find the area of the triangle below.

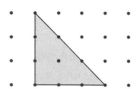

I can count the number of unit squares. △ABC has an area of 4.5 unit squares. I can also find the area by using the formula $A = \frac{1}{2}bh$, where the base and the height of the triangle are each 3 units in length.
$A = \frac{1}{2}(3)(3) = 4.5$ square units

hallar Vocabulario académico Usar la información dada y los datos relacionados para determinar o calcular un valor. Puedes usar algoritmos matemáticos, propiedades, fórmulas o una combinación de estos, así como otras estrategias matemáticas, cuando hallas un valor.

términos relacionados *calcular, descubrir, determinar*

ejemplo Halla el área del triángulo.

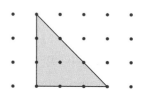

Puedo contar ei número de unidades cuadradas. El △ABC tiene un área de 4.5 unidades cuadradas. Puedo hallar el área usando la fórmula $A = \frac{1}{2}ba$, donde la base y la altura del triángulo miden 3 unidades de longitud respectivamente.
$A = \frac{1}{2}(3)(3) = 4.5$ unidades cuadradas

H **hypotenuse** The side of a right triangle that is opposite the right angle. The hypotenuse is the longest side of a right triangle. In the triangle below, the side labeled *c* is the hypotenuse.

hipotenusa El lado de un triángulo rectángulo que está opuesto al ángulo recto. La hipotenusa es el lado más largo de un triángulo rectángulo. En el triángulo de abajo, el lado rotulado *c* es la hipotenusa.

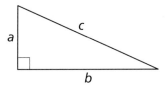

I **irrational number** A number that cannot be written as a quotient of two integers where the denominator is not 0. The decimal representation of an irrational number never ends and never shows a repeating pattern of a fixed number of digits. The numbers $\sqrt{2}$, $\sqrt{3}$, $\sqrt{5}$, and π are examples of irrational numbers.

número irracional Un número que no se puede escribir como el cociente de dos números enteros donde el denominador no es 0. La representación decimal de un número irracional nunca termina, y nunca muestra un patrón de un número fijo de dígitos que se repite. Los números $\sqrt{2}$, $\sqrt{3}$, $\sqrt{5}$, y π son ejemplos de números irracionales.

L **legs** The sides of a right triangle that are adjacent to the right angle. In the triangle above, the sides labeled *a* and *b* are legs.

catetos Los lados de un triángulo rectángulo que son adyacentes al ángulo recto. En el triángulo de arriba, los lados *a* y *b* son los catetos.

observe Academic Vocabulary

To notice or to examine carefully one or more characteristics of a particular object.

related terms *notice, examine, note, see*

sample What do you observe about the sum of the squares of the lengths of the legs of the right triangle in relationship to the length of the hypotenuse?

If I square the length of the hypotenuse, I get $5^2 = 25$. This is equal to the sum of the squares of the lengths of the legs of the triangle $3^2 + 4^2 = 9 + 16 = 25$.

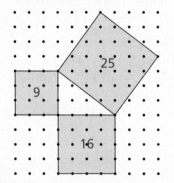

The area of the square built on the hypotenuse is equal to the sum of the areas of the squares built on the two legs of the right triangle.

observar Vocabulario académico

Notar o examinar con cuidado una o más características de un objeto determinado.

términos relacionados *notar, examinar, mirar, ver*

ejemplo ¿Qué observas sobre la suma de los cuadrados de las longitudes de los catetos del triángulo rectángulo con relación a la longitud de la hipotenusa?

Si elevo al cuadrado la longitud de la hipotenusa, obtengo $5^2 = 25$. Esto es igual a la suma de los cuadrados de las longitudes de los catetos del triángulo $3^2 + 4^2 = 9 + 16 = 25$.

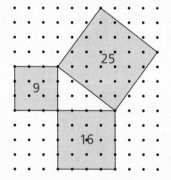

El área del cuadrado construido sobre la hipotenusa es igual a la suma de las áreas de los cuadrados construidos sobre los dos catetos del triángulo rectángulo.

obtuse triangle An obtuse triangle has one angle with a measure greater than 90°.

triángulo obtusángulo Un triángulo obtusángulo tiene un ángulo con una medida mayor que 90°.

P **perpendicular** Forming a right angle. For example, the sides of a right triangle that form the right angle are perpendicular.

perpendicular Que forma un ángulo recto. Por ejemplo, los lados de un triángulo rectángulo que forman el ángulo recto son perpendiculares.

Pythagorean Theorem A statement about the relationship among the lengths of the sides of a right triangle. The theorem states that if a and b are the lengths of the legs of a right triangle and c is the length of the hypotenuse, then $a^2 + b^2 = c^2$.

teorema de Pitágoras Un enunciado acerca de la relación que existe entre las longitudes de los lados de un triángulo rectángulo. El teorema enuncia que si a y b son las longitudes de los catetos de un triángulo rectángulo y c es la longitud de la hipotenusa, entonces $a^2 + b^2 = c^2$.

R **radius** A radius of a circle is the distance from the center of the circle to any point on the circle.

radio El radio de un círculo es la distancia que hay desde el centro del círculo a cualquier punto en el círculo.

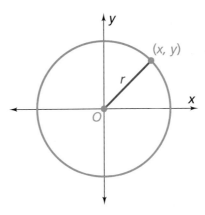

rational number A number that can be written as a quotient of two integers where the denominator is not 0. The decimal representation of a rational number either ends or repeats. Examples of rational numbers are $\frac{1}{2}$, $\frac{80}{99}$, 7, 0.2, and 0.191919 . . .

número racional Un número que se puede escribir como el cociente de dos números enteros donde el denominador no es 0. La representación decimal de un número racional termina o se repite. Ejemplos de números racionales son $\frac{1}{2}$, $\frac{80}{99}$, 7, 0.2 y 0.191919 . . .

real numbers The set of all rational numbers and all irrational numbers. The number line represents the set of real numbers.

números reales El conjunto de todos los números racionales y todos los números irracionales. La recta numérica representa el conjunto de los números reales.

repeating decimal A decimal with a pattern of a fixed number of digits that repeats forever, such as 0.3333333 . . . and 0.73737373 . . . . Repeating decimals are rational numbers.

decimal periódico Un número decimal con un patrón de un número fijo de dígitos que se repite infinitamente, como 0.3333333 . . . y 0.73737373 . . . Los decimales que se repiten son números racionales.

right triangle A right triangle is a triangle with one right angle.

triángulo rectángulo Un triángulo rectángulo es un triángulo que tiene un ángulo recto.

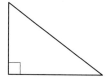

S **square root** If $A = s^2$, then s is the square root of A. For example, -3 and 3 are square roots of 9 because $3 \cdot 3 = 9$ and $-3 \cdot (-3) = 9$. The $\sqrt{}$ symbol is used to denote the positive square root. So, you write $\sqrt{9} = 3$. The positive square root of a number is the side length of a square that has that number as its area.

raíz cuadrada Si $A = s^2$, entonces s es la raíz cuadrada de A. Por ejemplo, -3 y 3 son raíces cuadradas de 9 porque $3 \cdot 3 = 9$ y $-3 \cdot (-3) = 9$. El símbolo $\sqrt{}$ se usa para indicar la raíz cuadrada positiva. Por eso, escribimos $\sqrt{9} = 3$. La raíz cuadrada positiva de un número es la longitud del lado de un cuadrado que tiene dicho número como su área.

T **terminating decimal** A decimal that ends, or terminates, such as 0.5 or 0.125. Terminating decimals are rational numbers.

decimal finito Un decimal que se acaba o termina, como 0.5 ó 0.125. Los decimales finitos son números racionales.

theorem A theorem is a general mathematical statement that has been proven true.

teorema Un teorema es un enunciado matemático general que se ha demostrado.

Index

accuracy, measurements and, 62

ACE
   analyzing triangles and
      circles, 88–102
   coordinate grids, 14–19
   Pythagorean Theorem,
      49–57
   squares, 29–35
   understanding real numbers
      and, 71–76

acute triangles, 38, 39–40

angle measures, 82

area, 3, 75, 105
   coordinate grids and, 13,
      18–19
   of pyramids, 76
   radius and, 98
   of rectangles, 89
   right triangles and, 55
   side lengths, 4
   of squares, 23, 24, 31
   of triangles, 16

baseball, 81

**Cartesian coordinate
   planes,** 85

circles
   Pythagorean Theorem and,
      85–87, 92–93, 102
   writing equations of, 103

**Common Core Mathematical
   Practices,** 5–6, 21, 37, 59,
      78, 104

cones, 52, 74

**converse, of Pythagorean
   Theorem,** 47

coordinate grids, 4
   ACE, 14–19
   finding areas, 13
   finding distances, 93, 106

locating points and finding
   distances, 10–11
Mathematical Reflections,
   20–21
shapes and, 12
squares and, 34
street maps and, 7–9

cube roots, 27–28, 32–33, 36

cubes, 74

cylinders, 52

decimals
   fractions and, 4
   representing decimals as
      fractions, 66–67, 72, 77
   representing fractions as
      decimals, 63–65, 71

diagonals, 72, 95, 107

distance, finding
   coordinate grids and, 10–11,
      14–15, 16, 20
   Pythagorean Theorem and,
      44–45, 50–51, 53–54, 58,
      88, 95
   right triangles and, 79–80, 99

division, 65

dot grids
   finding lengths with squares
      and, 25–26
   line segments and, 32
   Pythagorean Theorem, 44
   squares and, 22–23, 29

edge lengths, 32. *See also* side
   lengths

**Egyptian method for
   measuring angles,** 46–48

equilateral triangles, 82, 83, 97,
   100, 107

Explain Your Reasoning,
   106–107

45-45-90 triangles, 96

fractions
   decimals and, 4
   representing decimals as
      fractions, 66–67, 72, 77
   representing fractions as
      decimals, 63–65, 71

Glossary, 108–114

height, 90

hexagons, 29, 55

hypotenuse, 38, 49, 62, 71

Investigations
   analyzing triangles and
      circles, 79–87
   coordinate grids, 7–13
   Pythagorean Theorem,
      38–48
   squares, 22–28
   understanding real numbers,
      60–70

irrational numbers, 3, 4, 70,
   73, 77
   representing decimals as
      fractions, 72
   understanding real numbers
      and, 68–70

irregular shapes, 13, 16, 20

isosceles triangles, 84

legs, 38

length, 25–27. *See also* side
   lengths

lines
   coordinate grids and, 18
   equations for, 97

line segments
   equilateral triangles and, 82
   finding lengths with squares
      and, 25–26
   of squares, 32
   squares and, 30, 36
   triangles and, 90, 100

Looking Ahead, 2–3

Looking Back, 105–107

maps, coordinate grids and, 8–9, 19

Mathematical Highlights, 4

Mathematical Practices, 5–6

Mathematical Reflections
  analyzing triangles and circles, 103–104
  coordinate grids, 20–21
  Pythagorean Theorem, 58–59
  squares, 36–37
  understanding real numbers and, 77–78

negative numbers, 27, 30

nets, 51, 70

number lines, 4, 29, 35

obtuse triangles, 38, 39–40

parallelograms, 15, 18, 19, 35, 94

perimeter, 33, 89, 91

perpendicular lines, 18

points, locating, 10–11, 17–18

polygons, 15

prisms, 51, 52, 72

proofs, Pythagorean Theorem and, 4, 41–43

pyramids, 52, 74

Pythagoras, 41

Pythagorean Theorem, 3, 4, 38
  ACE, 49–57
  analyzing triangles and circles, 79–87
  Explain Your Reasoning, 106–107
  finding distances, 44–45
  Mathematical Reflections, 58–59
  proofs and, 41–43

right angles and, 46–48
right triangles and, 49
triangles and side lengths, 39–40
understanding real numbers, 60–70
Use Your Understanding, 105–106

quadrilaterals, 53, 94

radius, 54, 85, 86, 87, 98, 102

rational numbers, 4, 63–64, 70

real numbers, understanding
  ACE, 71–76
  irrational numbers and, 68–70
  Mathematical Reflections, 77–78
  Pythagorean Theorem and, 60
  representing decimals as fractions, 66–67
  representing fractions as decimals, 63–65
  the Wheel of Theodorus and, 61–62

reasoning, explaining your
  coordinate grids and, 11, 21
  Pythagorean Theorem, 59
  rational and irrational numbers, 70, 80
  squares and, 36, 37
  triangles and, 104
  understanding real numbers, 78

rectangles, 89, 94, 107

repeating decimals, 63, 64, 66, 68, 71, 77

rhombuses, 94

right angles, 46–48

right triangles, 3, 33, 107
  coordinate grids and, 15
  finding distances and, 79–80, 99
  45-45-90 triangles, 96

Pythagorean Theorem and, 38, 39–40, 83, 84
side lengths and, 51, 58
squares and, 49

shapes, coordinate grids and, 12

side lengths, 3, 32
  area and volume, 4
  equilateral triangles and, 82
  Pythagorean Theorem and, 38, 39–40, 50, 79–81, 105
  radius and, 98, 102
  right triangles and, 51, 58, 73
  squares and, 23–24, 31, 106, 107
  triangles and, 46–48
  volume and, 28
  Wheel of Theodorus, 71

square numbers, 56

square roots, 23–25, 29, 30, 36, 73

squares, 3, 22–23
  ACE, 29–35
  coordinate grids and, 12
  cube roots and, 27–28
  finding lengths with squares, 25–27
  Mathematical Reflections, 36–37
  properties of, 94
  right triangles and, 49
  side lengths and, 106, 107
  square roots and, 23–25

surface area and volume, 51, 76

tangrams, 94, 105

terminating decimals, 63, 64, 66, 68, 71, 77

Theodorus of Cyrene, 61

theorems. See Pythagorean Theorem

30-60-90 triangle, 83–84, 90, 91, 103

triangles
  area of, 16, 100
  coordinate grids and, 19
  Pythagorean Theorem and,
    38, 39–40, 82–84, 90–91
  similar triangles, 105
  squares and, 35
  Wheel of Theodorus, 61–62,
    71

"upright" squares, 34

Use Your Understanding,
  105–106

vertices, 12, 15, 34

volume, 4, 27, 51, 52, 74, 76

**Washington, D.C., coordinate
  grids and,** 7–9

Wheel of Theodorus, 61–62, 71

whole numbers, 25, 28, 29, 35,
  73

Wizard of Oz, The (movie), 84

x-**coordinate,** 9, 10

y-**coordinate,** 9, 10

Acknowledgments

Cover Design

Three Communication Design, Chicago

Text

084 Excerpt from "*The Wizard of Oz*" granted courtesy of Warner Bros. Entertainment Inc, ©1939. All Rights Reserved.

Photographs

Photo locators denoted as follows: Top (T), Center (C), Bottom (B), Left (L), Right (R), Background (Bkgd)

002 (CR) Erich Lessing/Art Resource, NY, (BR) David R. Frazier Photolibrary, Inc./Alamy; **003** Hfng/Shutterstock; **007** Encyclopedia/Corbis; **041** Getty Images/Thinkstock; **046** Erich Lessing/Art Resource, NY; **079** David R. Frazier Photolibrary, Inc./Alamy; **081** S.F. Hess California League/Baseball Cards/Library of Congress Prints and Photographs Division; **084** Warner Bros/Everett Collection, Inc.; **096** Huw Jones/Lonely Planet Images/Getty Images.

Growing, growing, growing

Exponential Functions

Lappan, Phillips, Fey, Friel

Growing, Growing, Growing

Exponential Functions

Looking Ahead 2

Mathematical Highlights 4

Mathematical Practices and Habits of Mind 5

1

Exponential Growth　　　　　　　　　　　　　7

1.1 **Making Ballots** Introducing Exponential Functions 7

1.2 **Requesting a Reward** Representing Exponential Functions 9

1.3 **Making a New Offer** Growth Factors 11

Ⓐ Ⓒ Ⓔ Homework 14

Mathematical Reflections 25

2

Examining Growth Patterns　　　　　　　　27

2.1 **Killer Plant Strikes Lake Victoria** y-Intercepts Other Than 1 28

2.2 **Growing Mold** Interpreting Equations for Exponential Functions 29

2.3 **Studying Snake Populations** Interpreting Graphs of
Exponential Functions 30

Ⓐ Ⓒ Ⓔ Homework 32

Mathematical Reflections 40

3 Growth Factors and Growth Rates   42

3.1 Reproducing Rabbits Fractional Growth Patterns 42

3.2 Investing for the Future Growth Rates 44

3.3 Making a Difference Connecting Growth Rate and Growth Factor 46

Ⓐ Ⓒ Ⓔ Homework 48

Mathematical Reflections 58

4 Exponential Decay   60

4.1 Making Smaller Ballots Introducing Exponential Decay 60

4.2 Fighting Fleas Representing Exponential Decay 62

4.3 Cooling Water Modeling Exponential Decay 64

Ⓐ Ⓒ Ⓔ Homework 66

Mathematical Reflections 74

5 Patterns With Exponents   76

5.1 Looking for Patterns Among Exponents 77

5.2 Rules of Exponents 78

5.3 Extending the Rules of Exponents 80

5.4 Operations With Scientific Notation 84

5.5 Revisiting Exponential Functions 86

Ⓐ Ⓒ Ⓔ Homework 88

Mathematical Reflections 102

Unit Project Half-Life 104

Looking Back 106

English/Spanish Glossary 109

Index 115

Acknowledgments 118

Looking Ahead

When the water hyacinth was introduced to Lake Victoria, it spread quickly over the lake's surface. At one point, the plant covered 769 square miles, and its area doubled every 15 days. **What** equation models this growth?

When Sam was in seventh grade, his aunt gave him a stamp worth $2,500. The value of the stamp increased by 6% each year for several years in a row. **What** was the value of Sam's stamp after four years?

What pattern of change would you expect to find in the temperature of a hot drink as time passes? **What** would a graph of the *(time, drink temperature)* data look like?

One of the most important uses of algebra is to model patterns of change. You are already familiar with linear patterns of change or linear functions. Linear patterns have constant differences and straight-line graphs. In a linear function, the y-value increases by a constant amount each time the x-value increases by 1.

In this Unit, you will study exponential patterns of change for exponential functions. Exponential growth patterns are fascinating because, although the values may change gradually at first, they eventually increase very rapidly. Patterns that decrease, or decay, exponentially may decrease quickly at first, but eventually they decrease very slowly.

Mathematical Highlights

Exponential Functions

In *Growing, Growing, Growing,* you will explore Exponential Functions, one of the most important types of nonlinear relationships.

The Investigations in this Unit will help you learn how to:

- Identify situations in which a quantity grows or decays exponentially

- Recognize the connections between the growth patterns in tables, graphs, and equations that represent exponential functions

- Construct equations to express the relationship between the variables in an exponential function in data tables, graphs, and problem situations

- Compare exponential and linear functions

- Develop and use rules for working with exponents, including scientific notation, to write and interpret equivalent expressions

- Solve problems about exponential growth and decay from a variety of different areas, including science and business

As you work on the Problems in this Unit, ask yourself questions about situations that involve nonlinear relationships such as:

How can I recognize whether the relationship between the variables is an exponential function?

What is the growth or decay factor?

What equation models the data in the table, graph, or problem situation?

What can I learn about this situation by studying a table or graph of the exponential function?

How can I answer questions about the problem situation by studying a table, graph, or equation that represents the exponential function?

Mathematical Practices and Habits of Mind

In the *Connected Mathematics* curriculum you will develop an understanding of important mathematical ideas by solving problems and reflecting on the mathematics involved. Every day, you will use "habits of mind" to make sense of problems and apply what you learn to new situations. Some of these habits are described by the *Common Core State Standards for Mathematical Practices* (MP).

MP1 Make sense of problems and persevere in solving them.
When using mathematics to solve a problem, it helps to think carefully about

- data and other facts you are given and what additional information you need to solve the problem;
- strategies you have used to solve similar problems and whether you could solve a related simpler problem first;
- how you could express the problem with equations, diagrams, or graphs;
- whether your answer makes sense.

MP2 Reason abstractly and quantitatively.
When you are asked to solve a problem, it often helps to

- focus first on the key mathematical ideas;
- check that your answer makes sense in the problem setting;
- use what you know about the problem setting to guide your mathematical reasoning.

MP3 Construct viable arguments and critique the reasoning of others.
When you are asked to explain why a conjecture is correct, you can

- show some examples that fit the claim and explain why they fit;
- show how a new result follows logically from known facts and principles.

When you believe a mathematical claim is incorrect, you can

- show one or more counterexamples—cases that don't fit the claim;
- find steps in the argument that do not follow logically from prior claims.

MP4 Model with mathematics.

When you are asked to solve problems, it often helps to

- think carefully about the numbers or geometric shapes that are the most important factors in the problem, then ask yourself how those factors are related to each other;
- express data and relationships in the problem with tables, graphs, diagrams, or equations, and check your result to see if it makes sense.

MP5 Use appropriate tools strategically.

When working on mathematical questions, you should always

- decide which tools are most helpful for solving the problem and why;
- try a different tool when you get stuck.

MP6 Attend to precision.

In every mathematical exploration or problem-solving task, it is important to

- think carefully about the required accuracy of results; is a number estimate or geometric sketch good enough, or is a precise value or drawing needed?
- report your discoveries with clear and correct mathematical language that can be understood by those to whom you are speaking or writing.

MP7 Look for and make use of structure.

In mathematical explorations and problem solving, it is often helpful to

- look for patterns that show how data points, numbers, or geometric shapes are related to each other;
- use patterns to make predictions.

MP8 Look for and express regularity in repeated reasoning.

When results of a repeated calculation show a pattern, it helps to

- express that pattern as a general rule that can be used in similar cases;
- look for shortcuts that will make the calculation simpler in other cases.

You will use all of the Mathematical Practices in this Unit. Sometimes, when you look at a Problem, it is obvious which practice is most helpful. At other times, you will decide on a practice to use during class explorations and discussions. After completing each Problem, ask yourself:

- What mathematics have I learned by solving this Problem?
- What Mathematical Practices were helpful in learning this mathematics?

Exponential Growth

In this Investigation, you will explore *exponential growth*. You will cut paper in half over and over to experience exponential growth. You will read a story about the land of Montarek. That story shows how exponential growth can be used. Finally, you will explore exponential patterns and compare them to linear growth patterns with tables, graphs, and equations.

1.1 Making Ballots
Introducing Exponential Functions

Chen is the secretary of the Student Government Association. He is making ballots for a meeting. Chen starts by cutting a sheet of paper in half. Then, he stacks the two pieces and cuts them in half again. With four pieces now, he stacks them and cuts them in half. By repeating this process, he makes smaller and smaller paper ballots.

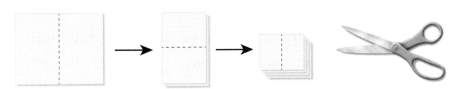

Common Core State Standards

8.F.A.2 Compare properties of two functions each represented in a different way (algebraically, graphically, numerically in tables, or by verbal descriptions).

8.F.A.3 Interpret the equation $y = mx + b$ as defining a linear function, whose graph is a straight line; give examples of functions that are not linear.

8.EE.A.3 Use numbers expressed in the form of a single digit times an integer power of 10 to estimate very large or very small quantities, and to express how many times as much one is than the other.

Also 8.EE.A.4, A-CED.A.1, A-CED.A.2, A-REI.B.3, F-IF.C.7, F-IF.C.7a, F-IF.C.7e, F-IF.C.9, F-BF.A.1, F-BF.A.1a, F-LE.A.1, F-LE.A.1a, F-LE.A.3, F-LE.B.5

After each cut, Chen counts the ballots and records the results in a table.

Number of Cuts	Number of Ballots
1	2
2	4
3	
4	
5	

He wants to predict the number of ballots after any number of cuts.

 Describe the pattern of change. How many ballots are there after *n* cuts?

Problem 1.1

A **1.** Make a table to show the number of ballots after each of the first 5 cuts.

   2. Look for a pattern in the way the number of ballots changes with each cut. Use your observations to extend your table to show the number of ballots for up to 10 cuts.

B **1.** Graph the data and write an equation that represents the relationship between the number of ballots and the number of cuts.

   2. How does the growth pattern show up in the graph and the equation?

   3. Is this relationship a linear function? Explain.

C **1.** Suppose Chen could make 20 cuts. How many ballots would he have? How many ballots would he have if he could make 40 cuts?

   2. How many cuts would it take to make 500 ballots?

A C E Homework starts on page 14.

1.2 Requesting a Reward
Representing Exponential Functions

When you found the number of ballots after 10, 20, and 40 cuts, you may have multiplied long strings of 2s. Instead of writing long product strings of the same factor, you can use **exponential form,** such as 2^5. You can write $2 \times 2 \times 2 \times 2 \times 2$ as 2^5, which is read "2 to the fifth power."

In the expression 2^5, 5 is the **exponent** and 2 is the **base.** When you evaluate 2^5, you get $2^5 = 2 \times 2 \times 2 \times 2 \times 2 = 32$. Since there are two ways to write 2^5, we call 32 the **standard form** and $2 \times 2 \times 2 \times 2 \times 2$ the **expanded form** of 2^5.

Stella used her calculator in Problem 1.1 to compute the number of ballots after 40 cuts. Calculators use shorthand for displaying very large numbers.

2^40

1.099511628E12

This is how the calculator displays $1.099511628 \times 10^{12}$

The number $1.099511628 \times 10^{12}$ is written in **scientific notation.**

This notation can be expanded as follows:

$$1.099511628 \times 10^{12} = 1.099511628 \times 1{,}000{,}000{,}000{,}000$$
$$= 1{,}099{,}511{,}628{,}000$$

The number $1{,}099{,}511{,}628{,}000$ is the standard form for the number $1.099511628 \times 10^{12}$ written in scientific notation.

The calculator above has approximated 2^{40} as accurately as it can with the number of digits it can store. A number written in scientific notation must be in the form:

(a number greater than or equal to 1 but less than 10) $\times$ *(a power of 10)*

As you explore the king's dilemma below, you can use scientific notation to express large numbers.

One day in the ancient kingdom of Montarek, a peasant saved the life of the king's daughter. The king was so grateful he told the peasant she could have any reward she desired. The peasant, the kingdom's chess champion, made an unusual request:

Plan 1—The Peasant's Plan

"I would like you to place 1 ruba on the first square of my chessboard, 2 rubas on the second square, 4 on the third square, 8 on the fourth square, and so on. Continue this pattern until you have covered all 64 squares. Each square should have twice as many rubas as the previous square."

The king replied, "Rubas are the least valuable coin in the kingdom. Surely you can think of a better reward." But the peasant insisted, so the king agreed to her request.

- Did the peasant make a wise choice? Explain.

Problem 1.2

A 1. Make a table showing the number of rubas the king will place on squares 1 through 10 of the chessboard.

2. Graph the points (*number of the square, number of rubas*) for squares 1 to 10.

3. Write an equation for the relationship between the number of the square *n* and the number of rubas *r*.

B 1. How does the number of rubas change from one square to the next?

2. How does the pattern of change you observed in the table show up in the graph? How does it show up in the equation?

C 1. Which square will have 2^{30} rubas? Explain.

2. What is the first square on which the king will place at least one million rubas? How many rubas will be on this square?

3. Larissa uses a calculator to compute the number of rubas on a square. When is the first time the answer is displayed in scientific notation?

D Compare the growth pattern to the growth pattern in Problem 1.1.

ACE Homework starts on page 14.

1.3 Making a New Offer
Growth Factors

The patterns of change in the number of ballots in Problem 1.1 and in the number of rubas in Problem 1.2 show **exponential growth.** In each case, you can find the value for any cut or square by multiplying the previous value by a fixed number. This fixed number is called the **growth factor.** These relationships are called **exponential functions.** The number of the cut or square is the *independent variable*. The number of pieces of paper or rubas on the square is the *dependent variable*.

- What are the growth factors for Problems 1.1 and 1.2?

The king told the queen about the reward he promised the peasant. The queen said, "You have promised her more money than the entire royal treasury! You must convince her to accept a different reward."

Plan 2—The King's New Plan

After much thought, the king came up with Plan 2. He would make a new board with only 16 squares. Then he would place 1 ruba on the first square and 3 rubas on the second. He drew a graph to show the number of rubas on the first five squares. He would continue this pattern until all 16 squares were filled.

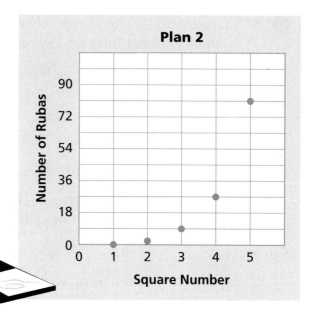

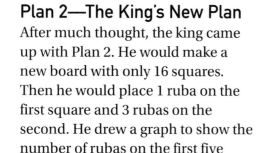

Plan 3—The Queen's Plan

The queen was unconvinced about the king's new plan. She devised Plan 3. Using a board with 12 squares, she would place 1 ruba on the first square. She would use the equation $r = 4^{n-1}$ to figure out how many rubas to put on each square. In the equation, r is the number of rubas on square n.

Problem 1.3

A 1. In the table below, Plan 1 is the reward the peasant requested. Plan 2 is the king's new plan. Plan 3 is the queen's plan. Copy and extend the table to show the number of rubas on squares 1 to 10 for each plan.

Reward Plans

Square Number	Number of Rubas		
	Plan 1	Plan 2	Plan 3
1	1	1	1
2	2	3	4
3	4	■	■
4	■	■	■

Problem 1.3 *continued*

2. **a.** What are the independent and dependent variables in each plan?

    b. How are the patterns of change in the number of rubas under Plans 2 and 3 similar to Plan 1? How are they different from Plan 1?

3. Do the growth patterns for Plans 2 and 3 represent exponential functions? If so, what is the growth factor for each? Explain.

B 1. Write an equation for the relationship between the number of the square n and the number of rubas r for Plan 2.

2. Make a graph of Plan 3 for $n = 1$ to 10. How does your graph compare to the graphs for Plans 1 and 2?

3. How is the growth factor represented in the equations and graphs for Plans 2 and 3?

C The king's financial advisor said that either Plan 2 or Plan 3 would devastate the royal treasury. She proposed a fourth plan.

Plan 4—The Financial Advisor's Plan

The advisor proposed Plan 4. The king would put 20 rubas on the first square, 25 on the second, 30 on the third, and so on. He would increase the number of rubas by 5 for each square. He would continue this pattern until all 64 squares are covered.

1. Compare the growth pattern of Plan 4 to Plans 1, 2, and 3. Is the pattern in Plan 4 an exponential function? Explain.

2. Write an equation that represents the relationship in Plan 4.

D For each plan, how many rubas are on the final square? List them from least to greatest.

A C E Homework starts on page 14.

Applications

1. Cut a sheet of paper into thirds. Stack the three pieces and cut the stack into thirds. Stack all of the pieces and cut the stack into thirds again.

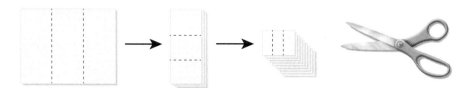

   a. Copy and complete this table to show the number of ballots after repeating this process five times.

   b. Suppose you continued this process. How many ballots would you have after 10 cuts? How many would you have after n cuts?

   c. How many cuts would it take to make at least one million ballots?

   Cutting Ballots

Cutting Processes	Number of Ballots
1	3
2	▩
3	▩
4	▩
5	▩

2. Chen, Lisa, Gabriel, and Artie each take a large piece of paper to make ballots. First, they cut the original piece of paper in half. Then, they cut each of those new pieces in half. Finally, they cut all of those pieces in half for a total of three cuts. They want to know how many ballots they will have without counting them. Each has a different conjecture. Who do you agree with? Explain.

   Chen's Conjecture The total number of ballots will be 2^{12} because as a group we made twelve total cuts.

   Lisa's Conjecture The total number will be 8^4 because each person will have eight ballots, and there are four of us.

   Gabriel's Conjecture The total number will be 4×2^3 because each person makes 2^3 ballots and there are four of us.

   Artie's Conjecture The total number can't be determined using a formula. You will have to count them piece by piece.

3. Angie is studying her family's history. She discovers records of ancestors 12 generations back. She wonders how many ancestors she has from the past 12 generations. She starts to make a diagram to help her figure this out. The diagram soon becomes very complex.

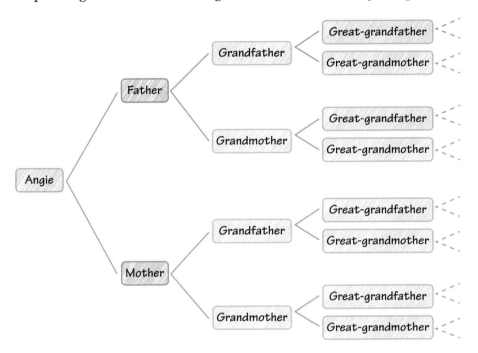

a. Make a table and a graph showing the number of ancestors in each of the 12 generations.

b. Write an equation for the number of ancestors a in a given generation n.

c. What is the total number of ancestors in all 12 generations?

4. Sarah was working on Problem 1.2. She found that there will be 2,147,483,648 rubas on square 32.

   a. How many rubas will be on square 33? How many will be on square 34? How many will be on square 35?

   b. Which square would have the number of rubas shown here?

   $$2{,}147{,}483{,}648 \cdot 2 \cdot 2 \cdot 2 \cdot 2 \cdot 2 \cdot 2 \cdot 2 \cdot 2 \cdot 2$$

   c. Use your calculator to do the multiplication in part (b). Do you notice anything strange about the answer your calculator gives? Explain.

   d. Write $2{,}147{,}483{,}648 \cdot 2 \cdot 2 \cdot 2 \cdot 2 \cdot 2 \cdot 2 \cdot 2 \cdot 2 \cdot 2$ in scientific notation.

   e. Write the numbers 2^{10}, 2^{20}, 2^{30}, 2^{40}, and 2^{50} in scientific notation.

   f. Explain how to write a large number in scientific notation.

For Exercises 5–7, write each number in scientific notation.

5. 100,000,000

6. 29,678,900,522

7. 11,950,500,000,000

For Exercises 8–10, write each number in standard form.

8. 6.43999001×10^8

9. 8.89234×10^5

10. $3.4348567000 \times 10^{10}$

11. What is the largest whole-number value of n that your calculator will display in standard notation?

   a. 3^n

   b. π^n

   c. 12^n

   d. 237^n

12. What is the smallest value of n that your calculator will display in scientific notation?

   a. 10^n

   b. 100^n

   c. $1000n^n$

13. Many single-celled organisms reproduce by dividing into two identical cells.

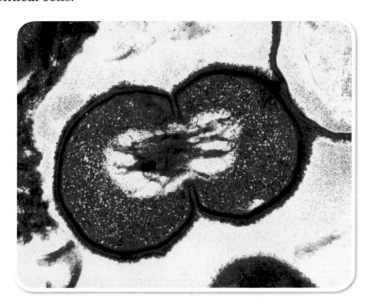

Suppose an amoeba (uh MEE buh) splits into two amoebas every half hour.

   a. A biologist starts an experiment with one amoeba. Make a table showing the number of amoebas she would have at the end of each hour over an 8-hour period.

   b. Write an equation for the number of amoebas a after t hours. Which variable is the independent variable? Dependent variable?

   c. How many hours will it take for the number of amoebas to reach one million?

   d. Make a graph of the data (*time, amoebas*) from part (a).

   e. What similarities do you notice in the pattern of change for the number of amoebas and the patterns of change for other situations in this Investigation? What differences do you notice?

14. Zak's uncle wants to donate money to Zak's school. He suggests three possible plans. Look for a pattern in each plan.

Plan 1 He will continue the pattern in this table until day 12.

School Donations

Day	1	2	3	4
Donation	$1	$2	$4	$8

Plan 2 He will continue the pattern in this table until day 10.

School Donations

Day	1	2	3	4
Donation	$1	$3	$9	$27

Plan 3 He will continue the pattern in this table until day 7.

School Donations

Day	1	2	3	4
Donation	$1	$4	$16	$64

a. Copy and extend each table to show how much money the school would receive each day.

b. For each plan, write an equation for the relationship between the day number n and the number of dollars donated d.

c. Are any of the relationships in Plans 1, 2, or 3 exponential functions? Explain.

d. Which plan would give the school the greatest total amount of money?

15. Carmelita is planning to swim in a charity swim-a-thon. Several relatives said they would sponsor her.

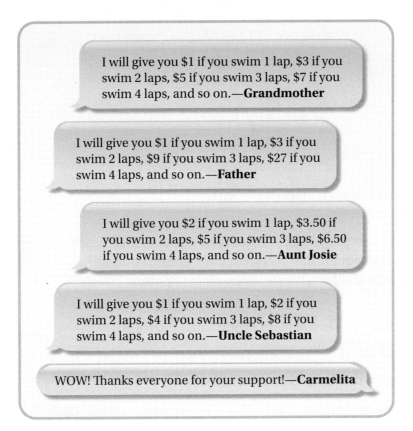

I will give you $1 if you swim 1 lap, $3 if you swim 2 laps, $5 if you swim 3 laps, $7 if you swim 4 laps, and so on.—**Grandmother**

I will give you $1 if you swim 1 lap, $3 if you swim 2 laps, $9 if you swim 3 laps, $27 if you swim 4 laps, and so on.—**Father**

I will give you $2 if you swim 1 lap, $3.50 if you swim 2 laps, $5 if you swim 3 laps, $6.50 if you swim 4 laps, and so on.—**Aunt Josie**

I will give you $1 if you swim 1 lap, $2 if you swim 2 laps, $4 if you swim 3 laps, $8 if you swim 4 laps, and so on.—**Uncle Sebastian**

WOW! Thanks everyone for your support!—**Carmelita**

a. Decide whether each donation pattern is an *exponential function, linear function,* or *neither.*

b. For each relative, write an equation for the total donation *d* if Carmelita swims *n* laps. Which variable is the independent variable? Dependent variable?

c. For each plan, tell how much money Carmelita will raise if she swims 20 laps.

16. The graphs below represent the equations $y = 2^x$ and $y = 2x + 1$.

Graph 1

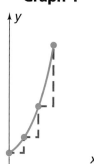

Graph 2

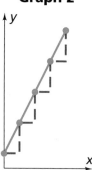

a. Tell which equation each graph represents. Explain your reasoning.

b. The dashed segments show the vertical and horizontal change between points at equal x intervals. For each graph, compare the vertical and horizontal change between pairs of points. What do you notice?

c. Does either equation represent an exponential function? A linear function? Explain.

For Exercises 17–21, study the pattern in each table.

a. Tell whether the relationship between x and y is a *linear function, exponential function,* or *neither*. Explain your reasoning.

b. If the relationship is a linear or exponential, give its equation.

17.

x	0	1	2	3	4	5
y	10	12.5	15	17.5	20	22.5

18.

x	0	1	2	3	4
y	1	6	36	216	1,296

19.

x	0	1	2	3	4	5	6	7	8
y	1	5	3	7	5	8	6	10	8

20.

x	0	1	2	3	4	5	6	7	8
y	2	4	8	16	32	64	128	256	512

21.

x	0	1	2	3	4	5
y	0	1	4	9	16	25

Connections

For Exercises 22–24, write each expression in exponential form.

22. $2 \times 2 \times 2 \times 2$

23. $10 \cdot 10 \cdot 10 \cdot 10 \cdot 10 \cdot 10 \cdot 10$

24. $2.5 \times 2.5 \times 2.5 \times 2.5 \times 2.5$

For Exercises 25–27, write each expression in standard form.

25. 2^{10} **26.** 10^2 **27.** 3^9

28. You know that $5^2 = 25$. How can you use this fact to evaluate 5^4?

29. The standard form for 5^{10} is 9,765,625. How can you use this fact to evaluate 5^{11}?

30. Multiple Choice Which expression is equal to one million?

     A. 10^6 **B.** 6^{10} **C.** 100^2 **D.** 2^{100}

31. Use exponents to write an expression for one billion (1,000,000,000).

For Exercises 32–34, decide whether each number is more or less than one million *without using a calculator* or multiplying. Explain how you found your answer. Use a calculator to check your answer.

32. 9^6 **33.** 3^{10} **34.** 11^6

For Exercises 35–40, write the number in exponential form using 2, 3, 4, or 5 for the base.

35. 125   **36.** 64   **37.** 81

38. 3,125   **39.** 1,024   **40.** 4,096

41. Refer to Problem 1.1. Suppose 250 sheets of paper is 1 inch high.

     a. How high would the stack of ballots be after 20 cuts? After 30 cuts?

     b. How many cuts would it take to make a stack 1 foot high?

     c. The average distance from Earth to the moon is about 240,000 miles. Which (if any) of the stacks in part (a) would reach the moon?

42. In Problem 1.2, suppose a Montarek ruba has the value of a modern U.S. penny. What are the dollar values of the rubas on squares 10, 20, 30, 40, 50, and 60?

43. A ruba has the same thickness as a modern U.S. penny (about 0.06 inch). Suppose the king had been able to reward the peasant by using Plan 1 (doubling the number of rubas in each square). What would be the height of the stack of rubas on square 64?

44. One of the king's advisors suggested another plan. Put 100 rubas on the first square of a chessboard, 125 on the second square, 150 on the third square, and so on, increasing the number of rubas by 25 for each square.

   a. Write an equation for the numbers of rubas r on square n. Explain the meanings of the numbers and variables in your equation.

   b. Describe the graph of this plan.

   c. What is the total number of rubas on the first 10 squares? The first 20 squares?

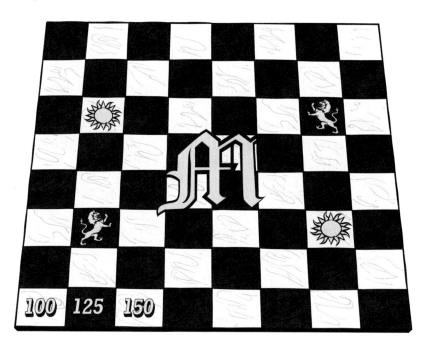

For Exercises 45–47, find the slope and y-intercept of the graph of each equation.

45. $y = 3x - 10$ **46.** $y = 1.5 - 5.6x$ **47.** $y = 15 + \dfrac{2}{5}x$

48. Write an equation whose line is less steep than the line represented by $y = 15 + \frac{2}{5}x$.

Extensions

49. Consider the two equations below.

Equation 1	Equation 2
$r = 3^n - 1$	$r = 3^{n-1}$

a. For each equation, find r when n is 2.

b. For each equation, find r when n is 10.

c. Explain why the equations give different values of r for the same value of n.

d. Do either of these equations represent an exponential function? Explain why.

50. The table below represents the number of ballots made by repeatedly cutting a sheet of paper in half.

Cutting Ballots

Number of Cuts	Number of Ballots
1	2
2	4
3	8
4	16

a. Write an equation for the pattern in the table.

b. Use your equation and the table to determine the value of 2^0.

c. What do you think b^0 should equal for any number b? For example, do you think 6^0 and 23^0 should equal? Explain.

51. The king tried to figure out the total number of rubas the peasant would receive under Plan 1. He noticed an interesting pattern.

   a. Extend and complete this table for the first 10 squares.

Reward Plan 1

Square	Number of Rubas on Square	Total Number of Rubas
1	1	1
2	2	3
3	4	7
4	▦	▦

   b. Describe the pattern of growth in the total number of rubas as the number of the square increases. Do either of these relationships represent an exponential function? Explain.

   c. Write an equation for the relationship between the number of the square n and the total number of rubas on the board t.

   d. When the total number of rubas reaches 1,000,000, how many squares will have rubas?

   e. Suppose the king had been able to give the peasant the reward she requested. How many rubas would she have received?

52. Refer to Plans 1–4 in Problem 1.3.

   a. Which plan should the king choose? Explain.

   b. Which plan should the peasant choose? Explain.

   c. Write an ending to the story of the king and the peasant.

Mathematical Reflections

In this Investigation, you explored situations in which the relationship between the two variables represented exponential functions. You saw how you could recognize patterns of exponential growth in tables, graphs, and equations.

Think about your answers to these questions. Discuss your ideas with other students and your teacher. Then write a summary of your findings in your notebook.

1. **Describe** an exponential growth pattern. Include key properties such as growth factors.

2. **How** are exponential functions similar to and different from the linear functions you worked with in earlier Units?

Common Core Mathematical Practices

As you worked on the Problems in this Investigation, you used prior knowledge to make sense of them. You also applied Mathematical Practices to solve the Problems. Think back over your work, the ways you thought about the Problems, and how you used Mathematical Practices.

Tori described her thoughts in the following way:

We wrote the equation, $r = \frac{1}{2} 2^n$ to represent the relationship between the number of rubas, r on square n in Problem 1.2. As the number of squares increase by 1, the number of rubas doubles.

We went backwards in the table to find the number of rubas on square 0. To find the number of rubas on square 0, we divided the number of rubas on square 1 by 2. One divided by two is $\frac{1}{2}$. $\frac{1}{2}$ is the y-intercept.

If you start with square 0, you get the number of rubas on the next square by multiplying the number of rubas on square 0 by 2. This process is repeated for the next square, etc.

So, on square n, you multiply $\frac{1}{2}$ by 2, n times. $\frac{1}{2} \times 2 \times 2 \times \ldots \times 2$ or $\frac{1}{2}(2^n)$.

Common Core Standards for Mathematical Practice

MP3 Construct viable arguments and critique the reasoning of others

 • What other Mathematical Practices can you identify in Tori's reasoning?

• Describe a Mathematical Practice that you and your classmates used to solve a different Problem in this Investigation.

Examining Growth Patterns

In Investigation 1, you learned to recognize exponential growth patterns. Now you are ready to take a closer look at the tables, graphs, and equations that represent exponential functions. You will explore this question:

- How do the starting value and growth factor show up in the table, graph, and equation that represent an exponential function?

For example, students at West Junior High wrote two equations to represent the reward in Plan 1 of Problem 1.2. Some students wrote $r = 2^{n-1}$ and others wrote $r = \frac{1}{2}\left(2^n\right)$. In both equations, r represents the number of rubas on square n.

- Are both equations correct? Explain.
- What is the value of r in both equations if $n = 1$? Does this make sense?
- What is the y-intercept for the graph of these equations?
- Do you think there is any value for n that will result in more than one value for r?

Common Core State Standards

8.F.A.1 Understand that a function is a rule that assigns to each input exactly one output. The graph of a function is the set of ordered pairs consisting of an input and the corresponding output.

8.F.B.5 Describe qualitatively the functional relationship between two quantities by analyzing a graph. Sketch a graph that exhibits the qualitative features of a function that has been described verbally.

Also N-Q.A.1, N-Q.A.2, A-SSE.A.1, A-SSE.A.1a, A-CED.A.1, A-CED.A.2, F-IF.C.7e, F-BF.A.1, F-BF.A.1a, F-LE.A.1, F-LE.A.1a, F-LE.A.2, F-LE.B.5

2.1 Killer Plant Strikes Lake Victoria
y-Intercepts Other Than 1

 Exponential functions occur in many real-life situations. For example, consider this story:

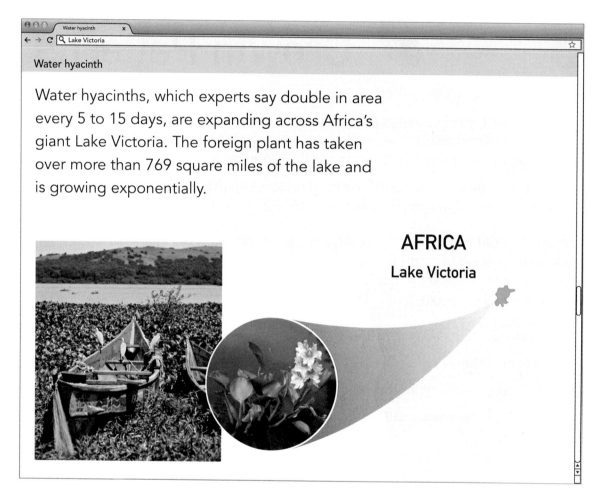

Water hyacinth

Water hyacinth

Water hyacinths, which experts say double in area every 5 to 15 days, are expanding across Africa's giant Lake Victoria. The foreign plant has taken over more than 769 square miles of the lake and is growing exponentially.

AFRICA

Lake Victoria

Little progress has been made to reverse the effects of the water hyacinths. Plants like the water hyacinth that grow and spread rapidly can affect native plants and fish. This in turn can affect the livelihood of fishermen. It can also impede rescue operations in case of a water disaster. To understand how such plants grow, you will look at a similar situation.

Problem 2.1

Ghost Lake is a popular site for fishermen, campers, and boaters. In recent years, a certain water plant has been growing on the lake at an alarming rate. The surface area of Ghost Lake is 25,000,000 square feet. At present, the plant covers 1,000 square feet of the lake. The Department of Natural Resources estimates that the area covered by the water plant is doubling every month.

A 1. Write an equation that represents the growth pattern of the plant.

2. Explain what information the variables and numbers in your equation represent.

3. Compare this equation to the equations in Investigation 1.

B 1. Make a graph of the equation.

2. How does this graph compare to the graphs of the exponential functions in Investigation 1?

3. Recall that a function is a relationship between two variables where, for each value of the independent variable, there is exactly one corresponding value of the dependent variable. Is the plant growth relationship a function? Justify your answer using a table, graph, or equation.

C 1. How much of the lake's surface will be covered at the end of a year by the plant?

2. How many months will it take for the plant to completely cover the surface of the lake?

A C E Homework starts on page 32.

2.2 Growing Mold
Interpreting Equations for Exponential Functions

Mold can spread rapidly. For example, the area covered by mold on a loaf of bread that is left out in warm weather grows exponentially.

Problem 2.2

Students at Magnolia Middle School conducted an experiment. They put a mixture of chicken bouillon (BOOL yahn), gelatin, and water in a shallow pan. Then they left it out to mold. Each day, the students recorded the area of the mold in square millimeters.

The students wrote the equation $m = 50\left(3^d\right)$ to model the growth of the mold. In this equation, m is the area of the mold in square millimeters after d days.

A For each part, answer the question and explain your reasoning.

   1. What is the area of the mold at the start of the experiment?

   2. What is the growth factor?

   3. What is the area of the mold after 5 days?

   4. On which day will the area of the mold reach 6,400 mm^2?

B An equation that represents an exponential function can be written in the form $y = a\left(b^x\right)$ where a and b are constant values.

   1. What is the value of b in the mold equation? What does this value represent? Does this make sense in this situation? Explain.

   2. What is the value of a in the mold equation? What does this value represent?

A C E Homework starts on page 32.

2.3 Studying Snake Populations
Interpreting Graphs of Exponential Functions

Garter snakes were introduced to a new area 4 years ago. The population is growing exponentially. The relationship between the number of snakes and the year is modeled with an exponential function.

Problem 2.3

A The graph shows the growth of the garter snake population.

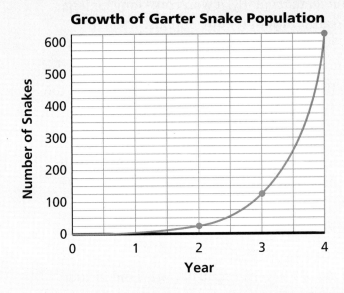

Growth of Garter Snake Population

(y-axis: Number of Snakes, from 0 to 600; x-axis: Year, from 0 to 4)

1. Find the snake population for years 2, 3, and 4.

2. Use the pattern in your answers from part (1) to estimate the population in Year 1. Explain your reasoning.

3. Explain how you can find the y-intercept for the graph.

B Explain how to find the growth factor for the population.

C Write an equation relating time t in years and population p. Explain what information the numbers in the equation represent.

D In what year is the population likely to reach 1,500?

E Amy and Chuck were discussing whether this relationship represented an exponential function. Who is correct? Explain why.

Amy's claim It is not a function. When the independent variable is 4, it looks like there is more than one dependent value associated with it.

OR

Chuck's claim It is a function. The scale used for the graph makes it difficult to read the values when the independent variable is 4.

 Homework starts on page 32.

Applications | Connections | Extensions

Applications

1. If you don't brush your teeth regularly, it won't take long for large colonies of bacteria to grow in your mouth. Suppose a single bacterium lands on your tooth and starts multiplying by a factor of 4 every hour.

   a. Write an equation that describes the number of bacteria b in the new colony after n hours.

   b. How many bacteria will be in the colony after 7 hours?

   c. How many bacteria will be in the colony after 8 hours? Explain how you can find this answer by using the answer from part (b) instead of the equation.

   d. After how many hours will there be at least 1,000,000 bacteria in the colony?

   e. Suppose that, instead of 1 bacterium, 50 bacteria land in your mouth. Write an equation that describes the number of bacteria b in this colony after n hours.

   f. Under the conditions of part (e), there will be 3,276,800 bacteria in this new colony after 8 hours. How many bacteria will there be after 9 hours and after 10 hours? Explain how you can find these answers without going back to the equation from part (e).

2. Loon Lake has a "killer plant" problem similar to Ghost Lake in Problem 2.1. Currently, 5,000 square feet of the lake is covered with the plant. The area covered is growing by a factor of 1.5 each year.

   a. Copy and complete the table to show the area covered by the plant for the next 5 years.

   b. The surface area of the lake is approximately 200,000 square feet. How long will it take before the lake is completely covered?

Growth of Loon Lake Plant

Year	Area Covered (sq. ft)
0	5,000
1	■
2	■
3	■
4	■
5	■

3. Leaping Liang just signed a contract with a women's basketball team. The contract guarantees her $20,000 the first year, $40,000 the second year, $80,000 the third year, $160,000 the fourth year, and so on, for 10 years.

   a. Make a table showing Liang's salary for each year of this contract.

   b. What is the total amount Liang will earn over the 10 years?

   c. Does the relationship between the number of years and salary represent an exponential function? Explain.

   d. Write an equation for Liang's salary *s* for any year *n* of her contract.

4. As a biology project, Talisha is studying the growth of a beetle population. She starts her experiment with 5 beetles. The next month she counts 15 beetles.

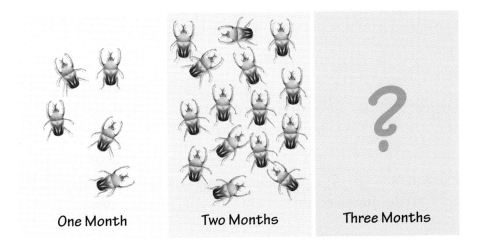

One Month   Two Months   Three Months

   a. Suppose the beetle population is growing linearly. How many beetles can Talisha expect to find after 2, 3, and 4 months?

   b. Suppose the beetle population is growing exponentially. How many beetles can Talisha expect to find after 2, 3, and 4 months?

   c. Write an equation for the number of beetles *b* after *m* months if the beetle population is growing linearly. Explain what information the variables and numbers represent.

   d. Write an equation for the number of beetles *b* after *m* months if the beetle population is growing exponentially. Explain what information the variables and numbers represent.

   e. How long will it take the beetle population to reach 200 if it is growing linearly?

   f. How long will it take the beetle population to reach 200 if it is growing exponentially?

5. Fruit flies are often used in genetic experiments because they reproduce very quickly. In 12 days, a pair of fruit flies can mature and produce a new generation. The table below shows the number of fruit flies in three generations of a laboratory colony.

Growth of Fruit-Fly Population

Generations	0	1	2	3
Number of Fruit Flies	2	120	7,200	432,000

a. Does this data represent an exponential function? If so, what is the growth factor for this fruit-fly population? Explain how you found your answers.

b. Suppose this growth pattern continues. How many fruit flies will be in the fifth generation?

c. Write an equation for the population p of generation g.

d. After how many generations will the population exceed one million?

6. A population of mice has a growth factor of 3. After 1 month, there are 36 mice. After 2 months, there are 108 mice.

a. How many mice were in the population initially (at 0 months)?

b. Write an equation for the population after any number of months. Explain what the numbers and variables in your equation mean.

7. Fido did not have fleas when his owners took him to the kennel. The number of fleas on Fido after he returned from the kennel grew according to the equation $f = 8(3^n)$, where f is the number of fleas and n is the number of weeks since he returned from the kennel. (Fido left the kennel at week 0.)

a. How many fleas did Fido pick up at the kennel?

b. Is the relationship represented by the equation an exponential function? If so, what is the growth factor for the number of fleas?

c. How many fleas will Fido have after 10 weeks if they are untreated?

8. Consider the equation $y = 150(2^x)$.

   a. Make a table of x and y-values for whole-number x-values from 0 to 5.

   b. What do the numbers 150 and 2 in the equation tell you about the relationship between the variables x and y?

For Exercises 9–12, find the growth factor and the y-intercept of the equation's graph.

9. $y = 300(3^x)$

10. $y = 300(3)^x$

11. $y = 6,500(2)^x$

12. $y = 2(7)^x$

13. The following graph represents the population growth of a certain kind of lizard.

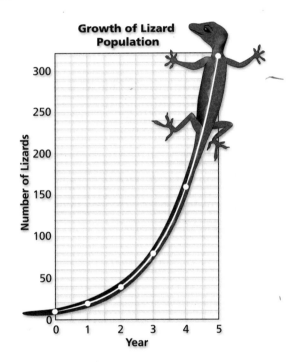

Growth of Lizard Population

a. What information does the point $(2, 40)$ on the graph tell you?

b. What information does the point $(1, 20)$ on the graph tell you?

c. When will the population exceed 100 lizards?

d. Explain how you can use the graph to find the growth factor for the population.

14. The following graphs show the population growth for two species. Each graph represents an exponential function.

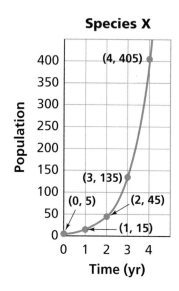

Species X

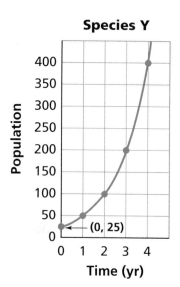

Species Y

a. Find the growth factors for the two species.

b. What is the y-intercept for the graph of Species X? Explain what this y-intercept tells you about the population.

c. What is the y-intercept for the graph of Species Y? Explain what this y-intercept tells you about the population.

d. Write an equation that describes the growth of Species X.

e. Write an equation that describes the growth of Species Y.

f. For which equation is (5, 1215) a solution?

Connections

15. **Multiple Choice** Choose the answer that best approximates 3^{20} in scientific notation.

A. 3.5×10^{-9} **B.** 8×10^3 **C.** 3×10^9 **D.** 3.5×10^9

16. **Multiple Choice** Choose the answer that is closest to 2.575×10^6.

F. 21^8 **G.** 12^6 **H.** 6^{12} **J.** 11^9

17. Approximate 5^{11} in scientific notation.

For Exercises 18–20, decide whether each number is less than or greater than one million without using a calculator. Explain.

18. 3^6

19. 9^5

20. 12^6

For Exercises 21–23, write the prime factorization of each number using exponents. Recall the prime factorization of 54 is $3 \times 3 \times 3 \times 2$. This can be written using exponents as $3^3 \times 2$.

21. 45

22. 144

23. 2,024

24. Consider the two equations below.

Equation 1	**Equation 2**
$y = 10 - 5x$	$y = (10)5^x$

a. What is the y-intercept of each equation?

b. For each equation, explain how you could use a table to find how the y-values change as the x-values increase. Describe the change.

c. Explain how you could use the equations to find how the y-values change as the x-values increase.

d. For each equation, explain how you could use a graph to find how the y-values change as the x-values increase.

For Exercises 25–28, write an equation for each line. Identify the slope and y-intercept.

25.
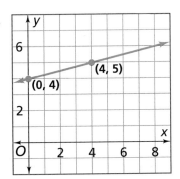

26.
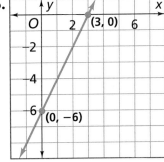

27.
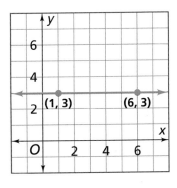

28.
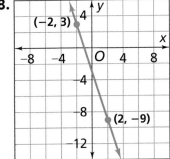

29. Maria enlarges a 2-cm-by-3-cm rectangle by a factor of 2 to get a 4-cm-by-6-cm rectangle. She then enlarges the 4-cm-by-6-cm rectangle by a factor of 2. She continues this process, enlarging each new rectangle by a factor of 2.

2 cm

3 cm

a. Copy and complete the table to show the dimensions, perimeter, and area of the rectangle after each enlargement.

Rectangle Changes

Enlargement	Dimensions (cm)	Perimeter (cm)	Area (cm²)
0 (original)	2 by 3	▦	▦
1	4 by 6	▦	▦
2	▦	▦	▦
3	▦	▦	▦
4	▦	▦	▦
5	▦	▦	▦

b. Is the pattern of growth for the perimeter linear, exponential, or neither? Explain.

c. Does the pattern of growth for the area represent a linear function, exponential function, or neither? Explain.

d. Write an equation for the perimeter P after n enlargements.

e. Write an equation for the area A after n enlargements.

f. How would your answers to parts (a)–(e) change if the copier were set to enlarge by a factor of 3?

For Exercises 30 and 31, Kele enlarged the figure below by a scale factor of 2. Ahmad enlarged the figure 250%.

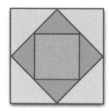

30. Who made the larger image?

31. Multiple Choice Which factor would give an image between Ahmad's image and Kele's image in size?

A. $\frac{2}{5}$ B. $\frac{3}{5}$ C. $\frac{9}{4}$ D. $\frac{10}{4}$

32. Companies sometimes describe part-time jobs by comparing them to full-time jobs. For example, a job that requires working half the number of hours of a full-time job is described as a $\frac{1}{2}$-time job or a 50%-time job. ACME, Inc. has three part-time job openings.

Order these jobs from the the most time to the the least time.

Extensions

33. a. Make a table and a graph for the equation $y = 1^x$.

   b. How are the patterns in the table and the graph of $y = 1^x$ similar to patterns you have observed for other exponential and linear functions? How are they different?

34. If you know that a graph represents an exponential function, you can find the equation for the function from two points on its graph. Find the equation of the exponential function whose graph passes through each pair of points. Explain.

   a. $(1, 6)$ and $(2, 12)$ **b.** $(2, 90)$ and $(3, 270)$

35. Leaping Liang plays basketball. A team promised her $1 million a year for the next 25 years. The same team offered Dribbling Dinara $1 the first year, $2 the second year, $4 the third year, $8 the fourth year, and so on, for 25 years.

   a. Suppose Liang and Dinara each accept the offers and play for 20 years. At the end of 20 years, who receives more money?

   b. Tell which player will receive more after 21 years, 22 years, 23 years, and 25 years.

   c. Do either of the two plans represent an exponential function? Explain.

Mathematical Reflections 2

In this Investigation, you studied quantities that grew exponentially. These patterns of growth represent exponential functions. You looked at how the values changed from one stage to the next, and you wrote equations to represent the relationship and used them to find the value of a quantity at any stage of growth.

You also graphed coordinate pairs from exponential functions and saw that there is a single output for each input. You sketched graphs from situations described in the Problems and analyzed graphs.

Think about your answers to these questions. Discuss your ideas with other students and your teacher. Then write a summary of your findings in your notebook.

1. **How** can you use a table, a graph, and an equation that represent an exponential function to find the y-intercept and growth factor for the function? Explain.

2. **How** can you use the y-intercept and growth factor to write an equation that represents an exponential function? Explain.

3. **How** would you change your answers to Questions 1 and 2 for a linear function?

Common Core Mathematical Practices

As you worked on the Problems in this Investigation, you used prior knowledge to make sense of them. You also applied Mathematical Practices to solve the Problems. Think back over your work, the ways you thought about the Problems, and how you used Mathematical Practices.

Jayden described his thoughts in the following way:

We noticed differences between the equations for the growth patterns. In Problem 2.1, the water plant on Ghost Lake equation had an additional factor before the base.

Equations in Investigation 1 were of the form $y =$ some number raised to an exponent. Examples are $y = 2^n$ and $y = 3^{n-1}$. These equations did not have a number in front of the bases, 2 and 3.

In Problem 2.1, there is a number in front of the 2^n. The equation is $a = 1,000(2^n)$. In this situation, we start tracking growth at $n = 0$ rather than $n = 1$. So, these graphs have a meaningful y-intercept.

....

Common Core Standards for Mathematical Practice

MP8 Look for and express regularity in repeated reasoning

- What other Mathematical Practices can you identify in Jayden's reasoning?

- Describe a Mathematical Practice that you and your classmates used to solve a different Problem in this Investigation.

3

Growth Factors and Growth Rates

In Investigation 2, you studied exponential growth of plants, mold, and a snake population. You used a whole-number growth factor and the starting value to write an equation and make predictions. In this Investigation, you will study exponential growth with fractional growth factors.

3.1 Reproducing Rabbits
Fractional Growth Patterns

In 1859, English settlers introduced a small number of rabbits to Australia. The rabbits had no natural predators in Australia, so they reproduced rapidly and ate grasses intended for sheep and cattle.

> ### Did You Know?
>
> **In the mid-1990s,** there were more than 300 million rabbits in Australia. The damage they caused cost Australian agriculture $600 million per year. In 1995, a deadly rabbit disease was deliberately spread, reducing the rabbit population by about half. However, because rabbits are developing immunity to the disease, the effects of this measure may not last.

Common Core State Standards

8.F.A.2 Compare properties of two functions each represented in a different way (algebraically, graphically, numerically in tables, or by verbal descriptions).

Also **8.F.A.1, 8.F.A.3, 8.F.B.5, A-SSE.A.1a, A-SSE.A.1b, A-CED.A.2, F-IF.B.4, F-IF.B.6, F-IF.C.8b, F-BF.A.1a, F-LE.A.1a, F-LE.A.1c, F-LE.A.2, F-LE.B.5**

Problem 3.1

Suppose biologists had counted the rabbits in Australia in the years after English settlers introduced them. The biologists might have collected data like those shown in the table.

A The table shows the rabbit population growing exponentially.

Growth of Rabbit Population

Time (yr)	Population
0	100
1	180
2	325
3	583
4	1,050

1. What is the growth factor? Explain how you found your answer.

2. Assume this growth pattern continued. Write an equation for the rabbit population p for any year n after the biologists first counted the rabbits. Explain what the numbers in your equation represent.

3. How many rabbits will there be after 10 years? How many will there be after 25 years? After 50 years?

4. In how many years will the rabbit population exceed one million?

B Suppose that, during a different time period, biologists could predict the rabbit population using the equation $p = 15(1.2)^n$, where p is the population in millions, and n is the number of years.

1. What is the growth factor?

2. What was the initial population?

3. In how many years will the initial population double?

4. What will the population be after 3 years? After how many more years will the population at 3 years double?

5. What will the population be after 10 years? After how many more years will the population at 10 years double?

6. How do the doubling times for parts (3)–(5) compare? Do you think the doubling time will be the same for this relationship no matter where you start the count? Explain your reasoning.

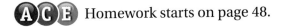 Homework starts on page 48.

3.2 Investing for the Future
Growth Rates

The yearly growth factor for one of the rabbit populations in Problem 3.1 is about 1.8. Suppose the population data fit the equation $p = 100(1.8)^n$ exactly. Then its table would look like the one below.

Growth of Rabbit Population

n	p
0	100
1	$100 \times 1.8 =$ **180**
2	$180 \times 1.8 =$ **324**
3	$324 \times 1.8 =$ **583.2**
4	$583.2 \times 1.8 =$ **1,049.76**

- Does it make sense to have a fractional part of a rabbit?

- What does this say about the reasonableness of the equation?

The *growth factor* 1.8 is the ratio of the population for a year divided by the population for the previous year. That is, the population for year $n + 1$ is 1.8 times the population for year n.

You can think of the growth factor in terms of a percent change. To find the percent change, compare the difference in population for two consecutive years, n and $n + 1$, with the population of year, n.

- From year 0 to year 1, the percent change is $\frac{180 - 100}{100} = \frac{80}{100} = 80\%$. The population of 100 rabbits in year 0 increased by 80%, resulting in $100 \times 80\% = 80$ additional rabbits.

- From year 1 to year 2, the percent change is $\frac{324 - 180}{180} = \frac{144}{180} = 80\%$. The population of 180 rabbits in year 1 increased by 80%, resulting in $180 \times 80\% = 144$ additional rabbits.

The percent increase is called the **growth rate.** In some growth situations, the growth rate is given instead of the growth factor. For example, changes in the value of investments are often expressed as percents.

- How are the growth rate 80% and the growth factor 1.8 related to each other?

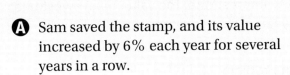

When Sam was in seventh grade, his aunt gave him a stamp worth $2,500. Sam considered selling the stamp, but his aunt told him that, if he saved it, it would increase in value.

A Sam saved the stamp, and its value increased by 6% each year for several years in a row.

  1. Make a table showing the value of the stamp each year for the five years after Sam's aunt gave it to him.

  2. Look at the pattern of growth from one year to the next. Is the value growing exponentially? Explain.

  3. Write an equation for the value v of Sam's stamp after n years.

  4. How many years will it take to double the value?

B Suppose the value of the stamp increased 4% each year instead of 6%.

  1. Make a table showing the value of the stamp each year for the five years after Sam's aunt gave it to him.

  2. What is the growth factor from one year to the next?

  3. Write an equation that represents the value of the stamp for any year.

  4. How many years will it take to double the value?

  5. How does the change in percent affect the graphs of the equations?

C **1.** Find the growth factor associated with each growth rate.

    a. 0%   **b.** 15%   **c.** 30%

    d. 75%   **e.** 100%   **f.** 150%

  2. How you can find the growth factor if you know the growth rate?

D **1.** Find the growth rate associated with each growth factor.

    a. 1.5   **b.** 1.25   **c.** 1.1   **d.** 1

  2. How can you find the growth rate if you know the growth factor?

A C E Homework starts on page 48.

Did You Know?

Some investors use a rule of thumb called the "Rule of 72" to approximate how long it will take the value of an investment to double. To use this rule, simply divide 72 by the annual interest rate.

For example, an investment at an 8% interest rate will take approximately $72 \div 8$, or 9, years to double. At a 10% interest rate, the value of an investment will double approximately every 7.2 years. This rule doesn't give you exact doubling times, only approximations.

• Do the doubling times you found in Problem 3.2 fit this rule?

3.3 Making a Difference
Connecting Growth Rate and Growth Factor

In Problem 3.2, the value of Sam's stamp increased by the same percent each year. However, each year, this percent was applied to the previous year's value. So, for example, the increase from year 1 to year 2 is 6% of $2,650, not 6% of the original $2,500. This type of change is called **compound growth.**

In this Problem, you will continue to explore compound growth. You will consider the effects of both the initial value and the growth factor on the value of an investment.

> ### *Problem* **3.3**
>
> Mrs. Ramos started college funds for her two granddaughters. She gave $1,250 to Cassie and $2,500 to Kaylee. Mrs. Ramos invested each fund in a 10-year bond that pays 4% interest a year.
>
> **A**   **1.** Write an equation to show the relationship between the number of years and the amount of money in each fund.
>
>   **2.** Make a table to show the amount in each fund for 0 to 10 years.
>
>   **3.** Compare the graphs of each equation you wrote in part (1).
>
>   **4. a.** How does the initial value of the fund affect the yearly value increases?
>
>   **b.** How does the initial value affect the growth factor?
>
>   **c.** How does the initial value affect the final value?
>
> **B**   A year later, Mrs. Ramos started a fund for Cassie's cousin, Matt. Cassie made this calculation to predict the value of Matt's fund several years from now:
>
> $$\text{Value} = \$2,000 \times 1.05 \times 1.05 \times 1.05 \times 1.05$$
>
>   **1.** What initial value, growth rate, growth factor, and number of years is Cassie assuming?
>
>   **2.** If the value continues to increase at this rate, how much would the fund be worth in one more year?
>
> **C**   Cassie's and Kaylee's other grandmother offers them a choice between college fund options.
>
>   **Option 1**   **Option 2**
>
> $1,000 at 3% interest per year $800 at 6% per year
>
>   Which is the better option? Explain your reasoning.

A C E Homework starts on page 48.

Applications

1. In parts of the United States, wolves are being reintroduced to wilderness areas where they had become extinct. Suppose 20 wolves are released in northern Michigan, and the yearly growth factor for this population is expected to be 1.2.

   a. Make a table showing the projected number of wolves at the end of each of the first 6 years.

   b. Write an equation that models the growth of the wolf population.

   c. How long will it take for the new wolf population to exceed 100?

2. This table shows the growth of the elk population in a state forest.

   a. The table shows that the elk population is growing exponentially. What is the growth factor? Explain how you found it.

   Growth of Elk Population

Time (yr)	Population
0	30
1	57
2	108
3	206
4	391
5	743

   b. Suppose this growth pattern continues. How many elk will there be after 10 years? How many elk will there be after 15 years?

   c. Write an equation you could use to predict the elk population p for any year n after the elk were first counted.

   d. In how many years will the population exceed one million?

3. Suppose there are 100 trout in a lake and the yearly growth factor for the population is 1.5. How long will it take for the number of trout to double?

4. Suppose there are 500,000 squirrels in a forest and the growth factor for the population is 1.6 per year. Write an equation you could use to find the squirrel population p in n years.

5. Multiple Choice The equation $p = 200(1.1)^t$ models the exponential growth of a population. The variable p is the population in millions and t is the time in years. How long will it take this population to double?

    A. 4 to 5 years   **B.** 5 to 6 years   **C.** 6 to 7 years   **D.** 7 to 8 years

In Exercises 6 and 7, the equation models the exponential growth of a population, where p is the population in millions and t is the time in years. Tell how much time it would take the population to double.

6. $p = 135(1.7)^t$ **7.** $p = 1{,}000(1.2)^t$

8. a. Fill in the table for each equation.

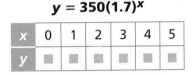

$y = 50(2.2)^x$

x	0	1	2	3	4	5
y						

$y = 350(1.7)^x$

x	0	1	2	3	4	5
y						

    b. What is the growth factor for each equation?

    c. Predict whether the graphs of these equations will ever cross.

    d. Estimate any points at which you think the graphs will cross.

9. Maya's grandfather opened a savings account for her when she was born. He opened the account with $100 and did not add or take out any money after that. The money in the account grows at a rate of 4% per year.

    a. Make a table to show the amount in the account from the time Maya was born until she turned 10.

    b. What is the growth factor for the account?

    c. Write an equation for the value of the account after any number of years.

Find the growth rate associated with the given growth factor.

10. 1.4

11. 1.9

12. 1.75

Find the growth factor associated with the given growth rate.

13. 45%

14. 90%

15. 31%

16. Suppose the price of an item increases by 25% per year. What is the growth factor for the price from year to year?

17. Currently, 1,000 students attend Greenville Middle School. The school can accommodate 1,300 students. The school board estimates that the student population will grow by 5% per year for the next several years.

   a. When will the population outgrow the present building?

   b. Suppose the school limits its growth to 50 students per year. How many years will it take for the population to outgrow the school?

18. Suppose that, for several years, the number of radios sold in the United States increased by 3% each year.

   a. Suppose one million radios sold in the first year of this time period. About how many radios sold in each of the next 6 years?

   b. Suppose only 100,000 radios sold in the first year. About how many radios sold in each of the next 6 years?

19. Suppose a movie ticket costs about $7, and inflation causes ticket prices to increase by 4.5% a year for the next several years.

   a. How much will a ticket cost 5 years from now?

   b. How much will a ticket cost 10 years from now? 30 years from now?

   c. How many years will it take for the cost of a ticket to exceed $26?

20. Find the growth rate (percent growth) for an exponential function represented by the equation $y = 30(2)^x$.

21. **Multiple Choice** Ms. Diaz wants to invest $500 in a savings bond. At which bank would her investment grow the most over 8 years?

   A. Bank 1: 7% annual interest for 8 years

   B. Bank 2: 2% annual interest for the first 4 years and 12% annual interest for the next four years

   C. Bank 3: 12% annual interest for the first 4 years and 2% annual interest for the next four years

   D. All three result in the same growth.

22. Oscar made the following calculation to predict the value of his baseball card collection several years from now:

$$\text{Value} = \$130 \times 1.07 \times 1.07 \times 1.07 \times 1.07 \times 1.07$$

   a. What initial value, growth rate, growth factor, and number of years is Oscar assuming?

   b. If the value continues to increase at this rate, how much would the collection be worth in three more years?

23. Carlos, Latanya, and Mila work in a biology laboratory. Each of them is responsible for a population of mice.

The growth factor for Carlos's population of mice is $\frac{3}{8}$.	The growth factor for Latanya's population of mice is 3.	The growth factor for Mila's population of mice is 125%.

   a. Whose mice are reproducing fastest?

   b. Whose mice are reproducing slowest?

Connections

Calculate each percent.

24. 120% of $3,000   **25.** 150% of $200   **26.** 133% of $2,500

For Exercises 27–30, tell whether the pattern represents exponential growth. Explain your reasoning. If the pattern is exponential, give the growth factor.

27. 1   1.1   1.21   1.331   1.4641   1.61051   1.771561

28. 3   5 $8\frac{1}{3}$ $13\frac{8}{9}$ $23\frac{4}{27}$

29. 3 $4\frac{2}{3}$ $6\frac{1}{3}$ 8 $9\frac{2}{3}$ $11\frac{1}{3}$

30. 2   6.4   20.5   66   210

31. A worker currently receives a yearly salary of $20,000.

a. Find the dollar values of a 3%, 4%, and 5% raise for this worker.

b. Find the worker's new annual salary for each raise in part (a).

c. Joanne says that she can find the new salary with a 3% raise in two ways:

Method 1
Add $20,000 to (3% of $20,000).

OR

Method 2
Find 103% of $20,000.

Explain why these two methods give the same result.

32. The graph shows the growth in the number of wireless subscribers in the United States from 1994 to 2009.

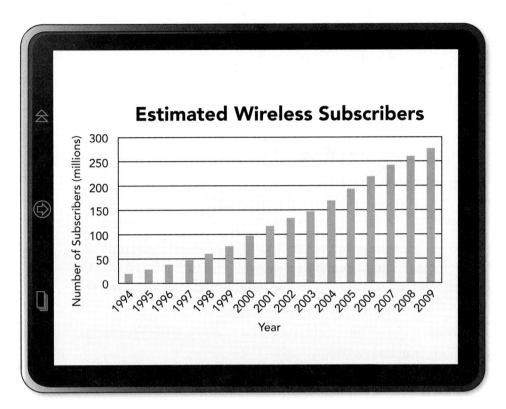

a. What do the bars in the graph represent?

b. What does the implied curve represent?

c. Describe the pattern of change in the total number of subscribers from 1994 to 2009. Could the pattern be modeled by an exponential function or a linear function? Explain.

d. The number of subscribers in 2010 was 300,520,098. In 2011, the number was 322,857,207. Do these numbers fit the pattern you described in part (c)? Explain.

e. If the U.S. population in 2010 was approximately 308 million, what might explain the number of subscriptions from 2011?

33. Refer to the drawing below.

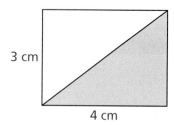

3 cm

4 cm

   a. What is the length of the diagonal? What is the area of the shaded region?

   b. Arturo enlarges the drawing to 110% of this size. Make a copy of the drawing on grid paper. What is the length of the diagonal in the enlarged drawing? What is the area of the shaded region?

   c. Arturo enlarges the enlargement to 110% of its size. He continues this process, enlarging each new drawing to 110% of its size. After five enlargements, what will be the length of the diagonal and the area of the shaded region?

   d. Arturo and Esteban are wondering if each enlargement is similar to the original figure.

Auturo's Conjecture

All the rectangles are similar because the ratio new width : new length is always 3 : 4. This ratio is the same as the ratio of the width to the length in the original figure.

Esteban's Conjecture

In part (a), the ratio diagonal length : area was different from the same ratio in part (b). Therefore, the figures are not similar.

   Which conjecture do you think is correct? Explain. Why is the other conjecture incorrect?

34. Kwan cuts lawns every summer to make money. One customer offers to give her a 3% raise next summer and a 4% raise the summer after that.

   Kwan says she would prefer to get a 4% raise next summer and a 3% raise the summer after that. She claims she will earn more money this way. Is she correct? Explain.

35. After graduating from high school, Kim accepts a job with a package delivery service, earning $9 per hour.

   a. How much will Kim earn in a year if she works 40 hours per week for 50 weeks and gets 2 weeks of paid vacation time?

   b. Write an equation showing the relationship between the number of weeks Kim works w and the amount she earns a.

   c. Kim writes the following equation: $9,000 = 360w$. What question is she trying to answer? What is the answer to that question?

   d. Suppose Kim works for the company for 10 years, receiving a 3% raise each year. Make a table showing how her annual income grows over this time period.

   e. When Kim was hired, her manager told her that instead of a 3% annual raise, she could choose to receive a $600 raise each year. How do the two raise plans compare over a 10-year period? Which plan do you think is better? Explain your answer.

36. Which represents faster growth, a growth factor of 2.5 or a growth rate of 25%?

37. Order these scale factors from least to greatest.

   130% $\frac{3}{2}$ 2 1.475

38. Christopher made a drawing that measures $8\frac{1}{2}$ by 11 inches. He needs to reduce it so it will fit into a space that measures $7\frac{1}{2}$ by 10 inches. What scale factor should he use to get a similar drawing that is small enough to fit? (Do not worry about getting it to fit perfectly.)

39. a. Match each growth rate from List 1 with the equivalent growth factor in List 2 if possible.

List 1

20%, 120%, 50%, 200%, 400%, 2%

List 2

1.5, 5, 1.2, 2.2, 4, 2, 1.02

   b. Order the growth rates from List 1 from least to greatest.

   c. Order the growth factors from List 2 from least to greatest.

Extensions

40. In Russia, shortly after the breakup of the Soviet Union, the yearly growth factor for inflation was 26. What growth rate (percent increase) is associated with this growth factor? We call this percent increase the *inflation rate*.

41. In 2000, the population of the United States was about 282 million and was growing exponentially at a rate of about 1% per year.

   a. At this growth rate, what will the population of the United States be in the year 2020?

   b. At this rate, how long will it take the population to double?

   c. The population in 2010 was about 308 million. How accurate was the growth rate?

42. Use the table to answer parts (a)–(d).

   a. One model of world population growth assumes the population grows exponentially. Based on the data in this table, what would be a reasonable growth factor for this model?

   b. Use your growth factor from part (a) to write an equation for the growth of the population at 5-year intervals beginning in 1955.

   c. Use your equation from part (b) to predict the year in which the population was double the 1955 population.

   d. Use your equation to predict when the population will be double the 2010 population.

World Population Growth

Year	Population (billions)
1955	2.76
1960	3.02
1965	3.33
1970	3.69
1975	4.07
1980	4.43
1985	4.83
1990	5.26
1995	5.67
2000	6.07
2005	6.46
2010	6.84

For Exercises 43–45, write an equation that represents the exponential function in each situation.

43. A population is initially 300. After 1 year, the population is 361.

44. A population has a yearly growth factor of 1.2. After 3 years, the population is 1,000.

45. The growth rate for an investment is 3% per year. After 2 years, the value of the investment is $2,560.

46. Suppose your calculator did not have an exponent key. You could find 1.5^{12} by entering:

$$1.5 \times 1.5 \times 1.5 \times 1.5 \times 1.5 \times 1.5 \times 1.5 \times 1.5 \times 1.5 \times 1.5 \times 1.5 \times 1.5$$

a. How could you evaluate 1.5^{12} with fewer keystrokes?

b. What is the fewest times you could press ☒ to evaluate 1.5^{12}?

47. Mr. Watson sold his boat for $10,000. He wants to invest the money.

Growth of $10,000 Investment at 4% Interest Compounded Quarterly

Time (mo)	Money in Account
0	$10,000
3	$10,100
6	$10,201
9	$10,303.01

a. How much money will Mr. Watson have after 1 year if he invests the $10,000 in an account that pays 4% interest per year?

b. Mr. Watson sees an advertisement for another type of savings account:

"4% interest per year compounded quarterly."

He asks the bank teller what "compounded quarterly" means. She explains that instead of giving him 4% of $10,000 at the end of one year, the bank will give him 1% at the end of each 3-month period (each quarter of a year).

If Mr. Watson invests his money at this bank, how much will be in his account at the end of one year?

c. Mr. Watson sees an advertisement for a different bank that offers 4% interest per year *compounded monthly*. (This means he will get $\frac{1}{12}$ of 4% interest every month.) How much money will he have at the end of the year if he invests his money at this bank?

d. Which account would have the most money at the end of one year? Explain.

Mathematical Reflections 3

In this Investigation, when you were given tables and descriptions of relationships, you explored exponential functions in which the growth factor was not a whole number. In some of these situations, the growth was described by giving the percent growth, or growth rate.

Think about these questions. Discuss your ideas with other students and your teacher. Then write a summary of your findings in your notebook.

1. Suppose you know the initial value for a population and the yearly growth rate.

   a. **How** can you determine the population several years from now?

   b. **How** is a growth rate related to the growth factor for the population?

   c. **How** can you use this information to write an equation that models the situation?

2. Suppose you know the initial value for a population and the yearly growth factor.

   a. **How** can you determine the population several years from now?

   b. **How** can you determine the yearly growth rate?

3. Suppose you know the equation that represents the exponential function relating the population p and the number of years n. **How** can you determine the doubling time for the population?

Common Core Mathematical Practices

As you worked on the Problems in this Investigation, you used prior knowledge to make sense of them. You also applied Mathematical Practices to solve the Problems. Think back over your work, the ways you thought about the Problems, and how you used Mathematical Practices.

Nick described his thoughts in the following way:

We thought that the growth of the rabbit population in Problem 3.1 represented an exponential function.

We compared the population from one year with the next year's population. We found that the ratio was not exactly, but was very close to, 1.8.

This data is experimental. Factors such as food availability and weather conditions could affect the growth of the population from year to year. So, we used 1.8 as an approximation of the growth rate.

Common Core Standards for Mathematical Practice
MP4 Model with mathematics

- What other Mathematical Practices can you identify in Nick's reasoning?

- Describe a Mathematical Practice that you and your classmates used to solve a different Problem in this Investigation.

Exponential Decay

The exponential functions you have studied so far have all involved quantities that increase. In this Investigation, you will explore quantities that decrease, or decay, exponentially as time passes.

4.1 Making Smaller Ballots
Introducing Exponential Decay

In Problem 1.1, you read about the ballots Chen is making. Chen cuts a sheet of paper in half. He stacks the two pieces and cuts them in half. Chen then stacks the resulting four pieces and cuts them in half, and so on.

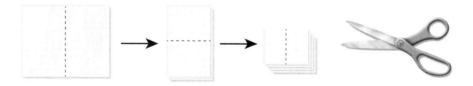

Common Core State Standards

8.F.A.2 Compare properties of two functions each represented in a different way (algebraically, graphically, numerically in tables, or by verbal descriptions).

8.F.A.3 Interpret the equation $y = mx + b$ as defining a linear function, whose graph is a straight line; give examples of functions that are not linear.

8.F.B.5 Describe qualitatively the functional relationship between two quantities by analyzing a graph . . . Sketch a graph that exhibits the qualitative features of a function that has been described verbally.

Also **8.F.A.1, A-SSE.A.1a, A-SSE.A.1b, A-CED.A.2, A-REI.D.10, F-IF.B.4, F-IF.B.6, F-IF.C.7e, F-BF.A.1a, F-LE.A.1a, F-LE.A.1c, F-LE.A.2, F-LE.B.5**

You investigated the pattern in the number of ballots each cut made. In this Problem, you will look at the pattern in the areas of the ballots.

Problem 4.1

A The paper Chen starts with has an area of 64 square inches. Copy and complete the table to show the area of a ballot after each of the first 10 cuts.

Areas of Ballots

Number of Cuts	Area (in.^{2})
0	64
1	32
2	16
3	■
4	■
5	■
6	■
7	■
8	■
9	■
10	■

B How does the area of a ballot change with each cut?

C Write an equation for the area A of a ballot after any cut n.

D Make a graph of the data.

E **1.** How is the pattern of change in the area different from the exponential growth patterns you studied? How is it similar?

   2. How is the pattern of change in the area different from linear patterns you studied? How is it similar?

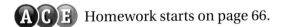 Homework starts on page 66.

4.2 Fighting Fleas
Representing Exponential Decay

 Exponential patterns like the one in Problem 4.1, in which a quantity decreases at each stage by a constant factor, show **exponential decay.** The factor the quantity is multiplied by at each stage is called the **decay factor.** A decay factor is always greater than 0 and less than 1. In Problem 4.1, the decay factor is $\frac{1}{2}$.

- Are exponential decay patterns also exponential functions? Explain.

After an animal receives flea medicine, the medicine breaks down in the animal's bloodstream. With each hour, there is less medicine in the blood.

A dog receives a 400-milligram dose of flea medicine. The table and graph show the amount of medicine in the dog's bloodstream each hour for 6 hours after the dose.

Breakdown of Medicine

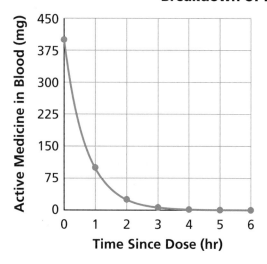

Time Since Dose (hr)	Active Medicine in Blood (mg)
0	400
1	100
2	25
3	6.25
4	1.5625
5	0.3907
6	0.0977

Problem 4.2

A Study the pattern of change in the graph and the table.

1. How does the amount of active medicine in the dog's blood change from one hour to the next?

2. Write an equation to model the relationship between the number of hours h since the dose is given and the milligrams of active medicine m.

3. How is the graph for this Problem similar to the graph you made in Problem 4.1? How is it different?

4. Does the relationship displayed in the table and graph represent an exponential function? Explain.

B 1. A different flea medicine breaks down at a rate of 20% per hour. This means that as each hour passes, 20% of the active medicine is used. This is the **rate of decay** of the medicine. The initial dose is 60 milligrams. Extend and complete this table to show the amount of active medicine in an animal's blood at the end of each hour for 6 hours.

Breakdown of Medicine

Time Since Dose (hr)	Active Medicine in Blood (mg)
0	60
1	▦
2	▦
⋮	⋮
6	▦

2. Make a graph using the table you completed in part (1).

3. For the medicine in part (1), Janelle wrote the equation $m = 60(0.8)^h$ to show the amount of active medicine m after h hours. Compare the quantities of active medicine in your table to the quantities given by Janelle's equation. Explain any similarities or differences.

4. Dwayne was confused by the terms *decay rate* (or *rate of decay*) and *decay factor*. He said:

> Because the rate of decay is 20%, the decay factor should be 0.2, and the equation should be $m = 60(0.2)^h$.

Do you agree with him? Explain.

5. Steven recalled that when the growth rate is 80%, the growth factor is 1.8 or 180%. How is the relationship between growth rate and growth factor similar to the relationship between decay rate and decay factor?

A C E Homework starts on page 66.

4.3 Cooling Water
Modeling Exponential Decay

Sometimes a cup of hot cocoa or tea is too hot to drink at first. So you must wait for it to cool.

- What pattern of change would you expect to find in the temperature of a hot drink as time passes?

- What shape would you expect for a graph of data (*time, drink temperature*)?

This experiment will help you explore these questions.

Equipment

- very hot water
- two thermometers
- a cup or mug for hot drinks
- a watch or clock

Directions

- Record air temperature.
- Fill the cup/mug with hot water.
- In a table, record the water temperature and room temperature at 5-minute intervals throughout your class period.

Problem 4.3

Ⓐ **1.** Complete the table with data from your experiment.

Hot Water Cooling

Time (min)	Water Temperature	Room Temperature
0	▦	▦
5	▦	▦
10	▦	▦
▦	▦	▦

Make a graph of your (*time, water temperature*) data.

2. Describe the pattern of change in the data. When did the water temperature change most rapidly? When did it change most slowly?

3. Is the relationship between time and water temperature an exponential decay relationship? Explain.

Ⓑ **1.** Add a column to your table. In this column, record the difference between the water temperature and the air temperature for each time value.

2. Make a graph of the (*time, temperature difference*) data. Compare this graph with the graph you made in Question A.

3. Describe the pattern of change in the data. When did the temperature difference change most rapidly? Most slowly?

4. Estimate the decay factor for the relationship between temperature difference and time in this experiment.

5. Write an equation for the (*time, temperature difference*) data. Your equation should allow you to predict the temperature difference at the end of any 5-minute interval.

Ⓒ **1.** What do you think the graph of the (*time, temperature difference*) data would look like if you had continued the experiment for several more hours?

2. What factors might affect the rate at which a cup of hot liquid cools?

3. What factors might introduce errors in the data you collect?

Ⓓ Compare the graphs in Questions A and B with the graphs in Problems 4.1 and 4.2. What similarities and differences do you observe?

Ⓐ Ⓒ Ⓔ Homework starts on page 66.

Applications

1. Chen, from Problem 4.1, finds that his ballots are very small after only a few cuts. He decides to start with a larger sheet of paper. The new paper has an area of 324 in.^{2}. Copy and complete this table to show the area of each ballot after each of the first 10 cuts.

Areas of Ballots

Number of Cuts	Area (in.^{2})
0	324
1	162
2	81
3	▦
4	▦
5	▦
6	▦
7	▦
8	▦
9	▦
10	▦

   a. Write an equation for the area A of a ballot after any cut n.

   b. With the smaller sheet of paper, the area of a ballot is 1 in.^{2} after 6 cuts. Start with the larger sheet. How many cuts does it take to get ballots this small?

   c. Chen wants to be able to make 12 cuts before getting ballots with an area of 1 in.^{2}. How large does his starting piece of paper need to be?

2. During the exploration of Problem 4.1, several groups of students in Mrs. Dole's class made a conjecture. They conjectured that the relationship between the number of cuts and the area of the ballot was an *inverse variation* relationship.

The class came up with two different arguments for why the relationship was not an inverse variation.

Argument 1

An inverse variation situation has a "factor-pair" relationship. Choose some constant number k. The two factors multiply to equal k, such as $yx = k$. For example, if the area of rectangle with length, l, and width, w, is 24,000 square feet, then $24,000 = lw$. This is an inverse variation.

In an exponential relationship, the values of the two variables x and y do not have this "factor-pair" relationship. For example, in Problem 4.1, the equation is $A = 64\left(\dfrac{1}{2}\right)^n$, but A and n do not multiply to get a constant number.

Argument 2

Any inverse variation will never have a y-intercept and this relationship does. Therefore, this relationship is not an inverse variation.

Which argument is correct? Explain why the students might have made this conjecture.

3. Latisha has a 24-inch string of licorice (LIK uh rish) to share with her friends. As each friend asks her for a piece, Latisha gives him or her half of what she has left. She doesn't eat any of the licorice herself.

a. Make a table showing the length of licorice Latisha has left each time she gives a piece away.

b. Make a graph of the data from part (a).

c. Suppose that, instead of half the licorice that is left each time, Latisha gives each friend 4 inches of licorice. Make a table and a graph for this situation.

d. Compare the tables and the graphs for the two situations. Explain the similarities and the differences.

4. Penicillin decays exponentially in the human body. Suppose you receive a 300-milligram dose of penicillin to combat strep throat. About 180 milligrams will remain active in your blood after 1 day.

    a. Assume the amount of penicillin active in your blood decreases exponentially. Make a table showing the amount of active penicillin in your blood for 7 days after a 300-milligram dose.

    b. Write an equation for the relationship between the number of days d since you took the penicillin and the amount of the medicine m remaining active in your blood.

    c. What is the equation for a 400-milligram dose?

For Exercises 5 and 6, tell whether the equation represents exponential decay or exponential growth. Explain your reasoning.

    5. $y = 0.8(2.1)^x$

    6. $y = 20(0.5)^x$

7. The graph below shows an exponential decay relationship.

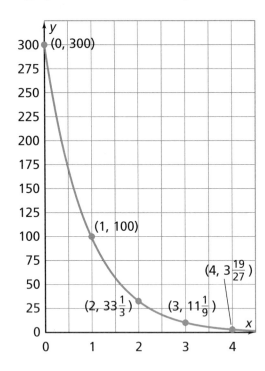

    a. Find the decay factor and the y-intercept.

    b. What is the equation for the graph?

For Exercises 8 and 9, use the table of values to determine the exponential decay equation. Then, find the decay factor and the decay rate.

8.

x	y
0	24
1	6
2	1.5
3	0.375
4	0.09375

9.

x	y
0	128
1	96
2	72
3	54

For Exercises 10–13, use Lara's conjecture below. Explain how you found your answer.

> ## Lara's Conjecture
> If you know the y-intercept and another point on the graph of an exponential function, then you can find all the other points.

10. The exponential decay graph has y-intercept $= 90$, and it passes through $(2, 10)$. When $x = 1$, what is y?

11. The exponential decay graph has y-intercept $= 40$, and it passes through $(2, 10)$. When $x = 4$, what is y?

12. The exponential decay graph has y-intercept $= 75$, and it passes through $(2, 3)$. When $x = -2$, what is y?

13. The exponential decay graph has y-intercept $= 64$, and it passes through $(3, 0.064)$. When $x = 2$, what is y?

14. Karen shops at Aquino's Groceries. Her bill came to $50 before tax. She used two of the coupons shown below.

Karen was expecting to save 10%, which is $5. The cashier rang up the two coupons. Karen was surprised when the total price rang up as $45.13 before tax. She was not sure why there was an extra $0.13 charge.

a. What would explain why the coupons did not take off 10% the way Karen expected?

b. Write an equation to represent the total amount Karen would spend based on the number of coupons she would use.

c. Karen had originally thought that if she used 10 coupons on her next trip to Aquino's Groceries she would save 50%. Her bill is still $50. How much would Karen actually spend?

d. How many coupons would you estimate it would take for Karen to get the $50 of groceries for free?

15. Hot coffee is poured into a cup and allowed to cool. The difference between coffee temperature and room temperature is recorded every minute for 10 minutes.

Cooling Coffee

Time (min)	0	1	2	3	4	5	6	7	8	9	10
Temperature Difference (°C)	80	72	65	58	52	47	43	38	34	31	28

a. Plot the data (*time, temperature difference*). Explain what the patterns in the table and the graph tell you about the rate at which the coffee cools.

b. Approximate the decay factor for this relationship.

c. Write an equation for the relationship between time and temperature difference.

d. About how long will it take the coffee to cool to room temperature? Explain.

16. The pizza in the ad for Mr. Costa's restaurant has a diameter of 5 inches.

   a. What are the circumference and area of the pizza in the ad?

   b. Mr. Costa reduces his ad to 90% of its original size. He then reduces the reduced ad to 90% of its size. He repeats this process five times. Extend and complete the table to show the diameter, circumference, and area of the pizza after each reduction.

Advertisement Pizza Sizes

Reduction Number	Diameter (in.)	Circumference (in.)	Area (in.²)
0	5	▪	▪
1	▪	▪	▪

   c. Write equations for the diameter, circumference, and area of the pizza after n reductions.

   d. How would your equations change if Mr. Costa had used a reduction setting of 75%?

   e. Express the decay factors from part (d) as fractions.

   f. Mr. Costa claims that when he uses the 90% reduction setting on the copier, he is reducing the size of the drawing by 10%. Is Mr. Costa correct? Explain.

17. Answer parts (a) and (b) without using your calculator.

   a. Which decay factor represents faster decay, 0.8 or 0.9?

   b. Order the following from least to greatest:

   0.9^4 0.9^2 90% $\frac{2}{10}$ $\frac{2}{9}$ 0.8^4 0.84

18. Natasha and Michaela are trying to find growth factors for exponential functions. They claim that if the independent variable is increasing by 1, then you divide the two corresponding y values to find the growth factor. For example, if (x_1, y_1) and (x_2, y_2) are two consecutive entries in the table, then the growth factor is $y_2 \div y_1$.

   a. Is their reasoning correct? Explain.

   b. Would this method work to find the growth pattern for a linear function? Explain.

Connections

For Exercises 19–22, write each number in scientific notation.

19. There are about 33,400,000,000,000,000,000,000 molecules in 1 gram of water.

20. There are about 25,000,000,000,000 red blood cells in the human body.

21. Earth is about 93,000,000 miles (150,000,000 km) from the sun.

22. The Milky Way galaxy is approximately 100,000 light years in diameter. It contains about 300,000,000,000 stars.

23. Consider these equations:

$$y = 0.75^x \qquad y = 0.25^x \qquad y = -0.5x + 1$$

  a. Sketch graphs of all three equations on one set of coordinate axes.

  b. What points, if any, do the three graphs have in common?

  c. In which graph does y decrease the fastest as x increases?

  d. How can you use your graphs to figure out which of the equations is not an example of exponential decay?

  e. How can you use the equations to figure out which is not an example of exponential decay?

24. A cricket is on the 0 point of a number line, hopping toward 1. She covers half the distance from her current location to 1 with each hop. So, she will be at $\frac{1}{2}$ after one hop, $\frac{3}{4}$ after two hops, and so on.

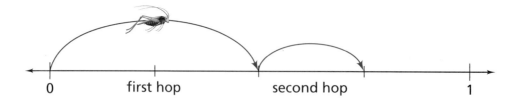

  a. Make a table showing the cricket's location for the first 10 hops.

  b. Where will the cricket be after n hops?

  c. Will the cricket ever get to 1? Explain.

Extensions

25. Freshly cut lumber, known as *green lumber*, contains water. If green lumber is used to build a house, it may crack, shrink, and warp as it dries. To avoid these problems, lumber is dried in a kiln that circulates air to remove moisture from the wood.

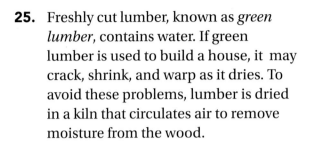

GREEN LUMBER KILN

ventilator — fans — heater

green lumber

Suppose that, in 1 week, a kiln removes $\frac{1}{3}$ of the moisture from a stack of lumber.

a. What fraction of the moisture remains in the lumber after 5 weeks in a kiln?

b. What fraction of the moisture has been removed from the lumber after 5 weeks?

c. Write an equation for the fraction of moisture m remaining in the lumber after w weeks.

d. Write an equation for the fraction of moisture m that has been removed from the lumber after w weeks.

e. Graph your equations from parts (c) and (d) on the same set of axes. Describe how the graphs are related.

f. A different kiln removes $\frac{1}{4}$ of the moisture from a stack of lumber each week. Write equations for the fraction of moisture remaining and the fraction of moisture removed after w weeks.

g. Graph your two equations from part (f) on the same set of axes. Describe how the graphs are related. How do they compare to the graphs from part (e)?

h. Green lumber is about 40% water by weight. The moisture content of lumber used to build houses is typically 10% or less. For each of the two kilns described above, how long should lumber be dried before it is used to build a house?

Mathematical Reflections

In this Investigation, you explored situations in which a quantity decayed by a constant percent rate per unit interval and graphed them. You constructed exponential decay functions given a graph, a description, or a table.

Think about these questions. Discuss your ideas with other students and your teacher. Then write a summary of your findings in your notebook.

1. **How** can you recognize an exponential decay pattern from the following?

   a. a table of data

   b. a graph

   c. an equation

2. **How** are exponential growth functions and exponential decay functions similar? **How** are they different?

3. **How** are exponential decay functions and decreasing linear functions similar? **How** are they different?

Common Core Mathematical Practices

As you worked on the Problems in this Investigation, you used prior knowledge to make sense of them. You also applied Mathematical Practices to solve the Problems. Think back over your work, the ways you thought about the Problems, and how you used Mathematical Practices.

Sophie described her thoughts in the following way:

We collected data to determine the pattern of change in the temperature of the water in a cup in Problem 4.3. We started with boiling water and checked the temperature every 5 minutes. Then, we compared the water temperature to the room temperature and recorded the difference.

We then fit a graph to the data. We used the equation to find an approximate decay factor.

This process was very similar to the one we used in determining bridge strength in the Thinking with Mathematical Models Unit.

....

Common Core Standards for Mathematical Practice
MP7 Look for and make use of structure

• What other Mathematical Practices can you identify in Sophie's reasoning?

• Describe a Mathematical Practice that you and your classmates used to solve a different Problem in this Investigation.

Patterns with Exponents

As you explored exponential functions in previous Investigations, you made tables of exponential growth. The table shows some values for $y = 2^n$. The y-values are given in both exponential and standard form.

The table shows interesting patterns. For example, Roxanne noticed that in each of the products below, the sum of the exponents of all the factors is the exponent for the product.

$$2^1 \times 2^2 = 2^3$$
$$2^2 \times 2^3 = 2^5$$

- Is Roxanne correct? Explain why or why not.

- Does Roxanne's pattern hold for any number b?
  For instance, what is the value of the expression $b^2 \times b^3$?

$y = 2^n$

x	y		
1	2^1	or	2
2	2^2	or	4
3	2^3	or	8
4	2^4	or	16
5	2^5	or	32
6	2^6	or	64
7	2^7	or	128
8	2^8	or	256

....

Common Core State Standards

8.EE.A.1 Know and apply the properties of integer exponents to generate equivalent numerical expressions.

8.EE.A.2. Use square root and cube root symbols to represent equations of the form $x^2 = p$ and $x^3 = p$. . . .

8.EE.A.4 Perform operations with numbers expressed in scientific notation, including problems where both decimal and scientific notation are used.

Also 8.F.A.3, A-SSE.A.1a, A-SSE.A.2, A-SSE.B.3c, N-RN.A.1, N-RN.A.2, F-IF.C.7e, F-IF.C.8b, F-LE.B.5

5.1 Looking for Patterns Among Exponents

The values of a^x for a given number a are called *powers of a*. You just looked at situations involving powers of 2. In Problem 5.1, you will explore patterns with powers of 2 and other numbers.

Problem 5.1

A Copy and complete this table.

x	1^x	2^x	3^x	4^x	5^x	6^x	7^x	8^x	9^x	10^x
1	1	2	■	■	■	■	■	■	■	■
2	1	4	■	■	■	■	■	■	■	■
3	1	8	■	■	■	■	■	■	■	■
4	1	16	■	■	■	■	■	■	■	■
5	1	32	■	■	■	■	■	■	■	■
6	1	64	■	■	■	■	■	■	■	■
7	1	128	■	■	■	■	■	■	■	■
8	1	256	■	■	■	■	■	■	■	■

B 1. Describe any patterns that you see in the rows and columns.

2. Give examples for your patterns.

3. Explain why your patterns are correct.

C Delmar noticed that if you extend the pattern upwards in the table for negative values of x, you get the values shown at the right.

1. Copy the table and extend it to include columns for 3^x through 10^x.

2. Delmar claims that $a^0 = 1$ and that $a^{-1} = \frac{1}{a}$ for any positive number a. Do you agree? Explain.

x	1^x	2^x
−2	1	$\frac{1}{4}$
−1	$\frac{1}{1} = 1$	$\frac{1}{2}$
0	1	1

A **C** **E** Homework starts on page 88.

5.2 Rules of Exponents

In Problem 5.1, you explored patterns among the values of a^x for different values of a. For example, Federico noticed that 64 appears three times in the powers table. It is in the column for 2^x, 4^x, and 8^x. He said this means that $2^6 = 4^3 = 8^2$.

- Explain why Federico's conclusion is true.

- Are there other numbers that appear more than once in the table?

- What other patterns do you notice in the table?

In Problem 5.2, you will look at patterns that lead to some important properties of exponents.

Problem 5.2

Use your table from Problem 5.1 to help you answer these questions.

A **1.** Write each of the following in expanded form. Then, write the answer in exponential form with a single base and power.

    a. $2^3 \times 2^2$ **b.** $3^4 \times 3^3$ **c.** $6^5 \times 6^5$

  2. What do you notice when you multiply two powers with the same base?

  3. Finish the following equation to express what you noticed. Explain why it is true.

$$a^m \times a^n = \blacksquare$$

B **1.** Rewrite each multiplication sentence as an equivalent division sentence.

    a. $3^3 \times 3^2 = 3^5$ **b.** $4^6 \times 4^5 = 4^{11}$ **c.** $5^8 \times 5^4 = 5^{12}$

  2. What do you notice when you divide two powers with the same base? Why do you think this happens?

  3. Finish the following equation to express what you noticed. Explain your reasoning. Assume $a \neq 0$.

$$\frac{a^m}{a^n} = \blacksquare$$

Problem 5.2 continued

C **1.** Write each of the following in expanded form. Then write the result in exponential form with a single base and power.

    a. $2^3 \times 5^3$ **b.** $5^2 \times 6^2$ **c.** $10^4 \times 2^4$

    2. What do you notice when you multiply two powers with the same exponent but different bases?

    3. Finish the following equation to express what you noticed. Explain.

$$a^m \times b^m = \blacksquare$$

D **1.** Mary says she can use the fact below to write a power raised to a power with a single base and power.

> I know that $(2^3)^2 = (2^3) \bullet (2^3)$.

    Use that fact to write each of the following with a single base and power.

    a. $(3^2)^2$ **b.** $(5^3)^3$ **c.** $(2^2)^4$

    2. What do you notice when you raise a power to a power?

    3. Finish the following equation to express what you know. Explain.

$$(a^m)^n = \blacksquare$$

E As he worked on Problem 5.1, Question C, Delmar made the following claim.

> $a^0 = 1$ and $a^{-1} = \dfrac{1}{a}$.

Use what you have learned in Questions A–D to show why each of the following is true for any nonzero value of a:

    1. $a^0 = 1$

    2. $a^{-1} = \frac{1}{a}$

    3. Finish the following equation.

$$a^{-m} = \blacksquare$$

A**C****E** Homework starts on page 88.

5.3 Extending the Rules of Exponents

In Problem 5.1 and Problem 5.2 you investigated rules for integral exponents and found the following to be true, where $x \neq 0$, $y \neq 0$, and m and n are integers.

$$x^m x^n = x^{m+n}$$

$$(x^m)^n = x^{mn}$$

$$(xy)^m = x^m y^m$$

$$\frac{x^m}{x^n} = x^{m-n}$$

$$x^{-1} = \frac{1}{x}$$

$$x^0 = 1$$

- Do these rules work for rational exponents?

Suppose a certain amoeba population quadruples every week. If you start with 1 amoeba, then the population y grows according to the relationship $y = 4^x$. The graph of this relationship appears below.

Amoeba Population Growth

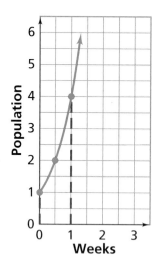

- Does it make sense to write $y = 4^{\frac{1}{2}}$?
- If so, what point does this correspond to on the graph?

The point $\left(\frac{1}{2}, 2\right)$ is the point on the graph that corresponds to an x-value of $\frac{1}{2}$. This means that $4^{\frac{1}{2}} = 2$. Chaska then reasons as follows.

> Since you already know that $\sqrt{4} = 2$, it must be true that $\sqrt{4} = 4^{\frac{1}{2}}$.

- Do the rules for adding exponents apply to the exponent $\frac{1}{2}$?
  For instance, is it true that $4^{\frac{1}{2}} \cdot 4^{\frac{1}{2}} = 4^{\frac{1}{2}+\frac{1}{2}} = 4$?

Chaska then thinks about other roots.

> I know that $\sqrt[3]{8} = 2$. So I conclude that the rule for
>
> the exponent $\frac{1}{2}$ can be extended to the exponent $\frac{1}{3}$.

- How can you write $\sqrt[3]{8} = 2$ using exponents?
- How can Chaska use the rules for exponents to confirm that $\sqrt[3]{8} \cdot \sqrt[3]{8} \cdot \sqrt[3]{8} = 8$?
- In general, the **nth root** of a number b is denoted by $\sqrt[n]{b}$ or $b^{\frac{1}{n}}$, where n is an integer greater than 1.
- Think about what Chaska found about the exponents $\frac{1}{2}$ and $\frac{1}{3}$.
  Is it true that $\sqrt[n]{x} = x^{\frac{1}{n}}$?

 - Do the other rules for exponents apply to exponents that are fractions?

In Problem 5.3, you will explore whether the rules for integral exponents apply for rational exponents.

Problem 5.3

A What does $16^{\frac{3}{2}}$ mean?

1. Mari, Latrell, and Jakayla came up with three different ways to think about $16^{\frac{3}{2}}$. Do any of these make sense? Explain.

Mari's Method

$$16^{\frac{3}{2}} = \left(16^{\frac{1}{2}}\right)^3$$
$$= (4)^3$$
$$= 64$$

Latrell's Method

$$16^{\frac{3}{2}} = (16^3)^{\frac{1}{2}}$$
$$= (4096)^{\frac{1}{2}}$$
$$\text{or } \sqrt{4096}$$
$$= 64$$

Jakayla's Method

$$16^{\frac{3}{2}} = 16^{1 + \frac{1}{2}}$$
$$= 16^1\left(16^{\frac{1}{2}}\right) \text{ or } 16\sqrt{16}$$
$$= 16(4)$$
$$= 64$$

2. Find the value of each of the following. Show your method.

   a. $8^{\frac{5}{3}}$ **b.** $125^{\frac{4}{3}}$

B **1.** Use what you learned about roots to compute each of the following.

   a. $4^{\frac{3}{2}} \cdot 4^{\frac{1}{2}}$ **b.** $4^{\frac{1}{3}} \cdot 2^{\frac{1}{3}}$ **c.** $\left(2^{\frac{5}{3}}\right)^3$ **d.** $\dfrac{25^{\frac{3}{2}}}{25^{\frac{1}{2}}}$

2. Use the rules for integral exponents to compute the answer in a different way for each of the expressions in part (1). Do you get the same numbers? Explain why or why not.

C Suppose that in Problem 1.2, R is the number of rubas on the nth square of a chessboard. Mari and Latrell came up with the following two equations for R.

Mari
$$R = \frac{1}{2}(2^n)$$

Latrell
$$R = 2^{n-1}$$

Which equation is correct? Explain.

Problem **5.3** *continued*

D Suppose that in Problem 1.4, the number of cuts is n and the area of each piece is A. Jakayla, Mari, and Latrell came up with three ways to express the exponential relationship.

Mari	Latrell	Jakayla
$A = \dfrac{64}{2^n}$	$A = 64(0.5^n)$	$A = 64(2^{-n})$

Are these all correct? Explain.

E Use the rules of exponents to write an equivalent expression for each of the following.

1. $x^{\frac{1}{2}} \cdot x^{\frac{3}{2}}$ **2.** $x^{\frac{2}{3}} \div x^{\frac{7}{6}}$ **3.** $\left(2x^{\frac{1}{2}}\right)^2$ **4.** $\left(16x^{\frac{4}{3}}\right)^{\frac{1}{2}}$

A C E Homework starts on page 88.

Did You Know?

Having only a single cell, amoebas are among the simplest organisms. Even so, amoebas and humans have common features. Both have DNA and cellular structure. The life cycle of an amoeba is typically a few days.

Most amoebas have no fixed shape and are so small that they cannot be seen with the naked eye. Yet there is one species, *Gromia sphaerica*, that is the size of a grape! The plural of amoeba is *amoebas* or *amoebae*.

5.4 Operations with Scientific Notation

Gray water is a term for wastewater that is reused without any treatment. For example, some people use the water that drains from their shower, bathtub, washing machine, or dishwasher to water their gardens. Reusing water in this way helps conserve an important resource.

The United States uses a huge amount of water. To get a sense of the amounts used for various purposes, consider the following figures from a recent year.

- A total of approximately 4.10×10^{11} gallons of water is used each day in the United States.

- Water for cooling electric power plants demands 2.01×10^{11} gallons per day.

- Irrigation uses about 1.28×10^{11} gallons of water per day.

- Livestock consumes about 2.14×10^{9} gallons of water per day.

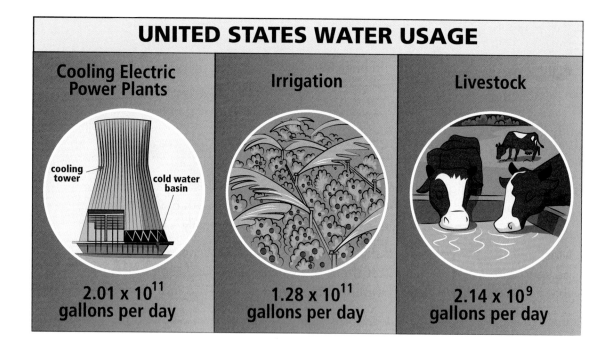

UNITED STATES WATER USAGE

Cooling Electric Power Plants
cooling tower
cold water basin
2.01×10^{11} gallons per day

Irrigation
1.28×10^{11} gallons per day

Livestock
2.14×10^{9} gallons per day

Gary and Judy are studying water use. They need to figure out how much water is used per person each day. The U.S. population in the same year was approximately 301,000,000. Assume that everyone uses the same amount of water each day.

- How much water is used per person each day?

Problem 5.4

A Gary and Judy are figuring out how much water each person uses per day. They used the following expression to find their answer: $(4.10 \times 10^{11}) \div (301{,}000{,}000)$. Each of them used a different method for carrying out the calculations. Consider their two methods for solving the problem.

Gary's Method

I thought of both numbers in millions. 10^6 is one million.
So $4.10 \times 10^{11} = 410{,}000 \times 10^6$, and $301{,}000{,}000 = 301 \times 10^6$.
Dividing gives me $410{,}000 \div 301 \approx 1{,}360$.
My result is $1{,}360$ gallons per person per day.

Judy's Method

I converted $301{,}000{,}000$ to 3.01×10^8. Then I rewrote the problem as

$$\frac{4.10 \times 10^{11}}{3.01 \times 10^8} = \frac{4.10}{3.01} \times \frac{10^{11}}{10^8} \approx 1.36 \times 10^3.$$

I know that $10^{11} \div 10^8$ equals 10^3 because $10^8 \cdot 10^3 = 10^{11}$.
So the answer is about 1.36×10^3 gallons per day for each person.

1. Which of these methods makes more sense to you? What other method could you use?

2. Do you use more than 1,000 gallons of water each day at home and at school? What might explain such a high average water use?

3. What other questions could you answer with the data given?

continued on the next page >

Problem 5.4 *continued*

B In Illinois, 11,600,000 people got their water from public supplies provided by cities and towns. Those people used 1.05×10^9 gallons of water each day.

    1. How many gallons of water per day did each person use?

    2. Compare the amount of water from public supplies to the amount used per person in all of the United States. What could account for the difference?

    3. Use your answer to Question B, part (1), to find the number of gallons each person in Illinois used *per second*. (There are 86,400 seconds in a day.) Write your answer in scientific notation.

C What percent of the water used in the United States each day went to each of the following? (Total use was 4.10×10^{11} gallons of water per day.)

    1. irrigation (1.28×10^{11} gallons of water per day)

    2. livestock (2.14×10^9 gallons of water per day)

D Use what you know about the rules of exponents and scientific notation to solve the following. Express your answer in scientific notation.

    1. $(4.0 \times 10^2) \times (3.5 \times 10^3)$

    2. $(2.0 \times 10^6) \div (2.5 \times 10^2)$

A C E Homework starts on page 88.

5.5 Revisiting Exponential Functions

You have studied situations that show patterns of exponential growth or exponential decay. All of these situations represent exponential functions that are modeled with equations of the form $y = a(b^x)$. In this equation, a is the starting value and b is the growth or decay factor.

 • What are the effects of a and b on the graph of the equation?

Problem 5.5

You can use your graphing calculator to explore how the values of *a* and *b* affect the graph of $y = a(b^x)$.

A   **1.** Let $a = 1$. Make a prediction about how the value of *b* affects the graph.

      2. Graph the four equations below in the same window. Use window settings that show *x*-values from 0 to 5 and *y*-values from 0 to 20.

$$y = 1.25^x \qquad y = 1.5^x \qquad y = 1.75^x \qquad y = 2^x$$

      What are the similarities in the graphs? What are the differences? Record your observations.

      3. Next, graph the three equations below in the same window. Use window settings that show $0 \le x \le 5$ and $0 \le y \le 1$.

$$y = 0.25^x \qquad\qquad y = 0.5^x \qquad\qquad y = 0.75^x$$

      Record your observations.

      4. Describe how you could predict the general shape of the graph of $y = b^x$ for a specific value of *b*.

B   Next, you will explore how the value of *a* affects the graph of $y = a(b^x)$. You may need to adjust the window settings as you work.

      1. Make a prediction about how the value of *a* affects the graph.

      2. Graph these equations in the same window. Record your observations.

$$y = 2(1.5)^x \qquad\qquad y = 3(1.5^x) \qquad\qquad y = 4(1.5^x)$$

      3. Graph these equations in the same window. Record your observations.

$$y = 2(0.5^x) \qquad\qquad y = 3(0.5^x) \qquad\qquad y = 4(0.5)^x$$

      4. Describe how the value of *a* affects the graph of an equation of the form $y = a(b^x)$.

C   You have explored the effects of *a* and *b* in the exponential equation $y = a(b^x)$. Compare those effects to the effects of *m* and *b* in the linear equation $y = mx + b$.

A **C** **E**   Homework starts on page 88.

Applications

1. Several students were working on Question A of Problem 5.1. They wondered what would happen if they extended their table. Do you agree or disagree with each conjecture below? Explain.

Heidi's conjecture:
The 1^x column will contain only ones.

Evan's conjecture:
The bottom right corner of any table will always have the largest value.

Roger's conjecture:
So far, every number in the 2 column is even. Eventually an odd number will show up if I extend the table far enough.

Jean's conjecture:
Any odd power (an odd row) will have all odd numbers in it.

Chaska's conjecture:
To get from one row to the next in the tens column multiply the number you have by 10. For example $10^5 = 100,000$, so $10^6 = 100,000 \times 10 = 1,000,000$.

Tim's conjecture:
The row where $x = 2$ will always have square numbers in it.

---

2. **Multiple Choice** Which expression is equivalent to $2^9 \times 2^{10}$?

   A. 2^{90} **B.** 2^{19} **C.** 4^{19} **D.** 2^{18}

Use the properties of exponents to write each expression as a single power. Check your answers.

3. $5^6 \times 8^6$ 4. $\left(7^5\right)^3$ 5. $\dfrac{8^{15}}{8^{10}}$

For Exercises 6–11, tell whether the statement is *true* or *false*. Explain.

6. $6^3 \times 6^5 = 6^8$ 7. $2^3 \times 3^2 = 6^5$

8. $3^8 = 9^4$ 9. $4^3 + 5^3 = 9^3$

10. $2^3 + 2^5 = 2^3(1 + 2^2)$ 11. $\dfrac{5^{12}}{5^4} = 5^3$

12. Multiple Choice Which number is the ones digit of $2^{10} \times 3^{10}$?

    F. 2   **G.** 4   **H.** 6   **J.** 8

For Exercises 13 and 14, find the ones digit of the product.

13. $4^{15} \times 3^{15}$

14. $7^{15} \times 4^{20}$

15. Manuela came to the following conclusion about power of 2.

> It must be true that $2^{10} = 2^4 \cdot 2^6$, because I can group
> $2 \cdot 2 \cdot 2 \cdot 2 \cdot 2 \cdot 2 \cdot 2 \cdot 2 \cdot 2 \cdot 2$ as
> $(2 \cdot 2 \cdot 2 \cdot 2) \cdot (2 \cdot 2 \cdot 2 \cdot 2 \cdot 2 \cdot 2)$

    a. Verify that Manuela is correct by evaluating both sides of the equation $2^{10} = 2^4 \cdot 2^6$.

    b. Use Manuela's idea of grouping factors to write three other expressions that are equivalent to 2^{10}. Evaluate each expression you find to verify that it is equivalent to 2^{10}.

    c. The standard form for 2^7 is 128, and the standard form for 2^5 is 32. Use these facts to evaluate 2^{12}. Explain your work.

    d. Test Manuela's idea to see if it works for exponential expressions with other bases, such as 3^8 or $(1.5)^{11}$. Test several cases. Give an argument supporting your conclusion.

For Exercises 16–21, tell whether each expression is equivalent to 1.25^{10}. Explain your reasoning.

16. $(1.25)^5 \cdot (1.25)^5$ **17.** $(1.25)^3 \times (1.25)^7$

18. $(1.25) \times 10$ **19.** $(1.25) + 10$

20. $(1.25^5)^2$ **21.** $(1.25)^5 \cdot (1.25)^2$

For Exercises 22–25, tell whether each expression is equivalent to $(1.5)^7$. Explain your reasoning.

22. $1.5^5 \times 1.5^2$

23. $1.5^3 \times 1.5^4$

24. 1.5×7

25. $(1.5) + 7$

26. Some students are trying to solve problems with rational exponents. Which of these solutions is correct?

Stu's Solution	Carrie's Solution
$81^{\frac{3}{4}} = \left(81^{\frac{1}{4}}\right)^3$	$125^{\frac{7}{3}} = 125^{\frac{6}{3}+\frac{1}{3}}$
$= (3^3)$	$= 125^2 \cdot 125^{\frac{1}{3}}$
$= 27$	$= 15{,}625 \cdot 5$
	$= 78{,}125$

For Exercises 27–30, use the properties of exponents to evaluate each expression.

27. $\left(756^{\frac{1}{7}}\right)^7$

28. $342^{\frac{5}{2}} \div 342^{\frac{3}{2}}$

29. $3^{35} \cdot 3^{-35}$

30. $\left(\frac{1}{2}\right)^{40} \cdot 2^{40}$

For Exercises 31–36, decide if each statement is *always true, always false,* or *sometimes true.* Explain.

31. $2^n \cdot 2^n = 2(2^n)$

32. $2^n \cdot 2^n = (2^n)^2$

33. 2^n is less than 2^{n-1}.

34. b^n is less than b^{n-1}.

35. For the expression 3^x, when x is negative, 3^x will be smaller than 1.

36. For the expression b^x, when x is negative, b^x will be smaller than 1.

37. In 1867, the United States of America purchased the territory of Alaska from the Russian Empire. Its 586,412 square miles cost $7.2 million. The United States paid roughly two cents per acre of land. Assume that the price of land in Alaska has increased in value by 5% a year since the purchase.

    a. Write an equation that represents the price per acre in the year n.

    b. What was the cost of an acre in 1900? In 2000?

    c. In what year did the cost reach approximately $1 per acre? $100 per acre?

    d. Gia calculated the cost per acre after n years on her calculator. She got the answer 2.453774647E28. For what year was she trying to find the cost?

38. Suppose n is the number of years after the United States purchased the territory of Alaska, in March of 1867. The equation $v = 7{,}200{,}000 \cdot (1.05)^n$ models the total value v of the territory. It is based on a 5% increase per year. Calculate the value of the territory during each month below. Explain what exponent you would use.

    a. April 1867   **b.** May 1867   **c.** September 1867

    d. June 1868   **e.** November 1868

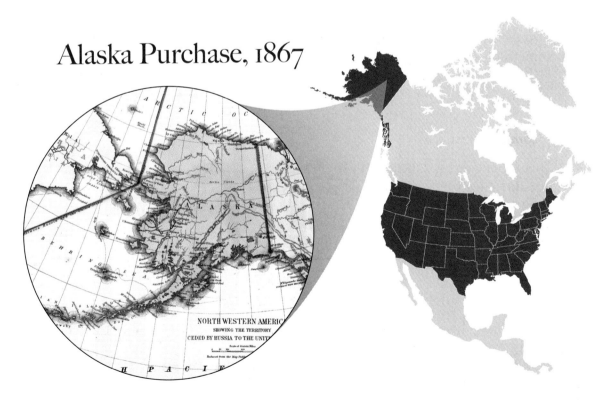

Alaska Purchase, 1867

39. Copy and complete this table.

Powers of Ten

Standard Form	Exponential Form
10,000	10^4
1,000	10^3
100	10^2
10	10^1
1	10^0
$\frac{1}{10} = 0.1$	10^{-1}
$\frac{1}{100} = 0.01$	10^{-2}
$\frac{1}{1{,}000} = 0.001$	■
$\frac{1}{10{,}000} = 0.0001$	■
■	10^{-5}
■	10^{-6}

40. Write each number in standard form as a decimal.

3×10^{-1} $\quad$ 1.5×10^{-2} $\quad$ 1.5×10^{-3}

41. If you use your calculator to compute $2 \div 2^{12}$, the display might show something like this:

4.8828125E⁻4

The display means 4.8828125×10^{-4}, which is a number in scientific notation. Scientific notation uses two parts. The first is a number greater than or equal to 1 but less than 10 (in this case, 4.8828125). The second is a power of 10 (in this case, 10^{-4}). You can convert 4.8828125×10^{-4} to standard form in this way.

$$4.8828125 \times 10^{-4} = 4.8828125 \times \frac{1}{10{,}000} = 0.00048828125$$

a. Write each number in standard notation.

1.2×10^{-1} $\quad$ 1.2×10^{-2} $\quad$ 1.2×10^{-3} $\quad$ 1.2×10^{-8}

b. Suppose you have the expression 1.2×10^{-n}, where n is any whole number greater than or equal to 1. Using what you discovered in part (a), explain how you would write the expression in standard notation.

42. Write each number in scientific notation.

    a. 2,000,000   **b.** 28,000,000   **c.** 19,900,000,000

    d. 0.12489   **e.** 0.0058421998   **f.** 0.0010201

43. When Tia divided 0.0000015 by 1,000,000 on her calculator, she got 1.5E−12, which means 1.5×10^{-12}.

    a. Write a different division problem that will give the result 1.5E−12 on your calculator.

    b. Write a multiplication problem that will give the result 1.5E−12 on your calculator.

44. The radius of the moon is about 1.74×10^{6} meters.

    a. Express the radius of the moon in standard notation.

    b. The largest circle that will fit on your textbook page has a radius of 10.795 cm. Express this radius in meters, using scientific notation.

    c. Suppose a circle has the same radius as the moon. By what scale factor would you reduce the circle to fit on your textbook page?

    d. Earth's moon is about the same size as Io, one of Jupiter's moons. What is the ratio of the moon's radius to the radius of Jupiter (6.99×10^{7} meters)?

Jupiter's moon, Io

45. The number 2^{7} is written in standard form as 128 and in scientific notation as 1.28×10^{2}. The number $\left(\frac{1}{2}\right)^{7}$, or $(0.5)^{7}$, is written in standard form as 0.0078125 and in scientific notation as 7.8125×10^{-3}. Write each number in scientific notation.

    a. 2^{8} **b.** $\left(\frac{1}{2}\right)^{8}$ **c.** 20^{8} **d.** $\left(\frac{1}{20}\right)^{8}$

46. a. The boxes in the table below represent decreasing *y*-values. The decay factor for the *y*-values is $\frac{1}{3}$. Copy and complete the table.

x	0	1	2	3	4	5	6	7	8
y	30	10	■	■	■	■	■	■	■

b. For *x* = 12, a calculator gives a *y*-value of 5.645029269E−5. What does that mean?

c. Write the *y*-values for *x* = 8, 9, 10, and 11 in scientific notation.

For Exercises 47–49, use the properties of exponents to show that each statement is true.

47. $\frac{1}{2}(2^n) = 2^{n-1}$

48. $4^{n-1} = \frac{1}{4}(4^n)$

49. $25(5^{n-2}) = 5^n$

50. Use the data from Problem 5.4 to answer the following questions. Write your final answer in scientific notation.

a. How many of gallons of water are used in the United States in a year?

b. About how many times greater is the amount of water used for irrigation than the amount used for livestock?

c. Suppose 80% of water is from *surface* sources. How many gallons of freshwater are removed *from the ground* each month?

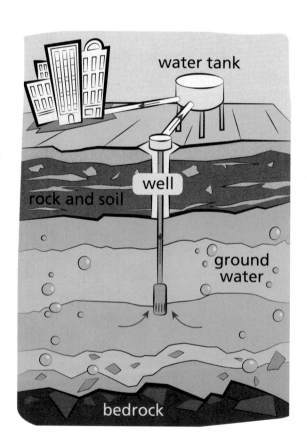

water tank

well

rock and soil

ground water

bedrock

For Exercises 51–57, rewrite each expression in scientific notation.

51. $(8.2 \times 10^2) \times (2.1 \times 10^5)$

52. $(2.0 \times 10^3) \times (3.5 \times 10^6) \times (3.0 \times 10^3)$

53. $(2.0 \times 10^8) \times (1.4 \times 10^{-10})$

54. $(5.95 \times 10^8) \div (1.70 \times 10^5)$

55. $(1.28 \times 10^6) \div (5.12 \times 10^7)$

56. $(2.8 \times 10^{-4}) \div (1.4 \times 10^4)$

57. $(3.6 \times 10^2) \div (9.0 \times 10^{-3})$

For Exercises 58–62, find the missing values in each equation. Choose values such that all numbers are written in correct scientific notation.

58. $(2.4 \times 10^3) \times (g \times 10^h) = 6.0 \times 10^{12}$

59. $(j \times 10^2) \times (1.8 \times 10^k) = 9.0 \times 10^1$

60. $(m \times 10^7) \div (2.4 \times 10^n) = 5.0 \times 10^4$

61. $(6.48 \times 10^6) \div (p \times 10^q) = 2.16 \times 10^{-2}$

62. $(r \times 10^s) \times (r \times 10^s) = 1.6 \times 10^5$

63. Without actually graphing these equations, describe and compare their graphs. Be as specific as you can.

$y = 4^x$ $\qquad$ $y = 0.25^x$ $\qquad$ $y = 10(4^x)$ $\qquad$ $y = 10(0.25^x)$

64. Explain how each of the graphs for the equations below will differ from the graph of $y = 2^x$.

a. $y = 5(2^x)$

b. $y = (5 \cdot 2)^x$

c. $y = \frac{1}{2}(2^x)$

d. $y = -1(2^x)$

e. $y = \left(\frac{1}{2}\right)^x$

65. Each graph below represents an exponential equation of the form $y = a(b^x)$.

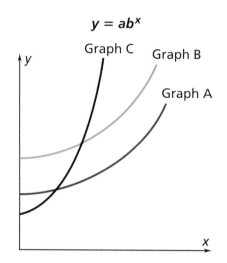

$y = ab^x$

Graph C   Graph B

Graph A

a. For which of the three functions is the value of a greatest?

b. For which of the three functions is the value of b greatest?

66. Grandville has a population of 1,000. Its population is expected to decrease by 4% a year for the next several years. Tinytown has a population of 100. Its population is expected to increase by 4% a year for the next several years. For parts (a)–(c), explain how you found each answer.

a. What is the population of each town after 5.5 years?

b. In how many years will Tinytown have a population of approximately 1,342? Explain your method.

c. Will the populations of the two towns ever be the same? Explain.

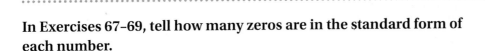

Connections

In Exercises 67–69, tell how many zeros are in the standard form of each number.

67. 10^{10}

68. 10^{50}

69. 10^{100}

In Exercises 70 and 71, find the least integer value of x that will make each statement true.

70. $9^6 < 10^x$

71. $3^{14} < 10^x$

In Exercises 72–74, identify the greater number in each pair.

72. 6^{10} or 7^{10}

73. 8^{10} or 10^8

74. 6^9 or 9^6

In Exercises 75 and 76, tell whether each statement is *true* or *false.* Do not do an exact calculation. Explain your reasoning.

75. $\left(1.56892 \times 10^5\right) - \left(2.3456 \times 10^4\right) < 0$

76. $\dfrac{3.96395 \times 10^5}{2.888211 \times 10^7} > 1$

77. Suppose you start with a unit cube (a cube with edges of length 1 unit). In parts (a)–(c), give the volume and surface area of the cube that results from the given transformation.

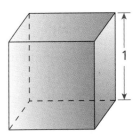

   a. Each edge length is doubled.

   b. Each edge length is tripled.

   c. Each edge is enlarged by a scale factor of 100.

78. Suppose you start with a cylinder that has a radius of 1 unit and a height of 1 unit. In parts (a)–(c), give the volume of the cylinder that results from the given transformation.

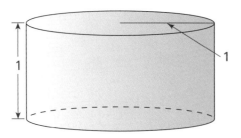

a. The radius and height are doubled.

b. The radius and height are tripled.

c. The radius and height are enlarged by a scale factor of 100.

79. a. Tell which of the following numbers are prime. (There may be more than one.)

$2^2 - 1$ $2^3 - 1$ $2^4 - 1$ $2^5 - 1$ $2^6 - 1$

b. Find another prime number that can be written in the form $2^n - 1$.

80. In parts (a)–(d), find the sum of the proper factors for each number.

a. 2^2

b. 2^3

c. 2^4

d. 2^5

e. What do you notice about the sums in parts (a)–(d)?

81. The expression $\frac{20}{10^2}$ can be written in many equivalent forms, including $\frac{2}{10}$, $\frac{1}{5}$, 0.2, and $\frac{2(10^2)}{10^3}$. In parts (a) and (b), write two equivalent forms for each expression.

a. $\dfrac{3(10)^5}{10^7}$

b. $\dfrac{5(10)^5}{25(10)^7}$

Extensions

In Exercises 82–86, predict the ones digit for the standard form of each number.

82. 7^{100}

83. 6^{200}

84. 17^{100}

85. 31^{10}

86. 12^{100}

For Exercises 87 and 88, find the value of a that makes each number sentence true.

87. $a^7 = 823{,}543$

88. $a^6 = 1{,}771{,}561$

89. Explain how you can use your calculator to find the ones digit of the standard form of 3^{30}.

90. Multiple Choice In the powers table you completed in Problem 5.1, look for patterns in the ones digit of square numbers. Which number is *not* a square number? Explain.

A. 289 **B.** 784 **C.** 1,392 **D.** 10,000

91. a. Find the sum for each row in the table below.

Sums of Powers of $\frac{1}{2}$

Row 1	$\frac{1}{2}$
Row 2	$\frac{1}{2} + \left(\frac{1}{2}\right)^2$
Row 3	$\frac{1}{2} + \left(\frac{1}{2}\right)^2 + \left(\frac{1}{2}\right)^3$
Row 4	$\frac{1}{2} + \left(\frac{1}{2}\right)^2 + \left(\frac{1}{2}\right)^3 + \left(\frac{1}{2}\right)^4$

b. Study the pattern. Suppose the pattern continues. Write the expression that would be in row 5 and evaluate the sum.

c. What would be the sum of the expression in row 10? What would you find if you evaluated the sum for row 20?

d. Describe the pattern of sums in words and with a symbolic expression.

e. For which row does the sum first exceed 0.9?

f. As the row number increases, the sum gets closer and closer to what number?

g. Celeste claims the pattern is related to the pattern of the areas of the ballots cut in Problem 4.1. She drew the picture below to explain her thinking.

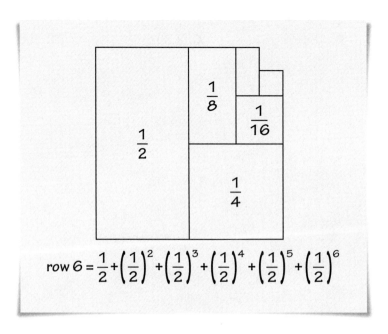

$$\text{row } 6 = \frac{1}{2} + \left(\frac{1}{2}\right)^2 + \left(\frac{1}{2}\right)^3 + \left(\frac{1}{2}\right)^4 + \left(\frac{1}{2}\right)^5 + \left(\frac{1}{2}\right)^6$$

What relationship do you think she has observed?

92. Chen, from Problem 4.1, decides to make his ballots starting with a sheet of paper with an area of 1 square foot.

   a. Copy and extend this table to show the area of each ballot after each of the first 8 cuts.

Areas of Ballots

Number of Cuts	Area (ft²)
0	1
1	$\frac{1}{2}$
2	$\frac{1}{4}$

   b. Write an equation for the area A of a ballot after any cut n.

   c. Use your equation to find the area of a ballot after 20 cuts. Write your answer in scientific notation.

93. In 1803, the United States bought the 828,000-square-mile Louisiana Purchase for $15,000,000. Suppose one of your ancestors was given 1 acre of the Louisiana Purchase. Assuming an annual increase in value of 4%, what was the value of this acre in 2003? (640 acres = 1 square mile)

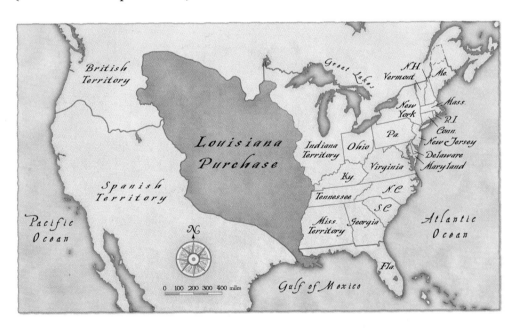

Mathematical Reflections 5

In this Investigation, you explored properties of exponents. You also looked at how the values of a and b affect the graph of $y = a(b^x)$. You made use of scientific notation to find relations among very large numbers. The following questions will help you summarize what you have learned.

Think about these questions. Discuss your ideas with other students and your teacher. Then write a summary of your findings in your notebook.

1. **a. Describe** some of the rules for operating with exponents.

    b. What is scientific notation? **What** are its practical applications?

2. **Describe** the effects of a and b on the graph of $y = a(b^x)$.

3. **Compare** exponential and linear functions. Include in your comparison information about their patterns of change, y-intercepts, whether the function is decreasing or increasing, and any other information you think is important. Include examples of how they are useful.

Common Core Mathematical Practices

As you worked on the Problems in this Investigation, you used prior knowledge to make sense of them. You also applied Mathematical Practices to solve the Problems. Think back over your work, the ways you thought about the Problems, and how you used Mathematical Practices.

Hector described his thoughts in the following way:

In Problem 5.4, we noticed that it is easy to use the rules of exponents to do multiplication when large numbers are expressed in scientific notation. Most of our group used a calculator anyway.

Since we were working with approximate data, we knew that our answers were also approximate.

We all used the graphing calculator in Problem 5.5. The calculator was faster for making the graphs so we could compare families of exponential functions.

....

Common Core Standards for Mathematical Practice
MP5 Use appropriate tools strategically

- What other Mathematical Practices can you identify in Hector's reasoning?

- Describe a Mathematical Practice that you and your classmates used to solve a different Problem in this Investigation.

Unit Project

Half-Life

Most things around you are composed of atoms that are stable. However, the atoms that make up *radioactive* substances are unstable. They break down in a process known as *radioactive decay*. From their decay, they emit radiation. At high levels, radiation can be dangerous.

Rates of decay vary from substance to substance. The term *half-life* describes the time it takes for half of the atoms in a radioactive sample to change into other more stable atoms. For example, the half-life of carbon-11 is 20 minutes. This means that 2,000 carbon-11 atoms are reduced to 1,000 carbon-11 atoms and 1,000 boron-11 atoms in 20 minutes. After 40 minutes, the carbon-11 atoms are reduced to 500 carbon-11 atoms and 1,500 boron-11 atoms.

Half-lives vary from a fraction of a second to billions of years. For example, the half-life of polonium-214 is 0.00016 seconds. The half-life of rubidium-87 is 49 billion years.

In this experiment, you will model the decay of a radioactive substance known as iodine-124. About $\frac{1}{6}$ of the atoms in a sample of iodine-124 decay each day. This experiment will help you determine the half-life of this substance.

Follow these steps to conduct your experiment:

- Use 100 cubes to represent 100 iodine-124 atoms. Mark one face of each cube.

- For the first day, place all 100 cubes in a container, shake the container, and pour the cubes onto the table.

- The cubes for which the mark is facing up represent atoms that have decayed. Remove these cubes, and record the number of cubes that remain.

- For the next day, place the remaining cubes in the container, shake the container, and pour the cubes onto the table.

- Repeat the last two steps until one cube or no cubes remain.

When you complete your experiment, answer the following questions.

1. a. In your experiment, how many days did it take to reduce the 100 iodine-124 atoms to 50 atoms? In other words, how many times did you have to roll the cubes until about 50 cubes remained?

   b. How many days did it take to reduce 50 iodine-124 atoms to 25 atoms?

   c. Based on your answers to parts (a) and (b), what is the half-life of iodine-124?

2. a. In a sample of real iodine-124, $\frac{1}{6}$ of the atoms decay after 1 day. What fraction of the atoms remain after 1 day?

   b. Suppose a sample contains 100 iodine-124 atoms. Use your answer from part (a) to write an equation for the number of atoms n remaining in the sample after d days.

   c. Use your equation to find the half-life of iodine-124.

   d. How does the half-life you found based on your equation compare to the half-life you found from your experiment?

3. a. Make up a problem involving a radioactive substance with a different rate of decay that can be modeled by an experiment involving cubes or other common objects. Describe the situation and your experiment.

   b. Conduct your experiment and record your results.

   c. Use your results to predict the half-life of your substance.

   d. Use what you know about the rate of decay to write an equation that models the decay of your substance.

   e. Use your equation to find the half-life of your substance.

Write a report that summarizes your findings about decay rates and half-lives. Your report should include tables and graphs justifying your answers to the questions above.

You developed your skills in recognizing and applying exponential relationships between variables by working on Problems in this Unit.

You wrote equations of the form $y = a(b^x)$ to describe exponential growth of populations and investments and exponential decay of medicines and radioactive materials. You used equations to produce tables and graphs of the relationships. You used those tables and graphs to make predictions and solve equations.

Use Your Understanding: Algebraic Reasoning

To test your understanding and skill in finding and applying exponential models, solve these problems. These problems arise as the student council at Lincoln Middle School plans a fundraising event.

The students want to have a quiz show called *Who Wants to Be Rich?* Contestants will be asked a series of questions. A contestant will play until he or she misses a question. The total prize money will grow with each question answered correctly.

1. Lucy proposes that a contestant receive $5 for answering the first question correctly. For each additional correct answer, the total prize would increase by $10.

   a. For Lucy's proposal, what equation gives the total prize *p* for correctly answering *n* questions?

   b. How many questions would a contestant need to answer correctly to win at least $50? To win at least $75? To win at least $100?

   c. Sketch a graph of the (n, p) data for $n = 1$ to 10.

2. Armando also thinks the first question should be worth \$5. However, he thinks a contestant's winnings should double with each subsequent correct answer.

    a. For Armando's proposal, what equation gives the total prize p for correctly answering n questions?

    b. How many questions will a contestant need to answer correctly to win at least \$50? To win at least \$75? To win at least \$100?

    c. Sketch a graph of the data (n, p) for $n = 1$ to 10.

3. The council decides that contestants for *Who Wants to Be Rich?* will be chosen by a random drawing. Students and guests at the fundraiser will buy tickets like the one below.

The purchaser will keep half of the ticket and add the other half to the entries for the drawing.

    a. To make the tickets, council members will take a large piece of paper and fold it in half many times to make a grid of small rectangles. How many rectangles will there be after n folds?

    b. The initial piece of paper will be a square with sides measuring 60 centimeters. What will be the area of each rectangle after n folds?

Decide whether each statement is *true* or *false*. Explain.

4. $3^5 \times 6^5 = 9^5$

5. $8^5 \times 4^6 = 2^{27}$

6. $\dfrac{2^0 \times 6^7}{3^7} = 2^7$

7. $8^{\frac{3}{2}} \times 2^{\frac{1}{2}} = 32$

8. $1.39 \times 10^{-5} = 139{,}000$

9. $1.099511 \times 10^6 = 1{,}099{,}511$

Explain Your Reasoning

To answer Questions 1–3, you had to use algebraic knowledge about number patterns, graphs, and equations. You had to recognize linear and exponential patterns from verbal descriptions and represent those patterns with equations and graphs.

10. How can you decide whether a data pattern can be modeled by an exponential equation of the form $y = a(b^x)$? How will the values of a and b relate to the data pattern?

11. Describe the possible shapes for graphs of exponential relationships. How can the shape of an exponential graph be predicted from the values of a and b in the equation?

12. How are the data patterns, graphs, and equations for exponential relationships similar to those for linear relationships? How are they different?

13. Describe the rules for exponents that you used in Questions 4–9. Choose one of the rules and explain why it works.

B   **base**   The number that is raised to a power in an exponential expression. In the expression 3^5, read "3 to the fifth power", 3 is the base and 5 is the exponent.

base   El número que se eleva a una potencia en una expresión exponencial. En la expresión 3^5, que se lee "3 elevado a la quinta potencia", 3 es la base y 5 es el exponente.

C   **compound growth**   Another term for exponential growth, usually used when talking about the monetary value of an investment. The change in the balance of a savings account shows compound growth because the bank pays interest not only on the original investment, but on the interest earned.

crecimiento compuesto   Otro término para crecimiento exponencial, normalmente usado para referirse al valor monetario de una inversión. El cambio en el saldo de una cuenta de ahorros muestra un crecimiento compuesto, ya que el banco paga intereses no sólo sobre la inversión original, sino sobre los intereses ganados.

D   **decay factor**   The constant factor that each value in an exponential decay pattern is multiplied by to get the next value. The decay factor is the base in an exponential decay equation, and is a number between 0 and 1. For example, in the equation $A = 64(0.5)^n$, where A is the area of a ballot and n is the number of cuts, the decay factor is 0.5. It indicates that the area of a ballot after any number of cuts is 0.5 times the area after the previous number of cuts. In a table of (x, y) values for an exponential decay relationship (with x-values increasing by 1), the decay factor is the ratio of any y-value to the previous y-value.

factor de disminución   El factor constante por el cual se multiplica cada valor en un patrón de disminución exponencial para obtener el valor siguiente. El factor de disminución es la base en una ecuación de disminución exponencial. Por ejemplo, en la ecuación $A = 64(0.5)^n$, donde A es el área de una papeleta y n es el número de cortes, el factor de disminución es 0.5. Esto indica que el área de una papeleta después de un número cualquiera de cortes es 0.5 veces el área después del número anterior de cortes. En una tabla de valores (x, y) para una relación de disminución exponencial (donde el valor x crece de a 1), el factor de disminución es la razón entre cualquier valor de y y su valor anterior.

decay rate   The percent decrease in an exponential decay pattern. In general, for an exponential pattern with decay factor b, the decay rate is $1 - b$.

tasa de disminución   El porcentaje de reducción en un patrón de disminución exponencial. En general, para un patrón exponencial con factor de disminución b, la tasa de disminución es $1 - b$.

decide Academic Vocabulary
To use the given information and any related facts to find a value or make a determination.

related terms *determine, find, conclude*

sample Study the pattern in the table. Decide whether the relationship is linear or exponential.

x	−1	0	1	2	3
y	−9	−7	−5	−3	−1

Each y-value Increases by 2 when each x-value Increases by 1. The relationship is linear.

decidir Vocabulario academico
Usar la información dada y los datos relacionados para hallar un valor o tomar una determinación.

terminos relacionados *decidir, hallar, calcular, concluir*

ejemplo ?Cual es una manera de determinar la descomposicion en factores primos de 27?

x	−1	0	1	2	3
y	−9	−7	−5	−3	−1

Cada valor de y aumenta en 2 cuando cada valor de x aumenta en 1. La relaclón es lineal.

---

describe Academic Vocabulary
To explain or tell in detail. A written description can contain facts and other information needed to communicate your answer. A diagram or a graph may also be included when you describe something.

related terms *explain, tell, present, detail*

sample Consider the following equations:

Equation 1 $y = 3x + 5$

Equation 2 $y = 5\left(3^x\right)$

Use a table to describe the change in *y*-values as the *x*-values increase in both equations.

x	0	1	2	3	4
y = 3x + 5	5	8	11	14	17
y = 5(3ˣ)	5	15	45	135	405

In y = 3x + 5, the value of y increases by 3 when x increases by 1. In y = 5(3ˣ), the value of y increases by a factor of 3 when x increases by 1.

describir Vocabulario academico Explicar usando detalles. Puedes describir una situacion usando palabras, numeros, graficas, tablas o cualquier combinacion de estos.

terminos relacionados *explicar, decir, presentar, dar detalles*

ejemplo Considera las siguintes ecuaciones.

Ecuacion 1 $y = 3x + 5$

Ecuacion 2 $y = 5\left(3^x\right)$

Usa una tabla para describir el cambio en los valores de *y* a medida que los valores de *x* se incrementan en ambas ecuaciones.

x	0	1	2	3	4
y = 3x + 5	5	8	11	14	17
y = 5(3ˣ)	5	15	45	135	405

In y = 3x + 5, el valor de y aumenta en 3 cuando x aumenta en 1. En y = 5(3ˣ), el valor de y aumenta por un factor de 3 cuando x aumenta en 1.

E **explain** Academic Vocabulary
To give facts and details that make an idea easier to understand. Explaining can involve a written summary supported by a diagram, chart, table, or any combination of these.

related terms *describe, justify, tell*

sample Etymologists are working with a population of mosquitoes that have a growth factor of 8. After 1 month there are 6,000 mosquitoes. In two months, there are 48,000 mosquitoes.

Write an equation for the population after any number of months. Explain each part of your equation.

I first find the initial population of mosquitoes by dividing 6,000 by 8 to get 750. I can then model the population growth with the equation $y = 750(8^m)$, where 750 represents the initial population, 8 is the growth factor, m is the number of months, and y is the population of mosquitoes after m months.

explicar Vocabulario academico
Dar hechos y detalles que hacen que una idea sea mas facil de comprender. Explicar puede implicar un resumen escrito apoyado por un diagrama, un grafica, una table o cualquier combatinacion de estos.

terminos relacionados *describir, justificar, decir*

ejemplo Los entomologos trabajan con una poblacion de mosquitos que tiene un factor de crecimiento de 8. Despues de 1 mes hay 6,000 mosquitos. En dos meses, hay 48,000 mosquitos.

Escribe una ecuacion para la poblacion despues de cualquier numero de meses. Explica cada parte de tu ecuacion.

Primero hallo la población inicial de mosquitos dividiendo 6,000 entre 8 para obtener 750. Luego puedo modelar el crecimiento de la población con la ecuación $y = 750(8^m)$, donde 750 representa la población inicial, 8 es el factor de crecimiento, m es el número de meses y y es la población de mosquitos luego de m meses.

exponent The small raised number that tells how many times a factor is used. For example, 5^3 means $5 \times 5 \times 5$. The 3 is the exponent.

exponente El pequeño número elevado que dice cuántas veces se usa un factor. Por ejemplo, 5^3 significa $5 \times 5 \times 5$. El 3 es el exponente.

exponential decay A pattern of decrease in which each value is found by multiplying the previous value by a constant factor greater than 0 and less than 1. For example, the pattern 27, 9, 3, 1, $\frac{1}{3}, \frac{1}{9}, \ldots$ shows exponential decay in which each value is $\frac{1}{3}$ times the previous value.

disminución exponencial Un patrón de disminución en el cual cada valor se calcula multiplicando el valor anterior por un factor constante mayor que 0 y menor que 1. Por ejemplo, el patrón 27, 9, 3, 1, $\frac{1}{3}, \frac{1}{9}, \ldots$ muestra una disminución exponencial en la que cada valor es $\frac{1}{3}$ del valor anterior.

exponential form A quantity expressed as a number raised to a power. In exponential form, 32 can be written as 2^5.

forma exponencial Una cantidad que se expresa como un número elevado a una potencia. En forma exponencial, 32 puede escribirse como 2^5.

exponential functions Relationships between two variables that are exponential. For example, the function represented by $y = 4^{n-1}$ for placing 1 ruba on square one, 4 rubas on square two, 16 rubas on square three, and so on, is an exponential function.

funciones exponenciales Relaciones entre dos variables que son exponenciales. Por ejemplo, la función representada por $y = 4^{n-1}$ para poner un ruba en el cuadro uno, cuatro rubas en el cuadro dos, dieciséis rubas en el cuadro tres y así sucesivamente, es una función exponencial.

exponential growth A pattern of increase in which each value is found by multiplying the previous value by a constant factor greater than 1. For example, the doubling pattern 1, 2, 4, 8, 16, 32, . . . shows exponential growth in which each value is 2 times the previous value.

crecimiento exponencial Un patrón de crecimiento en el cual cada valor se calcula multiplicando el valor anterior por un factor constante mayor que 1. Por ejemplo, el patrón 1, 2, 4, 8, 16, 32, . . . muestra un crecimiento exponencial en el que cada valor es el doble del valor anterior.

exponential relationship A relationship that shows exponential growth or decay.

relación exponencial Una relación que muestra crecimiento o disminución exponencial.

G **growth factor** The constant factor that each value in an exponential growth pattern is multiplied by to get the next value. The growth factor is the base in an exponential growth equation, and is a number greater than 1. For example, in the equation $A = 25(3)^d$, where A is the area of a patch of mold and d is the number of days, the growth factor is 3. It indicates that the area of the mold for any day is 3 times the area for the previous day. In a table of (x, y) values for an exponential growth relationship (with x-values increasing by 1), the growth factor is the ratio of any y-value to the previous y-value.

factor de crecimiento El factor constante por el cual se multiplica cada valor en un patrón de crecimiento exponencial para obtener el valor siguiente. El factor de crecimiento es la base en una ecuación de crecimiento exponencial. Por ejemplo, en la ecuación $A = 25(3)^d$, donde A es el área enmohecida y d es el número de días, el factor de crecimiento es 3. Esto indica que el área enmohecida en un día cualquiera es 3 veces el área del día anterior. En una tabla de valores (x, y) para una relación de crecimiento exponencial (donde el valor de x aumenta de a 1), el factor exponencial es la razón entre cualquier valor de y y su valor anterior.

growth rate The percent increase in an exponential growth pattern. For example, in Problem 3.1, the number of rabbits increased from 100 to 180 from year 0 to year 1, an 80% increase. From year 1 to year 2, the number of rabbits increased from 180 to 324, an 80% increase. The growth rate for this rabbit population is 80%. Interest, expressed as a percent, is a growth rate. For an exponential growth pattern with a growth factor of b, the growth rate is $b - 1$.

tasa de crecimiento El porcentaje de crecimiento en un patrón de crecimiento exponencial. Por ejemplo, en el Problema 3.1, el número de conejos aumentó de 100 a 180 del año 0 al año 1, un aumento del 80%. Del año 1 al año 2, el número de conejos aumentó de 180 a 324, un aumento del 80%. La tasa de crecimiento para esta población de conejos es del 80%. El interés, expresado como porcentaje, es una tasa de crecimiento. Para un patrón de crecimiento exponencial con un factor de crecimiento b, la tasa de crecimiento es $b - 1$.

N **nth root** The nth root of a number b is a number r which, when raised to the power of n, is equal to b. That is, $r^n = b$ and $\sqrt[n]{b} = b^{\frac{1}{n}} = r$.

raíz enésima La raíz enésima de un número b es un número erre que, cuando se eleva a la potencia n, es igual a b. Es decir, y $r^n = b$ a un $\sqrt[n]{b} = b^{\frac{1}{n}} = r$.

P **predict** Academic Vocabulary
To make an educated guess based on the analysis of real data.

related terms *estimate, expect*

sample Predict the ones digit for the expression 3^{11}.

3^1	3
3^2	9
3^3	27
3^4	81
3^5	243
3^6	729
3^7	2187
3^8	6561

The pattern for the ones digit of the powers of 3 is 3, 9, 7, 1, as the exponent increases by 1. If I continue the pattern, 3^9 will end with a 3, 3^{10} will end with a 9, and 3^{11} will end with a 7.

predecir Vocabulario academico
Hacer una conjectura informada basada en el analisis de datos reales.

terminos relacionados *estimar, esperar*

ejemplo Predice el digito de las unidades para la expresion 3^{11}.

3^1	3
3^2	9
3^3	27
3^4	81
3^5	243
3^6	729
3^7	2187
3^8	6561

El patrón para el dígito de las unidades de las potencias de 3 es 3, 9, 7, 1, a medida que el exponente aumenta en 1. Si continúo el patrón, 3^9 terminará con un 3, 3^{10} terminará con un 9, y 3^{11} terminará con un 7.

S **scientific notation** A short way to write very large or very small numbers. A number is in scientific notation if it is of the form $a \times 10^n$, where n is an integer and $1 \le a < 10$.

standard form The most common way we express quantities. For example, 27 is the standard form of 3^3.

notación científica Una manera corta de escribir números muy grandes o muy pequeños. Un número está e notación científica si está en la forma $a \times 10^n$, donde n es un entero y $1 \le a < 10$.

forma normal La manera más común de expresar una cantidad. Por ejemplo, 27 es la forma normal de 3^3.

Index

ACE
exponential decay, 66–73
exponential growth, 14–24
growth factors and growth rates, 48–57
growth patterns, 32–39
patterns with exponents, 88–101

algebraic reasoning, 106–107

amoebas, 83

area and perimeter
enlarging shapes and, 38, 54
exponential decay and, 61, 66–67, 71
patterns with exponents, 100

Ask Yourself, 4

bases, 9

calculators
exponential form and, 9, 16
exponents and, 57
scientific notation and, 17, 103

change, patterns of, 2. *See also* patterns with exponents
equations of, 23
exponential decay, 60–61, 64–65, 70, 74
and exponential functions, 18, 19
exponential growth, 8
growth factors and growth rates, 53
and linear functions, 19
tables and graphs, 20, 23–24

circles, 93

circumference, exponential decay and, 71

Common Core Mathematical Practices, 26, 41, 59, 75, 103

compound growth, 46–47, 57

decay factors, 94
exponential decay, 62–63, 68, 69, 70
fractions and, 71

decay rates, 63, 69, 104–105

dependent variables, 11, 13, 19, 31

diagonals, length of, 54

division, patterns with exponents and, 78

equations
compound growth, 47
decay rates, 107
exponential decay and, 61, 68, 70, 73
for exponential functions, 29–30, 57
exponential growth and, 11, 13, 15–16, 26, 34, 68
growth factors and growth rates, 36, 55, 58
growth patterns and, 27, 32, 33, 43
modeling growth, 2, 19
patterns of change, 23, 24
patterns with exponents, 81–83, 100
population growth, 48, 56
tables and graphs for, 39, 72, 86–87, 95
y-intercepts and, 37

equivalent form, 98

expanded form, 9, 78, 79

Explain Your Reasoning, 108

exponential decay, 4
ACE, 66–73
decay factors, 62–63
equations for exponential functions, 86–87
Mathematical Reflections, 74–75
modeling, 64–65
patterns of change, 60–61

exponential form, 9–11
calculators and, 16
exponential growth and, 21–22
patterns with exponents, 78, 79, 92

exponential functions
about, 7–8
equations of, 29–30, 39, 57
exponential decay and, 62
growth factors and, 11, 34
growth patterns and, 28–29
growth rates and, 50
linear functions and, 25, 108
and patterns of change, 3, 18, 19, 20
patterns with exponents, 86–87, 102
representing in exponential form, 9–11
tables and graphs for, 30–31, 40, 108

exponential growth, 4
ACE, 14–24
equations for exponential functions, 86–87
exponential decay and, 74
exponential functions, 7–11
growth factors and, 11–13, 48
Mathematical Reflections, 25–26
patterns and, 52

exponents, 37
ACE, 88–101
calculators and, 57
exponential form and, 9
exponential functions, 86–87
extending rules of, 80–83
Mathematical Reflections, 102–103
patterns with, 76–77
rules of, 78–79
scientific notation and, 84–86

factor-pair relationships, 67

factors, enlarging shapes and, 38

fractional growth patterns, 42–43

fractions, 71, 81, 82, 83

Glossary, 109–114

graphs and graphing. *See* tables and graphs

gray water, 84

growth, equations modeling, 2, 3, 7–13

growth factors, 7–11, 25, 44
exponential functions, 34, 40
exponential growth and, 52
population growth and, 48
y-intercepts and, 35–36

growth factors and growth rates
ACE, 48–57
compound growth, 46–47
fractional growth patterns, 42–43
growth rates, 44–46
independent variables and, 71
Mathematical Reflections, 48–57

growth patterns, 27
ACE, 32–39
equations for exponential functions, 29–30
graphs for exponential functions, 30–31
Mathematical Reflections, 40–41
y-intercepts, 28–29

growth rates, 44–46

half-life, 104–105

income growth, 55

independent variables, 11, 13, 19, 31, 71

inflation rate, 56

integral exponents, 80, 81

interest rates, 57

Investigations
exponential decay, 60–65
exponential growth, 7–13
growth factors and growth rates, 42–47
growth patterns, 27–31
patterns with exponents, 76–87

investment values
compound growth, 46–47, 57
growth factors and, 49
growth rates and, 44–45, 51
patterns with exponents, 91, 101

iodine-124, 106–107

linear functions
equations for exponential functions, 87
exponential decay and, 74
exponential functions and, 25, 108
exponential growth and, 8
growth patterns and, 33, 40
and patterns of change, 3, 19, 20
patterns with exponents, 102

lines, equations for, 37

Looking Ahead, 2–3

Looking Back, 106–108

Mathematical Highlights, 4

Mathematical Practices, 5–6

Mathematical Reflections
exponential decay, 74–75
exponential growth, 25–26
growth factors and growth rates, 48–57
growth patterns, 40–41
patterns with exponents, 102–103

medicine, exponential decay and, 62–63, 68

modeling strategies, exponential decay, 64–65

multiplication and division, 78

*n*th root, 81

operations strategies
patterns with exponents, 102
scientific notation and, 84–86

patterns. *See* change, patterns of; growth patterns

patterns with exponents, 76–77
ACE, 88–101
exponential functions, 86–87
extending rules of exponents, 80–83
Mathematical Reflections, 102–103
rules of exponents, 78–79
scientific notation and, 84–86

percentages, 52, 70

population growth
exponential functions, 57
exponential growth and, 49
fractional growth patterns, 42–43
growth factors and growth rates, 48, 51, 56, 58, 59
patterns with exponents, 80, 96

powers, patterns with exponents and, 77, 78, 79, 88–89
patterns with exponents, 99

prime factorization, 37

rabbits, population growth and, 42–43

radioactive decay, 104–105

radius, 93, 98

rates of decay. *See* decay rates

rational exponents, 80, 81, 90

ratios, 54

reasoning, explaining your.
  See also Mathematical
  Practices

  algebraic reasoning, 106–107
  compound growth, 47
  exponential decay and, 63,
    67, 68, 69, 75
  exponential functions, 39
  exponential growth and, 26
  growth factors and growth
    rates, 52, 53, 54, 59, 71
  growth patterns and, 30, 40,
    41
  patterns of change, 24
  patterns with exponents, 77,
    82, 89–90, 98, 103

rectangles, 38

roots, 81

Rule of 72, 46

scale factors, 55

  scientific notation, 4, 72
  calculators and, 17
  exponential form and, 9–10
  exponential growth and, 16
  patterns with exponents,
    92–93, 94, 95, 102

shapes, enlarging and
  reducing, 38, 54, 55, 71

side lengths, 99

similar figures, 54

slope, 22, 37

standard form, 9, 16, 21, 92,
  97, 99

sums, patterns with
  exponents, 100

surface area and volume, 97, 98

tables and graphs

  compound growth, 47
  for equations, 39, 72, 96
  exponential decay and, 61,
    62–63, 65, 67, 68, 70, 75
  for exponential functions,
    30–31, 40
  exponential growth and, 11,
    17–18
  growth factors and growth
    rates, 53
  growth patterns and, 27, 29,
    32–33
  growth rates and, 44–45
  patterns of change, 2, 20,
    23–24

patterns with exponents and,
  77, 80
population growth and, 44,
  48, 56
slope and y-intercepts, 22

Unit Project, 104–105

Use Your Understanding,
  106–107

variables
  dependent variables, 11, 13,
    19, 31
  exponential growth and, 49
  independent variables, 11,
    13, 19, 31, 71

y-intercepts
  equations and, 37
  exponential decay and, 67,
    68, 69
  exponential functions, 40
  graphs and graphing, 22
  growth factors and, 35–36
  growth patterns and, 27,
    28–29, 31
  patterns with exponents, 102

Acknowledgments

Text

028 Texas Christian University Press

"Killer Weed Strikes Lake Victoria" from CHRISTIAN SCIENCE MONITOR, JANUARY 12, 1998.

Photographs

Photo locators denoted as follows: Top (T), Center (C), Bottom (B), Left (L), Right (R), Background (Bkgd)

002 Jacques Jangoux/Alamy; **003** Andy Williams/Loop Images/Alamy; **017** Scott Camazine/Science Source; **028** (CL) Ocean/Corbis, (CR) Jacques Jangoux/Alamy; **029** David Toase/Photodisc/Getty Images; **080** XUNBIN PAN/Alamy; **091** (BL) Steven Wright/Shutterstock, (BR) Ridvan EFE/Shutterstock; **093** Picture Press/Alamy.

Frogs, Fleas, and Painted Cubes

Quadratic Functions

Lappan, Phillips, Fey, Friel

Frogs, Fleas, and Painted Cubes

Quadratic Functions

Looking Ahead 2

Mathematical Highlights 4

Mathematical Practices and Habits of Mind 5

1

Introduction to Quadratic Functions — 7

1.1 Staking a Claim Maximizing Area 8

1.2 Reading Graphs and Tables 9

1.3 Writing an Equation 12

ACE Homework 14

Mathematical Reflections 22

2

Quadratic Expressions — 24

2.1 Trading Land Representing Areas of Rectangles 24

2.2 Changing Dimensions The Distributive Property 28

2.3 Factoring Quadratic Expressions 32

2.4 Quadratic Functions and Their Graphs 36

ACE Homework 38

Mathematical Reflections 46

Quadratic Patterns of Change 48

3.1 Exploring Triangular Numbers 48

3.2 Counting Handshakes Another Quadratic Function 50

3.3 Examining Patterns of Change 51

3.4 Quadratic Functions and Patterns of Change 52

ACE Homework 55

Mathematical Reflections 68

Frogs Meet Fleas on a Cube: More Applications of Quadratic Functions 70

4.1 Tracking a Ball Interpreting a Table and an Equation 72

4.2 Measuring Jumps Comparing Quadratic Functions 73

4.3 Painted Cubes Looking at Several Functions 76

4.4 Putting It All Together Comparing Functions 78

ACE Homework 80

Mathematical Reflections 96

Looking Back 98

English/Spanish Glossary 101

Index 110

Acknowledgments 113

Looking Ahead

Suppose you travel to Mars to prospect a precious metal. You can claim any rectangular piece of land you can surround by 20 meters of laser fencing. **How** should you arrange your fencing to enclose the maximum area?

Suppose the circumference of a cross section of a tree is x feet. Is the relationship between the circumference and the area of the cross section linear, quadratic, exponential, or none of these?

A frog jumps straight up. Its height h in feet after t seconds is modeled by the equation $h = -16t^2 + 12t + 0.2$. **What** is the maximum height the frog reaches? **When** does the frog reach this height?

Mathematics is useful for solving practical problems in science, business, engineering, and economics. In earlier Units, you studied problems that could be modeled with linear and exponential functions, and with inverse variation. In this Unit, you will explore quadratic functions. Quadratic functions are found in many interesting situations, such as the height of a basketball thrown into the air, as well as those on the previous page.

Mathematical Highlights

Frogs, Fleas, and Painted Cubes

In *Frogs, Fleas, and Painted Cubes,* you will explore quadratic functions, an important type of nonlinear function.

You will learn how to

- Recognize patterns of change for quadratic relationships

- Write equations for quadratic functions represented in tables, graphs, and problem situations

- Connect quadratic equations to the patterns in tables and graphs of quadratic functions

- Use a quadratic equation to identify the maximum or minimum value, the *x*- and *y*-intercepts, line of symmetry, and other important features of the graph of a quadratic function

- Recognize equivalent quadratic expressions

- Use the Distributive Property to write equivalent quadratic expressions in factored and expanded form

- Use tables, graphs, and equations of quadratic functions to solve problems in a variety of situations from geometry, science, and business

- Compare properties of quadratic, linear, and exponential functions

When you encounter a new problem, it is a good idea to ask yourself questions. In this Unit, you might ask questions such as:

What are the independent and dependent variables?

How can I recognize whether the relationship between the variables is quadratic?

What equation models a quadratic function given in a table, graph, or problem context?

How can I answer questions about the problem situation by studying a table, graph, or equation representing a quadratic function?

Mathematical Practices and Habits of Mind

In the *Connected Mathematics* curriculum you will develop an understanding of important mathematical ideas by solving problems and reflecting on the mathematics involved. Every day, you will use "habits of mind" to make sense of problems and apply what you learn to new situations. Some of these habits are described by the *Common Core State Standards for Mathematical Practices* (MP).

MP1 Make sense of problems and persevere in solving them.

When using mathematics to solve a problem, it helps to think carefully about

- data and other facts you are given and what additional information you need to solve the problem;
- strategies you have used to solve similar problems and whether you could solve a related simpler problem first;
- how you could express the problem with equations, diagrams, or graphs;
- whether your answer makes sense.

MP2 Reason abstractly and quantitatively.

When you are asked to solve a problem, it often helps to

- focus first on the key mathematical ideas;
- check that your answer makes sense in the problem setting;
- use what you know about the problem setting to guide your mathematical reasoning.

MP3 Construct viable arguments and critique the reasoning of others.

When you are asked to explain why a conjecture is correct, you can

- show some examples that fit the claim and explain why they fit;
- show how a new result follows logically from known facts and principles.

When you believe a mathematical claim is incorrect, you can

- show one or more counterexamples—cases that don't fit the claim;
- find steps in the argument that do not follow logically from prior claims.

MP4 Model with mathematics.

When you are asked to solve problems, it often helps to

- think carefully about the numbers or geometric shapes that are the most important factors in the problem, then ask yourself how those factors are related to each other;
- express data and relationships in the problem with tables, graphs, diagrams, or equations, and check your result to see if it makes sense.

MP5 Use appropriate tools strategically.

When working on mathematical questions, you should always

- decide which tools are most helpful for solving the problem and why;
- try a different tool when you get stuck.

MP6 Attend to precision.

In every mathematical exploration or problem-solving task, it is important to

- think carefully about the required accuracy of results; is a number estimate or geometric sketch good enough, or is a precise value or drawing needed?
- report your discoveries with clear and correct mathematical language that can be understood by those to whom you are speaking or writing.

MP7 Look for and make use of structure.

In mathematical explorations and problem solving, it is often helpful to

- look for patterns that show how data points, numbers, or geometric shapes are related to each other;
- use patterns to make predictions.

MP8 Look for and express regularity in repeated reasoning.

When results of a repeated calculation show a pattern, it helps to

- express that pattern as a general rule that can be used in similar cases;
- look for shortcuts that will make the calculation simpler in other cases.

You will use all of the Mathematical Practices in this Unit. Sometimes, when you look at a Problem, it is obvious which practice is most helpful. At other times, you will decide on a practice to use during class explorations and discussions. After completing each Problem, ask yourself:

- What mathematics have I learned by solving this Problem?
- What Mathematical Practices were helpful in learning this mathematics?

Introduction to Quadratic Functions

In January of 1848, gold was discovered near Sacramento, California. By the spring of that year, a great gold rush had begun, bringing 500,000 new residents to California.

Throughout history, people have moved to particular areas of the world with the hopes of improving their lives.

- In 1867, prospectors headed to South Africa in search of diamonds.
- From 1860 to 1900, farmers headed to the American prairie where land was free.
- The 1901, Spindletop oil gusher brought drillers by the thousands to eastern Texas.

Prospectors and farmers had to stake claims on the land they wanted to work.

....

Common Core State Standards

A-SSE.A.1 Interpret expressions that represent a quantity in terms of its context.

A-CED.A.1 Create equations and inequalities in one variable . . .

F-IF.C.7a Graph linear and quadratic functions and show intercepts, maxima, and minima.

Also N-Q.A.1, A-SSE.A.1b, A-CED.A.2, A-REI.D.10, F-IF.B.4, F-IF.B.5, F-IF.C.7, F-IF.C.9, F-BF.A.1

1.1 Staking a Claim
Maximizing Area

Suppose it is the year 2100, and a rare and precious metal has just been discovered on Mars. You and hundreds of other adventurers travel to the planet to stake your claim. You are allowed to claim any rectangular piece of land that can be surrounded by 20 meters of laser fencing. You want to arrange your fencing to enclose the maximum area possible.

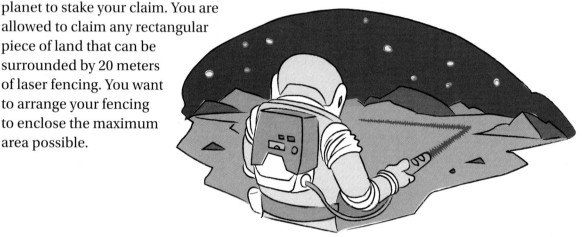

 What are the dimensions of a rectangle with the greatest area for a fixed perimeter?

Problem 1.1

A 1. Sketch several rectangles with a perimeter of 20 meters. Include some with small areas and some with large areas. Label the dimensions of each rectangle.

2. Make a table showing the length, width, and area for every rectangle with a perimeter of 20 meters and whole-number side lengths. Describe some patterns that you observe in the table.

3. Make a graph of the data (*length, area*). Describe the shape of the graph.

4. How does the pattern in the table appear in the graph?

B 1. What rectangle dimensions give the greatest possible area? Explain.

2. Suppose the dimensions were not restricted to whole numbers. Would this change your answer? Explain.

 Homework starts on page 14.

1.2 Reading Graphs and Tables

The relationship between length and area in Problem 1.1 is a **quadratic function.** Quadratic functions are characterized by their U-shaped graphs, which are called **parabolas.**

In Problem 1.1, the area depends on, or is a function of, the length. Recall that a relationship in which one variable depends on another is a *function.* Because the variable *area* depends on the length, it is called the **dependent variable.** The variable *length* is the **independent variable.**

You have studied other families of functions in earlier Units.

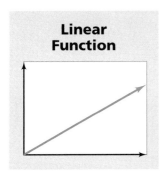

Linear Function

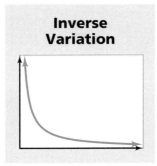

Inverse Variation

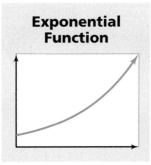

Exponential Function

- The distance covered by a van traveling at a constant speed is a function of time. The relationship between time and distance is a linear function.

- The time needed for a van to travel 200 miles is a function of the average speed of the van. The relationship between time and rate is an inverse variation.

- The value of an investment that grows at 4% per year is a function of the number of years. The relationship between the number of years and the value is an exponential function.

You have learned about important characteristics of these functions by studying tables, graphs, and equations that represent them. As you explore quadratic functions in this Unit, look for common patterns in the tables, graphs, and equations. In Problem 1.2, you will look for patterns in graphs and equations of quadratic functions.

Problem 1.2

Ⓐ The graph shows length and area data for rectangles with a fixed perimeter.

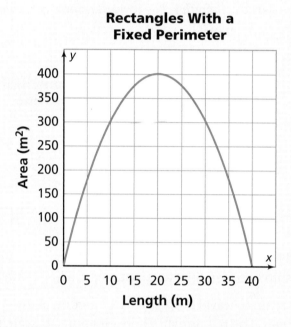

Rectangles With a Fixed Perimeter

1. Describe the shape of the graph and any special features you see.

2. What is the greatest area possible for a rectangle with this perimeter? What are the dimensions of this rectangle?

3. What is the area of the rectangle whose length is 10 meters? What is the area of the rectangle whose length is 30 meters? How are these rectangles related?

4. What are the dimensions of the rectangle with an area of 175 square meters?

5. What is the fixed perimeter for the rectangles represented by the graph? Explain how you found the perimeter.

Problem **1.2** *continued*

B Use the table to answer parts (1)–(5).

Rectangles With a Fixed Perimeter

Length (m)	Area (m²)
0	0
1	11
2	20
3	27
4	32
5	35
6	36
7	35
8	32
9	27
10	20
11	11
12	0

1. What patterns do you observe in the table? Compare these patterns with those you observed in the graph in Question A.

2. What is the fixed perimeter for the rectangles represented by this table? Explain.

3. What is the greatest area possible for a rectangle with this perimeter? What are the dimensions of this rectangle?

4. Estimate the dimensions of a rectangle with this fixed perimeter and an area of 16 square meters.

5. Suppose a rectangle with this perimeter has an area of 35.5 square meters. What are its dimensions?

C Based on Questions A and B, describe the change in area as the length increases by 1. Compare this pattern of change to those for linear and exponential functions and for inverse variation.

A C E Homework starts on page 14.

1.3 Writing an Equation

You used tables and graphs to represent relationships between length and area for rectangles with fixed perimeters. In this Problem, you will write equations for these functions.

You know that the formula for the area A of a rectangle with length ℓ and width w is $A = \ell w$ and the formula for perimeter P is $P = 2\ell + 2w$.

The rectangle below has a perimeter of 20 meters and a length of ℓ meters.

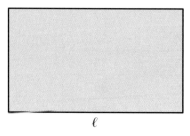

ℓ

- What equation represents the relationship between length ℓ and area A for a rectangle with a perimeter of 20 meters?

- How can you use the equation to find the maximum area?

Problem 1.3

A Consider rectangles with a perimeter of 60 meters.

  1. Sketch a rectangle to represent this situation. Label one side ℓ. Express the width in terms of ℓ.

  2. Write an equation for the area A in terms of ℓ.

  3. Make a table for your equation. Use your table to estimate the maximum area. What dimensions correspond to this area?

  4. Use data from your table to help you sketch a graph of the relationship between length and area.

  5. How can you use your graph to find the maximum area possible? How does your graph show the length that corresponds to the maximum area?

Problem 1.3 continued

B The equation for the areas of rectangles with a certain fixed perimeter is $A = \ell(35 - \ell)$, where ℓ is the length in meters.

  1. Draw a rectangle to represent this situation. Label one dimension ℓ. Label the other dimension in terms of ℓ.

  2. Make a table showing the length, width, and area for lengths of 0, 5, 10, 15, 20, 25, 30, and 35 meters. Does this table include the maximum area? Describe any patterns that you see.

  3. Describe the graph of this equation.

  4. What is the maximum area? What dimensions correspond to this maximum area? Explain.

  5. Describe two ways you could find the fixed perimeter. What is the perimeter?

C Suppose you know the perimeter of a rectangle. How can you write an equation for the area in terms of the length of a side?

D Study the graphs, tables, and equations for areas of rectangles with fixed perimeters. Which representation is most useful for finding the maximum area? Which is most useful for finding the fixed perimeter?

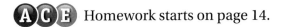 Homework starts on page 14.

Applications

1. Find the maximum area for a rectangle with a perimeter of 120 meters. Make your answer convincing by including these things:

   • Sketches of rectangles with a perimeter of 120 meters (Include rectangles that do not have the maximum area and the rectangle you think does have the maximum area.)

   • A table of lengths and areas for rectangles with a perimeter of 120 meters (Use increments of 5 meters for the lengths.)

   • A graph of the relationship between length and area

   Explain how each piece of evidence supports your answer.

2. What is the maximum area for a rectangle with a perimeter of 130 meters? As in Exercise 1, support your answer with sketches, a table, and a graph.

3. The graph shows the length and area of rectangles with a fixed perimeter. Use the graph for parts (a)–(e).

   a. Describe the shape of the graph and any special features.

   b. What is the maximum area for a rectangle with this fixed perimeter? What are the dimensions of this rectangle?

   c. Is there a rectangle with the least possible area? Explain.

   d. What is the area of a rectangle with a length of 3 centimeters?

   e. Describe two ways to find the fixed perimeter for the rectangles represented by the graph.

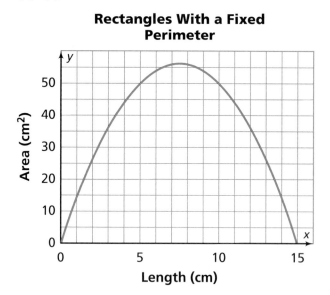

Rectangles With a Fixed Perimeter

4. Use the graph from Exercise 3. Make a table of values for the length and area.

    a. How is the shape of the graph reflected in the table?

    b. How can you use the table to find the maximum area and the dimensions of the rectangle with this area? Explain.

5. Hillsdale Farms wants to add a small, rectangular petting zoo for the public. They have a fixed amount of fencing to use for the zoo. This graph shows the lengths and areas of the rectangles they can make.

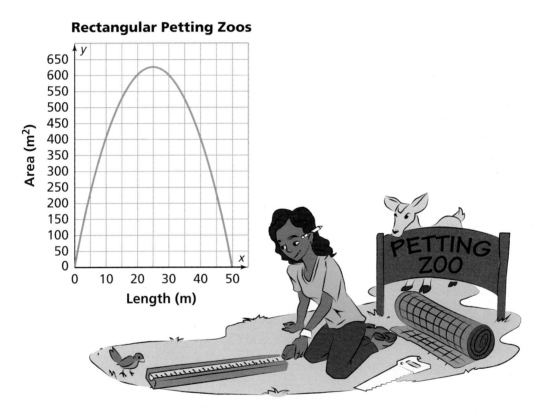

Rectangular Petting Zoos

    a. Describe the shape of the graph and any special features you observe.

    b. What is the greatest area possible for a rectangle with this perimeter? What are the dimensions of this rectangle?

    c. What is the area of the rectangle with a length of 10 meters? What is the area of the rectangle with a length of 40 meters? How are these rectangles related?

    d. What are the dimensions of the rectangle with an area of 600 square meters?

    e. What is the fixed amount of fencing available for the petting zoo? Explain.

6. The lifeguards at a beach want to place a rectangular boundary around the swimming area that can be used for water basketball. They have a fixed amount of rope to make the boundary. They use the table at the right to look at possible arrangements.

   a. What patterns do you observe in the table?

   b. What is the fixed perimeter for the possible swimming areas?

   c. Sketch a graph of the data (*length, area*). Describe the shape of the graph.

   d. Suppose the lifeguards make a rectangle with an area of 11.5 square meters. What are the dimensions of the rectangle?

   e. The lifeguards want to enclose the greatest area possible. What should be the dimensions of the swimming area?

Rectangular Swimming Area

Length (m)	Area (m²)
1	15
2	28
3	39
4	48
5	55
6	60
7	63
8	64
9	63
10	60
11	55
12	48
13	39
14	28
15	15

7. The equation for the areas of rectangles with a certain fixed perimeter is $A = \ell(20 - \ell)$, where ℓ is the length in meters.

   a. Describe the graph of this equation.

   b. What is the maximum area for a rectangle with this perimeter? What dimensions correspond to this area? Explain.

   c. A rectangle with this perimeter has a length of 15 meters. What is its area?

   d. Describe two ways you can find the perimeter. What is the perimeter?

8. A rectangle has a perimeter of 50 meters and a side length of ℓ.

   a. Express the other dimension of the rectangle in terms of ℓ.

   b. Write an equation for the area A in terms of ℓ.

   c. Sketch a graph of your equation and describe its shape.

   d. Use your equation to find the area of the rectangle with a length of 10 meters.

   e. How could you find the area in part (d) by using your graph?

   f. How could you find the area in part (d) by using a table?

   g. What is the maximum area possible for a rectangle with a perimeter of 50 meters? What are the dimensions of this rectangle?

9. A rectangle has a perimeter of 30 meters and a side length of ℓ.

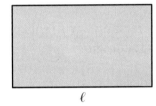

ℓ

   a. Express the other dimension of the rectangle in terms of ℓ.

   b. Write an equation for the area A in terms of ℓ.

   c. Make a graph of your equation and describe its shape.

   d. Use your equation to find the area of the rectangle with a length of 10 meters.

   e. How could you find the area in part (d) by using your graph?

   f. How could you find the area in part (d) by using a table?

   g. What is the maximum area possible for a rectangle with a perimeter of 30 meters? What are the dimensions of this rectangle?

10. **a.** Copy and complete the graph to show areas for rectangles with a fixed perimeter and lengths greater than 3 meters.

Rectangles With a Fixed Perimeter

b. Make a table of data for this situation.

c. What is the maximum area for a rectangle with this perimeter? What are the dimensions of this rectangle?

11. **Multiple Choice** Which equation describes the graph in Exercise 10?

A. $A = \ell(\ell - 6)$ **B.** $A = \ell(12 - \ell)$

C. $A = \ell(6 - \ell)$ **D.** $A = \ell(3 - \ell)$

12. **a.** Copy and complete the table to show areas for rectangles with a fixed perimeter and a length greater than 4 meters.

b. Make a graph of the relationship between length and area.

c. What are the dimensions of the rectangle with the maximum area?

13. **Multiple Choice** Which equation describes the data in the table in Exercise 12?

F. $A = \ell(8 - \ell)$ **G.** $A = \ell(16 - \ell)$

H. $A = \ell(4 - \ell)$ **J.** $A = \ell(\ell - 8)$

Rectangles With a Fixed Perimeter

Length (m)	Area (m²)
0	0
1	7
2	12
3	15
4	16
5	▪
6	▪
7	▪
8	▪

14. The equation $p = d(100 - d)$ gives the monthly profit p a photographer will earn if she charges d dollars for each print.

  a. Make a table and a graph for this equation.

  b. Estimate the price that will produce the maximum profit. Explain.

  c. How are the table and graph for this situation similar to those you made in Problem 1.1? How are they different?

Connections

15. Of all the rectangles with whole-number side lengths and an area of 20 square centimeters, which has the least perimeter? Explain.

16. **Multiple Choice** What does $2(-3 + 5) + 7 \times (-4) + (-1)$ equal?

  A. -55 **B.** -45 **C.** -31 **D.** -25

17. Eduardo's neighborhood association subdivided a large rectangular field into two playing fields as shown in the diagram.

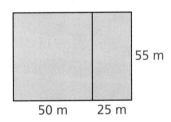

55 m

50 m   25 m

  a. Write expressions showing two ways you could calculate the area of the large field.

  b. Use the diagram and your expressions in part (a) to explain the Distributive Property.

For Exercises 18–21, use the Distributive Property to write the expression in expanded form. Then, simplify.

  18. $21(5 + 6)$ **19.** $2(35 + 1)$ **20.** $12(10 - 2)$ **21.** $9(3 + 5)$

For Exercises 22–24, use the Distributive Property to write the expression in factored form.

  22. $15 + 6$ **23.** $42 + 27$ **24.** $12 + 120$

For Exercises 25 and 26, solve each equation.

25. $5x - 30 = 95$

26. $22 + 4x = 152 - 9x$

For Exercises 27–30, do the following:

- Describe the pattern of change for each function.

- Describe how the pattern of change would look in a graph and in a table. Give as many details as you can without making a graph or table.

27. $y = 5x + 12$

28. $y = 10 - 3x$

29. $y = 3^x$

30. $y = \frac{15}{x}$

31. A rectangular soccer field has a perimeter of 400 yards. The equation $\ell = 200 - w$ represents the relationship between the length ℓ and width w of the field.

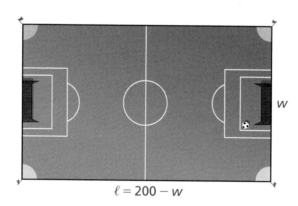

$\ell = 200 - w$

a. Explain why the equation is correct.

b. Is the relationship between length and width a quadratic function? Explain.

c. Suppose a field is a nonrectangular parallelogram with a perimeter of 400 yards. Is the relationship between the side lengths the same as it is for the rectangular field?

d. Suppose a field is a quadrilateral that is not a parallelogram. The perimeter of the field is 400 yards. Is the relationship between the side lengths the same as it is for the rectangular field?

32. Mr. DeAngelo is designing a school building. The music room floor will be a rectangle with an area of 1,200 square feet.

   a. Make a table showing a range of possible lengths and widths for the music room floor for ten different room arrangements.

   b. Add a column to your table for the perimeter of each rectangle.

   c. What patterns do you see in the perimeter column? What kinds of rectangles have large perimeters? What kinds have small perimeters?

   d. Write an equation you can use to calculate the length of the floor for any given width.

Extensions

33. A beach has a rectangular swimming area for toddlers. One side of the swimming area is the shore. Buoys and a rope with a length of 20 meters are used to form the other three sides.

   a. How should you arrange the rope to make a rectangle with the maximum area?

   b. In Problem 1.1, a fixed length of 20 meters is also used to form a rectangle. Compare the rectangle with maximum area in that Problem to the rectangle with maximum area in part (a). Are the shapes and areas of the rectangles the same? Explain.

   c. Make a graph relating the length and area for the possible rectangular swimming areas. How does the graph compare with the graph from Problem 1.1?

Mathematical Reflections

In this Investigation, you looked at the relationship between length and area for rectangles with a fixed perimeter. You learned that this relationship is a quadratic function. The following questions will help you summarize what you have learned.

Think about these questions. Discuss your ideas with other students and your teacher. Then write a summary of your findings in your notebook.

1. a. **Describe** the characteristics of graphs and tables of quadratic functions you have observed so far.

   b. **How** do the patterns in a graph of a quadratic function appear in the table of values for the function?

2. **Describe** two ways to find the maximum area for rectangles with a fixed perimeter.

3. **How** are tables, graphs, and equations for quadratic functions different from those for linear and exponential functions?

Common Core Mathematical Practices

As you worked on the Problems in this Investigation, you used prior knowledge to make sense of them. You also applied Mathematical Practices to solve the Problems. Think back over your work, the ways you thought about the Problems, and how you used Mathematical Practices.

Elena described her thoughts in the following way:

We noticed that the relationship between length and area was not an exponential or linear function. As the length increased by 1, the area did not grow by a constant factor or constant amount. The graph did not look like that of a linear or exponential function.

Common Core Standards for Mathematical Practice
MP7 Look for and make use of structure.

- What other Mathematical Practices can you identify in Elena's reasoning?

- Describe a Mathematical Practice that you and your classmates used to solve a different Problem in this Investigation.

Quadratic Expressions

In the last Problem, you used the lengths of rectangles with a fixed perimeter to write an expression that represents their area. *Length* was the independent variable, and *area* was the dependent variable. In this Investigation, you will continue to write expressions using area as a context.

2.1 Trading Land
Representing Areas of Rectangles

Suppose you give a friend two $1 bills, and your friend gives you eight quarters.

- Would you consider this a fair trade?

Common Core State Standards

A-SSE.A.1 Interpret expressions that represent a quantity in terms of its context.

F-IF.B.4 For a function that models a relationship between two quantities, interpret key features of graphs and tables in terms of the quantities, and sketch graphs showing key features given a verbal description of the relationship.

F-IF.C.8 Write a function defined by an expression in different but equivalent forms to reveal and explain different properties of the function.

Also A-SSE.A.1a, A-SSE.A.1b, A-SSE.B.2, A-SSE.B.3, A-CED.A.2, A-REI.D.10, F-IF.C.7, F-IF.C.7a, F-IF.C.8a, F-BF.A.1, F-BF.A.1a

Sometimes it is not this easy to determine whether a trade is fair. Consider the following situation:

A developer has purchased all the land on a mall site except for one square lot. The lot measures 125 meters on each side. In exchange for the lot, the developer offers its owner a lot on another site. The plan for this lot is shown below.

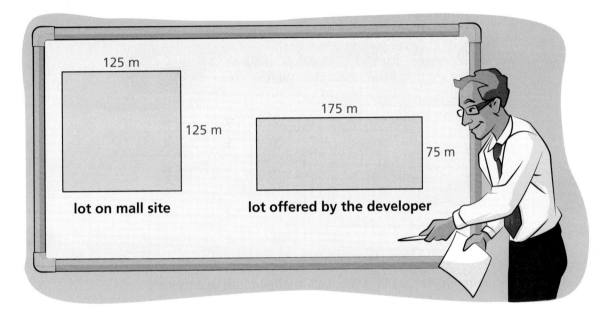

125 m

125 m

lot on mall site

175 m

75 m

lot offered by the developer

- Do you think this is a fair trade? Why or why not?

? How is the area of a square affected if one dimension is increased by *x* and the second dimension decreased by *x*? Explain.

In this Problem, you will look at a trade situation. See if you can find a pattern that will help you make predictions about more complex situations.

Problem 2.1

Suppose you trade a square lot for a rectangular lot. The length of the rectangular lot is 2 meters greater than the side length of the square lot, and the width is 2 meters less.

A 1. Copy and complete the table.

Original Square		New Rectangle			Difference of Areas (m²)
Side Length (m)	Area (m²)	Length (m)	Width (m)	Area (m²)	
2	4	4	0	0	4
3	9	5	1	5	4
4	▦	▦	▦	▦	▦
5	▦	▦	▦	▦	▦
6	▦	▦	▦	▦	▦
n	▦	▦	▦	▦	▦

2. Explain why the table starts with a side length of 2 meters, rather than 0 meters or 1 meter.

3. For each side length, tell how the areas of the new and original lots compare. For which side lengths, if any, is the trade fair?

Problem 2.1 *continued*

B **1.** Write an equation for the relationship between the side length n and the area A_1 of the original square.

2. Write an equation for the relationship between the side length n of the original square lot and the area A_2 of the new rectangular lot.

3. Carl claims there are two different expressions for the area of the new lot. Is this possible? Explain.

C **1.** On the same axes, sketch graphs of the area equations for both lots. For the independent variable, show values from −10 to 10. For the dependent variable, show values from −10 to 30.

2. Tell which part of each graph makes sense for the situation.

3. Describe any similarities and differences in the two graphs.

D **1.** Do either of the relationships represent quadratic functions? Explain.

2. Compare the graphs in this Problem to the graphs in Investigation 1. How are they alike? How are they different?

A C E Homework starts on page 38.

2.2 Changing Dimensions
The Distributive Property

In the last Problem, you looked at two expressions for the area of a rectangle: $(n - 2)(n + 2)$ and $n^2 - 4$. Because these two expressions describe the same area, they are equivalent. This means that $(n - 2)(n + 2) = n^2 - 4$ is true for every value of n.

Here is another example of equivalent expressions:

Suppose a square has sides of length x centimeters. One dimension of the square is increased by 3 centimeters to make a new rectangle.

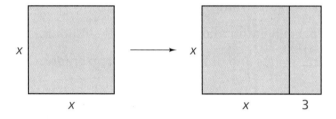

- How do the areas of the square and the new rectangle compare?

- Write two expressions for the area of the new rectangle. How do you know that the expressions are equivalent?

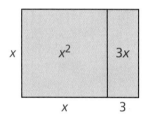

The expressions $x(x + 3)$ and $x^2 + 3x$ are examples of **quadratic expressions.** An expression in **factored form** is quadratic if it has exactly two *linear factors*, each with the variable raised to the first power. An expression in **expanded form** is quadratic if the highest power of the variable is 2. The expression $x(x + 3)$ is in factored form. The expression $x^2 + 3x$ is in expanded form.

The equation $x(x + 3) = x^2 + 3x$ is an example of the **Distributive Property,** which you studied in earlier Units. The Distributive Property says that, for any three numbers a, b, and c, $a(b + c) = ab + ac$.

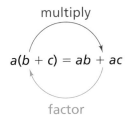

Area:
$a(b + c)$ or $ab + ac$

When you write $a(b + c)$ as $ab + ac$, you are multiplying, or writing the expression in expanded form. When you write $ab + ac$ as $a(b + c)$, you are factoring, or writing the expression in factored form.

multiply

$a(b + c) = ab + ac$

factor

- Can you use the Distributive Property to show that $(n - 2)(n + 2) = n^2 - 4$?

The **terms** $2x$ and $3x$ are **like terms.** You can use the Distributive Property to add like terms. For example, $2x + 3x = (2 + 3)x = 5x$.

In this Problem, you will explore what happens to the area of a square when one or both of its dimensions change. You can use the Distributive Property to write equivalent expressions for area in both factored form and expanded form.

Problem **2.2**

A Each rectangle is the result of changing one or more dimensions of a square. Each rectangle has been subdivided into two or four smaller rectangles. Write two expressions for the area of the rectangle outlined in red, one in factored form and one in expanded form.

1.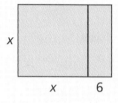

2.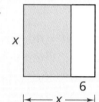

3.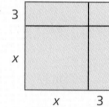

4.

5.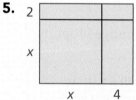

6.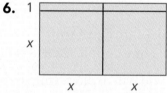

B Use a rectangle model to write each expression in expanded form.

1. $(x + 3)(x + 5)$

2. $(4 + x)(4 + x)$

3. $3x(x + 1)$

Problem 2.2 *continued*

C Carminda says she does not need a rectangle model to multiply $(x + 3)$ by $(x + 5)$. She uses the Distributive Property.

$$(x + 3)(x + 5) = (x + 3)x + (x + 3)5 \qquad (1)$$
$$= x^2 + 3x + 5x + 15 \qquad (2)$$
$$= x^2 + 8x + 15 \qquad (3)$$

1. Is Carminda correct? Explain what she did at each step.

2. Show how using the Distributive Property to multiply $(x + 3)$ and $(x + 5)$ is the same as using a rectangle model.

D Use the Distributive Property to write each expression in expanded form.

1. $(x + 5)(x + 5)$

2. $(x - 4)(x + 3)$

3. $2x(5 - x)$

4. $(2x + 1)(5 - x)$

5. $(n - 2)(n + 2)$

E Write each expression in expanded form.

1. $(x + 7)^2$

2. $(x - 7)^2$

3. $(2n - 5)^2$

4. $(2n + 5)^2$

5. After doing similar problems like these, Lydia claims that she sees a pattern that would help her expand expressions in less time. What pattern do you think she observes?

ACE Homework starts on page 38.

2.3 Factoring Quadratic Expressions

 Ms. Porath's class summarizes two ways to rewrite a factored expression, such as $(x + 2)(x + 6)$, in expanded form.

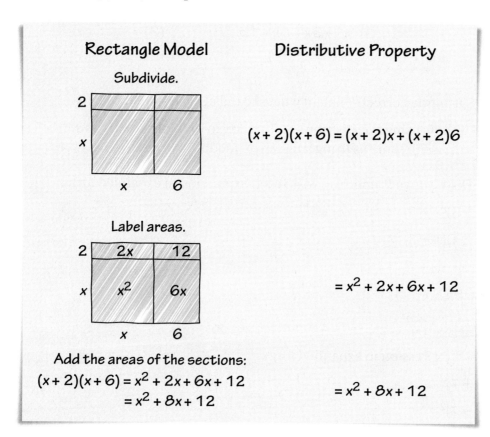

Rectangle Model　　　　**Distributive Property**

Subdivide.

$(x + 2)(x + 6) = (x + 2)x + (x + 2)6$

Label areas.

| 2 | 2x | 12 |
| x | x^2 | 6x |

$= x^2 + 2x + 6x + 12$

Add the areas of the sections:
$(x + 2)(x + 6) = x^2 + 2x + 6x + 12$
$= x^2 + 8x + 12$

$= x^2 + 8x + 12$

- How do these methods compare to the ones you and your classmates used?

In Problem 2.2, Question E, you expanded expressions like $(x + 3)^2$. The expression $(x + 3)^2$ is an example of a binomial squared. A **binomial** is an algebraic expression that is the sum or difference of two terms. For example, $x + 3$, $x - 4$, and $2x + 4$ are binomials. The two factors of a quadratic expression in factored form are examples of binomials. For example, in the factored form $(x + 2)(x + 6)$, $x + 2$ and $x + 6$ are binomials.

Lydia noticed the following pattern.

When you square a binomial, the expanded form has 3 terms.

$$(x + 3)^2 = x^2 + 6x + 9$$

- The first term is the square of the first term of the binomial: $x \cdot x$ or x^2

- The second term is twice the product of the two terms in the binomial: $2(x \cdot 3)$ or $6x$

- The third term is the square of the second term in the binomial: 3^2 or 9

- Is she correct? Explain.
- Is $x^2 + 8x + 12$ the square of a binomial? Explain.

You have used the Distributive Property to write quadratic expressions in expanded form. In the next Problem, you will use the Distributive Property to write expressions in factored form.

- How can you write an expanded expression, such as $x^2 + 8x + 12$, in factored form?

Problem 2.3

A **1.** Copy the diagram below. Replace each question mark with the correct length or area.

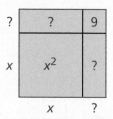

2. Write two expressions for the area of the rectangle outlined in red.

B Consider the expression $x^2 + bx + 8$.

1. Choose a value for b that gives an expression you can factor. Then, write the expression in factored form.

2. Compare your work with your classmates. Did everyone write the same expressions? Explain.

C For parts (1)–(3), find values of r and s that make the equations true.

1. $x^2 + 10x + 24 = (x + 6)(x + r)$

2. $x^2 + 11x + 24 = (x + s)(x + r)$

3. $x^2 + 25x + 24 = (x + r)(x + s)$

4. Describe the strategies you used to find the values of r and s in parts (1)–(3).

D Alyse sees a pattern in Question C. She says she can use the Distributive Property to factor the expression $x^2 + 10x + 16$. She writes:

$$x^2 + 10x + 16 = x^2 + 2x + 8x + 16 \qquad (1)$$
$$= x(x + 2) + 8(x + 2) \qquad (2)$$
$$= (x + 2)(x + 8) \qquad (3)$$

Is Alyse correct? Explain what she did at each step.

Problem **2.3** | *continued*

E Use the Distributive Property to factor each expression.

1. $x^2 + 5x + 2x + 10$

2. $x^2 + 11x + 10$

3. $x^2 + 3x - 10$

4. $x^2 - 8x + 15$

5. $15 - 14x - x^2$

6. $2x^2 + 7x + 5$

F Recall the expressions for the area of the rectangle in Problem 2.1: $n^2 - 4$ and $(n - 2)(n + 2)$. The expression $n^2 - 4$ is a **difference of squares.** After factoring and expanding quadratic expressions, the students in Mr. Towle's class claimed they could use the Distributive Property to show that the expressions for the area of the rectangle in Problem 2.1 were equivalent.

1. Are the students correct? Can you use the Distributive Property to show that $n^2 - 4 = (n - 2)(n + 2)$? Explain.

2. What are the factors of each expression?

a. $x^2 - 9$

b. $x^2 - 25$

A C E Homework starts on page 38.

2.4 Quadratic Functions and Their Graphs

In Investigation 1, you saw that graphs of equations of the form $y = x(a - x)$ are parabolas. You know that the graph of this equation is a parabola. You also know that the expressions $x(a - x)$ and $ax - x^2$ are equivalent expressions.

The **x-intercepts** of the graph below are $(0, 0)$ and $(a, 0)$. The **y-intercept** is $(0, 0)$. The graph has a *maximum point*. The y-coordinate of the maximum point is the **maximum value** of the function.

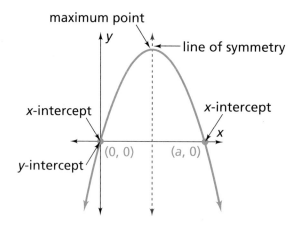

Some graphs, such as the graph of $y = -4 + x^2$, have a *minimum point*. The y-coordinate of the minimum point is the **minimum value** of the function.

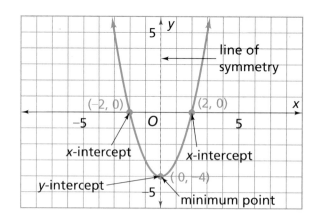

Milaka noticed that if you draw a vertical line from the minimum or maximum point to the x-axis and fold the graph along this line, the two halves of the parabola would match exactly. Her teacher said this line is called the **line of symmetry.**

- Does the line of symmetry divide the parabola into two identical parts? Explain.

In this Problem, you will explore the graphs of quadratic equations.

Problem 2.4

A The equations of several quadratic functions are given. For each function:

- Write an equivalent expression for y in expanded or factored form.
- Sketch a graph of the equation.
- Label the coordinates of the x- and y-intercepts.
- Label the maximum or minimum point.
- Draw the line of symmetry on your graph.

1. $y = x(x - 6)$ **2.** $y = 16 - x^2$

3. $y = x^2 + 6x + 9$ **4.** $y = x^2 + 9x + 20$

5. $y = x^2 + 5x - 14$ **6.** $y = (3 - x)(2 + x)$

B Without graphing, describe the graph of each equation. Give as many details as possible.

1. $y = x^2 + 8x + 12$ **2.** $y = (x + 3)(x - 3)$ **3.** $y = -x^2 + 6x$

4. Explain what features of the graph of a function, such as intercepts, maximum/minimum point, and line of symmetry, you can predict from an equation of the function. Describe how you can make these predictions.

ACE Homework starts on page 38.

Applications

1. A square has sides of length x centimeters. One dimension increases by 4 centimeters and the other decreases by 4 centimeters, forming a new rectangle.

   a. Make a table showing the side length and area of the square and the area of the new rectangle. Include whole-number x-values from 4 to 16.

   b. On the same axes, graph the data (x, *area*) for both the square and the rectangle.

   c. Suppose you want to compare the area of a square with the area of the corresponding new rectangle. Is it easier to use the table or the graph?

   d. Write equations for the area of the original square and the area of the new rectangle in terms of x.

   e. Use your calculator to graph both equations. Show values of x from -10 to 10. Copy the graphs onto your paper. Describe the relationship between the two graphs.

2. A square has sides of length x centimeters. One dimension increases by 5 centimeters, forming a new rectangle.

   a. Make a sketch to show the new rectangle.

   b. Write two expressions, one in factored form and one in expanded form, for the area of the new rectangle.

   c. Choose one of your expressions from part (b). Use it to write an equation for the area A of the new rectangle in terms of x. Then, graph the equation.

For Exercises 3 and 4, draw a divided rectangle whose area is represented by each expression. Label the lengths and area of each section. Then, write an equivalent expression in expanded form.

3. $x(x + 7)$

4. $x(x - 3)$

For Exercises 5–7, draw a divided rectangle whose area is represented by each expression. Label the lengths and area of each section. Then, write an equivalent expression in factored form.

5. $x^2 + 6x$ **6.** $x^2 - 8x$ **7.** $x^2 - x$

For Exercises 8–11, write the expression in factored form.

8. $x^2 + 10x$ **9.** $x^2 - 6x$ **10.** $x^2 + 11x$ **11.** $x^2 - 2x$

For Exercises 12–15, write the expression in expanded form.

12. $x(x + 1)$ **13.** $x(x - 10)$ **14.** $x(x + 6)$ **15.** $x(x - 15)$

For Exercises 16–20, write two expressions, one in factored form and one in expanded form, for the area of the rectangle outlined in red.

16.
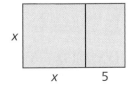

17.
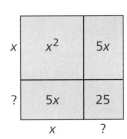

18.
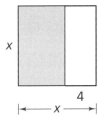

19.
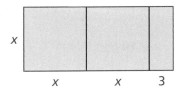

20.
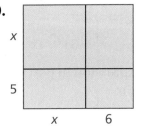

21. A square has sides of length x meters. Both dimensions increase by 5 meters, forming a new square.

    a. Make a sketch to show the new square.

    b. Write two expressions, one in factored form and one in expanded form, for the area of the new square.

    c. Choose one of your expressions from part (b). Use it to write an equation for the area A of the new square in terms of x. Then, graph the equation. Does the equation represent a quadratic function? Explain.

22. A square has sides of length x centimeters. One dimension increases by 4 centimeters and the other increases by 5 centimeters, forming a new rectangle.

   a. Make a sketch to show the new rectangle.

   b. Write two expressions, one in factored form and one in expanded form, for the area of the new rectangle.

   c. Choose one of your expressions from part (b). Use it to write an equation for the area A of the new square in terms of x. Then, graph the equation. Does the equation represent a quadratic function? Explain.

For Exercises 23–34, use the Distributive Property to write each expression in expanded form.

23. $(x - 3)(x + 4)$ **24.** $(x + 3)(x + 5)$ **25.** $x(x + 5)$

26. $(x - 2)(x - 6)$ **27.** $(x - 3)(x + 3)$ **28.** $(x - 3)(x + 5)$

29. $(2x + 1)(x + 1)$ **30.** $(x - 1)(7x + 1)$ **31.** $(x - 1)(3x - 3)$

32. $(x + 7)^2$ **33.** $(3x + 4)^2$ **34.** $(3x - 4)^2$

35. **a.** Draw and label a rectangle whose area is represented by each expression.

$$x^2 + 3x + 4x + 12 \qquad\qquad x^2 + 7x + 10$$

   b. For each expression in part (a), write an equivalent expression in factored form.

36. Write each expression in factored form.

   a. $x^2 + 13x + 12$ **b.** $x^2 - 13x + 12$ **c.** $x^2 + 8x + 12$

   d. $x^2 - 8x + 12$ **e.** $x^2 + 7x + 12$ **f.** $x^2 - 7x + 12$

   g. $x^2 + 11x - 12$ **h.** $x^2 - 11x - 12$ **i.** $x^2 + 4x - 12$

   j. $x^2 - 4x - 12$ **k.** $x^2 + x - 12$ **l.** $x^2 - x - 12$

37. Write each expression in expanded form. Look for a pattern. Make a generalization about the expanded form of expressions of the form $(x + a)(x + a)$.

    a. $(x + 1)(x + 1)$ **b.** $(x + 5)(x + 5)$ **c.** $(x - 5)(x - 5)$

38. Write each expression in expanded form. Look for a pattern. Make a generalization about the expanded form of expressions of the form $(x + a)(x - a)$.

    a. $(x + 1)(x - 1)$ **b.** $(x + 5)(x - 5)$ **c.** $(x + 1.5)(x - 1.5)$

39. Use your generalizations from Exercises 37 and 38 to write each of these expressions in factored form.

    a. $x^2 + 6x + 9$ **b.** $x^2 - 6x + 9$

    c. $x^2 - 9$ **d.** $x^2 - 16$

40. Write each expression in factored form.

    a. $2x^2 + 5x + 3$ **b.** $4x^2 - 9$ **c.** $4x^2 + 12x + 9$

41. Write each difference of squares in factored form.

    a. $x^2 - 49$ **b.** $4x^2 - 49$ **c.** $25x^2 - 1.44$

For Exercises 42–50, determine whether the equation represents a quadratic function *without* making a table or a graph. Explain.

42. $y = 5x + x^2$ **43.** $y = 2x + 8$ **44.** $y = (9 - x)x$

45. $y = 4x(3 + x)$ **46.** $y = 3^x$ **47.** $y = x^2 + 10x$

48. $y = x(x + 4)$ **49.** $y = 2(x + 4)$ **50.** $y = 7x + 10 + x^2$

51. Rewrite each equation in expanded form. Then, give the x- and y-intercepts, the coordinates of the maximum or minimum point, and the line of symmetry for the graph of each equation.

    a. $y = (x - 3)(x + 3)$ **b.** $y = x(x + 5)$ **c.** $y = (x + 3)(x + 5)$

    d. $y = (x - 3)(x + 5)$ **e.** $y = (x + 3)(x - 5)$ **f.** $y = x(x - 3)$

For Exercises 52 and 53, complete parts (a)–(e).

    a. Find an equivalent factored form of the equation.

    b. Identify the x- and y-intercepts for the graph of the equation.

    c. Find the coordinates of the maximum or minimum point.

    d. Find the line of symmetry.

    e. Tell which form of the equation can be used to predict the features in parts (b)–(d) without making a graph.

52. $y = x^2 + 5x + 6$ **53.** $y = x^2 - 25$

54. Darnell makes a rectangle from a square by doubling one dimension and adding 3 centimeters. He leaves the other dimension unchanged.

    a. Write an equation for the area A of the new rectangle in terms of the side length x of the original square.

    b. Graph your area equation.

    c. What are the x-intercepts of the graph? How can you find the x-intercepts from the graph? How can you find them from the equation?

Connections

55. The winner of the Jammin' Jelly jingle contest will receive $500. Antonia and her friends are writing a jingle. They plan to divide the prize money equally if they win.

    a. Suppose n friends write the winning jingle. How much prize money will each person receive?

    b. Describe the relationship between the number of friends and the prize money each friend receives.

    c. Write a question about this relationship that is easier to answer by making a graph. Write a question that is easier to answer by making a table. Write a question that is easier to answer by writing an equation.

    d. Is this relationship a quadratic function, a linear function, an exponential function, or an inverse variation? Explain.

56. The Stellar International Cellular long-distance company and the Call Any Time company have different charge plans.

   a. Represent each charge plan with an equation, a table, and a graph.

   b. For each plan, tell whether the relationship between calling time and monthly cost is a quadratic function, a linear function, an exponential function, or an inverse variation. How do your equation, table, and graph support your answer?

   c. For what number of minutes are the costs for the two plans equal?

57. A square has sides of length x centimeters.

   a. The square is enlarged by a scale factor of 2. What is the area of the enlarged square?

   b. How does the area of the original square compare with the area of the enlarged square?

   c. Is the new square similar to the original square? Explain.

58. A rectangle has dimensions of x centimeters and $(x + 1)$ centimeters.

   a. The rectangle is enlarged by a scale factor of 2. What is the area of the enlarged rectangle?

   b. How does the area of the original rectangle compare with the area of the enlarged rectangle?

   c. Is the new rectangle similar to the original rectangle? Explain.

59. Suppose the circumference of a cross section of a tree is x feet.

 a. What is the diameter in terms of x?

 b. What is the radius in terms of x?

 c. What is the area of the cross section in terms of x?

 d. Is the relationship between the circumference and the area of the cross section linear, quadratic, exponential, or none of these?

 e. Suppose the circumference of the cross section is 10 feet. What are the diameter, radius, and area of the cross section?

60. For each polygon, write formulas for the perimeter P and area A in terms of ℓ if it is possible. If it is not possible to write a formula, explain why.

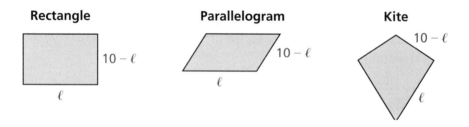

Rectangle **Parallelogram** **Kite**

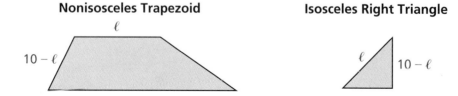

Nonisosceles Trapezoid **Isosceles Right Triangle**

61. a. Write the equation of the line that passes through the two points shown.

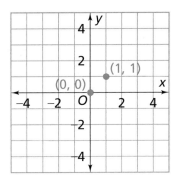

b. Is there a different line that can be drawn through these points? Explain.

For Exercises 62–65, evaluate the expression for the given values of x.

62. $x(x - 5)$ for $x = 2$ and $x = 3$

63. $3x^2 - x$ for $x = 1$ and $x = \frac{1}{3}$

64. $x^2 + 5x + 4$ for $x = 2$ and $x = -4$

65. $(x - 7)(x + 2)$ for $x = -2$ and $x = 2$

Extensions

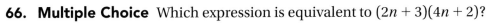

66. Multiple Choice Which expression is equivalent to $(2n + 3)(4n + 2)$?

A. $8n + 5$

B. $6n^2 + 7n + 4n + 5$

C. $8n^2 + 16n + 6$

D. $8n^2 + 6$

For Exercises 67 and 68, write each expression in factored form. You may want to draw a rectangle model.

67. $2x^2 + 3x + 1$

68. $4x^2 + 10x + 6$

69. Sketch graphs of the equations $y = x^2 + 2x$ and $y = x^2 + 2$.

a. How are the graphs similar?

b. How are the graphs different?

c. Find the y-intercept for each graph.

d. Find the x-intercepts for each graph if they exist. If there are no x-intercepts, explain why.

e. Do all quadratic functions have y-intercepts? Explain.

Mathematical Reflections 2

In this Investigation, you wrote quadratic expressions to represent areas of rectangles formed by changing the dimensions of a square. You rewrote expressions in different forms by using rectangular models and by using the Distributive Property. You looked at the equations and graphs of functions. The following questions will help you summarize what you have learned.

Think about these questions. Discuss your ideas with other students and your teacher. Then write a summary of your findings in your notebook.

1. Explain **how** you can use the Distributive Property to answer each question. Use examples to help with your explanations.

   a. Suppose a quadratic expression is in factored form. **How** can you find an equivalent expression in expanded form?

   b. Suppose a quadratic expression is in expanded form. **How** can you find an equivalent expression in factored form?

2. **Describe** what you know about the shape of the graph of a quadratic function. Include important features of the graph and describe how you can predict these features from the equation of the function.

Common Core Mathematical Practices

As you worked on the Problems in this Investigation, you used prior knowledge to make sense of them. You also applied Mathematical Practices to solve the Problems. Think back over your work, the ways you thought about the Problems, and how you used Mathematical Practices.

Hector described his thoughts in the following way:

We thought it was interesting how you can use equivalent expressions to represent the area of a rectangle in Problems 2.2 and 2.3. Le Von reminded us that the area model also represented the Distributive Property. In our group, we used the Distributive Property to factor or expand quadratic expressions. But we still thought that the area model might be helpful to factor more complex quadratic expressions.

....

Common Core Standards for Mathematical Practice

MP8 Look for and express regularity in repeated reasoning.

• What other Mathematical Practices can you identify in Hector's reasoning?

• Describe a Mathematical Practice that you and your classmates used to solve a different Problem in this Investigation.

Quadratic Patterns of Change

In previous Units, you studied patterns in linear and exponential functions. In this Investigation, you will look for patterns in quadratic functions as you solve some interesting counting problems.

- What patterns of change characterize linear and exponential functions?

- What patterns of change did you notice in the quadratic functions in Investigations 1 and 2?

3.1 Exploring Triangular Numbers

Study the pattern of dots.

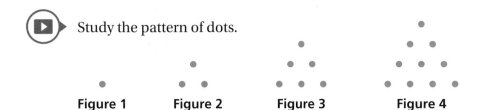

Figure 1   **Figure 2**   **Figure 3**   **Figure 4**

The numbers that represent the number of dots in each triangle are called **triangular numbers.** The first triangular number is 1, the second triangular number is 3, the third is 6, the fourth is 10, and so on.

> How many dots do you predict will be in Figure 5? In Figure *n*?

Common Core State Standards

A-SSE.A.2 Use the structure of an expression to identify ways to rewrite it.

F-IF.C.7 Graph functions expressed symbolically and show key features of the graph . . .

F-BF.A.1 Write a function that describes a relationship between two quantities.

Also A-SSE.A.1b, A-CED.A.2, A-REI.D.10, F-IF.B.4, F-IF.C.7a, F-IF.C.9, F-BF.A.1a, F-LE.A.1

Problem 3.1

You can also represent triangular numbers with patterns of squares. The number of squares in Figure n is the nth triangular number.

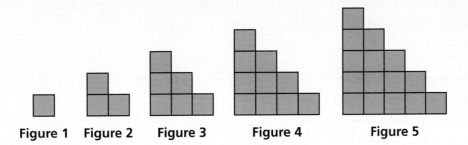

Figure 1 Figure 2 Figure 3 Figure 4 Figure 5

A **1.** What is the sixth triangular number? What is the tenth triangular number?

  2. Make a table of values (*figure number, triangular number*) for the first ten triangular numbers.

  3. Describe the pattern of change from one triangular number to the next.

  4. Describe how you can use the pattern in the table to find the 11th and 12th triangular numbers.

B **1.** Write an equation for the nth triangular number t. In other words, write an equation for the number of squares t in Figure n. Explain your reasoning.

  2. Use your equation to find the 11th and 12th triangular numbers.

C **1.** Use a calculator to graph your equation. Show n values from -5 to 5. Make a sketch of your graph.

  2. Does your graph represent the relationship you observed in the table? Explain.

  3. Does your equation represent a quadratic function? Explain.

  4. Compare this equation with the equations in Investigations 1 and 2.

ACE Homework starts on page 55.

3.2 Counting Handshakes
Another Quadratic Function

After a sporting event, the opposing teams often line up and shake hands. To celebrate their victory, members of the winning team may congratulate each other with a round of high fives.

 How many handshakes occur between two teams at the end of a game?

Problem 3.2

Consider three cases of greeting team members:

A **Case 1** Two teams have the same number of players. Each player on one team shakes hands with each player on the other team.

    1. How many handshakes will take place between two 5-player teams? Between two 10-player teams?

    2. Write an equation for the number of handshakes h between two n-player teams.

B **Case 2** One team has one fewer player than the other. Each player on one team shakes hands with each player on the other team.

    1. How many handshakes will take place between a 7-player team and a 6-player team? Between a 9-player team and an 8-player team?

    2. Write an equation for the number of handshakes h between an n-player team and an $(n - 1)$-player team.

C **Case 3** Each member of a team gives a high five to each teammate.

    1. How many high fives will take place among a team with 4 members? Among a team with 8 members?

    2. Write an equation for the number of high fives h among a team with n members.

D Compare the three equations from Questions A–C. Do they represent quadratic functions? Explain.

A C E Homework starts on page 55.

3.3 Examining Patterns of Change

In this Problem, you will examine the patterns of change that characterize quadratic relationships.

Problem 3.3

A Complete parts (1)–(2) for each case in Problem 3.2.

1. Make a table showing the number of players on each team and the number of handshakes or high fives. Include data for teams with 1 to 10 members.

2. Describe a pattern of change that can help you predict the numbers of handshakes or high fives for larger teams.

3. Compare the patterns in the three tables. How are the patterns similar? How are they different?

B 1. Use your calculator to graph the equations you wrote for the three cases in Problem 3.2. Show n values from -5 to 5. Make a sketch of the graph.

2. Compare the three graphs.

C 1. For each case, compare the table and its graph. Describe how the tables and graphs show the same pattern of change.

2. Do any of these patterns of change represent quadratic relationships? Explain.

3. Compare the patterns of change for the three cases with the patterns of change you observed in Investigations 1 and 2.

A C E Homework starts on page 55.

3.4 Quadratic Functions and Patterns of Change

You have used equations to model a variety of quadratic functions. You may have noticed some common characteristics of these equations. You have also observed patterns in the graphs and tables of quadratic functions.

To understand a function, it helps to look at how the value of the dependent variable changes each time the value of the independent variable increases by a fixed amount. For a linear function, the y-value increases by a constant amount each time the x-value increases by 1.

Look at this table for the linear function $y = 3x + 1$. The "first differences" are the differences between consecutive y-values.

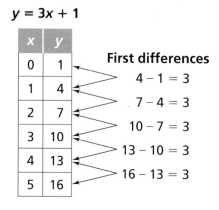

$y = 3x + 1$

Because the y-value increases by 3 each time the x-value increases by 1, the first differences for $y = 3x + 1$ are all a constant amount of 3.

The simplest quadratic function is $y = x^2$, and it is the rule for generating square numbers. In fact, the word *quadratic* comes from the Latin word for "square," *quadratus*.

The table shows that the first differences for $y = x^2$ are not constant.

$y = x^2$

x	y	First differences
0	0	
		$1 - 0 = 1$
1	1	
		$4 - 1 = 3$
2	4	
		$9 - 4 = 5$
3	9	
		$16 - 9 = 7$
4	16	
		$25 - 16 = 9$
5	25	

- What is the pattern of change for $y = x^2$?

Study the pattern of first and second differences for $y = x^2$.

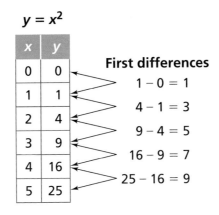

$y = x^2$

x	y	First differences	Second differences
0	0		
		$1 - 0 = 1$	
1	1		$3 - 1 = 2$
		$4 - 1 = 3$	
2	4		$5 - 3 = 2$
		$9 - 4 = 5$	
3	9		$7 - 5 = 2$
		$16 - 9 = 7$	
4	16		$9 - 7 = 2$
		$25 - 16 = 9$	
5	25		

(?) Will the tables for other quadratic functions show a similar pattern? Explain.

Problem **3.4**

Ⓐ **1.** Make a table of values for each quadratic equation below. Include integer values of x from -5 to 5. Show the first and second differences as is done for the table on the previous page.

a. $y = 2x(x + 3)$ 　　　　　　b. $y = 3x - x^2$

c. $y = (x - 2)^2$ 　　　　　　d. $y = x^2 + 5x + 6$

2. Consider the patterns of change in the values of y and in the first and second differences. In what ways are the patterns similar for the four tables? In what ways are they different?

3. What patterns of change seem to occur for quadratic functions?

Ⓑ **1.** Make a table of (x, y) values for each equation below. Show the first and second differences.

a. $y = x + 2$ 　　b. $y = 2x$ 　　c. $y = 2^x$ 　　d. $y = x^2$

2. Consider the patterns of change in the values of y and in the first and second differences. How are the patterns similar in all four tables? How are they different?

3. How can you use the patterns of change in tables to identify the type of function?

Ⓒ **1.** The introduction of this Problem shows that the second differences for the function $y = x^2$ are all 2. Is this true for all quadratic functions? Try some examples, such as $y = 2x^2$, $y = x^2 + 2$, $y = x^2 + 2x + 2$, and $y = 3x^2 + x$.

2. What information can you conclude about any quadratic function from a table of values?

Ⓐ Ⓒ Ⓔ Homework starts on page 55.

 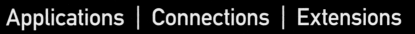
Applications

1. These dot patterns represent the first four *square numbers,* 1, 4, 9, and 16.

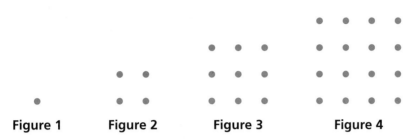

Figure 1   Figure 2   Figure 3   Figure 4

   a. What are the next two square numbers?

   b. Write an equation for the nth square number s.

   c. Make a table and a graph of (n, s) values for the first ten square numbers. Describe the pattern of change from one square number to the next.

2. The numbers of dots in the figures below are the first four *rectangular numbers.*

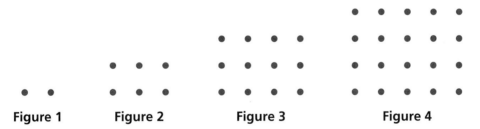

Figure 1   Figure 2   Figure 3   Figure 4

   a. What are the first four rectangular numbers?

   b. Find the next two rectangular numbers.

   c. Describe the pattern of change from one rectangular number to the next.

   d. Predict the seventh and eighth rectangular numbers.

   e. Write an equation for the nth rectangular number r.

3. In Problem 3.1, you looked at triangular numbers.

  a. What is the 18th triangular number?

  b. Is 210 a triangular number? Explain.

Did You Know?

Carl Friedrich Gauss (1777–1855) was a German mathematician and astronomer. When Gauss was about eight years old, his teacher asked his class to find the sum of the first 100 counting numbers. Gauss had the answer almost immediately!

Gauss realized that he could pair up the numbers as shown. Each pair has a sum of 101.

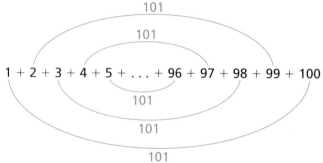

There are 100 numbers, so there are 50 pairs. This means the sum is

$50 \times 101 = 5{,}050 \left[\text{or } \frac{100}{2}(101) \text{ or } \frac{100}{2} \text{ (first number plus last number)}\right]$.

4. a. In Problem 3.1, you found an equation for the *n*th triangular number. Sam claims he can use this equation to find the sum of the first ten counting numbers. Explain why Sam is correct.

  b. What is the sum of the first ten counting numbers?

  c. What is the sum of the first 15 counting numbers?

  d. What is the sum of the first *n* counting numbers?

For Exercises 5–8, tell whether the number is a triangular number, a square number, a rectangular number, or none of these. Explain.

   5. 110   **6.** 66   **7.** 121   **8.** 60

  9. In a middle school math league, each team has six student members and two coaches.

     a. At the start of a match, the coaches and student members of one team exchange handshakes with the coaches and student members of the other team. How many handshakes occur?

     b. At the end of the match, the members and coaches of the winning team exchange high fives. How many high fives occur?

     c. The members of one team exchange handshakes with their coaches. How many handshakes occur?

 10. In a 100-meter race, five runners are from the United States and three runners are from Canada.

     a. How many handshakes occur if the runners from one country exchange handshakes with the runners from the other country?

     b. How many high fives occur if the runners from the United States exchange high fives?

 11. A company rents five offices in a building. There is a cable connecting each pair of offices.

     a. How many cables are there in all?

     b. Suppose the company rents two more offices. How many cables will they need in all?

     c. Compare this situation with Case 3 in Problem 3.2.

For Exercises 12–15, describe a situation that can be represented by the equation. Tell what the variables *p* and *n* represent in that situation.

   12. $p = n(n - 1)$ **13.** $p = 2n$

   14. $p = n(n - 2)$ **15.** $p = n(16 - n)$

   16. The graphs below represent situations you have looked at in this Unit.

Graph I   **Graph II**

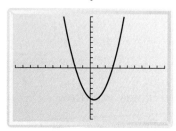 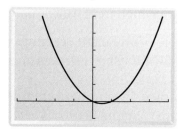

Graph III   **Graph IV**

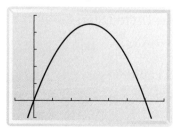 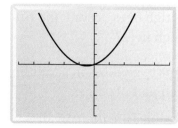

     a. Which graph might represent the number of high fives exchanged among a team with *n* players? Explain.

     b. Which graph might represent the areas of rectangles with a fixed perimeter?

     c. Which graph might represent the areas of a rectangle formed by increasing one dimension of a square by 2 centimeters and decreasing the other dimension by 3 centimeters?

     d. Which graph might represent a triangular-number pattern?

For Exercises 17–19, the tables represent quadratic functions. Copy and complete each table.

17.

x	y
0	0
1	1
2	3
3	6
4	▦
5	▦
6	▦

18.

x	y
0	0
1	3
2	8
3	15
4	▦
5	▦
6	▦

19.

x	y
0	0
1	4
2	6
3	6
4	▦
5	▦
6	▦

For Exercises 20–24, tell whether the table represents a quadratic function. If it does, tell whether the function has a maximum or minimum value.

20.

x	−3	−2	−1	0	1	2	3	4	5
y	−4	1	4	5	4	1	−4	−11	−18

21.

x	0	1	2	3	4	5	6	7	8
y	2	3	6	11	18	27	38	51	66

22.

x	0	1	2	3	4	5	6	7	8
y	0	−4	−6	−6	−4	0	6	14	24

23.

x	−4	−3	−2	−1	0	1	2	3	4
y	5	4	3	2	1	2	3	4	5

24.

x	−4	−3	−2	−1	0	1	2	3	4
y	18	10	4	0	−2	−2	0	4	10

25. **a.** For each equation, investigate the pattern of change in the y-values as the x-values increase or decrease at a constant rate. Describe the patterns you find.

$$y = 2x^2 \qquad\qquad y = 3x^2 \qquad\qquad y = \tfrac{1}{2}x^2 \qquad\qquad y = -2x^2$$

b. Use what you discovered in part (a) to predict the pattern of change for each of these equations.

$$y = 5x^2 \qquad\qquad y = -4x^2 \qquad\qquad y = \tfrac{1}{4}x^2 \qquad\qquad y = ax^2$$

26. Use the graph below.

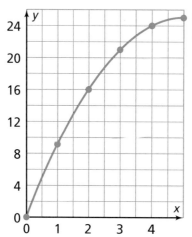

a. Make a table of (x, y) values for the six points shown on the graph.

b. The graph shows a quadratic function. Extend the graph to show x-values from 5 to 10. Explain how you know your graph is correct.

27. The graph shows a quadratic function. Extend the graph to show x-values from -4 to 0.

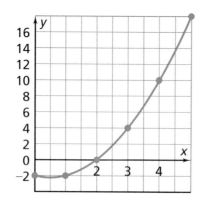

28. The table below shows a quadratic function. Extend the table to show
x-values from 0 to −5. Explain how you know your table is correct.

x	y
0	8
1	3
2	0
3	−1
4	0
5	3

Connections

29. **a.** Make sketches that show two ways of completing the rectangle
model below using whole numbers. For each sketch, express
the area of the large rectangle in both expanded form and
factored form.

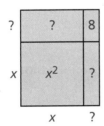

b. Is there more than one way to complete the rectangle model
below using whole numbers? Explain.

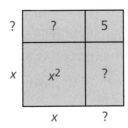

30. Write two equivalent expressions for the area of the rectangle outlined in red below.

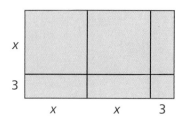

31. Consider these quadratic expressions.

$$2x^2 + 7x + 6 \qquad\qquad x^2 + 6x + 8$$

   a. For each expression, sketch a rectangle whose area represents the expression. Which expression is easier to present in a rectangle model? Why?

   b. Write each expression in factored form.

For Exercises 32–37, write the expression in expanded form.

32. $x(5 - x)$ 　　　　**33.** $(x + 1)(x + 3)$ 　　　　**34.** $(x - 1)(x + 3)$

35. $3x(x + 5)$ 　　　　**36.** $(2x + 1)(x + 3)$ 　　　　**37.** $(2x - 1)(x + 3)$

For Exercises 38–43, write the expression in factored form.

38. $x^2 - 9x + 8$ 　　　　**39.** $4x^2 - 6x$ 　　　　**40.** $3x^2 + 14x + 8$

41. $4x^2 + 6x$ 　　　　**42.** $4x^2 - x - 3$ 　　　　**43.** $x^3 - 2x^2 - 3x$

44. Min was having trouble factoring the expression in Exercise 40. Ricardo suggested that she use a rectangle model.

   a. Explain how a rectangle model can help Min factor the expression. Make a sketch to illustrate your explanation.

   b. How you can factor an expression without drawing a rectangle?

45. A diagonal of a polygon is a line segment connecting any two nonadjacent vertices. A quadrilateral has two diagonals like the one below.

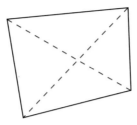

   a. How many diagonals does a pentagon have? How many does a hexagon have? A heptagon? An octagon?

   b. How many diagonals does an *n*-sided polygon have?

46. These "trains" are formed by joining identical squares.

Train 1   Train 2   Train 3   Train 4   Train 5

   a. How many rectangles are in each of the first five trains? For example, the diagram below shows the six rectangles in Train 3. (Remember, a square is a rectangle.)

   b. Make a table showing the number of rectangles in each of the first ten trains.

   c. How can you use the pattern of change in your table to find the number of rectangles in Train 15?

   d. Write an equation for the number of rectangles in Train *n*.

   e. Use your equation to find the number of rectangles in Train 15.

47. a. What is the area of the base of the can?

10 cm

10 cm

b. How many centimeter cubes or parts of cubes can fit in a single layer on the bottom of the can?

c. How many layers of this size would fill the can?

d. Use your answers to parts (a)–(c) to find the volume of the can.

e. The label on the lateral surface of the can is a rectangle with a height of 10 centimeters. What is the other dimension of the label?

f. What is the area of the label?

g. Use your answers to parts (a) and (f) to find the surface area of the can.

48. A company is trying to choose a box shape for a new product. It has narrowed the choices to the triangular prism and the cylinder shown below.

4 cm

3 cm

5 cm

4.24 cm

4.12 cm

a. Sketch a net for each box.

b. Find the surface area of each box.

c. Which box will require more cardboard to construct?

For Exercise 49–52, tell whether the pattern in each table represents a function that is linear, quadratic, exponential, or none of these.

49.

x	y
0	2
3	4
5	5
6	6
7	7
8	8
10	10

50.

x	y
−3	12
−2	7
−1	4
0	3
1	4
2	7
3	12

51.

x	y
0	1
2	9
5	243
6	729
7	2,187
8	6,561
10	59,049

52.

x	y
1	−2
2	0
3	3
4	8
5	15
6	24
7	14

53. Multiple Choice Which equation represents a quadratic relationship?

A. $y = (x − 1)(6 − 2)$

B. $y = 2x(3 − 2)$

C. $y = 2^x$

D. $y = x(x + 2)$

54. Multiple Choice Which equation has a graph with a minimum point at $(1, 4)$?

F. $y = −x^2 + 5$

G. $y = −x^2 + 5x$

H. $y = x^2 − 2x + 5$

J. $y = −x^2 + 7x − 10$

55. Write each expression in expanded form.

a. $−3x(2x − 1)$

b. $1.5x(6 − 2x)$

Extensions

56. You can use Gauss's method to find the sum of the whole numbers from 1 to 10 by writing the sum twice as shown and adding vertically.

$$1 + 2 + 3 + 4 + 5 + 6 + 7 + 8 + 9 + 10$$
$$\underline{10 + 9 + 8 + 7 + 6 + 5 + 4 + 3 + 2 + 1}$$
$$11 + 11 + 11 + 11 + 11 + 11 + 11 + 11 + 11 + 11$$

Each vertical sum of 11 occurs 10 times, or $10(11) = 110$. This result is twice the sum of the numbers from 1 to 10, so you divide by 2 to get $\frac{10(11)}{2} = \frac{110}{5} = 55$.

a. How can you use this idea to find $1 + 2 + 3 + \ldots + 99 + 100$?

b. How could you use this idea to find $1 + 2 + 3 + \ldots + n$ for any whole number n?

c. How is this method related to Gauss's method?

57. The patterns of dots below represent the first three *star numbers*.

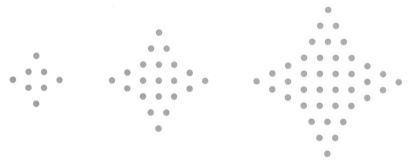

Figure 1   **Figure 2**   **Figure 3**

a. What are the first three star numbers?

b. Find the next three star numbers.

c. Write an equation you could use to calculate the *n*th star number.

58. In parts (a) and (b), explain your answers by drawing pictures or writing a convincing argument.

   a. Ten former classmates attend their class reunion. They all shake hands with each other. How many handshakes occur?

   b. A little later, two more classmates arrive. Suppose these two people shake hands with each other and the ten other classmates. How many new handshakes occur?

59. The pattern of dots below represents the first three *hexagonal numbers*.

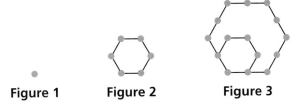

Figure 1 **Figure 2** **Figure 3**

   a. What are the first three hexagonal numbers?

   b. Find the next two hexagonal numbers.

   c. Write an equation you can use to calculate the *n*th hexagonal number.

60. There are 30 squares of various sizes in this 4-by-4 grid.

   a. Sixteen of the squares are the identical small squares that make up the grid. Find the other 14 squares. Draw pictures or give a description.

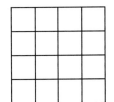

   b. How many squares are in an *n*-by-*n* grid? (**Hint:** Start with some simple cases and search for a pattern.)

61. Complete parts (a) and (b) for each equation.

$$y_1 = x + 1 \qquad\qquad y_2 = (x + 1)(x + 2)$$
$$y_3 = (x + 1)(x + 2)(x + 3) \qquad y_4 = (x + 1)(x + 2)(x + 3)(x + 4)$$

   a. Describe the shape of the graph of the equation. Include any special features.

   b. Describe the pattern of change between the variables.

Mathematical Reflections 3

In this Investigation, you counted handshakes and studied geometric patterns. You found that you can represent these situations with quadratic functions. The following questions will help you summarize what you have learned.

Think about these questions. Discuss your ideas with other students and your teacher. Then write a summary of your findings in your notebook.

1. **a.** In **what** ways is the triangular-number relationship similar to the relationships in the handshake problems? In what ways are these relationships different?

   b. In **what** ways are the quadratic functions in this Investigation similar to the quadratic functions in Investigations 1 and 2? In what ways are they different?

2. **a.** In a table of values for a quadratic function, **how** can you use the pattern of change to predict the next value?

   b. **How** can you use a table of values to decide if a function is quadratic?

3. **Compare** the patterns of change for linear, exponential, and quadratic functions.

Common Core Mathematical Practices

As you worked on the Problems in this Investigation, you used prior knowledge to make sense of them. You also applied Mathematical Practices to solve the Problems. Think back over your work, the ways you thought about the Problems, and how you used Mathematical Practices.

Ken described his thoughts in the following way:

A member of our group suggested that we could think of the triangular numbers as half of a rectangle with dimensions n and $n + 1$. He sketched diagrams to convince us that his reasoning was valid.

Another member of our group noticed that the first triangular number is 1. She explained that you add 2 to get the next triangular number. Then you add 3 to get the next number. You continue to add the next consecutive number to get the next triangular number. Both methods gave the same results for determining triangular numbers.

Common Core Standards for Mathematical Practice
MP2 Reason abstractly and quantitatively.

• What other Mathematical Practices can you identify in Ken's reasoning?

• Describe a Mathematical Practice that you and your classmates used to solve a different Problem in this Investigation.

Frogs Meet Fleas on a Cube: More Applications of Quadratic Functions

When you make a snowboard jump, gravity pulls you toward Earth. When you throw or kick a ball into the air, gravity brings it back down. For several hundred years, scientists have used mathematical models to describe and predict the effect of gravity on the position, velocity, and acceleration of falling objects.

Common Core State Standards

A-REI.D.10 Understand that the graph of an equation in two variables is the set of all its solutions plotted in the coordinate plane, often forming a curve (which could be a line).

F-IF.B.4 For a function that models a relationship between two quantities, interpret key features of graphs and tables in terms of the quantities, and sketch graphs showing key features given a verbal description of the relationship.

F-IF.C.7 Graph functions expressed symbolically and show key features of the graph, by hand in simple cases and using technology for more complicated cases.

F-IF.C.7a Graph linear and quadratic functions and show intercepts, maxima, and minima.

Also A-CED.A.2, F-IF.C.9, F-LE.A.1, F-LE.A.1a, F-LE.A.1b

Did You Know?

Aristotle, the ancient Greek philosopher and scientist, believed that heavier objects fall faster than lighter objects. In the late 1500s, the great Italian scientist Galileo challenged this idea.

It is said that, while observing a hailstorm, Galileo noticed that large and small hailstones hit the ground at the same time. If Aristotle were correct, this would happen only if the larger stones dropped from a higher point or if the smaller stones started falling first. Galileo didn't think either of these explanations was probable.

A famous story claims that Galileo proved that heavy and light objects fall at the same rate by climbing to the highest point he could find—the top of the Tower of Pisa—and dropping two objects simultaneously. Although they had different weights, the objects hit the ground at the same time.

4.1 Tracking a Ball
Interpreting a Table and an Equation

No matter how hard you throw or kick a ball into the air, gravity returns it to Earth. In this Problem, you will explore how the height of a thrown ball changes over time.

Problem 4.1

Suppose you throw a ball straight up in the air. This table shows how the height of the ball might change over time as it goes up and then returns to the ground.

A 1. Describe how the height of the ball changes over this 4-second time period.

2. Without actually making the graph, describe what the graph of these data would look like. Include as many important features as you can.

3. Do you think these data represent a quadratic function? Explain.

B The height h of the ball in feet after t seconds can be described by the equation $h = -16t^2 + 64t$.

1. Graph this equation on your calculator.

2. Does the graph match the description you gave in Question A? Explain.

3. When does the ball reach a height of about 58 feet? Explain.

4. Use the equation to find the height of the ball after 1.6 seconds.

5. When will the ball reach the ground? Explain.

Height of Thrown Ball

Time (seconds)	Height (feet)
0.00	0
0.25	15
0.50	28
0.75	39
1.00	48
1.25	55
1.50	60
1.75	63
2.00	64
2.25	63
2.50	60
2.75	55
3.00	48
3.25	39
3.50	28
3.75	15
4.00	0

 A C E Homework starts on page 80.

4.2 Measuring Jumps
Comparing Quadratic Functions

Many animals are known for their jumping abilities. Most frogs can jump several times their body length. Fleas are tiny, but they can easily leap onto a dog or a cat. Some humans have amazing jumping ability as well. Many professional basketball players have vertical leaps of more than 3 feet!

In Problem 4.1, the initial height of the ball is 0 feet. This is not very realistic because it means you would have to lie on the ground and release the ball without extending your arms. A more realistic equation for the height of the ball is $h = -16t^2 + 64t + 6$.

- Compare this equation with the equation in Problem 4.1.

- Use your calculator to make a table and a graph of this quadratic function.

- Compare your graph with the graph of the equation in Problem 4.1. Consider the following:

  - the maximum height reached by the ball

  - the x- and y-intercepts

  - the patterns of change in the height over time

- What information do the coefficients of t^2 and t, and the constant term, tell you about the graph of $h = -16t^2 + 64t + 6$?

Problem 4.2

A Suppose a frog, a flea, and a basketball player jump straight up. Their heights in feet after t seconds are modeled by these equations.

$$\text{Frog: } h = -16t^2 + 12t + 0.2$$
$$\text{Flea: } h = -16t^2 + 8t$$
$$\text{Basketball player: } h = -16t^2 + 16t + 6.5$$

1. Use your calculator to make tables and graphs of these three equations. Look at heights for time values between 0 seconds and 1 second. In your tables, use time intervals of 0.1 second.

2. What is the maximum height reached by each jumper? When is the maximum height reached?

3. How long does each jump last?

4. What do the **constant terms** 0.2 and 6.5 tell you about the frog and the basketball player? How is this information represented on the graph?

5. For each jumper, describe the pattern of change in the height over time. Explain how the pattern is reflected in the table and the graph.

B A jewelry maker would like to increase his profit by raising the price of his jade earrings. However, he knows that if he raises the price too high, he won't sell as many earrings and his profit will decrease.

The jewelry maker's business consultant develops the equation $P = 50s - s^2$ to predict the monthly profit P for a sales price s.

1. Make a table and a graph for this equation.

2. What do the equation, table, and graph suggest about the relationship between price and profit?

3. What price will bring the greatest profit?

4. How does this equation compare with the equations in Question A? How does it compare with other equations in this Unit?

 Homework starts on page 80.

Did You Know?

- The average flea weighs 0.000001 pound and is 2 to 3 millimeters long. It can pull 160,000 times its own weight and can jump 150 times its own length. This is equivalent to a human being pulling 24 million pounds and jumping nearly 1,000 feet!

- There are 3,000 known species and subspecies of fleas. Fleas are found on all land masses, including Antarctica.

- Most fleas make their homes on bats, rats, squirrels, and mice.

- The bubonic plague, which killed a quarter of Europe's population in the fourteenth century, was spread by rat fleas.

- Flea circuses originated about 300 years ago and were popular in the United States a century ago.

4.3 Painted Cubes
Looking at Several Functions

Leon invents a puzzle. He makes a large cube from 1,000 centimeter cubes.

He paints the faces of the large cube. When the paint dries, he separates the puzzle into the original centimeter cubes. The object of Leon's puzzle is to reassemble the cubes so no unpainted faces are showing.

When Leon examines the centimeter cubes, he notices that some are painted on only one face, some on two faces, and some on three faces. Many aren't painted at all.

> For any size of painted cube, what kind of equation tells you how many cubes will be painted on 1 face? 2 faces? 3 faces? 0 faces?

Problem **4.3**

In this Problem, you will investigate smaller versions of Leon's puzzle.

A 1. The cube at the right is made of centimeter cubes. The faces of this cube are painted. Suppose you broke the cube into centimeter cubes. How many centimeter cubes would be painted on

    a. three faces?   **b.** two faces?

    c. one face?   **d.** no faces?

Problem 4.3 *continued*

2. Answer the questions from part (1) for cubes with edges with lengths of 3, 4, 5, and 6 centimeters.

  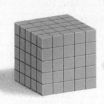 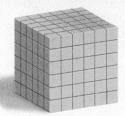

Organize your data in a table like the one below.

Edge Length of Large Cube	Number of Centimeter Cubes	Number of Centimeter Cubes Painted On			
		3 faces	2 faces	1 face	0 faces
2	▦	▦	▦	▦	▦
3	▦	▦	▦	▦	▦
4	▦	▦	▦	▦	▦
5	▦	▦	▦	▦	▦
6	▦	▦	▦	▦	▦

B Study the patterns in the table.

1. Describe the relationship between the edge length of the large cube and the total number of centimeter cubes.

2. Describe the relationship between the edge length of the large cube and the number of centimeter cubes painted on

   a. three faces   **b.** two faces

   c. one face   **d.** zero faces

3. Decide whether each relationship in parts (1) and (2) is a linear function, quadratic function, exponential function, or none of these.

C 1. Write an equation for each relationship in Question B. Tell what the variables and numbers in each equation mean.

2. Sketch the graph of each equation.

 Homework starts on page 80.

4.4 Putting It All Together
Comparing Functions

In prior Units, you looked at linear and exponential functions, and inverse variation. In this Problem, you will summarize your knowledge about all of these functions by sorting a variety of tables, graphs, and equations.

- What can you learn about a function from its graph?
- How are the features of a graph related to its equation?
- How can you determine if a function is linear, exponential, or quadratic?

Problem 4.4

For this Problem, you will be given some cards that have information about functions. Each card contains either an equation (E), a graph (G), function properties (P), or a table (T). Sort the cards into families that represent the same function. Then, complete Questions A–C for each family.

A Write a short summary about the family. Include as many details as you can.

B Make a new card that belongs to the family.

C Describe a problem that can be represented by the family.

A C E Homework starts on page 80.

$xy = 1$ E37	$y = x \cdot x^2$ E28	$y = 2^x$ E42
$y = (x + 2)^2$ E11	$y = x^2 + 4x + 4$ E35	$y = \frac{2}{1}x + 0$ E70

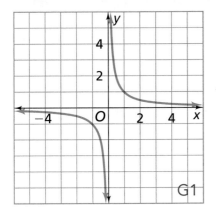

G1

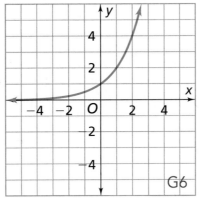

G6

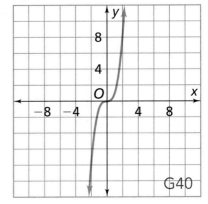

G40

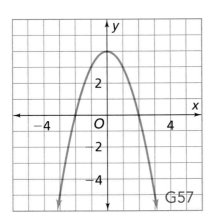

G57

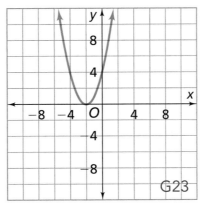

G23

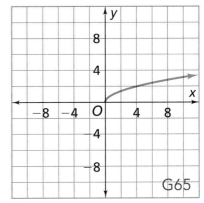

G65

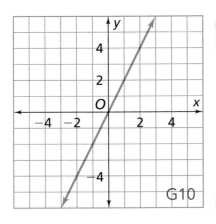

G10

Function Properties

- No maximum value
- No minimum value
- No x-intercepts
- No y-intercept
- Symmetric about origin
- Not defined at $x = 0$ or $y = 0$

P49

Function Properties

- No maximum value
- Minimum value at $x = 0$
- One x-intercept
- y-intercept at 0
- No symmetry
- Not defined at $x < 0$

P17

x	y
−2	−8
−1	−1
0	0
1	1
2	8
3	27

T64

x	y
−2	0
−1	3
0	4
1	3
2	0
3	−5

T69

x	y
0.5	3.75
−0.5	3.75
−4	−12
4	−12
5	−21
−5	−21

T21

x	y
1	2
2	4
4	8
8	16
16	32
32	64

T46

x	y
1	1
25	5
100	10
$\frac{1}{4}$	$\frac{1}{2}$
0.01	0.1

T29

x	y
−2	0.25
−1	0.5
0	1
1	2
2	4
3	8

T18

Applications

1. A signal flare is fired into the air from a boat. The height h of the flare in feet after t seconds is $h = -16t^2 + 160t$.

   a. How high will the flare travel? When will it reach this maximum height?

   b. When will the flare hit the water?

   c. Explain how you could use a table and a graph to answer the questions in parts (a) and (b).

2. A model rocket is launched from the top of a hill. The table shows how the rocket's height above ground level changes as it travels through the air.

   a. How high above ground level does the rocket travel? When does it reach this maximum height?

   b. From what height is the rocket launched?

   c. How long does it take the rocket to return to the top of the hill?

Height of Model Rocket

Time (seconds)	Height (feet)
0.00	84
0.25	99
0.50	112
0.75	123
1.00	132
1.25	139
1.50	144
1.75	147
2.00	148
2.25	147
2.50	144
2.75	139
3.00	132
3.25	123
3.50	112
3.75	99
4.00	84

3. A basketball player takes a shot. The graph shows the height of the ball starting when it leaves the player's hands.

Basketball Throws

a. Estimate the height of the ball when the player releases it.

b. When does the ball reach its maximum height? What is the maximum height?

c. How long does it take the ball to reach the basket (a height of 10 feet)?

4. The highest dive in the Olympic Games is from a 10-meter platform. The height h in meters of a diver t seconds after leaving the platform can be estimated by the equation $h = 10 + 4.9t - 4.9t^2$.

a. Make a table of the relationship between time and height.

b. Sketch a graph of the relationship between time and height.

c. When will the diver hit the water's surface? How can you find this answer by using your graph? How can you find this answer by using your table?

d. When will the diver be 5 meters above the water?

e. When is the diver falling at the fastest rate? How is this shown in the table? How is this shown in the graph?

5. Kelsey jumps from a diving board, springing up into the air and then dropping feet-first. The distance d in feet from her feet to the pool's surface t seconds after she jumps is $d = -16t^2 + 18t + 10$.

a. What is the maximum height of Kelsey's feet during this jump? When does the maximum height occur?

b. When do Kelsey's feet hit the water?

c. What does the constant term 10 in the equation tell you about Kelsey's jump?

6. The equation $h = -16t^2 + 48t + 8$ describes how the height h of a ball in feet changes over time t.

   a. What is the maximum height reached by the ball? Explain how you could use a table and a graph to find the answer.

   b. When does the ball hit the ground? Explain how you could use a table and a graph to find the answer.

   c. Describe the pattern of change in the height of the ball over time. Explain how this pattern would appear in a table and a graph.

   d. What does the constant term 8 mean in this context?

For Exercises 7–10, complete parts (a)–(d).

   a. Sketch a graph of the equation.

   b. Find the x- and y-intercepts. Label these points on your graph.

   c. Draw and label the line of symmetry.

   d. Label the coordinates of the maximum or minimum point.

7. $y = 9 - x^2$ 8. $y = 2x^2 - 4x$

9. $y = 6x - x^2$ 10. $y = x^2 + 6x + 8$

11. a. How can you tell from a quadratic equation whether the graph will have a maximum point or a minimum point?

   b. How are the x- and y-intercepts of the graph of a quadratic function related to its equation?

   c. How are the x- and y-intercepts related to the line of symmetry?

For Exercises 12–17, predict the shape of the graph of the equation. Give the maximum or minimum point, the x-intercepts, and the line of symmetry. Use a graphing calculator to check your predictions.

12. $y = x^2$ 13. $y = -x^2$ 14. $y = x^2 + 1$

15. $y = x^2 + 6x + 9$ 16. $y = x^2 - 2$ 17. $y = x(4 - x)$

18. A cube with edges of length 12 centimeters is built from centimeter cubes. The faces of the large cube are painted. How many of the centimeter cubes will have

a. three painted faces?

b. two painted faces?

c. one painted face?

d. no painted faces?

19. Four large cubes are built from centimeter cubes. The faces of each large cube are painted. In parts (a)–(d), determine the size of the large cube. Then, tell how many of its centimeter cubes have 0, 1, 2, and 3 painted faces.

a. For Cube A, 1,000 of the centimeter cubes have no painted faces.

b. For Cube B, 864 of the centimeter cubes have one painted face.

c. For Cube C, 132 of the centimeter cubes have two painted faces.

d. For Cube D, 8 of the centimeter cubes have three painted faces.

20. a. Copy and complete each table. Describe the pattern of change.

x	x
1	■
2	■
3	■
4	■
5	■

x	x^2
1	■
2	■
3	■
4	■
5	■

x	x^3
1	■
2	■
3	■
4	■
5	■

b. For each table, tell which column in the painted-cubes table in Problem 4.3 has a similar pattern. Explain.

21. Consider the functions described by these equations. Are any of them similar to functions in the painted-cubes situation? Explain.

$y_1 = 2(x - 1)$ $\qquad$ $y_2 = (x - 1)^3$ $\qquad$ $y_3 = 4(x - 1)^2$

For Exercises 22–25, match the equation with its graph. Then, give the line of symmetry for each graph and explain how to locate it.

22. $y = (x + 7)(x + 2)$

23. $y = x(x + 3)$

24. $y = (x - 4)(x + 6)$

25. $y = (x - 5)(x + 5)$

Graph A

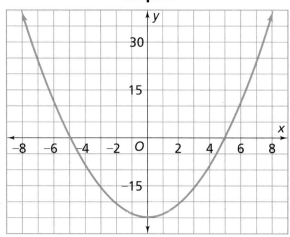

Graph B

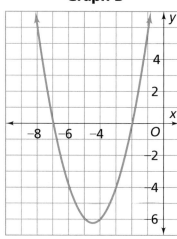

Graph C

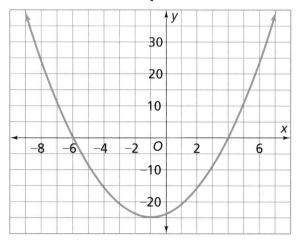

Graph D

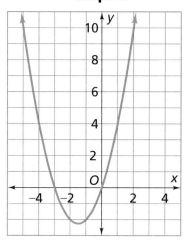

26. a. How are the graphs at the right similar?

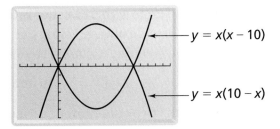
$y = x(x - 10)$
$y = x(10 - x)$

b. How are the graphs different?

c. The maximum value for $y = x(10 - x)$ occurs when $x = 5$. How can you find the y-coordinate of the maximum value?

d. The minimum value for $y = x(x - 10)$ occurs when $x = 5$. How can you find the y-coordinate of the minimum value?

27. Multiple Choice Which quadratic equation has x-intercepts at $(3, 0)$ and $(-1, 0)$?

A. $y = x^2 - 1x + 3$ **B.** $y = x^2 - 2x + 3$ **C.** $y = 3x^2 - 1x$ **D.** $y = x^2 - 2x - 3$

Connections

28. a. Describe the patterns of change in each table. (Look closely. You may find more than one.) Explain how you can use the patterns to find the missing entry.

Table 1

x	y
0	25
1	50
2	100
3	200
4	400
5	■

Table 2

x	y
-3	3
-2	6
-1	9
0	12
1	15
2	■

Table 3

x	y
2	6
3	12
4	20
5	30
6	42
7	■

Table 4

x	y
-2	21
-1	24
0	25
1	24
2	21
3	■

b. Tell which equation matches each table.

$y_1 = x^2 - 12$ $y_2 = x(x + 1)$ $y_3 = 25 - x^2$

$y_4 = (x)(x)(x)$ $y_5 = 3(x + 4)$ $y_6 = 25(2)^x$

c. Which tables represent quadratic functions? Explain.

d. Do any of the tables include the maximum y-value for the relationship?

e. Do any of the tables include the minimum y-value for the relationship?

29. A potter wants to increase her profits by changing the price of a particular style of vase. Using past sales data, she writes these two equations relating income I to selling price p:

$$I = (100 - p)p \text{ and } I = 100p - p^2$$

   a. Are the two equations equivalent? Explain.

   b. Show that $I = 100 - p^2$ is not equivalent to the original equations.

   c. It costs $350 to rent a booth at a craft fair. The potter's profit for the fair will be her income minus the cost of the booth. Write an equation for the profit M as a function of the price p.

   d. What price would give the maximum profit? What will the maximum profit be?

   e. For what prices will there be a profit rather than a loss?

30. Eggs are often sold by the dozen. When farmers send eggs to supermarkets, they often stack the eggs in bigger containers that are 12 eggs long, 12 eggs wide, and 12 eggs high.

   a. How many eggs are in each layer of the container?

   b. How many eggs are there in an entire container?

31. A square has sides of length x.

  a. Write formulas for the area A and perimeter P of the square in terms of x.

  b. Suppose the side lengths of the square are doubled. How do the area and perimeter change?

  c. How do the area and perimeter change if the side lengths are tripled?

  d. What is the perimeter of a square if its area is 36 square meters?

  e. Make a table of side length, perimeter, and area values for squares with whole-number side lengths from 0 to 12.

  f. Sketch graphs of the data (*side length, area*) and (*side length, perimeter*) from your table.

  g. Tell whether the patterns of change in the tables and graphs suggest linear, quadratic, or exponential functions, or none of these. Explain.

32. A cube has edges of length x.

  a. Write a formula for the volume V of the cube in terms of x.

  b. Suppose the edge lengths of the cube double. How does the volume change?

  c. How does the surface area and volume change if the edge lengths triple?

  d. Make a table for cubes with whole-number edge lengths from 0 to 12. Title the columns "Side Length," "Surface Area," and "Volume."

  e. Sketch graphs of the data (*edge length, surface area*) and (*edge length, volume*) from your table.

  f. Tell whether the patterns of change in the tables and graphs suggest linear, quadratic, or exponential functions, or none of these.

33. **a.** Find the areas of these circles.

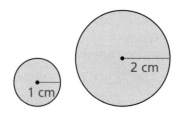

b. Copy and complete this table. Is the relationship between the area and the radius quadratic? Explain.

Radius (cm)	1	2	3	4	x
Area (cm²)	■	■	■	■	■

c. Below are nets for two cylinders with heights of 2 meters. Find the surface areas of the cylinders.

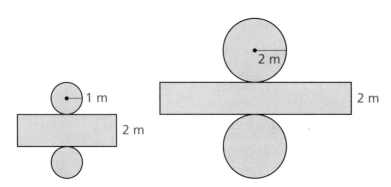

d. Copy and complete this table. Is the relationship between the surface area and the radius quadratic? Explain.

Radius (m)	1	2	3	4	x
Height (m)	2	2	2	2	2
Surface Area (m²)	■	■	■	■	■

34. Multiple Choice The equation $h = 4 + 63t - 16t^2$ represents the height h of a baseball in feet t seconds after it is hit. After how many seconds will the ball hit the ground?

A. 2 seconds   **B.** 4 seconds   **C.** 5 seconds   **D.** 15 seconds

35. a. Copy and complete the table to show surface areas of cylinders with equal radius and height. Use the nets shown.

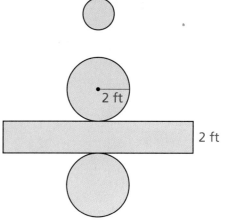

Radius (ft)	1	2	3	4	x
Height (ft)	1	2	3	4	x
Surface Area (ft²)	■	■	■	■	■

b. Is the relationship between surface area and radius a quadratic function? Explain.

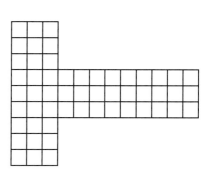

36. At the right is a net of a cube, divided into square units.

a. What is the edge length of the cube?

b. Find the surface area and volume of the cube.

c. Draw a net for a cube with a volume of 64 cubic units. What is the length of each edge of the cube? What is the surface area of the cube?

d. What formula relates the edge length of a cube to its volume? Is this relationship a quadratic function? Explain.

37. Silvio wants to gift wrap the cubic box shown. He has 10 square feet of wrapping paper. Is this enough to wrap the gift? Explain.

38. Multiple Choice Which table could represent a quadratic function?

F.

x	y
−3	−3
−2	−2
−1	−1
0	0
1	1
2	2
3	3

G.

x	y
−3	1
−2	2
−1	3
0	4
1	3
2	2
3	1

H.

x	y
1	0
2	2
3	6
4	12
5	20
6	30
7	42

J.

x	y
−1	10
0	7
1	4
2	1
3	4
4	7
5	10

39. Multiple Choice Suppose $y = x^2 - 4x$ and $y = 0$. What are all the possible values for x?

A. -4 **B.** 0 **C.** 4 or 0 **D.** -4 or 0

40. The cube buildings below are shown from the front right corner.

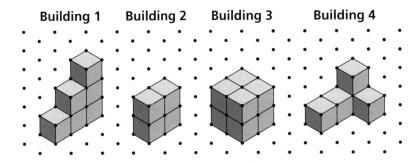

Building 1   Building 2   Building 3   Building 4

These drawings show the base outline, front view, and right view of Building 1. Draw these views for the other three buildings.

Base outline   Front view   Right view

41. Below are three views of a cube building. Draw a building that has all three views and has the greatest number of cubes possible. You may want to use isometric dot paper.

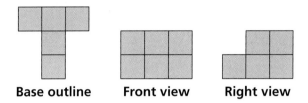

Base outline   Front view   Right view

42. Below are base plans for cube buildings. A *base plan* shows the shape of the building's base and the number of cubes in each stack.

Building 1

1	1	2
	3	1
	1	

Front

Building 2

1	1	2
	1	3
	1	

Front

Make a drawing of each building from the front right corner. You may want to use isometric dot paper.

For Exercises 43–46, evaluate the expression for the given values of *x*.

43. $x(x - 5)$ for $x = 5$ and $x = -5$

44. $3x^2 - x$ for $x = 1$ and $x = \frac{1}{3}$

45. $x^2 + 5x + 4$ for $x = 2$ and $x = -4$

46. $(x - 7)(x + 2)$ for $x = -2$ and $x = 2$

47. Match the equations, graphs, and properties. Each equation is given in factored form. The window of the graphs is shown at the right.

```
WINDOW  FORMAT
 Xmin=-5
 Xmax=5
 Xscl=1
 Ymin=-10
 Ymax=10
 Yscl=1
 Xres=1
```

Equations:

$y_1 = x^2$ $y_2 = x(x - 4)$

$y_3 = (x + 3)(x - 3)$ $y_4 = (x + 3)(x + 3)$

$y_5 = x(4 - x)$ $y_6 = x(x + 4)$

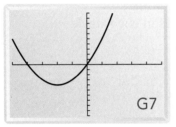 G7

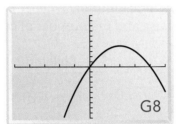 G8

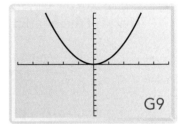 G9

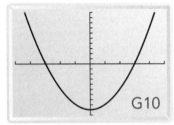 G10

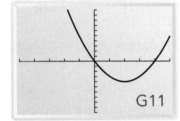 G11

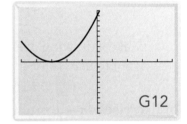 G12

Function Properties
- Two x-intercepts
- y-intercept $= -9$
- Line of symmetry:
  $x = 0$

P13

Function Properties
- Two x-intercepts
- y-intercept $= 0$
- Line of symmetry:
  $x = -2$

P14

Function Properties
- One x-intercept
- y-intercept $= 0$
- Line of symmetry:
  $x = 0$

P15

Function Properties
- Two x-intercepts
- y-intercept $= 0$
- Line of symmetry:
  $x = 2$

P16

Function Properties
- One x-intercept
- y-intercept $= 9$
- Line of symmetry:
  $x = -3$

P17

Function Properties
- Two x-intercepts
- y-intercept $= 0$
- Line of symmetry:
  $x = 2$

P18

48. Refer to Graphs G7 and G8 from Exercise 47. Without using your calculator, answer the following questions.

   a. Suppose parabola G7 is shifted 1 unit left. Write an equation for this new parabola.

   b. Suppose parabola G7 is shifted 4 units right. Write an equation for this new parabola.

   c. Can parabola G7 be transformed into parabola G8 by a shift to the right only? Explain.

Extensions

49. A puzzle involves a strip of seven squares, three pennies, and three nickels. The starting setup is shown.

To solve the puzzle, you must switch the positions of the coins so the nickels are on the left and the pennies are on the right. You can move a coin to an empty square by sliding it or by jumping it over one coin. You can move pennies only to the right and nickels only to the left.

You can make variations of this puzzle by changing the numbers of coins and the length of the strip. Each puzzle should have the same number of each type of coin and one empty square.

   a. Make drawings that show each move (slide or jump) required to solve puzzles with 1, 2, and 3 coins of each type. How many moves does it take to solve each puzzle?

   b. A puzzle with n nickels and n pennies can be solved with $n^2 + 2n$ moves. Use this expression to calculate the number of moves required to solve puzzles with 1, 2, 3, 4, 5, 6, 7, 8, 9, and 10 of each type of coin.

   c. Do your calculations for 1, 2, and 3 coins of each type from part (b) agree with the numbers you found in part (a)?

   d. By calculating first and second differences in the data from part (b), verify that the relationship between the number of moves and the number of each type of coin is quadratic.

Use the following information for Exercises 50–52.

A soccer coach wants to take her 20-player team to the state capital for a tournament. A travel company is organizing the trip. The cost will be $125 per student. The coach thinks this is too expensive, so she decides to invite other students to go along. For each extra student, the cost of the trip will be reduced by $1 per student.

50. The travel company's expenses for the trip are $75 per student. The remaining money is profit. What will the company's profit be if the following numbers of students go on the trip?

a. 20   **b.** 25   **c.** 60   **d.** 80

51. Let n represent the number of students who go on the trip. In parts (a)–(d), write an equation for the relationship described. It may help to make a table like the one shown here.

State Capital Trip

Number of Students	Price per Student	Travel Company's Income	Travel Company's Expenses	Travel Company's Profit
20	$125	$20 \times \$125 = \$2,500$	$20 \times \$75 = \$1,500$	$\$2,500 - \$1,500 = \$1,000$
21	$124	▓	▓	▓

a. the relationship between *the price per student* and n

b. the relationship between *the travel company's income* and n

c. the relationship between *the travel company's expenses* and n

d. the relationship between *the travel company's profit* and n

52. Use a calculator to make a table and a graph of the equation for the travel company's profit. Study the pattern of change in the profit as the number of students increases from 25 to 75.

a. What number of students gives the company the maximum profit?

b. What numbers of students guarantee the company will earn a profit?

c. What numbers of students will give the company a profit of at least $1,200?

53. The Terryton Tile Company makes floor tiles. One tile design uses grids of small, colored squares as in this 4 × 4 pattern.

a. Suppose you apply the same design rule to a 5 × 5 pattern. How many small squares will be blue? How many will be yellow? How many will be red?

b. How many small squares of each color will there be if you apply the rule to a 10 × 10 pattern?

c. How many small squares of each color will there be if you apply the rule to an n × n pattern?

d. What kinds of relationships between the side length of the pattern and the number of small squares of each color do the expressions in part (c) describe? Explain.

54. This prism is made from centimeter cubes. After the prism was built, its faces were painted. How many centimeter cubes have

a. no painted faces?   b. one painted face?

c. two painted faces?   d. three painted faces?

e. How many centimeter cubes are there in all?

Mathematical Reflections

In this Investigation, you explored the relationship between height and time for several situations. You also looked for common features in the tables, graphs, and equations of quadratic functions. These questions will help you summarize what you have learned.

Think about these questions. Discuss your ideas with other students and your teacher. Then write a summary of your findings in your notebook.

1. **Describe** three real-world situations that can be modeled by quadratic functions. For each situation, give examples of questions that quadratic representations help to answer.

2. **How** can you recognize a quadratic function from

   a. a table?

   b. a graph?

   c. an equation?

3. **What** clues in a problem situation indicate that a linear, exponential, or quadratic function is an appropriate model for the data in the problem?

Common Core Mathematical Practices

As you worked on the Problems in this Investigation, you used prior knowledge to make sense of them. You also applied Mathematical Practices to solve the Problems. Think back over your work, the ways you thought about the Problems, and how you used Mathematical Practices.

Sophie described her thoughts in the following way:

> In Problem 4.3, Zane noticed that the number of painted faces of the cube represents the surface area of the cube. Hank did not think this was true since the surface area of a cube is $6n^2$, where n is the side length of the cube.
>
> Some of us knew that we could prove that Zane's conjecture is true if we could show that the surface area equals the sum of the algebraic expressions for the number of painted faces. This means that $6n^2 = 8(3) + 12(n - 2)(2) + 6(n - 2)^2(1)$. We were able to use what we learned in this Unit to show that this is true.

Common Core Standards for Mathematical Practice

MP3 Construct viable arguments and critique the reasoning of others.

- What other Mathematical Practices can you identify in Sophie's reasoning?

- Describe a Mathematical Practice that you and your classmates used to solve a different Problem in this Investigation.

In this Unit, you studied quadratic functions. You learned to recognize quadratic patterns in graphs and tables and to write equations for those patterns. You answered questions about quadratic functions by solving equations and by finding maximum and minimum points on graphs.

Use Your Understanding: Algebraic Reasoning

Test your understanding and skill in working with quadratic relationships by solving these problems about a carnival.

1. In the game pictured at the right, players hit the end of a lever with a mallet, propelling a weight upward. The player wins a prize if the weight hits the bell at the top.

    The height h (in feet) of the weight t seconds after the mallet is struck is given by the equation $h = -16t^2 + bt$. The value of b depends on how hard the mallet hits the lever.

    a. Sketch the general shape of a graph of an equation of the form $h = -16t^2 + bt$.

    b. When Naomi plays, the weight rises 9 feet and falls back to the bottom in 1.5 seconds. Which table better matches this situation?

Table 1

Time (seconds)	0.0	0.25	0.5	0.75	1.0	1.25	1.5
Height (feet)	0	5	8	9	8	5	0

Table 2

Time (seconds)	0.0	0.25	0.5	0.75	1.0	1.25	1.5
Height (feet)	0	3	6	9	6	3	0

2. Wan's hit is just hard enough to cause the weight to touch the bell. This situation is modeled by $h = -16t^2 + 32t$.

    a. How high did the weight go?

    b. How long did it take the weight to return to the starting position?

    c. When was the weight 12 feet above the starting position?

3. The carnival is adding pony rides for young children. They have 180 feet of fence to build a rectangular pony corral.

    a. Let x represent the length of the pony corral in feet. Write an expression for the width in terms of x.

    b. Write an equation that shows how the area A of the corral is related to its length x.

    c. What length and width will give an area of 2,000 square feet? Write and solve an equation whose solution is the required length.

    d. What length and width will give the maximum area? Explain how you could use a table or graph to find this maximum area.

Explain Your Reasoning

To solve Problems 1–3, you used your knowledge of quadratic functions and of tables, graphs, and equations for quadratic situations.

4. Suppose the relationship between x and y is a quadratic function. What patterns would you expect to see

   a. in a table of (x, y) pairs?

   b. in a graph of (x, y) pairs?

   c. in an equation relating x and y?

5. How are the equations, tables, and graphs for quadratic relationships different from those for

   a. linear relationships?

   b. exponential relationships?

6. How can you tell whether the graph of a quadratic equation of the form $y = ax^2 + bx + c$ will have a maximum point or a minimum point?

7. What strategies can you use to solve quadratic equations such as $3x^2 - 5x + 3 = 0$ and $x^2 + 4x = 7$ by using

   a. a table of a quadratic function?

   b. a graph of a quadratic function?

English / Spanish Glossary

B **binomial** An algebraic expression that is the sum or difference of two terms. The expression $2x + 4$ is a binomial.

binomio Expresión algebraica que es la suma o diferencia de dos términos. La expresión $2x + 4$ es un binomio.

C **constant term** A number in an algebraic expression that is not multiplied by a variable. In the expanded form of a quadratic expression, $ax^2 + bx + c$, the constant term is the number c. The constant term in the expression $-16t^2 + 64t + 7$ is 7. The constant term in the expression $x^2 - 4$ is -4.

término constante Un número en una expresión algebraica que no está multiplicado por una variable. En la forma desarrollada de una expresión cuadrática, $ax^2 + bx + c$, el término constante es el número c. El término constante en la expresión $-16t^2 + 64t + 7$ es 7. El término constante en la expresión $x^2 - 4$ es -4.

D **dependent variable** One of the two variables in a relationship. Its value depends upon or is determined by the other variable called the *independent variable*. For example, the distance you travel on a car trip (dependent variable) depends on how long you drive (independent variable).

variable dependiente Una de las dos variables de una relación. Su valor depende o está determinado por el valor de la otra variable, llamada *variable independiente*. Por ejemplo, la distancia que recorres durante un viaje en carro (variable dependiente) depende de cuánto conduces (variable independiente).

describe Academic Vocabulary
To explain or tell in detail. A written description can contain facts and other information needed to communicate your answer. A diagram or a graph may also be included.

related terms *express, explain, illustrate*

sample Describe the graph of the equation $y = x^2 + 2x$.

The graph of $y = x^2 + 2x$ is a parabola that opens up. The minimum is located at $(-1, -1)$. The y-intercept and one of the x-intercepts is at the origin. The other x-intercept is located at $(-2, 0)$.

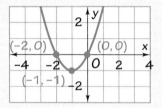

describir Vocabulario académico
Explicar o decir con detalle. Una descripción escrita puede contener datos y otra información necesaria para comunicar tu respuesta. También se puede incluir un diagrama o una gráfica.

términos relacionados *expresar, explicar, ilustrar*

ejemplo Describe la gráfica de la ecuación $y = x^2 + 2x$.

La gráfica de $y = x^2 + 2x$ es una parábola que se abre hacia arriba. El punto mínimo se localiza en $(-1, -1)$. El intercepto en y uno de los interceptos en x están en el origen. El otro intercepto en x se localiza en $(-2, 0)$.

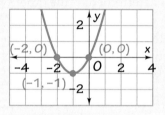

difference of squares An expression of the form $a^2 - b^2$. It can be factored as $(a + b)(a - b)$.

diferencia de cuadrados Una expresión de la forma $a^2 - b^2$. Se puede descomponer en factores de esta manera: $(a + b)(a - b)$.

Distributive Property For any three numbers a, b, and c, $a(b + c) = ab + ac$.

Propiedad distributiva Para tres números cualesquiera a, b y c, $a(b + c) = ab + ac$.

E **expanded form** The form of an expression composed of sums and differences of terms, rather than products of factors. The expressions $x^2 + 7x - 12$ and $x^2 + 2x$ are in expanded form.

forma desarrollada La forma de una expresión compuesta de sumas o diferencias de términos, en lugar de productos de factores. Las expresiones $x^2 + 7x - 12$ y $x^2 + 2x$ están representadas en forma desarrollada.

explain Academic Vocabulary
To give facts and details that make an idea easier to understand. Explaining something can involve a written summary supported by a diagram, chart, table, or any combination of these.

related terms *clarify, justify, tell*

sample Darla factored the expression $x^2 + 15x + 56$. Explain what she did.

$$x^2 + 15x + 56 = x^2 + 7x + 8x + 56 \qquad (1)$$
$$= x(x + 7) + 8(x + 7) \qquad (2)$$
$$= (x + 8)(x + 7) \qquad (3)$$

In Step 1, she rewrote 15x as the sum of 7x and 8x. In Step 2, she factored x from the first two terms and 8 from the last two terms. In Step 3, she factored (x + 7) from both terms.

explicar Vocabulario académico
Dar datos y detalles que hacen que una idea sea más fácil de comprender. Explicar puede implicar un resumen escrito apoyado por un diagrama, una gráfica, una tabla o una combinación de estos.

términos relacionados *aclarar, justificar, decir*

ejemplo Dora descompuso en factores la expresión $x^2 + 15x + 56$. Explica lo que hizo.

$$x^2 + 15x + 56 = x^2 + 7x + 8x + 56 \qquad (1)$$
$$= x(x + 7) + 8(x + 7) \qquad (2)$$
$$= (x + 8)(x + 7) \qquad (3)$$

En el Paso 1, volvió a escribir 15x como la suma de 7x y 8x. En el Paso 2, separó x como factor de los primeros dos términos y 8 de los últimos dos términos. En el Paso 3, separó (x + 7) de ambos términos.

F **factored form** The form of an expression composed of products of factors, rather than sums or differences of terms. The expressions $x(x - 2)$ and $(x + 3)(x + 4)$ are in factored form.

forma factorizada La forma de una expresión compuesta de productos de factores, en lugar de sumas o diferencias de términos. Las expresiones $x(x - 2)$ y $(x + 3)(x + 4)$ están representadas en forma factorizada.

independent variable One of the two variables in a relationship. Its value determines the value of the other variable called the *dependent variable*. If you organize a bike tour, for example, the number of people who register to go (independent variable) determines the cost for renting bikes (dependent variable).

variable independiente Una de las dos variables en una relación. Su valor determina el de la otra variable, llamada *variable dependiente*. Por ejemplo, si organizas un recorrido en bicicleta, el número de personas inscritas (variable independiente) determina el costo del alquiler de las bicicletas (variable dependiente).

like terms Terms with the same variable raised to the same power. In the expression $4x^2 + 3x - 2x^2 - 2x + 1$, $3x$ and $-2x$ are like terms, and $4x^2$ and $-2x^2$ are like terms.

términos semejantes Términos con la misma variable elevada a la misma potencia. En la expresión $4x^2 + 3x - 2x^2 - 2x + 1$, $3x$ y $-2x$ son términos semejantes, y $4x^2$ y $-2x^2$ también son términos semejantes.

line of symmetry A line that divides a graph or drawing into two halves that are mirror images of each other.

eje de simetría Recta que divide una gráfica o un dibujo en dos mitades en la que una es el reflejo de la otra.

linear term A part of an algebraic expression in expanded form in which the variable is raised to the first power. In the expression $4x^2 + 3x - 2x + 1$, $3x$ and $-2x$ are linear terms.

término lineal La parte de una expresión algebraica en forma desarrollada, en la que la variable está elevada a la primera potencia. En la expresión $4x^2 + 3x - 2x + 1$, $3x$ y $-2x$ son términos lineales.

maximum value of a function The greatest y-value of a function. If y is the height of a thrown object, then the maximum value of the height is the highest point the object reaches. If you throw a ball into the air, its height increases until it reaches the maximum height, and then its height decreases as it falls back to the ground. If y is the area of a rectangle with a fixed perimeter, then the maximum value of the area, or simply the maximum area, is the greatest area possible for a rectangle with that perimeter. In this Unit, you found that the maximum area for a rectangle with a perimeter of 20 meters is 25 square meters.

valor máximo de una función El mayor valor de y en una función. Si y es la altura de un objeto lanzado, entonces el valor máximo de la altura es la altura mayor que alcanza el objeto. Si lanzas una pelota al aire, su altura aumenta hasta que alcanza la altura máxima, y luego su altura disminuye a medida que cae hacia el suelo. Si y es el área de un rectángulo con un perímetro fijo, entonces el valor máximo del área, o simplemente el área máxima, es la mayor área posible para un rectángulo con ese perímetro. En esta unidad, estudiaste que el área máxima de un rectángulo con un perímetro de 20 metros es 25 metros cuadrados.

minimum value of a function The least *y*-value of a function. If *y* is the cost of an item, then the minimum value of the cost, or simply the minimum cost, is the least cost possible for the item.

valor mínimo de una función El valor menor de y en una función. Si *y* es el costo de un artículo, entonces el valor mínimo del costo, o simplemente el costo mínimo, es el menor costo posible para ese artículo.

P **parabola** The graph of a quadratic function. A parabola has a line of symmetry that passes through the maximum point if the graph opens downward or through the minimum point if the graph opens upward.

parábola La gráfica de una función cuadrática. Una parábola tiene un eje de simetría que pasa por el punto máximo si la gráfica se abre hacia abajo, o por el punto mínimo si la gráfica se abre hacia arriba.

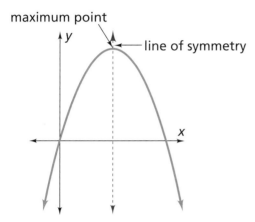

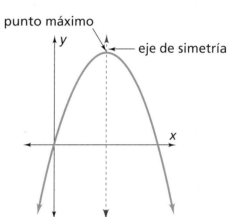

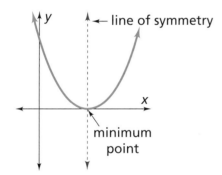

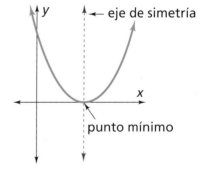

predict Academic Vocabulary
To make an educated guess based on the analysis of real data.

related terms *estimate, guess, expect*

sample Predict how many dots will be in Figure 8.

Figure 1   Figure 2   Figure 3   Figure 4

Figure 1 has 1 dot. Figure 2 has 2 + 1 = 3 dots. Figure 3 has 3 + 2 + 1 = 6 dots. Figure 4 has 4 + 3 + 2 + 1 = 10 dots. If the pattern continues, Figure 8 will have 8 + 7 + 6 + 5 + 4 + 3 + 2 + 1 = 36 dots.

predecir Vocabulario académico
Hacer una suposición basada en el análisis de datos reales.

términos relacionados *estimar, conjeturar, esperar*

ejemplo Predice cuántos puntos habrá en la Figura 8.

Figura 1   Figura 2   Figura 3   Figura 4

La Figura 1 tiene 1 punto. La Figura 2 tiene 2 + 1 = 3 puntos. La Figura 3 tiene 3 + 2 + 1 = 6 puntos. La Figura 4 tiene 4 + 3 + 2 + 1 = 10 puntos. Si el patrón continúa, la Figura 8 tendrá 8 + 7 + 6 + 5 + 4 + 3 + 2 + 1 = 36 puntos.

quadratic expression An expression that is equivalent to an expression of the form $ax^2 + bx + c$, where a, b, and c are numbers and $a \neq 0$. An expression in factored form is quadratic if it has exactly two linear factors, each with the variable raised to the first power. An expression in expanded form is quadratic if the highest power of the variable is 2. For example, $2x^2$, $3x^2 - 2x$, and $4x^2 + 2x - 7$ are all quadratic expressions. The expression $x(x - 2)$ is also a quadratic expression because $x(x - 2) = x^2 - 2x$. In this Unit, you used quadratic expressions to represent areas of rectangles for a fixed perimeter, the number of high fives between members of a team, and the path of a ball thrown into the air.

expresión cuadrática Una expresión que es equivalente a una expresión de la forma $ax^2 + bx + c$, donde a, b, y c son números y $a \neq 0$. Una expresión en forma factorizada es cuadrática si tiene exactamente dos factores lineales, cada uno con la variable elevada a la primera potencia. Una expresión en forma desarrollada es cuadrática si la potencia mayor de la variable es 2. Por ejemplo, $2x^2$, $3x^2 - 2x$, y $4x^2 + 2x - 7$ son expresiones cuadráticas. La expresión $x(x - 2)$ también es una expresión cuadrática porque $x(x - 2) = x^2 - 2x$. En esta unidad, usaste expresiones cuadráticas para representar áreas de rectángulos con un perímetro fijo, el número de saludos entre los miembros de un equipo y el recorrido de una pelota que se lanza al aire.

quadratic function A function between independent and dependent variables such that, as the dependent values increase by a constant amount, the successive (first) differences between the dependent values change by a constant amount. For example, in $y = x^2$, when x increases by 1, the first differences for y are 3, 5, 7, 9, . . . and then the second differences are 2, 2, 2, . . . The graphs of quadratic functions have the shape of a $\cup$ or upside down $\cup$ with a line of symmetry through a maximum or minimum point on the graph that is perpendicular to the x-axis.

función cuadrática La función entre las variables dependiente e independiente de modo que, a medida que aumentan los valores de la variable dependiente en una cantidad constante, las (primeras) diferencias sucesivas entre los valores dependientes cambian en una cantidad constante. Por ejemplo, en $y = x^2$, a medida que x aumenta en 1, las primeras diferencias para y son 3, 5, 7, 9, . . . y las segundas diferencias son 2, 2, 2, . . . Las gráficas de las funciones cuadráticas tienen forma de $\cup$ o $\cup$ invertida, con un eje de simetría que pasa por el punto máximo o el punto mínimo de la gráfica que es perpendicular al eje de las x.

quadratic term A part of an expression in expanded form in which the variable is raised to the second power. In the expression $4x^2 + 3x - 2x^2 - 2x + 1$, $4x^2$ and $-2x^2$ are quadratic terms.

término cuadrático Parte de una expresión en forma desarrollada en la que la variable está elevada a la segunda potencia. En la expresión $4x^2 + 3x - 2x^2 - 2x + 1$, $4x^2$ y $-2x^2$ son términos cuadráticos.

S **sketch** Academic Vocabulary
To draw a rough outline of something. When a sketch is asked for, it means that a drawing needs to be included in your response.

related terms *draw, illustrate*

sample The equation of the area of a rectangle is $A = w(20 - w)$, where w is the width of the rectangle in inches. Sketch a rectangle to represent the situation.

Label one side of the rectangle w inches and the other side $20 - w$ inches.

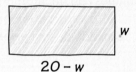

I sketched a graph of $A = w(20 - w)$ to show all of the possible areas of the rectangle.

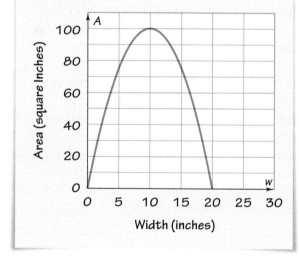

hacer un bosquejo Vocabulario académico
Dibujar un esbozo de algo. Cuando se pide un bosquejo, quiere decir que se debe incluir un dibujo en la respuesta.

términos relacionados *dibujar, ilustrar*

ejemplo La ecuación del área de un rectángulo es $A = a(20 - a)$, donde a es el ancho del rectángulo en pulgadas. Haz un bosquejo de un rectángulo y una gráfica para representar la situación.

Rotulo un lado del rectángulo a pulgads y el otro lado $20 - a$ pulgadas.

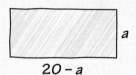

Hice el bosquejo de una gráfica de $A = a(20 - a)$ para mostrár todas las áreas posibles del rectángulo.

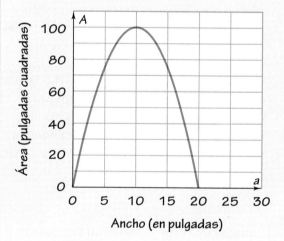

T **term** An expression that consists of either a number or a number multiplied by a variable raised to a power. In the expression $3x^2 - 2x + 10$, $3x^2$, $-2x$, and 10 are terms.

término Una expresión con un número o un número multiplicado por una variable elevada a una potencia. En la expresión $3x^2 - 2x + 10$, $3x^2$, $-2x$, y 10 son términos.

triangular number A number that gives the total number of dots in a triangular pattern. The first four triangular numbers are 1, 3, 6, and 10, the numbers of dots in Figures 1 through 4 below. The nth triangular number can be represented by the expression $\frac{n(n+1)}{2}$. The nth triangular number also represents the sum of the first n counting numbers.

número triangular Un número que da el número total de puntos en un patrón triangular. Los primeros cuatro números triangulares son 1, 3, 6 y 10, que es el número de puntos en las Figuras 1 a 4 a continuación. El enésimo número triangular se puede representar con la expresión $\frac{n(n+1)}{2}$. El enésimo número triangular también representa la suma de los n primeros números para contar.

Figure 1 **Figure 2** **Figure 3** **Figure 4**

X **x-intercept** The point where a graph crosses the x-axis. In the graph, the coordinates of the x-intercept are $(-4, 0)$.

intercepto en x El punto en el que la gráfica atraviesa el eje de las x. En la gráfica, las coordenadas del intercepto en x son $(-4, 0)$.

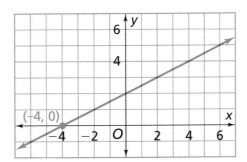

Y **y-intercept** The point where the graph crosses the y-axis. In a linear equation of the form $y = mx + b$, the y-intercept is the constant, b. In the graph, the coordinates of the y-intercept are $(0, 2)$.

intercepto en y El punto en que la gráfica atraviesa el eje de las y. En una ecuación lineal de la forma $y = mx + b$, el intercepto en y es la constante b. En la gráfica, las coordenadas del intercepto en y son $(0, 2)$.

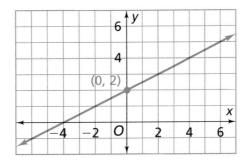

Index

ACE
applications of quadratic functions, 80–95
quadratic expressions, 38–45
quadratic functions, 14–21
quadratic patterns of change, 55–67

algebraic reasoning, 98–99

area and perimeter
applications of quadratic functions, 87, 88, 99
quadratic expressions and, 24–27
quadratic functions and, 8, 10–11, 19, 21
quadratic patterns of change and, 64
rectangles, 14–18, 22, 34
writing equations for, 12–13

Aristotle, 71

Ask Yourself, 4

binomials, 33

change, patterns of. *See also* quadratic patterns of change
applications of quadratic functions, 83, 85, 87
quadratic functions, 11, 20, 50, 52–54
quadratic relationships, 4, 51
triangular numbers, 48–49

circumference, 44

Common Core Mathematical Practices, 5–6, 23, 47, 69, 97

constant terms, 74

cubes, 89, 90–91, 97

dependent variables, 9

diagonals, 63

difference of squares, 35

Distributive Property
expanded form, 40
factoring quadratic expressions, 34–35
factors and factoring, 32
quadratic expressions, 4, 28–31, 46, 47
quadratic functions and, 19

dot patterns, 55

equations
applications of quadratic functions, 72, 73–74, 76, 77, 80–85, 86, 92, 93, 96
area of rectangles and, 13, 16–17, 27
for lines, 45
quadratic equations, 4, 19
quadratic functions and, 12–13, 18–19, 41, 50
quadratic patterns of change and, 63
quadratic relationships, 65, 94
sums and, 56
triangular numbers, 49

equivalent quadratic expressions, 4, 45
area of rectangles and, 28
expanded form, 38
factored form, 39, 46
rectangles and, 47, 62

expanded form
binomials, 33
Distributive Property, 40
equivalent quadratic expressions, 39–41
quadratic expressions, 19, 28, 29, 30, 31, 38–42, 46, 47, 62
quadratic patterns of change and, 65

Explain Your Reasoning, 100

exponential functions
comparing quadratic, linear, exponential, and inverse relationships, 78–79, 87, 96, 100
patterns of change, 68
quadratic functions and, 9, 11, 22, 23, 65
relationships and, 42

factored form
Common Core Mathematical Practices, 47
equivalent quadratic expressions, 39, 40, 41
quadratic expressions, 19, 28, 29, 38–42, 45, 46, 62

factoring quadratic expressions, 32–35

first differences, 52–53

fixed perimeter
area of rectangles and, 14–18
quadratic functions and, 10–11, 13, 14, 16, 22

fleas, 75

Galileo, 71

Gauss, Carl Friedrich, 56, 66

Glossary, 101–109

Gold Rush, 7

gravity, 70–71

hexagonal numbers, 66–67

independent variables, 9

inverse variation, 9, 11, 42, 78–79

Investigations
applications of quadratic functions, 70–79
quadratic expressions, 24–37
quadratic functions, 7–13
quadratic patterns of change, 48–54

land sections, 7, 8

like terms, 29

linear functions
applications of quadratic
functions, 87
comparing quadratic, linear,
exponential, and inverse
relationships, 78–79, 87,
96, 100
patterns of change, 48, 52, 68
quadratic functions and, 9,
11, 22, 23, 52, 65
relationships and, 42

lines, equations for, 45

lines of symmetry, 36, 37,
82, 84

Looking Ahead, 2–3

Looking Back, 98–100

Mathematical Highlights, 4

Mathematical Practices, 5–6

Mathematical Reflections
applications of quadratic
functions, 96–97
quadratic expressions, 46–47
quadratic functions, 22–23
quadratic patterns of change,
68–69

maximum and minimum
points, 82, 100

nets, 64, 89

parabolas, 9, 36, 37, 93

parallelograms, 20

patterns. *See also* change,
patterns of
applications of quadratic
functions, 77
dot patterns, 55
factoring quadratic
expressions, 34
quadratic functions and, 11,
16, 22

perimeter. *See* area and
perimeter

polygons, 44

prisms, 95

quadratic equations. *See*
equations

quadratic expressions, 4
ACE, 38–45
areas of rectangles, 24–27
Distributive Property, 28–31
factoring, 32–35
Mathematical Reflections,
46–47
quadratic functions and
their graphs, 36–37
rectangles and, 62

quadratic functions, 7
ACE, 14–21
equations, 41
graphs and graphing, 36–37,
46
Mathematical Reflections,
22–23
maximizing area, 8
quadratic patterns of change,
50, 52–54, 68
reading tables and graphs,
9–11
relationships and, 42
tables and graphs, 4, 59, 65
writing equations, 12–13

quadratic functions,
applications of
comparing quadratic
functions, 73–75
comparing quadratic, linear,
exponential, and inverse
relationships, 78–79
gravity and, 70–71
interpreting tables and
equations, 72
multiple functions, 76–77

quadratic patterns of change
ACE, 55–67
Mathematical Reflections,
68–69
quadratic functions, 50,
52–54
quadratic relationships, 51

triangular numbers, 48–49

quadratic relationships, 4, 51,
100

quadrilaterals, 20, 63

radius and diameter, 44, 88

reasoning, explaining your.
See also Mathematical
Practices; Mathematical
Reflections
algebraic reasoning, 98–99
area and perimeter, 15,
21, 25
area of rectangles and, 26
binomials, 33
quadratic expressions, 39
quadratic functions, 8, 10,
50, 100
quadratic functions and
their graphs, 45
quadratic patterns of change
and, 69

rectangles
area and perimeter, 14–18,
20, 21, 22, 99
equivalent quadratic
expressions, 47, 62
expanded form, 61
factored form, 61
factoring quadratic
expressions, 35
quadratic expressions,
24–27, 30, 38–42, 43
quadratic functions and, 8,
10–11
writing equations for, 12–13

rectangular numbers, 55, 57

second differences, 53

side lengths
applications of quadratic
functions, 87
area of rectangles and, 26, 27
quadratic functions and, 13
rectangles, 20

square numbers, 55, 57

squares, 38, 43

squaring binomials, 33

star numbers, 66–67

sums, equations and, 56

surface area and volume, 64, 87, 88, 89, 97

tables and graphs
applications of quadratic functions, 72, 77, 80–85, 92, 96, 98–99
area and perimeter, 38
area of rectangles and, 14–15, 16–17, 18, 21, 27

comparing quadratic, linear, exponential, and inverse relationships, 78–79
maximizing area and, 12, 13
patterns of change, 51
quadratic functions, 4, 9–11, 22, 59, 100
quadratic functions and their graphs, 36–37
quadratic patterns of change and, 58, 60–61
relationships and, 43
triangular numbers, 49

tables of values, 49

triangular numbers, 48–49, 56, 57, 68, 69

Use Your Understanding, 98–99

variables, 9

x-**intercepts,** 36, 37, 45, 82

x-**values,** 52–53, 54, 60

y-**intercepts,** 36, 37, 45, 82

y-**values,** 52–53, 54, 60

Acknowledgments

Cover Design

Three Communication Design, Chicago

Text

071 First paragraph of the "Did You Know" from Phytoon.com
Copyright © 2001–2002; Alinnov Science & Technology. All rights reserved.

071 Second paragraph of the "Did You Know" from Physicsweb.org
Copyright © 1996–2006 IOP Publishing Ltd. All rights reserved.

075 "Did You Know" from *The New York Times Magazine*, October 22, 1995.
Copyright © 1995 The New York Times Company.

081 Exercise 4 introduction is Copyright © 2006 The International Olympic
Committee.

Photographs

Photo locators denoted as follows: Top (T), Center (C), Bottom (B), Left (L),
Right (R), Background (Bkgd)

002 (CR) Mark Richards/PhotoEdit, (BR) F. Rauschenbach/Glow Images;
003 Radius Images/Alamy; **007** Photo Researchers, Inc.; **044** Mark Richards/
PhotoEdit; **070** Ipatov/Shutterstock; **071** Gavin Hellier/Jon Arnold Images Ltd/
Alamy; **073** F. Rauschenbach/Glow Images.

CONNECTED ✸ MATHEMATICS® 3

Butterflies, Pinwheels, and Wallpaper

Symmetry and Transformations

Lappan, Phillips, Fey, Friel

Butterflies, Pinwheels, and Wallpaper

Symmetry and Transformations

Looking Ahead 2

Mathematical Highlights 4

Mathematical Practices and Habits of Mind 5

1 Symmetry and Transformations · 7

1.1 Butterfly Symmetry Line Reflections 9

1.2 In a Spin Rotations 12

1.3 Sliding Around Translations 14

1.4 Properties of Transformations 16

Ⓐ Ⓒ Ⓔ Homework 18

Mathematical Reflections 28

2 Transformations and Congruence · 30

2.1 Connecting Congruent Polygons 31

2.2 Supporting the World Congruent Triangles I 32

2.3 Minimum Measurement Congruent Triangles II 34

Ⓐ Ⓒ Ⓔ Homework 38

Mathematical Reflections 48

Transforming Coordinates   50

3.1 Flipping on a Grid Coordinate Rules for Reflections 50

3.2 Sliding on a Grid Coordinate Rules for Translations 53

3.3 Spinning on a Grid Coordinate Rules for Rotations 54

3.4 A Special Property of Translations and Half-Turns 56

3.5 Parallel Lines, Transversals, and Angle Sums 58

Ⓐ Ⓒ Ⓔ Homework 61

Mathematical Reflections 73

Dilations and Similar Figures   75

4.1 Focus on Dilations 76

4.2 Return of Super Sleuth Similarity Transformations 79

4.3 Checking Similarity Without Transformations 81

4.4 Using Similar Triangles 84

Ⓐ Ⓒ Ⓔ Homework 86

Mathematical Reflections 95

Unit Project Making a Wreath and a Pinwheel 97

Looking Back 100

English/Spanish Glossary 103

Index 112

Acknowledgments 115

Looking Ahead

How could you move the wallpaper design so that it looks the same after the move?

Suppose you want to measure the distance across a pond from point *A* to point *B*. **How** could you locate points *C*, *D*, and *E* so that *AB* = *DE*?

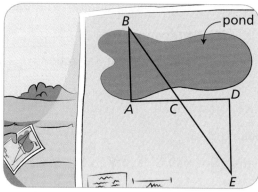

What coordinate rule for translation would "move" Mug 1 to the position of Mug 2?

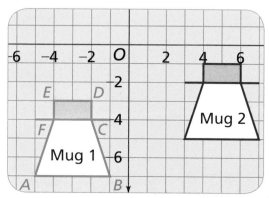

Geometric shapes give structure and style to natural and man-made objects that you see and use every day. To create and understand useful designs, it is helpful to know ways of making and describing shapes. In this Unit, you will develop your knowledge about symmetry, transformations, congruence, and similarity—four of the most important tools for thinking about geometric shapes.

Mathematical Highlights

Butterflies, Pinwheels, and Wallpaper

I n *Butterflies, Pinwheels, and Wallpaper,* you will learn how to

- Identify figures that have different kinds of symmetry

- Describe types of symmetry using reflections, rotations, and translations

- Use symmetry transformations to compare the size and shape of figures to see whether they are congruent or similar

- Identify congruent and similar triangles and quadrilaterals efficiently

- Use properties of congruent and similar triangles to solve problems about shapes and measurements

When you encounter a new problem, it is a good idea to ask yourself questions. In this Unit, you might ask questions such as:

How can I use symmetry to describe the shape and properties of figures in a design or a problem?

What figures in a pattern are congruent?

What parts of congruent figures will be matched by a congruence transformation?

What figures in a problem are similar?

Mathematical Practices and Habits of Mind

In the *Connected Mathematics* curriculum you will develop an understanding of important mathematical ideas by solving problems and reflecting on the mathematics involved. Every day, you will use "habits of mind" to make sense of problems and apply what you learn to new situations. Some of these habits are described by the *Common Core State Standards for Mathematical Practices* (MP).

MP1 Make sense of problems and persevere in solving them.

When using mathematics to solve a problem, it helps to think carefully about

- data and other facts you are given and what additional information you need to solve the problem;
- strategies you have used to solve similar problems and whether you could solve a related simpler problem first;
- how you could express the problem with equations, diagrams, or graphs;
- whether your answer makes sense.

MP2 Reason abstractly and quantitatively.

When you are asked to solve a problem, it often helps to

- focus first on the key mathematical ideas;
- check that your answer makes sense in the problem setting;
- use what you know about the problem setting to guide your mathematical reasoning.

MP3 Construct viable arguments and critique the reasoning of others.

When you are asked to explain why a conjecture is correct, you can

- show some examples that fit the claim and explain why they fit;
- show how a new result follows logically from known facts and principles.

When you believe a mathematical claim is incorrect, you can

- show one or more counterexamples—cases that don't fit the claim;
- find steps in the argument that do not follow logically from prior claims.

MP4 Model with mathematics.

When you are asked to solve problems, it often helps to

- think carefully about the numbers or geometric shapes that are the most important factors in the problem, then ask yourself how those factors are related to each other;
- express data and relationships in the problem with tables, graphs, diagrams, or equations, and check your result to see if it makes sense.

MP5 Use appropriate tools strategically.

When working on mathematical questions, you should always

- decide which tools are most helpful for solving the problem and why;
- try a different tool when you get stuck.

MP6 Attend to precision.

In every mathematical exploration or problem-solving task, it is important to

- think carefully about the required accuracy of results: is a number estimate or geometric sketch good enough, or is a precise value or drawing needed?
- report your discoveries with clear and correct mathematical language that can be understood by those to whom you are speaking or writing.

MP7 Look for and make use of structure.

In mathematical explorations and problem solving, it is often helpful to

- look for patterns that show how data points, numbers, or geometric shapes are related to each other;
- use patterns to make predictions.

MP8 Look for and express regularity in repeated reasoning.

When results of a repeated calculation show a pattern, it helps to

- express that pattern as a general rule that can be used in similar cases;
- look for shortcuts that will make the calculation simpler in other cases.

You will use all of the Mathematical Practices in this Unit. Sometimes, when you look at a Problem, it is obvious which practice is most helpful. At other times, you will decide on a practice to use during class explorations and discussions. After completing each Problem, ask yourself:

- What mathematics have I learned by solving this Problem?
- What Mathematical Practices were helpful in learning this mathematics?

Symmetry and Transformations

Symmetry is one of the most important and appealing features of shapes. Artists use symmetry to make designs that are pleasing to the eye. Architects use symmetry to make buildings balanced. Symmetry is also found in the structure of animals, plants, and everyday objects.

Common Core State Standards

8.G.A.1 Verify experimentally the properties of rotations, reflections, and translations:

8.G.A.1a Lines are taken to lines, and line segments to line segments of the same length.

8.G.A.1b Angles are taken to angles of the same measure.

8.G.A.1c Parallel lines are taken to parallel lines.

The butterfly, the pinwheel, and the piece of wallpaper, shown on this page and the next, illustrate three familiar forms of symmetry.

The butterfly has *reflectional symmetry*. You can make the butterfly design by reflecting, or flipping, a **basic design element** in a *line of symmetry* to make an image, or copy. The basic design element and its image form a design with reflectional symmetry.

- What is the basic design element for the butterfly design?
- Where is the line of symmetry?

The pinwheel has *rotational symmetry*. You can make the pinwheel design by rotating, or turning, a basic design element about a *center of rotation* to make one or more images. The basic design element and its images form a design with rotational symmetry.

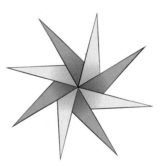

- What is the basic design element for the pinwheel design?
- How many copies do you need to complete the symmetric design?
- Where is the center of rotation?

The wallpaper design has *translational symmetry*. You can make the wallpaper design by translating, or sliding, a basic design element several times a certain distance and direction to make images. The basic design element and its images form a design with translational symmetry.

- What is the basic design element for the wallpaper design?

- What is the direction and distance of the translation?

The completed designs each have a different kind of symmetry. If you blinked just as someone flipped the butterfly design over the line of symmetry, the butterfly would look unchanged when you looked again. If you blinked just as someone turned the pinwheel 90 degrees about its center, the pinwheel would look unchanged when you looked again.

- If you blinked just as someone slid the wallpaper design, would the wallpaper look unchanged?

1.1 Butterfly Symmetry
Line Reflections

The butterfly shape has line or **reflectional symmetry.** You can make a design of your own with reflectional symmetry. Begin by drawing a basic design element and a **line of symmetry.** Then fold along the line, or use tracing paper, to locate the mirror images of key points.

The geometric operation, or **transformation,** that flips a figure and matches each point to an image point is called a **line reflection.** To identify the image of a point P, you can use prime notation (P'). You read P' as "P prime."

For example, you can make the symmetric figure below by reflecting pentagon *ABCDE* in line *m* to form *A′B′C′D′E′*. Together, the pentagons form a symmetric design.

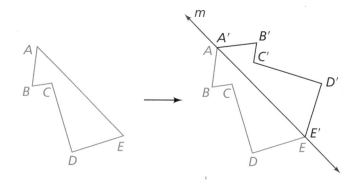

 • What is the relationship between each pair of symmetric points and the line of symmetry?

• How could you use that relationship to draw figures with line symmetry, without folding, tracing, or using a mirror?

To see how line reflections match parts of symmetric designs, it helps to do some drawing, folding, and measuring experiments. Using drawing tools, such as a ruler, an angle ruler, or a protractor, will help you discover important ideas about reflections.

Problem 1.1

Ⓐ Copy pentagon *ABCDE*, its image, *A′B′C′D′E′*, and the line of reflection, *m*.

1. Draw segments connecting each vertex of pentagon *ABCDE* to its image on pentagon *A′B′C′D′E′*.

2. Measure lengths and angles to see how the line of reflection is related to each segment you drew in part (1).

3. Describe the patterns in your measurements from part (2).

4. Which points are in the same location as their image under this reflection?

Problem 1.1 *continued*

B The design below has reflectional symmetry. How could you use only a pencil, a ruler, and an angle ruler or protractor to locate the line of symmetry?

C **1.** How could you use what you learned in Questions A and B to locate vertices J', K', L', and M', the images of vertices J, K, L, and M under a reflection in line n?

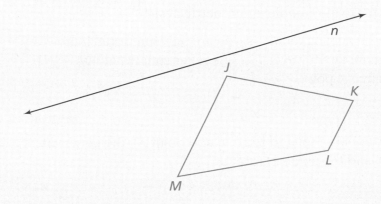

2. Is segment $K'L'$ the image of segment KL? In other words, when you reflect the points K and L to find points K' and L', does this reflection carry with it all the points between K and L, and locate them on segment $K'L'$? Explain.

3. Are the properties of the original quadrilateral $JKLM$ preserved in its image $J'K'L'M'$? Explain.

D Use your results from Questions A–C to complete this sentence: A reflection in line m matches each point X on a figure to an image point X' so that . . .

A C E Homework starts on page 18.

1.2 In a Spin
Rotations

The pinwheel design below has **rotational symmetry.** The transformation that turns a figure about a fixed point and matches each point to an image point is called a **rotation** about the **center of rotation.**

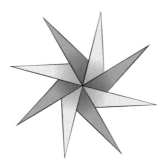

- What **angle of rotation** would rotate a basic design element so that the image makes the complete symmetric design?

- Is there a different basic design element and angle of rotation that you could use to make the complete symmetric design?

In most problems involving rotations, you are only interested in how key points of a design move. However, like line reflections, rotations match each point to an image point.

 How is each point *X* related to its image point *X'*, the center of rotation *O*, and the angle of rotation?

Using drawing tools, such as a ruler, angle ruler, or protractor, will help you discover important ideas about rotations.

Problem 1.2

A The compass star below has eight points that are labeled and a center of rotation *O*.

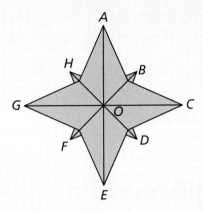

1. What is the smallest counterclockwise rotation (in degrees) that will rotate the star to a new position in which it looks unchanged?

2. **a.** Match each point on the compass star with the point that represents its image after the rotation in part (1).

   b. What is the image of segment *AO*? Of segment *HO*?

3. Describe the paths of points *A* and *H* on the compass star as they "move" from their original positions to their images.

4. Describe the relationship among any point *X*, its image, and the center of the compass star after the rotation in part (1).

5. Can you flip the compass star without changing its appearance? If so, what is the line of symmetry?

B Use the "flag" at the right as the basic design element. Using drawing tools, make designs that have rotational symmetries with the given angle of rotation.

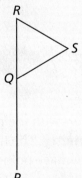

- In each case, specify the center of the rotation.

- If possible, find different ways to complete each of these tasks. Sketch the symmetric designs that would result from each strategy.

   1. 120° counterclockwise

   2. 90° counterclockwise

continued on the next page >

Problem **1.2** continued

C How is making a design with rotational symmetry like or unlike making a figure with reflectional symmetry?

D Use your results from Questions A–C to complete this sentence: A rotation of d degrees about point O matches each point X on a figure to an image point X' so that . . .

A C E Homework starts on page 18.

Homework starts on page 18.

1.3 Sliding Around
Translations

The wallpaper design below has neither reflectional symmetry nor rotational symmetry. However, it has a basic design element that repeats in a pattern. Suppose the wallpaper extended in all directions. Then you could slide the paper in several directions without changing what the eye would see.

Figures with the property of the wallpaper design have **translational symmetry.** The transformation that slides a figure and matches each point to an image point is called a **translation.**

? How could you describe a translation that matches the basic design element to an image?

Translations match a point on the plane to an image point. For reflections, you learned how each point and its image relate to the line of symmetry. For rotations, you learned how each point and its image relate to the center of rotation. In this Problem, you will learn how each point X is related to its image point X' after a translation.

Problem 1.3

A **1.** Diagrams 1 and 2 show polygon *GHJKLM* and its image under two different translations. On a copy of the diagrams:

- Locate and label the images G', H', J', K', L', and M' so that G' is the image of G, H' is the image of H, and so on.

- Draw segments from each vertex of *GHJKLM* to its image.

- Describe patterns relating the segments GG', HH', etc.

Diagram 1

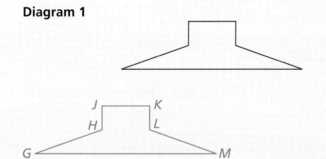

Diagram 2

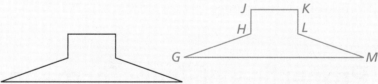

2. If you wanted to make a complete design with translational symmetry, how many images would you have to make?

continued on the next page >

Problem 1.3 *continued*

B Will drew a polygon and then drew an arrow to specify the distance and direction of a slide. How could you draw the image of the polygon under the specified translation?

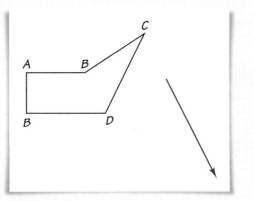

1. How do the corresponding vertices of the polygon and its image relate to each other? That is, what is the relationship between points *A* and *A'*, points *B* and *B'*, and so on?

2. How do the corresponding sides and angles of the polygon and its image relate to each other?

3. What shape is polygon *ABB'A'*? Explain.

4. Does the translation that matches point *A* to point *A'* and point *B* to point *B'* also match all the points on segment *AB* to points on segment *A'B'*? Explain.

C How is making a design with translational symmetry like or unlike making a design with reflectional or rotational symmetry?

D Use your results from Questions A–C to complete this sentence: A translation matches any two points *X* and *Y* on a figure to points *X'* and *Y'* so that . . .

ACE Homework starts on page 18.

1.4 Properties of Transformations

Reflections, rotations, and translations are useful in making symmetric designs from a basic design element. You can also use these ideas to show how one shape can be "moved" to fit onto another. To do so, it helps to know in advance what will change and what will stay the same.

The diagrams below show trapezoid *WXYZ* "moved" by a flip, turn, or a slide.

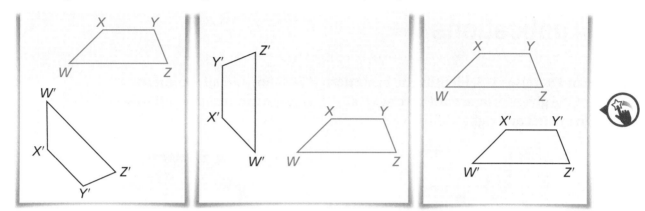

 • What transformations were used?

• How can you describe the details of each transformation?

• How is the shape, size, and position of the trapezoid affected?

In this Problem, you will summarize important ideas from Problems 1.1, 1.2, and 1.3. You will use these ideas in later Investigations.

Problem 1.4

Use the transformations of trapezoid *WXYZ* shown above.

A Describe each transformation with as much detail as you can. For example, give the reflection line, or the center of the rotation, or the direction and distance of the translation. Draw diagrams to support your answer.

B Suppose a reflection, a rotation, or a translation matches points *W* and *W'*, points *X* and *X'*, points *Y* and *Y'*, and points *Z* and *Z'*. In each case,

1. What distances are equal?

2. What angles are equal?

3. What line segments are parallel?

4. Which points and/or lines are "unmoved," if any?

5. Which properties of the original figure are preserved? Which properties change?

 Homework starts on page 18.

Applications

For Exercises 1–4, identify the basic design element and all symmetries of the given design. For Exercises 3 and 4, assume the design continues to the left and right without end.

1.

2.

3.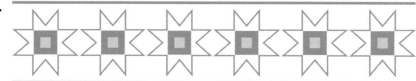

4.

5. On a copy of the diagram below, draw the image of triangle *ABC* after a reflection in line *m*. Describe how the vertices of the image relate to the corresponding vertices of the original triangle and the line of reflection.

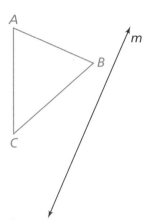

6. Quadrilateral $A'B'C'D'$ is a reflection image of quadrilateral *ABCD*.

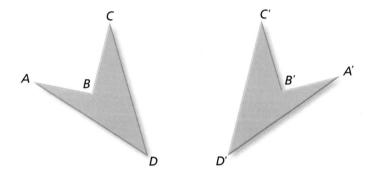

a. On a copy of the diagram, draw the line of reflection. Explain how you found it.

b. Describe the relationship between a point on the original figure and its image on $A'B'C'D'$.

7. Use the diagram at the right.

a. On a copy of the diagram, draw the image of polygon *PQRST* after a reflection in line *n*.

b. Does the resulting design have reflectional symmetry? Explain why or why not.

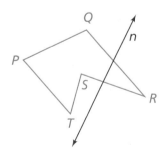

8. Use triangle *XYZ* below.

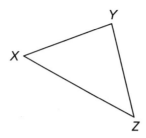

    a. On a copy of the diagram, draw the image of the triangle after a counterclockwise rotation of 90° about point *Z*.

    b. Describe how each vertex of the image relates to the corresponding vertex on the original triangle.

9. Use triangle *XYZ* and point *R* below.

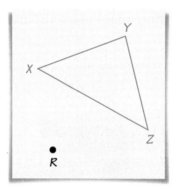

    a. On a copy of the diagram, draw the image of the triangle after a counterclockwise rotation of 90° about point *R*.

    b. Describe how each vertex of the image relates to the corresponding vertex on the original triangle.

10. Use polygon *FGHJK* at the right.

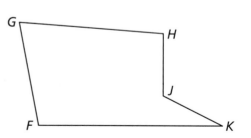

    a. On a copy of the diagram, draw the image of the polygon after a counterclockwise rotation of 180° about point *K*.

    b. Describe how each vertex of the image relates to the corresponding vertex on the original polygon.

11. Use triangle *PQR* and the arrow shown below.

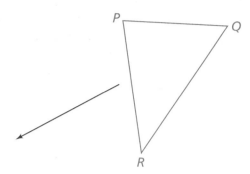

a. On a copy of the diagram, translate the triangle as indicated by the arrow.

b. Describe how each vertex of the image relates to the corresponding vertex on the original triangle.

12. The diagram at the right that shows a triangle and its image under a translation.

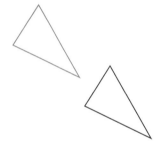

a. On a copy of the diagram, label the vertices of the two triangles *ABC* and *A'B'C'*, respectively, to indicate the correspondence of vertices by the translation.

b. Draw lines with an arrowhead at one end connecting pairs of corresponding vertices and explain what those lines have in common.

13. Use copies of the figure below for parts (a)–(c).

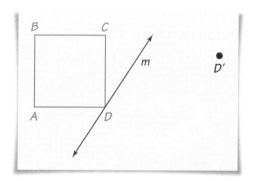

a. Draw the image of square *ABCD* under a reflection in line *m*.

b. Draw the image of square *ABCD* under a 45° counterclockwise rotation about point *A*.

c. Draw the image of square *ABCD* under a translation that matches point *D* to point *D'*.

Exercises 14–17 each give a figure and its image under a flip, turn, or slide. In each case, name the type of transformation used. For a flip, sketch the line of reflection. For a turn, locate the center and find the angle of rotation. For a slide, draw a line showing the direction and distance of the translation.

14.

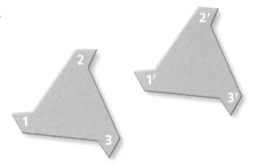

15.

16.

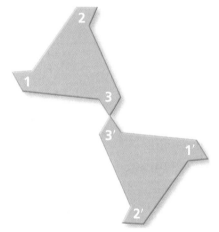

17.

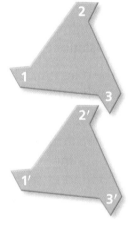

18. Quadrilateral *PQRS* is the image of parallelogram *ABCD* after a reflection and a translation. List all the properties of quadrilateral *PQRS* that you can infer from this fact.

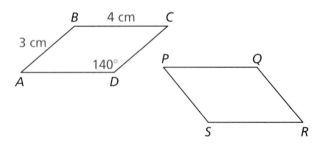

Connections

19. What symmetries does each capital letter have, if any?

A   B   C   D   E   F   G   H   I   J   K   L   M   N   O   P   Q   R   S   T   U   V   W   X   Y   Z

20. What symmetries does the rim have?

For Exercises 21–26, draw an example of each type of polygon. Draw all the lines of symmetry. If the polygon has rotational symmetry, identify the center and angle of rotation.

21. nonsquare rectangle

22. nonrectangular parallelogram

23. isosceles triangle

24. equilateral triangle

25. nonsquare rhombus

26. isosceles trapezoid

27. The rectangular prism and cylinder shown at the right both have a height of 4 centimeters. The diameter of the base of the cylinder is also 4 centimeters. Each figure is filled with a layer of centimeter cubes (some partial).

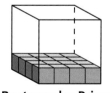
Rectangular Prism

Cylinder

    a. Describe the symmetries of the prism and the cylinder.

    b. How many layers of cubes will it take to fill the prism?

    c. What is the volume of the prism?

    d. How many cubes do you need to make one layer covering the bottom of the cylinder?

    e. What is the volume of the cylinder?

28. What kinds of symmetries do the following mathematical objects have?

   a. a number line

   b. a coordinate graph showing all four quadrants

   c. the graph of a quadratic function such as $y = x^2$

   d. the commutative properties of addition and multiplication

Extensions

29. Draw a rectangle like *ABCD* shown below and mark a point *P* outside of the rectangle.

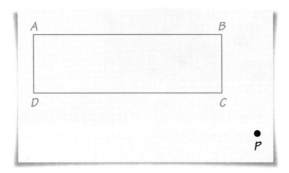

   a. Draw and label the image $A'B'C'D'$ of the rectangle under a counterclockwise rotation of 90° about point *P*.

   b. Describe the path each vertex of the rectangle travels in the rotation.

   c. Copy and complete the tables. Find the measurements indicated in the tables.

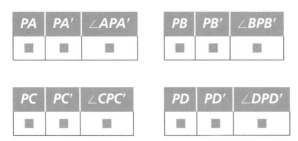

PA	PA'	∠APA'
■	■	■

PB	PB'	∠BPB'
■	■	■

PC	PC'	∠CPC'
■	■	■

PD	PD'	∠DPD'
■	■	■

d. Describe any patterns in the tables that relate the vertices of the original rectangle, the vertices of the image rectangle, and the center of rotation.

e. How would your answer to part (d) change if the angle of rotation were 120° instead of 90°?

The designs in Exercises 30–34 are actually first names. Describe the symmetries in each name. Then, write the name in standard lettering.

30.

31.

32.

33.

34.

35. Use the artistic technique illustrated in Exercises 30–34 to write your own name.

36. In this Investigation, you studied designs with reflectional, rotational, and translational symmetries. The design below is a bit different from those with the basic symmetries. Assume that the pattern continues to the left and right without end.

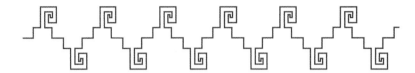

   a. Trace a basic design element with which you can produce the whole figure using only translations.

   b. Trace a smaller basic design element with which you can produce the whole figure using a combination of translations and line reflections.

37. Triangle *MBK* has its vertices on lines ℓ and *n*. Vertex *B* is the point of intersection of the lines.

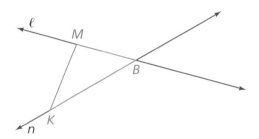

   a. On a copy of the diagram, sketch the image of triangle *MBK* under a rotation of 180° about point *B*. Locate and label image points M', B', and K'.

   b. What angle in triangle $M'B'K'$ corresponds to angle *MBK* in the original triangle?

   c. Make a conjecture about the angles formed where the two lines intersect. Test the conjecture with several other examples and see if you can find reasons for the pattern you observe.

38. Use a copy of the diagram below. Reflect triangle *ABC* over line ℓ. Label the image *A′B′C′*. Then, reflect triangle *A′B′C′* over line *m*. Label the image *A″B″C″*.

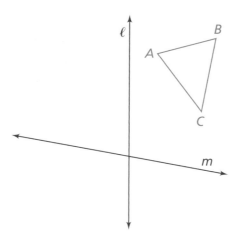

    a. Can you "move" triangle *ABC* exactly onto triangle *A″B″C″* with a single flip, turn, or slide? If so, describe the transformation.

    b. Experiment with reflecting figures in two intersecting lines. Make a conjecture based on your findings.

39. In the diagram below, lines *a* and *b* are parallel. On a copy of the diagram, reflect triangle *EFG* in line *a*. Label the image *E′F′G′*. Then, reflect triangle *E′F′G′* in line *b*. Label the image *E″F″G″*.

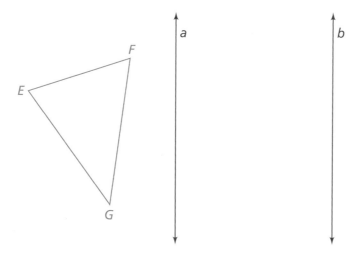

    a. Can you "move" triangle *EFG* exactly onto triangle *E″F″G″* with a single flip, turn, or slide? If so, describe the transformation.

    b. Experiment with reflecting figures in two parallel lines. Make a conjecture based on your findings.

Mathematical Reflections

In this Investigation, you used geometric transformations to describe and construct symmetric figures. The following questions will help you summarize what you have learned.

Think about these questions. Discuss your ideas with other students and your teacher. Then write a summary of your findings in your notebook.

1. **How** would you explain to someone how to make a design with

   a. reflectional symmetry?

   b. rotational symmetry?

   c. translational symmetry?

2. **How** are points and their images related by each of these geometric transformations?

   a. reflection in line *m*

   b. rotation of $d°$ about point *P*

   c. translation with distance and direction set by the segment from point *X* to point *X'*

3. **How** do reflections, rotations, and translations change the size and shape of line segments, angles, and/or polygons, if at all?

Common Core Mathematical Practices

As you worked on the Problems in this Investigation, you used prior knowledge to make sense of them. You also applied Mathematical Practices to solve the Problems. Think back over your work, the ways you thought about the Problems, and how you used Mathematical Practices.

Nick described his thoughts in the following way:

> In Problem 1.1, we used rulers to measure distances between points and their images so we could locate the line of symmetry of a design.
>
> We also used rulers to measure the distance between each vertex of a figure and a given reflection line so we could find the image.
>
> It turns out that you have to make sure that the distance from a point to the line is a perpendicular distance. If you do not check this with a protractor, the image is not accurate.

Common Core Standards for Mathematical Practice
MP5 Use appropriate tools strategically.

- What other Mathematical Practices can you identify in Nick's reasoning?

- Describe a Mathematical Practice that you and your classmates used to solve a different Problem in this Investigation.

Transformations and Congruence

You can use reflections, rotations, and translations to arrange copies of a basic design element in a symmetric pattern, as in the kaleidoscope patterns shown below.

- Can you find the basic design element in each kaleidoscope pattern?

- What transformations could you use on the basic design element to make the symmetric patterns?

Two figures that have the same size and shape are **congruent.** If you can flip, turn, and/or slide one figure exactly onto the other, the figures must be congruent. In this Investigation, you will compare the size and shape of geometric figures after a sequence of transformations.

....

Common Core State Standards

8.G.A.1 Verify experimentally the properties of rotations, reflections, and translations:

8.G.A.1a Lines are taken to lines, and line segments to line segments of the same length.

8.G.A.1b Angles are taken to angles of the same measure.

8.G.A.2 Understand that a two-dimensional figure is congruent to another if the second can be obtained from the first by a sequence of rotations, reflections, and translations; given two congruent figures, describe a sequence that exhibits the congruence between them.

2.1 Connecting Congruent Polygons

When two polygons are congruent, you can match the vertices in a way that pairs sides and angles of the same size. Quadrilaterals *ABCD* and *PQRS* are congruent.

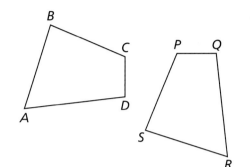

- What are the pairs of congruent sides and angles?

- How can you flip, turn, and/or slide one quadrilateral onto the other?

In this Problem, you will learn the standard language and symbols for describing congruent figures.

Problem 2.1

A Suppose you copied quadrilateral *ABCD* above, and moved the copy so that it fit exactly on quadrilateral *PQRS*. Copy and complete these statements to show which vertices correspond. The arrow means "corresponds to."

$A \rightarrow$ ▨ $B \rightarrow$ ▨ $C \rightarrow$ ▨ $D \rightarrow$ ▨

B The notation $\overline{AB}$ means "line segment *AB*." The symbol $\cong$ means "is congruent to." Copy and complete these statements to show which pairs of sides in the two quadrilaterals are congruent.

$\overline{AB} \cong$ ▨ $\overline{BC} \cong$ ▨ $\overline{CD} \cong$ ▨ $\overline{DA} \cong$ ▨

C The notation $\angle A$ means "angle *A*." Copy and complete these statements to show which angles are congruent.

$\angle A \cong$ ▨ $\angle B \cong$ ▨ $\angle C \cong$ ▨ $\angle D \cong$ ▨

D **1.** Use a copy of quadrilateral *ABCD*. Investigate combinations of reflections, rotations, and translations that will move the copy exactly onto quadrilateral *PQRS*. Describe the exact transformations that will accomplish this. Is there more than one way?

2. How could you rename quadrilateral *PQRS* so that the name shows how its vertices correspond to those of quadrilateral *ABCD*?

A C E Homework starts on page 38.

2.2 Supporting the World
Congruent Triangles I

In Problem 2.1, you matched quadrilateral *ABCD* to quadrilateral *PQRS*. One sequence of transformations that accomplishes this is shown below. Since you can "move" quadrilateral *ABCD* onto quadrilateral *RSPQ*, you know these shapes are congruent.

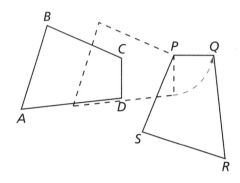

In this Problem, you are going to focus on congruent triangles. Triangles are a very special family of geometric figures. They are used in many construction projects to provide strength and stability for structures.

For example, this photograph of the George Washington Bridge, connecting New Jersey and New York City, shows congruent triangles in the bridge's towers.

Problem 2.2

For each pair of triangles:

- Inspect and measure parts of the figures to determine whether they are congruent.

- If the triangles are congruent, list the corresponding vertices.

- If the triangles are congruent, describe a sequence of transformations that would move one triangle onto the other.

A Are triangles *ABC* and *XYZ* congruent?

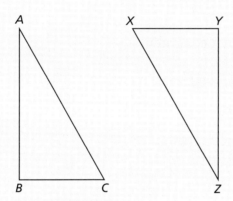

B Are triangles *DEF* and *STU* congruent?

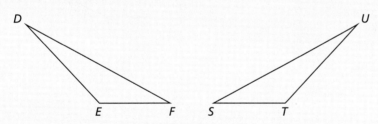

C Are triangles *GHI* and *VWX* congruent?

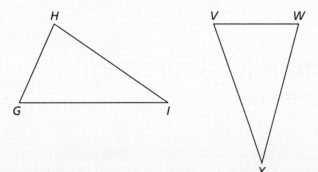

continued on the next page >

Problem **2.2** *continued*

D Are triangles *JKL* and *MNO* congruent?

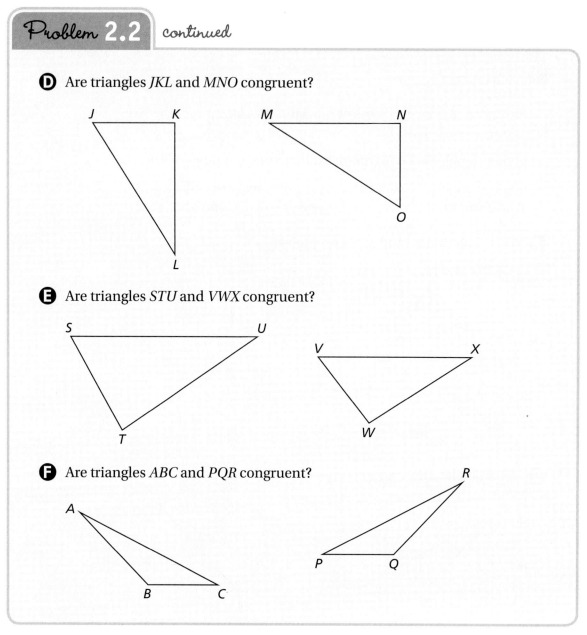

E Are triangles *STU* and *VWX* congruent?

F Are triangles *ABC* and *PQR* congruent?

 Homework starts on page 38.

2.3 Minimum Measurement
Congruent Triangles II

▶ In Problem 2.2, you might have noticed that it is not necessary to move one triangle onto the other to determine whether two triangles are congruent. If you know that the corresponding sides and angles are equal, you can conclude that the triangles are congruent.

For example, in triangles *ABC* and *RQP* below, ∠*A* ≅ ∠*R*, ∠*B* ≅ ∠*Q*, ∠*C* ≅ ∠*P*, $\overline{AB}$ ≅ $\overline{RQ}$, $\overline{BC}$ ≅ $\overline{QP}$, and $\overline{CA}$ ≅ $\overline{PR}$. Since all *corresponding parts* are congruent, the two triangles are congruent. Triangles *ABC* and *RQP* show a common way of marking congruent sides and angles. The sides with the same number of tic marks are congruent. The angles with the name number of arcs are congruent.

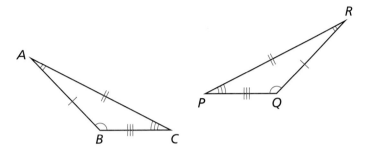

In this Problem, you will explore whether you need to know the measures of all the sides and angles of two triangles in order to determine congruence.

 Can you conclude that two triangles are congruent if you know the measures of only one, two, or three pairs of corresponding parts? Explain.

Problem 2.3

Consider the conditions described in Questions A–C. For each case, give an argument to support your answer. If the conditions are not enough to determine two triangles are congruent, give a counterexample.

A Can you be sure that two triangles are congruent if you know only

   1. one pair of congruent corresponding sides?

   2. one pair of congruent corresponding angles?

B Can you be sure that two triangles are congruent if you know only

   1. two pairs of congruent corresponding sides?

   2. two pairs of congruent corresponding angles?

   3. one pair of congruent corresponding sides and one pair of congruent corresponding angles?

continued on the next page >

Problem 2.3 continued

C Can you be sure that two triangles are congruent if you know

  1. two pairs of congruent corresponding angles and one pair of congruent corresponding sides as shown? Use your understanding of transformations to justify your answer.

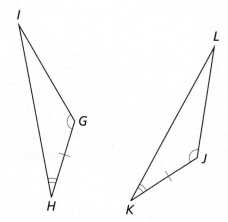

  2. two pairs of congruent corresponding sides and one pair of congruent corresponding angles as shown? Use your understanding of transformations to justify your answer.

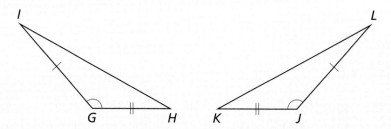

D Amy and Becky have different ideas about how to decide whether the conditions in Question C, part (2) are enough to show triangles are congruent.

  1. Amy flips triangle *GHI* as shown. She says you can translate the triangle so that $H \rightarrow K$ and $G \rightarrow J$. So all the measures in triangle *GHI* match measures in triangle *JKL*. Do you agree with Amy's reasoning? Explain.

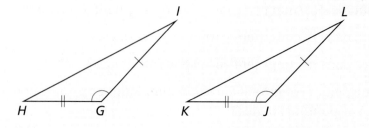

Problem **2.3** | *continued*

2. Becky thinks Amy should also explain why the translation matches *all* the sides and angles. She says that if you translate triangle *GHI* so that *G* → *J*, there will be two parallelograms in the figure. These parallelograms show her which corresponding angles and sides are congruent. What parallelograms does she see? How do these parallelograms help identify congruent corresponding sides and angles?

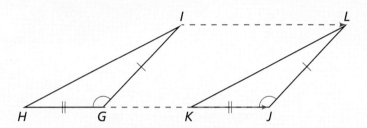

E 1. Can you be sure that two triangles are congruent if you know three pairs of congruent corresponding angles? Explain.

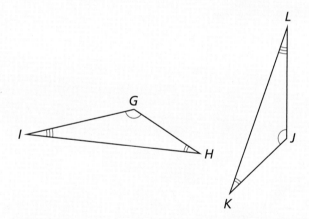

2. Are there any other combinations of three congruent corresponding parts that will guarantee two triangles are congruent? Make sketches to justify your answer.

3. Suppose two triangles appear to be *not* congruent. What is the minimum number of measures you should check to show they are not congruent?

A C E Homework starts on page 38.

Applications

In Exercises 1–4, the shapes in each pair are congruent. Match each vertex of the first shape to its corresponding vertex in the second shape.

1.

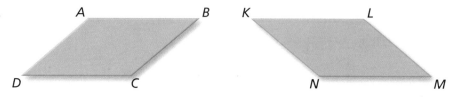

2.

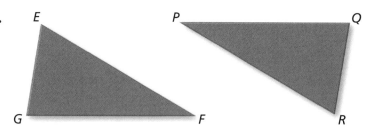

3. S

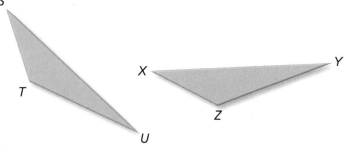

4.

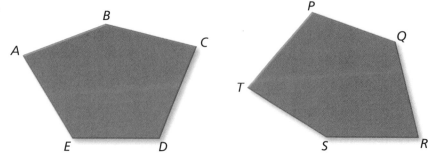

5. The figure below shows rectangle *JKLM* and its diagonals $\overline{JL}$ and $\overline{KM}$. List all pairs of congruent triangles in the figure, labeling each in a way that shows the corresponding vertices.

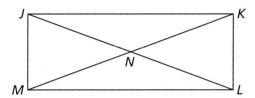

6. Select three different pairs of congruent triangles you identified in Exercise 5. Describe the flip, turn, and/or slide that would "move" one exactly onto the other.

For Exercises 7–12, decide whether you can tell that triangles in each pair are congruent based *only* on the given information.

7.

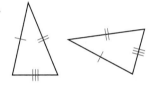

8.

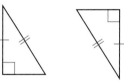

9.

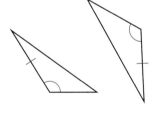

10.

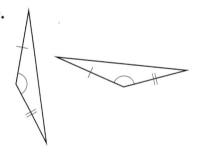

11.

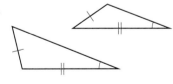

12.

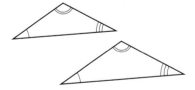

For Exercises 13–18, do the following for each pair of triangles.

- Inspect and measure parts of the figures to determine whether they are congruent.

- If the triangles are congruent, list the corresponding vertices.

- If the triangles are congruent, describe a sequence of transformations that would move one triangle onto the other.

13.

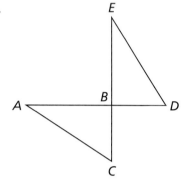

14.

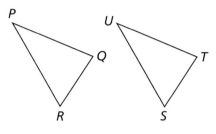

15.

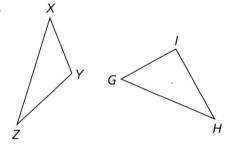

16.

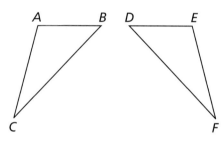

17.

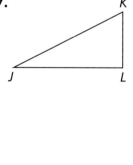

18.

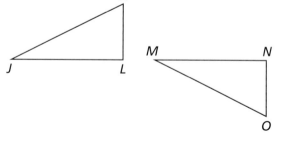

In Exercises 19–22, you are given a triangle *ABC* and information about another triangle, *DEF.* Tell whether triangle *DEF* is *definitely congruent* to triangle *ABC, possibly congruent* to triangle *ABC,* or *definitely not congruent* to triangle *ABC.* Explain your reasoning in each case.

19.

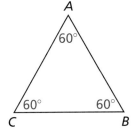

Angle *D*: 60°

Angle *E*: 60°

Angle *F*: 60°

20.

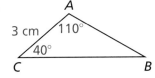

Angle *D*: 110°

Angle *E*: 40°

Side *DF*: 3 cm

21.

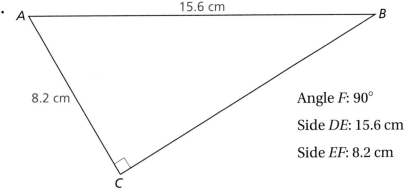

Angle *F*: 90°

Side *DE*: 15.6 cm

Side *EF*: 8.2 cm

22.

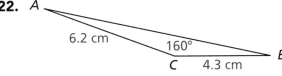

Angle F: 160°

Side *DF*: 4.3 cm

Side *EF*: 6.2 cm

Exercises 23–26 give different information for drawing the triangle below. Tell whether you would be certain to a draw a congruent copy of the triangle if you followed each set of directions.

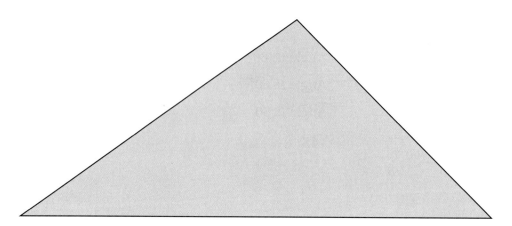

23. Draw ∠A with a measure of 35°, ∠B with a measure of 45°, and ∠C with a measure of 100°.

24. Draw ∠B with a measure of 45°, ∠C with a measure of 100°, and $\overline{AB}$ with a length of 5 inches.

25. Draw ∠B with a measure of 45°, $\overline{AB}$ with a length of 5 inches, and ∠A with a measure of 35°.

26. Draw ∠B with a measure of 45°, $\overline{AB}$ with a length of 5 inches, and $\overline{BC}$ with a length of 2.9 inches.

Connections

27. The kaleidoscope design at the right is composed of three congruent parts.

a. What is the shape of the basic design element for the symmetric pattern?

b. At what angle would you need to rotate the basic design element to complete the design?

28. Assume that the wallpaper design at the right extends without end in all directions.

a. Under what slide transformations would the design appear to be "unmoved" to a person who blinked while the transformation happened?

b. What basic design element could you use to produce the whole wallpaper design using only slide transformations?

c. What basic design element could you use to produce the whole wallpaper design using any transformation?

29. Are the circles shown below congruent? Explain your reasoning.

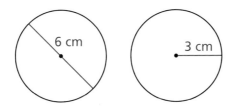

30. Use the rectangle and parallelogram at the right.

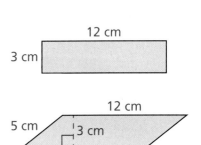

a. Find the perimeter and area of each figure.

b. Use your answers from part (a) and other examples, as needed, to justify your answers.

  i. If two shapes have the same perimeter, must the shapes be congruent?

  ii. If two shapes have the same area, must the shapes be congruent?

  iii. If two shapes have the same perimeter, must they have the same area?

  iv. If two shapes have the same area, must they have the same perimeter?

31. Suppose a friend asks you to draw a quadrilateral *ABCD* with
AB = 4 centimeters, ∠*B* = 120°, and *BC* = 3 centimeters.

a. Do you have enough information to draw the exact quadrilateral
your friend has in mind?

b. Suppose your friend also tells you that the quadrilateral is a
parallelogram. Will you be able to draw the exact shape with this
additional information?

c. What is the least amount of information about side lengths and
angle measures you would need to draw a quadrilateral *EFGH*
that is an exact copy of another quadrilateral *ABCD*?

32. Alejandro wants to build a footbridge directly across a pond from
point *A* to point *B*. He needs to find the length of $\overline{AB}$. He places
stakes at points *A*, *B*, and *C* to form a right triangle as shown in the
diagram below.

a. Where should Alejandro place the stakes for points *D* and *E* to
form a congruent triangle he can then measure?

b. What measurement will tell him the length of $\overline{AB}$?

33. Use triangle *ABC* below.

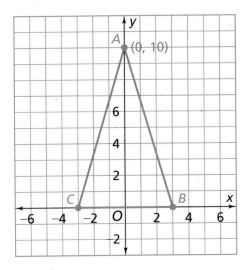

a. Explain how you know that $\triangle AOC \cong \triangle AOB$.

b. List the congruent corresponding sides and angles of the two figures.

34. Use trapezoid *PQRS* below.

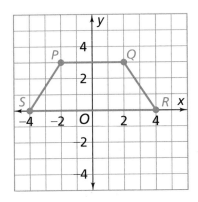

a. Explain how you know that $\overline{PS} \cong \overline{QR}$.

b. Explain how you know that $\angle P \cong \angle Q$ and $\angle S \cong \angle R$.

35. You know that triangles are rigid figures, but quadrilaterals are not.

   a. How is the rigidity of triangles related to the fact that when two triangles have three pairs of congruent corresponding sides, the triangles are congruent?

   b. How does this principle explain why braces are often used to help rectangular structures hold their shape?

 # Extensions

36. A teacher asks her students to explain whether or not the triangles shown below are congruent. One student argues that the triangles are congruent because there are two pairs of congruent corresponding sides and one pair of congruent corresponding angles. Do you agree or disagree? Explain.

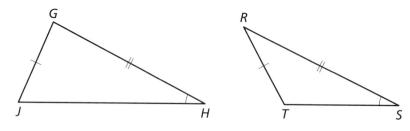

37. If two rectangles have the same area and the same perimeter, must they be congruent? Explore a variety of cases to develop a conjecture about this question.

38. In △*FGH* below, $\overline{FM}$ and $\overline{GN}$ are on lines of symmetry.

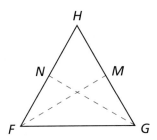

What does this symmetry tell you about

a. the angle measures in △*FGH*?

b. the side lengths in △*FGH*?

39. Pentagon *PQRST* has rotational symmetry about point *C* with an angle of rotation of 72°.

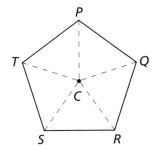

What does this symmetry tell you about

a. the angle measures of pentagon *PQRST*?

b. the side lengths of pentagon *PQRST*?

c. the segments from point *C* to each of the vertices?

40. In the figure below, $\overline{AB} \cong \overline{DE}$ and ∠*BAD* ≅ ∠*EDA*. Use this information to show that △*ABC* ≅ △*DEC*.

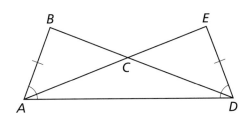

Mathematical Reflections 2

In this Investigation, you used geometric transformations to study congruence of figures. The following questions will help you summarize what you have learned.

Think about these questions. Discuss your ideas with other students and your teacher. Then write a summary of your findings in your notebook.

1. **How** can you find a sequence of flips, turns, and slides to "move" one figure exactly onto another to show that they are congruent?

2. **What** information about the sides and angles of two triangles will guarantee you can "move" one triangle onto the other?

3. **How** could you convince someone that two given triangles are *not* congruent?

Common Core Mathematical Practices

As you worked on the Problems in this Investigation, you used prior knowledge to make sense of them. You also applied Mathematical Practices to solve the Problems. Think back over your work, the ways you thought about the Problems, and how you used Mathematical Practices.

Shawna described her thoughts in the following way:

In Problem 2.2, we had to describe a sequence of transformations that would move one triangle onto another. It was challenging to break down the moves and describe exactly what was happening. We used tracing paper to show how two triangles match.

Once we knew the sequence of "moves" to make, we had to be very exact with the details. For flips, we provided the line of reflection. For turns, we provided the center and angle of rotation. For slides, we provided the direction and distance.

···

Common Core Standards for Mathematical Practice
MP6 Attend to precision.

- What other Mathematical Practices can you identify in Shawna's reasoning?

- Describe a Mathematical Practice that you and your classmates used to solve a different Problem in this Investigation.

Investigation 3

Transforming Coordinates

The computer programs that manage video displays for television shows and video games all use coordinate graphing systems. The axes and grid lines are hidden from view, but are essential to setting the color of the pixels that you see.

Rules for geometric transformations guide the movement of characters on the screen. In this Investigation, you will develop your understanding of coordinate rules for transformations and skill in using that knowledge to solve geometry problems.

3.1 Flipping on a Grid
Coordinate Rules for Reflections

When you draw a geometric figure on a grid, each point has a pair of coordinates. Most graphics programs have methods for moving figures from one position to another. The programs move key points (like vertices of polygons) first and then automatically fill in line segments to connect the key points. Recall that you followed this process to draw the Wump family in *Stretching and Shrinking*.

Common Core State Standards

8.G.A.2 Understand that a two-dimensional figure is congruent to another if the second can be obtained from the first by a sequence of rotations, reflections, and translations; given two congruent figures, describe a sequence that exhibits the congruence between them.

8.G.A.3 Describe the effect of dilations, translations, rotations, and reflections on two-dimensional figures using coordinates.

8.G.A.5 Use informal arguments to establish facts about the angle sum and exterior angle of triangles, about the angles created when parallel lines are cut by a transversal, and the angle-angle criterion for similarity of triangles.

Also 8.G.A.1, 8.G.A.1b, 8.G.A.1c

The diagram below shows a flag located in the first quadrant. Notice the labels on key points.

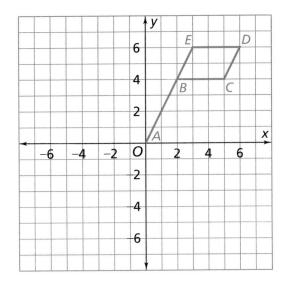

- How can you find the coordinates of the images of those key points under flips, turns, slides, and other sequences of transformations?

In this Problem, you will find rules to relate coordinates of key points on the flag to coordinates of their images after line reflections.

Problem 3.1

A Copy and complete the table showing the coordinates of points *A–E* and their images under a reflection in the *y*-axis.

Point	A	B	C	D	E
Original Coordinates	(0, 0)	(2, 4)	■	■	■
Coordinates After a Reflection	■	■	■	■	■

1. Write a rule relating coordinates of key points and their images after a reflection in the *y*-axis: $(x, y) \rightarrow (■, ■)$.

2. Would your rule give the correct coordinates if the flag started in the second, third, or fourth quadrant? Justify your answer with sketches and samples of coordinates that match.

3. **a.** Do any points remain unchanged under this reflection? Explain.

   b. Do the flag and its image make a symmetric design?

continued on the next page >

Problem **3.1** *continued*

B Copy and complete the table showing the coordinates of points *A–E* and their images under a reflection in the *x*-axis.

Point	A	B	C	D	E
Original Coordinates	(0, 0)	(2, 4)	▪	▪	▪
Coordinates After a Reflection	▪	▪	▪	▪	▪

1. Write a rule relating coordinates of key points and their images after a reflection in the *x*-axis: $(x, y) \rightarrow (▪, ▪)$.

2. Would your rule give the correct coordinates if the flag started in the second, third, or fourth quadrant? Justify your answer with sketches and samples of coordinates that match.

3. **a.** Do any points remain unchanged under this reflection? Explain.

   b. Do the flag and its image make a symmetric design?

C Copy and complete the table showing coordinates of points *A–E* and their images under a reflection in the line *y = x*.

Point	A	B	C	D	E
Original Coordinates	(0, 0)	(2, 4)	▪	▪	▪
Coordinates After a Reflection	▪	▪	▪	▪	▪

1. Write a rule relating coordinates of key points and their images after a reflection in the line $y = x$: $(x, y) \rightarrow (▪, ▪)$.

2. Would your rule give the correct coordinates if the flag started in the second, third, or fourth quadrant? Justify your answer with sketches and samples of coordinates that match.

 Homework starts on page 61.

3.2 Sliding on a Grid
Coordinate Rules for Translations

The diagram at the right shows four figures that look like Mug Wump with a hat. You can slide or translate Mug 1 to get the other three Mugs.

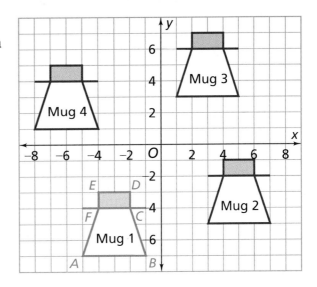

What coordinate rules for translations would "move" Mug 1 to the positions of the other Mugs?

Problem 3.2

Make a table of the coordinates of key points for Mug 1 and his images under the translations. Look for patterns.

Point	A	B	C	D	E	F
Coordinates of Mug 1	(−5, −7)	(−1, −7)	■	■	■	■
Coordinates of Mug 2	(3, −5)	■	■	■	■	■
Coordinates of Mug 3	■	■	■	■	■	■
Coordinates of Mug 4	■	■	■	■	■	■

A Write a rule showing how coordinates of key points on Mug 1 relate to their images after a translation to Mug 2: $(x, y) \rightarrow$ (■, ■).

B Write a rule showing how coordinates of key points on Mug 2 relate to their images after a translation to Mug 3: $(x, y) \rightarrow$ (■, ■).

continued on the next page >

Problem **3.2** *continued*

C Write a rule showing how coordinates of key points on Mug 3 relate to their images after a translation to Mug 4: $(x, y) \rightarrow (\blacksquare, \blacksquare)$.

D In Investigation 1, you learned that a translation of a segment, such as $\overline{AF}$, "moved" the segment to a *parallel* image segment.

    1. Find the image of $\overline{AF}$ on Mug 2, Mug 3, or Mug 4. Show that the image is parallel to $\overline{AF}$.

    2. How does the coordinate rule for any translation guarantee that a segment and its image will be parallel?

E Suppose a translation moves a figure *a* units horizontally and *b* units vertically on a coordinate grid. What rule describes the coordinates of each image point?

A C E Homework starts on page 61.

3.3 Spinning on a Grid
Coordinate Rules for Rotations

Look again at the flag in the first quadrant.

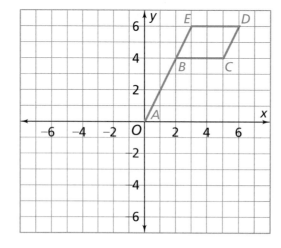

> **?** What coordinate rules for rotations would rotate the flag 90° or 180° counterclockwise about point *A*?

In this Problem, you will find rules relating coordinates of key points on the flag to coordinates of their images after quarter- and half-turn rotations.

Problem 3.3

A Rotate points *A–E* 90° counterclockwise about the origin. Copy and complete the table showing the coordinates of points *A′–E′*, which are the images of points *A–E*.

Point	A	B	C	D	E
Original Coordinates	(0, 0)	(2, 4)	▨	▨	▨
Coordinates After a 90° Rotation	▨	▨	▨	▨	▨

1. Write a rule for the pattern relating the coordinates of key points to the coordinates of their images after a rotation of 90°: $(x, y) \rightarrow (▨, ▨)$.

2. Would your rule give the correct coordinates if the flag started in the second, third, or fourth quadrant? Justify your answer with sketches and examples of coordinates that match.

3. **a.** Do any points remain unchanged under this rotation? Explain.

   b. Do the flag and its image make a symmetric design?

B Rotate points *A–E* another 90° counterclockwise about the origin so that they rotate a total of 180°. Copy and complete the table showing the coordinates of points *A″–E″*, which are the images of points *A′–E′*.

Point	A	B	C	D	E
Original Coordinates	(0, 0)	(2, 4)	▨	▨	▨
Coordinates After a 180° Rotation	▨	▨	▨	▨	▨

1. Write a rule for the pattern relating the coordinates of key points to the coordinates of their images after a rotation of 180°: $(x, y) \rightarrow (▨, ▨)$.

2. Would your rule give the correct coordinates if the flag started in the second, third, or fourth quadrant? Justify your answer with sketches and examples of coordinates that match.

 Homework starts on page 61.

3.4 A Special Property of Translations and Half-Turns

 When studying mathematical or scientific questions, asking yourself "What will happen if . . . ?" is helpful. In geometry, that means asking how properties of a figure will or will not change when you apply a transformation to it.

Your study of flips, turns, and slides showed that those transformations do not change the size or shape of a figure. Line segments "move" to line segments that are the same length. Angles "move" to angles of the same measure. In addition to these basic properties of transformations, translations and half-turn rotations have a special effect on lines.

The diagram below shows the effect of "moving" pentagon *ABCDE* in two ways. The first is a translation to pentagon *FGHIJ*. The second is a half-turn or 180° rotation about the origin to pentagon *KLMNO*.

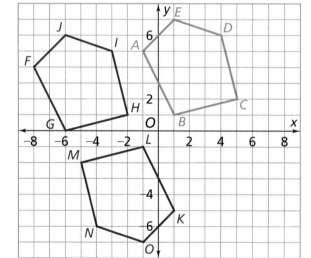

 • What is the special relationship among the corresponding sides of the three figures?

• How can you use the coordinates of the vertices to prove your conjecture?

In the Problem, you will discover and prove the special relationship among corresponding sides of pentagon *ABCDE* and its images after a translation and after a 180° rotation.

Problem 3.4

A Look at $\overline{AB}$ and its image after a translation, $\overline{FG}$.

1. In Investigation 1, you observed that a segment and its image after a translation appear to be congruent and parallel. Use the coordinates of the endpoints and slopes of lines to prove that your observation is correct.

2. Are other pairs of segments in pentagons *ABCDE* and *FGHIJ* related in the same way?

B Look at $\overline{AB}$ and its image after a half-turn, $\overline{KL}$.

1. How do the two segments appear to be related?

2. Use the coordinates of the endpoints to test your conjecture.

3. Are other pairs of segments in pentagons *ABCDE* and *KLMNO* related in the same way?

C Complete the following sentences to describe the pattern you found:

1. A translation "moves" every line *m* to a line *n* so that . . .

2. A half-turn "moves" every line *m* to a line *n* so that . . .

D If lines *m* and *n* are parallel, will it always be possible to find a translation or half-turn that "moves" one line onto the other? If so, what point should you choose for the center of the rotation? Explain.

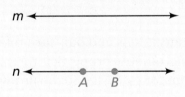

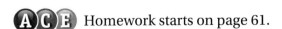

ACE Homework starts on page 61.

3.5 Parallel Lines, Transversals, and Angle Sums

In *Shapes and Designs*, you learned two very important and related properties of geometric figures.

> If a transversal cuts two parallel lines, many pairs of angles formed are congruent.

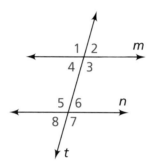

Angles 1, 3, 5, and 7 are congruent.
Angles 2, 4, 6, and 8 are congruent.

> In any triangle, the sum of the measures of the interior angles is equal to a straight angle, or 180°.

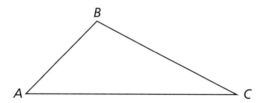

The sum of the measures of angles *A*, *B*, and *C* is 180°.

What you have learned about translations and half-turn rotations will help you explain why those two geometric properties are true. In this Problem, you will provide reasons for each step in the proofs of these two important properties.

Problem 3.5

For Questions A and B, use the diagram of the parallel lines and transversal on the previous page.

A Complete the following sentences to explain why angles 1, 3, 5, and 7 are congruent.

    1. Angles 1 and 3 are congruent because . . .

    2. Angles 5 and 7 are congruent because . . .

    3. What transformation "moves" angle 5 exactly onto angle 1? Explain.

    4. Are angles 1, 3, 5, and 7 all congruent? Explain.

B Construct an argument of your own to show that angles 2, 4, 6, and 8 are congruent.

C Use the transformations described below to explain why the sum of the measures of the interior angles of triangle *ABC* is 180°.

    1. Rotate triangle *ABC* 180° about point M_1, the midpoint of $\overline{AB}$. Mark any congruent corresponding angles and sides, and any parallel segments. Justify your claims.

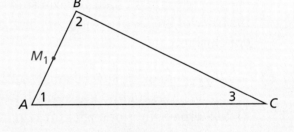

    2. Rotate triangle *ABC* 180° about point M_2, the midpoint of $\overline{BC}$. Mark any congruent corresponding angles and sides, and any parallel segments. Justify your claims.

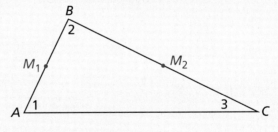

    3. How can you be sure that you have one straight line through point *B*, and not two nonparallel segments? Explain.

    4. How do triangle *ABC* and its images under 180° rotations about points M_1 and M_2 show that the sum of the measures of angles 1, 2, and 3 is 180°?

    5. Do you think this argument would work for any triangle? Explain.

continued on the next page >

Problem **3.5** *continued*

D Erin extended her drawing for Question C by continuing to rotate the images of triangle *ABC* around the midpoint of every side. The result is shown below.

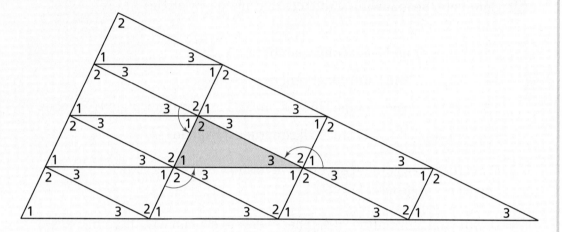

Erin says that if you know that the sum of the measures of the interior angles of a triangle is 180°, then you can show that the sum of the measures of the exterior angles of a triangle is 360°. How does her diagram support her conclusion?

E Another proof of the special angle-sum property of triangles uses a property of parallel lines cut by a transversal: If a transversal cuts two parallel lines, then alternate interior angles are congruent. In the diagram below, the line through point *B* is parallel to $\overline{AC}$.

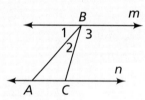

1. Which two angles are congruent because they are alternate interior angles formed by two parallel lines and a transversal?

2. How can you use this information about congruent angles to show that the sum of the measures of ∠*BAC*, ∠*ACB*, and ∠*ABC* is 180°?

A C E Homework starts on page 61.

Applications

For Exercises 1–7, make a copy of the figure below. Then, find the image of the figure after each transformation.

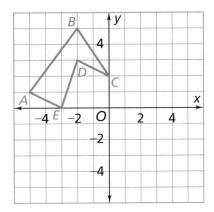

1. Copy and complete the table showing the coordinates of points *A–E* and their images after a reflection in the *y*-axis.

Point	A	B	C	D	E
Original Coordinates	(−5, 1)	(−2, 5)	■	■	■
Coordinates After a *y*-axis Reflection	■	■	■	■	■

   a. Draw the image.

   b. Write a rule relating coordinates of key points and their images after a reflection in the *y*-axis: $(x, y) \rightarrow (■, ■)$.

2. Add a row to your table from Exercise 1 to show the coordinates of points *A–E* and their images after a reflection in the *x*-axis.

   a. Draw the image.

   b. Write a rule relating coordinates of key points and their images after a reflection in the *x*-axis: $(x, y) \rightarrow (■, ■)$.

3. Add another row to your table from Exercise 1 to show the coordinates of points *A–E* and their images after a reflection in the *x*-axis, followed by a reflection in the *y*-axis.

   a. Draw the final image.

   b. Write a rule relating coordinates of key points and their images after both reflections: $(x, y) \rightarrow (\blacksquare, \blacksquare)$.

   c. What single transformation in this Investigation has the same effect as the sequence of two line reflections?

4. Copy and complete the table showing the coordinates of points *A–E* and their images after a translation that "moves" point *B* to point (3, 4).

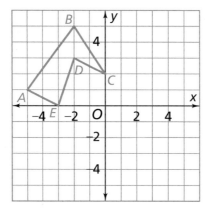

Point	A	B	C	D	E
Original Coordinates	(–5, 1)	(–2, 5)	▦	▦	▦
Coordinates After Translating *B* to (3, 4)	▦	▦	▦	▦	▦

   a. Draw the image.

   b. Write a rule relating coordinates of key points and their images after the translation: $(x, y) \rightarrow (\blacksquare, \blacksquare)$.

5. Add a row to your table from Exercise 4 to show the coordinates of points A–E and their images after the first translation, followed by a translation that "moves" point B' to (−1, 0).

  a. Draw the image.

  b. Write a rule relating coordinates of key points and their images after the second translation: $(x, y) \rightarrow (\blacksquare, \blacksquare)$.

  c. Write a rule relating coordinates of key points and their images after the sequence of the two translations: $(x, y) \rightarrow (\blacksquare, \blacksquare)$.

  d. What single transformation is equivalent to the sequence of the two translations?

6. Copy and complete the table showing the coordinates of points A–E and their images after a counterclockwise rotation of 90° about the origin.

Point	A	B	C	D	E
Original Coordinates	(−5, 1)	(−2, 5)	$\blacksquare$	$\blacksquare$	$\blacksquare$
Coordinates After a 90° Rotation	$\blacksquare$	$\blacksquare$	$\blacksquare$	$\blacksquare$	$\blacksquare$

  a. Draw the image.

  b. Write a rule relating coordinates of key points and their images after a rotation of 90°: $(x, y) \rightarrow (\blacksquare, \blacksquare)$.

7. Add a row to your table from Exercise 6 to show the coordinates of points A–E and their images after two counterclockwise rotations of 90° about the origin.

  a. Draw the final image.

  b. Write a rule relating coordinates of key points and their images after both rotations: $(x, y) \rightarrow (\blacksquare, \blacksquare)$.

  c. What single transformation is equivalent to the sequence of the two rotations?

8. **a.** Use triangle *ABC* shown in the diagram.

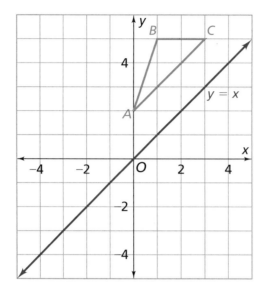

Copy and complete the table showing the coordinates of points *A–C* and their images after a reflection in the line *y = x*.

Point	A	B	C
Original Coordinates	▪	▪	▪
Coordinates After a Reflection in *y = x*	▪	▪	▪

b. Draw the image and label the vertices *A'*, *B'*, and *C'*.

c. Add a row to your table to show the coordinates of points *A–C* and their images after a reflection of triangle *A'B'C'* in the *x*-axis.

d. Draw the image and label the vertices *A"*, *B"*, and *C"*.

e. Draw the image of triangle *ABC* after the same two reflections, but in the reverse order. That is, reflect triangle *ABC* in the *x*-axis and then reflect its image, triangle *A'B'C'*, in the line *y = x*. What does the result suggest about the commutativity of a sequence of line reflections?

9. a. Use triangle *ABC* from Exercise 8. Draw triangle *ABC* on a coordinate grid.

  i. Translate A*BC* according to the rule $(x, y) \rightarrow (x + 2, y - 3)$. Label its image $A'B'C'$.

  ii. Translate *ABC* according to the rule $(x, y) \rightarrow (x - 4, y - 6)$. Label its image $A''B''C''$.

 b. Use the coordinates of the vertices of triangle *ABC* and its two images to compare the slopes of each pair of line segments.

  i. $\overline{AB}$ and $\overline{A'B'}$; $\overline{AC}$ and $\overline{A'C'}$; $\overline{CB}$ and $\overline{C'B'}$

  ii. $\overline{AB}$ and $\overline{A''B''}$; $\overline{AC}$ and $\overline{A''C''}$; $\overline{CB}$ and $\overline{C''B''}$

 c. What do your results from parts (a) and (b) say about the effect of translations on the slopes of lines? About the relationship between a line and its image under a translation?

10. a. Use triangle *ABC* from Exercise 8. Draw triangle *ABC* on a coordinate grid and its image after a 180° rotation about the origin. Label the image $A'B'C'$.

 b. Use the coordinates of the vertices of triangle *ABC* and its image to compare the slopes of each pair of line segments.

  i. $\overline{AB}$ and $\overline{A'B'}$ **ii.** $\overline{AC}$ and $\overline{A'C'}$ **iii.** $\overline{CB}$ and $\overline{C'B'}$

 c. What do your results from parts (a) and (b) say about the effect of half-turns or 180° rotations on the slopes of lines? About the relationship between a line and its image under a 180° rotation?

11. In the diagram below, lines L_1 and L_2 are parallel. What are the measures of angles *a–g*?

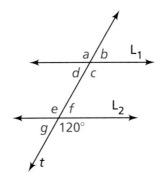

12. What are the measures of
angles *a* and *b* in the triangle
at the right?

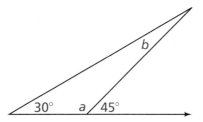

13. What is the value of *x* in the
diagram at the right?

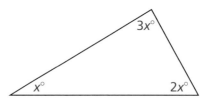

14. The diagram at the right
shows parallelogram *ABCD*
with one diagonal *DB*.
Assuming only that opposite
sides of any parallelogram
are parallel:

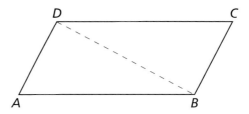

a. Which angles are congruent? How do you know?

b. How can you be sure that triangle *ABD* is congruent to triangle
ADB? What are the corresponding vertices, sides, and angles?

c. How does the congruence of triangles *ABD* and *ADB* imply that
the opposite angles of the parallelogram are congruent?

d. How does the congruence of triangles *ABD* and *ADB* guarantee
that, in a parallelogram, opposite sides are the same length?

15. The diagram below shows a rectangle with two diagonals.

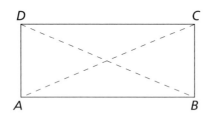

a. How can you be sure that triangle *ABC* is congruent to
triangle *BAD*?

b. Why does this congruence guarantee that, in a rectangle, the
diagonals are the same length?

Connections

16. Copy and complete the table of values for the function $y = -x^2$.
Remember: $-(-3)^2 = -9$.

x	−3	−2	−1	0	1	2	3
y	▨	▨	▨	▨	▨	▨	▨

   a. Use the table of values to graph the function $y = -x^2$.

   b. Describe the symmetries of the graph of the function $y = -x^2$.

17. Add a row to your table from Exercise 16 to show values of the
function $y = -x^2 + 4$.

   a. Use the values in the extended table. Graph $y = -x^2 + 4$ on the
same coordinate grid as $y = -x^2$ from Exercise 16.

   b. Write a coordinate rule that "moves"

      i. the graph of $y = -x^2$ to the position of the graph of $y = -x^2 + 4$.

      ii. the graph of $y = -x^2 + 4$ to the position of the graph of $y = -x^2$.

18. Complete the table of values for the function $y = |x|$.
Remember: $|-4| = |4| = 4$.

x	−4	−3	−2	−1	0	1	2	3	4
y	▨	▨	▨	▨	▨	▨	▨	▨	▨

   a. Use the table of values to graph the function $y = |x|$.

   b. Describe the symmetries of the graph of the function $y = |x|$.

19. Add a row to your table from Exercise 18 to show values of the
function $y = |x| - 3$.

   a. Use the values in the extended table. Graph $y = |x| - 3$ on the
same coordinate grid as $y = |x|$ from Exercise 18.

   b. Write a coordinate rule that "moves"

      i. the graph of $y = |x|$ to the position of the graph of $y = |x| - 3$.

      ii. the graph of $y = |x| - 3$ to the position of the graph of $y = |x|$.

20. Points *A* and *B* are on the *x*-axis.

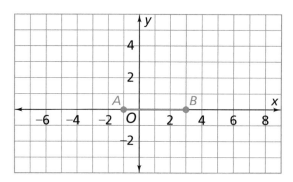

a. Compare the *x*-coordinates of points *A* and *B*.

b. Translate points *A* and *B* five units to right. Compare the *x*-coordinates of the image points.

c. Translate points *A* and *B* five units to left. Compare the *x*-coordinates of the image points.

d. Rotate points *A* and *B* 180° about the origin. Compare the *x*-coordinates of the image points.

e. Write a general rule about the effect of adding or subtracting a constant *c* from two integers, *a* and *b*. Complete the following sentence: If $a < b$, then when you add a constant *c* to *a* and *b* . . . .

f. Write a general rule about the effect of multiplying integers *a* and *b* by −1. Complete the following sentence: If $a < b$, then when you multiply each by −1 . . . .

For Exercises 21 and 22, describe the symmetries of each design.

21.

22.

23. **Multiple Choice** Squares, rectangles, and rhombuses are all types of parallelograms. Which of these statements is true for all parallelograms?

    A. The diagonals are congruent.

    B. Each diagonal divides the other in two congruent segments.

    C. The diagonals divide a parallelogram into four congruent triangles.

    D. The diagonals bisect the angles at each vertex.

24. What is the area of triangle ABC?

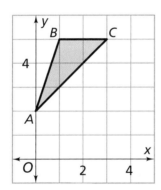

25. What are the side lengths and the perimeter of triangle ABC from Exercise 24?

Extensions

For Exercises 26–28, draw the figure on grid paper. Then, use symmetry transformations to draw a design that meets the given condition(s). Describe the transformations you used and the order in which you applied them.

26. a design that has at least two lines of symmetry

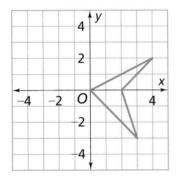

27. a design that has rotational symmetry

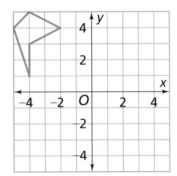

28. a design that has both reflectional and rotational symmetry

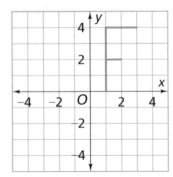

29. Multiple Choice Which of these statements is *not* true about the figure below if lines *m* and ℓ are parallel?

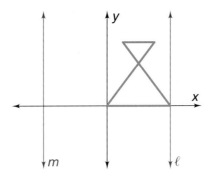

F. Reflecting the figure in the *y*-axis, and then reflecting the image in the *x*-axis, gives the same final image as rotating the figure 180° about the origin.

G. Reflecting the figure in line ℓ, and then reflecting the image in the *y*-axis, gives the same final image as reflecting the figure in line *m*.

H. Reflecting the figure in the *y*-axis and then rotating the image 180° about the origin gives the same final image as reflecting the figure in the *x*-axis.

J. Rotating the figure 90° counterclockwise about the origin and then rotating the image another 90° counterclockwise gives the same image as rotating the original image 180° about the origin.

30. Investigate what happens when you rotate a figure 180° about a point and then rotate the image 180° about a different point. Is the combination of the two rotations equivalent to a single transformation? Test several cases and make a conjecture about the result.

You might start your investigation with the figures below. Copy them onto grid paper. Rotate each polygon 180° about point C_1 and then 180° about point C_2.

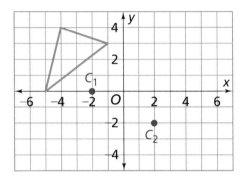 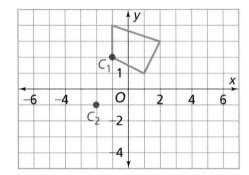

31. Plot points $P(-2, 4)$ and $Q(2, 1)$ on a coordinate grid.

   a. Find the coordinates of the points P' and Q' that are the images of points P and Q after a reflection in the x-axis. Then, use the Pythagorean Theorem to prove that $PQ = P'Q'$.

   b. Find coordinates of the points P'' and Q'' that are the images of points P and Q after a counterclockwise rotation of 180° about the origin. Then, prove that $PQ = P''Q''$.

   c. Find coordinates of the points P''' and Q''' that are the images of points P and Q after a translation with the rule $(x, y) \rightarrow (x + 3, y - 5)$. Then, prove that $PQ = P'''Q'''$.

Mathematical Reflections 3

In this Investigation, you used coordinate methods to study flips, turns, and slides. You also studied properties of parallel lines and properties of angles in triangles. The following questions will help you summarize what you have learned.

Think about these questions. Discuss your ideas with other students and your teacher. Then write a summary of your findings in your notebook.

1. **What** are the general forms of the coordinate rules for these transformations?

   a. reflection in the y-axis

   b. reflection in the x-axis

   c. counterclockwise rotation of 90° about the origin

   d. counterclockwise rotation of 180° about the origin

   e. translation that "moves" points a units horizontally and b units vertically

2. **What** is the effect of translations and half-turns on lines?

3. **How** has your knowledge of transformations changed or extended what you already knew about the angles formed by two parallel lines and a transversal?

4. **How** has your knowledge of transformations changed or extended what you already knew about the sum of the angle measures of a triangle?

Common Core Mathematical Practices

As you worked on the Problems in this Investigation, you used prior knowledge to make sense of them. You also applied Mathematical Practices to solve the Problems. Think back over your work, the ways you thought about the Problems, and how you used Mathematical Practices.

Tori described her thoughts in the following way:

In Problem 3.5, I really liked how understanding transformations helped me prove that the sum of the measures of the interior angles of a triangle is 180°, and the sum of the measures of the exterior angles is 360°. I remember showing this in *Shapes and Designs* by measuring angles.

Using transformations to show these results are always true, not just for the examples I drew and measured, was very satisfying. I like this way of reasoning better because it is visual, but does not depend on specific measurements.

....

Common Core Standards for Mathematical Practice

MP3 Construct viable arguments and critique the reasoning of others.

 • What other Mathematical Practices can you identify in Tori's reasoning?

• Describe a Mathematical Practice that you and your classmates used to solve a different Problem in this Investigation.

Dilations and Similar Figures

The Problems of the first three Investigations focused on ideas and techniques for recognizing and making symmetric patterns. They also focused on comparing figures to see if they have identical shape and size. You know, from earlier work in *Stretching and Shrinking*, that interesting things happen when you enlarge or reduce a figure.

For example, in one Investigation, you used a rubber band tool to enlarge the logo for a mystery club. In another Investigation, you compared various transformations of Mug Wump.

- Which characters are members of the Wump family, and which are impostors?

Common Core State Standards

8.EE.B.6 Use similar triangles to explain why the slope *m* is the same between any two distinct points on a non-vertical line in the coordinate plane . . .

8.G.A.4 Understand that a two-dimensional figure is similar to another if the second can be obtained from the first by a sequence of rotations, reflections, translations, and dilations; given two similar two-dimensional figures, describe a sequence that exhibits the similarity between them.

8.G.A.5 Use informal arguments to establish facts about the angle sum and exterior angle of triangles, about the angles created when parallel lines are cut by a transversal, and the angle-angle criterion for similarity of triangles.

Also 8.G.A.3

By measuring the figures that result from stretching or shrinking operations, you learned about **similarity transformations.** These are actions that change the size, but not the shape, of geometric figures. In this Investigation, you will review and extend your understanding of dilations and other similarity transformations.

4.1 Focus on Dilations

The key part of any similarity transformation is a **dilation.** The diagram below shows how a dilation, centered at point *P* with scale factor $\frac{3}{2}$ or 1.5, transforms triangle *ABC* to triangle *XYZ*. The two triangles are **similar figures.**

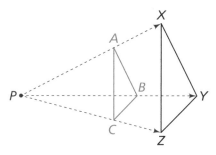

In everyday language, a "dilation" is usually an enlargement with a scale factor greater than 1. In mathematics, the scale factor of a dilation may be greater than or less than 1. A scale factor greater than 1 causes stretching, while a scale factor less than 1 causes shrinking. In fact, the diagram above also shows how a dilation with center *P* and scale factor $\frac{2}{3}$, or about 0.67, transforms triangle *XYZ* to triangle *ABC*.

 How do dilations affect the size and shape of the figures they transform?

In this Problem, you will review the properties of stretching and shrinking transformations by working with figures on a coordinate grid.

Problem 4.1

A Copy the figure below onto grid paper. Draw the image of quadrilateral *PQRS* after a dilation with center (0, 0) and scale factor 3. Label corresponding points *P′*, *Q′*, *R′*, and *S′*.

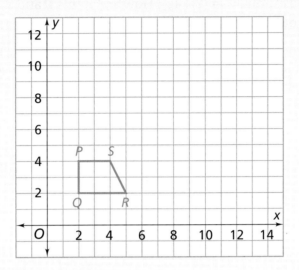

1. How do the side lengths of quadrilateral *P′Q′R′S′* compare to those of quadrilateral *PQRS*?

2. How do the angle measures of quadrilateral *P′Q′R′S′* compare to those of quadrilateral *PQRS*?

3. How does the perimeter of quadrilateral *P′Q′R′S′* compare to that of quadrilateral *PQRS*?

4. How does the area of quadrilateral *P′Q′R′S′* compare to that of quadrilateral *PQRS*?

5. How do the slopes of the sides of quadrilateral *P′Q′R′S′* compare to the slopes of the sides of quadrilateral *PQRS*?

6. What rule of the form $(x, y) \rightarrow (\blacksquare, \blacksquare)$ shows how coordinates of corresponding points are related under a dilation with center (0, 0) and scale factor 3?

continued on the next page >

Problem 4.1 continued

B On the drawing from Question A, draw $\overline{OP}$, $\overline{OP'}$, $\overline{OQ}$, and $\overline{OQ'}$.

   1. What similar triangles do you see? Explain.

   2. a. Suppose point $Z = (2z, 4z)$. How are points P and Z related to each other?

      b. Use coordinates to find the slopes of $\overline{OP}$, $\overline{OP'}$, $\overline{OZ}$, and $\overline{PZ}$. What do you notice? Explain why your discovery makes sense.

C Copy the figure below onto grid paper. Draw the image of quadrilateral *PQRS* after a dilation with center $(0, 0)$ and scale factor $\frac{1}{2}$.

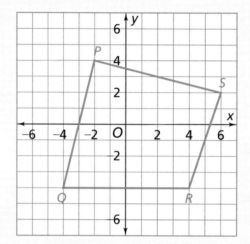

   1. How do the side lengths of quadrilateral $P'Q'R'S'$ compare to those of quadrilateral *PQRS*?

   2. How do the angle measures of quadrilateral $P'Q'R'S'$ compare to those of quadrilateral *PQRS*?

   3. How does the perimeter of quadrilateral $P'Q'R'S'$ compare to that of quadrilateral *PQRS*?

   4. How does the area of quadrilateral $P'Q'R'S'$ compare to that of quadrilateral *PQRS*?

   5. How do the slopes of the sides of quadrilateral $P'Q'R'S'$ compare to the slopes of the sides of quadrilateral *PQRS*?

   6. What rule of the form $(x, y) \rightarrow (\blacksquare, \blacksquare)$ shows how coordinates of corresponding points are related under a dilation with center $(0, 0)$ and scale factor $\frac{1}{2}$?

Problem **4.1** *continued*

D Use your results from Questions A and B to write conjectures about the effects of a dilation with scale factor k on a polygon. If necessary, try dilating a few more figures.

Begin your conjectures with: "When two polygons are related by a dilation with scale factor k, . . ."

E If you dilate a figure with reflectional or rotational symmetry, will the resulting image have the same symmetry? Explain.

A C E Homework starts on page 86.

4.2 Return of Super Sleuth
Similarity Transformations

Dilations transform geometric figures to larger or smaller versions of the same shape. The diagram below shows two versions of the "Super Sleuth" logo for the P. I. Middle School Mystery Club. They appear to be similar, but there is no obvious center or scale factor for a dilation that would stretch or shrink one image onto the other.

? What strategies could you use to check the similarity of the two figures?

If you can find a sequence of reflections, rotations, and/or translations that "move" one figure onto the other, then the two figures are congruent. In this Problem, you will decide if the same strategy works for testing the similarity of figures.

Problem 4.2

For each pair of polygons:

- Inspect and measure the parts of the figures to determine whether they are similar.

- If the figures are similar, list the corresponding vertices.

- If the figures are similar, describe a sequence of reflections, rotations, translations, and/or dilations that would move and then stretch or shrink one figure onto the other.

A Are triangles *ABC* and *PQR* similar?

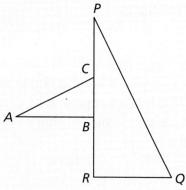

B Are rectangles *DEFG* and *STUV* similar?

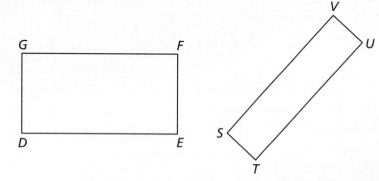

Problem 4.2 continued

C Are parallelograms *GHIJ* and *VWXY* similar?

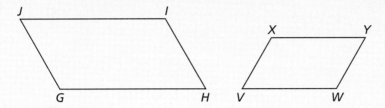

D What clues do you look for when identifying similar polygons?

A C E Homework starts on page 86.

4.3 Checking Similarity Without Transformations

In Investigation 2, you learned how to determine whether two triangles are congruent without actually "moving" one onto the other. That suggests there might be comparable strategies for testing the similarity of triangles.

If two triangles are similar, corresponding angles are congruent and the corresponding sides are related by a scale factor *k*.

For example, in triangles *ABC* and *XYZ*, you can measure to check that:

$$\angle X \cong \angle A \qquad XY = 2 \cdot AB$$
$$\angle Y \cong \angle B \qquad YZ = 2 \cdot BC$$
$$\angle Z \cong \angle C \qquad ZX = 2 \cdot CA$$

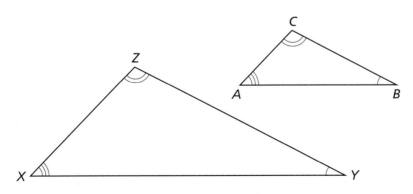

In this Problem, you will explore whether you need to measure all the sides and angles of the triangles to determine similarity.

 Can you conclude that two triangles are similar if you know the measures of only one, two, or three pairs of corresponding parts? Explain.

 Problem 4.3

The students at Palms Middle School have different ideas about whether they need to measure all the sides and angles of two triangles to determine similarity.

A Kevin and Ming think you only need to measure the angles of each triangle. They argue, "The angles give a polygon its shape. If two triangles have congruent corresponding angles, they will have the same shape and be similar."

Do you agree with their reasoning? Why or why not?

B Owen and Natasha agree that you need to measure angles, but have a different argument. They claim, "If two triangles have congruent corresponding angles, then you can flip, turn, and/or slide the smaller triangle onto the larger triangle as shown below. Then $\overline{AC}$ is parallel to $\overline{XZ}$, so a dilation centered at point Y will stretch triangle ABC exactly onto triangle XYZ. This proves that the original triangles are similar."

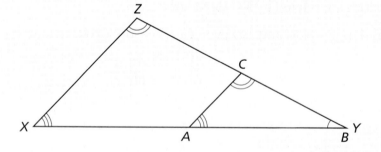

1. Do you agree with their reasoning? Why or why not?

2. How can they conclude that $\overline{AC}$ and $\overline{XZ}$ are parallel?

3. How can they conclude that a dilation centered at point Y would stretch triangle ABC onto triangle XYZ?

Problem **4.3** *continued*

C Kelly and Rico think you need to measure only two pairs of corresponding angles to guarantee similarity. They argue, "If you know the measures of two angles of a triangle, then you can subtract the sum of the two angles from 180° to find the measure of the third angle. If you know that the sum of two angles in one triangle is equal to the sum of two corresponding angles in another, then the third angles of those triangles must be equal in measure."

Do you agree with their reasoning? Why or why not?

D Complete this statement in a way that combines the ideas of the Palms Middle School students: If _____ angles in one triangle are equal in measure to _____ corresponding angles in another triangle, then . . .

E The shortcut for proving that two triangles are similar helps to verify other observations you might have made.

 1. In the figure below, the equation of the line is $y = ax + b$ and points P, Z, and W are on the line. Copy the diagram and find similar triangles. Explain why they are similar.

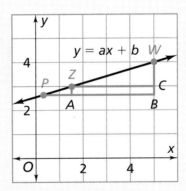

 2. How can you use the similar triangles to explain why the slope of $\overline{PZ}$ equals the slope of $\overline{PW}$ (or the slope of $\overline{ZW}$)? Explain.

A C E Homework starts on page 86.

4.4 Using Similar Triangles

 Similar triangles have the same shape, but are usually a different size. You can use the relationships between corresponding parts of similar triangles to solve measurement problems.

For example, the diagram below shows a method for calculating the height of an object that is difficult to measure directly. Place a mirror on a leveled spot at a convenient distance from the object. Back up from the mirror until you can see the reflection of the top of the object in the center of the mirror.

The two triangles in the diagram are similar. To find the object's height, you need to measure three distances and use similar triangles.

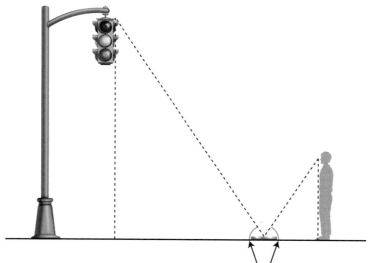

These angles are congruent because light reflects off a mirror at the same angle it hits the mirror.

Not drawn to scale

Problem 4.4

A Jim and Su use the mirror method to estimate the height of a traffic light near their school. They make the following measurements:

- height from the ground to Jim's eyes: 150 cm
- distance from the middle of the mirror to Jim's feet: 100 cm
- distance from the middle of the mirror to a point directly under the traffic signal: 450 cm

1. Sketch the situation to show the similar triangles formed. Label any parts of the triangles with the known measurements.

2. Explain how you know that the triangles are similar.

3. Use properties of similarity to estimate the height of the traffic light.

B Jim and Su also use the mirror method to estimate the height of the gymnasium in their school. They make the following measurements:

- height from the ground to Su's eyes: 130 cm
- distance from the middle of the mirror to Su's feet: 100 cm
- distance from the middle of the mirror to the gym wall: 9.5 m

1. Sketch the situation to show the similar triangles formed. Label any parts of the triangles with the known measurements.

2. Use properties of similarity to estimate the height of the gymnasium.

C Find an object that is too tall for you to measure directly. Use the mirror method to estimate its height. Make a sketch and explain how you used properties of similar triangles to estimate the height.

A C E Homework starts on page 86.

Applications

For Exercises 1–6, use the following figure.

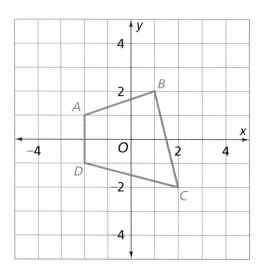

1. Copy the figure onto grid paper. Draw the image of quadrilateral *ABCD* under a dilation with center (0, 0) and scale factor 2. Label the image *A'B'C'D'*.

2. Find the side lengths of quadrilaterals *ABCD* and *A'B'C'D'*. How are the lengths of corresponding sides related?

3. Find the perimeters of quadrilaterals *ABCD* and *A'B'C'D'*. How are the two perimeters related?

4. Find the areas of quadrilaterals *ABCD* and *A'B'C'D'*. How are the two areas related?

5. Find the slopes of the sides of quadrilaterals *ABCD* and *A'B'C'D'*.

    a. How are the slopes of corresponding sides related?

    b. What does your answer to part (a) suggest about the relationship between a line and its image under a dilation?

6. What dilation would transform quadrilateral *A'B'C'D'* to quadrilateral *ABCD*?

For Exercises 7–10, suppose you dilate quadrilateral *ABCD* by a scale factor of 2. Then you flip, turn, or slide the image to quadrilateral *A″B″C″D″*.

7. Describe how the side lengths of quadrilateral *A″B″C″D″* are related to the side lengths of each quadrilateral.

   a. *ABCD*

   b. *A′B′C′D′*

8. Describe how the perimeter of quadrilateral *A″B″C″D″* is related to the perimeter of each quadrilateral.

   a. *ABCD*

   b. *A′B′C′D′*

9. Describe how the area of quadrilateral *A″B″C″D″* is related to the area of each quadrilateral.

   a. *ABCD*

   b. *A′B′C′D′*

10. Describe how the slopes of the sides of quadrilateral *A″B″C″D″* are related to the slopes of the sides of each quadrilateral.

   a. *ABCD*

   b. *A′B′C′D′*

For Exercises 11–15, tell whether the polygons in each pair are similar. For those that are similar, describe a sequence of flips, turns, slides, and/or dilations that would transform one to the other.

11.

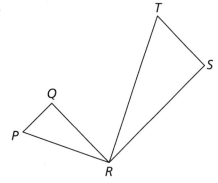

12.

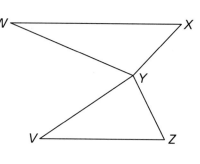

13.

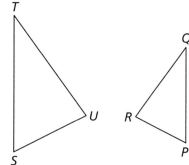

14.

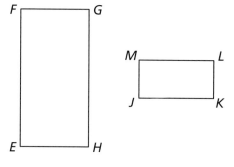

15.

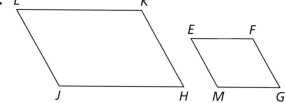

For Exercises 16–20, determine whether each statement is *true* or *false*. Justify your answer.

16. If $\angle P \cong \angle A$, $PQ = 2.5 \cdot AB$, and $PR = 2.5 \cdot AC$, you can conclude that the triangles are similar without measuring any more angles or sides.

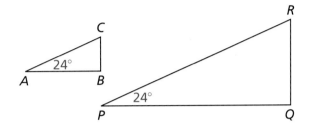

17. If $\overline{AB}$ is parallel to $\overline{DE}$, then triangles ABC and DEC are similar.

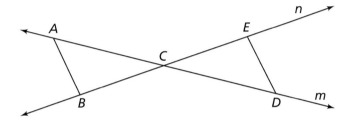

18. Any two equilateral triangles are similar to each other.

19. If corresponding angles of two polygons are congruent, then the polygons are similar.

20. Any two isosceles triangles are similar to each other.

21. Stan uses the mirror method to estimate the height of a building. His measurements are shown in the diagram below.

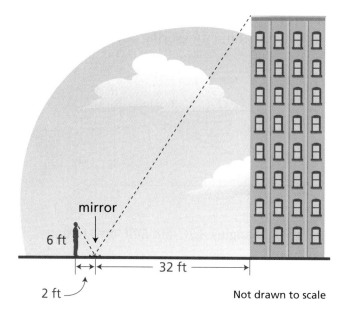

mirror

6 ft

2 ft

32 ft

Not drawn to scale

   a. How tall is the building?

   b. How do you know that your calculation is correct?

22. One afternoon, the building in Exercise 21 casts a shadow that is 10 feet long, while a nearby building casts a shadow that is 6 feet long.

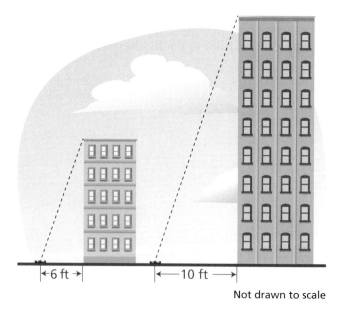

6 ft

10 ft

Not drawn to scale

   a. How tall is the shorter building?

   b. How do you know that your calculation is correct?

Connections

23. A sphere has a radius of 5 centimeters.

    a. What are the volume and surface area of the sphere?

    b. The sphere is dilated by a scale factor of 2.

        i. What is the surface area of the image?

        ii. What is the volume of the image?

    c. How can you find the answers to part (b) quickly by using your results from part (a)?

24. Consider the image of a figure after a dilation with center $(0, 0)$ and scale factor 1.5, followed by a dilation with center $(0, 0)$ and scale factor 4.

    a. What is the simplest coordinate rule that relates each point of the figure to its image after the two dilations?

    b. Suppose the order of the two dilations was reversed. Would the rule be different? Explain.

25. The figure below has reflectional symmetry in the y-axis.

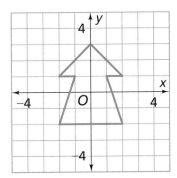

    a. Suppose the figure is dilated with scale factor 1.5 and center $(0, 0)$. Would the image have the same symmetry?

    b. Would the result be different with a different scale factor?

    c. Would the result be different if the center of dilation was outside the figure?

For Exercises 26 and 27, determine whether the given statement is *true* or *false*. Justify your answer.

  26. Any two squares are similar to each other.

  27. Any two rhombuses are similar to each other.

  28. The diagram below shows triangle *ABC* and its three images under a rotation of 180° about midpoints *M*, *N*, and *P*.

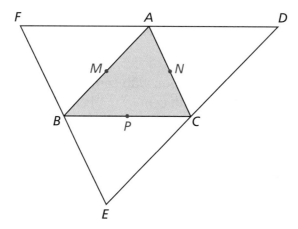

    a. Are any of the triangles in the diagram similar? If so, what is the scale factor? Explain.

    b. List all the parallelograms in the diagram. For each one, state why you think it is a parallelogram.

Extensions

29. Two students claim that you can determine whether two triangles are similar without measuring any angles. They say, "For example, if $XY = 2 \cdot AB$, $YZ = 2 \cdot BC$, and $ZX = 2 \cdot CA$, then triangles ABC and XYZ are similar."

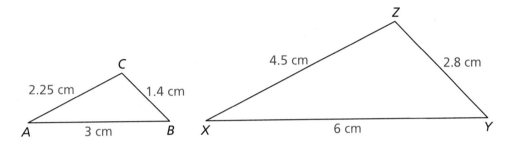

a. Do you think the students are correct? Explain.

b. Do you agree with their reasoning in the following proof? Explain why or why not.

> If triangles ABC and XYZ are similar, then the lengths of corresponding sides are proportional. That is, $\frac{XY}{AB} = \frac{YZ}{BC} = \frac{ZX}{CA} = 2$. If you dilate triangle ABC by a factor of 2, corresponding angles will be congruent. The image A′B′C′ will have side lengths that are congruent to those of triangle XYZ.
>
> So, triangle A'B'C' will be congruent to triangle XYZ and have congruent corresponding angles. This means that the angles of triangle ABC must be congruent to those of triangle XYZ, and the two triangles must be similar.

30. Suppose that a figure is transformed by two dilations, one after the other. The scale factors and centers of the two dilations are different. Will the final result be a dilation of the original figure with a different third center and scale factor?

Explore some simple cases to help you answer the question. For example, you might start with transformations of a simple triangle. Use centers of dilation (0, 0) and (1, 0) and scale factors 2 and 3.

31. Consider a one-directional dilation with rule $(x, y) \rightarrow (2x, y)$ instead of the basic dilation centered at the origin that "moves" $(x, y) \rightarrow (2x, 2y)$.

Experiment with a figure like the one below to see how the one-directional dilation works.

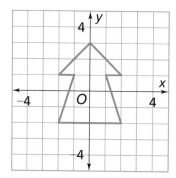

a. Does the transformation produce an image that is similar to the original figure?

b. How does the transformation affect the side lengths, angle measures, perimeter, and area of the figure?

c. How does the transformation affect the slopes of the sides of the figure?

Mathematical Reflections 4

In this Investigation, you used geometric transformations to study similarity of figures. The following questions will help you summarize what you have learned.

Think about these questions. Discuss your ideas with other students and your teacher. Then write a summary of your findings in your notebook.

1. **How** would you explain what it means for two geometric shapes to be similar using

   a. everyday words that most people could understand?

   b. technical terms of mathematics?

2. a. Suppose you dilate a polygon to form a figure of a different size. **How** will the side lengths, angle measures, perimeters, areas, and slopes of the sides of the two figures be alike? How will they be different?

   b. **How** has your knowledge of dilations changed or extended what you already knew about similarity?

3. **What** is the least amount of information you need in order to be sure that two triangles are similar?

4. **How** do you use similarity to find the side lengths of similar figures?

Common Core Mathematical Practices

As you worked on the Problems in this Investigation, you used prior knowledge to make sense of them. You also applied Mathematical Practices to solve the Problems. Think back over your work, the ways you thought about the Problems, and how you used Mathematical Practices.

Jayden described his thoughts in the following way:

In Problem 4.4, we applied what we knew about similar triangles to solve real-world problems. My group found the height of the flagpole outside the school by using the mirror method. We drew a diagram that showed how similar triangles model the situation. Then, we labeled the diagram with all the measurements we could find directly. Another group found the height of the school the same way, so we were able to compare our results to see if they made sense.

Common Core Standards for Mathematical Practice

MP4 Model with mathematics.

- What other Mathematical Practices can you identify in Jayden's reasoning?

- Describe a Mathematical Practice that you and your classmates used to solve a different Problem in this Investigation.

Unit Project

Making a Wreath and a Pinwheel

Origami is the Japanese art of paper folding. In this project, you will make an origami wreath and then transform your wreath into a pinwheel.

Materials

- 8 paper squares of the same size (4 paper squares in each of 2 colors gives a nice result)
- Scissors
- Ruler

Directions

The wreath is made by connecting eight folded squares. Follow these instructions to fold each square:

- Fold a paper square to make the creases as shown.

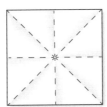

- Fold down the top corners of the square to make a "house." Then, fold the house in half so that the flaps are on the inside.

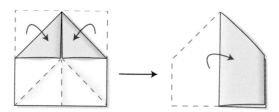

- Hold the "half-house" at its point, and push the bottom corner in along the folds to make a parallelogram.

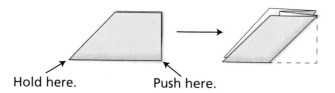

Hold here.   Push here.

Follow these steps to connect the eight pieces:

- Position two of the folded pieces as shown on the left below. (If you used different colors, use one piece of each color.) Slide the point of the right piece into the folded pocket of the left piece.

folded edge   folded edge

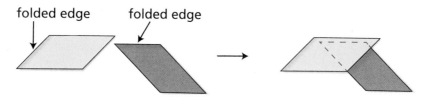

- Fold down the tips that extend over the inserted piece and tuck them into the valley formed by the folds of the inserted piece.

Fold these tips inward.   Tuck the tips into this pocket.

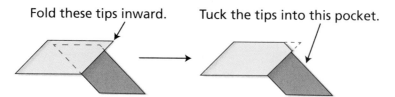

- Follow the steps on the previous page to attach the remaining folded pieces.

- Complete the wreath by connecting the last piece to the first piece, being careful to fold each flap over only one layer.

- To make a pinwheel, gently slide the sides of the wreath toward the center.

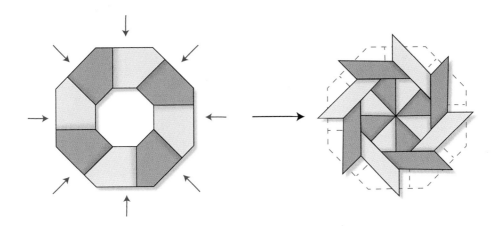

Study the drawings in the instructions for making the origami wreath and the pinwheel. Look for symmetries in the figures made at each stage.

1. Describe the reflectional and rotational symmetries of each figure.

   a. the square   **b.** the "house"   **c.** the "half-house"
   d. the parallelogram   **e.** the wreath   **f.** the pinwheel

2. Slide your pinwheel back into a wreath shape. If you gently push on a pair of opposite sides, you will get a pinwheel with only two "wings." Describe the reflectional and rotational symmetries of this figure.

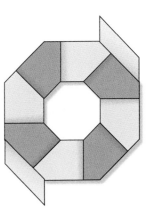

3. Slide your pinwheel back into a wreath shape. Gently push on opposite sides of the pinwheel to produce other shapes. Look at the shape of the center opening. What shapes can you make by pushing on the sides of the wreath?

In this Unit, you learned how to recognize and make symmetric figures. You learned how to use geometric transformations to compare the size and shape of figures. You also learned how to use coordinate grids to locate and show motion of figures.

Use Your Understanding: Algebraic Reasoning

Test your understanding of symmetry, transformations, congruence, and similarity by solving these problems about a home improvement project.

1. The wallpaper design below has been selected for the kitchen.

a. Describe the symmetries in the wallpaper pattern. Assume that the design continues in the same way horizontally and vertically.

b. The wallpaper pattern is made of two basic design elements. What is the smallest angle you can rotate each design element so that it looks the same as in its original position?

2. One of the square tiles for the kitchen floor is shown below.

   a. Describe all symmetries of the design on the tile.

   b. Identify the smallest basic design element that can be transformed to produce the entire design. Explain the transformations that will map that basic element onto all other parts of the design.

3. The living room rug has copies of the design at the right along its border. Here, the design is shown on a coordinate grid. Copy the figure onto grid paper. Draw the image of the design after each transformation.

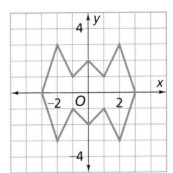

   a. a 90° counterclockwise rotation about the origin

   b. a reflection in the *y*-axis

   c. a translation with rule $(x, y) \rightarrow (x, y + 3)$

4. Consider triangle *ABC* below.

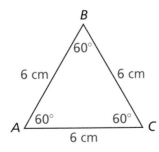

   a. What is the least number of side and/or angle measures needed to make a congruent copy of triangle *ABC*? Explain.

   b. What different combinations of side and angle measures could you use to make the congruent copy?

   c. If a friend claims that he has drawn a similar copy of triangle *ABC*, what measurements could you make to check that claim?

5. Line *k* is a line of symmetry for triangle *PQR*. What, if anything, does this tell you about each pair of parts of the figure?

   a. $\overline{PR}$ and $\overline{PQ}$

   b. $\angle Q$ and $\angle R$

   c. point *M* and $\overline{QR}$

   d. $\angle RPM$ and $\angle QPM$

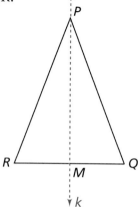

Explain Your Reasoning

Solving geometric problems requires using visual skills to see important patterns. However, you also need to be able to justify your conclusions.

6. How would you convince someone that a figure has the given symmetry?

   a. reflectional symmetry

   b. rotational symmetry

   c. translational symmetry

7. Suppose you have a figure and its image under a rotation. How could you find the center and angle of rotation that produced the image?

8. Suppose you have a figure and its image under a reflection. How could you find the line of reflection that produced the image?

9. Give some combinations of congruent sides and angles that will guarantee that two triangles are congruent. Then, give some combinations of congruent sides and angles that will *not* guarantee that two triangles are congruent.

10. Give some combinations of side and angle measures that will guarantee that two triangles are similar.

English / Spanish Glossary

A   **angle of rotation** The number of degrees that a figure rotates.

ángulo de rotación El número de grados que rota una figura.

B   **basic design element** A part of a pattern or design that, when transformed using at least one type of symmetry transformation, will produce the entire design.

elemento de diseño básico Parte de un patrón o diseño que, cuando se transforma usando un tipo de simetría de transformación, producirá el diseño completo.

C   **center of rotation** A fixed point about which a figure rotates.

centro de rotación Un punto fijo alrededor del cual rota una figura.

congruent figures Two figures are congruent if one is an image of the other under a translation, a reflection, a rotation, or some combination of these transformations. Put more simply, two figures are congruent if you can slide, flip, or turn one figure so it fits exactly on the other. The polygons below are congruent.

figuras congruentes Dos figuras son congruentes si una es la imagen de la otra sometida a una traslación, una reflexión, una rotación o a alguna combinación de estas transformaciones. Expresado de manera más sencilla, dos figuras son congruentes si puedes deslizar, voltear o rotar una figura para que coincida exactamente con la otra. Los siguientes polígonos son congruentes.

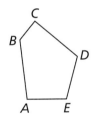 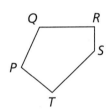

D **describe** Academic Vocabulary To explain or tell in detail. A written description can contain facts and other information needed to communicate your answer. A diagram or a graph may also be included.

related terms *express, explain, illustrate*

sample Describe the reflectional and rotational symmetries for the figure.

The figure has one vertical line of reflectional symmetry through its center. The figure cannot be rotated less than one full turn to any position so that it looks the same as it does in its original position. The figure does not have rotational symmetry.

describir Vocabulario académico Explicar o decir con detalle. Una descripción escrita puede contener datos y otra información necesaria para comunicar tu respuesta. También se puede incluir un diagrama o una gráfica.

términos relacionados *expresar, explicar, ilustrar*

ejemplo Describe las simetrías de reflexión y de rotación de la figura.

La figura tiene una recta vertical de simetría de reflexión a través de su centro. La figura no puede rotarse menos de una vuelta completa a cualquier posición de modo que se vea igual que en su posición original. La figura no tiene simetría de rotación.

---

dilation A transformation that enlarges or reduces a figure by a scale factor about a center point so that the original figure and its image are similar. If the scale factor is greater than 1, the dilation is an enlargement. If the scale factor is less than 1, the dilation is a reduction.

dilatación Una transformación que aumenta o reduce la figura en un factor de escala sobre un punto central para que la figura original y su imagen sean similares. Si el factor de escala es mayor que 1, la dilatación es un aumento. Si el factor de escala es menor que 1, la dilatación es una reducción.

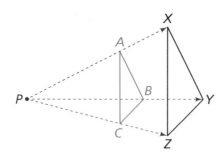

E **explain** Academic Vocabulary To give facts and details that make an idea easier to understand. Explaining something can involve a written summary supported by a diagram, chart, table, or any combination of these.

related terms *analyze, clarify, describe, justify, tell*

sample Are the triangles below congruent? Explain.

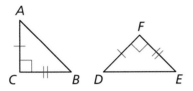

> The two triangles are congruent because the sides and the included angle of ΔABC are congruent to the two sides and the included angle of ΔDEF.

explicar Vocabulario académico Dar datos y detalles que hacen que una idea sea más fácil de comprender. Explicar puede incluir un resumen escrito apoyado por un diagrama, una gráfica, una tabla o una combinación de estos.

términos relacionados *analizar, aclarar, describir, justificar, decir*

ejemplo ¿Son congruentes los triángulos siguientes? Explica tu respuesta.

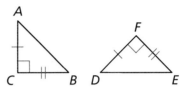

> Los dos triángulos son congruentes porque los dos lados y el ángulo incluido del ΔABC son congruentes con los dos lados y el ángulo incluido del ΔDEF.

I **identify** Academic Vocabulary To match a definition or a description to an object or to recognize something and be able to name it.

sample Identify the letter that has rotational symmetry.

A H V C

> The letter H has rotational symmetry because it can be turned 180 degrees to a position in which it looks the same as it does in the original position.

identificar Vocabulario académico Relacionar una definición o una descripción con un objeto, o bien, reconocer algo y ser capaz de nombrarlo.

ejemplo Identifica la letra que tiene simetría de rotación.

A H V C

> La letra H tiene simetría de rotación porque puede girarse 180 grados hasta una posición en la que se ve igual que en la posición original.

L **line of symmetry** A line of symmetry divides a figure into halves that are mirror images. Lines *WY* and *ZX* below are lines of symmetry.

eje de simetría El eje de simetría divide una figura en dos mitades en la que una es el reflejo de la otra. Las rectas *WY* y *ZX* que aparecen abajo son ejes de simetría.

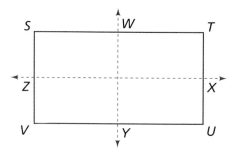

line reflection A transformation that maps each point of a figure to its mirror image, where a line acts as the mirror. Polygon *A′B′C′D′E′* below is the image of polygon *ABCDE* under a reflection in the line. If you drew a line segment from a point to its image, the segment would be perpendicular to, and bisected by, the line of reflection.

reflexión sobre un eje Una transformación en la que cada punto de una figura coincide con su imagen reflejada sobre un eje. El polígono *A′B′C′D′E′* que aparece abajo es la imagen del polígono *ABCDE* sometido a una reflexión sobre un eje. Si dibujaras un segmento de recta desde un punto hasta su imagen, el segmento sería perpendicular al eje de reflexión y estaría bisecado por este.

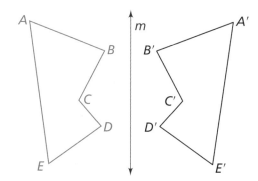

R **reflectional symmetry** A figure or design has reflectional symmetry if you can draw a line that divides the figure into halves that are mirror images. The line that divides the figure into halves is called the *line of symmetry*. The design below has reflectional symmetry about a vertical line through its center. Reflectional symmetry is sometimes referred to as *mirror symmetry* or *line symmetry*.

simetría de reflexión Una figura o diseño tiene simetría de reflexión si se puede dibujar una recta que divida la figura en dos mitades que sean imágenes reflejadas una de la otra. La recta que divide la figura en dos mitades se llama *eje de simetría*. El siguiente diseño tiene simetría de reflexión a ambos lados de una recta vertical que pasa por su centro. La simetría de reflexión a veces se conoce como *simetría axial*.

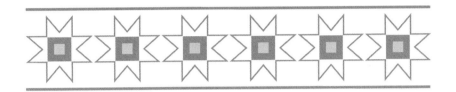

rotation A transformation that turns a figure counterclockwise about a point. Polygon *A'B'C'D'* below is the image of polygon *ABCD* under a 60° rotation about point *P*. If you drew a segment from a point on polygon *ABCD* to point *P* and another segment from the point's image to point *P*, the segments would be the same length and they would form a 60° angle.

rotación Una transformación en la que una figura gira alrededor de un punto en sentido contrario a las manecillas del reloj. El polígono *A'B'C'D'* que se muestra abajo es la imagen del polígono *ABCD* después de una rotación de 60° alrededor del punto *P*. Si se dibujara un segmento desde un punto en el polígono *ABCD* hasta el punto *P* y otro segmento desde la imagen del punto hasta el punto *P*, los segmentos tendrían la misma longitud y formarían un ángulo de 60°.

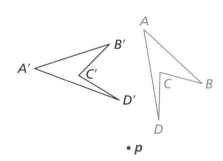

rotational symmetry A figure or design has rotational symmetry if it can be rotated less than a full turn about a point to a position in which it looks the same as the original. The design below has rotational symmetry with its center as the center of rotation and a 60° angle of rotation. This means that it can be rotated 60°, or any multiple of 60°, about its center point to produce an image that matches exactly with the original.

simetría de rotación Una figura o diseño tiene simetría de rotación si se puede rotar casi por completo alrededor de un punto hasta llegar a una posición en la que quede igual al dibujo original. El siguiente diseño tiene simetría de rotación: su centro es el centro de rotación y tiene un ángulo de rotación de 60°. Esto significa que se puede rotar 60°, o cualquier múltiplo de 60°, alrededor de su punto central para crear una imagen que coincida exactamente con la original.

S

similar figures Two figures are similar if one is an image of the other under a sequence of transformations that includes a dilation. If the scale factor is greater than 1, the side lengths of the image are greater than the corresponding side lengths of the original figure. If the scale factor is less than 1, the side lengths of the image are less than the corresponding side lengths of the original figure. If the scale factor is equal to 1, then the two figures are congruent.

figuras semejantes Dos figuras son semejantes si una de ellas es una imagen reflejada de la otra en una secuencia de transformaciones que incluye una dilatación. Si el factor de escala es mayor que 1, las longitudes de los lados de la imagen son mayores que las longitudes de los lados correspondientes de la figura original. Si el factor de escala es menor que 1, las longitudes de los lados de la imagen son menores que las longitudes de los lados correspondientes de la figura original. Si el factor de escala es igual a 1, entonces las dos figuras son congruentes.

similarity transformation A transformation that produces similar figures. The image of a figure under a similarity transformation, such as a dilation, has the same shape as the original figure, but may be a different size. A similarity transformation can also be a sequence of a rigid motion (reflection, rotation, or translation) and a dilation.

transformación de semejanza Una transformación que produce figuras semejantes. La imagen de una figura en una transformación de semejanza, como la dilatación, tiene la misma forma que la figura original, pero puede ser un tamaño diferente. Una transformación de semejanza también puede ser una secuencia de un movimiento rígido (reflexión, rotación o traslación) y una dilatación.

sketch Academic Vocabulary To draw a rough outline of something. When a sketch is asked for, it means that a drawing needs to be included in your response.

related terms *draw, illustrate*

sample Sketch the lines of symmetry for the figure.

A line of symmetry divides a figure into halves that are mirror images. I can sketch two lines of symmetry for the given figure.

hacer un bosquejo Vocabulario académico Dibujar un esbozo de algo. Cuando se pide un bosquejo, quiere decir que se debe incluir un dibujo en la respuesta.

términos relacionados *dibujar, ilustrar*

ejemplo Haz un bosquejo de los ejes de simetría de la figura.

Un eje de simetría divide una figura en mitades que son imágenes reflejadas. Puedo hacer el bosquejo de dos ejes de simetría para la figura dada.

symmetry An object or design has symmetry if part of it, the basic design element, can be transformed repeatedly, so that the design element and its copies produce the entire design. In this Unit, you learned about three types of symmetry. The butterfly below has *reflectional symmetry*, the pinwheel has *rotational symmetry*, and the wallpaper design has *translational symmetry*.

simetría Un objeto o diseño tiene simetría si parte del mismo, el elemento básico del diseño, puede transformarse repetidamente de manera que el elemento de diseño y sus copias produzcan el diseño completo. En esta Unidad, aprendiste tres tipos de simetría. La mariposa que ves a continuación tiene *simetría de reflexión*, el molinete tiene *simetría de rotación* y el diseño del papel tapiz tiene *simetría de traslación*.

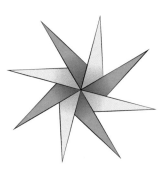

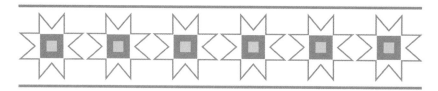

transformation A geometric operation that relates each point of a figure to an image point. The transformations you studied in this Unit—reflections, rotations, and translations—are symmetry transformations. A symmetry transformation produces an image that is identical in size and shape to the original figure.

transformación Una operación geométrica en la que cada punto de una figura coincide con un punto de su imagen. Las transformaciones que estudiaste en esta Unidad—reflexiones, rotaciones y traslaciones—son transformaciones de simetría. Una transformación de simetría da como resultado una imagen con el mismo tamaño y la misma forma que la figura original.

translation A transformation that slides each point on a figure to an image point a given distance and direction from the original point. Polygon $A'B'C'D'E'$ below is the image of polygon $ABCDE$ under a translation. If you drew line segments from two points to their respective image points, the segments would be parallel and they would have the same length.

traslación Una transformación que desliza cada punto de una figura hacia un punto de su imagen a determinada distancia y dirección del punto original. El polígono $A'B'C'D'E'$ que se observa a continuación es la imagen del polígono $ABCDE$ sometido a una traslación. Si dibujaras segmentos de recta desde dos puntos hasta los puntos correspondientes en su imagen, los segmentos serían paralelos y tendrían la misma longitud.

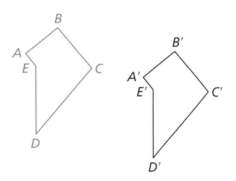

translational symmetry A design has translational symmetry if you can slide it to a position in which it looks exactly the same as it did in its original position. To describe translational symmetry, you need to specify the distance and direction of the translation. Below is part of a design that extends infinitely in all directions. This design has translational symmetry.

simetría de traslación Un diseño tiene simetría de traslación si se puede deslizar a una posición en la que luce exactamente igual que en la posición original. Para describir la simetría de traslación se debe especificar la distancia y la dirección de la traslación. La figura de abajo es parte de un diseño que se extiende infinitamente en todas las direcciones. Este diseño tiene simetría de traslación.

Index

ACE
    dilations and similar figures, 86–94
    symmetry and transformations, 18–27
    transformations and congruence, 38–47
    transforming coordinates, 61–72

algebraic reasoning, 100–102

angle measures
    congruent triangles, 101, 102
    dilations and similar figures, 89, 93, 94, 95
    triangles and, 58, 59, 60, 66

angle of rotation, 12, 102, 103
    kaleidoscope patterns, 42
    polygons and, 23
    rotational symmetry, 22, 49

angles
    angle sums, 58–60
    congruent triangles, 35–36, 41–42
    lines of symmetry and, 47
    notation and, 31
    translations and half-turns, 56

angle-sum property of triangles, 58–60, 65, 83

angle sums, transversals, and parallel lines, 58–60, 73

area and perimeter, 43–44, 69, 86–87, 94, 95

basic design elements, 103
    kaleidoscope patterns, 42
    reflectional symmetry and, 8
    symmetry and transformations, 18, 26, 69, 100–101
    transformations and congruence, 30

center of rotation, 12, 102, 103
    polygons and, 23
    rotational symmetry, 8, 13, 22, 49

circles, congruence and, 43

Common Core Mathematical Practices, 5–6, 29, 49, 74, 96

congruence, transformations and
    ACE, 38–47
    basic design elements, 30
    congruent polygons, 31
    congruent triangles, 32–37
    Mathematical Reflections, 48–49

congruent angles, 58, 59

congruent figures, 4, 103
    similarity transformations, 80
    triangles, 32–37, 38, 39–42, 45, 46–47, 48, 102

conjectures, 79

coordinate grids
    coordinate rules for reflections, 58–60
    dilations and similar figures, 77, 78
    symmetry and, 24
    transforming coordinates, 68, 70–72
    triangles, 64–65

coordinates, transforming
    ACE, 61–72
    coordinate rules for reflections, 50–52
    coordinate rules for rotations, 54–55
    coordinate rules for translations, 53–54
    Mathematical Reflections, 73–74

parallel lines, transversals, and angle sums, 58–60
    translations and half-turns, 56–57

corresponding parts
    congruent triangles and, 35–36, 37, 45
    similar figures and, 81–82, 83, 89
    similar triangles, 84, 93

dilations and similar figures, 104
    ACE, 86–94
    checking similarity without transformations, 81–83
    dilations, 76–79
    Mathematical Reflections, 95–96
    similarity transformations, 75–76, 79–81
    using similar triangles, 84–85

equilateral triangles, 89

Explain Your Reasoning, 102

geometric shapes, 3

Glossary, 103–111

graphs and graphing, 67

half-turns, translations and, 56–57, 72, 73

height, finding, 84–85, 90, 96

Investigations
    dilations and similar figures, 75–85
    symmetry and transformations, 7–17
    transformations and congruence, 30–49
    transforming coordinates, 50–60

isosceles triangles, 89

kaleidoscope patterns, 30, 42

line of reflection, 19, 22, 49

line reflections, 9–11, 26, 28, 106

line segments, 31, 56, 57

lines of symmetry, 9, 106
congruent triangles, 47, 102
polygons and, 23
reflectional symmetry and, 8, 11
rotational symmetry and, 13
transforming coordinates, 70

Looking Ahead, 2–3

Looking Back, 100–102

Mathematical Highlights, 4

Mathematical Practices, 5–6

Mathematical Reflections
dilations and similar figures, 95–96
symmetry and transformations, 28–29
transformations and congruence, 48–49
transforming coordinates, 73–74

measurement
congruent triangles, 40, 42, 44
similar triangles, 84–85, 90
symmetry and transformations, 29

mirror method, 84–85, 90, 96

notation, 31

number lines, 24

one-directional dilations, 94

origami project, 97–99

parallelograms
congruent angles, 66
congruent triangles and, 37
diagonals and, 69
dilations and similar figures, 92
similarity transformations, 81
transformations and congruence, 43, 44

parallel lines
angle-sum property of triangles, 60, 65
similar figures and, 89
transforming coordinates, 58–60, 71
translations and half-turns, 57
transversals and angle sums, 73

patterns. *See also* translational symmetry

pentagons, 47, 56–57

pinwheel project, 97–99

polygons
congruent polygons, 31, 38
dilations and similar figures, 88, 95
rotational symmetry, 20
similarity transformations, 80
symmetry and transformations, 23
translational symmetry, 16

Pythagorean Theorem, 72

quadratic functions, graphs of, 24

quadrilaterals
dilations and similar figures, 77, 78, 86–87
reflectional symmetry, 19
rigidity and, 46
transformations and congruence, 44

reasoning, explaining your
congruence and, 43
congruent angles, 59
congruent triangles, 36, 41
dilations and similar figures, 93, 96
similar figures and, 82, 83
symmetry and transformations, 29
transformations and congruence, 49, 102
transforming coordinates, 74

rectangles, 24–25, 43, 46, 66, 80

reflectional symmetry, 4, 9, 28, 102, 107
basic design elements and, 8, 101
dilations and similar figures, 91
line of reflection and, 22
line of symmetry and, 11
pinwheel project, 99
symmetry and transformations, 19
transforming coordinates, 71
triangles and, 27

reflections
coordinate rules for, 50–52, 73
coordinate rules for reflections, 61–62
triangles and, 64

rhombuses, 92

rigidity, 46

rotation, 107

rotational symmetry, 4, 12–14, 28, 102, 108
basic design elements and, 8, 100, 101
center and angle of rotation, 22
kaleidoscope patterns, 42
pentagons, 47
pinwheel project, 99
rectangles and, 24–25
symmetry and transformations, 20
transforming coordinates, 70, 71
triangles, 26

rotations
coordinate rules for, 54–55, 63, 73
symmetry and transformations, 12–14
translations and half-turns, 56–57, 72
triangles and, 59

rules, writing
  coordinate rules for
    reflections, 50–52, 61–62
  coordinate rules for
    rotations, 54–55, 63
  coordinate rules for
    translations, 53–54, 62–63
  graphing functions, 67
  transforming coordinates, 68

scale factors, 76, 77, 78, 86–87,
  91, 92, 94

side lengths
  congruent triangles, 35–36,
    41–42, 101, 102
  dilations and similar figures,
    86–87, 94, 95
  lines of symmetry and, 47

similar figures, 4
  ACE, 86–94
  checking similarity without
    transformations, 81–83
  dilations, 76–79
  Mathematical Reflections,
    95–96
  similarity transformations,
    75–76, 79–81
  using similar triangles, 84–85

**similarity, checking without
  transformations,** 81–83

similarity transformations,
  75–76, 79–81, 108

similar triangles, 78, 84–85, 90,
  96, 101, 102

slide transformations. *See*
  translational symmetry

slope, 83, 86–87, 94, 95

spheres, 91

squares, 21, 92

surface area and volume, 91

symmetry, 4, 69, 110. *See also*
  reflectional symmetry;
  rotational symmetry;
  translational symmetry

**symmetry and
  transformations,** 7
  ACE, 18–27
  basic design elements,
    100–101
  line reflections, 9–11
  Mathematical Reflections,
    28–29
  properties of
    transformations, 16–17
  rotations, 12–14
  translations, 14–16
  types of, 7–9

tables of values, 67

transformations, 4, 110
  basic design elements and,
    101
  dilations and similar figures,
    86–87, 88, 94
  line reflections, 9–10
  properties of, 16–17
  transforming coordinates,
    50–60

**transformations and
  congruence**
  ACE, 38–47
  basic design elements, 30
  congruent polygons, 31
  congruent triangles, 32–37,
    101–102
  Mathematical Reflections,
    48–49

**transformations and
  symmetry,** 7
  ACE, 18–27
  line reflections, 9–11
  Mathematical Reflections,
    28–29
  properties of
    transformations, 16–17
  rotations, 12–14
  translations, 14–16
  types of, 7–9

translational symmetry, 4, 22,
  28, 43, 49, 102, 111
  basic design elements and,
    9, 101

  coordinate rules for
    translations, 53
  patterns and, 14–15
  triangles, 21

translations, 111
  basic design elements, 26
  coordinate rules for, 53–54,
    62–63, 73
  symmetry and
    transformations, 14–16
  translations and half-turns,
    56–57, 72, 73

**transversals, parallel lines,
  and angle sums,** 58–60, 73

trapezoids, 17, 45

triangles
  angle measures, 58, 59, 60
  angle-sum property of
    triangles, 58–60
  area and perimeter, 69
  checking similarity without
    transformations, 82
  congruent triangles, 4,
    32–37, 38, 39–42, 45,
    46–47, 48, 102
  dilations and similar figures,
    92, 95
  reflectional symmetry, 19
  rigidity and, 46
  rotational symmetry, 20, 26
  similarity transformations,
    80
  similar triangles, 4, 78,
    84–85, 90, 96, 101, 102
  transformations and
    congruence, 101–102
  transforming coordinates,
    64–66
  translational symmetry, 21
  using similar triangles, 84–85

Unit Project, 97–99

Use Your Understanding,
  100–102

vertices, 31, 33, 38, 64, 65

wreath project, 97–99

Acknowledgments

Cover Design

Three Communication Design, Chicago

Photographs

Photo locators denoted as follows: Top (T), Center (C), Bottom (B), Left (L), Right (R), Background (Bkgd)

003 Jeffrey Greenberg/Photo Researchers, Inc.; **007** Florian Monheim/Roman von Götz/Bildarchiv Monheim GmbH/Alamy; **023** Nieuwenhoven/Fotolia; **032** rabbit75_fot/Fotolia.

Say It With Symbols

x
x + 5

Making Sense of Symbols

Lappan, Phillips, Fey, Friel

Say It With Symbols

Making Sense of Symbols

Looking Ahead 2

Mathematical Highlights 4

Mathematical Practices and Habits of Mind 5

1

Making Sense of Symbols: Equivalent Expressions 7

1.1 **Tiling Pools** Writing Equivalent Expressions 8

1.2 **Thinking in Different Ways** Determining Equivalence 10

1.3 **The Community Pool Problem** Interpreting Expressions 11

1.4 **Diving In** Revisiting the Distributive Property 12

ACE Homework 15

Mathematical Reflections 25

2

Combining Expressions 27

2.1 **Walking Together** Adding Expressions 27

2.2 **Predicting Profit** Substituting Expressions 29

2.3 **Making Candles** Volumes of Cylinders, Cones, and Spheres 31

2.4 **Selling Ice Cream** Solving Volume Problems 33

ACE Homework 34

Mathematical Reflections 44

Solving Equations   46

3.1 Selling Greeting Cards Solving Linear Equations 46

3.2 Comparing Costs Solving More Linear Equations 48

3.3 Factoring Quadratic Equations 50

3.4 Solving Quadratic Equations 52

ACE Homework 55

Mathematical Reflections 64

Looking Back at Functions   66

4.1 Pumping Water Looking at Patterns of Change 66

4.2 Area and Profit—What's the Connection? Using Equations 68

4.3 Generating Patterns Linear, Exponential, Quadratic 69

4.4 What's the Function? Modeling With Functions 70

ACE Homework 72

Mathematical Reflections 88

Reasoning With Symbols   90

5.1 Using Algebra to Solve a Puzzle 90

5.2 Odd and Even Revisited 91

5.3 Squaring Odd Numbers 94

ACE Homework 95

Mathematical Reflections 103

Unit Project Finding the Surface Area of Rod Stacks 105

Looking Back 107

English/Spanish Glossary 109

Index 114

Acknowledgments 119

Looking Ahead

In-ground swimming pools are often surrounded by borders of tiles. **How** many border tiles do you need to surround the pool?

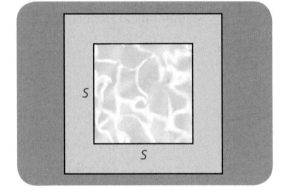

A school is selling ice cream served in souvenir cups for charity. The cup is cone-shaped with a height of 16 centimeters and a radius of 3 centimeters. The cup is filled and then topped with half a scoop of ice cream. **How** much ice cream do you need to make 75 cups?

You can approximate the height h of a pole-vaulter from the ground after t seconds with the equation $h = 32t - 16t^2$. **Will** the pole-vaulter clear a height of 17.5 feet?

You have used many powerful tools, including graphs, tables, and equations, to represent relationships among variables. Graphs allow you to see the shape of a relationship. They also help you identify intercepts and maximum and minimum points. Tables help you to observe patterns of change in the values of the variables. Equations give you an efficient way to generalize relationships.

In this Unit, you will focus on symbolic expressions and equations. You will see that different ways of reasoning about a situation can lead to different but equivalent expressions. You will use mathematical properties to rewrite expressions. You may discover that an equivalent expression allows you to think about a problem in a new way. And, you will learn new ways to solve equations. As you work through the Investigations, you will solve problems, such as the concession-stand profit at a water park, as well as those on the previous page.

Mathematical Highlights

Say It With Symbols

Algebra provides ideas and symbols for expressing information about quantitative variables and relationships. In *Say It With Symbols*, you will solve problems designed to develop your understanding and skill in using symbolic expressions and equations in algebra.

You will learn how to

- Represent patterns and relationships in symbolic forms

- Determine when different symbolic expressions are mathematically equivalent

- Write algebraic expressions in useful equivalent forms

- Combine symbolic expressions using algebraic operations to form new expressions

- Analyze expressions or equations to determine the patterns of change in the tables and graphs that the expression or equation represents

- Solve linear and quadratic equations using symbolic reasoning

- Use algebraic reasoning to validate generalizations and conjectures

When you encounter a new problem, it is a good idea to ask yourself questions. In this Unit, you might ask questions such as:

What expression or equation represents the pattern or relationship in a context?

Can you write an equivalent expression for a given expression to provide new information about a relationship?

What operations can transform a given equation or expression into an equivalent form that can be used to answer a question?

How can symbolic reasoning help confirm a conjecture?

Mathematical Practices and Habits of Mind

In the *Connected Mathematics* curriculum you will develop an understanding of important mathematical ideas by solving problems and reflecting on the mathematics involved. Every day, you will use "habits of mind" to make sense of problems and apply what you learn to new situations. Some of these habits are described by the *Common Core State Standards for Mathematical Practices* (MP).

MP1 Make sense of problems and persevere in solving them.

When using mathematics to solve a problem, it helps to think carefully about

- data and other facts you are given and what additional information you need to solve the problem;
- strategies you have used to solve similar problems and whether you could solve a related simpler problem first;
- how you could express the problem with equations, diagrams, or graphs;
- whether your answer makes sense.

MP2 Reason abstractly and quantitatively.

When you are asked to solve a problem, it often helps to

- focus first on the key mathematical ideas;
- check that your answer makes sense in the problem setting;
- use what you know about the problem setting to guide your mathematical reasoning.

MP3 Construct viable arguments and critique the reasoning of others.

When you are asked to explain why a conjecture is correct, you can

- show some examples that fit the claim and explain why they fit;
- show how a new result follows logically from known facts and principles.

When you believe a mathematical claim is incorrect, you can

- show one or more counterexamples—cases that don't fit the claim;
- find steps in the argument that do not follow logically from prior claims.

MP4 Model with mathematics.

When you are asked to solve problems, it often helps to

- think carefully about the numbers or geometric shapes that are the most important factors in the problem, then ask yourself how those factors are related to each other;
- express data and relationships in the problem with tables, graphs, diagrams, or equations, and check your result to see if it makes sense.

MP5 Use appropriate tools strategically.

When working on mathematical questions, you should always

- decide which tools are most helpful for solving the problem and why;
- try a different tool when you get stuck.

MP6 Attend to precision.

In every mathematical exploration or problem-solving task, it is important to

- think carefully about the required accuracy of results: is a number estimate or geometric sketch good enough, or is a precise value or drawing needed?
- report your discoveries with clear and correct mathematical language that can be understood by those to whom you are speaking or writing.

MP7 Look for and make use of structure.

In mathematical explorations and problem solving, it is often helpful to

- look for patterns that show how data points, numbers, or geometric shapes are related to each other;
- use patterns to make predictions.

MP8 Look for and express regularity in repeated reasoning.

When results of a repeated calculation show a pattern, it helps to

- express that pattern as a general rule that can be used in similar cases;
- look for shortcuts that will make the calculation simpler in other cases.

You will use all of the Mathematical Practices in this Unit. Sometimes, when you look at a Problem, it is obvious which practice is most helpful. At other times, you will decide on a practice to use during class explorations and discussions. After completing each Problem, ask yourself:

- What mathematics have I learned by solving this Problem?
- What Mathematical Practices were helpful in learning this mathematics?

Making Sense of Symbols: Equivalent Expressions

When you want to communicate an idea in words, you can express it in many ways. For example, all the statements below communicate the same information about Mika and Alberto.

> • Alberto is older than Mika.
>
> • Mika is younger than Alberto.
>
> • Alberto was born before Mika.
>
> • Mika was born after Alberto.

- Can you think of other ways to express the same idea?

You have written symbolic expressions and equations with variables to represent situations. Since you can usually think about a situation in more than one way, you can often express the situation in symbols in more than one way.

Common Core State Standards

8.EE.C.7 Solve linear equations in one variable.

8.EE.C.7b Solve linear equations with rational number coefficients, including equations whose solutions require expanding expressions using the distributive property and collecting like terms.

8.F.A.3 Interpret the equation $y = mx + b$ as defining a linear function, whose graph is a straight line; give examples of functions that are not linear.

Also A-SSE.A.1, A-SSE.A.1a, A-SSE.A.1b, A-SSE.A.2, A-SSE.B.3, A-CED.A.1, A-REI.B.3, F-IF.C.9, F-BF.A.1a

Consider the perimeter P of a rectangle with length L and width W.

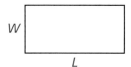

Alberto says the perimeter of the rectangle above is $P = 2(L + W)$. Mika says the perimeter is $P = 2L + 2W$.

- Why do you think Alberto used parentheses in his equation?

- Are both equations correct ways to represent perimeter? Explain.

Since $2(L + W)$ and $2L + 2W$ represent the same quantity (the perimeter of a rectangle), they are **equivalent expressions.** In this Investigation, you will explore situations in which a quantity can be described with different but equivalent expressions.

- How can you determine if two expressions are equivalent?

1.1   Tiling Pools
Writing Equivalent Expressions

 In-ground pools are often surrounded by borders of tiles. The Custom Pool Company gets orders for square pools of different sizes. For example, the pool below has side lengths of 3 feet and is surrounded by square border tiles. All Custom Pool border tiles measure 1 foot on each side.

 How many border tiles do you need to surround a square pool with side length s?

Problem 1.1

In order to calculate the number of tiles needed for a project, the Custom Pool manager wants an equation relating the number of border tiles to the size of the pool.

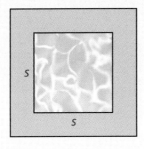

border tile

1 ft

1 ft

A **1.** Write an expression for the number of border tiles needed to surround a square pool with sides of length s feet.

2. Write a different but equivalent expression for the number of tiles needed to surround the square pool.

3. Explain why your two expressions for the number of border tiles are equivalent.

B **1.** Use each expression in Question A to write an equation for the number of border tiles N. Make a table and a graph for each equation.

2. Based on your table and graph, are the two expressions for the number of border tiles in Question A equivalent? Explain.

C Is the relationship between the side length of the pool and the number of border tiles linear or nonlinear? Explain.

A C E Homework starts on page 15.

1.2 Thinking in Different Ways
Determining Equivalence

When Takashi reported his ideas about an equation relating N and s in Problem 1.1, he made the following sketch.

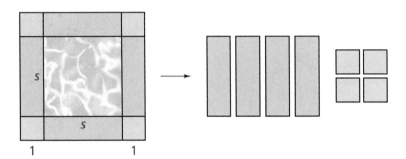

- What equation do you think Takashi wrote to relate N and s?

Problem 1.2

A Four students in Takashi's class came up with different equations for counting the number of border tiles. For each equation, make a sketch that shows how the student might have been thinking about the border of the pool.

    1. Stella's equation: $N = 4(s + 1)$

    2. Jeri's equation: $N = s + s + s + s + 4$

    3. Hank's equation: $N = 4(s + 2)$

    4. Sal's equation: $N = 2s + 2(s + 2)$

B Use each equation in Question A to find the number of border tiles needed for a square pool with a side length of 10 feet. Can you conclude from your results that all the expressions for the number of tiles are equivalent? Explain your reasoning.

C Which of the expressions for the number of border tiles in Question A represent Takashi's sketch? Explain.

A **C** **E** Homework starts on page 15.

1.3 The Community Pool Problem
Interpreting Expressions

In this Problem, you will interpret symbolic statements and use them to make predictions.

A community center is building a pool, part indoor and part outdoor. A diagram of the indoor part of the pool is shown. The indoor shape is made from a half-circle with radius x and a rectangle with length $4x$.

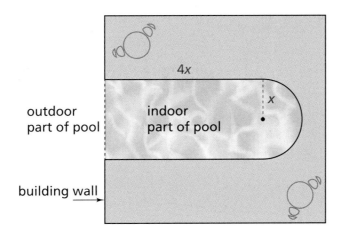

Problem 1.3

The exact dimensions of the pool are not available, but the area A of the whole pool is given by the equation:

$$A = x^2 + \frac{\pi x^2}{2} + 8x^2 + \frac{\pi x^2}{4}$$

A Which part of the expression for the area of the pool represents

    1. the area of the indoor part? Explain.

    2. the area of the outdoor part? Explain.

B **1.** Make a sketch of the outdoor part. Label the dimensions.

    2. If possible, draw another shape for the outdoor part of the pool. If not, explain why not.

continued on the next page >

Problem **1.3** *continued*

C Stella and Jeri each rewrote the expression for the area of the outdoor part of the pool to help them make a sketch.

Stella $x^2 + \frac{\pi x^2}{8} + \frac{\pi x^2}{8}$ **Jeri** $\left(\frac{1}{2}x\right)(2x) + \frac{\pi x^2}{4}$

1. Explain the reasoning that each person may have used to write their expression.

2. Decide if these expressions are equivalent to the original expression in Question A, part (2). Explain your reasoning.

D Does the equation for the area of the pool represent a linear or nonlinear function? Explain.

A C E Homework starts on page 15.

1.4 Diving In
Revisiting the Distributive Property

In Problems 1.1 and 1.2, you found patterns that could be represented by several different but equivalent symbolic expressions, such as:

$$4s + 4$$

$$4(s + 1)$$

$$s + s + s + s + 4$$

$$2s + 2(s + 2)$$

You can show the equivalence of these expressions with arrangements of the border tiles. You can also show that these expressions are equivalent by using properties of numbers and operations.

An important property is the **Distributive Property:**

For any real numbers a, b, and c:

$$a(b + c) = ab + ac \quad \text{and} \quad a(b - c) = ab - ac$$

For example, this property guarantees that $4(s + 1) = 4s + 4$ for any s.

We say that $a(b + c)$ and $4(s + 1)$ are in **factored form** and $ab + ac$ and $4s + 4$ are in **expanded form.**

The next problem revisits the Distributive Property.

Swimming pools are sometimes divided into sections that are used for different purposes. A pool may have a section for swimming laps and a section for diving, or a section for experienced swimmers and a section for small children.

Below are diagrams of pools with swimming and diving sections. The dimensions are in meters.

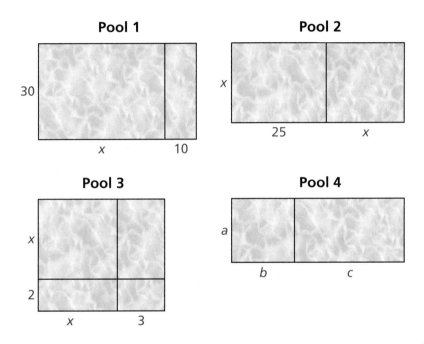

- For each pool, what are two different but equivalent expressions for the total area?

- How do these diagrams and expressions illustrate the Distributive Property? Explain.

The Distributive Property, as well as the Commutative Property and other properties for numbers, are useful for writing equivalent expressions. The **Commutative Property** states that for any real numbers a and b:

$$a + b = b + a \quad \text{and} \quad ab = ba$$

These properties were discussed in previous Units.

Problem 1.4

Ⓐ Use the Distributive Property to write each expression in expanded form.

1. $3(x + 5)$ **2.** $2(3x - 10)$

3. $2x(x + 5)$ **4.** $(x + 2)(x + 5)$

Ⓑ Use the Distributive Property to write each expression in factored form.

1. $12 + 24x$ **2.** $x + x + x + 6$

3. $x^2 + 3x$ **4.** $x^2 + 4x + 3$

Ⓒ The following expressions all represent the number of border tiles for a square pool with side length s.

$$4(s + 1) \qquad s + s + s + s + 4$$
$$2s + 2(s + 2) \qquad 4(s + 2) - 4$$
$$(s + 2)^2 - s^2 \qquad 2[2(s + 2) - 2]$$

Use the Distributive and Commutative properties to show that these expressions are equivalent.

Ⓓ Three of the following expressions are equivalent. Explain which expression is not equivalent to the other three.

1. $2x - 12x + 10$ **2.** $10 - x$

3. $10(1 - x)$ **4.** $\dfrac{20(-x + 1)}{2}$

Ⓔ Copy each equation. Insert one set of parentheses in the expression to the left of the equal sign so that it is equivalent to the expression to the right of the equal sign.

1. $6p + 2 - 2p = 4p + 12$ **2.** $6p + 2 - 2p = 6p$

ⒶⒸⒺ Homework starts on page 15.

Applications

1. **a.** How many 1-foot-square border tiles do you need to surround a pool that is 10 feet long and 5 feet wide?

    b. Write an expression for the number of border tiles needed to surround a pool L feet long and W feet wide.

    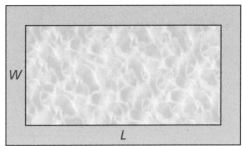

    c. Write a different but equivalent expression for the number of tiles needed in part (b). Explain why your expressions are equivalent.

2. A square hot tub has sides of length s feet. A tiler makes a border by placing 1-foot-square tiles along the edges of the tub and triangular tiles at the corners, as shown. The tiler makes the triangular tiles by cutting the square tiles in half along a diagonal.

    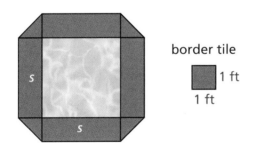

    border tile

    1 ft
    1 ft

    a. Suppose the hot tub has sides of length 7 feet. How many square tiles does the tiler need for the border?

    b. Write an expression for the number of square tiles N needed to build this border for a square tub with sides of length s feet.

    c. Write a different but equivalent expression for the number of tiles N. Explain why your expressions are equivalent.

    d. Is the relationship between the number of tiles and side length linear or nonlinear? Explain.

3. A rectangular pool is *L* feet long and *W* feet wide. A tiler makes a border by placing 1-foot-square tiles along the edges of the pool and triangular tiles on the corners, as shown. The tiler makes the triangular tiles by cutting the square tiles in half along a diagonal.

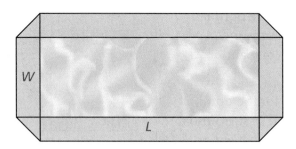

  a. Suppose the pool is 30 feet long and 20 feet wide. How many square tiles does the tiler need for the border?

  b. Write two expressions for the number of square tiles *N* needed to make this border for a pool *L* feet long and *W* feet wide.

  c. Explain why your two expressions are equivalent.

4. Below are three more expressions students wrote for the number of border tiles needed to surround the square pool in Problem 1.2.

$$4\left(\frac{s}{2}+\frac{s}{4}\right)+4 \qquad 2(s+0.5)+2(s+1.5) \qquad 4\left[\frac{s+(s+2)}{2}\right]$$

  a. Use each expression to find the number of border tiles *N* if *s* = 0.

  b. Do you think the expressions are equivalent? Explain.

  c. Use each expression to find the number of border tiles if *s* = 12. Has your answer to part (b) changed? Explain.

  d. What can you say about testing specific values as a method for determining whether two or more expressions are equivalent?

5. A square surrounds a circle with a radius *r*. Each expression represents the area of part of this figure. Describe the shape or region each area represents.

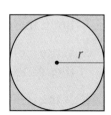

  a. $4r^2 - \pi r^2$ **b.** $4r^2 - \frac{\pi r^2}{4}$

6. The dimensions of a pool are shown below.

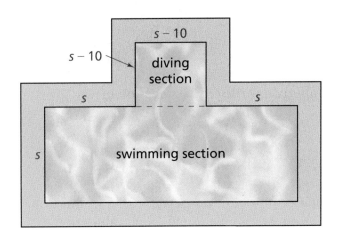

Each expression represents the surface area for part of the pool.

i. $s(3s - 10)$

ii. $(s - 10)^2$

iii. $2s^2 + s(s - 10)$

iv. $s^2 - 20s + 100$

a. Which expression(s) could represent the area of the diving section?

b. Which expression(s) could represent the area of the swimming section?

c. If you chose more than one expression for parts (a) and (b), show that they are equivalent.

d. Write an equation that represents the total surface area A of the pool.

e. What kind of relationship does the equation in part (d) represent?

For Exercises 7–9, complete parts (a)–(c).

a. For each expression, write an equation of the form $y = expression$. Make a table and a graph of the two equations. Show x values from -5 to 5 on the graph.

b. Based on your table and graph, tell whether you think the two expressions are equivalent.

c. If you think the expressions are equivalent, use the properties you have learned in this Investigation to verify their equivalence. If you think they are not equivalent, explain why.

7. $-3x + 6 + 5x$
   $6 + 2x$

8. $10 - 5x$
   $5x - 10$

9. $(3x + 4) + (2x - 3)$
   $5x + 1$

10. Use the Distributive Property to write each expression in expanded form.

a. $3(x + 7)$ **b.** $5(5 - x)$

c. $2(4x - 8)$ **d.** $(x + 4)(x + 2)$

11. Use the Distributive Property to write each expression in factored form.

a. $2x + 6$ **b.** $14 - 7x$

c. $2x - 10x$ **d.** $3x + 4x$

12. Use the Distributive and Commutative properties to determine whether each pair of expressions is equivalent for all values of x.

a. $3x + 7x$ and $10x$ **b.** $5x$ and $5x - 10x$

c. $4(1 + 2x) - 3x$ and $5x + 4$ **d.** $5 - 3(2 - 4x)$ and $-1 + 12x$

13. Here is one way Maleka proved that $2(s + 2) + 2s$ is equivalent to $4s + 4$.

$$
\begin{aligned}
(1) \quad 2(s + 2) + 2s &= 2s + 4 + 2s \\
(2) \quad &= 2s + 2s + 4 \\
(3) \quad &= (2 + 2)s + 4 \\
(4) \quad &= 4s + 4
\end{aligned}
$$

What properties of numbers and operations justify each step?

14. Find three equivalent expressions for $6x + 3$.

For Exercises 15–17, copy the statement. Insert parentheses on the left side of the equation, if necessary, to make the statement true for all values of p.

15. $7 + 5p - p = 11p$ **16.** $7 + 5p - p = 7$ **17.** $7 + 5p - p = 7 + 4p$

Connections

In Exercises 18–23, each expression represents the area of a rectangle. Draw a divided rectangle for each expression. Label the lengths and areas. For Exercises 18–20, write an equivalent expression in expanded form. For Exercises 21–23, write an equivalent expression in factored form.

18. $x(x + 6)$ **19.** $x(x - 6)$ **20.** $x(5 + 1)$

21. $x^2 + 4x$ **22.** $x^2 - 2x$ **23.** $3x + 4x$

24. A circular pool with a radius of 4 feet has a 1-foot border.

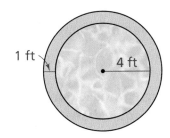

1 ft

4 ft

   a. What is the area of the circular pool?

   b. What is the area of the border?

   c. Write an expression for the area of a circular pool with a radius of r feet.

   d. Write an expression for the area of a 1-foot border around a circular pool with a radius of r feet.

25. Multiple Choice Which of the following expressions is equivalent to $m + m + m + m + m$?

     A. $m + 5$ **B.** $5m$ **C.** m^5 **D.** $5(m + 1)$

26. Multiple Choice Which of the following expressions is equivalent to $a - b$, where a and b are any numbers?

     F. $b - a$ **G.** $a + b$ **H.** $-a + b$ **I.** $-b + a$

27. Percy wants to write an equation for the number of tiles needed to surround a square pool with sides of length s feet. He makes a table for pools with sides of length 1, 2, 3, 4, and 5 feet. Then he uses the patterns in his table to write the equation $N = 8 + 4(s - 1)$.

Border Tiles

Side Length	1	2	3	4	5
Number of Tiles	8	12	16	20	24

   a. What patterns does Percy see in his table?

   b. Is Percy's expression for the number of tiles equivalent to $4(s + 1)$, Stella's expression in Problem 1.2? Explain.

Draw and label a rectangle whose area is represented by the expression. Then write an equivalent expression in expanded form.

   28. $(x + 1)(x + 4)$ **29.** $(x + 5)(x + 6)$ **30.** $3x(5 + 2)$

For Exercises 31–33, draw and label a rectangle whose area is represented by the expression. Then write an equivalent expression in factored form.

   31. $x^2 + x + 2x + 2$ **32.** $x^2 + 7x + 10$ **33.** $x^2 + 14x + 49$

34. Two expressions for the number of border tiles for the pool below are given. Sketch a picture that illustrates each expression.

$$2(s + 0.5) + 2(s + 1.5) \qquad 4\left[\frac{s + (s + 2)}{2}\right]$$

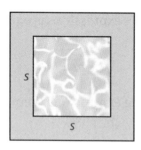

border tile

1 ft

1 ft

Find the sum or difference.

35. $\frac{5}{7} - \frac{1}{3}$

36. $\frac{5}{2} + \frac{1}{3}$

37. $\frac{1}{2}x + \frac{1}{2}x$

38. $\frac{2}{3}x - \frac{1}{2}x$

Find the sum, difference, product, or quotient.

39. 2×14

40. $-2 - (-14)$

41. $-2 \div (-14)$

42. $-6 \times (-11)$

43. $-6 + 11$

44. $6 - 11$

45. $-18(3x)$

46. $\frac{-24x}{-8}$

47. $-18x \div 3$

Find the greatest common factor for each pair of numbers.

48. 35 and 40

49. 36 and 12

50. 100 and 25

51. 42 and 9

52. Below is a diagram of Otter Middle School's outdoor track. The shape of the interior region (shaded green) is a rectangle with a half-circle at each end.

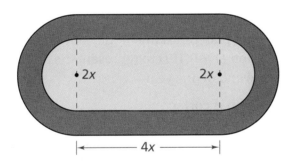

a. Find an expression that represents the area of the interior region.

b. Find the perimeter of the interior region as if you wanted to put a fence around it. Explain how you found your answer.

c. Write an expression equivalent to the one in part (b).

53. For Problem 1.2, Percy wrote the expression $8 + 4(s - 1)$ to represent the number of border tiles needed to surround a square pool with side length s.

   a. Is this expression equivalent to the other expressions? Explain.

   b. Four students used Percy's expression to calculate the number of border tiles needed for a pool with a side length of 6 feet. Which student performed the calculations correctly?

Stella	Hank
$8 + 4(6 - 1) = 8 + 24 - 1$ $= 31 \text{ tiles}$	$8 + 4(6 - 1) = 8 + 4(5)$ $= 8 + 20$ $= 28 \text{ tiles}$

Takashi	Jackie
$8 + 4(6 - 1) = 12 + (6 - 1)$ $= 12 + 5$ $= 17 \text{ tiles}$	$8 + 4(6 - 1) = 12(6 - 1)$ $= 12(5)$ $= 60 \text{ tiles}$

54. Meiko invests D dollars in a money-market account that earns 10% interest per year. She does not plan on taking money out during the year. She writes the expression $D + 0.10D$ to represent the amount of money in the account at the end of one year.

   a. Explain why this expression is correct.

   b. Write an equivalent expression in factored form.

   c. Suppose Meiko invested $1,500. How much money will she have in her account at the end of one year?

For Exercises 55 and 56, use this information: The ski club is planning a trip for winter break. They write the equation $C = 200 + 10N$ to estimate the cost in dollars C of the trip for N students.

55. Duncan and Corey both use the equation to estimate the cost for 50 students. Duncan says the cost is $10,500$, and Corey says it is 700.

    a. Whose estimate is correct? Show your work.

    b. How do you think Duncan and Corey found such different estimates if they both used the same equation?

56. a. Suppose 20 students go on the trip. What is the cost per student?

    b. Write an equation for the cost per student S when N students go on the trip.

    c. Use your equation to find the cost per student when 40 students go on the trip.

57. Below are two students' calculations for writing an equivalent expression for $10 - 4(x - 1) + 11 \times 3$.

    a. Which student performed the calculations correctly?

    b. What mistakes did the other student make?

Sarah

$$10 - 4(x - 1) + 11 \times 3 = 10 - 4x + 4 + 11 \times 3$$
$$= 10 - 4x + 4 + 33$$
$$= 10 - 4x + 37$$
$$= 10 + 37 - 4x$$
$$= 47 - 4x$$

Emily

$$10 - 4(x - 1) + 11 \times 3 = 10 - 4x + 4 + 11 \times 3$$
$$= 10 - 4x + 15 \times 3$$
$$= 25 - 4x \times 3$$
$$= 25 - 12x$$

Extensions

For Exercises 58 and 59, write an equation for the number of 1 foot-by-1 foot tiles *N* needed to surround each pool based on the width *w* of the border. The diagrams below show each pool surrounded by a border of widths 1, 2, and 3.

58.

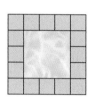 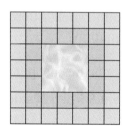 

59.

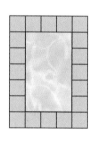 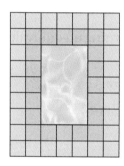 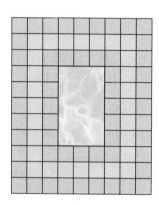

60. The expression puzzles below all start with the original expression $2n - 3 + 4n + 6n + 1$. Each one ends with a different expression.

Expression Puzzles

Puzzle	Original Expression	Desired Result
1	$2n - 3 + 4n + 6n + 1$	$12n - 5$
2	$2n - 3 + 4n + 6n + 1$	$12n + 3$
3	$2n - 3 + 4n + 6n + 1$	$12n - 2$
4	$2n - 3 + 4n + 6n + 1$	$n + 1$

    a. Solve each puzzle by inserting one set of parentheses in the original expression so that it is equivalent to the desired result.

    b. Show that your expression is equivalent to the desired result. Justify each step.

Mathematical Reflections

1

In this Investigation, you found different but equivalent expressions to represent a quantity in a relationship. The following questions will help you summarize what you have learned.

Think about these questions. Discuss your ideas with other students and your teacher. Then write a summary of your findings in your notebook.

1. **What** does it mean to say that two expressions are equivalent?

2. **Explain** how you can use the Distributive Property to write equivalent expressions.

3. **Explain** how you can use the Distributive and Commutative properties to show that two or more expressions are equivalent.

Common Core Mathematical Practices

As you worked on the Problems in this Investigation, you used prior knowledge to make sense of them. You also applied Mathematical Practices to solve the Problems. Think back over your work, the ways you thought about the Problems, and how you used Mathematical Practices.

Hector described his thoughts in the following way:

In Problem 1.1, we found many different but equivalent expressions to represent the number of unit tiles needed to surround a pool. When the teacher asked if there were more, Jon said there were an infinite number.

Jon showed how you could multiply the term $4n$ in the expression $4n + 4$ by 3 and then divide by 3 to get $\frac{3(4n)}{3} + 4$. He then showed how you could multiply $4n$ by 4 and then divide by 4 to get $\frac{4(4n)}{4} + 4$. Both expressions are equivalent to $4n + 4$. You could do this with any number, so there are an infinite number of equivalent expressions.

....

Common Core Standards for Mathematical Practice

MP7 Look for and make use of structure.

• What other Mathematical Practices can you identify in Hector's reasoning?

• Describe a Mathematical Practice that you and your classmates used to solve a different Problem in this Investigation.

Combining Expressions

In the last Investigation, you found several ways to write equivalent expressions to describe a quantity. You also learned several ways to show that two expressions are equivalent. You will continue to answer these questions about two or more expressions:

- Are the expressions equivalent? Why?

- If expressions are equivalent, what information does each expression represent?

You will also look at ways to write new equations and to answer this question:

- What are the advantages and disadvantages of using one equation rather than two or more equations to represent a situation?

2.1 Walking Together
Adding Expressions

In *Moving Straight Ahead,* Leanne, Gilberto, and Alana enter a walkathon as a team. This means that they each will walk the same number of kilometers. The walkathon organizers offer a prize to the three-person team that raises the most money.

Common Core State Standards

8.F.A.3 Interpret the equation $y = mx + b$ as defining a linear function, whose graph is a straight line; give examples of functions that are not linear.

8.G.C.9 Know the formulas for the volumes of cones, cylinders, and spheres and use them to solve real-world and mathematical problems.

Also 8.EE.C.7, 8.EE.C.7b, 8.F.A.1, 8.F.A.2, N-Q.A.1, N-Q.A.2, A-SSE.A.1, A-SSE.A.1a, A-SSE.A.1b, A-SSE.A.2, A-SSE.B.3, A-CED.A.1, A-REI.B.3, F-IF.C.9, F-BF.A.1, F-BF.A.1a

The individual pledges for each student are as follows:

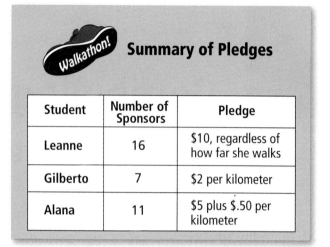

Summary of Pledges

Student	Number of Sponsors	Pledge
Leanne	16	$10, regardless of how far she walks
Gilberto	7	$2 per kilometer
Alana	11	$5 plus $.50 per kilometer

Problem 2.1

A **1.** Write equations to represent the money M that each student will raise for walking x kilometers.

    a. $M_{\text{Leanne}} = $ ■

    b. $M_{\text{Gilberto}} = $ ■

    c. $M_{\text{Alana}} = $ ■

  2. Write an equation for the total amount of money M_{total} the three-person team will raise for walking x kilometers.

B **1.** Write an expression that is equivalent to the expression for the total amount of money raised by the team in Question A, part (2). Explain why it is equivalent.

  2. What information does this new expression represent about the situation?

  3. Suppose each person walks 10 kilometers. Explain which expression(s) you would use to calculate the total amount of money raised.

C Is the relationship between kilometers walked and total money raised linear or nonlinear? Explain.

A C E Homework starts on page 34.

2.2 Predicting Profit
Substituting Expressions

The manager of the Water Town amusement park uses data collected over the past several years to write equations that will help her make predictions about the daily operations of the park.

The daily concession-stand profit in dollars P depends on the number of visitors V. The manager writes the equation below to model this relationship:

$$P = 2.50V - 500$$

She uses the equation below to predict the number of visitors V based on the probability of rain R.

$$V = 600 - 500R$$

- What information might each of the numbers in the equations represent?

- What units should you use with the expression $-500R$? The expression $600 - 500R$?

> **?** Can you write an equation to represent profit in terms of the probability of rain? What units would you use with this equation? Explain.

Problem 2.2

A 1. Suppose the probability of rain is 25%. What profit can the concession stand expect? Explain.

2. What is the probability of rain if the profit expected is $625? Explain your reasoning.

B 1. Write an equation you can use to predict the concession-stand profit P based on the probability of rain R.

2. Use your equation to predict profit when the probability of rain is 25%. Compare your answer with your result in Question A, part (1).

continued on the next page >

Problem **2.2** *continued*

C 1. Write an equivalent expression for the profit in Question B. Explain why the two expressions are equivalent.

2. What probability of rain predicts a profit of $625? Compare your answer with your result in Question A, part (2).

3. Predict the profit when the probability of rain is 0%. Does your answer make sense? Explain.

4. Predict the profit when the probability of rain is 100%. Does your answer make sense?

D Do the equations in Questions B and C represent a linear or nonlinear function? Explain.

A C E Homework starts on page 34.

Did You Know?
....

The calculation of the quarterback rating in the National Football League (NFL™) uses a series of equations:

Completion Rating: $CR = 5\left(\dfrac{\text{completions}}{\text{attempts}}\right) - 1.5$

Yards Rating: $YR = \dfrac{\dfrac{\text{yards}}{\text{attempts}} - 3}{4}$

Touchdown Rating: $TR = 20\left(\dfrac{\text{touchdowns}}{\text{attempts}}\right)$

Interception Rating: $IR = \dfrac{19 - 2\left(\dfrac{\text{interceptions}}{\text{attempts}}\right)}{8}$

OVERALL RATING $= 100\left(\dfrac{CR + YR + TR + IR}{6}\right)$

2.3 Making Candles
Volumes of Cylinders, Cones, and Spheres

Rocky Middle School is sponsoring a charity event. They plan to make and sell candles at the outdoor market in the city.

Andy's committee is in charge of designing the candles. They designed three different shapes of candles: a sphere, a cone, and a cylinder. The molds for the three types of candles have the same radius and height.

? What is the relationship among the volumes of these three candles?

Problem 2.3

A Isaiah tried to figure out how much wax to buy to make the cylindrical candle, but he forgot the formula for the volume of a cylinder. Noah claims that to find the volume of a rectangular prism, you need to know the number of unit cubes in one layer of the prism and the prism's height. He thinks the same idea works for finding the volume of a cylinder.

1. Is Noah correct? Write an expression to find the volume of a rectangular prism.

2. Will this method work for finding the volume of a cylinder? Explain why or why not.

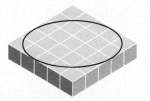

continued on the next page >

Problem **2.3** *continued*

B Andy decided to explore the relationship among the volumes of the three candle designs. He used plastic containers in the shape of a cylinder, cone, and sphere. The containers have the same height h and inside radius r, which means that the inside diameter of the sphere is equal to the height. Andy tried to find relationships among the three containers.

1. Write the relationships among the three containers in words and then as algebraic equations.

2. Use the relationships in part (1) to write an expression for finding the volume of

   a. a cone with height h and radius r.

   b. a sphere with radius r.

C The price of each candle is based on the cost of wax plus markup for profit. If the cylindrical candle sells for $12, what should the prices of the other two candles be?

D Andy decides to sell cylindrical candles with a radius of 3 inches and a height of 1.25 feet.

1. How much liquid wax does Andy need to make the candle?

2. Describe the dimensions of a rectangular candle that uses the same amount of wax.

A C E Homework starts on page 34.

2.4 Selling Ice Cream
Solving Volume Problems

Rocky Middle School also plans to sell ice cream at the charity event. They expect to sell about 100 scoops of ice cream. The ice cream comes in cylindrical cartons. Ester's committee must decide how many cartons to buy for the event.

Problem 2.4

A Use the formulas from Problem 2.3 and the following information.

- A carton of ice cream has a radius of 11 centimeters and a height of 30 centimeters.

- A scoop of ice cream has a radius of 3 centimeters.

How many cartons of ice cream should Ester order to make 100 scoops?

B Ester finds 50 souvenir glass cups left over from the last charity event. The cup is cone-shaped and has a height of 16 centimeters and a radius of 3 centimeters. The cup is filled and then topped with half a scoop of ice cream.

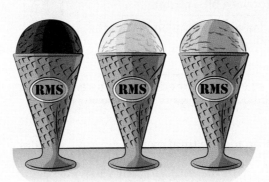

1. How much ice cream do you need to make 50 cups?

2. If the 50 cups are in addition to the 100 scoops from Question A, how many more cartons of ice cream must Ester order?

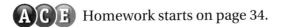 Homework starts on page 34.

Applications

1. The student council is organizing a T-shirt sale to raise money
    for a local charity. They make the following estimates of expenses
    and income:

    -   Expense of $250 for advertising
    -   Income of $12 for each T-shirt
    -   Expense of $4.25 for each T-shirt
    -   Income of $150 from a sponsor

    a. Write an equation for the income I for selling n T-shirts.

    b. Write an equation for the expenses E for selling n T-shirts.

    c. Suppose the student council sells 100 T-shirts. What is
        their profit?

    d. Write an equation for the profit P made for selling n T-shirts.

**For Exercises 2–5, use the following information: In *Variables and
Patterns*, several students were planning a bike tour. They estimated
the following expenses and incomes.**

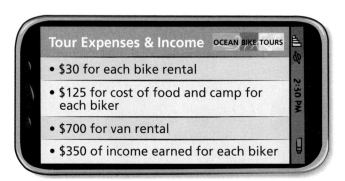

Tour Expenses & Income OCEAN BIKE TOURS

- $30 for each bike rental
- $125 for cost of food and camp for each biker
- $700 for van rental
- $350 of income earned for each biker

2. a. Write an equation for the total expenses E for n bikers.

    b. Write an equation for the total income I for n bikers.

    c. Write an equation for the profit P for n bikers.

    d. Find the profit for 25 bikers.

    e. Suppose the profit is $1,055. How many bikers went on the trip?

    f. Does the profit equation represent a linear, quadratic, or
        exponential function, or none of these? Explain.

3. **Multiple Choice** Suppose someone donates a van at no charge. Which equation represents the total expenses?

   A. $E = 125 + 30$ **B.** $E = 125n + 30n$

   C. $E = 155$ **D.** $E = 155 + n$

4. **Multiple Choice** Suppose students use their own bikes. Which equation represents the total expenses? (Assume they will rent a van.)

   F. $E = 125n + 700$ **G.** $E = 125 + 700 + n$

   H. $E = 825n$ **J.** $E = 350n + 125n + 700$

5. **Multiple Choice** Suppose students use their own bikes. Which equation represents the profit? (Assume they will rent a van.)

   A. $P = 350 - (125 + 700 + n)$ **B.** $P = 350n - 125n + 700$

   C. $P = 350n - (125n + 700)$ **D.** $P = 350 - 125n - 700$

For Exercises 6–8, recall the equations from Problem 2.2,
$P = 2.50V - 500$ **and** $V = 600 - 500R.$

6. Suppose the probability of rain is 50%. What profit can the concession stand expect to make?

7. What is the probability of rain if the profit expected is $100?

8. The manager estimates the daily employee-bonus fund B (in dollars) from the number of visitors V using the equation $B = 100 + 0.50V.$

   a. Suppose the probability of rain is 30%. What is the daily employee-bonus fund?

   b. Write an equation that relates the employee-bonus fund B to the probability of rain R.

   c. Suppose the probability of rain is 50%. Use your equation to calculate the employee-bonus fund.

   d. Suppose the daily employee-bonus fund is $375. What is the probability of rain?

9. A park manager claims that the profit P for a concession stand depends on the number of visitors V, and that the number of visitors depends on the day's high temperature T (in degrees Fahrenheit). The following equations represent the manager's claims:

$$P = 4.25V - 300$$
$$V = 50(T - 45)$$

a. Suppose 1,000 people visit the park one day. Predict the high temperature on that day.

b. Write an expression for profit based on temperature.

c. Write an expression for profit that is equivalent to the one in part (b). Explain what information the numbers and variables represent.

d. Find the profit if the temperature is 70°F.

10. Explain what happens to the volume of a cylinder when

a. the radius is doubled.

b. the height is doubled.

11. Explain what happens to the volume of a cone when

a. the radius is doubled.

b. the height is doubled.

12. Explain what happens to the volume of a sphere when

a. the radius is doubled.

b. the radius is tripled.

c. the radius is quadrupled (multiplied by 4).

13. The astronomy observatory pictured below has a diameter of 10 feet.

   a. What is the area of the floor?

   b. Write a general algebraic expression for the area of the floor.

   c. The observatory is made of a 3-foot-tall cylinder and half of a sphere (also called a *hemisphere*). What is the volume of the space inside the observatory?

   d. Write a general algebraic expression for the volume of the space inside the observatory.

14. The Jackson Middle School model rocket club drew the model rocket design below. The rocket is made from a cylinder and a cone. Write an expression to represent the volume of the rocket.

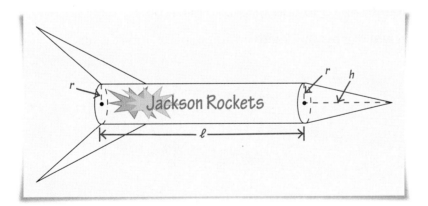

15. Ted made the model submarine shown below for his science class. Write an algebraic expression for the volume of Ted's submarine.

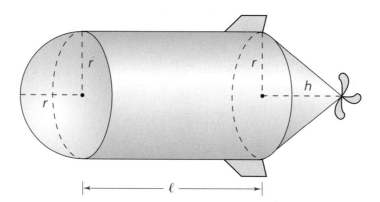

16. The pyramid and rectangular prism have the same base and height.

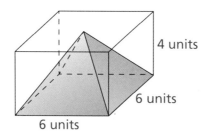

4 units

6 units

6 units

   a. Find the volume of the pyramid.

   b. Draw a pyramid with a volume of $\frac{1}{3}(8)$ cubic units.
      Hint: You might find it easier to draw the related prism first.

   c. Draw a pyramid with a volume of $\frac{1}{3}(27)$ cubic units.

   d. Find the height of a pyramid with a volume of $9x^3$ cubic units.

Connections

17. **Multiple Choice** Which statement is *false* when *a, b,* and *c* are different real numbers?

 F. $(a + b) + c = a + (b + c)$ **G.** $ab = ba$

 H. $(ab)c = a(bc)$ **J.** $a - b = b - a$

For Exercises 18–20, use the Distributive Property and sketch a rectangle to show the equivalence of the two expressions.

18. $x(x + 5)$ and $x^2 + 5x$

19. $(2 + x)(2 + 3x)$ and $4 + 8x + 3x^2$

20. $(x + 2)(2x + 3)$ and $2x^2 + 7x + 6$

21. A student's solution for $11x - 12 = 30 + 5x$ is shown below. Some steps are missing in the solution.

$$11x - 12 = 30 + 5x$$
$$11x = 42 + 5x$$
$$6x = 42$$
$$x = 7$$

 a. Copy the steps above. Fill in the missing steps.

 b. How can you check that $x = 7$ is the correct solution?

 c. Explain how you could use a graph or a table to solve the original equation for x.

22. In the following graph, line ℓ_1 represents the income for selling n soccer balls. Line ℓ_2 represents the expenses for manufacturing n soccer balls.

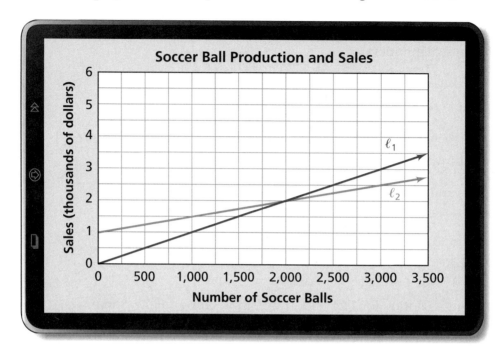

a. What is the start-up expense (the expense before any soccer balls are produced) for manufacturing the soccer balls?
Note: The vertical axis is in *thousands* of dollars.

b. What are the expenses and income for producing and selling 500 balls? 1,000 balls? 3,000 balls? Explain.

c. What is the profit for producing and selling 500 balls? 1,000 balls? 3,000 balls? Explain.

d. What is the break-even point? Give the number of soccer balls and the expenses.

e. Write equations for the expenses, income, and profit. Explain what the numbers and variables in each equation represent.

f. Suppose the manufacturer produces and sells 1,750 soccer balls. Use the equations in part (e) to find the profit.

g. Suppose the profit is $\$10,000$. Use the equations in part (e) to find the number of soccer balls produced and sold.

For Exercises 23–28, use properties of equality to solve each equation. Check your solution.

23. $7x + 15 = 12x + 5$

24. $7x + 15 = 5 + 12x$

25. $-3x + 5 = 2x - 10$

26. $14 - 3x = 1.5x + 5$

27. $9 - 4x = \frac{3 + x}{2}$

28. $-3(x + 5) = \frac{2x - 10}{3}$

29. The writing club wants to publish a book of students' short stories, poems, and essays. A member of the club contacts two local printers to get bids on the cost of printing the books.

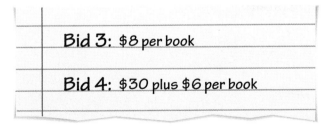

Bid 1: $100 plus $4 per book

Bid 2: $25 plus $7 per book

a. Make a table of values (*number of books printed, cost*) for each bid. Use your table to find the number of books for which the two bids are equal. Explain how you found your answer.

b. Make a graph of the two equations. Use your graph to find the number of books for which the two bids are equal. Explain.

c. For what numbers of books is Bid 1 less than Bid 2? Explain.

30. Use the information about printing costs from Exercise 29.

a. For each bid, find the cost of printing 75 books.

b. Suppose the cost cannot exceed $300. For each bid, find the greatest number of books that can be printed. Explain.

31. The writing club decides to request bids from two more printers.

Bid 3: $8 per book

Bid 4: $30 plus $6 per book

For what number of books does Bid 3 equal Bid 4? Explain.

Simplify each expression. Then explain how the expression could represent a volume calculation.

32. $3.14 \times 4.25^2 \times 5.5$

33. $\frac{1}{3} \times 3.14 \times 4.25^2 \times 5.5$

34. $\frac{4}{3} \times 3.14 \times 4.25^3$

35. $\frac{1}{3} \times 3.14 \times 4.25^2 \times 5.5 + \frac{4}{6} \times 3.14 \times 4.25^3$

36. $3.14 \times 4.25^2 \times 5.5 + \frac{4}{6} \times 3.14 \times 4.25^3$

37. $3.14 \times 4.25^2 \times 5.5 + \frac{1}{3} \times 3.14 \times 4.25^2 \times 3.5$

38. $3.14 \times 4.25^2 \times 5.5 - \frac{4}{6} \times 3.14 \times 4.25^3$

39. $3.14 \times 4.25^2 \times 5.5 - \frac{1}{3} \times 3.14 \times 4.25^2 \times 3.5$

Extensions

40. The Phillips Concert Hall staff estimates their concession stand profits P_C and admission profits P_A with the following equations, where x is the number of people attending (in hundreds):

$$P_C = 15x - 500$$
$$P_A = 106x - x^2$$

The concession-stand profits include revenue from advertising and the sale of food and souvenirs. The admission profits are based on the difference of ticket sales and cost.

  a. Write an equation for the total profit for P in terms of the number of people x (in hundreds).

  b. What is the maximum profit? How many people must attend in order to achieve the maximum profit?

For Exercises 41–43, suppose you slice the three-dimensional figure as indicated. Describe the shape of the face that results from the slice.

41. a. vertical slice

b. horizontal slice

42. a. vertical slice

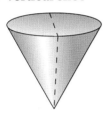

b. horizontal slice

43. a. vertical slice

b. horizontal slice

Mathematical Reflections 2

In this Investigation, you combined expressions or substituted an equivalent expression for a quantity to make new expressions. You wrote expressions to represent the relationships among the volumes of cylinders, cones, and spheres. You also used these expressions to make predictions. The following questions will help you summarize what you have learned.

Think about these questions. Discuss your ideas with other students and your teacher. Then write a summary of your findings in your notebook.

1. **Describe** a situation in which it is helpful to add expressions to form a new expression. Explain how you can combine the expressions.

2. **Describe** a situation in which it is helpful to substitute an equivalent expression for a quantity in an equation.

3. **What** are the advantages and disadvantages of working with one equation rather than two or more equations in a given situation?

4. Write an expression that represents the volume of each three-dimensional figure. **Explain** your reasoning.

   a. cylinder

   b. cone

   c. sphere

Common Core Mathematical Practices

As you worked on the Problems in this Investigation, you used prior knowledge to make sense of them. You also applied Mathematical Practices to solve the Problems. Think back over your work, the ways you thought about the Problems, and how you used Mathematical Practices.

Elena described her thoughts in the following way:

We discovered an efficient way to find the profit in Problem 2.2. The profit P depends on the number of visitors V that attend the park. The equation $P = 2.50V - 500$ represents profit. The number of visitors depends on the probability of rain R. The equation $V = 600 - 500R$ represents the number of visitors.

We substituted the expression for the number of visitors written in terms of the probability of rain $(600 - 500R)$ for V in the equation that represents profit. Using one equation reduced the number of calculations that we had to do.

Common Core Standards for Mathematical Practice
MP6 Attend to precision.

- What other Mathematical Practices can you identify in Elena's reasoning?

- Describe a Mathematical Practice that you and your classmates used to solve a different Problem in this Investigation.

Investigation 3

Solving Equations

A problem often requires finding solutions to equations. In previous Units, you developed strategies for solving linear and quadratic equations. In this Investigation, you will use the properties of real numbers to extend these strategies.

3.1 Selling Greeting Cards
Solving Linear Equations

 The steps below show one way to solve $100 + 4x = 25 + 7x$ for x.

$$100 + 4x = 25 + 7x$$
$$(1) \quad 100 + 4x - 4x = 25 + 7x - 4x$$
$$(2) \quad 100 = 25 + 3x$$
$$(3) \quad 100 - 25 = 25 + 3x - 25$$
$$(4) \quad 75 = 3x$$
$$(5) \quad \frac{75}{3} = \frac{3x}{3}$$
$$(6) \quad 25 = x$$

Common Core State Standards

8.EE.C.7a Give examples of linear equations in one variable with one solution, infinitely many solutions, or no solutions . . .

8.EE.C.8b Solve systems of two linear equations in two variables algebraically, and estimate solutions by graphing the equations. Solve simple cases by inspection.

Also 8.EE.A.2, 8.EE.C.7, 8.EE.C.7b, 8.EE.C.8, 8.EE.C.8a, 8.EE.C.8c, 8.F.A.1, N-Q.A.1, N-Q.A.2, A-SSE.A.1, A-SSE.A.1a, A-SSE.A.1b, A-SSE.A.2, A-SSE.B.3, A-SSE.B.3a, A-CED.A.1, A-CED.A.2, A-REI.A.1, A-REI.B.3, A-REI.B.4, A-REI.B.4b, A-REI.C.6, A-REI.D.10, A-REI.D.11

- How could you explain Steps 1, 3, and 5 in the solution?

- The solution begins by subtracting $4x$ from each side of the equation. Could you begin with a different first step? Explain.

- How can you check that $x = 25$ is the correct solution?

- Can you describe another method for finding the solution to the equation?

The preceding example uses the **properties of equality** that you learned in the Grade 7 Unit *Moving Straight Ahead.*

- You can add or subtract the same quantity from each side of an equation to write an equivalent equation.

- You can multiply or divide each side of an equation by the same nonzero quantity to write an equivalent equation.

You can use these properties as well as the Distributive and Commutative properties to solve equations.

Problem 3.1

A The school choir is selling boxes of greeting cards to raise money for a trip. The equation for the profit in dollars P in terms of the number of boxes sold s is

$$P = 5s - (100 + 2s)$$

1. What information do the expressions $5s$ and $100 + 2s$ represent in the situation? What information do 100 and $2s$ represent?

2. Use the equation to find the number of boxes the choir must sell to make a $200 profit. Explain.

3. How many boxes must the choir sell to break even? Explain.

4. Write a simpler expression for profit. Explain how your expression is equivalent to the original expression for profit.

5. One of the choir members wrote the following expression for profit: $5s - 2(50 + s)$. Explain whether this expression is equivalent to the original expression for profit.

B Describe how to solve an equation that has parentheses such as $200 = 5s - (100 + 2s)$ without using a table or graph.

continued on the next page >

Problem **3.1** *continued*

C Solve each equation for *x* when $y = 0$. Check your solutions.

1. $y = 5 + 2(3 + 4x)$ **2.** $y = 5 - 2(3 + 4x)$

3. $y = 5 + 2(3 - 4x)$ **4.** $y = 5 - 2(3 - 4x)$

A C E Homework starts on page 55.

3.2 Comparing Costs
Solving More Linear Equations

Ms. Lucero wants to install tiles around her square swimming pool. She finds the following two advertisements for tile companies.

COVER *and* **SURROUND IT**

$1,000 for design and delivery

$25 per tile after 12 tiles

TILE and **Beyond**

• $740 for design and delivery

• $32 per tile after 10 tiles

The equations below show the estimated costs *C* (in dollars) of buying and installing *N* border tiles.

      Cover and Surround It: $C_C = 1{,}000 + 25(N - 12)$

      Tile and Beyond: $C_T = 740 + 32(N - 10)$

You can use *subscripts* to show different uses for a variable: C_C means cost for *Cover and Surround It*; C_T means cost for *Tile and Beyond*.

- Do the equations make sense, given the description above for each company's charges? Explain.

- Is the cost of *Tile and Beyond* always cheaper than the cost of *Cover and Surround It*? Explain.

Ms. Lucero wants to know when the costs of each company were equal.

- How can Ms. Lucero use the equation $C_C = C_T$ to answer her question?

Problem 3.2

Ⓐ **1.** Without using a table or graph, find the number of tiles for which the two costs are equal.

2. How can you check that your solution is correct?

3. How can you use a graph or table to find the number of tiles for which the two costs are equal?

4. For what numbers of tiles is *Tile and Beyond* cheaper than *Cover and Surround It* ($C_T < C_C$)? Explain your reasoning.

Ⓑ Use the strategies that you developed in Problem 3.1 and in Question A to solve each equation for *x*. Check your solutions.

1. $3x = 5 + 2(3 + 4x)$

2. $3x = 5 - 2(3 + 4x)$

3. $10 + 3x = 2(3 + 4x) + 5$

4. $7 + 3(1 - x) = 5 - 2(3 - 4x)$

5. For what values of *x* is the inequality $10 + 3x > 2(3 + 4x) + 5$ true?

Ⓒ For each pair of equations,

- Find the values of *x* that make $y_1 = y_2$ without using a table or graph.

- State whether the linear equation $y_1 = y_2$ has a finite number of solutions, an infinite number of solutions, or no solutions.

- Graph the pair of equations.

- Use the graph to help explain your solution.

1. $y_1 = 3(2x - 5)$ and $y_2 = 2(3x - 1) + x$

2. $y_1 = 3(2x - 5)$ and $y_2 = 2(3x - 1) + 7$

3. $y_1 = 3(2x - 5)$ and $y_2 = 2(3x - 1) - 13$

Ⓐ Ⓒ Ⓔ Homework starts on page 55.

3.3 Factoring Quadratic Equations

Sometimes mathematical problems that appear to be different are actually the same. Finding the x-intercepts of the graph of $y = x^2 + 5x$ is the same as solving the equation $x^2 + 5x = 0$. The *solutions* to $x^2 + 5x = 0$ are also called the **roots** of the equation. In *Frogs, Fleas, and Painted Cubes*, you found the solutions or roots by using a table or graph of $y = x^2 + 5x$ as shown.

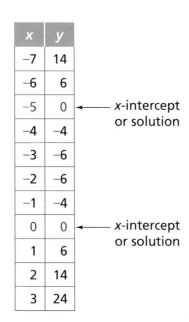

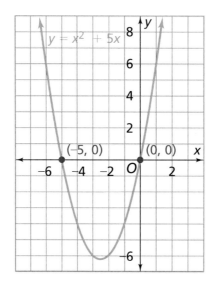

- What is the factored form of $x^2 + 5x$?

- What is the relationship between the factored form of $x^2 + 5x$ and the x-intercepts of the graph of $y = x^2 + 5x$? Explain.

To factor the expression $x^2 + 5x + 6$, Trevor draws the area model shown.

- Does the model represent $x^2 + 5x + 6$?

- What are the factors of $x^2 + 5x + 6$?

- What are the x-intercepts of the graph of $y = x^2 + 5x + 6$?

- What is the relationship between the x-intercepts of the graph of $y = x^2 + 5x + 6$ and the factored form of $x^2 + 5x + 6$?

Algebra provides important tools, such as factoring, that can help solve quadratic equations such as $x^2 + 5x = 0$ without using tables or graphs. Before using this tool, you need to review how to write quadratic expressions in factored form.

Problem 3.3

A Jakai suggests the method below to factor $x^2 + 8x + 12$.

> • Find factor pairs of 12, such as 1 and 12, 2 and 6, 3 and 4, −1 and −12, −2 and −6, and −3 and −4.
>
> • Find the factor pair whose sum is 8; 2 + 6 = 8.
>
> • Write the factored form: (x + 2)(x + 6).

1. Use an area model to show why Jakai's method works for the expression $x^2 + 8x + 12$.

2. Could Jakai have used another factor pair, such as 1 and 12 or 3 and 4, to make an area model for the expression $x^2 + 8x + 12$? Explain.

B Use a method similar to Jakai's to write each expression in factored form. Show why each factored form is correct.

1. $x^2 + 5x + 4$ **2.** $x^2 - 5x + 4$

3. $x^2 - 3x - 4$ **4.** $x^2 + 4x + 4$

C **1.** Examine the following expressions. How are they similar to and different from those in Question B?

a. $x^2 + 4x$ **b.** $4x^2 + 32x$

c. $6x^2 - 4x$ **d.** $x^2 - 4$

2. Will Jakai's method for factoring work on these expressions? If so, use his method to write them in factored form. If not, find another way to write each in factored form.

continued on the next page >

Problem **3.3**   *continued*

D   **1.** Examine the following expressions. How are they similar to and different from those in Question B?

     a. $2x^2 + 8x + 8$ **b.** $4x^2 + 4x + 1$ **c.** $2x^2 + 9x + 4$

   2. Will Jakai's method work on these expressions? If so, write them in factored form. If not, find another way to write each in factored form. Explain why your expression is equivalent to the original expression.

 Homework starts on page 55.

3.4   Solving Quadratic Equations

In the last Problem, you explored ways to write quadratic expressions in factored form. In this Problem, you will use the factored form to find solutions to quadratic equations.

- If you know that the product of two numbers is zero, what can you say about the numbers?

- How can you solve the equation $0 = x^2 + 8x + 12$ by factoring?

First, write $x^2 + 8x + 12$ in factored form to get $(x + 2)(x + 6)$. This expression is the product of two linear factors.

- When $0 = (x + 2)(x + 6)$, what must be true about one or both of the linear factors?

- How can this information help you find the solutions to $0 = (x + 2)(x + 6)$?

- How can this information help you find the x-intercepts of the graph of $y = x^2 + 8x + 12$?

Problem 3.4

Ⓐ **1.** Write $x^2 + 10x + 24$ in factored form.

2. How can you use the factored form to solve $x^2 + 10x + 24 = 0$ for x?

3. Explain how the solutions to $0 = x^2 + 10x + 24$ relate to the graph of $y = x^2 + 10x + 24$.

Ⓑ Solve each equation for x without making a table or graph.

1. $0 = (x + 1)(2x + 7)$　　　**2.** $0 = (5 - x)(x - 2)$

3. $0 = x^2 + 6x + 9$　　　　**4.** $0 = x^2 - 16$

5. $0 = x^2 + 10x + 16$　　　**6.** $0 = 2x^2 + 7x + 6$

7. How can you check your solution without using a table or a graph.

Ⓒ Solve each equation for x without making a table or graph. Check your answers.

1. $0 = x(9 - x)$　　　　**2.** $0 = -3x(2x + 5)$

3. $0 = 2x^2 + 32x$　　　　**4.** $0 = 18x - 9x^2$

Ⓓ You can approximate the height h of a pole-vaulter from the ground after t seconds with the equation $h = 32t - 16t^2$.

1. Suppose the pole-vaulter writes the equation $0 = 32t - 16t^2$. What information is the pole-vaulter looking for?

2. The pole-vaulter wants to clear a height of 17.5 feet. Will the pole-vaulter clear the desired height? Explain.

ⒶⒸⒺ Homework starts on page 55.

Did You Know?

You can find the solutions to many quadratic equations by using tables or graphs. Sometimes, however, these methods will only give approximate answers. For example, the solutions to the equation $x^2 - 2 = 0$ are $x = \sqrt{2}$ and $x = -\sqrt{2}$. Using a table or graph, you get only an approximation for $\sqrt{2}$.

You could try a factoring method similar to those used in this Investigation. However, the probability of being able to readily factor any quadratic expression $ax^2 + bx + c$, where a, b, and c are real numbers, is small.

The Greeks used a geometric method to solve quadratic equations in around 300 B.C. There is evidence that mathematicians from India had

François Viète

methods for solving these equations in around 500 B.C., but their methods remain unknown.

For years, mathematicians tried to find a general solution to $ax^2 + bx + c = 0$. In a book published in 1591, François Viète was the first person to develop a formula for finding the roots of a quadratic equation. It is called the *quadratic formula* and is given below.

$$x = \frac{-b \pm \sqrt{b^2 - 4ac}}{2a}$$

This formula can be used to solve any quadratic equation. You will learn more about this formula in *Function Junction*.

Applications

1. The organizers of a walkathon discuss expenses and income. They make the following estimates:

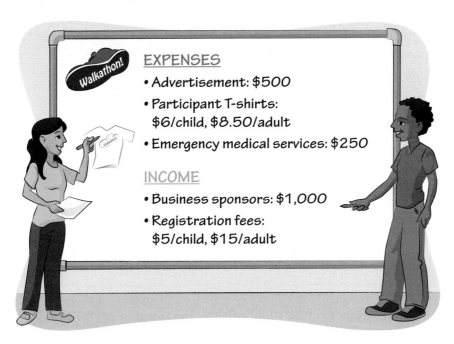

EXPENSES
- Advertisement: $500
- Participant T-shirts: $6/child, $8.50/adult
- Emergency medical services: $250

INCOME
- Business sponsors: $1,000
- Registration fees: $5/child, $15/adult

a. Suppose 30 adults and 40 children participate in the walkathon. Find the total income, the total expenses, and the profit. Show your work.

b. Write an equation showing the profit *P* in the form:

P = (expression for income) − (expression for expenses).

c. Write another expression for profit that is equivalent to the one in part (b).

d. Suppose 30 adults and 40 children participate. Use your equation from parts (b) or (c) to find the profit. Compare your answer to the profit you calculated in part (a).

e. Suppose 100 children participate and the profit is $1,099. How many adults participated? Show your work.

2. Marcel and Kirsten each try to simplify the following equation:

$$P = (1,000 + 5c + 15a) - (500 + 6c + 8.50a + 250)$$

They are both incorrect. Study the steps in their reasoning and identify their mistakes.

a.
> ## Marcel
>
> $P = (1,000 + 5c + 15a) - (500 + 6c + 8.50a + 250)$
> $= 1,000 + 5c + 15a - 500 + 6c + 8.50a + 250$
> $= 1,000 - 500 + 250 + 5c + 6c + 15a + 8.50a$
> $= 750 + 11c + 23.50a$ ✗

b.
> ## Kirsten
>
> $P = (1,000 + 5c + 15a) - (500 + 6c + 8.50a + 250)$
> $= 1,000 + 5c + 15a - 500 - 6c - 8.50a - 250$
> $= 1,000 - 500 - 250 + 5c - 6c + 15a - 8.50a$
> $= 250 + c + 6.50a$ ✗

3. According to the equation $V = 200 + 50(T - 70)$, the number of visitors V to a park depends on the day's high temperature T (in degrees Fahrenheit). Suppose 1,000 people visited the park one day. Predict that day's high temperature.

Solve each equation for x using the techniques that you developed in Problem 3.1. Check your solutions.

4. $10 + 2(3 + 2x) = 0$ 5. $10 - 2(3 + 2x) = 0$

6. $10 + 2(3 - 2x) = 0$ 7. $10 - 2(3 - 2x) = 0$

8. The two companies from Problem 3.2 decide to lower their costs for a Fourth of July sale. The equations below show the lower estimated costs C (in dollars) of buying and installing N border tiles.

Cover and Surround It: $C_C = 750 + 22(N - 12)$

Tile and Beyond: $C_T = 650 + 30(N - 10)$

a. Without using a table or graph, find the number of tiles for which the cost estimates from the two companies are equal.

b. How can you check that your solution is correct?

c. Explain how a graph or table could be used to find the number of tiles for which the costs are equal.

d. For what numbers of tiles is *Tile and Beyond* cheaper than *Cover and Surround It*? Explain your reasoning.

e. Write another expression that is equivalent to the expression for *Tile and Beyond*'s cost estimate (C_T). Explain what information the variables and numbers represent.

9. The school choir from Problem 3.1 has the profit plan $P = 5s - (100 + 2s)$. The school band also sells greeting cards. The equation for the band's profit is $P = 4s - 2(10 + s)$. Find the number of boxes that each group must sell to have equal profits.

Solve each equation for x without using tables or graphs. Check your solutions.

10. $8x + 16 = 6x$

11. $8(x + 2) = 6x$

12. $6 + 8(x + 2) = 6x$

13. $4 + 5(x + 2) = 7x$

14. $2x - 3(x + 6) = -4(x - 1)$

15. $2 - 3(x + 4) = 9 - (3 + 2x)$

16. $2.75 - 7.75(5 - 2x) = 26$

17. $\frac{1}{2}x + 4 = \frac{2}{3}x$

For Exercises 18–23, solve each equation and state whether it has
a finite number of solutions, an infinite number of solutions, or no
solutions. Then explain how the solution is represented by the graph
of two equations.

18. $3(2x - 5) = 5(x - 4)$

19. $3(2x - 5) = 6(x - 4) + 9$

20. $3(2x - 5) = 5(x - 4) + 5$

21. $3(2x - 5) = 5(x - 4) + x$

22. $3(2x - 5) = 5(x - 4) + x + 5$

23. $5 - 2(x - 1) = 2(3 - x) + 7$

24. Write each product in expanded form.

   a. $(x - 2)(x + 2)$

   b. $(x - 5)(x + 5)$

   c. $(x - 4)(x + 4)$

   d. $(x - 12)(x + 12)$

25. Write each quadratic expression in factored form.

   a. $x^2 + 5x + 4$

   b. $8 + x^2 + 6x$

   c. $x^2 - 7x + 10$

   d. $x^2 + 7x$

   e. $x^2 - 6 + 5x$

   f. $2x^2 - 5x - 12$

   g. $x^2 - 7x - 8$

   h. $x^2 - 5x$

26. Write each quadratic expression in factored form.

   a. $x^2 - 9$

   b. $x^2 - 36$

   c. $x^2 - 49$

   d. $x^2 - 400$

   e. $x^2 - 64$

   f. $x^2 - 144$

For Exercises 27–29, solve each equation for x. Check your solutions by
using a calculator to make tables or graphs.

27. $x^2 + 1.5x = 0$

28. $x^2 + 6x + 8 = 0$

29. $8x - x^2 = 0$

30. The equation $H = -16t^2 + 8t$ describes the height of a flea's
jump (in feet) after t seconds.

   a. Is the equation linear, quadratic, or exponential?

   b. Write an expression that is equivalent to $-16t^2 + 8t$.

   c. Without using a graph or a table, find the time when the flea lands
on the ground. Explain how you found your answer.

31. Use an area model to factor each expression.

    a. $x^2 + 8x + 15$ **b.** $x^2 - 9$ **c.** $2x^2 + 5x + 3$

32. Use your answers to Exercise 31 to solve each equation.

    a. $x^2 + 8x + 15 = 0$ **b.** $x^2 - 9 = 0$ **c.** $2x^2 + 5x + 3 = 0$

In Exercises 33 and 34, each solution contains an error.

- Find the error, and correct the solution.

- How would you help a student who made this error?

33.

$$6x^2 - x = 1$$

Solution

$$6x^2 - x - 1 = 0$$
$$(3x - 1)(2x + 1) = 0$$
$$3x - 1 = 0 \text{ or } 2x + 1 = 0$$
$$x = \frac{1}{3} \text{ or } x = -\frac{1}{2} \quad \textbf{✗}$$

34.

$$24n^2 - 16n = 0$$

Solution

$$24n^2 - 16n = 0$$
$$24n^2 = 16n$$
$$n = \frac{16}{24} \text{ or } n = \frac{2}{3} \quad \textbf{✗}$$

Connections

35. In Problem 3.1, the equation for profit P, in terms of the number of boxes sold s, is $P = 5s - (100 + 2s)$. The number of boxes sold also depends on the number of choir members.

    a. Suppose each member sells 11 boxes. Write an equation that will predict profit from the number of choir members n.
    Hint: First find an expression for the number of boxes sold.

    b. Write an equivalent expression for profit in part (a). Explain what the variables and numbers represent.

    c. Suppose the choir has 47 members. What is the profit?

    d. Suppose the profit is $1,088. How many choir members are there?

    e. In part (d), how many boxes were sold?

36. The equations $N = 2s + 2(s + 2)$ and $N = 4(s + 2) - 4$ both represent the number of 1-foot square border tiles needed to surround a square pool with sides of length s feet.

   a. Suppose $N = 48$. Solve $N = 2s + 2(s + 2)$ for s.

   b. Suppose $N = 48$. Solve $N = 4(s + 2) - 4$ for s.

   c. How do your answers for parts (a) and (b) compare? Explain.

37. Multiple Choice If $\frac{3}{4}(x - 4) = 12$, what is the value of x?

   A. 6   **B.** 8   **C.** $18\frac{1}{3}$ **D.** 20

38. Multiple Choice What is the value of $x^2(7 - x) + 1$ when $x = 5$?

   F. 201   **G.** 75   **H.** 51   **J.** 28

39. In Problem 3.2, you found the number of tiles for which the cost estimates for the two companies were equal. What is the side length of the largest square pool that can be surrounded by that number of tiles? Explain your reasoning.

For Exercises 40 and 41, use the Distributive and Commutative properties to simplify each expression. Check that the original expression and your simplified expression are equivalent by testing several x values in both expressions.

   40. $2(9x + 15) - (8 + 2x)$ **41.** $(7x - 12) - 2(3x + 10)$

42. You can write quadratic expressions in factored and expanded forms. Which form would you use for each of the following? Explain.

   a. to determine whether a quadratic relationship has a maximum point or a minimum point

   b. to find the x- and y-intercepts of a quadratic relationship

   c. to find the line of symmetry for a quadratic relationship

   d. to find the coordinates of the maximum or minimum point for a quadratic relationship

Each figure in Exercises 43–47 has an area of 24 square meters. Find each labeled dimension.

43.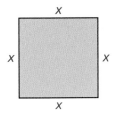

44.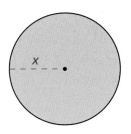

45.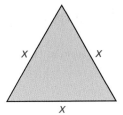

46.

47.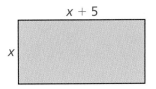

48. An oil company ships oil in spherical tanks that are 3 meters in diameter. The company now wants to ship oil in cylindrical tanks that are 4 meters high but have the same volume as the spheres. What radius must the cylindrical tanks have?

Same Volume
Not drawn to scale

49. Write a quadratic equation that has

a. one solution (one x-intercept)

b. two solutions (two x-intercepts)

50. John wants to know if he can bounce a superball over his house. You can approximate the height h of the superball on one bounce with the equation $h = 48t - 16t^2$, where t is the number of seconds after the ball hits the ground.

a. How long is the ball in the air?

b. Suppose his house is 30 feet tall. Will the ball make it over his house? Explain.

51. Each team in a lacrosse league must play each of the other teams twice. The number of games g played in a league with n teams is $g = n^2 - n$. What are the x-intercepts for the graph of this equation? Explain what information they represent.

52. The height (in feet) of an arch above a point x feet from one of its bases is approximated by the equation $y = 0.2x(1{,}000 - x)$. What is the maximum height of the arch? Explain.

Extensions

For Exercises 53 and 54, find the value of c for which $x = 3$ is the solution to the equation.

53. $3x + c = 2x - 2c$

54. $3x + c = cx - 2$

55. Write two linear equations that have the solution $x = 3$. Are there more than two equations with a solution of $x = 3$? Explain.

56. Insert parentheses into the expression $13 = 3 + 5x - 2 - 2x + 5$ so that the solution to the equation is $x = 1$.

57. Write the following expressions in expanded form.

   a. $(x - 2)(x + 2)$
                    b. $(x - 12.5)(x + 12.5)$

   c. $\left(x - \sqrt{5}\right)\left(x + \sqrt{5}\right)$
          d. $\left(x - \sqrt{2}\right)\left(x + \sqrt{2}\right)$

58. Factor.

   a. $x^2 - 100$
                      b. $x^2 - 1.44$

   c. $x^2 - 7$
                        d. $x^2 - 24$

59. Use the quadratic formula from the *Did You Know?* after Problem 3.4 to solve each equation.

   a. $x^2 - 6x + 8 = 0$
                b. $-x^2 - x + 6 = 0$

   c. $10 - 7x + x^2 = 0$
             d. $4x^2 - x = 0$

   e. $2x^2 - 12x + 18 = 0$
         f. $3x + x^2 - 4 = 0$

60. The graphs of $y = 1.5x + 6$ and $y = -2x + 15$ are shown at the right. The scale on the x-axis is 1, and the scale on the y-axis is 3.

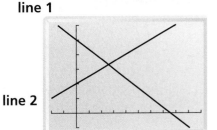

line 1

line 2

   a. Is $y = 1.5x + 6$ or $y = -2x + 15$ the equation of line 1?

   b. Find the coordinates of the point of intersection of the two lines.

   c. How could you find the answer to part (b) without using a graph or a table?

   d. What values of x satisfy the inequality $1.5x + 6 < -2x + 15$? How is your answer shown on the graph?

   e. What values of x satisfy the inequality $1.5x + 6 > -2x + 15$? How is your answer shown on the graph?

61. Use the graph of $y = x^2 - 9x$ at the right. The scale on the x-axis is 1. The scale on the y-axis is 2.

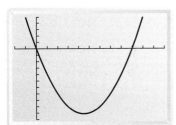

   a. What are the coordinates of the x-intercepts?

   b. How could you find the answer to part (a) without using a graph or a table?

   c. What values of x satisfy the inequality $x^2 - 9x < 0$? How is your answer shown on the graph?

   d. What values of x satisfy the inequality $x^2 - 9x > 0$? How is your answer shown on the graph?

   e. What is the minimum y-value? What x-value corresponds to this minimum y-value?

Use what you have learned in this Investigation to solve each equation. Show your work and check your solutions.

62. $x^2 + 5x + 7 = 1$ **63.** $x^2 + 6x + 15 = 6$

Mathematical Reflections 3

In this Investigation, you learned methods for solving linear and quadratic equations. The following questions will help you summarize what you have learned.

Think about these questions. Discuss your ideas with other students and your teacher. Then write a summary of your findings in your notebook.

1. **a. Describe** some general strategies for solving linear equations, including those with parentheses. Give examples that illustrate your strategies.

   b. Describe how you can tell if a linear equation has a finite number of solutions, an infinite number of solutions, or no solutions.

2. **Describe** some strategies for solving quadratic equations of the form $ax^2 + bx + c = 0$. Give examples.

3. **How** are the solutions of linear and quadratic equations related to graphs of the equations?

Common Core Mathematical Practices

As you worked on the Problems in this Investigation, you used prior knowledge to make sense of them. You also applied Mathematical Practices to solve the Problems. Think back over your work, the ways you thought about the Problems, and how you used Mathematical Practices.

Sophie described her thoughts in the following way:

In Problem 3.4, we learned that the linear factors of a quadratic equation reveal the x-intercepts of its graph. First, we rewrite the quadratic equation in factored form. Then, we set the equation equal to 0. The solutions of the equation are the x-intercepts of its graph. Now we can use linear factors to help us sketch the graphs of quadratic equations.

Common Core Standards for Mathematical Practice

MP8 Look for and express regularity in repeated reasoning.

- What other Mathematical Practices can you identify in Sophie's reasoning?

- Describe a Mathematical Practice that you and your classmates used to solve a different Problem in this Investigation.

Looking Back at Functions

Throughout your work in algebra, you have identified patterns of change between variables as linear, exponential, and quadratic functions. You have used tables, graphs, and equations to represent and reason about these functions. In this Unit, you have found that writing equivalent expressions for a quantity or variable can reveal new information about a situation. This Investigation will help pull these ideas together.

4.1 Pumping Water
Looking at Patterns of Change

Magnolia Middle School needs to empty their pool for resealing. Ms. Theodora's math class decides to collect data on the amount of water in the pool and the time it takes to empty it.

Common Core State Standards

8.F.A.3 Interpret the equation $y = mx + b$ as defining a linear function, whose graph is a straight line; give examples of functions that are not linear.

8.F.B.5 Describe qualitatively the functional relationship between two quantities by analyzing a graph (e.g., where the function is increasing or decreasing, linear or nonlinear). Sketch a graph that exhibits the qualitative features of a function that has been described verbally.

Also 8.EE.C.7, 8.EE.C.7b, 8.F.A.1, 8.F.B.4, N-Q.A.1, N-Q.A.2, A-SSE.A.1, A-SSE.A.1a, A-SSE.A.1b, A-SSE.A.2, A-SSE.B.3, A-SSE.B.3a, A-CED.A.1, A-CED.A.2, A-REI.B.3, A-REI.B.4, A-REI.B.4b, F-IF.C.9, F-BF.A.1, F-BF.A.1a, F-LE.A.1, F-LE.A.2, F-LE.B.5

The class writes the following equation to represent the amount of water w (in gallons) in the pool after t hours.

$$w = -250(t - 5)$$

- What information does the -250 represent?

- What units should you use for -250?

- What information does $(t - 5)$ represent? What units should you use for $(t - 5)$?

- What units should you use for $-250(t - 5)$? Explain.

Problem 4.1

A Answer the following questions. Explain your reasoning.

    1. How many gallons of water are pumped out each hour?

    2. How long will it take to empty the pool?

    3. How many gallons of water are in the pool at the start?

B **1.** Write an expression for the amount of water in the tank after t hours that is equivalent to the original expression.

    2. What information does this new expression tell you about the amount of water in the tank?

    3. Which expression is more useful in this situation? Explain.

C **1.** Describe the pattern of change in the relationship between the two variables w and t.

    2. Without graphing the equation, describe the shape of the graph. Include as much information as you can.

D Suppose the equation for the amount of water w (in gallons) in the pool after t hours is $w = -450(2t - 7)$.

    1. How many gallons of water are pumped out each hour?

    2. How long will it take to empty the pool?

    3. How many gallons of water are in the pool at the start?

    4. Write an expression that is equivalent to $-450(2t - 7)$. Which expression is more useful? Explain.

A C E Homework starts on page 72.

4.2 Area and Profit—What's the Connection?

Using Equations

In the next Problem, you will explore two familiar situations that have an interesting connection. Tony and Paco will operate the water tube concession stand at Water Town. Tony is responsible for designing the building that will store the tubes. Paco is responsible for deciding the rental fee for the tubes.

Problem 4.2

A Every concession stand must have a rectangular floor space and a perimeter of 88 meters. Tony wants the greatest area possible.

   1. Write an equation for the area in terms of the length.

   2. What is the maximum area for the rectangular floor space?

B Paco knows that on a typical day, the number of tube rentals n is related to the rental price for each tube p. Records from other water parks suggest:

- If the tubes are free (rental price = 0), there will be 54 rentals.

- Each increase of $1 in rental price will result in one fewer tube rented.

Paco uses this information to write the following equations:

      Equation 1 $n = 54 - (1)p$

      Equation 2 $I = np$, where I is the daily income

   1. Do these equations make sense? Explain.

   2. Write an equation for income in terms of the number of rentals n.

   3. The expense for storage and maintenance of each rented tube is $10 per day. Write an equation for daily profit D in terms of the number of rentals n.

   4. What number of rentals produces the maximum daily profit? What is the maximum profit? What price produces the maximum daily profit?

   5. Compare the equation in part (3) to the equation in Question A, part (1).

A C E   Homework starts on page 72.

4.3 Generating Patterns
Linear, Exponential, Quadratic

In this Problem, you are given two data points for a linear, exponential, and quadratic relationship. You will use these points to find more data points. Then you will write an equation for each relationship.

(?) Is it always possible to find a linear, exponential, or quadratic equation from two given points? Can you find more than one equation?

Problem 4.3

A The first two rows in a table of numbers are given below. Write four more numbers in each column to make a linear relationship, an exponential relationship, and a quadratic relationship.

Data Points

x	Linear y	Exponential y	Quadratic y
1	1	1	1
2	4	4	4
3	▢	▢	▢
4	▢	▢	▢
5	▢	▢	▢
6	▢	▢	▢

B Explain why the pattern in each column is correct.

C **1.** Write an equation for each relationship. Explain what information the variables and numbers represent.

2. Compare your equations with those of your classmates. Do you all have the same equations? What properties of each kind of function helped you construct the table and equation for each?

 Homework starts on page 72.

4.4 What's the Function?
Modeling With Functions

In the following Problem, you are given descriptions of situations. You will decide if each situation can represent a linear, quadratic, exponential, or inverse variation relationship.

Problem 4.4

Ⓐ For each of the following situations:

- Determine whether the situation can represent a linear function, a quadratic function, an exponential function, an inverse variation, or none of these.

- Write an equation that represents the function.

- Write a problem that you can solve using the equation. Then, solve the problem.

(1) A cylinder has a height of 16 inches. Consider the relationship between the volume and the radius of the cylinder.

(2) A rectangle has an area of 24 square inches. Consider the relationship between the width and the length of the rectangle.

(3) A laptop costs $800 and loses 50% of its value each year. Consider the relationship between the value of the laptop and time.

(4) Tim sells magazines for a fundraiser. His first customer buys 2 magazines. With his second customer, his sales total 4 magazines. With his fourth customer, his sales total 8 magazines. With his eighth customer, his sales total 16 magazines. Consider the relationship between the number of magazines sold and the number of customers.

(5) A cylinder has a radius of 4 inches. Consider the relationship between the volume and the height of the cylinder.

Problem 4.4 continued

(6) Jorge keeps track of the number of people who visit his new Web site each day. On the first day, he has 3 visitors. On the second day, he has 9 visitors. On the third day, he has 27 visitors. On the fourth day, he has 81 visitors. Suppose this pattern continues. Consider the relationship between the day number and the number of visitors.

(7) Unit squares are arranged as shown below. Figure 1 has one rectangle. Figure 2 has 3 rectangles. Figure 3 has 6 rectangles, and so on. Consider the relationship between the number of rectangles and the figure number.

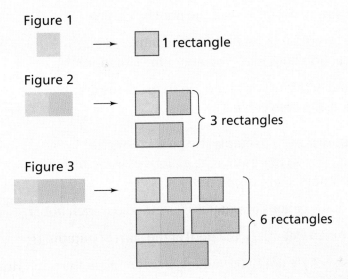

(8) A basketball manufacturer needs to know the relationship between the volume of the ball and its radius. Consider the relationship between the volume of a sphere and its radius.

B Without graphing the relationship, describe the shapes of the graphs for the relationships in Question A. Give as much detail as possible, including patterns of change, intercepts, and maximum and minimum points.

A C E Homework starts on page 72.

 Applications

1. A pump is used to empty a swimming pool. The equation $w = -275t + 1{,}925$ represents the gallons of water w that remain in the pool t hours after pumping starts.

   a. How many gallons of water are pumped out each hour?

   b. How much water is in the pool at the start of pumping?

   c. Suppose there are 1,100 gallons of water left in the pool. How long has the pump been running?

   d. After how many hours will the pool be empty?

   e. Write an equation that is equivalent to $w = -275t + 1{,}925$. What information does it tell you about the situation?

   f. Without graphing, describe the shape of the graph of the relationship between w and t.

2. A new pump is used to empty the pool in Exercise 1. The equation $w = -275(2t - 7)$ represents the gallons of water w that remain in the pool t hours after pumping starts.

   a. How many gallons of water are pumped out each hour?

   b. How much water is in the pool at the start of pumping?

   c. Suppose there are 1,000 gallons of water left in the pool. How long has the pump been running?

   d. After how many hours will the pool be empty?

   e. Write an equation that is equivalent to $w = -275(2t - 7)$. What information does it tell you about the situation?

3. A truck has a broken fuel gauge. Luckily, the driver keeps a record of mileage and gas consumption. The driver uses the data to write an equation for the relationship between the number of gallons of gas in the tank g and the number of miles driven m since the last fill-up.

$$g = 25 - \frac{1}{15}m$$

   a. How many gallons of gasoline are in a full tank? Explain.

   b. Suppose the driver travels 50 miles after filling the tank. How much gas is left?

   c. After filling the tank, how many miles can the driver travel before 5 gallons remain?

   d. After filling the tank, how many miles can the driver travel before the tank is empty?

   e. How many miles does the driver have to travel in order to use 1 gallon of gas? Explain.

   f. In the equation, what do the numbers 25 and $\frac{1}{15}$ tell you about the situation?

4. A middle school orders some yearbooks. Their bill is shown below.

Yearbook Printer 123 Publishing Drive • Paperville, MA 02689

INVOICE # 090480

QUANTITY	DESCRIPTION	COST
400	Middle School Yearbook	$2,500
	TOTAL	$2,500

The school gives some free copies to the yearbook advisor and staff. They sell the rest to students. The equation below tells how close the school is to paying for the printing bill.

$$y = 2,500 - 15(N - 8)$$

Describe what information the numbers and variables represent in this situation.

5. A farmer has 240 meters of fence. The farmer wants to build a rectangular fence that encloses the greatest possible land area.

   a. Write an equation for the fenced area A in terms of the length ℓ of the rectangular plot.

   b. What are the dimensions of the rectangle with the greatest area?

   c. Describe how you could find the information in part (b) from a graph of the equation.

   d. Does the equation for area represent a linear, quadratic, or exponential function, or none of these? Explain.

6. In Exercise 5, suppose the farmer uses the 240 meters of fence to enclose a rectangular plot on only three sides and uses a creek as the boundary of the fourth side.

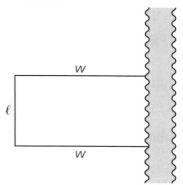

   a. Write an equation for the fenced area A in terms of the length ℓ of the rectangular plot.

   b. What are the dimensions of the rectangle with the greatest area?

   c. Does the equation represent a linear, quadratic, or exponential function, or none of these? Explain.

7. The math club is selling posters to advertise National Algebra Day. The following equation represents the profits *P* they expect for selling *n* posters at *x* dollars each.

$$P = xn - 6n$$

They also know that the number of posters *n* sold depends on the selling price *x*, which is represented by this equation:

$$n = 20 - x$$

a. Write an equation for profit in terms of the number of posters sold. **Hint:** First solve the equation $n = 20 - x$ for *x*.

b. What is the profit for selling 10 posters?

c. What is the selling price of the posters in part (b)?

d. What is the greatest possible profit?

8. The tables below represent the projected growth of certain species of deer. Use the three tables to answer parts (a)–(c).

Table 1

Year	Deer
2010	1,000
2011	1,030
2012	1,061
2013	1,093
2014	1,126

Table 2

Year	Deer
2010	1,000
2011	1,030
2012	1,060
2013	1,090
2014	1,120

Table 3

Year	Deer
2010	1,000
2011	3,000
2012	9,000
2013	27,000
2014	81,000

a. Describe the growth represented in each table. Do any of these patterns represent linear, exponential, or quadratic functions?

b. Write an equation for each pattern that represents a linear, exponential, or quadratic function.

c. Does any table show a population of deer growing at a rate of 3% per year? Explain.

9. The Department of Natural Resources is collecting data on three different species of animals. They find that these species show different patterns of population growth. They write the equations below to represent the population P of each species after t years.

Species 1	Species 2	Species 3
$P_1 = 10{,}000 + 100t$	$P_2 = 10(3^t)$	$P_3 = 800 + 10t^2$

a. Describe what information the numbers and variables represent in each equation.

b. Describe the pattern of growth for each species. Explain how the patterns differ.

c. Pick any two species. After how many years will the populations of the two species be equal? Explain how you got your answer.

10. Suppose the figures shown are made with toothpicks.

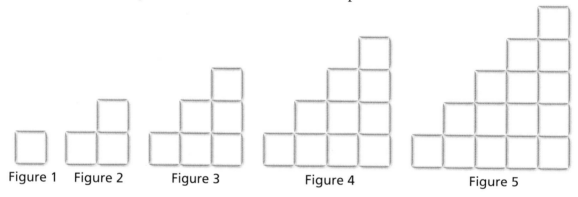

Figure 1   Figure 2   Figure 3   Figure 4   Figure 5

a. What patterns in the set of figures do you notice?

b. How many toothpicks do you need to make Figure 7?

c. Is the relationship between the perimeter and the figure number a linear, quadratic, or exponential function? Explain.

d. Is the relationship between the total number of toothpicks and the figure number a linear, quadratic, or exponential function?

e. Write an equation to represent the perimeter of Figure N. Explain your rule.

f. Write an equation to represent the total number of toothpicks needed to make Figure N. Explain your rule.

Use the four graphs to answer Exercises 11–13.

Graph 1

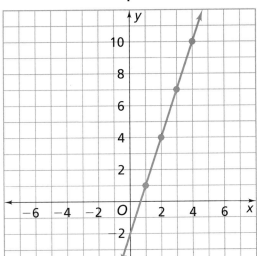

Graph 2

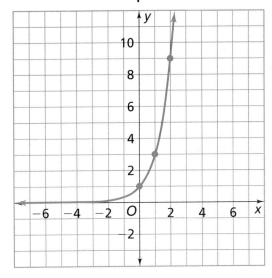

Graph 3

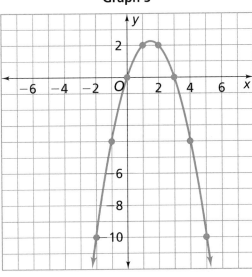

Graph 4

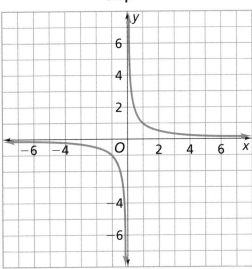

11. Which graph represents a linear function? A quadratic function? An exponential function?

12. Make a table of y-values for $x = 1, 2, 3, \ldots 6$ for each function.

13. Write an equation for each function. Describe your strategy.

Match each equation below with one of the graphs.

Graph A

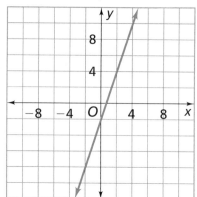

Graph B

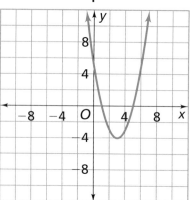

Graph C

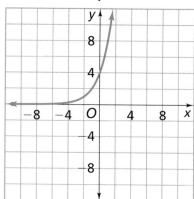

Graph D

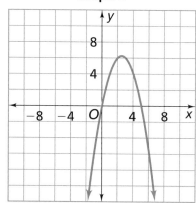

Graph E

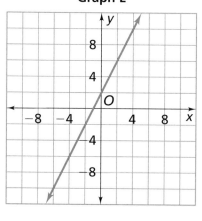

Graph F

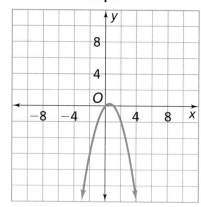

Graph G

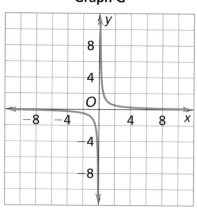

14. $y = \frac{1}{x}$

15. $y = x(5 - x)$

16. $y = (x - 1)(x - 5)$

17. $y = x(1 - x)$

18. $y = 2 + 2x$

19. $y = 5(2^x)$

20. $y = -2 + 3x$

21. For parts (a)–(c), use the set of equations below.

(1) $y = x^2 + 8x$ (4) $y = 2(x - 3) + 6$ (7) $y = 0.25^x$

(2) $y = 2x$ (5) $y = x(x + 8)$ (8) $y = 17 + x(x + 3)$

(3) $y = 4^{x-1}$ (6) $y = 0.25(4^x)$ (9) $y = (x + 1)(x + 17)$

a. Which equations represent linear, quadratic, or exponential functions?

b. Find any equations that represent the same function.

c. Without graphing the equation, describe the shape of the graph of each equation in part (b). Give as much detail as possible, including patterns of change, intercepts, and maximum and minimum points.

22. Pick a linear, quadratic, and exponential equation from Exercise 21. Describe a problem that can be represented by each equation.

23. Use the following equations for parts (a)–(c).

(1) $y = x^2 + 8x + 16$ (10) $y = (4x - 3)(x + 1)$

(2) $y = \frac{1}{3}(3^x)$ (11) $y = 20x - 4x^2$

(3) $y = 10 - 2x$ (12) $y = x^2$

(4) $y = 2x^3 + 5$ (13) $y = 3^{x-1}$

(5) $y = (x^2 + 1)(x^2 + 3)$ (14) $y = 16 - 2(x + 3)$

(6) $y = 0.5^x$ (15) $y = 4x^2 - x - 3$

(7) $y = 22 - 2x$ (16) $y = x + \frac{1}{x}$

(8) $y = \frac{3}{x}$ (17) $y = 4x(5 - x)$

(9) $y = (x + 4)(x + 4)$ (18) $y = 2(x - 3) + 6(1 - x)$

a. Which equations represent functions that are linear? Exponential? Quadratic?

b. For each function in part (a), find those equations that represent the same function.

c. Without graphing the equation, describe the shape of the graph of those equations in part (b). Give as much detail as possible, including patterns of change, intercepts, and maximum and minimum points.

24. Pick one linear, one quadratic, and one exponential equation from Exercise 23. Describe a problem that can be represented by each equation.

Connections

25. Betty's Bakery sells giant cookies for $1.00 each. This price is not high enough for the bakery to earn a profit anymore. Betty must raise the price, but she does not want to lose customers by raising the price too high or too quickly. She considers the following three plans.

> **Plan 1** Raise the price by $.05 each week until the price reaches $1.80.
>
> **Plan 2** Raise the price by 5% each week until the price reaches $1.80.
>
> **Plan 3** Raise the price by the same amount each week for 8 weeks. The price reaches $1.80 in the eighth week.

a. Make a table of prices for each plan. How many weeks will it take for the price to reach $1.80 under each plan?

b. Graph the data for each plan on the same coordinate grid. Compare the shapes of the graphs. What do the shapes mean in terms of changing the cookie price?

c. Are any of the graphs linear? Explain.

d. Which plan do you think Betty should implement? Give reasons for your choice.

26. Betty suspects that someone is stealing her chocolate chips.

a. There are one million chocolate chips in a new canister. Betty uses about 40,000 chips each day. How many days should the canister last?

b. Make a graph that shows the relationship between the number of days after Betty opens a new canister and the number of chips that should be in the canister at the end of each day.

c. Write an equation for the relationship from part (b).

d. After Betty opens a new canister, she begins keeping track of the chips at the end of each day. A gauge on the side of the chip canister allows Betty to estimate the remaining number of chips. Make a graph of the data below. Compare the graph with your graph from part (b). Are Betty's suspicions justified? Explain.

Chocolate Chip Daily Count

Day	1	2	3	4	5	6	7	8
Number of Chips Left (thousands)	800	640	512	410	330	260	210	170

27. Since Betty raised her prices, cookie sales have fallen. She calls in a business consultant who suggests conducting a customer survey. The survey asks, "Which price are you willing to pay for a cookie?" Here are the results:

Cookie Price Survey

Price	$1.75	$1.50	$1.25	$1.00
Number of Customers	100	117	140	175

a. Make a graph of the data. Draw a line or curve that models the trend.

b. Use your graph to predict the number of customers willing to pay $1.35 and the number willing to pay $2.00.

c. Do you think predictions based on your graph are accurate? Explain.

d. Consider your work in past Units. What situation from your previous work has a graph similar to this one?

28. Sabrina uses an area model to find the product $(x + 2)(x + 3)$.

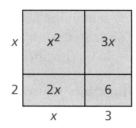

Tara uses the Distributive Property to multiply $(x + 2)(x + 3)$.

$$(x + 2)(x + 3) = (x + 2)x + (x + 2)3$$
$$= x^2 + 2x + 3x + 6$$
$$= x^2 + x(2 + 3) + 6$$
$$= x^2 + 5x + 6$$

a. Explain each step in Tara's method.

b. Explain how Tara's method relates to Sabrina's area model.

c. Use the Distributive Property to find each product.

   i. $(x + 5)(x + 3)$ **ii.** $(x + 4)(x + 1)$ **iii.** $(x - 2)(x + 4)$

29. a. A soccer team has 21 players. Suppose each player shakes hands with each of the other players. How many handshakes will take place?

   b. Write an equation for the number of handshakes h among a team with n players.

   c. Write an expression for the number of handshakes that is equivalent to the one in part (b).

30. a. Write an expression that is equivalent to $(x + 2)(x + 5)$.

   b. Explain two methods for checking equivalence.

31. For the equation $y = (x + 2)(x + 5)$, find each of the following. Explain how you found each.

   a. y-intercept   **b.** x-intercept(s)

   c. maximum or minimum point   **d.** line of symmetry

For Exercises 32–37, find an equivalent expression.

32. $x^2 \cdot x^3$

33. $x \cdot x^0 \cdot x^5$

34. $\dfrac{x^2 \cdot x^3}{x}$

35. $\dfrac{x^8}{x^5}$

36. $\dfrac{x^5}{x^8}$

37. $\dfrac{4x^8}{2x^5}$

38. Mary's salary is $30,000 per year. What would be her new salary given each condition?

   a. She gets a 15% raise.

   b. Her salary grows by a factor of 1.12.

   c. Her salary increases by 110%.

39. Examine the three different cylinders.

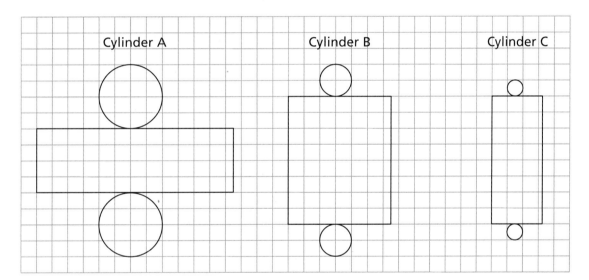

   a. Compare the three cylinders.

   b. Estimate the surface area of each cylinder. Which cylinder has the greatest surface area? Explain.

   c. Which cylinder has the greatest volume? Explain.

40. The equation $d = -16t^2 + 16t + 6.5$ represents the distance d, in feet, from the ground to the top of a basketball player's head t seconds after the player jumps. Find the distance to the top of the player's head after

a. 0.1 second.   **b.** 0.3 second.   **c.** 1 second.

d. What operations did you perform to calculate your answers in parts (a)–(c)? In what order did you perform the operations?

41. A bacteria colony begins with 5,000 bacteria. The population doubles every hour. This pattern of exponential growth can be modeled by the equation $b = 5,000(2^t)$, where b is the number of bacteria and t is the number of hours.

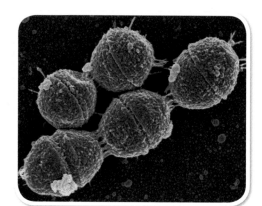

a. What is the population of the colony after 3 hours? After 5 hours?

b. What mathematical operations did you perform to calculate your answers in part (a)? In what order did you perform these operations?

For Exercises 42–47, write an expression equivalent to the given expression.

42. $5 - 6(x + 10) - 4$

43. $-3(x - 4) - (x + 3)$

44. $x(x + 2) - 5x + 6$

45. $6x^2 + 5x(x - 10) + 10$

46. $\frac{1}{2}x^2 + \frac{1}{4}x^2 + x^2 + 3x$

47. $7x^2 - 3.5x + 0.75x - 8$

48. Write an equation for

a. y in terms of z given $y = 6x + 10$ and $x = 2z - 7$.

b. P in terms of n given $P = xn - 6n$ and $x = 12 - n$.

c. A in terms of w given $A = \ell w$ and $\ell = 15 - w$.

Give an equation for each function.

49. a parabola with x-intercepts $(-3, 0)$ and $(2, 0)$

50. a line with a slope of -4 and an x-intercept of $(2, 0)$

51. an exponential function with a scale factor of 1.25

52. a. Sketch each equation below on the same coordinate grid.

$$y = 4x^2 \qquad y = -4x^2 \qquad y = \tfrac{1}{4}x^2 \qquad y = -\tfrac{1}{4}x^2$$

b. What is the effect of a change in the value of a on the graph of the equation $y = ax^2$?

53. a. Sketch each equation below on the same coordinate grid.

$$y = 4x^2 + 5 \qquad y = 4x^2 - 5 \qquad y = 4x^2 + 3 \qquad y = 4x^2 - 3$$

b. What is the effect of a change in the value of c on the graph of the equation $y = 4x^2 + c$?

54. You want to attach an anchor wire for a flagpole to the top of the pole and anchor it to the ground at a distance that is half the height of the pole. What is the height of the tallest flagpole you can support with a 60-foot anchor wire?

55. The figures show cones inside cylinders. Each cone shares the same radius and height as the cylinder containing it. Which cone has a volume of $3\pi x^2$ cubic units? Explain.

Cone 1

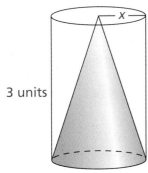

3 units

Cone 2

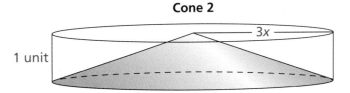

1 unit

Extensions

56. Caley's cell phone company offers two different monthly billing options for local phone service.

> **Plan 1** $25 for up to 100 minutes, plus $.50 for each extra minute
>
> **Plan 2** $50 for an unlimited number of minutes

a. Suppose Caley uses 200 minutes each month. What is the best option for him? Explain.

b. For what number of minutes are the costs of the two plans equal? Explain.

c. Write an equation for each plan. Describe how the variables and numbers represent the growth patterns of the plans.

d. Graph each equation on the same coordinate grid. Describe how the graphs describe the growth patterns of the phone plans.

57. A quarterback's statistics for one season are shown below. Use the equations and the statistics to find his overall rating that season.

Completion Rating: $CR = 5\left(\dfrac{\text{completions}}{\text{attempts}}\right) - 1.5$

Yards Rating: $YR = \dfrac{\dfrac{\text{yards}}{\text{attempts}} - 3}{4}$

Touchdown Rating: $TR = 20\left(\dfrac{\text{touchdowns}}{\text{attempts}}\right)$

Interception Rating: $IR = \dfrac{19 - 2\left(\dfrac{\text{interceptions}}{\text{attempts}}\right)}{8}$

OVERALL RATING $= 100\left(\dfrac{CR + YR + TR + IR}{6}\right)$

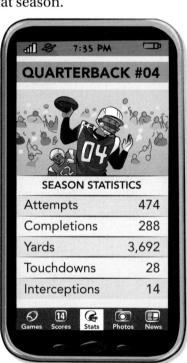

7:35 PM

QUARTERBACK #04

04

SEASON STATISTICS

Attempts	474
Completions	288
Yards	3,692
Touchdowns	28
Interceptions	14

Games Scores Stats Photos News

58. The equation below represents the space s in feet between cars that is considered safe given the average velocity v in feet per second on a busy street.

$$s = \frac{v^2}{32} + v + 18$$

   a. Suppose a car travels at a rate of 44 feet per second. How far should it be from the car ahead of it in order to be safe?

   b. What is 44 feet per second in miles per hour?

   c. Suppose a taxi is 100 feet behind a car. At what velocity is it safe for the taxi to be traveling in feet per second? In miles per hour?

59. Below is the graph of $y = (x + 2)(x - 1)(x - 5)$.

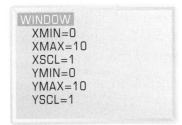
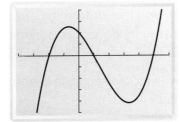

   a. What are the solutions to $(x + 2)(x - 1)(x - 5) = 0$? How are the solutions shown on the graph?

   b. What values of x satisfy the inequality $(x + 2)(x - 1)(x - 5) < 0$? How is your answer shown on the graph?

   c. How can you find the answer to part (b) without using the graph? **Hint:** Use what you know about multiplying positive and negative numbers.

60. a. Graph $y = x^2 + 4$. Is it possible to find x when $y = 0$? Explain.

   b. Give two examples of a quadratic equation ($ax^2 + bx + c = 0$, where a, b, and c are real numbers) with no solution.

   c. Give two examples of quadratic equations with 1 solution.

   d. Give two examples of quadratic equations with 2 solutions.

Mathematical Reflections 4

In this Investigation, you studied equations that represent linear, exponential, or quadratic functions. You also used expanded or factored expressions for y to make predictions about the shapes of the graphs of these functions. The following questions will help you summarize what you have learned.

Think about these questions. Discuss your ideas with other students and your teacher. Then write a summary of your findings in your notebook.

1. **Describe** how you can tell whether an equation is a linear, an exponential, or a quadratic function.

2. **Describe** how you can determine specific features of the graph of a function from its equation. Include its shape, x- and y-intercepts, maximum and minimum points, and patterns of change.

3. **Describe** how you can recognize which function to use to solve an applied problem.

Common Core Mathematical Practices

As you worked on the Problems in this Investigation, you used prior knowledge to make sense of them. You also applied Mathematical Practices to solve the Problems. Think back over your work, the ways you thought about the Problems, and how you used Mathematical Practices.

Ken described his thoughts in the following way:

When Jim and I were working on Problem 4.2, we were wondering how maximum area related to finding maximum profit. We thought that "maximum" was the connection and that each relationship was a quadratic function. We were correct.

We found a quadratic equation to represent the relationship between the two variables in each situation. The equations were exactly the same except for the variables. The equations were $A = 44\ell - \ell^2$ and $D = 44n - n^2$.

Common Core Standards for Mathematical Practice
MP2 Reason abstractly and quantitatively.

• What other Mathematical Practices can you identify in Ken's reasoning?

• Describe a Mathematical Practice that you and your classmates used to solve a different Problem in this Investigation.

Investigation 5

Reasoning With Symbols

You have looked at patterns and made conjectures and predictions. You have given informal arguments to support your conjectures. In this Investigation, you will look at how algebra can help you justify some of your conjectures by providing evidence or proof.

5.1 Using Algebra to Solve a Puzzle

People receive a lot of information by email. Some emails are useful, while others are for fun. A puzzle similar to the one below appeared in several emails in a recent year.

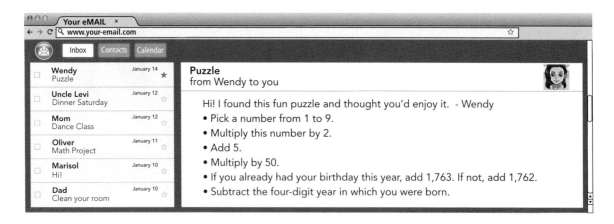

Inbox | Contacts | Calendar

Wendy — January 14
Puzzle

Uncle Levi — January 12
Dinner Saturday

Mom — January 12
Dance Class

Oliver — January 11
Math Project

Marisol — January 10
Hi!

Dad — January 10
Clean your room

Puzzle
from Wendy to you

Hi! I found this fun puzzle and thought you'd enjoy it. - Wendy
• Pick a number from 1 to 9.
• Multiply this number by 2.
• Add 5.
• Multiply by 50.
• If you already had your birthday this year, add 1,763. If not, add 1,762.
• Subtract the four-digit year in which you were born.

Common Core State Standards

8.EE.C.7b Solve linear equations with rational number coefficients, including equations whose solutions require expanding expressions using the distributive property and collecting like terms.

Also 8.F.A.1, 8.F.A.2, 8.F.B.4, N-RN.B.3, A-SSE.A.1, A-SSE.A.1a, A-SSE.A.1b, A-SSE.A.2, A-SSE.B.3, A-CED.A.1, A-CED.A.2, F-BF.A.1

Problem 5.1

On February 1, 2013, Elizabeth shared the puzzle shown on the previous page with her classmates. She told them, "If you tell me your answer, I will tell you how old you are."

(A) 1. Work through the steps using the date above.

2. You should have a three-digit number. Look at the first digit and the last two digits. What information do these numbers represent?

(B) Let *n* represent the number you chose in the first step. Repeat the steps with *n*. Use mathematical statements to explain why the puzzle works.

(C) Will the puzzle work for the current year? If not, how can you change the steps to make it work?

A C E Homework starts on page 95.

5.2 Odd and Even Revisited

In *Prime Time*, you looked at factors and multiples. You explored several conjectures about even and odd whole numbers, including:

> The sum of two even whole numbers is even.

> The sum of an even whole number and odd whole number is odd.

- Are these conjectures true for odd and even integers?

- How might you convince a friend that these conjectures are true?

Daphne claims that the algebraic expression 2*n*, where *n* is any integer, will produce all even integers.

- Is Daphne correct? Explain.

- What symbolic expression will produce all odd integers? Explain why it works.

Problem 5.2

Rachel offers the following argument for showing that the sum of two even integers is even.

> • Let *n* and *m* represent any two integers.
>
> • Then 2*n* and 2*m* are two even integers.
>
> • 2*n* + 2*m* is the sum of two even integers.
>
> • And 2*n* + 2*m* = 2(*n* + *m*).
>
> • 2(*n* + *m*) is an even integer.
>
> • So, the sum of two even integers is even.

A Study Rachel's argument. Provide reasons for each step. Does her argument prove the conjecture that the sum of any two even integers is an even integer? Explain.

B Bianca offers the following argument:

> • Show two even numbers as rectangular arrays with one dimension equal to 2. Let *n* and *m* represent any two integers.
>
>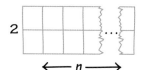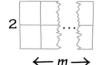
>
> • Then you can represent the sum of the two numbers as a single array with a dimension equal to 2.
>
>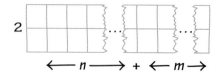

Does Bianca's argument prove the conjecture about the sum of two even numbers? Explain.

Problem 5.2 *continued*

C Show that the following conjectures are true.

1. The sum of an odd integer and an even integer is odd.

2. The product of an even integer and an odd integer is even.

D Rachel thinks that she may be able to use reasoning similar to Question A to convince Bianca that the product of two rational numbers is rational.

Let $\frac{a}{b}$ and $\frac{c}{d}$ be rational numbers, where a, b, c, and d are integers, $b \neq 0$, and $d \neq 0$.

1. How could Rachel convince Bianca that the product of two rational numbers is rational?

2. How could Rachel convince Bianca that the sum or difference of two rational numbers is rational?

E Rachel wonders about sums and products of rational and irrational numbers. Help her justify her claims.

1. Rachel thinks that the sum of a rational number p and an irrational number q is irrational. Is it possible that $p + q = s$, where s is a rational number? Does thinking about the same relationship as $q = s - p$ help? Explain.

2. Rachel thinks that the product of a rational number p and an irrational number q is irrational. Is it possible that $pq = y$, where y is a rational number? Explain.

ACE Homework starts on page 95.

5.3 Squaring Odd Numbers

In this Problem, you will operate on odd numbers and look for patterns.

Problem 5.3

A Perform the following operations on the first eight odd numbers. Record your information in a table.

- Pick an odd number.
- Square it.
- Subtract 1.

B What patterns do you see in the resulting numbers?

C Make conjectures about these numbers. Explain why your conjectures are true for any odd number.

A C E Homework starts on page 95.

Applications

Maria presents several number puzzles to her friends. She asks them to pick a number and to perform various operations on it. She then predicts the result. For Exercises 1 and 2, show why the puzzles work.

1.

Puzzle 1

- Pick a number.
- Double it.
- Add 6.
- Divide by 2.
- Subtract the number you picked.

Maria claims the result is 3.

2.

Puzzle 2

- Pick a number.
- Add 4.
- Multiply by 2.
- Subtract 6.
- Divide by 2.
- Subtract the number you picked.

Maria claims the result is 1.

3. a. Design a puzzle similar to Maria's puzzles. Try it on a friend.

   b. Explain why your puzzle works.

Show that the following conjectures are true.

4. The sum of two odd integers is even.

5. The product of two even integers is even.

6. The product of two odd integers is odd.

7. Look at the product of three consecutive whole numbers. For example:

$$1 \times 2 \times 3 \qquad 2 \times 3 \times 4 \qquad 3 \times 4 \times 5$$

a. What pattern do you see?

b. Make a conjecture about the product of three consecutive whole numbers. Show that your conjecture is true.

8. Look at the product of four consecutive whole numbers.

a. What patterns do you see?

b. Make a conjecture about the product of four consecutive whole numbers. Show that your conjecture is true.

9. Determine whether each sum or product is rational or irrational.

a. $0.\overline{3} + 0.\overline{234}$

b. $\sqrt{2} + 3$

c. $5 \cdot \sqrt{7}$

d. $6\sqrt{36}$

e. $\frac{987}{123} + \frac{123}{987}$

f. $\frac{26}{78} \cdot \frac{68}{17}$

10. a. Are the following numbers divisible by 2? Explain.

$$10,034 \qquad\qquad 69,883$$

b. How can you determine whether a number is divisible by 2? Explain.

11. Look at several numbers that are divisible by 4. What patterns do you notice among these numbers that can help you determine whether a number is divisible by 4? Explain.

12. Look at several numbers that are divisible by 5. What patterns do you notice among these numbers that can help you determine whether a number is divisible by 5? Explain.

Connections

13. Study the sequence of cube buildings below.

- What pattern do you notice?

- Use the pattern to construct the next building in the sequence.

- Think about your steps as you construct your building. The labels below show one way you might think about the pattern.

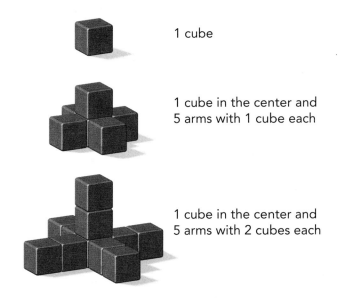

1 cube

1 cube in the center and 5 arms with 1 cube each

1 cube in the center and 5 arms with 2 cubes each

a. Describe a pattern you see in the cube buildings.

b. Use your pattern to write an expression for the number of cubes in the *n*th building, where *n* is an integer.

c. Use your expression to find the number of cubes in the fifth building.

d. Use the Distributive and Commutative properties to write an expression equivalent to the one in part (b). Does this expression suggest another pattern in the cube buildings? Explain.

e. Look for a different pattern in the buildings. Describe the pattern and use it to write a different expression for the number of cubes in the *n*th building.

Suppose a chess tournament has n participants. Each participant plays each of the other participants twice.

14. **a.** Find the total number of games played for tournaments with 2, 3, 4, 5, and 6 participants.

   b. Look for a pattern in your data. Use the pattern to write an expression for the number of games played in a tournament with n participants.

15. Gina used a table to answer Exercise 14. Make a table like the one below to record wins (W) and losses (L) for a tournament with n participants.

Game 1

	P_1	P_2	P_3	...	P_n
P_1					
P_2					
P_3					
...					
P_n					

Game 2

   a. How many cells should your table have?

   b. How many cells in the table will not be used? Explain.

   c. Use your answers from parts (a) and (b) to write an expression for the total number of games played.

   d. Compare your expressions for the total number of games played in Exercises 14(b) and 15(c).

Solve each equation for x without using a table or a graph.

16. $(x - 4)(x + 3) = 0$ **17.** $x^2 + 4x = 0$

18. $x^2 + 9x + 20 = 0$ **19.** $x^2 + 7x - 8 = 0$

20. $x^2 - 11x + 10 = 0$ **21.** $x^2 - 6x - 27 = 0$

22. $x^2 - 25 = 0$ **23.** $x^2 - 100 = 0$

24. $2x^2 + 3x + 1 = 0$ **25.** $3x^2 + 10x + 8 = 0$

For Exercises 26–29, answer parts (a) and (b) below.

   a. Write two different but equivalent expressions for each situation. Show that the expressions are equivalent.

   b. Write a problem that can be solved by substituting a value into your expressions. Then solve your problem.

26. Suppose you go on an 8-hour car trip. For the first 6 hours, you travel at an average rate of r miles per hour on the highway. For the last 2 hours, you travel at an average rate of 30 mph slower in the city. Find the distance traveled.

27. A bag contains only dimes and quarters. The bag has 1,000 coins. Find the amount of money in the bag.

28. The length of a rectangular pool is 4 feet longer than twice the width. Find the area of the pool.

29. For a concert, there are x reserved and $(4,000 - x)$ general tickets. Find the amount of money collected for the concert given the prices below.

30. The height of a ball (in feet) t seconds after it is thrown is $h = -16t^2 + 48t$. Find parts (a)–(c) without using a table or graph.

   a. the height of the ball after 2 seconds

   b. the maximum height of the ball

   c. the total time the ball is in the air

   d. How could you use a table or graph to answer parts (a)–(c)? Explain.

For each expression, write an equation of the form $y = expression$.
Determine whether the two expressions are equivalent.

    a. with a table and graph

    b. without a table or graph

31. $9x - 5(x - 3) - 20$ and $5 - 4x$

32. $(10x - 5) - (4x + 2)$ and $10x - 5 - 4x + 2$

For Exercises 33–37, complete each table. Decide whether the
relationship is linear, quadratic, exponential, or none of these.

33.

x	-7	-5	-3	5
$y = 4(x - 7) + 6$	▪	▪	▪	▪

34.

x	-7	-5	-3	5
$y = -3 - 7(x + 9)$	▪	▪	▪	▪

35.

x	-7	-5	-3	5
$y = 2(3)^x$	▪	▪	▪	▪

36.

x	-7	-5	-3	5
$y = 3x^2 - x - 1$	▪	▪	▪	▪

37.

x	-7	-5	-3	5
$y = 5(x - 2)(x + 3)$	▪	▪	▪	▪

38. For Exercises 33 and 34, write an equivalent expression for y that
would make the calculations easier.

39. Study the pattern in each table. Write an equation for those that are linear, exponential, or quadratic. Otherwise, write *none of these*.

Table 1

x	y
−2	15
0	9
2	3
3	0
4	−3

Table 2

x	y
0	−16
1	−15
2	−12
3	−7
4	0

Table 3

x	y
−2	2
−1	1
0	0
1	1
2	2

Table 4

x	y
0	3
1	12
2	48
3	192
4	768

Table 5

x	y
1	4
2	2
3	$\frac{4}{3}$
4	1
5	$\frac{4}{5}$

40. Suppose triangle *ABC* is a right triangle and the lengths of its two legs are integers.

    a. Can the perimeter be a rational number? If so, give an example. If not, justify why it cannot be a rational number.

    b. Can the perimeter be an irrational number? If so, give an example. If not, justify why it cannot be an irrational number.

41. A 30-60-90 triangle has a hypotenuse that is an integer.

    a. Can the perimeter be a rational number? If so, give an example. If not, justify why it cannot be a rational number.

    b. Can the perimeter be an irrational number? If so, give an example. If not, justify why it cannot be an irrational number.

Extensions

42.   **a.** Find the next statement for the following pattern.

$$1^2 + 2^2 = 3^2 - 2^2$$

$$2^2 + 3^2 = 7^2 - 6^2$$

$$3^2 + 4^2 = 13^2 - 12^2$$

$$4^2 + 5^2 = 21^2 - 20^2$$

    b. Make a conjecture about these statements.

    c. Show that your conjecture is correct.

43. For many years, mathematicians have been looking for a way to generate prime numbers. One of their proposed rules follows.

$$P = n^2 - n + 41$$

The rule suggests that if n is a whole number, then $n^2 - n + 41$ is a prime number.

George claims the rule is not true because he tested it for several values of n and found one that did not yield a prime number.

   a. Test the rule for several values of n. Is each result prime?

   b. Is George correct? Explain.

44. Find an example for each conjecture.

   a. The sum of two irrational numbers is an integer.

   b. The sum of two irrational numbers is rational, but not an integer.

   c. The sum of two irrational numbers is irrational.

45. Look at several numbers that are divisible by 3. What patterns do you notice among these numbers that can help you determine whether a number is divisible by 3? Explain.

46. Look at several numbers that are divisible by 6. What patterns do you notice among these numbers that can help you determine whether a number is divisible by 6? Explain.

47. Judy thinks she knows a quick way to square any number whose last digit is 5. For example, 25 squared is 625.

> **Example: 25**
>
> • Look at the digit to the left of 5. Multiply it by the number that is one greater than it. (Example: 2 x 3 = 6)
>
> • Write the product followed by 25. This is equal to the square of the number. (Example: 625 = 25²)

   a. Try this squaring method on two other numbers that end in 5.

   b. Explain why this method works.

Mathematical Reflections 5

In this Investigation, you made conjectures about patterns that you observed and represented these conjectures in symbolic statements. You also found ways to show that your conjectures were valid. The following questions will help you summarize what you have learned.

Think about these questions. Discuss your ideas with other students and your teacher. Then write a summary of your findings in your notebook.

1. **Describe** how and why you could use symbolic statements to represent relationships and conjectures.

2. **Describe** how you can show that your conjectures are correct.

Common Core Mathematical Practices

As you worked on the Problems in this Investigation, you used prior knowledge to make sense of them. You also applied Mathematical Practices to solve the Problems. Think back over your work, the ways you thought about the Problems, and how you used Mathematical Practices.

Shawna described her thoughts in the following way:

The number puzzle in Problem 5.1 was cool. We used algebraic statements for each step to show why the puzzle worked. We also had to use our knowledge of place value to interpret some of the steps, particularly the last one, which solved the mystery.

Common Core Standards for Mathematical Practices
MP2 Reason abstractly and quantitatively.

• What other Mathematical Practices can you identify in Shawna's reasoning?

• Describe a Mathematical Practice that you and your classmates used to solve a different Problem in this Investigation.

Unit Project

Finding the Surface Area of Rod Stacks

In this Unit Project, you will find different ways to find the surface area of colored rod stacks.

Part 1: Staircase Stacks

1. Choose a rod length to use to make a staircase stack. Use one of the unit rods to determine the dimensions of your chosen rod.

2. Stack several rods of this length as shown. Each rod is one unit high and one unit wide and is staggered one unit.

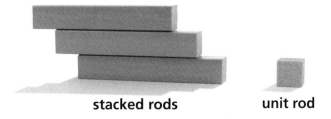

stacked rods   **unit rod**

   Find the surface area of one rod, a stack of two rods, a stack of three rods, and so on. Describe a pattern that you see in the surface areas of the stacks you made.

3. Write an equation that shows the relationship between the surface area A and the number of rods n in the stack. Explain.

4. Repeat Exercises 1–3 for two other rod lengths.

5. Find a student who used rods of the same length for Exercises 1–3 and whose expression for area from Exercise 3 looks different from yours. Are your expressions equivalent? Explain.

6. a. Make a table with columns for rod length and surface area equation. Complete the table for rod lengths 2 through 10. You will need to find students who used rods that you did not use.

   b. Do the equations in your table represent linear, quadratic, or exponential relationships? Explain.

   c. Write an equation for the surface area A of any stack of n rods of length ℓ.

   d. Use your equation from part (c) to find the surface area of a stack of 50 rods of length 10.

Part 2: Finding the Surface Area of a Rectangular Prism

Suppose rods of length 4 are stacked to form a rectangular prism as shown below right.

7. What are the dimensions of the prism?

8. Find an equation for the surface area of the prism.

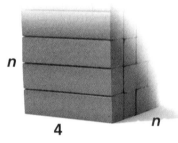

9. Suppose the prism is 10 rods high and 10 rods wide. What is the surface area of the prism?

10. How would the equation change if the rod length were a length other than 4?

11. Is the relationship between the surface area and the number of rods in a prism stack linear, quadratic, exponential, or none of these? Explain.

Write a report about the results you found for rod stacks and rod prisms. Explain how you found the equations for surface area in each case. Use diagrams to show what you did and what you found.

Looking Back

In this Unit, you learned and practiced the standard rules for writing and interpreting symbolic expressions in algebra. You used properties of numbers and operations to write algebraic expressions in equivalent forms and to solve linear and quadratic equations with algebraic reasoning. You also identified which function to use to solve a problem.

Use Your Understanding: Symbols

Test your understanding and skill in the use of algebraic notation and reasoning by solving these problems about managing a concert tour.

The promoter pays appearance fees to each group on the concert program. Some groups also get a portion of the ticket sales.

- The lead group earns $15,000, plus $5 for every ticket sold.

- The second group earns $1,500, plus $1.50 for every ticket sold.

- The third group earns $1,250 flat.

  1. For parts (a)–(c), use E for the promoter's expenses and t for the number of tickets sold.

  a. Write an equation to show payments to each group.

  b. Write an equation to show payment to the lead group and the combined payments to the other groups.

  c. Write an equivalent equation different from parts (a) and (b) to show the simplest calculation of the total amount paid to the performers.

  2. Tickets cost $25, $30, and $40.

  a. Write an equation that shows how the promoter's income from ticket sales I depends on the number of each type of ticket sold x, y, and z.

  b. The promoter sells 5,000 tickets at $25, 3,000 tickets at $30, and 950 tickets at $40. Find the average income for each ticket.

  c. Write an equation that shows how the average income for each ticket sold V depends on the variables x, y, z, and t.

3. Square tiles were used to make the pattern below.

  a. Write an equation for the number of tiles T needed to make the nth figure. Explain.

  b. Find an equivalent expression for the number of tiles in part (a). Explain why they are equivalent.

  c. Write an equation for the perimeter P of the nth figure.

  d. Identify and describe the figure in the pattern that can be made with exactly 420 tiles.

  e. Describe the relationship represented by the equations in parts (a) and (c). Do any of these represent linear, exponential, or quadratic functions? Explain.

4. A company packages its three beverages in containers of different shapes: a cylinder, a cone, and a sphere. Mary compares the costs of the drinks. She arranges the data in a table. Which drink is the best buy? Explain.

Beverage Containers

Shape	Cylinder	Cone	Sphere
Height	6 in.	10 in.	6 in.
Diameter	4 in.	6 in.	6 in.
Cost	$1.25	$1.40	$1.30

Explain Your Reasoning

When you solve problems by writing and operating on symbolic expressions, you should be able to explain your reasoning.

  5. How can writing two different equivalent expressions for a situation be helpful?

  6. How can solving a linear or quadratic equation be helpful?

  7. How can a symbolic statement be helpful in expressing a general relationship or conjecture?

English/Spanish Glossary

C   **Commutative Property of Addition** A mathematical property that states that the order in which quantities are added does not matter. It states that $a + b = b + a$ for any two real numbers a and b. For example, $5 + 7 = 7 + 5$ and $2x + 4 = 4 + 2x$.

propiedad conmutativa de la suma Una propiedad matemática que establece que el orden en que se suman las cantidades no tiene importancia. Esta propiedad establece que para dos números reales cualesquiera a y b, $a + b = b + a$. Por ejemplo, $5 + 7 = 7 + 5$ y $2x + 4 = 4 + 2x$.

Commutative Property of Multiplication A mathematical property that states that the order in which quantities are multiplied does not matter. It states that $ab = ba$ for any two real numbers a and b. For example, $5 \times 7 = 7 \times 5$ and $2x(4) = (4)2x$.

propiedad conmutativa de la multiplicación Una propiedad matemática que establece que el orden en que se multiplican los factores no tiene importancia. Esta propiedad establece que para dos números reales cualesquiera a y b, $ab = ba$. Por ejemplo, $5 \times 7 = 7 \times 5$ y $2x(4) = (4)2x$.

D   **describe** Academic Vocabulary
To explain or tell in detail. A written description can contain facts and other information needed to communicate your answer. A diagram or a graph may also be included.

related terms *express, explain, illustrate*

sample Without graphing, describe the shape of the graph of the equation $y = 2x^2 + 1$.

describir Vocabulario académico
Explicar o decir con detalle. Una descripción escrita puede contener datos y otra información necesaria para comunicar tu respuesta. También se puede incluir un diagrama o una gráfica.

términos relacionados *expresar, explicar, ilustrar*

ejemplo Sin hacer una gráfica, describe la forma de la gráfica de la ecuación $y = 2x^2 + 1$.

> The equation is quadratic, so the graph is a parabola. The graph opens upward because 2 is positive. It is narrower than the graph of $y = x^2$ because the absolute value of 2 is greater than 1.

> La ecuación es cuadrática, por tanto la gráfica es una parábola. La gráfica se abre hacia arriba porque 2 es positivo. Es más estrecha que la gráfica de $y = x^2$ porque el valor absoluto de 2 es mayor que 1.

Distributive Property A mathematical property used to rewrite expressions involving addition and multiplication. The Distributive Property states that for any three real numbers a, b, and c, $a(b + c) = ab + ac$. If an expression is written as a factor multiplied by a sum, you can use the Distributive Property to *multiply* the factor by each term in the sum.

$$4(5 + x) = 4(5) + 4(x) = 20 + 4x$$

If an expression is written as a sum of terms and the terms have a common factor, you can use the Distributive Property to rewrite the expression as the common factor multiplied by a sum. This process is called *factoring*.

$$20 + 4x = 4(5) + 4(x) = 4(5 + x)$$

propiedad distributiva Una propiedad matemática que se usa para volver a escribir expresiones que incluyen la suma y la multiplicación. La propiedad distributiva establece que para tres números reales cualesquiera a, b y c, $a(b + c) = ab + ac$. Si una expresión está escrita como un factor multiplicado por una suma, se puede usar la propiedad distributiva para *multiplicar* el factor por cada término de la suma.

$$4(5 + x) = 4(5) + 4(x) = 20 + 4x$$

Si una expresión se escribe como una suma de términos y los términos tienen un factor común, se puede usar la propiedad distributiva para volver a escribir la expresión como el factor común multiplicado por una suma. Este proceso se llama *descomponer en factores*.

$$20 + 4x = 4(5) + 4(x) = 4(5 + x)$$

E **equivalent expressions** Expressions that represent the same quantity. For example, $2 + 5$, $3 + 4$, and 7 are equivalent expressions. You can apply the Distributive Property to $2(x + 3)$ to write the equivalent expression $2x + 6$. You can apply the Commutative Property to $2x + 6$ to write the equivalent expression $6 + 2x$.

expresiones equivalentes Expresiones que representan la misma cantidad. Por ejemplo, $2 + 5$, $3 + 4$ y 7 son expresiones equivalentes. Puedes aplicar la propiedad distributiva a $2(x + 3)$ para escribir la expresión equivalente $2x + 6$. Puedes aplicar la propiedad conmutativa a $2x + 6$ para escribir la expresión equivalente $6 + 2x$.

estimate Academic Vocabulary
To find an approximate answer.

related terms *guess, predict*

sample A partial net of a cone is shown below. Estimate the lateral surface area of the cone.

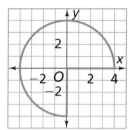

I can count the number of unit squares. The net has three equal sections. I estimate one of the sections to be about 13 square units, so the total is about 39 square units.

expanded form The form of an expression made up of sums or differences of terms rather than products of factors. The expressions $x^2 + 7x + 12$ and $x^2 + 2x$ are in expanded form.

Hacer una estimación Vocabulario académico Hallar una respuesta aproximada.

términos relacionados *suponer, predecir*

ejemplo A continuación se muestra el modelo plano parcial de un cono. Estima el área total lateral del cono.

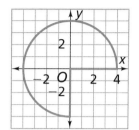

Puedo contar el número de unidades cuadradas. El modelo plano tiene tres secciones iguales. Estimo que una de las secciones tiene aproximadamente 13 unidades cuadradas, por tanto, el total es aproximadamente 39 unidades cuadradas.

forma desarrollada La forma de una expresión compuesta de sumas o diferencias de términos en vez de productos de factores. Las expresiones $x^2 + 7x + 12$ y $x^2 + 2x$ están representadas en forma desarrollada.

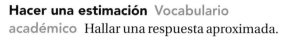

explain Academic Vocabulary

To give facts and details that make an idea easier to understand. Explaining can involve a written summary supported by a diagram, chart, table, or a combination of these.

related terms *analyze, clarify, describe, justify, tell*

sample The equation shows the relationship between the number of gallons g of water in a tank and the number of minutes m a shower is on.

$$g = 50 - 2.5m$$

How many gallons of water are in a full tank before the shower begins? Explain.

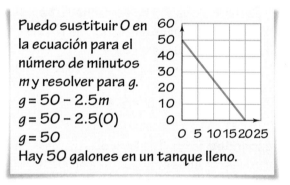

I can substitute 0 into the equation for the number of minutes m and solve for g.
$g = 50 - 2.5m$
$g = 50 - 2.5(0)$
$g = 50$
There are 50 gallons in a full tank.

explicar Vocabulario académico

Dar hechos y detalles que hacen que una idea sea más fácil de comprender. Explicar puede incluir un resumen escrito apoyado por un diagrama, una gráfica, una tabla o una combinación de estos.

términos relacionados *analizar, aclarar, describir, justificar, decir*

ejemplo La ecuación muestra la relación entre el número de galones g de agua en un tanque y el número de minutos m que una ducha ha estado funcionando.

$$g = 50 - 2.5m$$

¿Cuántos galones de agua hay en un tanque lleno antes de que comience la ducha? Explícalo.

Puedo sustituir 0 en la ecuación para el número de minutos m y resolver para g.
$g = 50 - 2.5m$
$g = 50 - 2.5(0)$
$g = 50$
Hay 50 galones en un tanque lleno.

F **factored form** The form of an expression made up of products of factors rather than sums or differences of terms. The expressions $(x + 3)(x + 4)$ and $x(x + 2)$ are in factored form.

forma factorizada Una expresión compuesta de productos de factores, en vez de sumas o diferencias de términos. Las expresiones $(x + 3)(x + 4)$ y $x(x + 2)$ están representadas en forma factorizada.

P **properties of equality** The properties of equality state that if you add or subtract the same quantity from each side of an equation, the two sides of the equation remain equal. If you multiply or divide each side of an equation by the same nonzero quantity, the two sides of the equation remain equal.

propiedades de la igualdad Las propiedades de la igualdad establecen que si se suma o resta la misma cantidad a ambos lados de una ecuación, los dos lados de la ecuación se mantienen iguales. Si se multiplica o divide ambos lados de una ecuación por el mismo número distinto de cero, los dos lados de la ecuación se mantienen iguales.

R **roots** The roots of a two-variable equation are the values of x that make y equal 0. For example, the roots of $y = x^2 + 5x$ are -5 and 0 because $(-5)^2 + 5(-5) = 0$ and $0^2 + 5(0) = 0$. The roots of $y = x^2 + 5x$ are the solutions to the equation $0 = x^2 + 5x$. The roots of a two-variable equation are the x-intercepts of its graph.

raíces Las raíces de una ecuación de dos variables son los valores de x que hacen que y sea igual a 0. Por ejemplo, las raíces de $y = x^2 + 5x$ son -5 y 0 porque $(-5)^2 + 5(-5) = 0$ y $0^2 + 5(0) = 0$. Las raíces de $y = x^2 + 5x$ son las soluciones de la ecuación $0 = x^2 + 5x$. Las raíces de una ecuación de dos variables son los interceptos en x de su gráfica.

S **solve** Academic Vocabulary
To determine the value or values that make a given statement true. Several methods and strategies can be used to solve a problem including estimating, isolating the variable, drawing a graph, or using a table of values.

related terms *find, graph*

sample Solve the equation $0 = x^2 + 6x - 7$ for x.

The equation is quadratic. I can solve the equation by factoring the right side of the equation into two factors and setting each factor equal to zero.
$0 = x^2 + 6x - 7$
$0 = (x + 7)(x - 1)$

$x + 7 = 0$ or $x - 1 = 0$
$x = -7$ or $x = 1$
I can also solve the quadratic by graphing and identifying the x-intercepts at $(-7, 0)$ and $(1, 0)$.

resolver Vocabulario académico
Determinar el valor o valores que hacen verdadero un enunciado. Se pueden usar varios métodos o estrategias para resolver un problema, entre ellos la estimación, aislar la variable, hacer una gráfica o usar una tabla de valores.

términos relacionados *hallar, hacer una gráfica*

ejemplo Resuelve la ecuación $0 = x^2 + 6x - 7$ para x.

La ecuación es cuadrática. Puedo resolver la ecuación descomponiendo en factores el lado derecho de la ecuación en dos factores y estabieciendo cada factor igual a cero.
$0 = x^2 + 6x - 7$
$0 = (x + 7)(x - 1)$

$x + 7 = 0$ or $x - 1 = 0$
$x = -7$ or $x = 1$
También puedo resolver la ecuación cuadrática al hacer una gráfica e identificar los interceptos en x en $(-7, 0)$ y $(1, 0)$.

Index

ACE
  combining expressions, 34–43
  equivalent expressions, 15–24
  functions, 72–87
  reasoning with symbols, 95–102
  solving equations, 55–63

addition and subtraction, 27–28, 44, 47

algebra, solving puzzles with, 90–91, 95, 104

algebraic expressions, 91, 107

algebraic reasoning, 4, 107

area and perimeter
  algebraic expressions and, 37
  determining equivalence, 10
  equations and, 24, 68, 108
  equivalent expressions and, 8–9, 13, 15–17, 19, 20, 21
  finding, 61
  functions and, 70, 76, 89
  interpreting symbolic expressions and, 10–11
  rational and irrational numbers and, 101
  reasoning with symbols and, 99
  rectangles, 74
  surface area, 83

area models, 50, 52, 59, 82

Ask Yourself, 4

circles, 61

Common Core Mathematical Practices, 5–6, 26, 45, 65, 89, 104

commutative properties
  Distributive Property and, 18

equivalent expressions and, 13, 14, 25
  expressions and, 97
  solving equations and, 47, 60

Commutative Property of Addition, 109

Commutative Property of Multiplication, 109

cones, 31–32, 33, 36, 43, 44, 108. See also cylinders, cones, and spheres

conjectures
  about patterns, 103
  odd and even numbers, 91, 92, 93, 95
  patterns and, 101
  products of whole numbers, 96
  rational and irrational numbers, 102
  squaring odd numbers, 94
  symbolic reasoning and, 4, 108

coordinate grids, 63, 80, 85, 86

cost data
  equations and, 86
  equivalent expressions and, 23
  modeling with functions, 70
  solving equations and, 48–49, 57, 60
  substituting expressions, 29–30

cube buildings, 97

cubic functions, 70

cylinders, cones, and spheres
  faces of, 43
  income and expense data, 108
  volume of, 31–32, 33, 36, 37–38, 44, 61, 70, 83, 85

data points, equations and, 69

differences, 21, 93

distance, finding, 84

Distributive Property
  defined, 110
  equivalent expressions, 12–14, 18, 25, 39, 47
  expressions and, 97
  multiplication and, 82
  solving equations and, 60

division, whole numbers, 96, 102

equations
  area and perimeter, 17, 24
  combining expressions, 44
  finding surface area and, 105–106
  functions and, 68, 70, 77, 78, 82
  income and expense data, 34, 35, 36, 40, 107
  patterns and, 72–73, 80–81, 108
  properties of equality, 41
  reasoning with symbols and, 98
  relationships among variables, 3
  speed and distance data, 87
  substituting expressions, 29–30
  tables and graphs and, 39, 87
  time, rate, and distance, 84
  writing equivalent expressions, 9, 10, 84

equations, solving
  ACE, 55–63
  factoring quadratic equations, 50–52
  linear equations, 46–49
  Mathematical Reflections, 64–65
  solving quadratic equations, 52–54

equivalence, determining, 10, 17, 82, 100

equivalent expressions
ACE, 15–24
algebraic expressions, 107
defined, 110
determining equivalence, 10, 27, 100
Distributive Property and, 12–14, 39
finding, 83
interpreting expressions, 11–12
Mathematical Reflections, 15–24, 44
patterns and, 67, 72, 108
properties of equality and, 47
reasoning with symbols and, 7–8, 99
simplifying expressions and, 60
solving equations and, 57, 59, 100
substituting expressions, 30
symbolic expressions, 3, 4, 108
writing equations, 82
writing equivalent expressions, 8–9, 84

estimation
cost data, 23, 48, 57, 60
defined, 111
income and expense data, 34, 35, 42, 55
surface area and volume, 83

even numbers. *See* odd and even numbers

expanded form
defined, 111
Distributive Property and, 12, 14, 18
equivalent expressions and, 19, 20
products and, 58
quadratic expressions, 60
solving equations and, 62
tables and graphs, 88

exponential equations, 58

exponential functions
area and perimeter, 74, 76, 108
equations and, 79–80, 88
patterns of change, 75
profits and, 34
scale factors, 84
tables and graphs, 77

exponential growth, 84

exponential relationships, 69, 70, 100, 101, 106

expression puzzles, 24

expressions. *See also* equivalent expressions
integers and, 97
interpreting, 11–12
simplifying, 42, 56, 60

expressions, combining
ACE, 34–43
adding expressions, 27–28
cylinders, cones, and spheres, 31–32
Mathematical Reflections, 44–45
solving volume problems, 33
substituting expressions, 29–30

faces, of cylinders, cones, and spheres, 43

factored form, 112
area models and, 59
Distributive Property and, 12, 14, 18
equivalent expressions and, 19, 20, 22
quadratic equations, 50, 51–52, 65
quadratic expressions, 58, 60
solving equations and, 52–53, 54, 62
tables and graphs, 88

factor pairs, 52

fractions, 21

functions
ACE, 72–87

area and perimeter and, 76
linear, quadratic, and exponential relationships, 69
Mathematical Reflections, 88–89
modeling with functions, 70–71
patterns of change and, 66–67
using equations, 68
writing equations, 84

geometric methods, for solving quadratic equations, 54

Glossary, 109–113

graphs. *See* tables and graphs

greatest common factors, 21

growth patterns, 86

growth rates, 75–76, 84

height
of cylinders, cones, and spheres, 85
modeling with functions, 70, 85
reasoning with symbols and, 99
solving equations and, 53, 58, 61, 62
volume and, 32, 36, 38

hemispheres, 37

hypotenuse, 101

income and expense data. *See also* profits
algebraic reasoning, 107
combining expressions, 34, 35, 36
cylinders, cones, and spheres, 108
equations and, 55, 68, 75
functions and, 80
tables and graphs, 40
tables of values, 41
variables and, 73

inequalities, 49, 63, 87

integers, 91–93, 101, 102

interest rates, 22

inverse variation relationships, 70

Investigations
> combining expressions, 27–33
> equivalent expressions, 7–14
> functions, 66–71
> reasoning with symbols, 90–94
> solving equations, 46–54

irrational numbers, 93, 96, 101

linear equations
> algebraic reasoning, 107
> solving equations, 46–49
> solving equations and, 58, 62, 64
> symbolic expressions, 108
> symbolic reasoning and, 4

linear factors, 52, 65

linear functions
> area and perimeter, 74, 76, 108
> equations and, 79–80, 88
> equivalent expressions and, 12
> patterns of change, 75
> profits and, 34
> substituting expressions, 30
> tables and graphs, 77, 80

linear relationships
> adding expressions, 28
> equations and, 69, 101
> equivalent expressions and, 9, 15
> finding surface area and, 106
> identifying, 100
> modeling with functions, 70

lines of symmetry, 60, 82

Looking Ahead, 2–3

Looking Back, 107–108

Mathematical Highlights, 4

Mathematical Practices, 5–6

Mathematical Reflections
> combining expressions, 44–45
> equivalent expressions, 15–24
> functions, 88–89
> reasoning with symbols, 103–104
> solving equations, 64–65

mathematical statements, 91

maximum and minimum points, 60, 63, 71, 82, 88

modeling strategies, 70–71, 85

multiples of 5, squares of, 102

multiplication and division, 26, 47, 82

National Football League (NFL), 30

negative numbers, 87

nonlinear functions, 12, 30

nonlinear relationships, 9, 15, 28

odd and even numbers, 91–93, 94, 95, 96

parabolas, 84

parentheses, 14, 18, 47, 62, 64

patterns
> conjectures and, 101, 103
> cube buildings and, 97
> division and, 96, 102
> equations and, 101, 108
> equivalent expressions and, 20
> finding surface area and, 105–106
> linear, quadratic, and exponential relationships, 69
> modeling with functions, 70, 71
> reasoning with symbols, 98
> squaring odd numbers, 94
> symbolic expressions and, 12
> whole numbers and, 96

patterns of change
> equations and, 80–81, 88
> functions and, 66–67, 71
> relationships among variables, 75, 76, 83
> symbolic expressions and, 4

points of intersection, 63

positive numbers, 87

predictions
> combining expressions and, 29–30, 44
> equations and, 36, 56, 59
> number puzzles, 95
> prices, 81
> symbolic statements and, 11
> tables and graphs, 81

price data, 81, 99

prime numbers, 102

probabilities, 29–30, 35, 45

products, 21
> area models and, 82
> expanded form and, 58
> odd and even numbers, 93, 95
> rational and irrational numbers, 96
> solving quadratic equations, 52
> whole numbers, 96

profits
> combining expressions, 45
> finding volume and, 32
> functions and, 80
> income and expense data, 34, 35, 36, 40, 42
> quadratic functions, 89
> solving equations and, 47–48, 55, 57, 59, 75
> substituting expressions, 29–30
> using equations, 68

properties of equality, 41, 47, 112

properties of real numbers, 46

puzzles
   expression puzzles, 24
   solving with algebra, 90–91,
      95, 104

pyramids, 38

quadratic equations
   algebraic reasoning, 107
   factoring, 50–52
   number of solutions, 61
   relationships among
      variables, 89
   solving equations, 52–54, 58,
      64, 65, 87
   symbolic expressions, 108
   symbolic reasoning and, 4

quadratic expressions, 58, 60

quadratic formula, 54, 62

quadratic functions
   area and perimeter, 74, 76,
      89, 108
   equations and, 79–80, 88
   patterns of change, 75
   profits and, 34, 89
   tables and graphs, 77

quadratic relationships
   equations and, 69
   finding surface area and, 106
   identifying, 100
   modeling with functions, 70
   writing equations, 101

quotients, 21

radius
   cylinders, cones, and
      spheres, 85
   equivalent expressions and,
      16, 19
   finding volume and, 32, 33,
      36
   modeling with functions, 70,
      71

**rational and irrational
   numbers,** 93, 96, 101, 102

real numbers, 39, 46, 54

reasoning, explaining your
   area and perimeter and, 76

equivalent expressions and,
      9, 10, 11, 15, 16, 17, 26, 39
   expression puzzles, 24
   expressions and, 97
   factoring quadratic
      equations, 50
   finding surface area and,
      105, 106
   finding volume and, 31, 44
   income and expense data,
      40, 108
   linear, quadratic, and
      exponential relationships,
      69
   odd and even numbers, 91, 93
   patterns of change, 67
   quadratic functions, 89
   reasoning with symbols, 98,
      102
   solving equations and, 57,
      58, 60
   solving puzzles with algebra,
      104
   squaring odd numbers, 94
   symbolic expressions, 108

rectangles, 39, 61, 68, 70, 71, 74

rectangular prisms, 31, 38, 106

roots, 50, 54, 112

scale, graphs and, 63

scale factors, 84

side lengths, 8, 9, 10, 14, 15, 20,
   22, 60

slope, 84

solutions, number of
   linear equations and, 49
   quadratic equations, 61, 87
   solving equations and, 58, 64

speed and distance data, 87, 99

spheres, 44. *See also* cylinders,
   cones, and spheres
   faces of, 43
   income and expense data,
      108
   modeling with functions, 71
   volume of, 31–32, 36, 61

sports statistics, 30, 86

squares, 61

squaring numbers, 94, 102

staircase stacks, 105–106

subscripts, 48

substitutions, 29–30, 44, 45, 99

sums
   fractions and, 21
   odd and even numbers, 91,
      92, 93, 95
   rational and irrational
      numbers, 96, 102

surface area, 83, 105–106

symbolic expressions
   area and perimeter and,
      10–11
   explaining your reasoning,
      108
   odd and even numbers, 91
   patterns and, 12

symbolic statements, 11, 103

symbols, reasoning with
   ACE, 95–102
   Mathematical Reflections,
      103–104
   odd and even numbers,
      91–93
   solving puzzles with algebra,
      90–91
   squaring odd numbers, 94

tables and graphs
   area and perimeter, 74
   determining equivalence,
      100
   equations and, 69, 87
   equivalent expressions and,
      17, 20
   factoring quadratic
      equations, 50
   finding surface area and, 106
   functions and, 71, 77–78, 79
   growth patterns, 86
   income and expense data,
      40, 41, 108
   linear equations and, 49

patterns of change, 67, 72, 75, 81

price data, 80

reasoning with symbols, 98, 99

relationships among variables, 3

solving equations and, 39, 54, 57, 58, 62, 63, 64, 65

squaring odd numbers, 94

writing equivalent expressions and, 9

tables of values, 41, 77

temperature data, 36

time, rate, and distance, 84

triangles, 61, 101

unit cubes, 31

Unit Project, 105–106

units of measurement, 67

unit squares, 71

Use Your Understanding, 107–108

variables

growth patterns and, 86

income and expense data and, 73

patterns of change and, 75, 76

quadratic equations, 89

relationships among, 3, 9, 31–32, 105–106

Viète, François, 54

volume

combining expressions, 33

of cylinders, cones, and spheres, 31–32, 44, 61, 83, 85

of cylinders, cones, and spheres and, 37–38

modeling with functions, 70, 71

of prisms and pyramids, 38

simplifying expressions and, 42

whole numbers, 91–93, 96, 102

writing equations, 24, 27, 28

writing expressions, 8–9, 28

x-intercepts

equations, 62, 65, 82, 88

modeling with functions, 71

parabolas, 84

quadratic equations, 50, 52

quadratic expressions, 60

slope and, 84

y-intercepts

equations, 82, 88

factoring quadratic equations, 50

modeling with functions, 71

quadratic expressions, 60

zero, 52, 53, 58

Acknowledgments

Cover Design

Three Communication Design, Chicago

Text

National Football League

030, 086 "*National Football League Passer Rating Formula*" from WWW.NFL.COM. Used by permission.

Photographs

Photo locators denoted as follows: Top (T), Center (C), Bottom (B), Left (L), Right (R), Background (Bkgd)

002 Dennis MacDonald/PhotoEdit; **003** Leonid Serebrennikov/Alamy; **053** Dennis MacDonald/PhotoEdit; **054** The Art Gallery Collection/Alamy; **084** Dr. Gary Gaugler/Science Source.

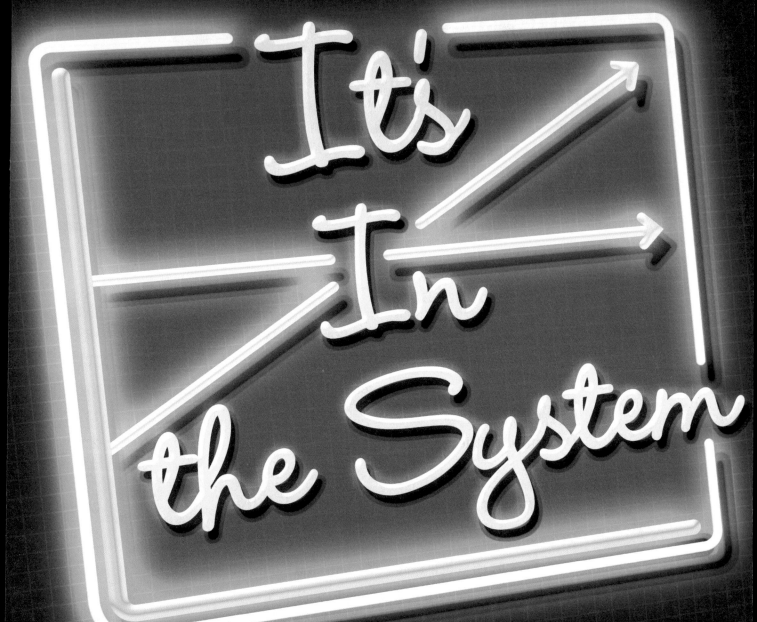

It's
In
the System

Systems of
Linear Equations
and Inequalities

Lappan, Phillips, Fey, Friel

It's In the System

Systems of Linear Equations and Inequalities

Looking Ahead 2

Mathematical Highlights 4

Mathematical Practices and Habits of Mind 5

1 Linear Equations With Two Variables 7

1.1 Shirts and Caps Solving Equations With Two Variables 8

1.2 Connecting $Ax + By = C$ and $y = mx + b$ 10

1.3 Booster Club Members Intersecting Lines 11

ACE Homework 13

Mathematical Reflections 22

2 Solving Linear Systems Symbolically 24

2.1 Shirts and Caps Again Solving Systems With $y = mx + b$ 25

2.2 Taco Truck Lunch Solving Systems by Combining Equations I 27

2.3 Solving Systems by Combining Equations II 30

ACE Homework 32

Mathematical Reflections 45

3 Systems of Functions and Inequalities   47

3.1 Comparing Security Services Linear Inequalities 48

3.2 Solving Linear Inequalities Symbolically 50

3.3 Operating at a Profit Systems of Lines and Curves 51

Ⓐ Ⓒ Ⓔ Homework 54

Mathematical Reflections 61

4 Systems of Linear Inequalities   63

4.1 Limiting Driving Miles Inequalities With Two Variables 63

4.2 What Makes a Car Green? Solving Inequalities by Graphing I 65

4.3 Feasible Points Solving Inequalities by Graphing II 67

4.4 Miles of Emissions Systems of Linear Inequalities 70

Ⓐ Ⓒ Ⓔ Homework 72

Mathematical Reflections 77

Looking Back 79

English/Spanish Glossary 81

Index 86

Acknowledgments 89

Looking Ahead

Pablo, Jasmine, and their brothers visit a taco truck for lunch. Pablo and his brother order 6 tacos and 2 drinks for $9. Jasmine and her brother order 4 tacos and 2 drinks for $7. **What** is the price of one taco and the price of one drink?

The owners of a shopping center get bids from two security companies. Super Locks charges $3,975 plus $6 per day. Fail Safe charges $995 plus $17.95 per day. For **what** number of days will Super Locks cost less than Fail Safe?

A family wants to drive their car and SUV at most 1,000 miles each month. **What** are some pairs (*car miles, SUV miles*) that meet this condition?

In this Unit, you will apply and extend what you have learned about the properties of equality, linear equations, and methods for solving equations and inequalities. You will learn graphic and symbolic methods for solving systems of linear equations and inequalities. As you work in this Unit, you will solve problems about admission fees for various events, as well as those on the previous page.

Mathematical Highlights

It's In the System

In this Unit, you will write and solve systems of linear equations and inequalities that model real-world situations. The methods for solving these algebraic systems combine graphic and algebraic reasoning from earlier *Connected Mathematics* Units.

You will learn how to

- Solve linear equations and systems of linear equations with two variables

- Solve linear inequalities and systems of inequalities with two variables

- Use systems of linear equations and inequalities to solve problems

When you encounter a new problem, it is a good idea to ask yourself questions. In this Unit, you might ask questions such as:

What are the variables in this problem?

Does the problem call for solving a system of equations or inequalities relating those variables?

What strategy will be most effective in solving the system?

Mathematical Practices and Habits of Mind

In the *Connected Mathematics* curriculum you will develop an understanding of important mathematical ideas by solving problems and reflecting on the mathematics involved. Every day, you will use "habits of mind" to make sense of problems and apply what you learn to new situations. Some of these habits are described by the *Common Core State Standards for Mathematical Practices* (MP).

MP1 Make sense of problems and persevere in solving them.

When using mathematics to solve a problem, it helps to think carefully about

- data and other facts you are given and what additional information you need to solve the problem;
- strategies you have used to solve similar problems and whether you could solve a related simpler problem first;
- how you could express the problem with equations, diagrams, or graphs;
- whether your answer makes sense.

MP2 Reason abstractly and quantitatively.

When you are asked to solve a problem, it often helps to

- focus first on the key mathematical ideas;
- check that your answer makes sense in the problem setting;
- use what you know about the problem setting to guide your mathematical reasoning.

MP3 Construct viable arguments and critique the reasoning of others.

When you are asked to explain why a conjecture is correct, you can

- show some examples that fit the claim and explain why they fit;
- show how a new result follows logically from known facts and principles.

When you believe a mathematical claim is incorrect, you can

- show one or more counterexamples—cases that don't fit the claim;
- find steps in the argument that do not follow logically from prior claims.

MP4 Model with mathematics.

When you are asked to solve problems, it often helps to

- think carefully about the numbers or geometric shapes that are the most important factors in the problem, then ask yourself how those factors are related to each other;
- express data and relationships in the problem with tables, graphs, diagrams, or equations, and check your result to see if it makes sense.

MP5 Use appropriate tools strategically.

When working on mathematical questions, you should always

- decide which tools are most helpful for solving the problem and why;
- try a different tool when you get stuck.

MP6 Attend to precision.

In every mathematical exploration or problem-solving task, it is important to

- think carefully about the required accuracy of results; is a number estimate or geometric sketch good enough, or is a precise value or drawing needed?
- report your discoveries with clear and correct mathematical language that can be understood by those to whom you are speaking or writing.

MP7 Look for and make use of structure.

In mathematical explorations and problem solving, it is often helpful to

- look for patterns that show how data points, numbers, or geometric shapes are related to each other;
- use patterns to make predictions.

MP8 Look for and express regularity in repeated reasoning.

When results of a repeated calculation show a pattern, it helps to

- express that pattern as a general rule that can be used in similar cases;
- look for shortcuts that will make the calculation simpler in other cases.

You will use all of the Mathematical Practices in this Unit. Sometimes, when you look at a Problem, it is obvious which practice is most helpful. At other times, you will decide on a practice to use during class explorations and discussions. After completing each Problem, ask yourself:

- What mathematics have I learned by solving this Problem?
- What Mathematical Practices were helpful in learning this mathematics?

Linear Equations With Two Variables

Solving equations is one of the most common and useful tasks in mathematics. In earlier Units, you learned how to solve

- linear equations, such as $3x + 5 = 17$.
- proportions, such as $\frac{3}{5} = \frac{6}{x}$.
- quadratic equations, such as $x^2 - 5x + 6 = 0$.
- exponential equations, such as $2^{x+1} = 64$.

The Problems of this Investigation pose a new challenge. You will learn to solve linear equations, such as $3x + 5y = 11$, that have two variables.

- What does a solution for this equation look like?
- What does a graph of this equation look like?

......

Common Core State Standards

8.EE.C.8 Analyze and solve pairs of simultaneous linear equations.

8.EE.C.8a Understand that solutions to a system of two linear equations in two variables correspond to points of intersection of their graphs, because points of intersection satisfy both equations simultaneously.

8.EE.C.8b Solve systems of two linear equations in two variables algebraically, and estimate solutions by graphing the equations. Solve simple cases by inspection.

8.EE.C.8c Solve real-world and mathematical problems leading to two linear equations in two variables.

Also 8.F.A.3, A-CED.A.2, A-CED.A.3, A-CED.A.4, A-REI.B.3, A-REI.C.6, A-REI.D.10

1.1 Shirts and Caps
Solving Equations With Two Variables

The eighth-graders are selling T-shirts and caps to raise money for their end-of-year party. The profit from the fundraiser depends on the number of caps and the number of T-shirts sold.

PROFIT
• $5 profit per T-shirt
• $10 profit per cap

GOAL
• Raise $600

Problem 1.1

To plan for the fundraiser, class officers need to know how many T-shirts and caps to order and sell.

A Find the profit *P* if the students sell

1. 15 shirts and 10 caps.

2. 12 shirts and 20 caps.

3. 30 shirts and 50 caps.

4. *s* shirts and *c* caps.

Problem **1.1** *continued*

B **1.** Find five pairs of numbers for shirt and cap sales that will allow the students to make a profit of exactly $600.

2. Each answer from part (1) can be written as an ordered pair of numbers (s, c). The ordered pairs (s, c), which represent points on a graph, are *solutions* of the equation $5s + 10c = 600$. Plot the ordered pairs on a coordinate grid like the one below.

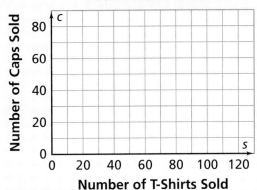

Fundraiser Sales

3. Use the graph to find three other ordered pairs that meet the profit goal.

4. Suppose the number of T-shirts sold was on the vertical axis and the number of caps sold was on the horizontal axis. Would the solutions change? Explain.

C For each equation

- find five solution pairs (x, y), including some with negative values.

- plot the solutions on a coordinate grid and draw the graph showing all possible solutions.

1. $x + y = 10$ **2.** $x - 2y = -4$

3. $-2x + y = 3$ **4.** $-3x + 2y = -4$

D Make a conjecture about the shape of the graph for any equation in the form $Ax + By = C$, where A, B, and C are fixed numbers. Explain why your conjecture is true.

A C E Homework starts on page 13.

1.2 Connecting $Ax + By = C$ and $y = mx + b$

There are two common forms of linear equations with two variables.

- When the values of one variable depend on those of another, it is common to express the relationship as $y = mx + b$. This equation is in **slope-intercept form.**

- When the values of the two variables combine to produce a fixed third quantity, you can express the relationship as $Ax + By = C$. This equation is in **standard form.** The equations in Problem 1.1 are in standard form.

The graph of each type of equation is a straight line. Since you know a lot about the graphs of **linear functions,** it is natural to ask: Given an equation in one form, can you rewrite the equation in the other form?

As you work on this Problem, look for connections between the two forms of linear equations.

Problem 1.2

Ⓐ Four students tried to write $12x + 3y = 9$ in equivalent $y = mx + b$ form. Did each student get an equation equivalent to the original $Ax + By = C$ form? If so, explain the reasoning for each step. If not, tell what errors the student made.

Jared

$12x + 3y = 9$
$\quad 3y = -12x + 9 \qquad (1)$
$\quad\ y = -4x + 3 \qquad (2)$

Molly

$12x + 3y = 9$
$\quad 3y = 9 - 12x \qquad (1)$
$\quad\ y = 3 - 12x \qquad (2)$
$\quad\ y = -12x + 3 \qquad (3)$

Mia

$12x + 3y = 9$
$\quad 4x + y = 3 \qquad (1)$
$\quad\ y = 3 - 4x \qquad (2)$
$\quad\ y = -4x + 3 \qquad (3)$

Ali

$12x + 3y = 9$
$\quad 3y = 9 - 12x \qquad (1)$
$\quad\ y = 3 - 4x \qquad (2)$
$\quad\ y = 4x - 3 \qquad (3)$

Problem **1.2** *continued*

B Write each equation in $y = mx + b$ form.

1. $x - y = 4$ **2.** $2x + y = 9$

3. $8x + 4y = -12$ **4.** $c = ax + dy$

C Write each equation in $Ax + By = C$ form.

1. $y = 5 - 3x$ **2.** $y = \frac{3}{4}x + \frac{1}{4}$

3. $x = 2y - 3$ **4.** $fy + 3 = gx - 15$

D Write a linear equation in slope-intercept form or standard form to represent each situation. Then, explain why your choice is the best representation.

1. Mary is selling popcorn for $5.00 per bucket and hotdogs for $4.75 each. After one hour, she makes $72.50.

2. Matt is in charge of selling roses for the Valentine's Day dance. The roses sell for $3.75 each. He estimates that the expenses for the roses are $25.00. Matt wants to write an equation for the profit.

3. Kaylee is mixing paint for an art project. She mixes 5 ounces of green paint with every 3 ounces of white paint. She needs 50 ounces of the paint mixture.

 Homework starts on page 13.

1.3 Booster Club Members
Intersecting Lines

At a school band concert, Christopher and Celine sell memberships for the band's booster club. An adult membership costs $10, and a student membership costs $5. At the end of the evening, the students had sold 50 memberships for a total of $400. The club president asked,

• How many of the new members are adults and how many are students?

You can answer the question by writing and solving equations that represent the question and the given information.

Problem 1.3

A Let *a* represent the number of $10 adult memberships and *s* represent the number of $5 student memberships.

1. What equation relates *a* and *s* to the $400 income total? Explain what each term of the equation represents.

2. Find three solutions for your equation from part (1).

3. What equation relates *a* and *s* to the total of 50 new members? Explain what each term of the equation represents.

4. Find three solutions for your equation from part (3).

5. Are there any pairs of values for *a* and *s* that satisfy both equations?

B 1. Graph the two equations from Question A on a grid like the one at the right. Does it matter which variable goes on which axis? Explain.

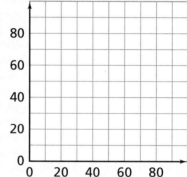

2. Determine the coordinates of the intersection point. Explain what the coordinates tell you about the numbers of adult and student memberships sold.

3. Could there be a common solution for the two equations that is *not* shown on your graph?

4. Describe situations you have studied in previous Units that are similar to this Problem.

The two equations you wrote to model the conditions of this Problem are called a **system of linear equations.** The coordinates of the intersection point satisfy both equations. These coordinates are the **solution of the system.**

C Use graphic or symbolic methods to solve each system of linear equations. Check your answer.

1. $x + y = 4$ and $x - y = -2$ 2. $2x + y = -1$ and $x - 2y = 7$

3. $-2x + y = 3$ and $-4x + 2y = 6$ 4. $-2x + y = 3$ and $-4x + 2y = 10$

 Homework starts on page 13.

Applications

1. For a fundraiser, students sell calendars and posters.

   a. What equation shows how the income I for the fundraiser depends on the number of calendars c and the number of posters p that are sold?

   b. What is the income if students sell 25 calendars and 18 posters?

   c. What is the income if students sell 12 calendars and 15 posters?

   d. What is the income if students sell 20 calendars and 12 posters?

   e. Find three combinations of calendar sales and poster sales that will give an income of exactly $100.

   f. Each answer in part (e) can be written as an ordered pair (c, p). Plot the ordered pairs on a coordinate grid.

   g. Use your graph to estimate three other (c, p) pairs that would meet the $100 goal.

2. Kateri saves her quarters and dimes. She plans to exchange the coins for paper money when the total value equals $10.

   a. How many coins does she need to make $10 if all the coins are quarters? If all the coins are dimes?

   b. What equation relates the number of quarters x and the number of dimes y to the goal of $10?

   c. Use the answers from part (a) to help you draw a graph showing all solutions to the equation.

   d. Use the graph to find five combinations of dimes and quarters that will allow Kateri to reach her goal.

3. Students in Eric's gym class must cover a distance of 1,600 meters by running or walking. Most students run part of the way and walk part of the way. Eric can run at an average speed of 200 meters per minute and walk at an average speed of 80 meters per minute.

    a. Suppose Eric runs for 4 minutes and walks for 8 minutes. How close is he to the 1,600-meter goal?

    b. Write an equation for the distance d Eric will cover if he runs for x minutes and walks for y minutes.

    c. Find three combinations of running and walking times for which Eric would cover 1,600 meters.

    d. Plot the ordered pairs from part (c) on a graph. Use the graph to estimate several other combinations of running and walking times for which Eric would cover 1,600 meters.

4. Kevin said that if you triple his age, the result will be 1 less than his mother's age.

    a. Which, if any, of these equations shows the relationship between Kevin's age x and his mother's age y? Choose all that are correct.

$$3x - y = 1 \qquad y - 3x = 1 \qquad 3x + 1 = y \qquad 3x = 1 - y$$

    b. Find three pairs of values (x, y) that satisfy the equation relating Kevin's age and his mother's age. Plot these ordered pairs, and draw the line through the points.

    c. Use the graph to estimate three other ordered pairs that satisfy the equation. Use the equation to check the estimates.

Find three pairs of values (x, y) that satisfy each equation. Plot those points and use the pattern to find two more solution pairs. (Hint: What is y if $x = 0$? What is x if $y = 0$?)

5. $6 = 3x - 2y$ 6. $10 = x + 2y$

7. $2x + y = 6$ 8. $-3x + 4y = -4$

Write the equation in equivalent $Ax + By = C$ form. Then, identify the x-intercept, y-intercept, and slope.

9. $y = 4x - 2$ 10. $y = -3x + 5$ 11. $y = x - 7$

12. $y = 5x + 3$ 13. $y = -8x - 12$ 14. $y = -9x + 5$

For Exercises 15–20, write the equation in $y = mx + b$ form. Identify the x-intercept, y-intercept, and slope.

15. $-2x - y = -5$

16. $6x + 3y = -9$

17. $x - y = 4$

18. $3x + 4y = 12$

19. $-7x + 2y = -16$

20. $x - 5y = 55$

21. Look back over your work for Exercises 9–20. Look for patterns relating the standard form of the equation, $Ax + By = C$, to the x-intercept, y-intercept, and slope.

a. Write a general formula for calculating the x-intercept from the values of A, B, and C.

b. Write a general formula for calculating the y-intercept from the values of A, B, and C.

c. Write a general formula for calculating the slope from the values of A, B, and C.

22. Tell which line below is the graph of each equation in parts (a)–(d). Explain.

a. $2x + 3y = 9$

b. $3x - 4y = 12$

c. $x - 3y = 6$

d. $3x + 2y = 6$

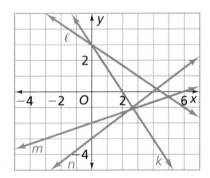

23. In Exercise 1, suppose the goal is to raise $\$600$. One equation relating the calendar and poster sales to the $\$600$ goal is $3c + 2p = 600$. Suppose the company donating the calendars and posters said they would provide a total of 250 items.

a. What equation relates c and p to the 250 items donated?

b. Graph both equations on the same grid. Find the coordinates of the intersection point. Explain what these coordinates tell you about the fundraising situation.

24. In Exercise 2, one equation relating Kateri's quarters and dimes to her goal of $10(1,000$ cents) is $25x + 10y = 1,000$. Suppose Kateri collects 70 coins to reach her goal.

   a. What equation relates x and y to the number of coins Kateri collected?

   b. Graph both equations on the same grid. Find the coordinates of the intersection point. Explain what these coordinates tell you about this situation.

25. In Exercise 3, one equation relating the times Eric spends running and walking to reach the goal of covering 1,600 meters is $200x + 80y = 1,600$. Suppose Eric runs and walks for a total of 12 minutes to reach his goal.

   a. What equation relates x and y to Eric's total time?

   b. Graph both equations on the same grid. Find the coordinates of the intersection point. Explain what these coordinates tell you about this situation.

26. In Exercise 4, one equation relating the ages of Kevin and his mother is $y - 3x = 1$. The sum of Kevin's age and his mother's age is 61 years.

   a. What equation relates Kevin's and his mother's ages to the total of their ages?

   b. Graph both equations on the same grid. Find the coordinates of the intersection point. Explain what these coordinates tell you about the ages of Kevin and his mother.

27. Use graphing methods to solve each system of equations. (**Hint:** If you are using a graphing calculator, you can determine a good graphing window by first finding the x- and y-intercepts of each graph.)

   a. $x - y = -4$ and $x + y = 6$

   b. $-2x + y = 3$ and $x + 2y = -9$

   c. $-2x + y = 1$ and $4x - 2y = 6$

Connections

For Exercises 28–33, solve the inequality. Then, write the solution using symbols, write the solution using words, and graph the solution on a number line.

28. $x + 3 < 5$

29. $x - 12 > -4$

30. $14 + x \leq -2$

31. $2x + 7 \geq -3$

32. $7x + 3 \leq -17 + 2x$

33. $-3 - 4x \geq 5x + 24$

34. The cost C to make T-shirts for a softball team is represented by the equation $C = 24 + 6N$, where N represents the number of T-shirts.

    a. Find the coordinates of a point that lies on the graph of this equation. Explain what the coordinates mean in this context.

    b. Find the coordinates of a point above the line. Explain what the coordinates mean in this context.

    c. Find the coordinates of a point below the line. Explain what the coordinates mean in this context.

35.   **a.** Which of the following points lies on the line $y = 4x - 3$? Describe where the other three points are located in relation to the line.

        (2, 1)   (2, 2)   (2, 5)   (2, 8)

    b. Find another point that lies on the line $y = 4x - 3$. Find three more points that lie above the line.

    c. The points $(-2, -11)$ and $(3, 9)$ lie on the graph of $y = 4x - 3$. Use this information to find two points that make the inequality $y < 4x - 3$ true, and two points that make the inequality $y > 4x - 3$ true.

Write an equation of a line parallel to the given line.

36. $y = 4x + 6$

37. $-6x + y = 3$

38. $x + y = 9$

39. $x + 4y = -20$

40. $y = -\frac{3}{4}x - 2$

41. $7x + y = -12$

For Exercises 42–47, write an equation of a line perpendicular to the given line.

42. $y = -4x + 2$

43. $y = -\frac{2}{3}x - 7$

44. $y = 6x + 12$

45. $-2x + y = -1$

46. $x - 4y = 20$

47. $2x + 3y = 8$

48. Tell whether each ordered pair is a solution of $3x - 5y = 15$. Show how you know.

a. $(-2, -4)$ **b.** $(0, -3)$ **c.** $(-10, 9)$

d. $(-5, -6)$ **e.** $(-10, -9)$ **f.** $(-4, -5.4)$

49. The angle measures of the triangle are $x°$, $y°$, and $z°$.

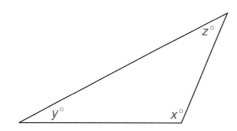

a. What equation shows how z depends on x and y?

b. Find five combinations of values for x and y for which the value of z is 40.

50. Multiple Choice Suppose k, m, and n are numbers and $k = m + n$. Which of the following statements must be true?

A. $k - m = n$ **B.** $m - k = n$

C. $2k = 2m + n$ **D.** $-n = k + m$

51. Multiple Choice Which equation is equivalent to $3x + 5y = 15$?

F. $3x = 5y + 15$ **G.** $x = -5y + 5$

H. $y = 0.6x + 3$ **J.** $y = -0.6x + 3$

52. Suppose you are given the linear equation $Ax + By = C$.

a. What is the slope of every line parallel to this line?

b. What is the slope of every line perpendicular to this line?

53. You will need two sheets of grid paper and two different cans with paper labels (for example, clam chowder and stewed tomatoes cans). On grid paper, trace the top and bottom of each can. Cut these out. Now carefully remove the labels and trace these on grid paper.

    a. Estimate and compare the surface areas of the cans. (**Hint:** The surface area of a can = label + top + bottom or S.A. = $\ell w + 2\pi r^2$.)

    b. After Joel removes his two labels, he notices that the labels are the exact same size and shape. Explain how this can happen.

54. Multiple Choice Which values are solutions of the quadratic equation $x^2 + 8x - 33 = 0$?

    A. $x = -11$ and $x = -3$

    B. $x = 11$ and $x = -3$

    C. $x = -11$ and $x = 3$

    D. $x = 11$ and $x = 3$

55. Use the graph of $y = x^2 + 8x - 33$ to find the solution of each inequality.

    a. $x^2 + 8x - 33 > 0$ **b.** $x^2 + 8x - 33 < 0$

56. Tell whether each line has a slope of $-\frac{1}{2}$.

    a. $y = \frac{-1}{-2}x + 3$ **b.** $y = \frac{-1}{2}x + 3$

    c. $y = \frac{1}{-2}x + 3$ **d.** $y = -\frac{1}{2}x + 3$

57. a. What shape will this net make if it is cut out and folded?

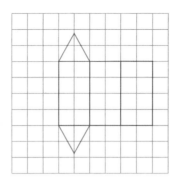

b. Find the surface area of the shape.

c. Find the volume of the shape.

Without graphing, decide whether the lines are *parallel, perpendicular,* or *neither.*

58. $3x + 6y = 12$ and $y = 10 + \frac{-1}{2}x$

59. $y = -x + 5$ and $y = x + 5$

60. $y = 2 - 5x$ and $y = -5x + 2$

61. $y = -3 + 5x$ and $y = \frac{-x}{5} + 3$

62. $10x + 5y = 20$ and $y = 10x + 20$

Extensions

63. Jasmine wants to run a marathon. She knows she will have to walk some of the 26.2 miles, but she wants to finish in 5 hours. She plans to run 10-minute miles and walk 15-minute miles. Let x represent the number of minutes Jasmine runs. Let y represent the number of minutes she walks.

    a. What equation relates x and y to the goal of completing the race in 5 hours?

    b. What equation relates x and y to the goal of covering 26.2 miles?

    c. For each equation, find several ordered-pair solutions (x, y). Then, plot the points with those coordinates and use the pattern to draw a graph of the equation. Graph both equations on the same grid.

    d. Use the graphs to estimate the combination of running and walking times that will allow Jasmine to complete the marathon in exactly 5 hours.

64. In Exercise 63, suppose Jasmine decides she wants to finish the marathon in less than 5 hours.

    a. Find five combinations of running and walking times that give a total time of less than 5 hours.

    b. Express the condition that the total running and walking times must be less than 5 hours as an inequality.

    c. Make a graph of all the solutions of the inequality.

    d. Graph the linear equation from Exercise 63, part (b) on the same grid as the inequality. Explain how the result shows Jasmine's options for running and walking times if she wants to finish the marathon in 5 hours or less.

Mathematical Reflections

In this Investigation, you used coordinate graphs to display solutions of linear equations in the form $Ax + By = C$ and to find solutions of systems of linear equations. The following questions will help you summarize what you have learned.

Think about these questions. Discuss your ideas with other students and your teacher. Then write a summary of your findings in your notebook.

1. **What** pattern will result from plotting all points (x, y) that satisfy an equation in the form $Ax + By = C$?

2. **How** can you change linear equations in the form $Ax + By = C$ to $y = mx + b$ form and vice versa? Explain when one form might be more useful than the other.

3. **How** can you use a graph to find values of x and y that satisfy systems of two linear equations in the form $Ax + By = C$?

Common Core Mathematical Practices

As you worked on the Problems in this Investigation, you used prior knowledge to make sense of them. You also applied Mathematical Practices to solve the Problems. Think back over your work, the ways you thought about the Problems, and how you used Mathematical Practices.

Ken described his thoughts in the following way:

> In Problem 1.2, we wrote the equation $12x + 3y = 9$ as $y = 3 - 4x$ because we knew they were equivalent. We noticed that each form highlights a different part of the same equation.
>
> If the value of one variable depended on another, the $y = mx + b$ form was more useful because the variable y was already isolated.
>
> If the values of the two variables combined to produce a fixed value, the $Ax + Bx = C$ form was more useful because the constant was isolated.
>
> **Common Core Standards for Mathematical Practice**
> **MP7** Look for and make use of structure.

- What other Mathematical Practices can you identify in Ken's reasoning?

- Describe a Mathematical Practice that you and your classmates used to solve a different Problem in this Investigation.

Solving Linear Systems Symbolically

Your work in Investigation 1 revealed key facts about solving linear equations.

- The solutions of equations in the form $Ax + By = C$ are ordered pairs of numbers.

- The graph of the solutions for an equation $Ax + By = C$ is a straight line.

- The solution of a system of two linear equations is the coordinates of the point where the lines intersect.

In *Say It With Symbols,* you solved systems of equations, such as the following:

> Ms. Lucero wants to install tiles around her square swimming pool. The equations below show the estimated costs C (in dollars) of buying and installing N border tiles.
>
> *Cover and Surround It:* $C_C = 1{,}000 + 25(N - 12)$
>
> *Tile and Beyond:* $C_T = 740 + 32(N - 10)$
>
> For what number of tiles are the costs of the two companies equal?

Common Core State Standards

8.EE.C.8 Analyze and solve pairs of simultaneous linear equations.

8.EE.C.8a Understand that solutions to a system of two linear equations in two variables correspond to points of intersection of their graphs, because points of intersection satisfy both equations simultaneously.

8.EE.C.8c Solve real-world and mathematical problems leading to two linear equations in two variables.

Also **8.EE.C.8b, A-CED.A.2, A-CED.A.3, A-CED.A.4, A-REI.B.3, A-REI.C.5, A-REI.C.6, A-REI.D.10**

You can write the two equations as a system of two linear equations:

$$\begin{cases} C_C = 1{,}000 + 25(N - 12) \\ C_T = 740 + 32(N - 10) \end{cases}$$

You found solutions of this system in two ways by

- setting $C_C = C_T$ and solving for N. Then, you substituted N into one of the equations to find the cost.

- graphing the pair of equations. Then, you found the coordinates (C, N) of the intersection point of the two lines. The ordered pair is called the solution of the system. When you substitute the coordinates into each equation, the resulting statement is true.

Finding an exact solution is not always easy to do from a graph of the pair of linear equations. In this Investigation, you will develop symbolic methods for solving systems of linear equations.

2.1 Shirts and Caps Again
Solving Systems With $y = mx + b$

Recall the T-shirt and cap sale from Investigation 1.

PROFIT
- $5 profit per T-shirt
- $10 profit per cap

GOAL
- Raise $600

DAY 1
- 18 items sold
- $125 profit earned

- What two equations represent the relationship between the number of shirts sold and the number of caps sold?

- How can you find the number of shirts and the number of caps sold? Explain your reasoning.

Problem 2.1

A Check Nyla and Jimfa's solution strategies below.

Nyla

Write a system of two linear equations.

$$\begin{cases} c + s = 18 \\ 10c + 5s = 125 \end{cases}$$

Write equivalent equations.

$$\begin{cases} c = 18 - s \\ c = \dfrac{1}{10}(125 - 5s) \end{cases} \text{ or}$$

$$\begin{cases} c = 18 - s \\ c = 12.5 - 0.5s \end{cases}$$

Graph the two equations. The solution of the system is the point where the graphs of the equations meet.

Jimfa

Write a system of two linear equations.

$$\begin{cases} c + s = 18 \\ 10c + 5s = 125 \end{cases}$$

Write equivalent equations.

$$\begin{cases} c = -s + 18 \\ c = -0.5s + 12.5 \end{cases}$$

Write one linear equation.

$$-0.5s + 12.5 = -s + 18$$

Solve the linear equation for s. Then find the related value of c.

1. Do you agree with Nyla's reasoning? If not, explain why. If so, solve the system using her method.

2. Do you agree with Jimfa's reasoning? If not, explain why. If so, solve the system using his method.

3. How many shirts and caps did the class sell? Explain your reasoning.

B Use symbolic methods to find values of x and y that satisfy each system. Check your solution by substituting the values into the equations and showing that the resulting statements are true.

1. $\begin{cases} y = 1.5x - 0.4 \\ y = 0.3x + 5 \end{cases}$

2. $\begin{cases} x + y = 3 \\ x - y = -5 \end{cases}$

3. $\begin{cases} 3x - y = 30 \\ x + y = 14 \end{cases}$

4. $\begin{cases} x + 6y = 15 \\ -x + 4y = 5 \end{cases}$

5. $\begin{cases} x - y = -5 \\ -2x + 2y = 10 \end{cases}$

6. $\begin{cases} x - y = -5 \\ -2x + 2y = 8 \end{cases}$

Problem 2.1 *continued*

C Ming and Eun Mi discuss how to solve the system. $\begin{cases} x + y = 3 \\ x - y = -5 \end{cases}$

Ming says it would be easier to solve the system by writing each equation in the equivalent form $x = ny + c$. Eun Mi says it would be easier to solve the system by writing each equation in the equivalent form $y = mx + b$. Who is correct? Explain.

A C E Homework starts on page 32.

2.2 Taco Truck Lunch
Solving Systems by Combining Equations I

In Problem 2.1, you developed strategies for solving systems of equations by writing each equation in the equivalent form $y = mx + b$ or $x = ny + c$. Then you found the solution of the system by graphing or by solving one linear equation for x or y.

In this Problem, you will learn another strategy for solving linear systems.

Pablo and Jasmine each took their brothers out for lunch. They stopped at a taco truck where the prices were not posted.

After placing their orders, they compared what they bought with the total cost for each order.

Pablo and his brother got 6 tacos and 2 drinks for $9.

- Can you use this information to find the price of one taco? Of one drink? Explain.

Jasmine and her brother got 4 tacos and 2 drinks for $7.

- Does the additional information help you find the price of one taco? Of one drink? Explain.

? What is the price of one taco and the price of one drink? Explain your reasoning.

Problem **2.2**

A Pablo's younger brother Pedro used the orders and total prices to find the price of each taco and each drink.

When asked how he figured out the prices, Pedro said, "It's kind of like what we did in school with coins and pouches." Then he made the following sketch.

1. How does the sketch help you find the price of one taco and the price of one drink?

2. Find another way to use Pedro's sketch to solve the problem.

Problem **2.2** *continued*

B Pablo and Jasmine had just started studying systems of linear equations in algebra. They looked at Pedro's drawing and said, "We could write that as a system of equations."

1. Write an equation that represents the cost of Pablo's order and one that represents the cost of Jasmine's order. Use t for the price of each taco and d for the price of each drink.

2. What operations with the equations from part (1) match your way of using Pedro's sketch to find the prices t and d? Why do the operations make sense?

C In algebra class the next day, Pablo and Jasmine tried to solve the system of linear equations. $\begin{cases} x + 4y = 11 \\ x + y = 5 \end{cases}$

1. How could they represent the system with a sketch similar to the one Pedro drew of the taco truck orders?

2. How could the sketch and reasoning about the equations lead them to a solution of the system?

D Use diagrams or reasoning about equations to solve each system.

1. $\begin{cases} 3x + y = 4 \\ x + y = 5 \end{cases}$
2. $\begin{cases} 3x + 2y = 4 \\ x + 2y = 6 \end{cases}$

A**C****E** Homework starts on page 32.

2.3 Solving Systems by Combining Equations II

Pablo and Jasmine showed their method for solving systems of linear equations. Their teacher then asked the class how they would solve the following system using the methods from Problem 2.2.

$$\begin{cases} 2x - y = 4 \\ x + y = 5 \end{cases}$$

Their classmate Samantha offered the following solution:

If $2x - y = 4$ and $x + y = 5$, then

$$(2x - y) + (x + y) = 4 + 5 \qquad (1)$$
$$3x = 9 \qquad (2)$$
$$x = 3 \qquad (3)$$
$$3 + y = 5 \qquad (4)$$
$$y = 2 \qquad (5)$$

- What reasoning justifies each step of her solution?

- Is her solution correct? Why or why not?

Pablo said, "Jasmine and I combined equations by subtracting equals from equals." Samantha said, "In my method, I combined equations by adding equals to equals." You will use both methods in this Problem.

Problem 2.3

A Use the methods of Pablo and Jasmine, and Samantha to solve each system.

1. $\begin{cases} -x + 4y = 2 \\ x + 2y = 5 \end{cases}$

2. $\begin{cases} 2x + 3y = 4 \\ 5x + 3y = -8 \end{cases}$

3. $\begin{cases} 2x - 3y = 4 \\ 5x - 3y = 7 \end{cases}$

4. $\begin{cases} 3x + 2y = 10 \\ 4x - y = 6 \end{cases}$

B In the T-shirt and cap sale, the equation $5s + 10c = 125$ related profit to the number of shirts and caps sold.

1. Find five solutions of the equation.

2. Samantha said, "If we had doubled the price of each item, we would have doubled the profit for the same numbers of shirts and caps sold." Do you agree with her reasoning? Why or why not?

3. Write Samantha's new equation. Check whether the solutions from part (1) are also solutions of the new equation.

C 1. Is System B below equivalent to System A? Explain.

System A

$\begin{cases} 3x + 2y = 10 \\ 4x - y = 6 \end{cases}$

System B

$\begin{cases} 3x + 2y = 10 \\ 8x - 2y = 12 \end{cases}$

2. Use the combination method to solve System B.

3. Check that your solution also satisfies System A.

D For each system:

- Write an equivalent system that is easy to solve using the combination method.

- Solve the system.

- Check that your solution also satisfies the original system.

1. $\begin{cases} 2x + 2y = 5 \\ 3x - 6y = 12 \end{cases}$

2. $\begin{cases} x + 3y = 4 \\ 4x + 5y = 2 \end{cases}$

3. $\begin{cases} 2x + y = 5 \\ 3x - 2y = 15 \end{cases}$

4. $\begin{cases} -x + 2y = 5 \\ 5x - 10y = 11 \end{cases}$

A C E Homework starts on page 32.

Applications

1. A school is planning a Saturday Back-to-School Festival to raise funds for the school art and music programs. Some of the planned activities are a ring toss, frog jump, basketball free throws, and a golf putting green. The organizers are considering two pricing plans.

> Plan 1: $5 admission fee, $1 per game
>
> Plan 2: $2.50 admission fee, $1.50 per game

   a. Write equations that show how the cost *y* for playing the games at the festival depends on the number of games *x* that a participant chooses to play.

   b. Estimate the coordinates of the intersection point of the graphs of the two equations. Check to see if those coordinates are an exact solution of both equations.

   c. Use the expressions in the two cost equations to write and solve a single linear equation for the *x*-coordinate of the intersection point. Then use that *x*-value to find the *y*-coordinate of the intersection point.

   d. For what number of games would Plan 1 be a better deal for participants than Plan 2?

2. In Exercise 1, suppose the two pricing plans changed as follows. Complete parts (a)–(d) based on these two plans.

> Plan 1: $4.50 admission fee, $1 per game
>
> Plan 2: $3.50 admission fee, $1 per game

Solve each system of equations.

3. $\begin{cases} y = 6x + 4 \\ y = 4x - 2 \end{cases}$

4. $\begin{cases} y = 3x + 7 \\ y = 5x - 7 \end{cases}$

5. $\begin{cases} y = -2x - 9 \\ y = 12x + 19 \end{cases}$

6. $\begin{cases} y = -x + 16 \\ y = -x - 8 \end{cases}$

7. $\begin{cases} y = 17x - 6 \\ y = 12x + 44 \end{cases}$

8. $\begin{cases} y = -20x + 14 \\ y = -8x - 44 \end{cases}$

For Exercises 9–14, write the equation in $y = mx + b$ form.

9. $4x + 6y + 12 = 0$

10. $-7x + 9y + 4 = 0$

11. $-4x - 2y - 6 = 0$

12. $-x + 4y = 0$

13. $2x - 2y + 2 = 0$

14. $25x + 5y - 15 = 0$

15. A sixth-grade class sells pennants and flags. They earn $1 profit for each pennant sold and $6 profit for each flag sold. They sell 50 items in total for a profit of $115.

   a. Write two equations that represent the relationship between the number of pennants sold p and the number of flags sold f.

   b. How many pennants and how many flags were sold?

16. A seventh-grade class sells mouse pads and cell phone cases with their school logo on them. The class earns $2 profit for each mouse pad sold and $4 profit for each cell phone case sold. They sell 100 items in total for a profit of $268.

   a. Write two equations that represent the relationship between the number of mouse pads sold m and the number of cell phone cases sold c.

   b. How many mouse pads and how many cell phone cases were sold?

17. Write a system of equations that you can use to find the two numbers.

   a. Two numbers have a sum of 119 and a difference of 25.

   b. Two numbers have a sum of 71 and a difference of 37.

   c. Two numbers have a sum of 32 and a difference of 60.

   d. Two numbers have a sum of 180 and a difference of 45.

   e. If you know the sum and difference of two numbers, how can you use this information to find one of the two missing numbers? How do you find the second missing number?

18. On a hot summer day, Jay set up a lemonade stand. He kept track of how many glasses he sold on his phone.

   a. Write two equations that relate the number of large glasses sold *l* and the number of small glasses sold *s*.

   b. Solve the system of equations.

   c. How many small glasses were sold?

   d. How many large glasses were sold?

Pablo and Jasmine decide to try some other food trucks after eating at the taco truck in Problem 2.2. For Exercises 19–22, do the following.

   a. Write two equations based on the information.

   b. Solve the system of equations to determine the price of 1 serving of food and the price of 1 drink or bag of chips.

19. Pablo buys 3 servings of jambalaya and 2 drinks for $18.00. Jasmine buys 1 serving of jambalaya and 2 drinks for $9.00.

20. Pablo buys 4 sandwiches and 4 bags of chips for $24.00. Jasmine buys 8 sandwiches and 4 bags of chips for $43.00.

21. Pablo buys 3 loaves of zucchini bread and 5 cups of tea for $15.00. Jasmine buys 5 loaves of zucchini bread and 3 cups of tea for $21.00.

22. Pablo buys 6 apple pies and 2 juices for $39.00. Jasmine buys 2 apple pies and 4 juices for $18.00.

Solve each system by using the combination method.

23. $\begin{cases} 3x - 2y = 12 \\ -3x + 8y = -6 \end{cases}$
   24. $\begin{cases} 4x + 9y = 7 \\ 4x - 9y = 9 \end{cases}$
   25. $\begin{cases} 12x - 14y = -8 \\ -8x - 14y = 52 \end{cases}$

26. $\begin{cases} 5x + 15y = 10 \\ 5x - 10y = -40 \end{cases}$
   27. $\begin{cases} -6x - 4y = 21 \\ -6x + 3y = 0 \end{cases}$
   28. $\begin{cases} 2x - 3y = 14 \\ -x + 3y = -6 \end{cases}$

29. $\begin{cases} 3x + 2y = 17 \\ -2x - y = -12 \end{cases}$
   30. $\begin{cases} 4x + 3y = 18 \\ 3x + 4y = 3 \end{cases}$
   31. $\begin{cases} -2x + 6y = 42 \\ 4x - 3y = -12 \end{cases}$

32. Students in Mr. Coutley's class are playing the game "guess the date." For example, one student chooses a date (April 16), writes the date as an ordered pair (4, 16), and gives two clues.

Clue 1 "If I add the month number and the day number, the sum is 20."

Clue 2 "If I double the month number and add it to the day number, the sum is 24."

The other students try to determine the date based on the two clues. Find the date that each student is thinking of by writing and solving a system of two equations.

ANDREW

First Clue: If I double the month number and add it to double the day number, the sum is 26.

Second Clue: If I double the month number and then subtract double the day number, the difference is –18.

First Clue: If I double the month number and add the day number, the sum is 26.

Second Clue: If I multiply the month number by 10 and then subtract the day number, the difference is 10.

LARA

MARTHA

First Clue: The sum of triple the month number and double the day number is 62.

Second Clue: The difference of double the month number and the day number is 4.

First Clue: The sum of four times the month number and the day number is 42.

Second Clue: The sum of the month number and four times the day number is 33.

AHNA

Connections

For Exercises 33–38, solve the equation. Check the solution.

33. $3x + 12 = 24$

34. $-7x - 13 = 15$

35. $8 - 2x = 30$

36. $-7 + 9x = 38$

37. $-4 - 6x = -22$

38. $8x + 17 = -15$

39. For each part (a)–(f), find the value of y when $x = -2$.

   a. $y = 3x - 7$

   b. $3x - 2y = 10$

   c. $7x - 4y = 12$

   d. $x = 4y - 2$

   e. $3 = 2x - y$

   f. $12 = -3x - 4y$

Write an equation of the line satisfying the given conditions.

40. slope $= -4$, y-intercept $= 3$

41. slope $= \frac{2}{3}$, passes through the point $(3, 4)$

42. slope $= -3$, y-intercept $= 2$

43. passes through the points $(5, 4)$ and $(1, 7)$

For Exercises 44–49, identify the slope and y-intercept of the line.

44. $3x + 2y = 4$

45. $4x - 8y = 12$

46. $x - y = 7$

47. $y = 4x - 8$

48. $2y = 4x + 6$

49. $y = 9$

50. Two lines can intersect at 0 points (if they are parallel), 1 point, or an infinite number of points (if they are the same). In parts (a)–(d), give all the possible numbers of intersection points for the two figures. Make sketches to illustrate the possibilities.

   a. a circle and a straight line

   b. two circles

   c. a circle and a triangle

   d. a circle and a rectangle

51. A **chord** is a line segment joining two points on a **circle.** $\overline{AC}$ is a chord in the diagram at the right.

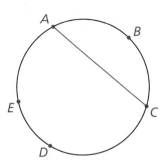

    a. How many chords can you draw by joining the labeled points on this circle?

    b. How many points inside the circle are intersection points of two or more of the chords from part (a)?

    c. The chords cut the circle into several nonoverlapping regions. How many regions are formed?

52. Multiple Choice Which point is *not* on the graph of $2x - 5y = 13$?

    A. $(9, 1)$ **B.** $(4, -1)$ **C.** $(0, 3.2)$ **D.** $(6.5, 0)$

53. The cylinder below represents an air conditioner with a radius of x feet and height of 2 feet.

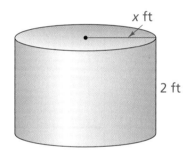

    a. Draw a net of a cover for the air conditioner. The top and sides need to be covered, but not the bottom.

    b. Which equation below represents the area of the cover? Which represents the volume?

$$y = 2\pi x^2 \qquad\qquad y = \pi x^2 + 4\pi x$$
$$y = 2x^3 \qquad\qquad y = \pi x(x + 4)$$

54. Multiple Choice Kaya wants to fence off part of her yard for a garden. She has 150 feet of fencing. She wants a rectangular garden with a length 1.5 times its width. Which system represents these conditions?

    F. $\begin{cases} 1.5w = \ell \\ w + \ell = 150 \end{cases}$ **G.** $\begin{cases} w = 1.5\ell \\ w + \ell = 150 \end{cases}$

    H. $\begin{cases} 2w = 3\ell \\ w + \ell = 75 \end{cases}$ **J.** $\begin{cases} 3w = 2\ell \\ 2(w + \ell) = 150 \end{cases}$

55. Multiple Choice Which equation shows how to find one dimension of the garden described in Exercise 54?

A. $2.5w = 150$ **B.** $2.5\ell = 150$

C. $2w = 3(75 - w)$ **D.** $5w = 150$

For Exercises 56–59, write an equation that represents each line on the graph. Then, solve the system of equations symbolically.

56.

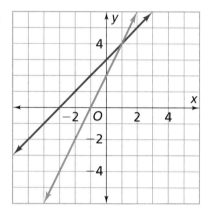

57.

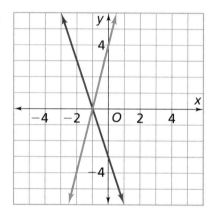

58.

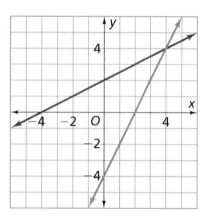

59.

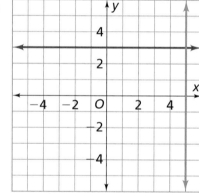

60. How does the solution of each system of equations in Exercises 56–59 relate to its the graph?

Write a system of equations that has each solution.

61. $x = 3, y = 2$ **62.** $x = 0, y = 0$

63. $x = -4, y = -2$ **64.** $x = \frac{1}{2}, y = \frac{1}{4}$

For Exercises 65–68, tell whether the table represents a linear, quadratic, exponential, or inverse variation relationship. Write an equation for the relationship.

65.

x	0	1	2	3	4	5	6	7
y	0	−3	−4	−3	0	5	12	21

66.

x	−1	0	1	2	3	4	5	6
y	$\frac{1}{3}$	1	3	9	27	81	243	729

67.

x	1	3	4	6	9	10	12	18
y	2	8	11	17	26	29	35	53

68.

x	1	2	3	4	6	8	10	12
y	12	6	4	3	2	1.5	1.2	1

69. Use the tables of four linear equations.

Line a

x	−3	−2	−1	0
y	6	2	−2	−6

Line b

x	−3	−1	0	4
y	−6	−2	0	8

Line c

x	−3	1	0	3
y	6	2	3	0

Line d

x	4	6	8	10
y	5	6	7	8

What is the solution of the system of equations formed by

  a. lines *a* and *b*?   **b.** lines *a* and *c*?   **c.** lines *a* and *d*?

  d. lines *b* and *c*?   **e.** lines *b* and *d*?   **f.** lines *c* and *d*?

Solve each equation for *x*.

70. $5(x + 4) - 2x = 5 + 6x + 2x$ **71.** $2(x + 2) - 6x = 6x + 8 - 2x$

72. $x^2 - 7x + 12 = 0$ **73.** $x^2 + 5x - 6 = 0$

74. Match each equation with its corresponding graph below.

  a. $y = 2^{x-1}$ **b.** $y = -x^2 + 2x + 8$ **c.** $y = (x + 2)(x - 4)$

  d. $y = 2^x$ **e.** $y = 2x^2$ **f.** $25 = x^2 + y^2$

Graph 1

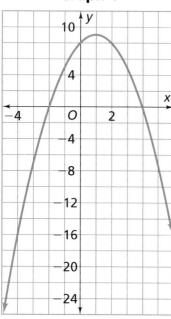

Graph 2

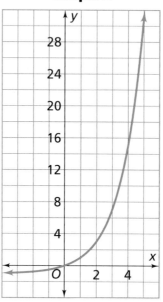

Graph 3

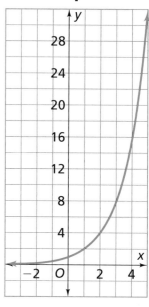

Graph 4

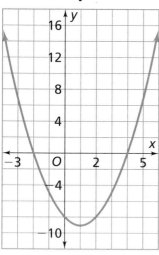

Graph 5

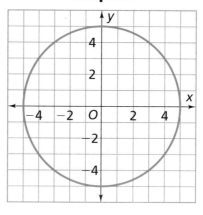

Graph 6

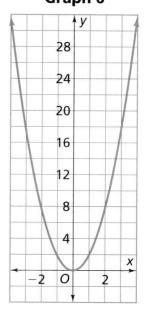

Extensions

75. Antonia and Marissa both babysit. Antonia charges $5.50 an hour. Marissa charges a base rate of $20.00, plus $.50 an hour.

  a. For each girl, write an equation showing how the charge depends on babysitting time.

  b. For what times are Marissa's charges less than Antonia's?

  c. Is there a time for which Antonia and Marissa charge the same amount?

76. Raj's age is 1 year less than twice Sarah's age. Toni's age is 2 years less than three times Sarah's age.

  a. Suppose Sarah's age is s years. What is Raj's age in terms of s?

  b. How old is Toni in terms of s?

  c. How old are Raj, Sarah, and Toni if the sum of their ages is 21?

77. Melissa and Trevor sell candy bars to raise money for a class field trip. Trevor sells 1 more than five times as many candy bars as Melissa sells. Together they sell 49 candy bars.

  a. Let m represent the number of candy bars Melissa sells. Let t represent the number of candy bars Trevor sells. Write a linear system to represent this situation.

  b. Solve your system to find the number of candy bars each student sells.

78. Solve each system by writing each equation in the equivalent form $y = mx + b$ or by using the combination method. You may get some interesting results. In each case, graph the equations and explain what the results indicate about the solution.

  a. $\begin{cases} x - 2y = 3 \\ -3x + 6y = -6 \end{cases}$

  b. $\begin{cases} x - y = 4 \\ -x + y = -4 \end{cases}$

  c. $\begin{cases} 2x - 3y = 4 \\ 4x - 6y = 7 \end{cases}$

  d. $\begin{cases} 4x - 6y = 4 \\ -6x + 9y = -6 \end{cases}$

79. The equation of the line is $y = \frac{4}{3}x$. The equation of the circle is $x^2 + y^2 = 25$.

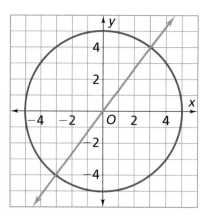

You can find the intersection points by solving the system below. Modify the combination method to solve the system.

$$\begin{cases} y = \frac{4}{3}x \\ x^2 + y^2 = 25 \end{cases}$$

80. In Investigation 1, you learned that the solution of a system of linear equations is the intersection point of their graphs. Determine the maximum number of intersection points for the graphs of each type of function given.

   a. a quadratic function and a linear function

   b. a quadratic function and a different quadratic function

   c. a cubic function and a linear function

   d. an inverse variation and a linear function

   e. Which pairs of functions in parts (a)–(d) might not have an intersection?

81. Write a system in the form $\begin{cases} ax + by = c \\ dx + ey = f \end{cases}$ that has the given solution.

   a. $(3, 7)$

   b. $(-2, 3)$

   c. no solution

82. Consider these equivalent systems.

$$\begin{cases} 2y - 3x = 0 \\ y + x = 75 \end{cases} \quad \text{and} \quad \begin{cases} 2y - 3x = 0 \\ 3y + 3x = 225 \end{cases}$$

    a. Do the four equations in these two systems represent four different lines? Explain.

    b. Adding the two equations in the second system gives $5y = 225$, or $y = 45$. Does $y = 45$ represent the same line as either equation in the system? Does its graph have anything in common with the lines in the system?

    c. If you add the two equations in the first system, you get $3y - 2x = 75$. Does this equation represent the same line as either equation in the system? Does its graph have anything in common with the lines in the system?

    d. What conjectures can you make about the results of adding any two linear equations? Consider the following questions:

       • Will the result be a linear equation?

       • Will the graph of the new equation have anything in common with the graphs of the original equations?

83. During math class, Mr. Krajewski gives Ben the following system.

$$\begin{cases} -3x - 6y + z = -7 \\ 6x + 3y - z = 6 \\ -9x - 3y + z = -7 \end{cases}$$

Ben thinks that he can solve the system if he adds the first equation to the second equation.

    a. Why do you think Ben adds the two equations?

    b. Is there another pair of equations Ben should add together?

    c. Find the values of x, y, and z that satisfy the three equations.

84. A baking company makes two kinds of Sweeties, regular and double-stuffed.

a. How many wafers are in one serving of regular Sweeties? How many wafers are in one serving of double-stuffed Sweeties?

b. Let w represent the number of Calories in each wafer and f represent the number of Calories in each layer of filling.

i. What equation shows the relationship between w, f, and the number of Calories in one serving of regular Sweeties?

ii. What equation shows the relationship between w, f, and the number of Calories in one serving of double-stuffed Sweeties?

c. Solve the system of equations from part (b) to find the number of Calories in each Sweetie wafer and each layer of filling.

Mathematical Reflections 2

In this Investigation, you learned several strategies for finding solutions of systems of linear equations. The following questions will help you summarize what you have learned.

Think about these questions. Discuss your ideas with other students and your teacher. Then write a summary of your findings in your notebook.

1. **What** is the goal in solving a system of linear equations?

2. **What** strategies can you use to solve a system of linear equations?

3. **How** can you check a possible solution of a system of linear equations?

Common Core Mathematical Practices

As you worked on the Problems in this Investigation, you used prior knowledge to make sense of them. You also applied Mathematical Practices to solve the Problems. Think back over your work, the ways you thought about the Problems, and how you used Mathematical Practices.

Tori described her thoughts in the following way:

When we were solving systems of equations in Problem 2.1, some of us graphed the equations and some of us used symbolic methods. We were surprised that both of these methods gave the same results.

Both methods showed that the system in Question B, part (6) had no solution. The lines were parallel. The system in Question B, part (5) produced the same line, which means that the system had an infinite number of solutions. Then we remembered that we studied similar situations in *Moving Straight Ahead* for linear equations.

· ·

Common Core Standards for Mathematical Practice

MP8 Look for and express regularity in repeated reasoning.

- What other Mathematical Practices can you identify in Tori's reasoning?

- Describe a Mathematical Practice that you and your classmates used to solve a different Problem in this Investigation.

Systems of Functions and Inequalities

Many businesses have contracts with private companies to provide security alarms and to respond to break-ins. Suppose the owners of a shopping center get bids from two reliable security companies.

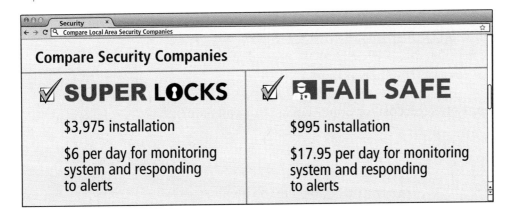

- How could you use linear functions to compare the costs for the two security companies?

- What patterns do you expect to see in the graphs of these functions?

- How can you use a graph to answer questions about which company offers the best price?

Common Core State Standards

8.EE.C.8a Understand that solutions to a system of two linear equations in two variables correspond to points of intersection of their graphs, because points of intersection satisfy both equations simultaneously.

8.EE.C.8c Solve real-world and mathematical problems leading to two linear equations in two variables.

Also A-CED.A.1, A-CED.A.2, A-CED.A.3, A-REI.B.3, A-REI.B.4, A-REI.B.4b, A-REI.C.7, A-REI.D.10, A-REI.D.12

3.1 Comparing Security Services
Linear Inequalities

The cost of security services from Super Locks and Fail Safe depends on the number of days that the company provides service. The graph below shows the bids for both companies.

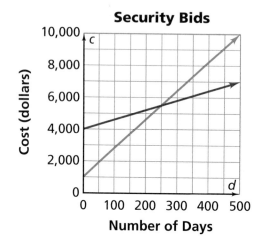

Security Bids

- Which line represents the cost for Super Locks? For Fail Safe?

Problem 3.1

A Use the graph above to estimate the answers to these questions. Explain your reasoning in each case.

1. For what number of days will the costs for the two companies be the same? What is that cost?

2. For what numbers of days will Super Locks cost less than Fail Safe?

3. For what numbers of days will Fail Safe cost less than Super Locks?

B 1. For each company, write an equation for the cost c for d days of security services.

2. For Question A, parts (1)–(3), write an equation or inequality that you can use to answer each question.

Problem 3.1 *continued*

C Solve each equation or inequality by graphing a pair of linear functions.

1. $2x + 1 = 0.5x + 4$ 2. $2x + 1 < 0.5x + 4$ 3. $2x + 1 > 0.5x + 4$

4. $x - 2 = 6 - x$ 5. $x - 2 > 6 - x$ 6. $x - 2 < 6 - x$

7. $3x + 4 = 13$ 8. $3x + 4 \leq 13$ 9. $3x + 4 \geq 13$

D Francis recalls that he used number-line graphs to show solutions of inequalities in *Moving Straight Ahead*. For Question C, part (8) he graphed the solutions of the inequality $3x + 4 \leq 13$ on a number line, as shown below. The solutions are $x \leq 3$.

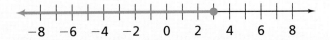

He used the number-line graph shown below to represent the solutions of the inequality $3x + 4 < 13$. The solutions are $x < 3$.

1. How do the solutions of $3x + 4 \leq 13$ on a coordinate grid relate to the solutions on a number line?

2. Draw number-line graphs to represent solutions of each inequality.

   a. $2x + 1 < 0.5x + 4$

   b. $2x + 1 > 0.5x + 4$

   c. $2x + 1 \geq 0.5x + 4$

A C E Homework starts on page 54.

3.2 Solving Linear Inequalities Symbolically

Graphing methods are helpful for estimating solutions of inequalities. If you want exact results, you can use symbolic reasoning.

You already know how to use properties of equality to solve linear equations. To solve **linear inequalities**, you will learn to use the properties of operations on inequalities.

Problem 3.2

A Suppose that two numbers q and r are related by the inequality $q < r$. Draw a number line such as the one below.

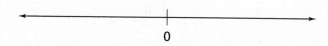

0

Locate points to represent the numbers q and r when

1. both q and r are positive numbers.

2. both q and r are negative numbers.

3. one number is negative and the other is positive.

B Suppose $q < r$.

- Complete each statement below with an inequality symbol ($<$ or $>$) so that the result is true for all values of q and r.

- Use the number-line graphs from Question A and ideas about geometric transformations to explain each answer.

- If it is not possible to write an inequality statement that is true for all values of q and r, give examples to show why that is the case.

1. $q + 23 \blacksquare r + 23$ 2. $q - 35 \blacksquare r - 23$ 3. $14q \blacksquare 14r$

4. $-6q \blacksquare -6r$ 5. $\dfrac{q}{5} \blacksquare \dfrac{r}{5}$ 6. $\dfrac{q}{-3} \blacksquare \dfrac{r}{-3}$

C What do your results from Question B suggest about how working with inequalities is similar to and different from working with equations?

Problem **3.2** *continued*

D Use symbolic reasoning to solve each inequality. Then, make a number-line graph to show the solutions.

1. $3x + 17 < 47$

2. $43 < 8x - 9$

3. $-6x + 9 < 25$

4. $14x - 23 < 5x + 13$

5. $18 < -4x + 2$

6. $3{,}975 + 6x < 995 + 17.95x$

A C E Homework starts on page 54.

3.3 Operating at a Profit
Systems of Lines and Curves

In the last Problem, you found that working with linear inequalities was similar to working with linear equations when operations involved positive numbers. When operations involved negative numbers, some differences occurred. Hector summarizes the results below:

If $p < q$ and a is positive, then
$$p + a < q + a$$
$$p - a < q - a$$
$$ap < aq$$

If $p < q$ and b is negative, then
$$p + b < q + b$$
$$p - b < q - b$$
$$bp > bq$$

In *Variables and Patterns* and *Say It With Symbols,* you studied the business plans of students who operate bicycle tours. The income and operating costs of the business both depend on the number of customers *n*.

Income	**Operating Cost**
$I = 400n - 10n^2$	$C = 150n + 1{,}000$

You found ways to find the break-even point, which is when income equals operating cost. You can also find the break-even point by thinking about these two equations as a system of functions.

- When would the tour business make a profit?

- When would it lose money?

- When would it simply break even?

- How can you use symbolic reasoning to solve this system of equations to answer these questions?

As with linear systems, it helps to begin with graphs that model the business conditions. Then, you can use symbolic reasoning to find the exact values of the coordinates of the points that answer your questions.

Problem 3.3

 A 1. Graph the income and cost functions on the same coordinate grid with the number of customers *n* on the horizontal axis.

2. Write an equation or inequality relating the two functions that you could use to answer each question.

 a. For what numbers of customers will income equal operating costs?

 b. For what numbers of customers will operating costs exceed income?

 c. For what numbers of customers will income exceed operating costs?

3. a. Use your graphs from part (1) to estimate solutions of the equations and inequalities you wrote in part (2). Explain how you know that your estimates are reasonably accurate.

 b. Describe how you could find exact solutions of the equations and inequalities from part (2).

Problem 3.3 *continued*

B Use ideas from your work in Question A to solve the following equations and inequalities.

1. $x^2 - 4x + 4 = 2x - 1$

2. $x^2 - 4x + 4 < 2x - 1$

3. $x^2 - 4x + 4 > 2x - 1$

4. $-x^2 + 4x + 2 = x - 2$

5. $-x^2 + 4x + 2 < x - 2$

6. $-x^2 + 4x + 2 > x - 2$

C In *Looking for Pythagoras*, you learned that the points on the graph of a circle with radius r and center $(0, 0)$ are solutions of the equation $x^2 + y^2 = r^2$. Use this fact to estimate the solutions of the systems of equations shown in the graph below.

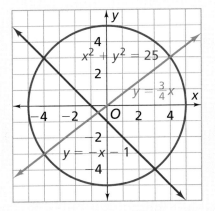

1. $\begin{cases} x^2 + y^2 = 25 \\ y = \frac{3}{4}x \end{cases}$

2. $\begin{cases} x^2 + y^2 = 25 \\ y = -x - 1 \end{cases}$

3. Describe how you could find exact solutions of the systems in parts (1) and (2).

ACE Homework starts on page 54.

Applications

1. Sam needs to rent a car for a one-week trip in Oregon. He is considering two companies.

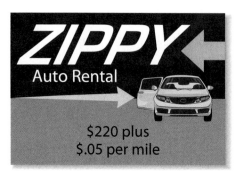

A+ Auto Rental

$175 plus $.10 per mile

ZIPPY Auto Rental

$220 plus $.05 per mile

   a. Write an equation relating the rental cost for each company to the number of miles driven.

   b. Graph the equations.

   c. Under what circumstances is the rental cost the same for both companies? What is that cost?

   d. Under what circumstances is renting from Zippy cheaper than renting from A+?

   e. Suppose Sam rents a car from A+ and drives 225 miles. What is his rental cost?

2. Mariana lives 1,250 meters from school. Ming lives 800 meters from school. Both students leave for school at the same time. Mariana walks at an average speed of 70 meters per minute, while Ming walks at an average speed of 40 meters per minute. Mariana's route takes her past Ming's house.

   a. Write equations that show Mariana and Ming's distances from school t minutes after they leave their homes.

   Answer parts (b)–(d) by writing and solving equations or inequalities.

   b. When, if ever, will Mariana catch up with Ming?

   c. How long will Mariana remain behind Ming?

   d. At what times is the distance between the two students less than 20 meters?

3. Suppose s and t are two numbers and that $s > t$. Determine whether each inequality must be true.

    a. $s + 15 > t + 15$

    b. $s - (-22) > t - (-22)$

    c. $s \times 0 > t \times 0$

    d. $\frac{s}{-6} > \frac{t}{-6}$

    e. $\frac{s}{6} > \frac{t}{6}$

    f. $s(-3) < t(-4)$

For Exercises 4–7, solve the inequality. Then, graph the solution on a number line.

4. $12 < 7x - 2$

5. $2x + 12 > 32$

6. $4x - 17 \leq 31$

7. $-16x - 12 > 14 - 10x$

8. Use the graph below to estimate solutions for the inequalities and equations in parts (a)-(f). Then, use symbolic reasoning to check your estimates.

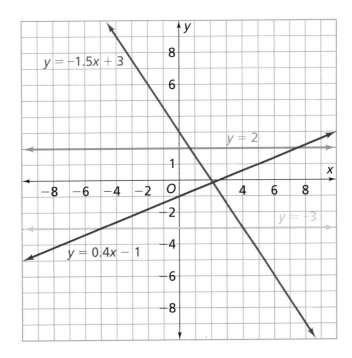

    a. $0.4x - 1 > 2$

    b. $0.4x - 1 > -3$

    c. $-1.5x + 3 > 2$

    d. $-1.5x + 3 < -3$

    e. $-1.5x + 3 = 0.4x - 1$

    f. $-1.5x + 3 > 0.4x - 1$

9. When a soccer ball is kicked into the air, its height h in feet at any time t seconds later can be estimated by the function $h = -16t^2 + 32t$. For each question, write and solve an equation or inequality.

   a. When does the ball return to the ground ($h = 0$ feet)?

   b. When is the ball 12 feet above the ground?

   c. When is the ball at least 12 feet above the ground?

   d. When is the ball at most 12 feet above the ground?

   e. When is the ball 16 feet above the ground?

10. Solve each equation or inequality. Sketch the graphs of the functions that are associated with each equation or inequality. Explain how to find the solutions using the graphs.

   a. $-x^2 + 4x - 4 = -2x + 4$

   b. $-x^2 + 4x - 4 < -2x + 4$

   c. $-x^2 + 4x - 4 > -2x + 4$

   d. $x^2 - 5x = 6$

   e. $x^2 - 5x < 6$

   f. $x^2 - 5x > 6$

11. The graph below shows a circle with radius 4 and two lines intersecting the circle.

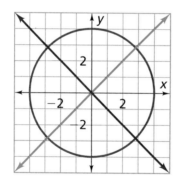

   • Estimate the solution(s) of the systems of equations using the graph.

   • Check your estimates by substituting them into the equations.

   • Find exact solution(s) of each system.

   a. $\begin{cases} x^2 + y^2 = 16 \\ y = x \end{cases}$

   b. $\begin{cases} x^2 + y^2 = 16 \\ y = -x \end{cases}$

Connections

Calculate the *y*-value for the given *x*-value.

12. $y = 3x + 2$ when $x = -2$

13. $y = -3x + 4$ when $x = 9$

14. $y = \frac{1}{2}x - 4$ when $x = 24$

15. $y = -5x - 7$ when $x = \frac{1}{5}$

16. $y = \frac{2}{3}x - 12$ when $x = -18$

17. $y = -\frac{1}{4}x - \frac{3}{4}$ when $x = -6$

Graph the system of equations and estimate the point of intersection. Then, use symbolic reasoning to check whether your estimate is accurate.

18. $y = 2x + 4$ and $y = \frac{1}{2}x - 2$

19. $y = x + 5$ and $y = -3x + 3$

20. $y = 3$ and $y = 6x - 3$

21. $x = 2$ and $y = -\frac{2}{5}x + 4$

Write an equation for the line satisfying the given conditions.

22. slope $= 2$, *y*-intercept $= -3$

23. slope $= -4$, passes through $(0, 1.5)$

24. passes through $(-2, 1)$ and $(4, -3)$

25. passes through $(4, 0)$ and $(0, 3)$

Identify the slope, *x*-intercept, and *y*-intercept of the line.

26. $y = 7x - 3$

27. $y = -3x + 4$

28. $y = \frac{2}{3}x + 12$

29. $y = -\frac{1}{4}x - 5$

30. $y = \frac{3}{4} - 17x$

31. $y = -\frac{2}{3}(x + 10)$

**For Exercises 32–37, copy each pair of expressions. Insert <, >, or =
to make a true statement.**

32. $-18 \div (-3)$ ■ $-24 \div (-4)$

33. $1{,}750(-12)$ ■ $1{,}749(-12)$

34. $5(18 - 24)$ ■ $90 - (-120)$

35. $-8(-5)$ ■ $-7(-5)$

36. $4[-3 - (-7)]$ ■ $4(-3) - 4(-7)$

37. $-5(-4)^2$ ■ $-4(-5)^2$

38. Write an equation or inequality that tells whether each point is
inside, outside, or on the circle with a radius of 10 and centered
at $(0, 0)$.

a. $(6, 8)$ **b.** $(7, 7)$ **c.** $(-7, -7)$

d. $(-6, 8)$ **e.** $(-7, 8)$ **f.** $(-7, -8)$

**For Exercises 39–44, copy each pair of fractions. Insert <, >, or = to
make a true statement.**

39. $\frac{6}{8}$ ■ $\frac{-18}{24}$

40. $\frac{6}{8}$ ■ $\frac{7}{9}$

41. $\frac{6}{8}$ ■ $\frac{-7}{9}$

42. $\frac{6}{8}$ ■ $\frac{-18}{-24}$

43. $\frac{6}{8}$ ■ $\frac{-7}{-9}$

44. $\frac{8}{6}$ ■ $\frac{-9}{7}$

45. Use the figures below for parts (a)–(f). Insert <, >, or = to make
true statements.

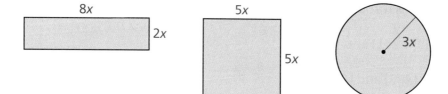

a. perimeter of square ■ perimeter of rectangle

b. area of square ■ area of rectangle

c. perimeter of square ■ circumference of circle

d. area of square ■ area of circle

e. perimeter of rectangle ■ circumference of circle

f. area of rectangle ■ area of circle

46. The gender of a newborn child is nearly equally likely to be a boy or a girl. Consider the patterns likely to occur in a family with three children.

Note: In the following statements, $P(Q)$ is used to indicate the probability that event Q occurs.

Copy parts (a)–(d). Insert $<$, $=$, or $>$ to make true statements.

a. $P(\text{all boys})$ ■ $P(\text{all girls})$

b. $P(\text{exactly one boy})$ ■ $P(\text{exactly 2 girls})$

c. $P(BGB)$ ■ $P(BBG)$

d. $P(\text{two boys and one girl})$ ■ $P(\text{all girls})$

47. Multiple Choice If $w = 3x + c$, what is the value of x?

A. 3

B. $\dfrac{w - c}{3}$

C. $w - c$

D. $\dfrac{w + c}{3}$

48. Suppose $\frac{a}{b}$ and $\frac{c}{d}$ are two nonzero fractions and $\frac{a}{b} < \frac{c}{d}$.

a. Give an example of values of a, b, c, and d that satisfy $\frac{a}{b} < \frac{c}{d}$ and also $\frac{b}{a} < \frac{d}{c}$.

b. Give an example of values of a, b, c, and d that satisfy $\frac{a}{b} < \frac{c}{d}$ and also $\frac{b}{a} > \frac{d}{c}$.

49. Multiple Choice Which function's graph is perpendicular to the graph of $y = 2.5x + 4$?

A. $y = 2.5x$

B. $y = 0.4x$

C. $y = -0.4x$

D. $y = -2.5x$

50. Use a table or graph of $y = 5(2^x)$ to estimate the solution of the inequality $5(2^x) > 1,000$.

For Exercises 51–56, write the expression for x in factored form. Then, find the x- and y-intercepts for the graph of the function.

51. $y = x^2 + 4x$ **52.** $y = x^2 + 4x + 4$ **53.** $y = x^2 + 3x - 10$

54. $y = x^2 - 8x + 16$ **55.** $y = x^2 - 4$ **56.** $y = x^2 + 4x + 3$

57. Multiple Choice Which expression is the factored form of $x + 2x + 6$?

F. $3x + 6$ **G.** $2(x + 3)$ **H.** $3(x + 2)$ **J.** $3(x + 6)$

Extensions

58. In parts (a)–(d), find values of x that satisfy the given conditions. Then, graph the solution on a number line.

    a. $x + 7 < 4$ *or* $x + 3 > 9$
       (**Hint:** Find the x-values that satisfy one inequality or the other, or both.)

    b. $3x + 4 < 13$ *and* $12 < 6x$
       (**Hint:** Find the x-values that satisfy both inequalities.)

    c. $5x - 6 > 2x + 18$ *or* $-3x + 5 > 8x - 39$

    d. $-11x - 7 < -7x + 33$ *and* $9 + 2x > 11x$

59. Suppose m and n are positive whole numbers and $m < n$. Tell whether each statement is always true.

    a. $2^m < 2^n$ **b.** $m^2 < n^2$ **c.** $0.5^m < 0.5^n$ **d.** $\frac{1}{m} < \frac{1}{n}$

60. Solve these quadratic inequalities.
    (**Hint:** Use a graph or table of $y = 5x^2 + 7$ to estimate the solutions. Then adapt the reasoning used to solve linear inequalities to check the accuracy of your estimates.)

    a. $5x^2 + 7 \leq 87$ **b.** $5x^2 + 7 > 87$

61. Solve these exponential inequalities.
    (**Hint:** Use a graph or table of $y = 2(3^x) - 8$ to estimate the solutions. Then adapt the reasoning used to solve linear inequalities to check the accuracy of your estimates.)

    a. $2(3^x) - 8 < 46$ **b.** $2(3^x) - 8 > 10$

Mathematical Reflections 3

In this Investigation, you learned graphic and symbolic methods for solving systems of linear equations and linear inequalities. The following questions will help you summarize what you have learned.

Think about these questions. Discuss your ideas with other students and your teacher. Then write a summary of your findings in your notebook.

1. **How** can you use coordinate graphs to solve linear equations such as $ax + b = cx + d$ and linear inequalities such as $ax + b < cx + d$?

2. **How** can you use symbolic reasoning to solve inequalities such as $ax + b < cx + d$?

3. **What** strategies can you use to solve systems of equations and inequalities that involve linear and quadratic functions or lines and circles?

Common Core Mathematical Practices

As you worked on the Problems in this Investigation, you used prior knowledge to make sense of them. You also applied Mathematical Practices to solve the Problems. Think back over your work, the ways you thought about the Problems, and how you used Mathematical Practices.

Sophie described her thoughts in the following way:

> Our group had a discussion about which representation we thought was most useful for finding solutions of a system with one linear and one quadratic function. We used both graphical and symbolic methods.
>
> Several of us thought that the graphs provided a powerful visual picture of what the symbols represented. This was similar to systems of linear equations. The graphs illustrated why sometimes there are only two solutions, one solution, or no solution.

Common Core Standards for Mathematical Practice
MP5 Use appropriate tools strategically.

- What other Mathematical Practices can you identify in Sophie's reasoning?

- Describe a Mathematical Practice that you and your classmates used to solve a different Problem in this Investigation.

Investigation 4

Systems of Linear Inequalities

Investigation 3 focused on strategies for solving inequalities with one variable such as $3x + 4 < 13$ and $14x - 23 < 5x + 13$. Many problems, however, involve two or more variables.

In earlier Investigations, you applied your knowledge of simple linear equations to solve equations or systems of equations with two variables. You can also apply what you have learned about simple inequalities to solve inequalities or systems of inequalities with two variables in the form $Ax + By < C$.

4.1 Limiting Driving Miles
Inequalities With Two Variables

Automobiles are a major source of air pollution. When Jarod studied the effects of this pollution on global climate change, he decided to take a look at his family's driving habits. His family has two vehicles, a car and an SUV. His parents estimate that the family drives about 1,200 miles each month. They decide to try to limit their driving to no more than 1,000 miles each month.

• What are the variables in the situation? How are they related?

Common Core State Standards

8.EE.C.8b Solve systems of two linear equations in two variables algebraically, and estimate solutions by graphing the equations. Solve simple cases by inspection.

8.EE.C.8c Solve real-world and mathematical problems leading to two linear equations in two variables.

A-CED.A.3 Represent constraints by equations or inequalities, and by systems of equations and/or inequalities, and interpret solutions as viable or non-viable options in a modeling context.

Also A-CED.A.2, A-REI.C.6, A-REI.D.10, A-REI.D.12

Problem 4.1

Ⓐ 1. Find ten possible pairs (*car miles, SUV miles*) that give a total of no more than 1,000 miles.

2. On a copy of the grid below, plot the ten points you found in part (1).

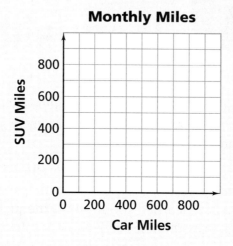

Monthly Miles

3. Are there other possible pairs (*car miles, SUV miles*) that give a total of no more than 1,000 miles? Explain.

4. A *region* is a part of a graph or plane. Describe the region where points representing totals of no more than 1,000 miles are located.

5. In what region are the points that meet the goal of less than 1,000 miles per month? How does this region compare to the region in part (4)?

Ⓑ Suppose Jarod's family wants to limit their driving to no more than 800 miles per month.

1. Draw a graph of pairs (*car miles, SUV miles*) that meet this condition.

2. Describe the region of the graph that includes all the points that represent driving no more than 800 miles.

Problem **4.1** *continued*

C Let *c* represent the number of miles driven using the car. Let *s* represent the number of miles driven using the SUV. Write inequalities to model the following situations.

1. a total of no more than 1,000 miles driven using both vehicles

2. a total of no more than 800 miles driven using both vehicles

3. How are the inequalities you wrote in parts (1) and (2) related to your work in Questions A and B?

 Homework starts on page 72.

4.2 What Makes a Car Green?
Solving Inequalities by Graphing I

Carbon dioxide (CO_2) is a major factor in global climate change. Jarod finds out the amount of CO_2 that his family's vehicles emit.

This SUV emits 1.25 pounds of carbon dioxide per mile.

This car emits 0.75 pounds of carbon dioxide per mile.

- Suppose Jarod's family wants to limit CO_2 emissions from their car and SUV to *at most* 600 pounds per month. What inequality would model this condition?

- What would a graph of the solutions for this inequality look like?

Problem 4.2

A Suppose Jarod's family wants their total CO_2 emissions to be *exactly* 600 pounds per month.

   1. Give six examples of pairs (*car miles, SUV miles*) that meet this condition.

   2. Write an equation to model this condition.

   3. Graph your equation.

B Suppose the family wants to limit their total CO_2 emissions to at most 600 pounds per month.

   1. Write an inequality that describes the possibilities for the number of miles they can drive that meet this condition.

   2. What is one solution (*car miles, SUV miles*) that meets this condition?

   3. Draw a graph displaying the solutions of your inequality from part (1). Describe the regions.

C Soo's family has a minivan and a hybrid car. The minivan emits 1.2 pounds of CO_2 per mile. The hybrid car emits 0.5 pounds of CO_2 per mile. The family wants to limit their total emissions to at most 500 pounds per month.

   1. The family plans to drive both vehicles. Write an inequality to describe the possibilities for the number of miles they can drive each vehicle.

   2. Draw a graph displaying the pairs (*minivan miles, hybrid miles*) that satisfy the inequality you wrote in part (1).

A C E Homework starts on page 72.

4.3 Feasible Points
Solving Inequalities by Graphing II

In Problem 4.2, you graphed ordered pairs of driving mileage that would limit CO_2 emissions by Jarod and Soo's families. You discovered that the solutions of the inequalities are triangular regions. You also had to consider the fact that mileage and emission data cannot be negative numbers. In other words, all **feasible points** are in the first quadrant.

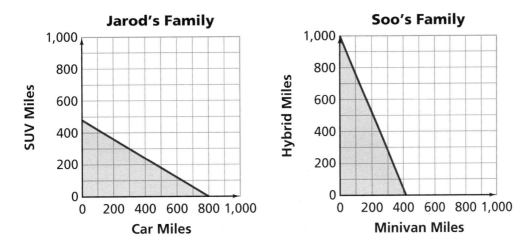

Some inequalities have solutions that are not limited to positive numbers. For example, one solution for $3x + 5y > 15$ is $(-1, 5)$. The region of feasible points for such inequalities will be different from those for the CO_2 emission problems.

Use what you have learned about graphs of linear inequalities to explore the possible shapes of feasible regions.

Problem **4.3**

A Match each inequality with its graph, if possible. The solutions are shown by the shaded region. Be prepared to explain your strategies for matching the inequalities and graphs.

1. $y - 3x \geq 6$ **2.** $x - 3y \geq 6$ **3.** $3x + y \leq 6$

4. $x + 3y \leq 6$ **5.** $x - 3y \leq 6$ **6.** $y \geq -3x$

7. $y \leq -3x$ **8.** $x \geq -3$ **9.** $y \geq -3$

a.

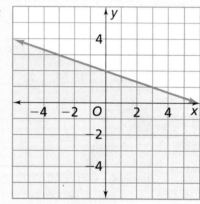

b.

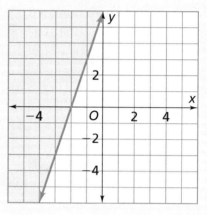

c.

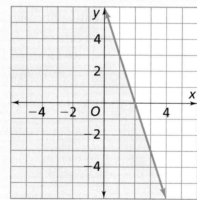

d.

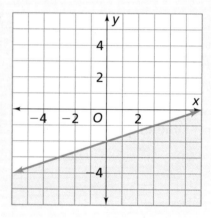

Problem **4.3**   *continued*

e.
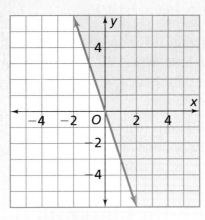

f.
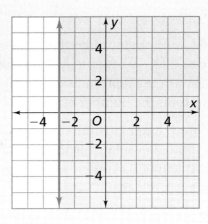

g.
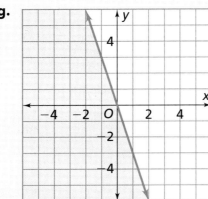

h.
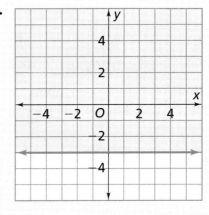

B Refer to the inequalities in parts (1)–(4) of Question A.

1. Rewrite each inequality in either $y \leq mx + b$ or $y \geq mx + b$ form.

2. Compare these forms of the inequalities with their graphs. Explain how these forms help you determine which region should be shaded.

C Consider the inequality $y < 3x + 6$.

1. Does the pair (2, 12) satisfy the inequality? Explain.

2. At the right is the graph of $y < 3x + 6$. How is this graph different from the graphs in Question A? What is the reason for this difference?

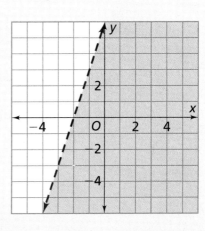

A C E Homework starts on page 72.

4.4 Miles of Emissions
Systems of Linear Inequalities

Jarod's family determines that, on average, they drive their SUV more than twice as many miles as they drive their car. Jarod writes the inequality $s > 2c$, where s represents the number of miles they drive the SUV, and c represents the number of miles they drive the car.

The family agrees to limit the total CO_2 emissions to less than 600 pounds per month. Recalling that the car emits 0.75 pounds of CO_2 per mile and the SUV emits 1.25 pounds of CO_2 per mile, Jarod writes the inequality $0.75c + 1.25s < 600$.

Together, the two inequalities form a **system of linear inequalities.**

$$\begin{cases} s > 2c \\ 0.75c + 1.25s < 600 \end{cases}$$

- What pairs (c, s) are solutions of both inequalities in the system?

Use what you have learned about solving linear inequalities with two variables to develop a strategy for solving systems of inequalities.

Problem 4.4

Ⓐ 1. Why is the system of two inequalities above an accurate model of the conditions that Jarod's family wants to satisfy?

2. How would the system change if Jarod's family agrees to total emissions that are at most 600 pounds rather than less than 600 pounds?

Ⓑ 1. Graph the inequalities $0.75c + 1.25s < 600$ and $s > 2c$ on the same coordinate grid.

2. Where on the graph are the points that satisfy both conditions? Find three solution pairs (c, s) for the system. Can Jarod's family drive a total of 800 miles under these conditions?

Problem 4.4 *continued*

C Adsila's family has a car and an SUV that emit the same amount of CO_2 as the vehicles Jarod's family drives. Adsila's family drives the car *at least* three times as much as the SUV. They want to limit total CO_2 emissions to at most 400 pounds per month. Adsila draws the following graph to see how they can reach their goal.

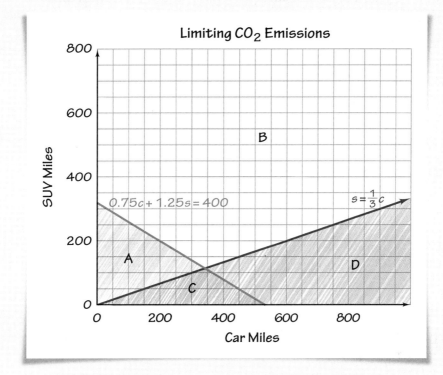

1. Describe the information that the points in Regions A, B, C, and D represent in terms of the situation.

2. In which region(s) are the points that satisfy both conditions?

A C E Homework starts on page 72.

Applications

1. Ana has a car and a motorcycle. She wants to limit the combined mileage of the two vehicles to at most 500 miles per month.

   a. Write an inequality to model this condition.

   b. Draw a graph of all the pairs (*car miles, motorcycle miles*) that satisfy this condition.

   c. What strategy did you use to draw your graph?

2. A developer plans to build housing for at least 50 families. He wants to build some single-family houses and some four-family apartment buildings.

   a. Write an inequality to model this situation.

   b. Draw a graph to display the possible pairs of the number of single-family houses and the number of apartments the developer can build.

3. The Simon family's car emits 0.75 pounds of CO_2 per mile. Their minivan emits 1.25 pounds of CO_2 per mile. The Simons want to limit their emissions to at most 400 pounds per month.

   a. Write an inequality to model this condition.

   b. Draw a graph of all the pairs (*car miles, minivan miles*) that satisfy this condition.

4. Math Club members are selling games and puzzles. They make a profit of $10 per game and $8 per puzzle. They would like to make a profit of at least $200.

   a. What are some possibilities for the number of games and the number of puzzles the Math Club can sell to reach its goal?

   b. Write an inequality to model this situation.

   c. Draw a graph of all the pairs (*number of games, number of puzzles*) that meet the goal.

For Exercises 5–7, find three pairs (x, y) that satisfy the inequality and three pairs (x, y) that do not. Then, draw a graph showing all the solutions.

5. $x - 4y \geq 8$

6. $4x - y \leq 8$

7. $x - 4y < 8$

8. For parts (a)–(d), graph the inequality.

    a. $x \geq 8 + 4y$

    b. $x \geq 4$

    c. $y \leq -2$

    d. $2x - 4y \geq 8$

9. Math Club members want to advertise their fundraiser each week in the school paper. They know that a front-page ad is more effective than an ad inside the paper. They have a $30 advertising budget. It costs $2 for each front-page ad and $1 for each inside-page ad. The club wants to advertise at least 20 times.

    a. What are some possibilities for the number of front-page ads and the number of inside-page ads the club can place?

    b. Write a system of linear inequalities to model this situation.

    c. Graph your system of inequalities. Be sure it is clear which region shows the solution.

10. The Science Club can spend at most $400 on a field trip to a dinosaur exhibit. It has enough chaperones to allow at most 100 students to go on the trip.

    a. How many students 12 years and under can go on the trip if no students over 12 years go?

    b. How many students over 12 years can go on the trip if no students 12 years or under go?

    c. Write a system of linear inequalities to model this situation.

    d. Graph your system of inequalities. Be sure it is clear which region shows the solution.

DINO exhibit

$3 for students 12 years and under

$6 for students over 12 years

Find three pairs (x, y) that satisfy the system of inequalities and three pairs (x, y) that do not. Then, draw a graph showing all the solutions.

11. $\begin{cases} 4x + 6y \le 24 \\ x + 5y \le 10 \end{cases}$

12. $\begin{cases} 2x - y \le 4 \\ -x + y > -1 \end{cases}$

Connections

For Exercises 13 and 14, use a graph to estimate the solution of the system of equations. Check the estimated solution and revise your answer if necessary.

13. $\begin{cases} x + y = 18 \\ 3x - y = 10 \end{cases}$

14. $\begin{cases} 80x + 40y = 400 \\ 20x + 80y = 420 \end{cases}$

15. Multiple Choice What is the greatest whole-number value of x for which $4x < 14$?

A. 3 **B.** 4 **C.** 11 **D.** 14

16. The parks commission in the town of Euclid decides to build a triangular park with one side that is 400 feet long.

a. What are some possibilities for the lengths of the other sides? Explain.

b. The city planner wrote these inequalities.

$$x + y > 400 \qquad x + 400 > y \qquad y + 400 > x$$

The variables x and y represent possible lengths for the other two sides of the triangle. Why do these inequalities make sense? Why does the planner need all three inequalities to describe the situation?

c. Graph the three inequalities from part (b) on the same grid. Describe the region that represents all the possible lengths for the other sides of the park.

d. Give a pair of lengths for the other two sides of the park. Explain how to find this answer by using your graph from part (c).

e. Give a possible pair of lengths that could *not* be the other two side lengths. Explain how to find this answer using your graph from part (c).

17. Robin wants to make a smoothie out of milk, strawberry yogurt, and ice. She finds this nutritional information:

MILK
Nutrition Facts
Serving Size 1 cup

Calories   100
Protein   9g

STRAWBERRY YOGURT
Nutrition Facts
Serving Size   1 cup

Calories   190
Protein   13g

ICE
Nutrition Facts
Serving Size 1 cup

Calories   0
Protein   0g

Robin wants her smoothie to have about 335 Calories and 24 grams of protein.

  a. Write a system of equations to model the conditions for Robin's smoothie.

  b. Graph the equations from part (a).

  c. How much yogurt and milk should Robin use to make her smoothie? Explain.

18. Kadian also wants a milk-and-yogurt smoothie. She uses the nutritional information from Exercise 17. She wants her smoothie to have at most 400 Calories and at least 20 grams of protein.

  a. Write a system of inequalities to model the conditions for Kadian's smoothie.

  b. Graph the system of inequalities. Be sure it is clear which region shows the solution.

  c. Use your graph from part (b) to describe some combinations of milk and yogurt amounts Kadian could use for her smoothie.

Extensions

19. Carolina wants to make a smoothie out of milk, strawberry yogurt, and ice. She uses the following nutritional information:

MILK
Nutrition Facts
Serving Size   1 cup
Calories   100
Protein   9g
Calcium   306mg

STRAWBERRY YOGURT
Nutrition Facts
Serving Size   1 cup
Calories   190
Protein   13g
Calcium   415mg

ICE
Nutrition Facts
Serving Size   1 cup
Calories   0
Protein   0g
Calcium   0mg

She wants her smoothie to have at most 400 Calories, at least 20 grams of protein, and at least 700 milligrams of calcium.

a. Write a system of inequalities to model the conditions for Carolina's smoothie.

b. Graph the system of inequalities. Be sure it is clear which region shows the solution.

c. What are some combinations (*milk, yogurt*) Carolina might choose?

20. Suppose you are making a smoothie. What nutrients are important to you? Would you like your smoothie to be a good source of vitamin C, calcium, fiber, protein, or Calories? What ingredients would you like in your smoothie? Write guidelines for your smoothie. Use nutritional information about the ingredients from a reliable source. Then write a system of inequalities to help you decide how much of each ingredient to include.

Mathematical Reflections 4

In this Investigation, you explored situations that could be modeled with linear inequalities involving two variables. You also solved systems of linear inequalities to find values that satisfied several conditions. The following questions will help you to summarize what you have learned.

Think about these questions. Discuss your ideas with other students and your teacher. Then write a summary of your findings in your notebook.

1. Suppose you are given one linear inequality with two variables. **How** could you use a graph to find solutions of the inequality?

2. Suppose you were given a system of two linear inequalities. **How** could you use a graph to find solutions of the system?

Common Core Mathematical Practices

As you worked on the Problems in this Investigation, you used prior knowledge to make sense of them. You also applied Mathematical Practices to solve the Problems. Think back over your work, the ways you thought about the Problems, and how you used Mathematical Practices.

Jayden described his thoughts in the following way:

In our group, Jen and Nick had a suggestion for solving a system of linear inequalities in Problem 4.4. They said that you could combine the methods we used for solving a system of linear equations and solving a linear inequality.

We graphed the equation of the line associated with each inequality. Then, we found the regions that satisfied both inequalities.

Common Core Standards for Mathematical Practice
MP2 Reason abstractly and quantitatively.

• What other Mathematical Practices can you identify in Jayden's reasoning?

• Describe a Mathematical Practice that you and your classmates used to solve a different Problem in this Investigation.

In this Unit, you extended your ability to use algebraic equations and inequalities to solve problems. In particular, you learned how to solve systems of linear equations and inequalities.

Use Your Understanding: Systems

Check your understanding of concepts and methods for solving systems of equations and inequalities by solving the following problems.

1. To encourage attendance to Talent Night, a school offers discounted tickets to students wearing school colors. In all, 250 tickets are sold for a total of $2,100.

Talent Night Tickets

Full Price: $9
Discounted: $6

   a. Let x represent the number of full-price tickets sold. Let y represent the number of discounted tickets sold. Write a system of equations to represent the information about the ticket sales.

   b. Solve the system of equations in two ways.
      - Use a graph to estimate.
      - Use the combination method.

2. The Pep Club sells popcorn and juice at basketball games. The club earns $1.20 for each bag of popcorn and $.80 for each cup of juice.

   a. The club's goal is to earn at least $50 at each game. Let x represent the number of bags of popcorn sold. Let y represent the number of cups of juice sold. Write an inequality to represent the club's goal.

   b. Find at least five pairs (x, y) that satisfy the inequality in part (a). Sketch a graph that represents all the solutions.

   c. The club must buy supplies. They spend $.15 for each bag and $.20 for each cup. Suppose the club can spend at most $15 on supplies for each game. Write an inequality for this constraint.

   d. Find at least five pairs (x, y) that satisfy the inequality in part (c). Sketch a graph of the inequality on the same grid you used in part (b). Label the region that shows the pairs (x, y) that satisfy both constraints.

Explain Your Reasoning

In this Unit, you used graphs and symbolic reasoning to solve systems of equations and inequalities.

3. Consider systems of linear equations in the form $\begin{cases} Ax + By = C \\ Dx + Ey = F \end{cases}$.

   a. Describe the solution of each equation as it is represented on a graph.

   b. Describe the solution of the system as it is represented on a graph.

   c. What numbers of solutions are possible for a system in this form? How are these possibilities shown by the graphs?

   d. How can you solve such a system by using the combination method?

   e. How can you check the solution of a system?

4. Describe the solution graph for each type of inequality.

   a. an inequality with one variable in the form $Ax + B < C$

   b. an inequality with two variables in the form $Ax + By < C$

   c. a system of linear inequalities with two variables in the form
   $\begin{cases} Ax + By < C \\ Dx + Ey < F \end{cases}$

C **chord** A line segment with endpoints on a circle. Segments *CD* and *AB* in the diagram below are chords.

cuerda Segmento de recta cuyos extremos están sobre un círculo. Los segmentos *CD* y *AB* en el diagrama de abajo son cuerdas.

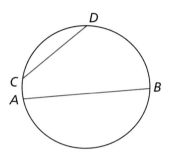

circle A geometric figure consisting of all points *P* that are a fixed distance *r* from a point *C*, called the center of the circle.

círculo Figura geométrica en la que todos los puntos *P* están a una distancia fija *r* de un punto *C*, llamado el centro del círculo.

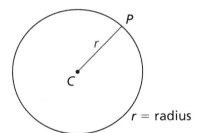

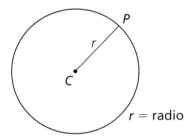

compare Academic Vocabulary

To tell or show how two things are alike and different.

related terms *analyze, relate*

sample Compare the slopes of the lines $-6x + y = 12$ and $2y = 12x + 3$.

> I can write the equations of both lines in slope-intercept form to find their slopes.
>
> $-6x + y = 12$ $2y = 12x + 3$
>
> $y = 6x + 12$ $y = 6x + \dfrac{3}{2}$
>
> The slopes are equal. The lines are parallel since they have the same slope but a different y-intercept.

comparar Vocabulario académico

Decir o mostrar en qué se parecen y en qué se diferencian dos cosas.

términos relacionados *analizar, relacionar*

ejemplo Compara las pendientes de las rectas $-6x + y = 12$ y $2y = 12x + 3$.

> Puedo escribir las ecuaciones de ambas rectas en la forma pendiente-intercepto para hallar sus pendientes.
>
> $-6x + y = 12$ $2y = 12x + 3$
>
> $y = 6x + 12$ $y = 6x + \dfrac{3}{2}$
>
> Las pendientes son iguales. Las rectas son paralelas puesto que tienen la misma pendiente, pero un intercepto en y diferente.

D **decide** Academic Vocabulary

To use the given information and related facts to find a value or make a determination.

related terms *determine, find, conclude*

sample Decide whether to use a graph or the combination method to solve the system. Then solve the system.
$$\begin{cases} x - y = 8 \\ 3x + y = 4 \end{cases}$$

> The coefficients of y in the two equations are opposites, so the combination method is a good method.
>
> $(x - y) + (3x + y) = 8 + 4$
>
> $4x = 12$
>
> $x = 3$
>
> $x - y = 8$
>
> $3 - y = 8$
>
> $-y = 5$
>
> $y = -5$
>
> The solution to the system is (3, −5).

decidir Vocabulario académico

Usar la información dada y los datos relacionados para hallar un valor o tomar una determinación.

términos relacionados *determinar, hallar, concluir*

ejemplo Decide si debes usar una gráfica o el método de combinación para resolver el sistema. Luego, resuelve el sistema.
$$\begin{cases} x - y = 8 \\ 3x + y = 4 \end{cases}$$

> Los coeficientes de y en las dos ecuaciones son opuestos, así que el método de combinación es un buen método.
>
> $(x - y) + (3x + y) = 8 + 4$
>
> $4x = 12$
>
> $x = 3$
>
> $x - y = 8$
>
> $3 - y = 8$
>
> $-y = 5$
>
> $y = -5$
>
> La solución del sistema es (3, −5).

E **explain** Academic Vocabulary

To give facts and details that make an idea easier to understand. Explaining can involve a written summary supported by a diagram, chart, table, or a combination of these.

related terms *analyze, clarify, describe, justify, tell*

sample What is the length of segment *OP*? Explain your reasoning.

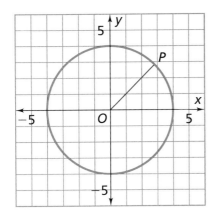

Segment *OP* is a radius of the circle because it connects the center of the circle to a point on the circle. The center of the circle is at the origin and the point (4, 0) lies on the circle. So, the length of the radius is 4 units. Since the lengths of all radii of a given circle are equal, segment *OP* is also 4 units in length.

explicar Vocabulario académico

Proporcionar datos y detalles que hagan que una idea sea más fácil de comprender. Explicar puede incluir un resumen escrito apoyado por un diagrama, una gráfica, una tabla o una combinación de estos.

términos relacionados *analizar, aclarar, describir, justificar, decir*

ejemplo ¿Cuál es la longitud del segmento *OP*? Explica tu razonamiento.

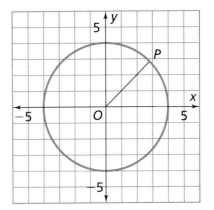

El segmento *OP* es un radio del círculo porque conecta el centro del círculo con un punto en el círculo. El centro del círculo está en el origen y el punto (4, 0) se encuentra en el círculo. Así que la longitud del radio es de 4 unidades. Puesto que las longitudes de todos los radios de un círculo dado son iguales, segmento *OP* tambien tiene 4 unidades de longitud.

F **feasible points** The set of all solutions that satisfy an equation, an inequality, or a system.

puntos factibles El conjunto de todas las soluciones que satisfacen una ecuación, una desigualdad o un sistema.

identify Academic Vocabulary
To match a definition or a description to an object or to recognize something and be able to name it.

related terms *name, find, classify*

sample Identify the y-intercept of the line $4x - 2y = 10$.

> I can find the y-intercept of the line by setting x = 0 and solving for y.
> $4x - 2y = 10$
> $4(0) - 2y = 10$
> $-2y = 10$
> $y = -5$
> The y-intercept of the line is –5.

identificar Vocabulario académico
Relacionar una definición o una descripción con un objeto, o bien, reconocer algo y ser capaz de nombrarlo.

términos relacionados *nombrar, hallar, clasificar*

ejemplo Identifica el intercepto en y de la recta $4x - 2y = 10$.

> Puedo hallar el intercepto en y de la recta estableciendo que x = 0 y hallando el valor de y.
> $4x - 2y = 10$
> $4(0) - 2y = 10$
> $-2y = 10$
> $y = -5$
> El intercepto en y de la recta es –5.

linear equation in slope-intercept form The slope-intercept form of a linear equation is $y = mx + b$, where m is the slope and b is the y-intercept.

ecuación lineal en forma pendiente-intercepto La forma pendiente-intercepto de una ecuación lineal es $y = mx + b$, donde m es la pendiente y b es el intercepto en y.

linear equation in standard form The standard form of a linear equation is $Ax + By = C$, where A, B, and C are integers and A and B are not both zero. The equation $6x + 3y = 12$ is in standard form. Although the slope-intercept form, $y = mx + b$, is common and useful, it is not considered the "standard form."

ecuación lineal en forma estándar La forma estándar de una ecuación lineal es $Ax + By = C$, donde A, B, y C son enteros y A y B son distintos de cero. La ecuación $6x + 3y = 12$ está en forma estándar. Aunque la forma pendiente-intercepto, $y = mx + b$, es común y útil, no se considera como la "forma estándar."

linear function A function whose graph is a line.

función lineal Una función cuya gráfica es una recta.

linear inequality A mathematical sentence, such as $Ax + By + C < Dx + Ey + F$, which expresses a relationship of inequality between two quantities, each of which is a linear expression. For example, $y < -2x + 4$ and $6x + 3y \geq 12$ are linear inequalities, as are $x < 3$ and $2x + 3 < 7x$.

desigualdad lineal Un enunciado matemático, como $Ax + By + C < Dx + Ey + F$, que expresa una relación de desigualdad entre dos cantidades, cada una de las cuales es una expresión lineal. Por ejemplo, $y < -2x + 4$ y $6x + 3y \geq 12$ son desigualdades lineales, como también lo son $x < 3$ y $2x + 3 < 7x$.

S **solution of the system** A set of values for the variables that makes all the equations or inequalities true.

solución del sistema Un conjunto de valores para las variables que hace que todas las ecuaciones o desigualdades sean verdaderas.

system of linear equations Two or more linear equations that represent constraints on the variables used. A solution of a system of equations is a pair of values that satisfies all the equations in the system. For example, the ordered pair $(1, 2)$ is the solution of the system because it satisfies both equations.

$$\begin{cases} 6x + 3y = 12 \\ -2x + y = 0 \end{cases}$$

sistema de ecuaciones lineales Dos o más ecuaciones lineales que representan limitaciones en las variables usadas. La solución de un sistema de ecuaciones es un par de valores que satisface todas las ecuaciones del sistema. Por ejemplo, el par ordenado $(1, 2)$ es la solución del sistema porque satisface ambas ecuaciones.

$$\begin{cases} 6x + 3y = 12 \\ -2x + y = 0 \end{cases}$$

system of linear inequalities Two or more linear inequalities that represent constraints on the variables used. A solution of a system of inequalities is a pair of values that satisfies all the inequalities in the system. The solution of the system

$$\begin{cases} 6x + 3y < 12 \\ -2x + y > 0 \end{cases}$$

is indicated by region A in the graph below. All the points in this region satisfy *both* inequalities. The points in region B satisfy $-2x + y > 0$, but *not* $6x + 3y < 12$. The points in region C satisfy $6x + 3y < 12$, but *not* $-2x + y > 0$. The points in the unshaded region do not satisfy either inequality.

sistema de desigualdades lineales Dos o más desigualdades lineales que representan limitaciones en las variables usadas. La solución de un sistema de desigualdades es un par de valores que satisface todas las desigualdades en el sistema. La solución del sistema

$$\begin{cases} 6x + 3y < 12 \\ -2x + y > 0 \end{cases}$$

está indicada por la región A en la gráfica de abajo. Todos los puntos de esta región satisfacen *ambas* desigualdades. Los puntos de la región B satisfacen $-2x + y > 0$, pero *no* $6x + 3y < 12$. Los puntos de la región C satisfacen $6x + 3y < 12$, pero *no* $-2x + y > 0$. Los puntos de la región sin sombrear no satisfacen ninguna desigualdad.

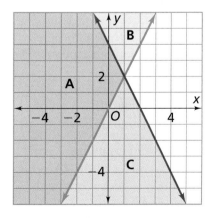

Index

ACE
>   linear equations with two
>   variables, 13–21
>   solving linear systems
>   symbolically, 32–33
>   systems of functions and
>   inequalities, 54–60
>   systems of linear
>   inequalities, 72–76

addition, solving linear
>   **systems symbolically**
>   **and,** 43

age data, 14, 16, 41

angle measures, 18

area and perimeter, 37–38, 58

Ask Yourself, 4

$Ax + By < C$ **form,** 63, 80

$Ax + By = C$ **form**
>   forms of linear equations, 9,
>   10–11
>   linear equations with two
>   variables, 14, 15, 18, 23
>   solving linear systems
>   symbolically, 22, 24, 42
>   systems of linear equations
>   and inequalities, 80

break-even points, 52

chords, 37, 81

circles
>   defined, 81
>   solving linear systems
>   symbolically, 36, 37, 42
>   systems of functions and
>   inequalities, 53, 56, 58, 61

circumference, 58

combining equations, 27–31,
>   34, 79

Common Core Mathematical
>   **Practices,** 5–6, 23, 46,
>   61, 78

conjectures, 9, 43

coordinate grids, 9, 13, 49, 52,
>   70

cost data, 17, 24–25, 48, 54, 73

cubic functions, 42

cylinders, 37

differences, 33

equivalent equations, 26, 27

equivalent systems, 31, 43

estimation
>   graphs and graphing, 50
>   inequalities with two
>   variables, 63
>   surface area and, 19
>   systems of functions and
>   inequalities, 48, 53, 55, 56,
>   57, 59
>   systems of linear
>   inequalities, 74

Explain Your Reasoning, 80

exponential equations, 7

exponential inequalities, 60

exponential relationships, 39

factored form, 60

feasible points, 67–69, 83

fractions, 58

functions. *See* systems of
>   functions and inequalities

Glossary, 81–85

graphic methods. *See* graphs
>   and graphing

graphs and graphing
> $Ax + By = C$ form, 24
>   forms of linear equations
>   and, 10
>   inequalities with two
>   variables, 64, 72–74

intersecting lines and, 12
linear equations with two
>   variables, 7, 9, 13, 14, 15,
>   16, 17, 19, 21, 22
solving inequalities, 55,
>   65–69
solving linear equations and
>   inequalities, 61
solving linear systems
>   symbolically, 38, 40, 41,
>   43, 46
systems of functions and
>   inequalities, 47, 48, 49, 52,
>   53, 54, 56, 57, 59, 60, 62
systems of linear equations,
>   25, 79
systems of linear equations
>   and inequalities, 79, 80
systems of linear
>   inequalities, 70, 71, 74, 75,
>   76, 77, 78, 80

height and time, 56

income and expense data, 13,
>   25–26, 52, 73

inequalities. *See also* linear
>   inequalities
>   linear equations with two
>   variables, 17, 19, 21
>   solving by graphing, 55,
>   65–69
>   with two variables, 63–65,
>   72–74, 77

inequality symbols, 50, 58

intersecting lines
>   linear equations with two
>   variables, 11–12
>   linear inequalities, 48
>   solving linear systems
>   symbolically, 32, 36, 38, 42
>   systems of functions and
>   inequalities, 56
>   systems of linear equations,
>   24

intersection points
    linear equations with two
      variables, 12, 15, 16
    solving linear systems
      symbolically, 24, 25, 26,
      32, 36, 37, 42
    systems of functions and
      inequalities, 57

inverse variations, 39, 42

Investigations
    linear equations with two
      variables, 7–12
    solving linear systems
      symbolically, 24–31
    systems of functions and
      inequalities, 47–53
    systems of linear
      inequalities, 63–71

linear equations, 3, 4, 61, 84.
    See also systems of linear
    equations

**linear equations with two
    variables**
    ACE, 13–21
    forms of, 10–11
    intersecting lines, 11–12
    Mathematical Reflections,
      13–21
    solving, 7, 8–9

linear functions
    defined, 84
    graphs and graphing, 49
    linear equations with two
      variables, 10
    solving linear systems
      symbolically, 42
    systems of functions and
      inequalities, 47, 61, 62

linear inequalities, 4, 48–49,
    50–51, 61, 84. *See also*
    systems of functions and
    inequalities; systems of
    linear inequalities

linear relationships, 39

**linear systems, solving
    symbolically,** 24–25

ACE, 32–33
Mathematical Reflections,
    45–46
solving by combining
    equations, 27–31
solving with $y = mx + b$
    form, 25–27

lines
    equations for, 36, 57, 78
    systems of functions and
      inequalities, 61

lines and curves, systems of,
    51–53

Looking Ahead, 2–3

Looking Back, 79–80

Mathematical Highlights, 4

Mathematical Practices, 5–6

Mathematical Reflections
    linear equations with two
      variables, 13–21
    solving linear systems
      symbolically, 45–46
    systems of functions and
      inequalities, 61–62
    systems of linear
      inequalities, 77–78

negative numbers, 50, 51

nets, 20

number lines, 17, 49, 50, 51, 55

ordered pairs
    $Ax + By = C$ form, 24
    inequalities with two
      variables, 72
    linear equations with two
      variables, 9, 13, 14, 21
    solving linear systems
      symbolically, 35
    systems of linear
      inequalities, 64, 66, 70, 74,
      75, 76, 80

parallel lines, 17, 18, 20, 46

patterns
    $Ax + By = C$ form, 22
    linear equations with two
      variables, 14, 21

systems of functions and
    inequalities, 47, 59

perpendicular lines, 18, 20

points. *See also* intersection
    points
    chords and, 37
    feasible points, 67–69
    inequalities with two
      variables, 64
    linear equations with two
      variables, 9, 14, 15, 16, 17,
      21
    systems of functions and
      inequalities, 50, 52, 53, 58
    systems of linear
      inequalities, 70, 71

positive numbers, 50, 51, 67

price data, 27–29, 32

profits
    solving linear equations with
      two variables, 8–9
    solving linear systems
      symbolically, 31, 33, 34, 41
    systems of functions and
      inequalities, 51–53

properties of equality, 3

proportions, 7

quadratic equations, 7, 19

quadratic functions, 42, 61, 62

quadratic inequalities, 60

quadratic relationships, 39

radius, 53, 56, 58

reasoning, explaining your
    forms of linear equations
      and, 10, 11
    linear equations and
      inequalities, 80
    linear equations with two
      variables, 9, 15, 19, 23
    solving linear systems
      symbolically, 25, 26, 28,
      30, 46
    systems of functions and
      inequalities, 53

systems of linear inequalities, 78

rectangles, 36, 58

regions
inequalities with two variables, 64
solving inequalities, 66
systems of linear inequalities, 71, 73, 75, 76, 78, 80

relationships among variables. *See* variables

sales data, 79–80

serving data, 44

side lengths, 74

slope, 15, 18, 19, 36, 57

slope-intercept form, 10–11, 15, 22, 84

solution of the system, 12, 85

solutions, writing, 17

speed and distance data, 14, 16, 21, 54

squares, 58

standard form, 10–11, 14, 22, 84

substitutions, 25

sums, 33

surface area and volume, 19, 20

symbolic methods
linear equations with two variables, 17
solving linear inequalities symbolically, 50–51, 61

solving linear systems symbolically, 24–31
systems of functions and inequalities, 55, 62
systems of linear equations and inequalities, 3, 80

systems of functions and inequalities, 47
ACE, 54–60
linear inequalities, 48–49
Mathematical Reflections, 61–62
solving linear inequalities symbolically, 50–51
systems of lines and curves, 51–53

systems of linear equations, 4, 79–80, 85
graphs and graphing, 16
intersecting lines and, 12
solving linear systems symbolically, 24–25, 26, 27–29, 38

systems of linear inequalities, 4, 79–80, 85
about, 70–71
ACE, 72–76
inequalities with two variables, 63–65
Mathematical Reflections, 77–78
solving inequalities by graphing, 65–69

systems of lines and curves, 51–53

tables of values, relationships among variables and, 39

triangles, 74

Use Your Understanding, 79–80

variables
inequalities with two variables, 63–65, 72–74, 77
solving equations and, 4
solving linear equations with two variables, 7, 8–9
solving linear systems symbolically, 33
standard form and slope-intercept form, 23

volume. *See* surface area and volume

whole-number values, 74

$x = ny + c$ **form,** 27

x**-intercepts,** 14, 15, 16, 32, 57, 60

x**-values,** 57, 60

$y = mx + b$ **form**
linear equations with two variables, 10–11, 15, 22, 23
solving linear systems symbolically, 25–27, 33, 41

y**-intercepts**
linear equations with two variables, 14, 15, 16
solving linear systems symbolically, 32, 36
systems of functions and inequalities, 57, 60

y**-values,** 57

Acknowledgments

Cover Design

Three Communication Design, Chicago

Photographs

Photo locators denoted as follows: Top (T), Center (C), Bottom (B), Left (L), Right (R), Background (Bkgd)

003 VisionsofAmerica/Joe Sohm/Digital Vision/Getty Images.

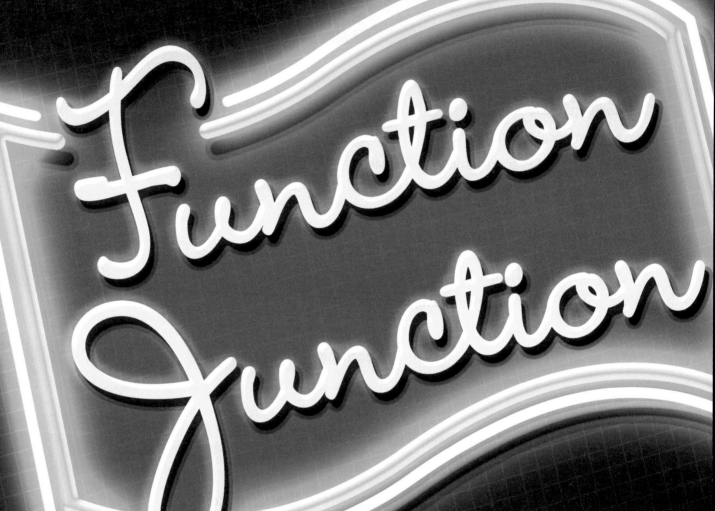

The Families
of Functions

Lappan, Phillips, Fey, Friel

Function Junction

The Families of Functions

Looking Ahead 2

Mathematical Highlights 4

Mathematical Practices and Habits of Mind 5

1

The Families of Functions

The Families of Functions 7

1.1 Filling Functions 8

1.2 Domain, Range, and Function Notation 10

1.3 Taxi Fares, Time Payments, and Step Functions 12

1.4 Piecewise-Defined Functions 14

1.5 Inverse Functions 17

ACE Homework 20

Mathematical Reflections 30

2

Arithmetic and Geometric Sequences

Arithmetic and Geometric Sequences 32

2.1 Arithmetic Sequences 33

2.2 Geometric Sequences 37

ACE Homework 41

Mathematical Reflections 47

3

Transforming Graphs, Equations, and Functions   49

3.1 Sliding Up and Down Vertical Translations of Functions 50

3.2 Stretching and Flipping Up and Down Multiplicative Transformations of Functions 52

3.3 Sliding Left and Right Horizontal Translations of Functions 54

3.4 Getting From Here to There Transforming $y = x^2$ 56

ACE Homework 58

Mathematical Reflections 61

4

Solving Quadratic Equations Algebraically   63

4.1 Applying Square Roots 64

4.2 Completing the Square 66

4.3 The Quadratic Formula 70

4.4 Complex Numbers 73

ACE Homework 76

Mathematical Reflections 83

5

Polynomial Expressions, Functions, and Equations   85

5.1 Properties of Polynomial Expressions and Functions 86

5.2 Combining Profit Functions Operating With Polynomials I 90

5.3 Product Time Operating With Polynomials II 92

5.4 The Factor Game Revisited 94

ACE Homework 96

Mathematical Reflections 101

Looking Back 103

English/Spanish Glossary 106

Index 113

Acknowledgments 118

Looking Ahead

Taxi fares are often calculated with a function. **What** sort of graph would you expect for such a function? **What** units and scale make sense for this graph?

RATES
$5.00 for distances one mile or less and $2.00 for each additional mile or part of a mile

TAXI
RATE

On television quiz shows, the payoff increases for each correct answer. Suppose the pattern continues. **What** are the next five payoffs you expect?

Odd$ Are

$100

$300

$500

The graph at the right has a different shape than any of the linear, quadratic, exponential, or inverse functions you have studied before. **What** kind of algebraic function has a graph like this?

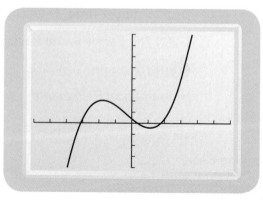

In other Units, you looked for important relationships between variables. You represented those relationships with algebraic expressions, equations, and graphs. You used those representations to solve Problems. Some of those Problems were about amusements park rides such as Bumper Cars, the Sky Dive, and wood-frame and steel-frame roller coasters.

Working on the Problems of this Unit will extend your understanding of functions and their representations. You will study new forms of mathematical notation. You will explore new families of functions and new techniques for transforming expressions to equivalent forms and solving equations. Finally, you will learn about an extension of the real number system.

Mathematical Highlights

The Families of Functions

Functions have been a major theme throughout all of your work with algebra. In *Function Junction* you will take a deeper look at functions and explore new functions.

The Investigations in this Unit will help you learn how to

- Determine the domain and range of functions and the $f(x)$ notation for expressing functions

- Examine numeric and graphic properties of step and piecewise-defined functions

- Investigate properties and uses of inverse functions

- Investigate properties and applications of arithmetic and geometric sequences

- Explore the relationships between functions with graphs connected by transformations such as translations and dilations

- Express quadratic functions in equivalent vertex form and use that new form to solve equations and sketch graphs

- Develop a formula for solving any quadratic equation

- Explore the meaning and operations of complex numbers

- Use polynomial expressions and functions to model and to answer questions about data patterns and graphs that cannot be represented with linear, quadratic, inverse variation, or exponential functions

As you work through the Problems of this Unit, it will be helpful to keep asking yourself questions such as these:

What are the variables in the situation and how are they related?

What familiar type of function could be used to model the relationship of variables, or is something new required?

How are algebraic expressions and graphs of the relationship between variables connected to each other?

How can the algebraic expression for a function be written in a form that makes it easier to sketch or analyze a graph or solve an equation?

Common Core State Standards
Mathematical Practices and Habits of Mind

In the *Connected Mathematics* curriculum you will develop an understanding of important mathematical ideas by solving problems and reflecting on the mathematics involved. Every day, you will use "habits of mind" to make sense of problems and apply what you learn to new situations. Some of these habits are described by the *Common Core State Standards for Mathematical Practices* (MP).

MP1 Make sense of problems and persevere in solving them.

When using mathematics to solve a problem, it helps to think carefully about

- data and other facts you are given and what additional information you need to solve the problem;
- strategies you have used to solve similar problems and whether you could solve a related simpler problem first;
- how you could express the problem with equations, diagrams, or graphs;
- whether your answer makes sense.

MP2 Reason abstractly and quantitatively.

When you are asked to solve a problem, it often helps to

- focus first on the key mathematical ideas;
- check that your answer makes sense in the problem setting;
- use what you know about the problem setting to guide your mathematical reasoning.

MP3 Construct viable arguments and critique the reasoning of others.

When you are asked to explain why a conjecture is correct, you can

- show some examples that fit the claim and explain why they fit;
- show how a new result follows logically from known facts and principles.

When you believe a mathematical claim is incorrect, you can

- show one or more counterexamples—cases that don't fit the claim;
- find steps in the argument that do not follow logically from prior claims.

MP4 **Model with mathematics.**

When you are asked to solve problems, it often helps to

- think carefully about the numbers or geometric shapes that are the most important factors in the problem, then ask yourself how those factors are related to each other;
- express data and relationships in the problem with tables, graphs, diagrams, or equations, and check your result to see if it makes sense.

MP5 **Use appropriate tools strategically.**

When working on mathematical questions, you should always

- decide which tools are most helpful for solving the problem and why;
- try a different tool when you get stuck.

MP6 **Attend to precision.**

In every mathematical exploration or problem-solving task, it is important to

- think carefully about the required accuracy of results: is a number estimate or geometric sketch good enough, or is a precise value or drawing needed?
- report your discoveries with clear and correct mathematical language that can be understood by those to whom you are speaking or writing.

MP7 **Look for and make use of structure.**

In mathematical explorations and problem solving, it is often helpful to

- look for patterns that show how data points, numbers, or geometric shapes are related to each other;
- use patterns to make predictions.

MP8 **Look for and express regularity in repeated reasoning.**

When results of a repeated calculation show a pattern, it helps to

- express that pattern as a general rule that can be used in similar cases;
- look for shortcuts that will make the calculation simpler in other cases.

You will use all of the Mathematical Practices in this Unit. Sometimes, when you look at a Problem, it is obvious which practice is most helpful. At other times, you will decide on a practice to use during class explorations and discussions. After completing each Problem, ask yourself:

- What mathematics have I learned by solving this Problem?
- What Mathematical Practices were helpful in learning this mathematics?

The Families of Functions

In earlier Units you studied real-world situations that involved relationships between variables. Here are some examples:

- Distance traveled by riders on a bike tour related to the time riding
- Area of a rectangular piece of land with a fixed perimeter related to the width
- Strength of a bridge related to the length
- Area of ballots cut from a piece of paper related to the number of cuts

In each situation you asked these questions:

- What are the variable quantities?
- What measurement units are appropriate for the situation?

Common Core State Standards

F-IF.A.1 Understand that a function from one set (called the domain) to another set (called the range) assigns to each element of the domain exactly one element of the range.

F-IF.C.7b Graph square root, cube root, and piecewise-defined functions, including step functions and absolute value functions.

F-BF.B.4a Solve an equation of the form $f(x) = c$ for a simple function f that has an inverse and write an expression for the inverse.

Also N-Q.A.1, N-Q.A.2, F-IF.A.2, F-IF.B.4, F-IF.B.5, F-IF.B.6

The relationships in the examples from earlier Units are called *functions*. Some of the types of functions you studied are expressed with equations:

- Linear functions, with equations in the form $y = mx + b$
- Quadratic functions, with equations in the form $y = ax^2 + bx + c$
- Inverse variation functions, with equations in the form $y = \frac{k}{x}$
- Exponential functions, with equations in the form $y = a(b^x)$

In each case, every value of the independent variable x is related to exactly one value of the dependent variable y. Any relationship between variables with that property is called a **function**. Many functions have rules that are quite different from those that you have studied so far.

The Problems in this Investigation introduce the standard terminology and notation for functions. You will also study new families of special functions.

1.1 Filling Functions

Not all functions can be defined by simple algebraic rules. Suppose you fill each of these containers with water flowing in at a constant rate. Then you study the results.

- What variables does this situation suggest?
- What are the best units to measure the quantities involved?
- What would tables, graphs, or equations of each of the functions related to filling these containers look like?

Look at each container pictured above. The height of water at any time depends on the length of time the water has been flowing into it. There is exactly one water height at each point in time. So height is a function of time.

Problem 1.1

A Match each of these (*time, water height*) graphs to one of the containers on the preceding page. Explain why each graph shows the rate of filling for one of the containers. Assume the water flows at a constant rate.

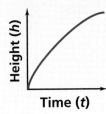
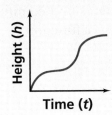
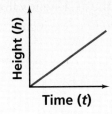

B Sketch containers that would have functions for rate of filling that would match these graphs.

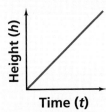
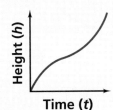
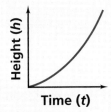

C The drawings below show a two-dimensional view of containers that have a constant dimension of 1 inch from front to back. Again, the water flows at a constant rate. Sketch graphs of the functions for rate of filling for these containers.

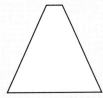
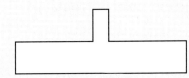

D Do the graphs in Questions A–C represent any functions you have seen in previous Units? Explain.

E Delsin and Christina are analyzing the graphs from Question C. Delsin says those graphs show volume as a function of time. Christina says that graphs showing how volume changes over time would be three identical graphs. They would be linear graphs for all three containers. She thinks the graphs show how height changes over time. Who is right? Explain.

A C E Homework starts on page 20.

1.2 Domain, Range, and Function Notation

The drawing below shows the side view of a lab flask that you might use in chemistry class. The graph shows how the height of water in the flask changes with time as a steady flow of water is poured into it. The relation between the *height* of the water and *time* is a function.

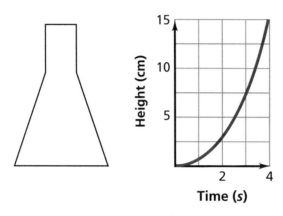

Mathematicians use two special terms, *domain* and *range*, to describe any function.

- The **domain** of a function is the set of all possible values for the input variable. For the filling function, the domain is the set of all times for which there is a related height.

- The **range** of a function is the set of all possible values for the output variable. For the filling function, the range is the set of heights from zero to the top of the container.

A function assigns to each element of the domain exactly one element of the range. The assignment process is commonly written in symbolic form. The notation $h(t)$ is read, "the value of height h at time t." The equation $h(2) = 3$ tells you that the height of the water in the flask is 3 centimeters after 2 seconds of pouring. The notation $h(t)$ does *not* mean h times t.

- What is the domain of the height function shown in the graph?

- What range makes sense for the function shown in the graph?

- What is each equation asking and what value would you insert to make it a true statement?

$$h(0) = \blacksquare \qquad h(2) = \blacksquare \qquad h(\blacksquare) = 1 \qquad h(\blacksquare) = 10$$

Function notation *f(x)* is another way of expressing rules for functions. For example, the function $y = 1.5x - 4$ can be written as $f(x) = 1.5x - 4$. The notation shows the relationships between the independent and dependent variables in a short form. The sentence $f(10) = 11$ tells you that the value of y is 11 when the value of x is 10.

Problem 1.2

Ⓐ For each of the following examples, describe a domain and a range that make sense for the function. Then use function notation to complete the given sentences.

1. **a.** Suppose $f(x) = 1.5x - 4$. What are the domain and range of $f(x)$?

    b. $f(3) = \blacksquare$ **c.** $f(-2) = \blacksquare$ **d.** $f(\blacksquare) = 5$

    e. $f(\blacksquare) = -1$ **f.** $f(n) = \blacksquare$ **g.** $f(x + 1) = \blacksquare$

2. **a.** Suppose $g(x) = \sqrt{x}$. What are the domain and range of $g(x)$?

    b. $g(9) = \blacksquare$ **c.** $g(49) = \blacksquare$ **d.** $g(\blacksquare) = 5$

    e. $g(t) = \blacksquare$ **f.** $g(x - 5) = \blacksquare$

3. **a.** Suppose $h(x) = 5(2^x)$. What are the domain and range of $h(x)$?

    b. $h(-3) = \blacksquare$ **c.** $h(0) = \blacksquare$ **d.** $h(\blacksquare) = 40$

    e. $h(m) = \blacksquare$ **f.** $h(3x) = \blacksquare$

Ⓑ The graph of any function f is the set of all points with coordinates $(x, f(x))$, or the set of all points (x, y) that satisfy the equation $y = f(x)$. Sketch graphs of the three functions defined in Part A.

Ⓒ Not all relationships between variables are functions. For example, the next table shows age in years and height in inches of students on a middle school basketball team.

Heights and Ages

Age (years)	11	11	12	12	12	13	13	13	13	14
Height (inches)	60	58	62	67	62	65	68	72	68	70

Why is *height* not a function of *age* in this case?

ⒶⒸⒺ Homework starts on page 20.

1.3 Taxi Fares, Time Payments, and Step Functions

In many important applications of mathematics a function is defined in words. However, it may not be easy to write a simple algebraic expression for that function. For example, the fare for riding in a taxicab might be calculated with a function such as the one described on the cab below:

RATES

$5.00 for distances one mile or less and $2.00 for each additional mile or part of a mile

In this taxi you would pay $5.00 for any trip 1 mile or less in length. You'd pay $7.00 for any trip longer than 1 mile but not longer than 2 miles. You'd pay $9.00 for any trip longer than 2 miles but not longer than 3 miles, and so on.

- Suppose you made a table and graph for the function relating taxicab fare to distance traveled. What patterns would you expect to see?

Analyzing relationships like the taxicab fare scheme is easier if you calculate some sample values and look for a pattern.

Problem 1.3

 1. Complete the table at the right to show taxicab fares for trips from 1 to 8 miles.

Taxi Fares

Distance (mi)	1	2	3	4	5	6	7	8
Fare ($)	5	7	■	■	■	■	■	■

2. Graph the data points in the table of sample taxi fares. Complete the graph so it shows the fares for any distances between 0 and 8 miles.

3. Does the completed graph represent a function? If not, why not? If it does, what are its domain and range?

Problem 1.3 *continued*

B When stores want to sell things quickly, they offer deals that spread payments over many months with 0% interest. Suppose that you buy a new bicycle for $240. You get a deal that requires $10 monthly payments.

   1. Complete the following table to show the unpaid balance for months 0 to 7.

Account Balance

Month	0	1	2	3	4	5	6	7
Unpaid Balance ($)	240	230	▨	▨	▨	▨	▨	▨

   2. Graph the data points in the table of unpaid balances. Then complete the graph so it shows the unpaid balance at any time between 0 and 7 months.

   3. Does the completed graph represent a function? If not, why not? If it does, what are its domain and range?

C In many quantitative problems it makes sense to round numbers to a nearby whole-number value. There are three common ways to do this rounding:

   • The *standard rounding rule* takes the integer closest to x, with values exactly halfway between integers rounded up

   • The *ceiling rule* takes the nearest integer greater than or equal to x

   • The *floor rule* takes the nearest integer less than or equal to x

   1. Complete the following table of values for the standard, ceiling, and floor rounding rules.

Comparing Standard, Ceiling, and Floor Functions

x	−3.25	−2.75	−0.5	0.6	1.7	2.21	3.5
Standard	▨	▨	▨	▨	▨	▨	▨
Ceiling	▨	▨	▨	▨	▨	▨	▨
Floor	▨	▨	▨	▨	▨	▨	▨

   2. Pick one of the three rules and draw a graph of its values for $x = -3$ to $x = 3$.

   3. Do any of the rules define functions? If not, why not? If so, what are the domain(s) and range(s)?

continued on the next page >

Problem 1.3 *continued*

> **D** The relationships between variables that you analyzed in Questions A–C are examples of a special type of functions called **step functions.**
>
>   **1.** How do the graphs show why the step function name makes sense?
>
>   **2.** Why it is hard to give an algebraic expression for calculating values of such functions?

A **C** **E** Homework starts on page 20.

1.4 Piecewise-Defined Functions

Suppose the container below has constant width from front to back. Water pours into it at a constant rate.

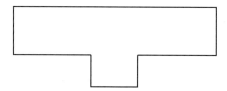

- How rapidly will the water level rise?

- What sort of graph would you expect for the function relating water height to time?

- What kind of algebraic rule would express the height function?

There is a function that describes the rate at which water fills the container pictured above. You can write rules that relate the dependent and independent variables for that function. However, the rules or expressions for that function and others like it are different on different pieces of the domain. Such relationships are called **piecewise-defined functions.**

The following Problem will enhance your understanding of piecewise-defined functions. You will work with some function rules that are stated in words and others given as algebraic expressions.

Problem 1.4

A The graph below models the rate at which the water level would rise in the container pictured to its left.

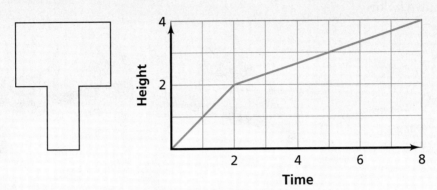

1. Why does it make sense that the graph should consist of two different linear pieces?

2. What algebraic expressions would you use to model the pieces of the rate of filling function?

B The absolute value function has the following piecewise definition:

$$|x| = \begin{cases} x \ if \ x \geq 0 \\ -x \ if \ x < 0 \end{cases}$$

1. Copy and complete this table of values for the absolute value function $v(x) = |x|$.

x	−3	−2.5	−2	−1.5	−1	0	1	1.5	2	2.5	3
$v(x) = \|x\|$	3	▪	▪	▪	▪	▪	▪	▪	▪	▪	▪

2. Use the data for the points $\left(x, |x|\right)$ to draw a graph of $v(x)$.

C Use results from Question B to draw graphs of these variations on the absolute value function.

1. $a(x) = |x| + 1$

2. $b(x) = |x| - 2$

3. $c(x) = v(x) - 1$

4. Explain how these graphs are related to the graph of $v(x) = |x|$.

continued on the next page >

Problem **1.4** *continued*

D Competitors in iron-man triathlon races swim, bicycle, and run a total of 140.6 miles. Suppose that one racer's pace in each part of the race was as shown below.

Swimming
Distance: 2.4 miles
Time: 2 hours

Biking
Distance: 112 miles
Time: 8 hours

Running
Distance: 26.2 miles
Time: 4 hours

1. What were the racer's average speeds for swimming, biking, and running?

2. Sketch a graph showing the racer's progress over the whole race. Assume that the pace on each segment of the race is constant .

3. What are the domain and range of the function graphed in part (2)?

4. Based on your graph, estimate the racer's average rate for the entire triathlon.

A C E Homework starts on page 20.

1.5 Inverse Functions

If an airplane averages 500 miles per hour in flight, you know that the time and distance traveled are related. Look at the two tables below. Numbers in the first table show distance as a function of time. Numbers in the second table show time as a function of distance.

The equations $d = 500t$ and $f(t) = 500t$ both show how distance traveled is related to time in flight.

Using units of measure helps to keep track of the domain and range. Here is an example.

2,000 miles = 500 mph × 4 hours

Time and Distance

Time (hours)	Distance (miles)
0	0
1	500
2	1,000
3	1,500
4	2,000
■	■
t	$500t$

The equations $t = d \div 500$ and $g(d) = d \div 500$ both show how time in flight is related to distance traveled.

- How do units of measure help make sense of this sentence?

  4 hours = 2,000 miles ÷ 500 mph

Distance and Time

Distance (miles)	Time (hours)
0	0
500	1
1,000	2
1,500	3
2,000	4
■	■
d	■

The functions $f(x) = 500x$ and $g(x) = x \div 500$ are related in a very special and useful way. The function $g(x)$ is the **inverse function** of $f(x)$, and $f(x)$ is the inverse function of $g(x)$.

- Why does the term *inverse* make sense in describing how functions $f(x)$ and $g(x)$ are related?

Working on this Problem will develop your ability to find and use inverses of familiar functions.

Problem 1.5

For the situations described in Questions A–E, do the following:

- Write an equation that shows how the two variables are related.

- Use function notation to write an equation that shows the same relationship.

- Write the equation and function that show the inverse relationship of the two variables.

- Explain what the function and its inverse tell about the related variables.

A A bus averages 50 miles per hour on the highway. How is the distance covered *d*, in miles, related to the driving time *t*, in hours?

B A gas station offers the price shown in the advertisement below. How is the price per gallon on Tuesday *T* related to the price *D* on other days of the week?

GASOLINE SERVICE

100 Main Street

TUESDAYS ARE SPECIAL!

Get **20¢** off the
regular price per gallon.

C The typical customer at the Spartan Deli buys food that costs $7.50. How is the Deli's daily income *I* related to the number of customers *n*?

D 1. The Spartan Deli has operating expenses of $850 per day. How is the Deli's daily profit *P* related to the number of customers *n*?

   2. Amy thinks that the answer for the inverse is $n = P \div 7.50 + 850$. Becky says that the units needed for the expression on the right side of this equation would not give a number of people. Who do you agree with? Explain.

Problem **1.5** *continued*

E How is the area A of any square related to the length s of its sides?

F For any function $f(x)$, the inverse function is shown by the function notation $f^{-1}(x)$. The notation $f^{-1}(x)$ is read, "f inverse of x."

Suppose a function $f(x)$ tells the range value corresponding to each domain value. Then the inverse of that function reverses this relationship. Values that were in the domain are now in the range, and vice versa.

Find inverses for the functions below and explain how you know that your answers are correct.

Hint: You might find it helpful to write each function as an equation using y to name the dependent variable. For example, $f(x) = 3x$ could be written as $y = 3x$. Then the task is to find an expression that shows how to calculate x when given y.

1. $f(x) = 3x$

2. $g(x) = x + 7$

3. $h(x) = 3x + 7$

4. $j(x) = x - 7$

5. $k(x) = x^2$

6. $m(x) = \frac{1}{x}$

7. $n(x) = x^3$

G For each function in Question F, do the following:

• Describe the domain and range of the function.

• Describe the domain and range of the inverse function.

• Explain any ways that the domain of the original function must be limited if it is to have the proposed inverse.

• Sketch a graph of the function and a graph of its inverse. Use separate coordinate axes for each pair of graphs.

A C E Homework starts on page 20.

Applications

1. Suppose each container below is filled at a constant rate with water. Match each container with the graph that represents the relationship between the height of the water in the container and time.

Container 1 **Container 2** **Container 3**

Graph 1 **Graph 2** **Graph 3**

2. The graphs below show the pattern of time and distance traveled by two school buses. Make a copy of each graph. On copies of each graph mark the following intervals:

   • when the bus is speeding up

   • when the bus is slowing down

   • when the bus is moving at a constant speed

   • when the bus is stopped

   a. Bus A

   b. Bus B

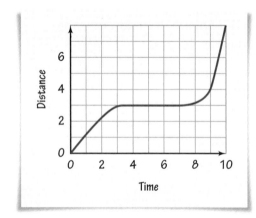

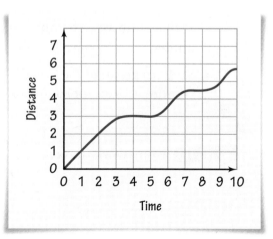

3. Ocean water levels rise and fall with a tidal period of about 12 hours. The graph below shows water depth at the end of a pier in a seacoast city.

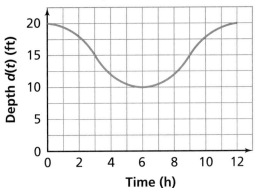

Water Depth Over Twelve Hours

The function $d(t)$ gives water depth at time t hours after midnight. Use the graph to complete the following sentences and explain what each sentence tells about water depth.

   a. $d(0) = $ ▨

   b. $d(2) = $ ▨

   c. $d(4) = $ ▨

   d. $d(6) = $ ▨

   e. $d(9) = $ ▨

   f. $d(▨) = 15$

4. What are the domain and range of the function for water depth shown above?

Complete the sentences to give correct statements.

5. $f(x) = -2x + 5$

   a. $f(7) = $ ▨   **b.** $f(-3) = $ ▨   **c.** $f(▨) = 17$

6. $g(x) = x^2 + 5x$

   a. $g(7) = $ ▨   **b.** $g(-3) = $ ▨   **c.** $g(▨) = 6$

7. $h(x) = 4(0.5)^x$

   a. $h(2) = $ ▨   **b.** $h(-1) = $ ▨   **c.** $h(▨) = 4$

8. Describe the domain and range for the functions $f(x) = -2x + 5$, $g(x) = x^2 + 5x$, and $h(x) = 4(0.5^x)$.

9. For each function, sketch the graph and describe the domain and range.

    a. $f(x) = 4x + 5$ **b.** $g(x) = x^2 + 2$ **c.** $h(x) = 2^x$ **d.** $j(x) = \frac{1}{x}$

10. Determine if the relationship in each table shows that y is a function of x.

a.

x	2	3	4	5	6
y	4	7	10	13	16

b.

x	3	4	1	-1	2
y	4	3	-1	1	2

c.

x	0	2	4	3	0
y	1	3	5	7	9

d.

x	-4	-3	-1	1	2
y	0	1	1	1	0

For Exercises 11 and 12, use the graphs below.

$f(x)$ $g(x)$ $h(x)$

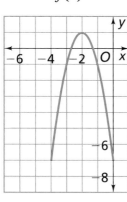 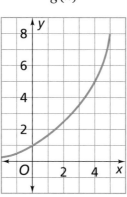 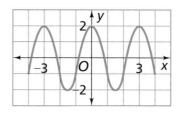

11. Identify the domain and range of each function.

12. Use the graphs to complete these sentences that use function notation.

    a. $f(-4) = \blacksquare$ **b.** $g(4) = \blacksquare$ **c.** $h(1) = \blacksquare$

    d. $f(\blacksquare) = 1$ **e.** $g(\blacksquare) = 1$ **f.** $h(\blacksquare) = 2$

13. The fee for airport parking is shown below. For parts (a)–(f), calculate the cost of parking $c(t)$ for the given times.

   a. $c(0.5)$ **b.** $c(1.0)$ **c.** $c(2.5)$

   d. $c(5.0)$ **e.** $c(5.5)$ **f.** $c(8.0)$

   g. Draw a graph showing the charges for any time from 0 to 8 hours.

14. Multiple Choice At Akihito's school, lunches cost $1.25. Akihito starts the school year with a school lunch account balance of $100. Which graph best represents the pattern of change in Akihito's account balance during a typical week?

A.

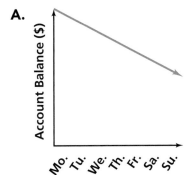

B.

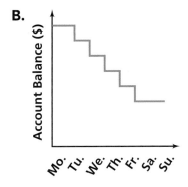

C.

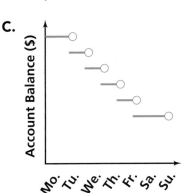

D. None of these

15. Suppose $r(x)$ is the function that applies the standard rounding rule to numbers. Also, $c(x)$ applies the ceiling rule for rounding, and $f(x)$ applies the floor rule for rounding. Complete the following sentences to give correct statements.

a. $r(1.6) = $ ■

b. $c(1.6) = $ ■

c. $f(1.6) = $ ■

d. $r(-1.6) = $ ■

e. $c(-1.6) = $ ■

f. $f(-1.6) = $ ■

g. $r(-1.3) = $ ■

h. $c(-1.3) = $ ■

i. $f(-1.3) = $ ■

j. $r(■) = -2$

k. $c(■) = -2$

m. $f(■) = -2$

16. Graph each of the following piecewise functions.

a.
$$y = \begin{bmatrix} x^2 \ if \ x \le 0 \\ 3x \ if \ x > 0 \end{bmatrix}$$

b.
$$y = \begin{bmatrix} \frac{1}{2}x + 4 \ if \ x < 0 \\ -\frac{1}{2}x + 4 \ if \ x \ge 0 \end{bmatrix}$$

c.
$$y = \begin{bmatrix} 4 \ if \ x < 2 \\ 2^x \ if \ x \ge 2 \end{bmatrix}$$

17. The figure and graph below show the function for rate of filling for the container from Problem 1.4.

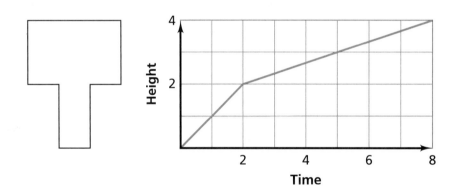

Suppose that the height of the water is measured in inches and the filling time in seconds. At what rate is water height rising during the following intervals?

a. the first two seconds

b. the time from 2 to 8 seconds

18. Desheng and Chelsea are trying to write a piecewise function rule for the following graph.

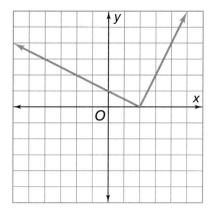

Desheng says the y-intercept is 1, the slope of the left part is $-\frac{1}{2}$, and the slope of the right part is 2. He writes the following function rule.

$$y = \begin{bmatrix} -\frac{1}{2}x + 1 \; if \; x < 2 \\ 2x + 1 \; if \; x \geq 2 \end{bmatrix}$$

Chelsea says the left part of the graph has slope $-\frac{1}{2}$ and y-intercept of 1. The right part of the graph has slope 2. It would have a y-intercept of -4 if the graph extended to intersect the y-axis. She writes the following function rule.

$$y = \begin{bmatrix} -\frac{1}{2}x + 1 \; if \; x \leq 2 \\ 2x - 4 \; if \; x > 2 \end{bmatrix}$$

Whose reasoning is correct? Explain.

19. Find inverses for these functions.

     a. $f(x) = 6x$ **b.** $g(x) = x - 4$ **c.** $h(x) = 6x - 4$

     d. $j(x) = \sqrt{x}$ **e.** $k(x) = 4x^2$ **f.** $m(x) = -\frac{3}{x}$

20. For each function in Exercise 19, do the following.

- Describe the domain and range of the function.

- Describe the domain and range of the inverse function.

- Explain any ways that the domain of the inverse function differs from the domain of original function. (In what ways must the domain of the inverse function be limited?)

Connections

21. For $f(x) = \sqrt{x}$, evaluate each of the following.

    a. $f(121)$ **b.** $f\left(\frac{1}{4}\right)$ **c.** $f(m^2)$ **d.** $f(4q^2)$

22. For $f(x) = 4^x$, complete the following sentences.

    a. $f(4) = \blacksquare$ **b.** $f(-2) = \blacksquare$ **c.** $f(\blacksquare) = 1$

    d. $f(\blacksquare) = 2$ **e.** $f(a) = \blacksquare$ **f.** $f(b + 2) = \blacksquare$

23. For $g(x) = x^2$, evaluate each of the following expressions.

    a. $g(3)$ **b.** $g\left(\frac{1}{2}\right)$ **c.** $g(-d)$ **d.** $g\left(\frac{n}{2m}\right)$

24. For $j(x) = \frac{1}{2}x$, evaluate each of the following expressions.

    a. $j(-7)$ **b.** $j(0)$ **c.** $j(2s)$ **d.** $j\left(\frac{r}{t}\right)$

25. Linear, quadratic, and exponential functions all have as their domains the set of real numbers.

    a. Why is the domain of $r(x) = \sqrt{x}$ not all real numbers?

    b. Why is the domain of $s(x) = \frac{1}{x}$ not all real numbers?

26. Many variables in your life change as time passes. Tell whether any of the following changes shows a pattern like a step function. **Hint:** More than one pattern may be a step function.

    a. your height

    b. the price of a one-scoop cone of ice cream

    c. your age in years

    d. the number of questions left to answer as you work on homework

27. For each of the following numeric equations, write the other equations in the fact family.

    a. $7 + 12 = 19$ **b.** $4 \times 3 = 12$

28. Addition and subtraction are inverse operations. Multiplication and division are also inverse operations. How do those inverse operation labels relate to the inverse functions in Problem 1.5?

29. Solve each of these equations using ideas about fact families and inverse operations.

    a. $x + 7 = 12$ **b.** $5x = 35$ **c.** $5x + 7 = 82$

    d. $\frac{7}{x} = 12$ **e.** $\frac{9}{x-2} = 3$ **f.** $\frac{5}{x} + 7 = 8$

Extensions

30. a. Copy and complete the following table of values.

Variations of the Ceiling Rounding Function $c(x)$

x	0	0.25	0.5	0.75	1.0	1.25	1.5	1.75	2.0	2.25	2.5
c(x) − x											
x − c(x)											

    b. Using data in the table, draw a graph of $c(x) - c$ from $x = 0$ to $x = 5$.

    c. Using data in the table, draw a graph of $c - c(x)$ from $x = 0$ to $x = 5$.

    d. What can you conclude from the two graphs?

31. a. Copy and complete the following table of values.

Variations of the Floor Rounding Function $f(x)$

x	0	0.25	0.5	0.75	1.0	1.25	1.5	1.75	2.0	2.25	2.5
f(x) − x											
x − f(x)											

    b. Using data in the table, draw a graph of $f(x) - f$ from $x = 0$ to $x = 5$.

    c. Using data in the table, draw a graph of $f - f(x)$ from $x = 0$ to $x = 5$.

    d. What can you conclude from the two graphs?

32. What are the domain and range of the ceiling function $c(x)$?

33. Sketch graphs for each of these pairs of functions for $x = 0$ to $x = 5$. Draw the line $y = x$ on each graph. Then describe the relationship of the pair of inverse function graphs to the $y = x$ line.

    a. $f(x) = 2x$ and $g(x) = 0.5x$

    b. $h(x) = x^2$ and $j(x) = \sqrt{x}$

34. Describe functions with these domains and ranges.

    a. domain: all real numbers
       range: all real numbers greater than or equal to zero

    b. domain: all real numbers
       range: all integers

    c. domain: all nonnegative real numbers
       range: all nonpositive real numbers

35. Connie and Margaret are given the following extra credit problem: For $g(x) = 2x + 4$, find $g(g(1))$.

Connie's Method	OR	Margaret's Method
$g(g(1))$ is the same as $(g(1))^2$ So, $g(1) = 2(1) + 4 = 6$ which means that $(g(1))^2 = 6^2 = 36$.		$g(1) = 2(1) + 4 = 6$ This means that $g(g(1)) = g(6)$ $g(6) = 2(6) + 4 = 16$

    Which of these methods is correct? Explain.

36. **a.** Suppose $f(x) = 5x + 35$ and $g(x) = 5(2^x)$. Find the point where the graphs of $y = f(x)$ and $y = g(x)$ intersect.

    b. Explain why the x-coordinates of the points where the graphs of the equations $y = f(x)$ and $y = g(x)$ intersect are the solutions of the equation $f(x) = g(x)$.

37. Scott and Jim are driving from Gilbertville to Rivertown. The cities are 30 miles apart. Halfway between them is an intersection with the road east to Delmore City. You can see Scott and Jim's route on the diagram below. They are traveling at 60 mph (miles per hour).

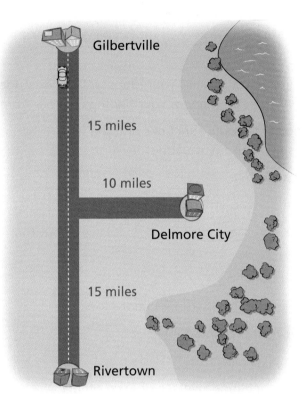

Gilbertville

15 miles

10 miles

Delmore City

15 miles

Rivertown

a. Suppose that Scott and Jim measure distance in miles along the roads shown and time in minutes. Write a piecewise function rule for the function relating distance d from Delmore City to time t.

b. Draw a graph that shows how far they are from Delmore City at any time in their trip from Gilbertville to Rivertown.

c. Suppose that you measure distance "as the crow flies," rather than along the roads that are shown. How would that change the function rule and graph?

Mathematical Reflections

In this Investigation, you used tables, graphs, and algebraic expressions to represent and study a variety of functions relating variables. The questions below will help you summarize what you have learned.

Think about these questions. Discuss your ideas with other students and your teacher. Then write a summary of your findings in your notebook.

1. This Investigation was about functions and the ways that mathematicians think and write about them.

   a. What is a function?

   b. What are the domain and range of a function?

   c. What does a statement such as $f(6) = 23$ say about the function $f(x)$?

2. **a. What** is a step function?

   b. Describe what graphs of step functions look like.

3. **a. What** is a piecewise-defined function?

   b. Give an example to illustrate this idea.

4. **a. When** are two functions inverses of each other?

   b. What example would you give to illustrate this idea?

Common Core Mathematical Practices

As you worked on the Problems in this Investigation, you used prior knowledge to make sense of them. You also applied Mathematical Practices to solve the Problems. Think back over your work, the ways you thought about the Problems, and how you used Mathematical Practices.

Tori described her thoughts in the following way:

> In Problem 2 of this Investigation, we learned how to use the terms *domain* and *range*. They describe the possible values for independent and dependent variables in a relationship.
>
> We learned how to use $f(x)$ notation to specify rules for functions and values to be calculated.
>
> We also learned how the terms *step function* and *piecewise function* explain the patterns of change in those kinds of relationships.
>
> **Common Core Standards for Mathematical Practice**
> **MP6** Attend to precision.

 • What other Mathematical Practices can you identify in Tori's reasoning?

• Describe a Mathematical Practice that you and your classmates used to solve a different Problem in this Investigation.

Arithmetic and Geometric Sequences

Quiz shows have long been a popular feature of television programming. In most such shows, the payoff for correct answers increases as the difficulty of questions increases.

Here are payoff patterns from two different shows. The payoffs on *Odds Are* increase from $100 to $300 to $500 to $700 to $900 and so on. The payoffs on *Double or Nothing* increase from $50 to $100 to $200 to $400 to $800 and so on.

- If the patterns in those examples continue, what are the next five payoffs you would expect for each game?

- Which game do you think would give the greater total payoff if a contestant got ten straight questions correct?

Common Core State Standards

F-IF.A.3 Recognize that sequences are functions, sometimes defined recursively, whose domain is a subset of the integers.

F-BF.A.1a. Determine an explicit expression, a recursive process, or steps for calculation from a context.

F-BF.A.2 Write arithmetic and geometric sequences both recursively and with an explicit formula, use them to model situations, and translate between the two forms.

Also F-IF.A.2, F-LE.A.2

You probably recognize that the two quiz show payoff schemes look like the outputs of linear and exponential functions. In these examples, the domains of the functions are restricted to the whole numbers 1, 2, 3, 4, . . . Mathematicians call such special functions **sequences.**

The number patterns that occur in the quiz show payoff schemes are examples of *arithmetic sequences* and *geometric sequences*. Understanding sequences will develop your ability to recognize these special number patterns. You will also learn to express them as functions, and to use the functions for solving problems.

2.1 Arithmetic Sequences

The payoff scheme for the *Odds Are* game begins an **arithmetic sequence.** It can be modeled with a function $a(n)$ having a domain that is the whole numbers 1, 2, 3, 4, . . . The numbers in the sequence are called *terms*.

Note on Notation For example, in the sequence 100, 300, 500, 700, 900, . . . the fourth term is $a(4) = 700$. The term $a(n)$ is called the *n*th term, and $a(n + 1)$ is the next term. In this example, $a(n+1)$ is obtained by adding 200 to $a(n)$.

In a sequence, the value of a term can be determined from the previous term. Generating each term of a sequence from the previous term is called a *recursive* process.

• What are the key properties of arithmetic sequences?

• How are arithmetic sequences related to linear functions?

In the following Problem, look for patterns relating each term of an arithmetic sequence to the next. Then try to find a way of calculating any term in such a sequence.

Problem 2.1

(A) 1. Copy and complete the table below. Follow the linear function pattern suggested by the first five values of $a(n)$.

***Odds Are* Payoff Function**

n	1	2	3	4	5	6	7	8	9	10
$a(n)$	100	300	500	700	900	▪	▪	▪	▪	▪

2. What is the relationship between each term in the sequence and the next? Express the relationship as an equation relating each term $a(n)$ and the next term $a(n+1)$.

3. What algebraic expression shows how to calculate $a(n)$ for any value of n, without finding every term in the sequence?

4. How are the answers to parts (1) and (2) related to each other?

(B) Adsila applied for a summer job at a snack bar. The boss told her, "You will get better at the job with experience. So the hourly pay will increase steadily." He showed her this table.

Snack Bar Wages

Week n	1	2	3	4	5	6	7	8	9	10
Hourly Wage $p(n)$	$5.00	$5.50	$6.00	$6.50	$7.00	▪	▪	▪	▪	▪

1. Complete the table of values for the hourly pay function $p(n)$. Follow the linear function pattern suggested by the first five values.

2. What is the relationship between each term in the sequence and the next? Express the relationship as an equation relating $p(n)$ and $p(n+1)$.

3. What expression shows how to calculate $p(n)$ for any n, without finding every term in the sequence?

4. How are the answers to parts (2) and (3) related to each other?

Problem 2.1 *continued*

C In Problem 1.3 you studied the way monthly payments of $10 reduce an amount owed. The payments were for a bicycle that cost $240. The amounts owed $d(n)$ form a sequence that begins 240, 230, 220, ... So terms in the sequence are $d(1) = 240$, $d(2) = 230$, and so on.

   1. What is the relationship between each term in the sequence and the next? Express the relationship as an equation relating $d(n)$ and $d(n + 1)$.

   2. What expression shows how to calculate $d(n)$ for any value of n, without finding every term in the sequence?

   3. How are the answers to parts (1) and (2) related to each other?

D The following tables show number patterns that are arithmetic sequences. In each case, do the following.

- Complete the table of values for the function in a way that continues the linear pattern.

- Describe the relationship between each term and the next in the sequence. Then write an equation to show that relationship.

- Write an algebraic expression that shows how to calculate the nth term in the sequence.

- Explain how the equation for the nth term in the sequence is connected to the equation that relates term n to term $(n + 1)$.

1.

n	1	2	3	4	5	6	7	8	9	10
$j(n)$	−7	−5	−3	−1	1	■	■	■	■	■

2.

n	1	2	3	4	5	6	7	8	9	10
$g(n)$	$\frac{1}{2}$	$\frac{2}{3}$	$\frac{5}{6}$	1	$\frac{7}{6}$	■	■	■	■	■

3.

n	1	2	3	4	5	6	7	8	9	10
$h(n)$	−1	0.75	2.50	4.25	6.00	■	■	■	■	■

continued on the next page >

Problem **2.1** *continued*

E Consider properties shared by the sequences in Questions A–D.

1. What kind of equation relates $f(n + 1)$ and $f(n)$ in each case?

2. What kind of expression shows how to calculate $f(n)$ directly in each case?

3. How are the answers to parts (1) and (2) related to each other?

4. How would you define an arithmetic sequence?

F Not all number patterns are arithmetic sequences.

1. On another television quiz show, the payoffs in the first part of the game are as follows:

$100, $500, $1,000, $2,000, $3,000, $5,000, $7,000, $10,000, $15,000, and $25,000

How is this sequence of numbers different from the sequences in Questions A–D?

2. The lines on a football field are 10 yards apart. The marking on each line is the distance to the nearest goal line. After a muddy football game, a field looks like this drawing.

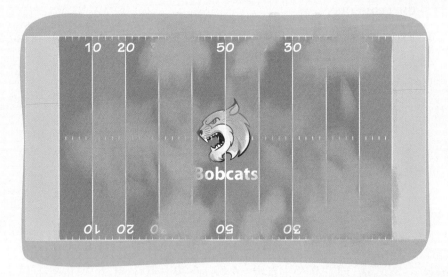

The yard line markers start from one goal line 10, 20, 30, 40, 50, . . . How does this sequence continue? How is the resulting pattern different from the examples in Questions A–D?

 Homework starts on page 41.

2.2 Geometric Sequences

The payoffs for the *Double or Nothing* quiz show are 50, 100, 200, 400, 800, ... The sequence is an example of a **geometric sequence**. It also can be modeled with an exponential function $g(n)$ having a domain that is the whole numbers 1, 2, 3, 4, ... As you examine situations that involve geometric sequences, ask yourself these questions:

- What are the key properties of geometric sequences?
- How are geometric sequences related to exponential functions?

In the following Problem, look for a pattern relating each term of the sequence to the next. Then find a way to calculate any term in the sequence.

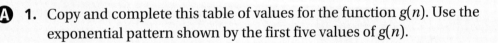

Problem 2.2

A **1.** Copy and complete this table of values for the function $g(n)$. Use the exponential pattern shown by the first five values of $g(n)$.

n	1	2	3	4	5	6	7	8	9	10
g(n)	50	100	200	400	800	▪	▪	▪	▪	▪

2. Daniela answers the fifteenth question correctly. What is her payoff?

3. What is the relationship between each term in the sequence and the next? That is, what equation relates $g(n)$ and $g(n + 1)$ in every case?

4. What expression shows how to calculate $g(n)$ for any value of n, without finding every term in the sequence?

5. How are the answers to parts (1) and (2) related to each other?

continued on the next page >

Problem 2.2 continued

B Jakayla applies for a summer job at a swimming pool. The manager wants workers who stay the whole season. So the hourly pay increases each week as shown in the table.

Swimming Pool Wages

Week n	1	2	3	4	5	6	7	8	9	10
Hourly Wage $p(n)$	$2.00	$3.00	$4.50	$6.75	▦	▦	▦	▦	▦	▦

1. Copy and complete the table of values for the hourly pay function $p(n)$. Use the exponential pattern that you think the manager has in mind.

2. What is the relationship between each term in the sequence and the next? That is, what equation relates $p(n)$ and $p(n + 1)$ in every case?

3. What expression shows how to calculate $p(n)$ for any value of n?

4. How are the answers to parts (3) and (4) related to each other?

C Suppose a sports tournament has 128 teams at the start. In each round, half the teams are eliminated. The number of teams remaining in each round is a sequence. That sequence is shown in the table below.

Teams in Tournament

Round n	1	2	3	4	5	6	7
Teams $t(n)$	128	64	32	▦	▦	▦	▦

1. Complete the table to show the number of teams in rounds 4 through 7. In which round is the championship game played?

2. What is the relationship between each term in the sequence and the next? That is, what equation relates $t(n)$ and $t(n + 1)$ in every case?

3. What expression shows how to calculate $t(n)$ for any value of n?

4. How are the sequence properties in parts (2) and (3) related to each other?

Problem 2.2 *continued*

D The following number patterns are the beginnings of geometric sequences. In each case, do the following.

- Copy and complete the table of values for the function. Continue the pattern shown by the first five entries.

- Describe the relationship between each term and the next in the sequence. Then write an equation to show that relationship.

- Write an equation that shows how to calculate any term in the sequence.

- Explain how the equation for the nth term in the sequence is connected to the equation that relates term n to term $(n + 1)$.

1.

n	1	2	3	4	5	6	7	8
$f(n)$	−1	−3	−9	−27	−81	■	■	■

2.

n	1	2	3	4	5	6	7	8
$g(n)$	2	$\frac{4}{3}$	$\frac{8}{9}$	$\frac{16}{27}$	$\frac{32}{81}$	■	■	■

3.

n	1	2	3	4	5	6	7	8	9	10
$h(n)$	−1	2	−4	8	−16	■	■	■	■	■

E Describe properties shared by the geometric sequences in Questions A–D.

1. What kind of equation relates $f(n + 1)$ and $f(n)$ in each case?

2. What kind of expression shows how to calculate $f(n)$ directly in each case?

3. How are the sequence properties in parts (1) and (2) related to each other?

4. How would you define a geometric sequence?

continued on the next page >

Problem **2.2** *continued*

F The number pattern that starts 1, 1, 2, 3, 5, 8, 13, 21, 34, 55, . . . is known to mathematicians as the *Fibonacci Sequence*. It is named after an Italian mathematician who lived more than 800 years ago.

1. Explain why the Fibonacci numbers are neither an arithmetic sequence nor a geometric sequence.

2. Study the pattern shown above and calculate the next five terms of the Fibonacci Sequence.

3. As given above, the first two terms of the Fibonacci Sequence are $f(1) = 1$ and $f(2) = 1$. Complete the equation $f(n) = \blacksquare$ to show how any other term $f(n)$ of the Fibonacci Sequence can be calculated.

A C E Homework starts on page 41.

Did You Know?

The name *Fibonacci* means "son of Bonacci." Leonardo Fibonacci was an Italian businessman who lived from about 1170 to 1250. He traveled widely through Greece and the Middle East. In his travels he picked up many ideas from Indian and Arabic mathematics.

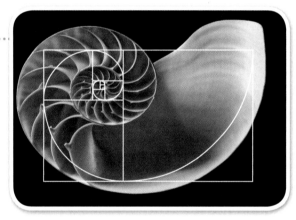

Fibonacci published those ideas in a 1202 book titled *Liber abbaci*. There he described methods for base-ten numeration, arithmetic algorithms, and the solution of algebraic problems.

The Fibonacci Sequence was used as an early model for how some things in nature grow. For example, the Fibbonacci Sequence can be seen in the growth of a chambered nautilus shell.

Applications

For each arithmetic sequence in Exercises 1–3, do the following.

   a. Complete the table.

   b. Write the equation that relates each term $a(n)$ to the next term $a(n + 1)$.

   c. Write the algebraic expression that shows how to calculate $a(n)$ for any n, without finding the previous terms.

1.

n	1	2	3	4	5	6	7	8	9	10
a(n)	275	310	345	380	▨	▨	▨	▨	▨	▨

2.

n	1	2	3	4	5	6	7	8	9	10
a(n)	$\frac{1}{4}$	$\frac{5}{8}$	1	$\frac{11}{8}$	▨	▨	▨	▨	▨	▨

3.

n	1	2	3	4	5	6	7	8	9	10
a(n)	68	▨	▨	26	▨	−2	▨	▨	▨	▨

4. Latrell volunteers at a local charity. The first week he works a total of 2 hours (for training). Each week after the first, he volunteers $3\frac{1}{2}$ hours.

Suppose $t(n)$ represents the total number of hours worked during weeks 1 through n.

   a. Write an equation that represents the relationship between $t(n)$ and $t(n + 1)$.

   b. How many hours does Latrell volunteer in 1 year (52 weeks)?

5. An arithmetic sequence can be represented with this equation: $a(n + 1) = 12 + a(n)$. For $n = 5$, $a(5) = 72$. What is $a(0)$? What is $a(10)$?

6. The algebraic expression $4n + 2$ represents the value of the nth term in an arithmetic sequence. What equation relates $a(n)$ and $a(n + 1)$?

For Exercises 7–16, study each number pattern to see if it begins an arithmetic sequence, a geometric sequence, or neither. For those that begin either an arithmetic sequence or a geometric sequence, do the following.

- **Tell which type of sequence, arithmetic or geometric, is shown**

- **Write an equation relating $s(n)$ and $s(n + 1)$**

- **Write an algebraic expression for a function $s(n)$ that shows how to find any term in the sequence beyond those already given**

7. $-5, 1, 7, 13, 19, 25, 31, \ldots$

8. $16, 13, 10, 7, 4, 1, -2, \ldots$

9. $10, 8, 6, 4, 2, 0, 0, 0, \ldots$

10. $5, -10, 20, -40, 80, -160, \ldots$

11. $3, 4.5, 6, 7.5, 9, 10.5, 12, \ldots$

12. $3, 2, 1, 0, 1, 2, 3, 2, 1, \ldots$

13. $27, 18, 12, 8, \frac{16}{3}, \frac{32}{9}, \frac{64}{27}, \ldots$

14. $4, 4, 4, 4, 4, \ldots$

15. $1, -1, 1, -1, 1, -1, 1, \ldots$

16. $1, 5, 25, 125, 625, 3125, \ldots$

For Exercises 17–21, answer the question that is asked. Then study each number pattern that satisfies the given conditions. For those that are arithmetic or geometric sequences, do the following.

- State whether the sequence is arithmetic or geometric

- Write an equation relating $s(n)$ and $s(n + 1)$

- Write an algebraic expression for a function $s(n)$ that shows how to find any term in the sequence

- Explain how the equation for the nth term in the sequence is connected to the equation that relates term n to term $(n + 1)$

17. On a game show, payoffs for correct responses in each question category increase as follows: $200, $400, $600, $800, $1,000. What is the total amount of money that can be won by correct answers for all questions of a category?

18. When two rivals played a round of golf they agreed to the following payoff sequence. The winner of the first hole earns 5 cents. The winner of the next hole wins 10 cents. The payoff doubles for each hole thereafter. What is the payoff for winning the 18th hole?

19. An airplane cruising at an altitude of 40,000 feet begins its descent to land. It loses altitude at a rate of 1,500 feet per minute. How long will it take to reach the ground?

20. On a 100-point multiple-choice test, the point value of each question depends on the number of questions. The 100 points are divided equally among the questions. For example, on a test with two questions, each question counts for 50 points. How many questions are on a test if each question counts for 5 points?

21. Hana wins $10,000 in the lottery. She puts the money in a bank account that pays interest of 5% once each year. How long will it take that account to grow to $20,000?

Connections

22. The sequence of prime numbers begins 2, 3, 5, 7, ...
Suppose $p(n)$ is the nth prime number.

   a. What are $p(10)$ and $p(15)$?

   b. For what value of n is $p(n) = 41$?

   c. Is the sequence of prime numbers an arithmetic sequence, a geometric sequence, or neither?

23. Look for a pattern in this sequence of fractions: $\frac{1}{2}, \frac{2}{3}, \frac{3}{4}, \frac{4}{5}, \frac{5}{6}, \frac{6}{7}, \ldots$

   a. What are the values of $f(10)$ and $f(15)$?

   b. What expression for the function $f(n)$ will generate the fractions in the pattern for any whole number n?

   c. For what value of n is $f(n) = \frac{23}{24}$?

   d. Is the sequence of fractions an arithmetic sequence, a geometric sequence, or neither?

24. Study the sequence of decimal place values that begins
0.0001, 0.001, 0.01, 0.1, 1, 10, 100, 1,000, ...

   a. Is the sequence of numbers an arithmetic sequence, a geometric sequence, or neither?

   b. What expression for the function $d(n)$ will generate the numbers in the pattern for any whole number n?

25. The sum of degree measures for interior angles of a convex polygon is given by a linear equation. For a polygon with n sides, that equation is $s(n) = 180(n - 2)$ for $n = 3, 4, 5, \ldots$

   a. What are the values of $s(3)$, $s(4)$, $s(5)$, and $s(6)$?

   b. Is the sequence of angle sums an arithmetic sequence, a geometric sequence, or neither?

   c. Find $s(1)$ and $s(2)$. Explain why these values make sense in the sequence of numbers but do not make sense for polygons.

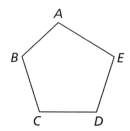

For a pentagon,
$m\angle A + m\angle B + m\angle C + m\angle D + m\angle E = 180°(n - 2)$
$= 540°$

26. Determine whether each function family will generate arithmetic sequences when their domains are restricted to the positive integers 1, 2, 3, 4, 5, ...?

   a. linear functions $f(x) = mx + b$

   b. quadratic functions $g(x) = ax^2 + bx + c$

   c. exponential functions $h(x) = a(b^x)$

   d. inverse variation functions $j(x) = \frac{k}{x}$

   e. Which types of functions will generate geometric sequences when their domains are restricted to the positive integers 1, 2, 3, 4, 5, ...?

Extensions

27. One way to determine whether a pattern might be a geometric sequence is to look at the ratio of successive terms $\frac{f(n)}{f(n-1)}$.

   a. Copy the table below and calculate ratios to complete it. Give answers as decimals accurate to 2 places.

Ratios for Terms of the Fibonacci Sequence

n	1	2	3	4	5	6	7	8	9	10
$f(n)$	1	1	2	3	5	8	13	21	34	55
$\frac{f(n)}{f(n-1)}$	■	■	■	■	■	■	■	■	■	■

   b. Mathematicians have proven that as terms of the Fibonacci Sequence continue, the ratio $\frac{f(n)}{f(n-1)}$ gets closer and closer to the number $\frac{1+\sqrt{5}}{2}$. This number is called the *golden ratio*. Do your results in part (a) support that claim?

28. A sequence begins 1, 2, ... and obeys the equation $g(n) = g(n-1) - g(n-2)$. Find the first 10 terms of the sequence.

In the Odds Are quiz show your total payoff will be the sum of the payoffs for all questions answered correctly. For example, if you answer the first three questions correctly, your payoff will be

$$S_3 = 100 + 300 + 500 \quad \text{so} \quad S_3 = a_1 + a_2 + a_3$$

For any sequences with terms $a_1 + a_2 + a_3, \ldots$ there is a related sequence of partial sums $S_1, S_2, S_3, \ldots$ defined in the same way.

29. For each arithmetic sequence in parts (a)–(c), write seven terms of the associated sequence of partial sums. Then tell whether that sequence of partial sums is an arithmetic sequence or some other familiar type of sequence.

   a. $1, 2, 3, 4, 5, 6, 7, \ldots$

   b. $5, 10, 15, 20, 25, 30, 35, \ldots$

   c. $20, 15, 10, 5, 0, -5, -10, \ldots$

   d. The sum of the first n terms of any arithmetic sequence is given by the formula $S_n = \left(\frac{n}{2}\right)(a_1 + a_n)$. Use the formula to find the sum of the first seven terms in each arithmetic sequence of parts (a)–(c). Compare your results from using the formula with your results from adding the first seven terms.

30. For each geometric sequence in parts (a)–(c), write seven terms of the associated sequence of partial sums. Then tell whether that sequence of partial sums is a geometric sequence or some other familiar type of sequence.

   a. $1, 2, 4, 8, 16, 32, 64, \ldots$

   b. $729, 243, 81, 27, 9, 3, 1, \ldots$

   c. $1, -2, 4, -8, 16, -32, 64, \ldots$

   d. The sum of the first n terms of any geometric sequence is given by the formula $S_n = a_1\left(\frac{1 - r^n}{1 - r}\right)$. In this formula, the first term is a_1, and the common ratio r relates successive terms. Use the formula to find the sum of the first seven terms in each geometric sequence of parts (a)–(c). Compare your results from using the formula with your results from adding the first seven terms.

Mathematical Reflections 2

In this Investigation, you studied a variety of number patterns that were examples of arithmetic and geometric sequences. The questions below will help you summarize what you have learned.

Think about these questions. Discuss your ideas with other students and your teacher. Then write a summary of your findings in your notebook.

1. **a. Describe** the defining properties of an arithmetic sequence.

   b. What examples would you give to illustrate the idea for someone?

2. **a. Describe** the defining properties of a geometric sequence.

   b. What examples would you give to illustrate the idea for someone?

3. **How** are arithmetic and geometric sequences related to linear and exponential functions?

Common Core Mathematical Practices

As you worked on the Problems in this Investigation, you used prior knowledge to make sense of them. You also applied Mathematical Practices to solve the Problems. Think back over your work, the ways you thought about the Problems, and how you used Mathematical Practices.

Nick described his thoughts in the following way:

> When we worked with the number sequence −100, 100, 300, 500, . . . it helped to model the pattern in two ways.
>
> The equation $a(n + 1) − a(n) = 200$ showed the constant difference between terms. The equation $a(n) = −300 + 200n$ showed the same constant difference and the first term.
>
> ···
> **Common Core Standards for Mathematical Practice**
> **MP4** Model with mathematics.

 • What other Mathematical Practices can you identify in Nick's reasoning?

• Describe a Mathematical Practice that you and your classmates used to solve a different Problem in this Investigation.

3 Transforming Graphs, Equations, and Functions

In earlier work you have studied many examples of quadratic functions. Their rules used a variety of algebraic expressions in the form $ax^2 + bx + c$. The following diagram shows graphs of several examples, including a simple quadratic function, $f(x) = x^2$. All quadratic function graphs and expressions can be produced by transformations of the graph and expression for the function $f(x) = x^2$.

Four Quadratic Functions

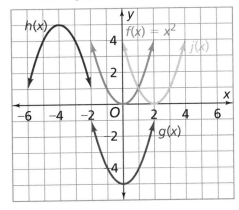

The Problems of this Investigation will develop your ability to apply transformations for quadratic functions. These transformations can be applied to other important families of functions. The explanations of how the equations and graphs transform will draw on what you know about geometric transformations and their coordinate rules.

....

Common Core State Standards

F-IF.C.7a Graph linear and quadratic functions and show intercepts, maxima, and minima.

F-IF.C.9 Compare properties of two functions each represented in a different way (algebraically, graphically, numerically, in tables, or by verbal descriptions).

F-BF.B.3 Identify the effect on the graph of replacing $f(x)$ by $f(x) + k$, $k\,f(x)$, $f(kx)$, and $f(x + k)$ for specific values of k (both positive and negative); find the value of k given the graphs. Experiment with cases and illustrate an explanation of the effects on the graph using technology.

Also A-SSE.B.3b, F-IF.B.4

3.1 Sliding Up and Down
Vertical Translations of Functions

The next diagram shows graphs of three functions. Their graphs are related to each other by translation up and down.

Three Quadratic Functions

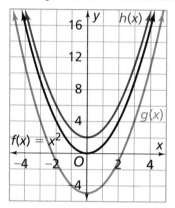

- What are the coordinate rules for translating the graph of *f(x)* onto the graphs of *g(x)* and *h(x)*?

- Can you use information from these coordinate rules to write algebraic expressions for calculating values of *g(x)* and *h(x)*?

Problem 3.1

A Complete a table of sample values for the functions $f(x)$, $g(x)$, and $h(x)$ graphed above.

Values for Three Quadratic Functions

x	−4	−3	−2	−1	0	1	2	3	4
$f(x) = x^2$	16	9	4	▪	▪	▪	▪	▪	▪
$g(x)$	▪	▪	▪	▪	▪	▪	▪	▪	▪
$h(x)$	▪	▪	▪	▪	▪	▪	▪	▪	▪

Problem 3.1 *continued*

B Write rules for translations that map the graph of $f(x) = x^2$ onto the other two graphs.

    1. $f(x) \rightarrow g(x)$ has rule $(x, y) \rightarrow (\blacksquare, \blacksquare)$.

    2. $f(x) \rightarrow h(x)$ has rule $(x, y) \rightarrow (\blacksquare, \blacksquare)$.

C Based on the results of your work in Questions A and B:

    1. What algebraic expression shows how to calculate values for $g(x)$?

    2. What algebraic expression shows how to calculate values for $h(x)$?

D This diagram shows graphs of four linear functions, including $f(x) = x$.

Four Linear Functions

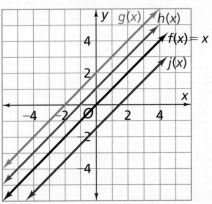

For $g(x)$, $h(x)$, and $j(x)$:

- Write the rule for the translation that maps the graph of $f(x) = x$ onto it.

- Write an algebraic expression that shows how to calculate values for the second function.

E Suppose that you are studying two functions $f(x)$ and $g(x)$. Using the rule $(x, y) \rightarrow (x, y + k)$, you can translate $f(x)$ onto $g(x)$. What equation relates the values of $f(x)$ and $g(x)$ for all values of x?

A C E Homework starts on page 58.

3.2 Stretching and Flipping Up and Down

Multiplicative Transformations of Functions

Suppose that you transformed the graph of $y = x^2$ by mapping each point (x, y) to the image point (x, ky). The image graph would be related to the original graph. The next diagram shows graphs of two quadratic functions related to $f(x) = x^2$ in that way.

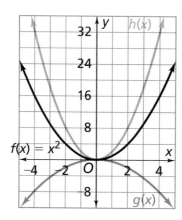

 Can you see a way to find algebraic expressions for calculating output values of the functions $g(x)$ and $h(x)$?

Study the functions in the diagram. Think about how stretching or shrinking a graph vertically changes its algebraic expression. Compare the new algebraic expression to the old expression.

Problem 3.2

A Complete a table of sample values for the functions $f(x)$, $g(x)$, and $h(x)$ graphed above.

x	−4	−3	−2	−1	0	1	2	3	4
$f(x) = x^2$	16	9	4	1	0	1	4	9	16
$g(x)$	■	■	■	■	0	■	■	■	■
$h(x)$	■	■	■	■	0	■	■	■	■

Problem **3.2** *continued*

B Write rules that map $f(x) = x^2$ onto the other graphs.

    1. $f(x) \rightarrow g(x)$ has rule $(x, y) \rightarrow (\blacksquare, \blacksquare)$.

    2. $f(x) \rightarrow h(x)$ has rule $(x, y) \rightarrow (\blacksquare, \blacksquare)$.

C Based on the results of your work in Questions A and B:

    1. What algebraic expression could you use for calculating values of $g(x)$?

    2. What algebraic expression could you use for calculating values of $h(x)$?

D The graph of a piecewise-defined function $s(t)$ is shown below.

s(t)

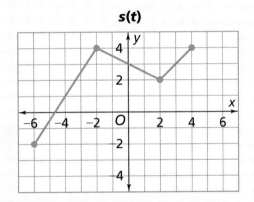

On the same coordinate grid, graph functions $p(t)$, $q(t)$, and $r(t)$ with these properties:

    1. $p(t) = 3s(t)$ for all values of t.

    2. $q(t) = 0.5s(t)$ for all values of t.

    3. $r(t) = -s(t)$ for all values of t.

E Study the effects of changing constants in the algebraic expression for the linear function $f(x) = ax$. Do the same for the quadratic function $g(x) = bx^2$. Use a graphing calculator or a technology tool.

F Two functions are related by the equation $g(x) = kf(x)$ for all values of x. How are their graphs related?

A **C** **E** Homework starts on page 58.

3.3 Sliding Left and Right
Horizontal Translations of Functions

In Problem 3.1, you discovered how algebraic expressions are related if the graphs of those functions are related by translating vertically. There are similar connections between functions if their graphs are related by horizontal translations.

$f(x) = x^2$ and Two Translations

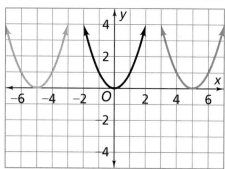

- How can you write algebraic expressions for calculating values of the other two functions?

The relationship between functions with graphs that are vertical translations of each other was clear. For horizontal translations, there is a different relationship between functions and graphs. See if you can determine a pattern as you work through the Problem.

Problem 3.3

Ⓐ The functions with graphs shown above are translations of $f(x) = x^2$ with rules $g(x) = (x + 5)^2$ and $h(x) = (x - 5)^2$.

1. Which is the graph of $g(x)$? $h(x)$? Explain.

2. Sketch by hand graphs of $j(x) = (x + 3)^2$ and $k(x) = (x - 2.5)^2$. Explain how you know that your sketches are accurate. Test your thinking with a graphing calculator or online tool. Adjust your ideas as needed.

Problem **3.3** *continued*

B Use the diagram below.

1. Which graph represents the function $g(x) = f(x + 3)$ for all x? Explain.

2. Which graph represents the function $h(x) = f(x - 3)$ for all x? Explain.

Two Horizontal Translations of Piecewise-Defined Function $f(x)$

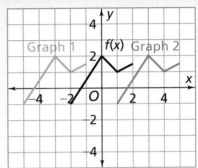

C Think about your results for Questions A and B. Suppose you are given a graph of a function $f(x)$ and a positive number k. Explain what you could say about the shape and location of graphs for these related functions.

1. $g(x) = f(x - k)$ for all x.

2. $h(x) = f(x + k)$ for all x.

D 1. Match each graph with the function it represents. Do not use a graphing calculator or online graphing tool. Justify your reasoning.

$f(x) = (x - 3)^2 - 1$

$g(x) = (x + 3)^2 - 4$

$h(x) = -(x + 2)^2 + 9$

$j(x) = -(x - 2)^2 + 4$

Graphs of Four Functions

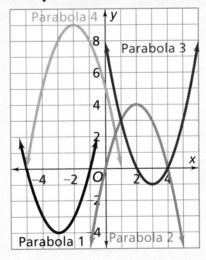

2. Explain the effects of changing a, b, and c in $f(x) = a(x - b)^2 + c$. Use a graphing calculator or online software to test the changes.

continued on the next page >

Problem 3.3 *continued*

E If m and k are positive numbers, explain what you could say about the shape and location of graphs for these related functions.

1. $r(x) = f(x + k) + m$ for all x.   **2.** $s(x) = f(x - k) + m$ for all x.

3. $t(x) = f(x - k) - m$ for all x.   **4.** $u(x) = f(x + k) - m$ for all x.

Ⓐ Ⓒ Ⓔ Homework starts on page 58.

3.4 Getting From Here to There
Transforming $y = x^2$

In Problems 3.1, 3.2, and 3.3 you discovered how changes in quadratic function rules lead to changes in their graphs. Suppose a, b, and c represent any positive numbers. You should be able to predict the shape and location for any graph in the forms:

- $f(x) = a(x + b)^2 + c$
- $g(x) = a(x + b)^2 - c$
- $h(x) = a(x - b)^2 + c$
- $j(x) = a(x - b)^2 - c$

Think back to your work in *Frogs, Fleas, and Painted Cubes*. In that Unit, you first solved problems involving quadratic expressions and graphs. You located the lines of symmetry and maximum or minimum points of those graphs.

Think more about the relationship between function rules and graphs for quadratic functions. The following Problem provides an opportunity to further develop and extend your understanding.

Problem 3.4

Answer the questions below. Check your ideas by graphing the function.

A For each of these functions, find the line of symmetry. Identify the coordinates of the maximum or minimum point on its graph. Write down any patterns you notice.

1. $f(x) = x^2$ **2.** $g(x) = x^2 + 3$ **3.** $h(x) = x^2 - 5$

4. $f(x) = -x^2$ **5.** $g(x) = -x^2 + 3$ **6.** $h(x) = -x^2 - 5$

Problem 3.4 continued

B For each of these functions, find the line of symmetry. Identify the coordinates of the maximum or minimum point on its graph. Write down any patterns you notice.

1. $f(x) = (x - 4)^2$ **2.** $g(x) = (x + 3)^2$

3. $h(x) = (x - 4)^2 - 5$ **4.** $j(x) = (x + 3)^2 - 1$

5. $k(x) = -(x - 4)^2 - 5$ **6.** $h(x) = -(x + 3)^2 + 2$

C For each of these functions, find the line of symmetry. Identify the coordinates of the maximum or minimum point on its graph. Write down any patterns you notice.

1. $f(x) = 2x^2$ **2.** $g(x) = 4x^2 + 3$

3. $h(x) = -3x^2 - 5$ **4.** $j(x) = 0.5(x - 4)^2$

5. $k(x) = 2(x + 3)^2$ **6.** $m(x) = -3(x - 4)^2$

7. $j(x) = 0.5(x - 4)^2 + 2$ **8.** $k(x) = -2(x + 3)^2 - 1$

9. $m(x) = -3(x - 4)^2 - 5$

D Suppose a and b are non-negative numbers (i.e. $a \geq 0$ and $b \geq 0$). For parts (1)–(4), find the following:

- line of symmetry

- coordinates of the maximum or minimum point on the graph

1. $f(x) = a(x + b)^2 + c$ **2.** $f(x) = a(x - b)^2 + c$

3. $f(x) = -a(x + b)^2 + c$ **4.** $f(x) = -a(x - b)^2 + c$

Note on Notation The functions in parts (1)–(4) differ only by where the positive and negative signs are placed in their rules. The symbol $\pm$ can be used to express all four cases in a short form. The notation "± 5" means "+5 or −5". The notation "$\pm a$" means "the number a and its additive inverse." So, "$f(x) = \pm a(x \pm b)^2 + c$" indicates four different cases.

E The maximum or minimum point on the graph of a quadratic function is called the *vertex*. Why do you think $f(x) = a(x \pm b)^2 \pm c$ is called the *vertex form* of a quadratic function?

A C E Homework starts on page 58.

Applications

Exercises 1–9 refer to the graph of a function $f(x)$.
On copies of the graph, draw graphs of these functions.

Graph of f(x)

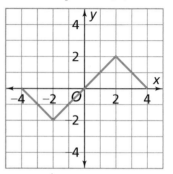

1. $g(x) = f(x) + 2$

2. $h(x) = f(x) - 1$

3. $j(x) = 0.5f(x)$

4. $k(x) = 1.5f(x)$

5. $m(x) = -2f(x)$

6. $n(x) = f(x - 1)$

7. $p(x) = f(x + 0.5)$

8. $q(x) = -2f(x) + 1$

9. $r(x) = f(x - 1) + 2$

10. Match each function with its graph. Explain how you made each
match. Give coordinates of the maximum or minimum point on each
graph. Be prepared to explain how you can find that information
from just the function rule.

a. $a(x) = x^2$

b. $b(x) = (x - 2)^2$

c. $c(x) = -(x - 2)^2 - 2$

d. $d(x) = (x + 2)^2 - 2$

e. $e(x) = 0.5x^2$

f. $f(x) = 1.5x^2$

g. $g(x) = -(x - 3)^2$

h. $h(x) = -x^2 - 2$

Parabolas 1 and 2

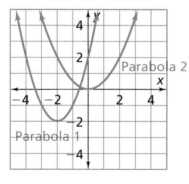

Parabolas 3 and 4

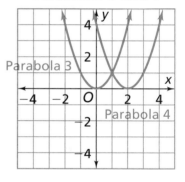

Parabolas 5 and 6

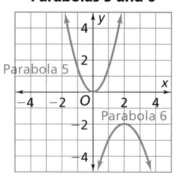

Parabolas 7 and 8

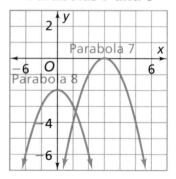

Connections

Exercises 11–15 refer to the following figure.

Five Transformations of a Flag

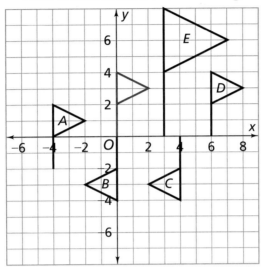

For each flag:

- Give the coordinate rule $(x, y) \rightarrow (\blacksquare, \blacksquare)$ for the transformation that maps the red flag to the given flag.

- Identify the kind of transformation(s) involved.

11. Flag A

12. Flag B

13. Flag C

14. Flag D

15. Flag E

Extensions

16. The function $f(x) = x^2 - 4x - 5$ can also be expressed as $f(x) = (x - 5)(x + 1)$ and $f(x) = (x - 2)^2 - 9$.

    a. Use algebraic reasoning to show that the three expressions are equivalent.

    b. Find the y-intercept, x-intercept(s), line of symmetry, and maximum or minimum point on the graph of $f(x)$. Explain which algebraic expression makes each calculation easiest.

17. a. Suppose $g(x) = f(2x)$ when $f(x) = x^2 - 4x - 5$. Find the standard expression for $g(x)$.

    Hint: Replace each occurrence of x in $x^2 - 4x - 5$ with $2x$. Simplify the result.

    b. Sketch a graph that shows both $f(x)$ and $g(x) = f(2x)$ on the same axes.

    c. Find the y-intercept, x-intercept(s), line of symmetry, and maximum or minimum point on the graph of $g(x)$.

    d. How does replacement of x with $2x$ seem to change the graph of $f(x)$? The properties of $f(x)$?

18. a. Suppose $g(x) = f(0.5x)$ when $f(x) = x^2 - 4x - 5$. Find the standard expression for $g(x)$.

    b. Sketch a graph that shows both $f(x)$ and $g(x) = f(0.5x)$ on the same axes.

    c. Find the y-intercept, x-intercept(s), line of symmetry, and maximum or minimum point on the graph of $g(x)$.

    d. How does replacement of x with $0.5x$ seem to change the graph of $f(x)$? The properties of $f(x)$?

19. Think about your work on Exercises 17–18. How do you think the graph of $g(x) = f(kx)$ is related to that of $f(x)$?

20. Test your conjecture in Exercise 19. Draw and compare graphs of these pairs of functions.

    a. $f(x) = x^2$ and $f(3x) = (3x)^2$

    b. $f(x) = x^2 - 1$ and $f(0.5x) = (0.5x)^2 - 1$

    c. $f(x) = x^2 - 6x$ and $f(2x) = 4x^2 - 12x$

Mathematical Reflections 3

In this Investigation, you studied the relationships between functions whose graphs are related by various familiar geometric transformations. These questions will help you summarize what you have learned.

Think about your answers. Discuss your ideas with other students and your teacher. Then write a summary of your findings in your notebook.

1. **How** will the rule for a function $f(x)$ change if the graph is:

   a. Translated up or down by k?

   b. Stretched away from or toward the x-axis by a factor of k?

   c. Translated left or right by k?

2. **How** does the vertex form of a quadratic equation like $f(x) = (x - h)^2 + k$ (where h and k are positive numbers) help to sketch the graph of the function?

Common Core Mathematical Practices

As you worked on the Problems in this Investigation, you used prior knowledge to make sense of them. You also applied Mathematical Practices to solve the Problems. Think back over your work, the ways you thought about the Problems, and how you used Mathematical Practices.

Shawna described her thoughts in the following way:

In Problem 3.3 we had trouble understanding why the graph of $f(x + 3)$ would be 3 units left of the graph of $f(x)$.

We looked at several examples, like $g(x) = (x + 1.5)^2$ and $h(x) = (x - 1.5)^2$. We could see that the graph of $g(x)$ would be 1.5 units left of $f(x) = x^2$, but we could not figure out why.

Eventually we figured out the meaning of the function rule $g(x) = f(x + 3)$. Each point on the graph of $g(x)$ is the same height as a corresponding point on the graph of $f(x)$. The graph of $f(x)$, however, is 3 units to the right. So the graph of $g(x)$ must be identical to that of $f(x)$, but 3 units to the left.

It might be easier to just memorize this, but it we wanted to understand why it worked.

··

Common Core Standards for Mathematical Practice

MP1 Make sense of problems and persevere in solving them.

- What other Mathematical Practices can you identify in Shawna's reasoning?

- Describe a Mathematical Practice that you and your classmates used to solve a different Problem.

Solving Quadratic Equations Algebraically

In *Frogs, Fleas and Painted Cubes*, you learned to solve quadratic equations such as $(x - 2)(x - 1) = 0$. You also learned that you can write quadratic functions in different ways using equivalent expressions. Each equivalent form of the expression provides different information about the function.

Three Forms of Quadratic Functions

Form:	Standard	Factored	Vertex
Function	$f(x) = ax^2 + bx + c$	$g(x) = (x - m)(x - n)$	$h(x) = a(x - p)^2 + q$
Characteristics Revealed	y-intercept at $(0, c)$	zeros at $(m, 0)$ and $(n, 0)$	vertex at (p, q)
Example	$f(x) = 2x^2 + 4x + 1$ has y-intercept $(0, 1)$.	$g(x) = (x - 3)(x - 4)$ has zeros $(3, 0)$, $(4, 0)$.	$h(x) = (x - 3)^2 + 1$ has vertex $(3, 1)$.

$f(x) = 2x^2 + 4x + 1$

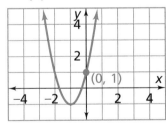

$g(x) = (x - 3)(x - 4)$

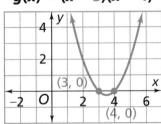

$h(x) = (x - 3)^2 + 1$

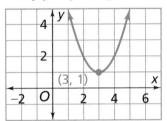

Common Core State Standards

A-SSE.B.3b Complete the square in a quadratic expression to reveal the maximum or minimum value of the function it defines.

A-REI.B.4b Solve quadratic equations by inspection, taking square roots, completing the square, the quadratic formula, and factoring, as appropriate to the initial form of the equation. Recognize when the quadratic formula gives complex solutions and write them as $a \pm bi$ for real numbers a and b.

Also A-REI.B.4, A-REI.B.4a, A-SSE.A.1b, A-SSE.B.3, F-IF.C.8a

You can use your knowledge of different quadratic forms to find more strategies for solving quadratic equations. Graphing is one possible strategy for solving.

$f(x) = x^2$ and $g(x) = (x - 3)^2$

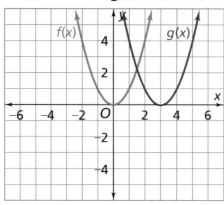

- If $f(x) = x^2$, how would you solve $x^2 = 4$ from the graph of $f(x)$?

- If $g(x) = (x - 3)^2$, how would you solve $(x - 3)^2 = 4$ from the graph of $g(x)$?

- What points on $f(x)$ and $g(x)$ correspond to your solutions?

- How are these points related?

4.1 Applying Square Roots

Anita says she can solve $x^2 = 4$ and $(x - 3)^2 = 4$ without using a graph. She calls her strategy, *Take the Square Root*. Her work is shown below.

> **Take the Square Root**
> $x^2 = 4$
> $\sqrt{x^2} = \sqrt{4}$
> $x = 2$

Tawanda says she can amend Anita's strategy so it finds both solutions for $x^2 = 4$.

> **Amended Strategy**
> $x^2 = 4$
> $\sqrt{x^2} = \pm\sqrt{4}$
> $x = \sqrt{4}$ or $x = -\sqrt{4}$
> $x = 2$ or $x = -2$

Tawanda is using one of the *properties of equality*. The property states that you can take the square root of both sides of an equation. If you do, then the new equation formed has the same solutions as the original equation.

- Using Tawanda's amended strategy, what are the algebraic solutions for $(x - 3)^2 = 4$?

- How do these algebraic solutions compare to the graphical solutions for $(x - 3)^2 = 4$?

- Can you use Anita's amended *Take the Square Root* strategy to solve any quadratic equation?

As you use algebraic and graphing strategies to solve quadratic equations, look for connections among your strategies.

Problem 4.1

A **1.** Use a symbolic method to solve these equations.

    a. $(x + 1)^2 = 9$ **b.** $(x - 3)^2 = 0.25$ **c.** $(x + 0.5)^2 = 4$

2. **a.** Graph $h(x) = (x + 1)^2$ using a graphing tool. Where on the graph do you look for the solutions for $(x + 1)^2 = 9$? What are the solutions?

    b. Graph $j(x) = (x + 1)^2 - 9$ using a graphing tool. Where on the graph do you look for the solutions for $(x + 1)^2 - 9 = 0$? Give the solutions.

    c. How are the graphical solutions for $(x + 1)^2 = 9$ and $(x + 1)^2 - 9 = 0$ related to each other?

3. Solve symbolically. Then check your solutions graphically. In each case, explain how your solutions relate to the line of symmetry.

    a. $(x - 3)^2 - 4 = 0$ **b.** $(x - 3)^2 - 2 = 0$

B Kailey says she could have solved $(x + 1)^2 = 9$ without graphing or taking square roots. She calls her method a *Factoring Strategy*.

Factoring Strategy

$$(x + 1)^2 = 9$$
$$(x + 1)(x + 1) = 9$$
$$x^2 + 2x + 1 = 9$$
$$x^2 + 2x - 8 = 0$$
$$(x + 4)(x - 2) = 0$$

How does Kailey finish her method? Do her solutions agree with your answer to Question A, part (1)?

continued on the next page >

Problem **4.1** *continued*

C Use Kailey's method or Anita's method to solve these quadratic equations. If neither strategy works, explain why.

1. $(x + 4)^2 = 25$ 2. $(x - 4)^2 = 5$

3. $x^2 + 8x - 9 = 0$ 4. $x^2 + 8x + 7 = 0$

5. $x^2 - 6x + 9 = 0$ 6. $(x + 2)^2 = 2$

7. $x^2 + 4x + 4 = 2$ 8. $x^2 + 4x = 4$

D When does Kailey's factoring method work? When does Anita's square root method work? When does graphing work?

A C E Homework starts on page 76.

4.2 Completing the Square

In Problem 4.1, you were able to solve many different quadratic equations. Some equations, however, cannot be solved using the symbolic methods discussed in Problem 4.1. Consider the quadratic equation below.

$$x^2 + 4x = 4 \text{ or } x^2 + 4x - 4 = 0$$

- Suppose $f(x) = x^2 + 4x - 4$. What do we know about the graph of this function?

Suppose you could write this function in vertex form. Then you would know more about the graph of this function. Start by plotting some points and drawing a graph. You can then determine the vertex form from the graph you drew.

f(x) = x² + 4x − 4

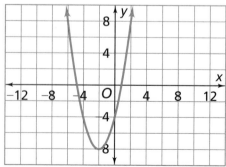

- Explain how you can tell the vertex form of the function is $f(x) = (x + 2)^2 - 8$ from the graph.

- How can you use the graph to find the solutions for $(x + 2)^2 - 8 = 0$?

From the vertex form of the equation you can find solutions for $(x + 2)^2 - 8 = 0$ symbolically.

$$(x + 2)^2 = 8$$
$$\sqrt{(x + 2)^2} = \pm\sqrt{8}$$
$$(x + 2) = \sqrt{8} \quad \text{or} \quad (x + 2) = -\sqrt{8}$$
$$x = -2 + \sqrt{8} \quad \text{or} \quad x = -2 - \sqrt{8}$$

- How are these solutions like or unlike the solutions you found graphically?

- How are these solutions related to the line of symmetry of the graph of $f(x)$?

- How can we take any quadratic equation, like $x^2 + 4x - 4 = 0$, and rewrite it in a vertex form?

There is a way to write any quadratic equation in a vertex form. The key is to recognize the pattern for the expanded form of a perfect square like $(x + 2)^2$.

Problem 4.2

A In parts (1) and (2), look for patterns that help you recognize perfect square quadratic expressions.

1. Write each expression in equivalent standard form, $ax^2 + bx + c$.

a. $(x + 1)^2$ **b.** $(x - 3)^2$ **c.** $(x + 6)^2$ **d.** $(x - 0.2)^2$

2. Write each of these expressions in equivalent factored form.

a. $x^2 + 8x + 16$ **b.** $x^2 + 6x + 9$

c. $x^2 - 18x + 81$ **d.** $x^2 - 10x + 25$

3. a. What value of c would make $x^2 + 12x + c$ a perfect square? Explain your reasoning.

    b. What value of b would make $x^2 + bx + 49$ a perfect square? Explain your reasoning.

B Brendan can use the pattern for $(x + a)^2$ to rewrite any quadratic expression in vertex form. Then he uses the vertex form to solve any quadratic equation. For example, he wants to solve $x^2 + 4x + 3 = 0$. His work is shown below.

$$x^2 + 4x + 3 = 0$$
"$x^2 + 4x$" looks like the beginning of the perfect square $x^2 + 4x + 4$.
$$x^2 + 4x + 4 - 4 + 3 = 0$$

1. Is this still equivalent to $x^2 + 4x + 3 = 0$? Explain.

2. Next he writes
$$(x^2 + 4x + 4) - 4 + 3 = 0$$
$$(x + 2)^2 - 1 = 0$$

Where did the "-1" come from?

3. How would you finish Brendan's method?

Problem **4.2** | *continued*

C Try Brendan's method on the following quadratic equations.

1. $x^2 + 6x + 5 = 0$ **2.** $x^2 - 8x + 11 = 0$

3. $x^2 + 4x - 4 = 0$ **4.** $x^2 - 6x - 1 = 0$

D Brendan's method for rewriting $x^2 + 4x + 3 = 0$ involves adding a 4 and subtracting a 4 on the left side of the equation. He ends up with $(x + 2)^2 - 1$ in place of $x^2 + 4x - 3$. The diagram shows a square with sides $(x + 2)$ and area $(x + 2)^2$.

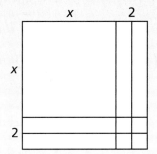

1. a. On a copy of the square, locate $(x + 2)^2 - 1$ in the picture. Shade this in one color.

   b. Explain how this picture shows that $x^2 + 4x + 3$ and $(x + 2)^2 - 1$ are equivalent.

2. Make a sketch that shows that $(x + 3)^2 - 2$ and $x^2 + 6x + 7$ are equivalent.

3. Use the sketch below to find an equivalent expression for $x^2 + 8x + 3$.

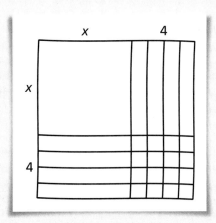

4. Draw a square that will help you find an equivalent expression in vertex form for $x^2 + 6x + 8$.

5. Consider the standard form for quadratic expressions, $x^2 + bx + c$. Is it always possible to find an equivalent expression in vertex form? Explain.

6. How does completing the square in a quadratic expression reveal the maximum or minimum value of the related quadratic function?

A C E Homework starts on page 76.

4.3 The Quadratic Formula

The quadratic equation $x^2 - 6x + 4 = 0$ can be written in equivalent vertex form as $(x - 3)^2 - 5 = 0$. This leads to a solution of the equation symbolically and graphically.

$$f(x) = (x - 3)^2 - 5$$

$$(x - 3)^2 - 5 = 0$$
$$(x - 3)^2 = 5$$
$$x - 3 = \pm\sqrt{5}$$
$$x = 3 \pm \sqrt{5}$$
$$x \approx 5.24 \text{ or}$$
$$x \approx 0.76$$

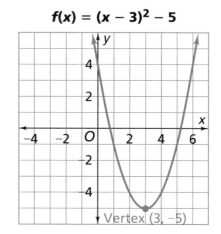

- Why are $x = 5.24$ and $x = 0.76$ approximate solutions for $x^2 - 6x + 4 = 0$?

- How are the exact solutions $3 + \sqrt{5}$ and $3 - \sqrt{5}$ represented on the graph?

- You can complete the square to rewrite $f(x) = x^2 - 6x + 4$ as $f(x) = (x - 3)^2 - 5$. How does that identify the zeros and the maximum or minimum point of the function?

This approach to solving quadratic equations works when it only takes a few steps to find the vertex form of the given quadratic expression. There are many cases, however, where this same approach requires many more steps. Let us now consider a more efficient method.

Completing the square is more complicated when the coefficient of the x^2 is not 1. Consider $3x^2 + 5x + 1 = 0$.

Mathematicians have developed a general formula to solve quadratic equations. This formula is called the **Quadratic Formula.** This formula calculates the solutions to any quadratic equation in the form $ax^2 + bx + c = 0$ when $a \neq 0$. The formula says solutions will be:

$$x = \frac{-b}{2a} + \frac{\sqrt{b^2 - 4ac}}{2a} \text{ and } x = \frac{-b}{2a} - \frac{\sqrt{b^2 - 4ac}}{2a}$$

The Quadratic Formula may look like a complicated procedure for solving equations. It is only a matter of matching and substituting the coefficients. Then you perform the arithmetic using the Order of Operations.

- Explain how the formula gives these solutions to the equation $3x^2 + 5x + 1 = 0$.

$$x = \frac{-5}{6} + \frac{\sqrt{13}}{6} \text{ and } x = \frac{-5}{6} - \frac{\sqrt{13}}{6}.$$

Problem 4.3

A In parts (1)–(6), use the Quadratic Formula to solve these quadratic equations.

1. $2x^2 + 9x + 6 = 0$

2. $4x^2 + 3x - 5 = 0$

3. $-3x^2 + 5x + 1 = 0$

4. $-2x^2 + 7x - 6 = 0$

5. $12 + 18x + 4x^2 = 0$

6. $-3x + 4x^2 - 5 = 0$

continued on the next page >

Problem 4.3 *continued*

B You can also use **completing the square** to solve all of the equations in Question A. However, this process would take many steps. You can use completing the square to develop the Quadratic Formula. This formula can be used to solve any quadratic equation. To see why the formula works, Kalvin starts with an example.

1. Kalvin begins to solve $2x^2 + 9x + 6 = 0$ by completing the square. His work is shown below.

$$2x^2 + 9x + 6 = 0$$

$$2\left(x^2 + \frac{9}{2}x + 3\right) = 0 \quad \text{Factor 2 out of each}$$
$$\text{term on the left.}$$

$$x^2 + \frac{9}{2}x + 3 = 0$$

Need to write above equation in vertex form.

$$x^2 + \frac{9}{2}x + \left(\frac{9}{4}\right)^2 - \left(\frac{9}{4}\right)^2 + 3 = 0$$

Complete this to find solutions for x.

2. Follow the same logic Kalvin used in part (1). Complete the reasoning on both sides of the table. Provide reasons for each step.

Developing the Quadratic Formula

$2x^2 + 9x + 6 = 0$	$ax^2 + bx + c = 0$	Reasons
$2\left(x^2 + \left(\frac{9}{2}\right)x + 3\right) = 0$	$a\left(x^2 + \left(\frac{b}{a}\right)x + \frac{c}{a}\right) = 0$	■
$x^2 + \left(\frac{9}{2}\right)x + 3 = 0$	$x^2 + \left(\frac{b}{a}\right)x + \frac{c}{a} = 0$	■
$x^2 + \left(\frac{9}{2}\right)x + \left(\frac{9}{4}\right)^2 - \left(\frac{9}{4}\right)^2 + 3 = 0$	$x^2 + \left(\frac{b}{a}\right)x + \left(\frac{b}{2a}\right)^2 - \left(\frac{b}{2a}\right)^2 + \frac{c}{a} = 0$	■
$\left(x + \frac{9}{4}\right)^2 - \frac{33}{16} = 0$	$(x + ■)^2 - ■ = 0$	■
■	■	■
■	■	■
$x = ■$ or $x = ■$	$x = ■$ or $x = ■$	■

Problem 4.3 *continued*

C Choose a different strategy to solve each of these quadratic equations, if possible.

1. $(x - 4)^2 - 9 = 0$ **2.** $2x^2 + 5x - 2 = 0$

3. $x^2 + 1 = 0$ **4.** $x^2 - 8x - 9 = 0$

ACE Homework starts on page 76.

4.4 Complex Numbers

The Quadratic Formula gives an algorithm for solving any quadratic equation in the form $ax^2 + bx + c = 0$. Sometimes you get strange results when using the formula. Consider the equation $x^2 + 4x + 5 = 0$. According to the Quadratic Formula, the solutions to that equation should be

$$x = -2 + \frac{\sqrt{-4}}{2} \text{ and } x = -2 - \frac{\sqrt{-4}}{2}.$$

The solutions require the square roots of negative numbers. What is that number? Is it a real number?

The graph of $f(x) = x^2 + 4x + 5$ shows the problem from another view.

f(x) = x² + 4x + 5

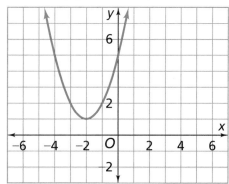

The seemingly impossible calculation required to solve $x^2 + 4x + 5 = 0$ puzzled mathematicians for thousands of years. Eventually, they decided to extend the number system. The extended number system includes the real numbers and numbers like $\sqrt{-1}$. The process began with defining a solution to the equation $x^2 + 1 = 0$.

If $x^2 + 1 = 0$, then $x^2 = -1$.

So $x = \pm\sqrt{-1}$.

In order to have a solution, we need to define a new number. This number requires the property that its square is equal to -1. We write it as the imaginary number i, where $i = \sqrt{-1}$.

All previous mathematics had suggested the impossibility of such a number. The table below shows some numbers that result from the extension of the number system.

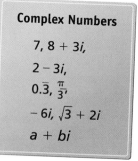

Real Numbers	Imaginary Numbers	Complex Numbers
$3, \sqrt{5},$	$i = \sqrt{-1}$	$7, 8 + 3i,$
$\frac{\pi}{3}, 2.7, \frac{4}{9},$	$7i, -i\sqrt{2},$	$2 - 3i,$
$-\sqrt{7}, 0.\overline{3}$	$6i + 7i$	$0.\overline{3}, \frac{\pi}{3},$
$a + bi\ (b = 0)$	$a + bi\ (a = 0)$	$-6i, \sqrt{3} + 2i$
		$a + bi$

The set of real numbers and the **imaginary numbers** is called the set of **complex numbers.**

  Do the operations for real numbers apply to complex numbers?

You will get some ideas about the complex number system and its operations by answering the questions that follow.

Problem 4.4

A In this Question, you will use the fact that $\sqrt{-1} = i$.

1. Explain why $(2i)^2 = -4$, so $2i$ is a square root of -4.

2. Explain why $(-3i)^2 = -9$, so $-3i$ is a square root of -9.

3. Use i to write $\sqrt{-49}$ as a complex number.

4. Use i to write $\sqrt{-\frac{4}{9}}$ as a complex number.

B 1. Explain why it makes sense that $7i + 11i = 18i$ and, in general, $bi + di = (b + d)i$.

2. Write the sum $(5 + 3i) + (6 + 4i)$ as a number in the form $a + bi$.

3. Write the difference $(5 + 3i) - (6 + 4i)$ as a number in the form $a + bi$.

C Apply what you know about multiplying binomials and the imaginary number i to find each product. Write these products as a complex number in the form $a + bi$.

1. $(5 + 3i)(6 + 4i)$

2. $(5 - 3i)(6 + 4i)$

3. $(5 + 3i)^2$

D Use the Quadratic Formula to solve these equations. Write your answers as complex numbers in the form $a + bi$.

1. $x^2 + 2x + 2 = 0$

2. $x^2 - 4x + 13 = 0$

3. $-x^2 + 8x - 17 = 0$

4. $x^2 + 6x + 11 = 0$

E For each equation from Question D, graph the corresponding quadratic function. Explain how you can tell from the graph of a quadratic function whether the related equation will have real or imaginary solutions.

A**C****E** Homework starts on page 76.

Applications

1. Solve for x.

   a. $(x - 3)^2 - 1 = 0$ **b.** $(x + 1)^2 - 4 = 0$

   c. $(x - 1)^2 - 3 = 0$ **d.** $(x + 1)^2 - 1 = 0$

   e. $4(x + 1)^2 - 4 = 0$ **f.** $4(x - 1)^2 - 3 = 0$

2. The functions below correspond to the equations you solved in Exercise 1. Use information about the vertex form and the zeroes you found in Exercise 1. Match each function to the correct graph. Explain your thinking in each case.

   a. $a(x) = (x - 3)^2 - 1$ **b.** $b(x) = (x + 1)^2 - 4$ **c.** $c(x) = (x - 1)^2 - 3$

   d. $d(x) = (x + 1)^2 - 1$ **e.** $e(x) = 4(x + 1)^2 - 4$ **f.** $f(x) = 4(x - 1)^2 - 3$

   Parabola 1

   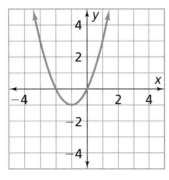

   Parabola 2

   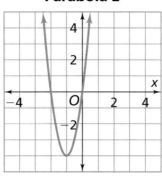

   Parabola 3

   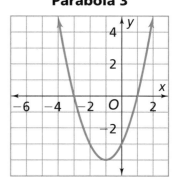

   Parabola 4

   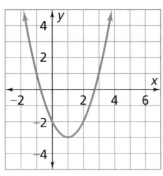

   Parabola 5

   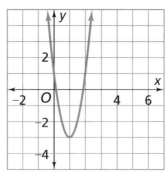

   Parabola 6

   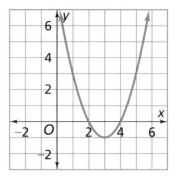

In Exercises 3–8, expand each expression to give a perfect square trinomial.

3. $(x + 7)^2$

4. $(x - 7)^2$

5. $(2x + 7)^2$

6. $(2x - 7)^2$

7. $(x + p)^2$

8. $\left(x + \dfrac{q}{s}\right)^2$

For Exercises 9–14, each quadratic function is in standard form.

- Complete the square to write each function in vertex form.
- Identify coordinates of the maximum or minimum point.
- Identify the x-intercept(s) and y-intercept.
- State which form is more convenient to identify coordinates of the maximum/minimum point, x-intercept(s), and y-intercept.

9. $f(x) = x^2 + 2x - 3$

10. $g(x) = x^2 - 4x - 5$

11. $h(x) = x^2 - 6x + 5$

12. $j(x) = x^2 + 4x + 2$

13. $k(x) = -x^2 + 3x - 1$

14. $l(x) = -x^2 + 8x - 5$

For Exercises 15–20, use the Quadratic Formula to solve the equations. Give both the exact result provided by the formula and a decimal approximation, where appropriate.

15. $5x^2 + 10x - 15 = 0$

16. $3x^2 + 2x - 7 = 0$

17. $-4x^2 + 5x - 1 = 0$

18. $7x + 3x^2 = -3$

19. $0 = 2 + 3x + x^2$

20. $3x^2 - 2 = 6x$

21. Solve the equation $x^2 - 6x + 13 = 0$. Write the solutions as complex numbers in the form $a + bi$ and $a - bi$ if needed.

Write the result of the indicated sum, difference, or product in the form of a single complex number $a + bi$.

22. $(3 + 7i) + (13 - 4i)$

23. $(3 + 7i) - (13 - 4i)$

24. $(3 + 7i)(13 - 4i)$

25. $(3 + 7i)(3 - 7i)$

Connections

26. Bianca's teacher asks her students to find a quadratic function that has zeroes at $(-2, 0)$ and $(0, 0)$.

a. Bianca says that there is only one quadratic function that fits this description. She makes the following table of values for her function. Is $f(x)$ a quadratic function? Explain.

x	-2	-1	0	1	2	3
f(x)	0	-1	0	3	8	15

b. Aleshanee says she can make a different table and different graph, with the same zeroes. Is $g(x)$ a quadratic function? Explain.

x	-2	-1	0	1	2	3
g(x)	0	-4	0	12	32	60

c. How are $f(x)$ and $g(x)$ related to each other?

27. Write expressions in vertex form, $a(x - b)^2 + c$, for functions with these properties.

a. minimum point at $(3, -5)$

b. maximum point at $(1, 4)$

c. minimum point at $(-3, 1)$

d. maximum point at $(-5, -2)$

28. Write equations that have these properties.

a. solutions are whole numbers

b. solutions are integers, but not whole numbers

c. solutions are real numbers, but not rational numbers

d. solutions are complex numbers, but not real numbers

29. In each pair of calculations, write the two results in simplest possible equivalent form. Explain how the reasoning in each case is based on number system properties.

  a. $(3 + 2i) + (7 - 3i)$ and $(3 + 2x) + (7 - 3x)$

  b. $(3 + 2i) - (7 - 3i)$ and $(3 + 2x) - (7 - 3x)$

  c. $(3 + 2i)(7 - 3i)$ and $(3 + 2x)(7 - 3x)$

  d. $-(7 - 3i)$ and $-(7 - 3x)$

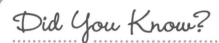

Did You Know?

In 1806, J. R. Argand developed a method for displaying complex numbers graphically. Any complex number could be displayed as a point in the coordinate plane. His method, called the *Argand Diagram*, relates the *x*-axis (real axis) with the *y*-axis (imaginary axis).
The *x*-values are real numbers *a*.
The *y*-values are imaginary numbers *bi*.

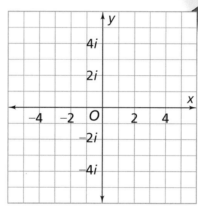

---

30. On a copy of the coordinate plane shown above, label each point with the complex number it represents.

  a. $3 + 2i$ **b.** $4 - 3i$ **c.** $-2 + 4i$ **d.** $-4 - 3i$

31. Name the geometric transformations that map points representing any complex number as indicated.

  a. $(3 + 2i) \to (3 - 2i)$ and, in general, $(a + bi) \to (a - bi)$

  b. $(3 + 2i) \to (-3 + 2i)$ and, in general, $(a + bi) \to (-a + bi)$

  c. $(3 + 2i) \to (-3 - 2i)$ and, in general, $(a + bi) \to (-a - bi)$

  d. $(3 + 2i) \to (7 + 5i)$ and, in general, $(a + bi) \to (a + 4) + (b + 3)i$

Extensions

32. The following tables each show a quadratic relationship.

x	−2	−1	0	1	2	3
f(x)	0	−1	0	3	8	15

x	−2	−1	0	1	2	3
g(x)	0	−2	0	6	16	30

a. For each table, find the function that represents the table.

b. How are the functions related to each other?

33. Alejandro and Latasia are solving the equation $4x^2 + 32x + 60 = 0$. Their methods are shown below.

Alejandro's Method

$4x^2 + 32x + 60 = 0$
$(2x + 10)(2x + 6) = 0$

OR

Latasia's Method

$4x^2 + 32x + 60 = 0$
$4(x^2 + 8x + 15) = 0$
$x^2 + 8x + 15 = 0$
$(x + 5)(x + 3) = 0$

a. What are the solutions for x using Latasia's Method?

b. What are the solutions for x using Alejandro's Method?

c. Which of the two methods is correct (*Latasia's, Alejandro's, both, or neither*)?

34. Hai and Jenna were asked to use the *completing the square* strategy to solve the equation $4x^2 + 16x - 48 = 0$.

Hai's Method

First, factor 4 from the left side to get
$$4(x^2 + 4x - 12) = 0$$

Then, solve $x^2 + 4x - 12 = 0$ like this:
$$x^2 + 4x + \blacksquare = 12$$
$$x^2 + 4x + 4 = 16$$
$$(x + 2)^2 = 16$$
$$x + 2 = 4 \text{ or } x + 2 = -4$$
$$x = -2 \text{ or } x = -6$$

OR

Jenna's Method

$$4x^2 + 16x + \blacksquare = 48$$
$$4x^2 + 16x + 64 = 48 + 64$$
$$(2x + 8)^2 = 112$$
$$2x + 8 = \pm\sqrt{112}$$
$$2x = -8 \pm\sqrt{112}$$
$$x = \frac{-8 \pm\sqrt{112}}{2}$$

Which of these two methods is correct? Explain.

35. a. You can use ideas from the Quadratic Formula proof to complete the square. These ideas cover all cases where the coefficient of x^2 is a number other than 1. Explain why each step in the process below is justified.

Step 1 $ax^2 + bx + c = a\left(x^2 + \frac{b}{a}x\right) + c$

Step 2 $= a\left(x^2 + \frac{b}{a}x + \left(\frac{b}{2a}\right)^2 - \left(\frac{b}{2a}\right)^2\right) + c$

Step 3 $= a\left(x^2 + \frac{b}{a}x + \frac{b^2}{4a^2} - \frac{b^2}{4a^2}\right) + c$

Step 4 $= a\left(x^2 + \frac{b}{a}x + \frac{b^2}{4a^2}\right) + \left(c - \frac{b^2}{4a}\right)$

Step 5 $= a\left(x + \frac{b}{2a}\right)^2 + \left(c - \frac{b^2}{4a}\right)$

b. Follow each step in the process demonstrated above to complete the square for the expression $2x^2 + 6x + 5$.

36. Use Step 5 in the process demonstrated in Exercise 35 to write each quadratic expression in equivalent vertex form.

a. $3x^2 + 5x + 7$ **b.** $-3x^2 + 5x - 7$ **c.** $6x^2 - 5x + 4$

37. For any complex number $a + bi$, the number $a - bi$ is called its **complex conjugate**. Show that the product of a complex number and its complex conjugate is always a real number. Simplify each expression below.

a. $(3 + 2i)(3 - 2i)$ **b.** $(-3 - 2i)(-3 + 2i)$ **c.** $(a + bi)(a - bi)$

38. The relationship of each complex number to its complex conjugate can be used to define division of complex numbers.

a. Explain why each step in this calculation of $(3 + 4i) \div (1 + 2i)$ makes sense.

Step 1 $\quad \dfrac{3 + 4i}{1 + 2i} = \dfrac{3 + 4i}{1 + 2i} \cdot \dfrac{1 - 2i}{1 - 2i}$

Step 2 $\quad\quad\quad = \dfrac{(3 + 4i)(1 - 2i)}{(1 + 2i)(1 - 2i)}$

Step 3 $\quad\quad\quad = \dfrac{11 - 2i}{5}$

Step 4 $\quad\quad\quad = \dfrac{11}{5} - \dfrac{2}{5}i$

b. Write $(3 + 4i) \div (1 - 2i)$ in standard complex number form $a + bi$.

c. Write $(3 - 4i) \div (1 + 2i)$ in standard complex number form $a + bi$.

39. Xavier applied what he knew about adding fractions to problems with variables in the denominator. For example, Xavier recalled that when adding $\frac{2}{3} + \frac{1}{5}$, the common denominator is $15 = 3 \cdot 5$. He used this strategy to find the sum $\frac{2}{3} + \frac{1}{a}$.

$$\text{Step 1} \quad \frac{2}{3} + \frac{1}{a} = \left(\frac{a}{a} \cdot \frac{2}{3}\right) + \left(\frac{3}{3} \cdot \frac{1}{a}\right)$$

$$\text{Step 2} \quad\quad\quad = \frac{2a}{3a} + \frac{3}{3a}$$

$$\text{Step 3} \quad\quad\quad = \frac{2a + 3}{3a}$$

Is Xavier's method correct? Explain.

40. Use a strategy similar to Exercise 39 to write each sum as a single fraction.

a. $\dfrac{5}{b} + \dfrac{2}{5}$ **b.** $\dfrac{3}{d} + \dfrac{2}{c}$ **c.** $\dfrac{1}{a} + \dfrac{1}{4a^2}$

Mathematical Reflections 4

In this Investigation, you used algebraic reasoning to write quadratic expressions in equivalent vertex form. You developed the Quadratic Formula for solving quadratic equations. You also developed basic ideas about complex numbers. These questions will help you summarize what you have learned.

Think about your answers. Discuss your ideas with other students and your teacher. Then write a summary of your findings in your notebook.

1. **What** are the key steps in writing a quadratic expression like $x^2 + 6x + 11$ in vertex form?

2. **How** does the Quadratic Formula help to solve equations in the form $ax^2 + bx + c = 0$?

3. **What** methods do you have for solving quadratic equations, other than the Quadratic Formula?

4. **What** are the complex numbers? **How** are they added, subtracted, and multiplied?

Common Core Mathematical Practices

As you worked on the Problems in this Investigation, you used prior knowledge to make sense of them. You also applied Mathematical Practices to solve the Problems. Think back over your work, the ways you thought about the Problems, and how you used Mathematical Practices.

Hector described his thoughts in the following way:

We could solve quadratic equations like $(x - a)^2 = b$, by taking square roots of both sides. There are two solutions, $x = a + \sqrt{b}$ and $x = a - \sqrt{b}$. That was only useful for solving some quadratic equations.

We soon found out how to write any quadratic equation in this form. This process is called completing the square.

Once we understood the pattern of steps, we could do this every time. The steps are not difficult, but there are several of them.

We were glad that there was a formula that captured all of the steps at once.

Common Core Standards for Mathematical Practice

MP7 Look for and make use of structure.

• What other Mathematical Practices can you identify in Hector's reasoning?

• Describe a Mathematical Practice that you and your classmates used to solve a different Problem in this Investigation.

Polynomial Expressions, Functions, and Equations

Linear and quadratic functions, equations, and graphs are very familiar mathematical models. Situations occur when these functions are not good models for patterns in data. Consider the graph below.

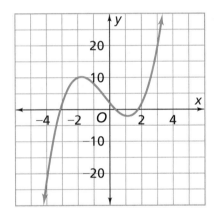

We cannot fit a linear, quadratic, exponential, or inverse variation function to model its shape.

You can produce graphs with more "hills" and "valleys" than quadratic graphs. You can extend those functions to include terms involving x^3, x^4, and even higher powers. For example, the function with graph shown above is $f(x) = x^3 + x^2 - 6x + 2$. The algebraic expression $x^3 + x^2 - 6x + 2$ is called a *polynomial*.

· ·

Common Core State Standards

A-APR.A.1 Understand that polynomials form a system analogous to the integers, namely, they are closed under the operations of addition, subtraction, and multiplication; add, subtract, and multiply polynomials.

F-IF.B.4. For a function that models a relationship between two quantities, interpret key features of graphs and tables in terms of the quantities, and sketch graphs showing key features given a verbal description of the relationship.

F-BF.A.1b. Combine standard function types using arithmetic operations.

Also F-IF.C.7a, F-IF.C.8a, F-IF.C.9

In general, a **polynomial** expression has the following form.

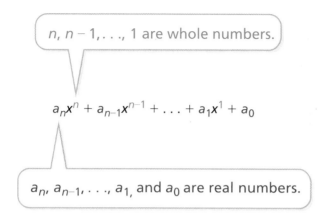

n, n − 1, . . ., 1 are whole numbers.

$$a_nx^n + a_{n-1}x^{n-1} + \ldots + a_1x^1 + a_0$$

$a_n, a_{n-1}, \ldots, a_1,$ and a_0 are real numbers.

In the polynomial expression $x^3 + x^2 - 6x + 2$, the value of n is 3 and the coefficients are $a_3 = 1$, $a_2 = 1$, $a_1 = -6$, and $a_0 = 2$.

In the polynomial expression $5x^4 - 3x^2 + 4x - 7$, the value of n is 4 and the coefficients are $a_4 = 5$, $a_3 = 0$, $a_2 = -3$, $a_1 = 4$, and $a_0 = -7$.

A **polynomial function** is a function with a rule given by a polynomial expression.

The Problems of this Investigation will develop your understanding and skill in operating with polynomials. You will also graph polynomial functions and solve polynomial equations.

5.1 Properties of Polynomial Expressions and Functions

One of the most important characteristics of any polynomial expression is its degree. The **degree of a polynomial** is the greatest exponent of the variable that occurs in the expression. For example, a quadratic polynomial has degree 2. A polynomial with degree 3 is called a cubic polynomial. A polynomial with degree 4 is called a quartic polynomial.

Knowing the degree of a polynomial helps in predicting the shape of its graph. The degree of a polynomial also predicts solutions of related equations. Examine the graph of $f(x) = x^3 + x^2 - 6x + 2$ below.

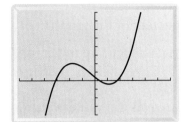

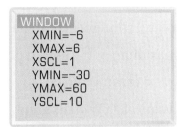

WINDOW
XMIN=-6
XMAX=6
XSCL=1
YMIN=-30
YMAX=60
YSCL=10

- How does the graph help you estimate solutions of the equation $x^3 + x^2 - 6x + 2 = 0$?

- How does the graph help you to identify intervals on which values of the function $f(x) = x^3 + x^2 - 6x + 2$ are increasing or decreasing?

- How does the graph help you to identify *local maximum* or *local minimum* points?

A calculator or computer graphing tool is useful in exploring properties of polynomial functions. You can see how changes in a polynomial lead to changes in the graph.

The zeros of a function tell you the x-intercepts of the graph. You can find the zeros for a function $p(x)$ by solving the equation $p(x) = 0$.

Problem 5.1

A For each of the following quadratic functions,

- Sketch a graph.

- Estimate or find exact coordinates of the maximum or minimum point.

- Identify intervals on the x-axis where function values are increasing and where function values are decreasing.

- Estimate or find exact coordinates for the x- and y-intercepts.

- Give the equation of the line of symmetry of the graph.

1. $f(x) = (x + 3)^2$ **2.** $g(x) = -x^2 + 3x + 4$

3. $h(x) = (x - 3)^2 - 9$ **4.** $j(x) = -x^2 + 5x - 6$

continued on the next page >

Problem 5.1 *continued*

B For any quadratic polynomial function:

1. How many x- and y-intercepts can be expected for the graph?

2. How many maximum or minimum points can occur on the graph?

3. Where is the line of symmetry for the graph located?

4. How do the value of $f(x)$ and its graph change as the value of x grows very large in absolute value?

C For each of the following cubic polynomial functions,

- Sketch a graph.

- Estimate coordinates of the local maximum or minimum points.

- Identify intervals on the x-axis where function values are increasing and where function values are decreasing.

- Estimate coordinates for the x- and y-intercepts.

- Give the equation for any line of symmetry of the graph.

1. $f(x) = x^3 + x^2 - 2x - 3$

2. $g(x) = -x^3 + x^2 - 2x - 3$

3. $h(x) = -x^3 - x^2 + 2x$

4. $j(x) = x^3$

D Use your graphing tool to explore other cubic polynomials. Then make conjectures about answers to the following questions about any such function.

1. How many x- and y-intercepts can be expected for the graph?

2. How many local maximum or minimum points can occur on the graph?

3. How many lines of symmetry does the graph have? Where are these lines located?

4. How do the value of $f(x)$ and its graph change as the value of x grows very large in absolute value?

Problem 5.1 *continued*

E Think about your work with linear, quadratic, and cubic polynomials. Make conjectures about answers to the following questions about quartic polynomial functions. Quartic polynomials are rules in the form $f(x) = a_4x^4 + a_3x^3 + a_2x^2 + a_1x + a_0$. Test your ideas by graphing a variety of examples of such functions.

1. How many x- and y-intercepts would you expect for the graph?

2. How many maximum or minimum points can occur on the graph?

3. How many lines of symmetry are there for the graph?

4. How do the value of $f(x)$ and its graph change as the value of x grows very large in absolute value?

F The degree of any polynomial tells instantly some important information about its graph.

1. What common symmetry do you see in the graphs of $f(x) = x^2$, $g(x) = x^4$, and $h(x) = x^6$?

2. What common symmetry do you see in the graphs of $j(x) = x$, $k(x) = x^3$, and $m(x) = x^5$?

3. Any function for which $f(x) = f(-x)$ for all x is called an even function.

   a. Explain why each function in Part 1 is an even function.

   b. Explain why the graph of any even function will have the same symmetry as the examples in Part 1.

4. Any function for which $f(-x) = -f(x)$ for all x is called an odd function.

   a. Explain why each function in Part 2 is an odd function.

   b. Explain why the graph of any odd function will have the same symmetry as the examples in Part 2.

A C E Homework starts on page 96.

5.2 Combining Profit Functions: Operating With Polynomials I

Amusement parks make money by charging for rides such as roller coasters, bumper cars, and water slides. They also make money from restaurants and stands that sell pretzels, ice cream, or lemonade. Profits of each type depend on the number of customers at the park.

Suppose that managers of the *Sahara Adventure Park* predict daily profit (in \$100 units) as a function of the number of customers (in units of 100 customers) with two polynomial functions $R(n)$ and $F(n)$.

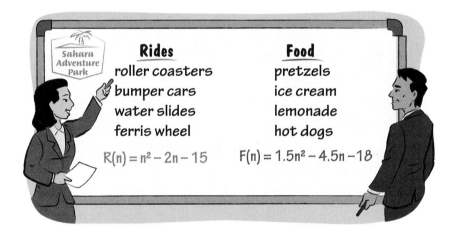

- What do the graphs of these functions look like?

- What do they tell about profit prospects for each part of the business?

- What single quadratic polynomial shows the total profit, $T(n)$, for the park on a day with n hundred customers?

- What single quadratic polynomial shows the difference in profit, $D(n)$, for the two sources of income on a day with n hundred customers?

Combining quadratic polynomials by addition and subtraction can provide information about profits at *Sahara Adventure Park*. Operations with those polynomials are similar to operations with multi-digit numbers.

Problem 5.2

Ⓐ Explore the connection between polynomials and decimal numbers by answering the following questions.

1. Evaluate these expressions when $x = 10$.

   a. $5x$

   b. $3x^2$

   c. $4x^3$

   d. $7x^4$

   e. $6x^5$

   f. $6x^5 + 7x^4 + 4x^3 + 3x^2 + 5x + 8$

2. Write polynomial expressions for functions with these values.

   a. $p(10) = 2{,}357$

   b. $q(10) = 15{,}042$

   c. $r(10) = 754{,}302$

3. In part (2) you found $p(x)$ for which $p(10) = 2{,}357$ and $q(x)$ for which $q(10) = 15{,}042$.

   a. Write the rule for $r(x) = p(x) + q(x)$ as a single polynomial.

   b. Find the value of $r(10) = p(10) + q(10)$, using the expression in part (a).

4. How is adding decimal numbers like adding polynomials?

Ⓑ Write each of these sums and differences of polynomials in standard polynomial form.

1. $(x^2 + 2x - 5) + (4x^2 - 7x + 12)$

2. $(x^2 + 2x - 5) - (4x^2 - 7x + 12)$

3. $(2x - 5) + (7x^2 + 3x + 4)$

4. $(2x - 5) - (7x^2 + 4)$

5. $(x^3 + 7x^2 + 3x + 4) + (-3x^4 - 7x^2 + 9)$

6. $(x^3 + 7x^2 + 3x + 4) - (-3x^4 - 7x^2 + 9)$

Ⓒ What general strategy can be applied to find the sum or difference of two polynomials. How is that strategy justified?

continued on the next page >

Problem 5.2 *continued*

D Find the sum of the two quadratic profit functions $R(n)$ and $F(n)$ at *Sahara Adventure Park*. Use graphs and/or algebraic reasoning to answer these questions.

1. For what number of customers will the park have maximum total loss (i.e., minimum profit)? What is that loss?

2. According to the model, there is no maximum profit. Explain why this is true.

3. How many customers are needed for the park to break even ($0 profit)?

 Homework starts on page 96.

5.3 Product Time: Operating With Polynomials II

You can apply whole number arithmetic and properties of operations to develop an algorithm for polynomial multiplication.

Problem 5.3

A Calculate these number products. Be prepared to explain and justify the strategy you used in each case.

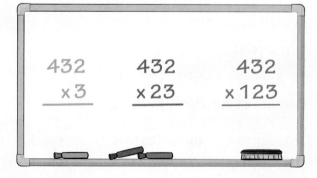

$$\begin{array}{r} 432 \\ \times\ 3 \\ \hline \end{array} \qquad \begin{array}{r} 432 \\ \times\ 23 \\ \hline \end{array} \qquad \begin{array}{r} 432 \\ \times\ 123 \\ \hline \end{array}$$

Problem 5.3

B **1.** Show why $(98)(70)$ is the same as $(100 - 2)(70)$.

  2. Show why $(98)(73)$ is the same as $(100 - 2)(70 + 3)$.

C Write each of these products in simplest possible standard polynomial form. Be prepared to explain and justify the strategy you used in each case.

  1. $(x^2 - 4)(7x)$ **2.** $(x^2 - 4)(7x + 3)$

  3. $(2x - 5)(7x^2 + 3x + 4)$ **4.** $(x^3 + 6x^2 + 3x + 4)(7x^2)$

  5. $(x^3 + 7x^2 + 3x + 4)(7x^2 + 9)$ **6.** $(x^2 + 3x + 4)(7x^2 + x - 2)$

D What general strategy can be applied to find the product of two polynomials? How is that strategy justified?

E The sum, difference, and product of any two integers is always another integer. Mathematicians say that the system of integers is closed under the operations of addition, subtraction, and multiplication. Is the same thing true of the system of polynomials? That is, will the sum, difference, or product of two polynomials always be another polynomial?

F **1.** Consider the case of $f(x) = (x^2 - 4)(x - 5)$, which has equivalent expression $f(x) = x^3 - 5x^2 - 4x + 20$. Which algebraic expression for the function makes it easier to predict these features of the graph?

  a. the y-intercept   **b.** the x-intercepts

  2. a. Find the zeros of $f(x)$.   **b.** Sketch a rough graph of $f(x)$.

  3. Consider the case of $g(x) = (x - 4)(x + 5)(x - 1)$, which has equivalent expression $g(x) = x^3 - 21x + 20$. Which algebraic expression for the function makes it easier to predict these features of the graph?

  a. the y-intercept   **b.** the x-intercepts

  4. a. Find the zeros of $g(x)$.   **b.** Sketch a rough graph of $g(x)$.

A C E Homework starts on page 96.

5.4 The Factor Game Revisited

In Problem 1.1 of *Prime Time*, you played the *Factor Game* with small whole numbers. You have learned a lot of mathematics since this first Problem. Throughout *Connected Mathematics*, factoring with whole numbers and algebraic expressions has remained an important skill.

Playing the *Factor Game II* applies what you know about polynomial expressions. To play the game, you need a *Factor Game II* board and colored pens or markers.

Factor Game II

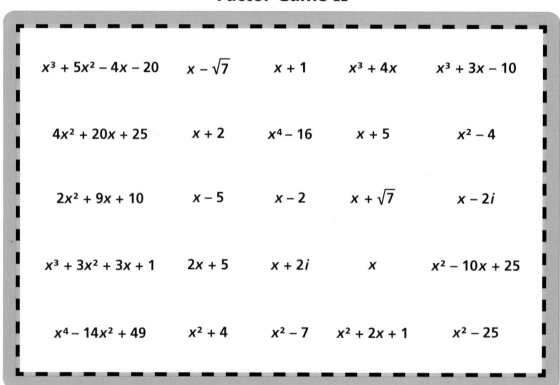

$x^3 + 5x^2 - 4x - 20$	$x - \sqrt{7}$	$x + 1$	$x^3 + 4x$	$x^3 + 3x - 10$
$4x^2 + 20x + 25$	$x + 2$	$x^4 - 16$	$x + 5$	$x^2 - 4$
$2x^2 + 9x + 10$	$x - 5$	$x - 2$	$x + \sqrt{7}$	$x - 2i$
$x^3 + 3x^2 + 3x + 1$	$2x + 5$	$x + 2i$	x	$x^2 - 10x + 25$
$x^4 - 14x^2 + 49$	$x^2 + 4$	$x^2 - 7$	$x^2 + 2x + 1$	$x^2 - 25$

Factor Game II

Rules

1. Player A chooses an expression on the game board and circles it.

2. Using the same color, Player A circles all the proper factors of Player A's expression.

3. Player B circles a new expression. Player B circles all of the factors that are not already circled.

4. The players take turns choosing expressions and circling factors.

5. If a player chooses an expression with no uncircled factors, that player loses their current turn and scores no points.

6. The game ends when there are no expressions left with uncircled factors.

7. Each player counts the number of expressions that he or she circled. The player with the greater total wins.

Problem 5.4

Play the *Factor Game II* several times with a partner. Look for interesting patterns and strategies that might help you win. Make notes on your observations.

A 1. Examine the *Factor Game II* board. For which polynomials are there no factors on the board? Explain how you know.

2. Which factor pairs are easy to recognize? Explain.

3. Are there factors on the board for which there is no product on the board?

4. For which polynomials is it most challenging to find factors? Explain.

B Which polynomials are likely to have the most factors? Explain.

C There are three cubic and two quartic polynomials on the board. What strategies did you use to decide on likely factors for these polynomials?

D Is there a polynomial on the board that is *both* of the following?

• a factor of another polynomial on the board

• a product of two or more other polynomials on the board

Explain your reasoning.

 Homework starts on page 96.

Applications | Connections | Extensions

Applications

For Exercises 1–5,

- Sketch a graph of the function for $-4 \leq x \leq 4$.

- Estimate coordinates of the local maximum or minimum point(s).

- Identify the intervals for x when the function values are increasing. Identify when the function is decreasing.

- Estimate coordinates for the x- and y-intercepts.

1. $f(x) = -0.1x^3 + 1$

2. $g(x) = 0.2x^4 - 10$

3. $h(x) = x^3 - x^2 - 2x$

4. $j(x) = -x^3 + x^2 + 2x + 5$

5. $k(x) = x^4 - 10x^2 + 9$

Write the sums and differences as equivalent standard polynomial expressions.

6. $(x^2 - x - 2) + (3x^2 + 5x + 10)$

7. $(3x^2 - 4x + 7) - (5x^2 - x)$

8. $(5x^3 + 3x^2 + 4x - 3) + (x^3 - 7x^2 - 4x + 1)$

9. $(x^3 - 7x^2 - 4x + 1) - (5x^3 + 3x^2 + 4x - 3)$

10. $(3x^3 + 5x^2 + 10) + (7x^4 + 5x^3 - 10x^2 + 4x)$

For Exercises 11–15 write the products as equivalent standard polynomial expressions.

11. $(3x + 4)(5x - 1)$

12. $(3x^2 + 5x + 10)(2x - 3)$

13. $(x^2 - x - 2)(3x^2 + 4x + 1)$

14. $(x^3 - 7x^2 - 4x + 1)(3x + 4)$

15. $(5x^3 + 3x^2 + 4x - 3)(x^2 + 7)$

Connections

16. If $c(x) = x^3$, find the values for $c^{-1}(x)$

    a. $c^{-1}(8)$ **b.** $c^{-1}(27)$

    c. $c^{-1}(-8)$ **d.** $c^{-1}(-64)$

17. If $q(x) = x^4$, find the values for $q^{-1}(x)$

    a. $q^{-1}(16)$ **b.** $q^{-1}(81)$

    c. $q^{-1}(1)$ **d.** $q^{-1}(-16)$

18. On a copy of the graph below, sketch graphs of these variations on the basic cubic function.

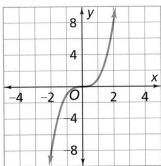

    a. $f(x) = x^3 + 2$ **b.** $g(x) = (x - 2)^3$ **c.** $h(x) = 0.5x^3$

19. On a copy of the graph of $q(x) = x^4$ sketch graphs of these variations on the basic quartic function.

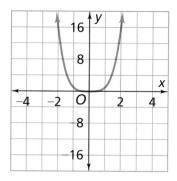

a. $f(x) = x^4 - 5$

b. $g(x) = (x + 1)^4$

c. $h(x) = 0.2x^4$

20. In *Frogs, Fleas, and Painted Cubes,* you studied the number of colored faces on unit cubes that are assembled to make a larger cube with sides of length n whose 6 faces are then painted.

a. Explain why the total number of unit cubes required to make such a larger cube with sides of length n must be n^3.

b. Explain why the number of cubes with 3 painted faces is 8.

c. Explain why the number of cubes with 2 painted faces is $12(n - 2)$.

d. Explain why the number of cubes with only 1 painted face is $6(n - 2)^2$.

e. Explain why the number of cubes with no painted faces is $(n - 2)^3$.

Extensions

21. Amami solved the quadratic equation $x^2 - 7x - 18 = 0$. His work is shown below.

$$x^2 - 7x - 18 = 0$$
$$(x + 2)(x - 9) = 0$$
$$x = -2 \text{ or } x = 9$$

   a. Why is the equation $x^2 - 7x - 18 = 0$ equivalent to $(x + 2)(x - 9) = 0$?

   b. How do you know that the equation $(x + 2)(x - 9) = 0$ has solutions -2 and 9?

   c. How can you check that $x = -2$ and $x = 9$ are solutions of $x^2 - 7x - 18 = 0$?

22. Larisa solved the equation $x^3 - 7x^2 - 18x = 0$. Her work is shown below.

$$x^3 - 7x^2 - 18x = 0$$
$$x(x^2 - 7x - 18) = 0$$
$$x = 0, \ x = -2 \text{ or } x = 9$$

   a. Why is the equation $x^3 - 7x^2 - 18x = 0$ equivalent to $x(x^2 - 7x - 18) = 0$?

   b. How do you know that the equation $x(x^2 - 7x - 18) = 0$ has solutions 0, -2, and 9?

   c. How can you check those solutions in the equation $x^3 - 7x^2 - 18x = 0$?

23. Use reasoning like that developed in Exercises 21 and 22 to solve these equations.

   a. $x^3 - 3x^2 + 2x = 0$

   b. $x^4 + 4x^3 + 3x^2 = 0$

   c. $x^3 - 9x = 0$

24. Write polynomial functions with these properties.

    a. $p(6) = 0$; $p(-1) = 0$; $p(0) = 0$

    b. $q(4) = 0$; $q(-3) = 0$; $q(7) = 0$

    c. $r(-3) = 0$; $r(-1) = 0$; $r(1) = 0$; $r(4) = 0$

    d. Anita, Cameron, and Ervin each drew a graph for part (c).

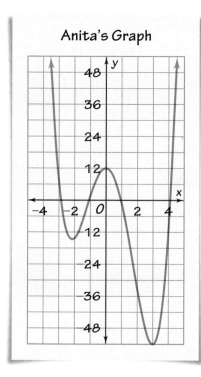

Anita's Graph

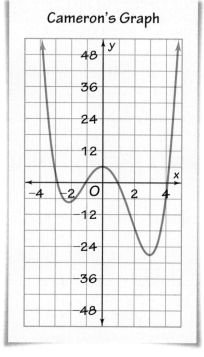

Cameron's Graph

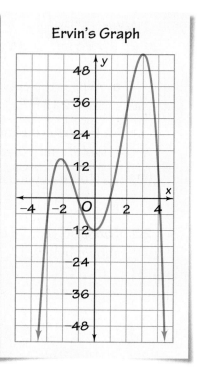

Ervin's Graph

       How do you think Cameron's function rule is different from Anita's function rule? How do you think Ervin's function rule is different from Anita's function rule?

25. Use what you know about quadratic equations to solve polynomial equations of degree 4. In each case, apply the fact that $x^4 = (x^2)^2$.

    a. How do you know that the equation $x^4 - 16 = 0$ is equivalent to the equation $(x^2 + 4)(x^2 - 4) = 0$?

    b. How do you know that the only real number solutions of $(x^2 + 4)(x^2 - 4) = 0$ are 2 and -2? What complex number solutions are there for the equation?

    c. Solve $x^4 - 81 = 0$. Give both real and complex number solutions.

    d. How do you know that $x^4 - 5x^2 + 6 = 0$ is equivalent to $(x^2 - 3)(x^2 - 2) = 0$? What does that second equivalent equation tell you about the solutions to $x^4 - 5x^2 + 6 = 0$?

Mathematical Reflections 5

In this Investigation, you studied the properties of polynomial functions, expressions, and graphs. You developed strategies for adding, subtracting, and multiplying polynomial expressions. These questions will help you summarize what you have learned.

Think about your answers. Discuss your ideas with other students and your teacher. Then write a summary of your findings in your notebook.

1. **What** are polynomial expressions and functions?

2. **How** can one analyze the graph of a polynomial function $p(x)$ to discover

   a. solutions to the equations $p(x) = 0$?

   b. intervals on which values of the function are increasing or decreasing?

   c. points that show relative maximum or minimum values of the function?

3. **What** strategies give standard polynomial expressions for

   a. the sum or difference of two polynomials?

   b. the product of two polynomials?

Common Core Mathematical Practices

As you worked on the Problems in this Investigation, you used prior knowledge to make sense of them. You also applied Mathematical Practices to solve the Problems. Think back over your work, the ways you thought about the Problems, and how you used Mathematical Practices.

Elena described her thoughts in the following way:

> We wanted to discover patterns in the graphs of degree 3 and 4 polynomials. It was helpful to have graphing software to test many examples.
>
> We also wanted to develop algorithms for addition, subtraction, and multiplication of polynomials. It was important to recall connections to what we knew about decimal operations.
>
> We also discovered that we could apply general properties of the number system to operations with polynomials.

Common Core Standards for Mathematical Practice

MP5 Use appropriate tools strategically.

- What other Mathematical Practices can you identify in Elena's reasoning?

- Describe a Mathematical Practice that you and your classmates used to solve a different Problem in this Investigation.

Looking Back

In this Unit, you extended your understanding and skill in work with mathematical functions, expressions, equations, and graphs. You learned new function concepts such as domain, range, and inverses. You learned how to use $f(x)$ notation for describing functions.

You also studied examples of step, piecewise, and polynomial functions. You discovered the special properties of arithmetic and geometric sequences.

You saw how information about quadratic functions can be revealed by transforming graphs and writing expressions in vertex form. You developed a formula for solving any quadratic equation. Finally, you used that formula as a starting point for development of the complex number system.

Use Your Understanding: The Functions Five Game

Now it is time to test your understanding of those new mathematical ideas and techniques. Challenge yourself or other students in your class to play the Functions Five Game.

You will use game cards like the ones shown below. The cards have mathematical properties that you will match to functions.

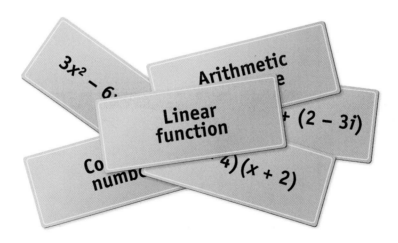

The Functions Five Game Board is shown below. You will match the properties on the cards to the functions in the cells. To make the property cards, write each of the properties listed on the facing page on a separate card. Then choose the game you want to play from the options described at the bottom of the facing page.

Game Board

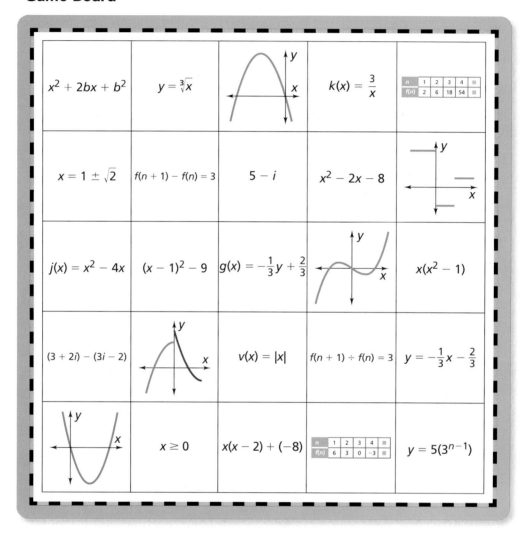

Properties

- Linear function
- Geometric sequence
- $g(x) = -(x + 2)^2 + 4$
- Degree 3 polynomial
- Inverse of $h(x) = -3x - 2$
- $(3 + 2i)(1 - i)$
- $(x - 4)(x + 2)$
- Arithmetic sequence
- Piecewise-defined function
- $3x^2 - 6x - 3 = 0$
- Perfect square trinomial
- $(x, y) \rightarrow (x - 2, y + 4)$
  for graph of $y = -x^2$
- Vertex form of a quadratic

- Complex number
- Step function
- Inverse of $y = x^3$
- $f(x) = (x - 2)^2 - 4$
- Quadratic function
- Domain of $r(x) = \sqrt{x}$
- $(3 + 2i) + (2 - 3i)$
- Inverse of $r(x) = \frac{3}{x}$
- Inverse variation function
- Formula for area of a square
- Exponential function
- $(x, y) \rightarrow (x + 2, y - 4)$
  for graph of $y = x^2$

Most cards can be matched with two or more cells on the game board. As a result, the Functions Five Game can be played in several different ways.

Rules

Option 1: Solitaire Study the game board and the set of game cards. Try to find a way to check off every cell on the board with the least number of cards.

Option 2: Five-by-Five Functions Each player or team picks a card and marks all of the cells on the game board that match the directions on the card. Then take turns. The winner is the player who has the most correct matches after each player has drawn five cards.

Option 3: Functions Five Follow the same directions as in Option 2. Play until one player or team has marked five cells in a row, column, or diagonal.

Option 4: Fickle Functions Follow the same directions as in Option 3. When a card is drawn, each player can only choose one corresponding cell on the game board that matches the directions on the card.

English / Spanish Glossary

A **arithmetic sequence** A number sequence formed by adding a fixed number to each previous term to find the next term. The fixed number is called the common difference.

example 4, 7, 10, 13, ...

progresión aritmética Una secuencia de números que se forma al sumar un número fijo a cada término anterior para hallar el siguiente término. El número fijo se conoce como diferencia común.

ejemplo 4, 7, 10, 13, ...

C **compare** Academic Vocabulary
To tell or show how two things are alike or different.

related terms *analyze, relate*

sample Compare the graph of $f(x) = x^2$ with the graph of $g(x) = -(x-2)^2 - 1$.

comparar Vocabulario académico
Decir o mostrar en qué se parecen y en qué se diferencian dos cosas.

términos relacionados *analizar, relacionar*

ejemplo Compara la gráfica de $f(x) = x^2$ con la gráfica de $g(x) = -(x-2)^2 - 1$.

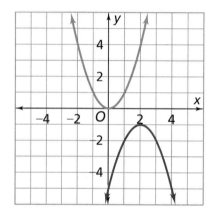

The graph of $g(x) = -(x-2)^2 - 1$ has the same shape as $f(x) = x^2$. The graph of $g(x)$ is a vertical flip of the graph of $f(x) = x^2$, translated 2 units right and 1 unit down.

La gráfica de $g(x) = -(x-2)^2 - 1$ tiene la misma forma que $f(x) = x^2$. La gráfica de $g(x)$ es una inversión vertical de la gráfica de $f(x) = x^2$, trasladada 2 unidades a la derecha y 1 unidad hacia abajo.

completing the square The process of writing any given quadratic expression in equivalent form $a(x-b)^2 + c$. Completing the square turns every quadratic equation into the form $(x-p)^2 = q$.

completar un cuadrado El proceso de escribir cualquier expresión cuadrática dada en la forma equivalente $a(x-b)^2 + c$. Cuando se completa un cuadrado, cualquier ecuación cuadrática a la forma $(x-p)^2 = q$.

complex conjugates Number pairs in the form $a + bi$ and $a - bi$ are complex conjugates.

conjugados complejos Los pares de números de la forma $a + bi$ y $a - bi$ son conjugados complejos.

complex numbers The set of numbers that can be written in the form $a + bi$ where a and b are real numbers and i is the number whose square is -1. 7, $6 + i$, and $-2i$ are examples of complex numbers.

números complejos El conjunto de números que se puede escribir en la forma $a + bi$, donde a y b son números reales e i es el número cuyo cuadrado es -1. 7, $6 + i$, y $-2i$ son ejemplos de numeros complejos.

D **degree of a polynomial** The highest power of the variable in monomial terms of the expression.

grado de un polinomio El grado más alto de la variable en términos monomios de la expresión.

describe Academic Vocabulary
To explain or tell in detail. A written description can contain facts and other information needed to communicate your answer. A diagram or a graph may also be included.

describir Vocabulario académico
Explicar o decir con detalle. Una descripción escrita puede contener datos y otro tipo de información necesaria para comunicar tu respuesta. También puede incluir un diagrama o una gráfica.

related terms *express, explain*

términos relacionados *expresar, explicar*

sample Describe how to calculate the nth term in the following sequence: $19, 11, 3, -5, -13, -21, \ldots$

ejemplo Describe cómo calcular el *enésimo* término en la siguiente progresión: $19, 11, 3, -5, -13, -21, \ldots$

The sequence $19, 11, 3, -5, -13, -21, \ldots$ is an arithmetic sequence with common difference -8. Using the formula $a_n = a_1 + (n - 1)d$, we can substitute 19 for a_1 and -8 for d. We now have $A_n = 19 + (n - 1)(-8)$, or more simply, $A_n = -8n + 27$, which finds the nth term.

La progresión $19, 11, 3, -5, -13, -21, \ldots$ es una progresión aritmética con la diferencia común -8. Usando la fórmula $a_n = a_1 + (n - 1)d$, podemos sustituir 19 por a_1 y -8 por d. Ahora tenemos $A_n = 19 + (n - 1)(-8)$, o de manera más simple, $A_n = -8n + 27$, que halla el *enésimo* término.

domain (of a relation or a function)
The set of possible values for the input or independent variable.

dominio (de una relación o una función)
El conjunto de valores posibles para la entrada o la variable independiente.

E explain Academic Vocabulary
To give facts and details that make an idea easier to understand. Explaining can involve a written summary supported by a diagram, chart, table, or a combination of these.

related terms *describe, show, justify*

sample Using the diagram below, explain why the expressions $x^2 + 4x + 3$ and $(x + 2)^2 - 1$ are equivalent.

explicar Vocabulario académico Dar datos y detalles que hacen que una idea sea más fácil de comprender. Explicar puede implicar un resumen escrito apoyado por un diagrama, una gráfica, una tabla o una combinación de estos.

términos relacionados *describir, mostrar, justificar*

ejemplo Usando el diagrama de abajo, explica por qué las expresiones $x^2 + 4x + 3$ y $(x + 2)^2 - 1$ son equivalentes.

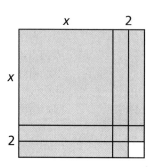

The diagram models $(x + 2)^2$ with a unit square missing from the right hand corner. The tiles in the diagram can be rearranged so that the length is x + 3 and the width is x + 1, which gives the area of $x^2 + 4x + 3$. Since the areas are equal, the expressions are also equivalent.

El diagrama representa $(x + 2)^2$ con una unidad cuadrada que falta en la esquina derecha. Los azulejos del diagrama se pueden volver a ordenar de manera que la longitud sea x + 3 y el ancho sea x + 1, que da el área de $x^2 + 4x + 3$. Dado que las áreas son iguales, las expresiones también son equivalentes.

F function A relationship between two variables in which the value of one variable depends on the value of the other variable.

función Una relación entre dos variables en la que el valor de una variable depende del valor de la otra.

function notation An expression in the form $f(x)$ that represents the value of the dependent variable when the independent variable is x. The notation is read 'f of x'.

notación de una función Una expresión en la forma $f(x)$ que representa el valor de la variable dependiente cuando la variable independiente es x. La notación se lee como "f de x".

function rule An equation that describes a function.

regla de la función Una ecuación que describe una función.

G geometric sequence A number sequence in which each term is multiplied by the same factor to find the next term.

example $9, 3, 1, \frac{1}{3}, \ldots$

progresión geométrica Una secuencia numérica en la que cada término se multiplica por el mismo factor para hallar el siguiente término.

ejemplo $9, 3, 1, \frac{1}{3}, \ldots$

I imaginary number Any number of the form bi, where b is a real number, and $b \neq 0$.

número imaginario Cualquier número de la forma bi, donde b es un número real y $b \neq 0$.

imaginary unit The complex number i whose square is -1.

unidad imaginaria El número complejo i cuyo cuadrado es -1.

inverse function If a function $f(x)$ pairs each input value a with a unique output value b, then the inverse of $f(x)$ is the function that pairs each b with a. The inverse of $f(x)$ is written as $f^{-1}(x)$.

If $f(x) = 3x + 2$, then $f^{-1}(x) = \frac{x-2}{3}$ because, for example, $f(4) = 14$ and $f^{-1}(14) = 4$, and so on.

función inversa Si una función $f(x)$ empareja cada valor de entrada a con un valor de salida único b, entonces el inverso de $f(x)$ es la función que empareja cada b con a. El inverso de $f(x)$ se escribe como $f^{-1}(x)$.

Si $f(x) = 3x + 2$, entonces $f^{-1}(x) = \frac{x-2}{3}$ porque, por ejemplo, $f(4) = 14$ y $f^{-1}(14) = 4$ y así sucesivamente.

L local maximum The value $f(k)$ of a function $f(x)$ that is greater than all other values of that function in some neighborhood of $x = k$. Local maximum points are represented by hilltops on graphs of $f(x)$. In the graph shown below, $(-1, 32)$ is a local maximum.

máximo local El valor $f(k)$ de una función $f(x)$ que es mayor que todos los demás valores de esa función en la vecindad de $x = k$. Los puntos máximos locales están representados por colinas en las gráficas de $f(x)$. En la gráfica que se muestra a continuación, $(-1, 32)$ es un máximo local.

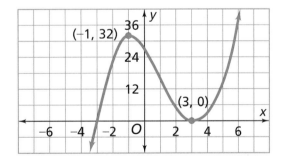

local minimum The value $f(x)$ of a function $f(x)$ that is less than all other values of that function in some neighborhood of $x = k$. Local minimum points are represented by valley bottoms on graphs of $f(x)$. In the graph shown above, $(3, 0)$ is a local minimum.

mínimo local El valor $f(x)$ de una función $f(x)$ que es menor que todos los demás valores de esa función en la vecindad de $x = k$. Los puntos mínimos locales están representados por fondos de valles en las gráficas de $f(x)$. En la gráfica que se muestra más arriba, $(3, 0)$ es un mínimo local.

P **piecewise-defined function** A function that has different rules for different parts of its domain.

función de fragmentos Una función que tiene reglas diferentes para diferentes partes de su dominio.

polynomial An algebraic expression in the form $a_n x^n + a_{n-1} x^{n-1} + \ldots + a_1 x^1 + a_0$, where n is a whole number and the coefficients a_n, a_{n-1}, a_1, and a_0 are numbers.

example $2x^2$, $3x + 7$, 28, and $-7x^3 - 2x^2 + 9$ are all polynomials.

polinomio Una expresión algebraica en la forma $a_n x^n + a_{n-1} x^{n-1} + \ldots + a_1 x^1 + a_0$, donde n es un número entero y los coeficientes a_n, a_{n-1}, a_1, y a_0 son números.

ejemplo $2x^2$, $3x + 7$, 28, y $-7x^3 - 2x^2 + 9$ son todos polinomios.

polynomial function A function with a rule represented in the form $f(x) = a_n x^n + a_{n-1} x^{n-1} + \ldots + a_1 x^1 + a_0$.

example $f(x) = x^3 + x^2 - 6x + 2$

función polinomial Una función con una regla representada en la forma $f(x) = a_n x^n + a_{n-1} x^{n-1} + \ldots + a_1 x^1 + a_0$.

ejemplo $f(x) = x^3 + x^2 - 6x + 2$

Q **Quadratic Formula** If $ax^2 + bx + c = 0$ and $a \neq 0$, then $x = \frac{-b}{2a} \pm \frac{\sqrt{b^2 - 4ac}}{2a}$.

fórmula cuadrática Si $ax^2 + bx + c = 0$ y $a \neq 0$, entonces $x = \frac{-b}{2a} \pm \frac{\sqrt{b^2 - 4ac}}{2a}$.

$$2x^2 + 10x + 12 = 0$$
$$x = \frac{-b}{2a} \pm \frac{\sqrt{b^2 - 4ac}}{2a}$$
$$x = \frac{-10}{2(2)} \pm \frac{\sqrt{10^2 - 4(2)(12)}}{2(2)}$$
$$x = \frac{-10}{4} \pm \frac{\sqrt{4}}{4}$$
$$x = \frac{-10}{4} + \frac{2}{4} \text{ or } x = \frac{-10}{4} - \frac{2}{4}$$
$$x = -2 \text{ or } -3$$

R **range (of a relation or a function)** The set of possible values for the output or dependent variable.

rango (de una relacion o funcion) El conjunto de los valores posibles para la salida o la variable dependiente.

represent Academic Vocabulary
To stand for or take the place of something else. Symbols, equations, charts, and tables are often used to represent particular situations.

related terms *symbolize, stand for*

sample Represent the table of values below as a graph and a function rule.

x	−3	−2	−1	0	1	2	3	4
y	6	1	−2	−3	−2	1	6	13

representar Vocabulario académico
Significar o tomar el lugar de algo más. Los símbolos, las ecuaciones, las gráficas y las tablas a menudo se usan para representar situaciones particulares.

términos relacionados *simbolizar, significar*

ejemplo Representa la siguiente tabla de valores como una gráfica y como una regla de la función.

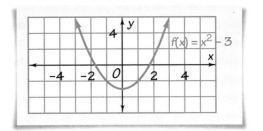

S **sequence** An ordered list of numbers that often forms a pattern.

progresión Lista ordenada de números que muchas veces forma un patron.

solving quadratic equations The process of finding the values of the variable that make the quadratic equation true. Methods for solving quadratic equations include factoring, completing the square, using the Quadratic Formula, and graphing.

resolver ecuaciones cuadráticas
El proceso de encontrar los valores de la variable que hacen que la ecuación cuadrática sea verdadera. Los métodos para resolver las ecuaciones cuadráticas incluyen descomponer en factores, completar un cuadrado, usar la fórmula cuadrática y hacer gráficas.

step function A function that pairs every number in an interval with a single value. The graph of a step function can look like the steps of a staircase.

función escalón Una función que empareja cada número de un intervalo con un solo valor. La gráfica de una función escalón se puede parecer a los peldaños de una escalera.

V **vertex form** The vertex form of a quadratic function is $f(x) = a(x-p)^2 + q$, where $a \neq 0$ and (p, q) is the coordinate of the vertex of the function.

example $f(x) = (x+1)^2 - 2$
The vertex is $(-1, -2)$.

forma vértice La forma vértice de una función cuadrática es $f(x) = a(x-p)^2 + q$, donde $a \neq 0$ y (p, q) es la coordenada del vértice de la función.

ejemplo $f(x) = (x+1)^2 - 2$
El vértice es $(-1, -2)$.

Z **zeros of a function** The values of x for which $f(x)$ is equal to 0. For example, the zeros of the function $f(x) = x^2 - 9$ are -3 and 3 because $f(-3) = 0$ and $f(3) = 0$. The zeros of a function are the x-intercepts of the graph of the function. The graph of $f(x) = x^2 - 9$ has x-intercepts at $(-3, 0)$ and $(3, 0)$.

ceros de una función Los valores de x para los que $f(x)$ es igual a 0. Por ejemplo, los ceros de la función $f(x) = x^2 - 9$ son -3 y 3 porque $f(-3) = 0$ y $f(3) = 0$. Los ceros de una función son los interceptos en x de la gráfica de una función. La gráfica de $f(x) = x^2 - 9$ tiene interceptos en x en $(-3, 0)$ y $(3, 0)$.

Index

absolute value functions, 15

ACE
arithmetic and geometric
sequences, 41–46
families of functions, 20–29
polynomial expressions,
functions, and equations,
96–100
solving quadratic equations
algebraically, 76–82
transforming graphs,
equations, and functions,
58–60

addition
complex numbers, 83
polynomial expressions,
functions, and equations,
90, 101, 102

algebraic expressions
arithmetic and geometric
sequences, 34, 35–36, 41,
42
functions and, 4
horizontal translations, 54
multiplicative
transformations, 52, 53
quadratic functions, 49
transforming graphs,
equations, and functions,
60
vertical translations, 51

angle sums, 44

area and perimeter, inverse
functions and, 19

Argand diagrams, 79

arithmetic and geometric
sequences, 103
ACE, 41–46
arithmetic sequences, 33–36
geometric sequences, 37–40
Mathematical Reflections,
47–48
patterns and, 32–33

arithmetic sequences, 4,
33–36, 41–42, 105, 106

Ask Yourself, 4

average speed, 16

binomials, complex numbers
and, 75

ceiling rounding function, 13,
24, 27, 28

coefficients, 71, 81

Common Core Mathematical
Practices, 5–6, 31, 48, 62,
84, 102

completing the square, 66–69,
72, 81, 84, 106

complex conjugates, 82, 107

complex numbers, 4, 107
Argand diagram, 79
complex conjugates, 82
Functions Five game, 105
polynomial expressions,
functions, and equations,
100
quadratic formula and, 103
solving quadratic equations
algebraically, 73–75, 77,
78, 83

conjectures, 88, 89

constants, changing, 53

coordinate rules, 50

cubic polynomials, 86, 88, 89,
97

decimals, 91, 102

degrees of a polynomial,
86–87, 89, 105, 107

dependent variables, 11

differences, 75, 77, 91–92, 96

dilations, 4

distance. See time and distance

domain, 103, 107
arithmetic and geometric
sequences, 45
ceiling rounding function, 28
families of functions, 4, 10,
11, 22, 30
Functions Five game, 105
inverse functions and, 19, 25
linear, quadratic, and
exponential functions, 26
piecewise-defined functions,
16
taxi fares, 12
variables and, 31

equations, arithmetic and
geometric sequences, 39,
41–42, 43

equivalent expressions, 68, 69,
96, 97, 99

equivalent forms, 79

estimation
families of functions, 16
polynomial expressions,
functions, and equations,
87, 88, 96
solving quadratic equations
algebraically, 77

even functions, 89

expanded form, 67

exponential functions, 8
arithmetic and geometric
sequences, 33, 37, 45, 47
domains, 26
Functions Five game, 105
polynomial expressions,
functions, and equations,
85

expressions, simplifying, 82

extended number system, 74

faces, 98

fact families, equations and, 27

factored form, of quadratic functions, 63, 68

Factor Game II, 94–95

factor pairs, 95

factors and factoring, 65–66

Fibonacci sequence, 40, 45

filling functions, 8–9, 15, 20, 24

flags, 59

floor rounding function, 13, 24, 27

formulas
  arithmetic and geometric sequences, 46
  quadratic equations and, 4
  quadratic formula, 70–73, 75, 77, 81, 83, 103, 110

fractions, 82

function notation $f(x)$, 4, 11, 22, 31, 33, 103, 108

function rules
  defined, 108
  piecewise-defined functions, 14, 25, 29
  polynomial expressions, functions, and equations, 86, 91, 100
  transforming graphs, equations, and functions, 56, 58, 61, 62

functions, absolute value, 15

functions, ceiling rounding, 13, 24, 27, 28

functions, defined, 108

functions, even. *See* even functions

functions, exponential, 8
  arithmetic and geometric sequences, 33, 37, 45, 47
  domains, 26
  Functions Five game, 105

polynomial expressions, functions, and equations, 85

functions, families of, 7–8, 103
  ACE, 20–29
  domain, range, and function notation $f(x)$, 10–11
  filling functions, 8–9
  inverse functions, 17–19
  Mathematical Reflections, 30–31
  piecewise-defined functions, 14–16
  taxi fares, time payments, and step functions, 12–14

functions, filling, 8–9, 15, 20, 24

functions, floor rounding, 13, 24, 27

functions, height, 8–9, 10, 11, 20, 24

functions, inverse, 4, 25, 103, 109
  families of functions, 17–19, 30
  Functions Five game, 105
  graphs and graphing, 28

functions, inverse variation, 8, 45, 85, 105

functions, linear, 8
  arithmetic and geometric sequences, 33, 45, 47
  domains, 26
  Functions Five game, 105
  multiplicative transformations, 53
  polynomial expressions, functions, and equations, 85
  vertical translations, 51

functions, odd. *See* odd functions

functions, piecewise-defined, 4, 24–25, 103, 110
  families of functions, 14–16, 30, 31
  Functions Five game, 105
  horizontal translations, 55

functions, quadratic, 8, 103
  arithmetic sequences, 45
  domains, 26
  forms of, 63–64
  Functions Five game, 105
  graphs and graphing, 49
  multiplicative transformations, 52
  polynomial expressions, functions, and equations, 85
  vertex forms, 57

functions, step, 4, 103, 111
  families of functions, 14, 30, 31
  Functions Five game, 105
  patterns and, 26

functions, time, 8–9, 10, 20

functions, zeros of, 63, 70, 76, 78, 87, 111

Functions Five game, 103–105

games
  Factor Game II, 94–95
  Functions Five game, 103–105

geometric sequences, 4, 37–40, 105, 109. *See also* arithmetic and geometric sequences

geometric transformations, 79

Glossary, 106–111

graphs, equations, and functions, transforming, 49
  ACE, 58–60
  horizontal translations, 54–56
  Mathematical Reflections, 61–62
  multiplicative transformations, 52–53
  transforming $y = x^2$, 54–56
  vertical translations, 50–51

graphs and graphing
  algebraic functions and, 2
  arithmetic sequences, 34, 35

completing the square, 66

complex numbers, 73, 75

domain and range, 11, 22

families of functions, 8, 12, 13–14

filling functions and, 9

geometric sequences, 37–38

horizontal translations, 54, 55–56

inverse functions, 19, 28

multiplicative transformations, 52, 53

piecewise-defined functions, 15, 16, 25, 29

polynomial expressions, functions, and equations, 85, 87, 89, 93, 96, 97–98, 100, 101, 102

quadratic functions, 63–64

solving quadratic equations algebraically, 76

square roots and, 65

step functions, 30

time and distance, 20, 21

time payments, 23

transforming $y = x^2$, 56

vertical translations, 50, 51

height functions, 8–9, 10, 11, 20, 24

horizontal translations, 54–56, 61

imaginary numbers, 74, 75, 79, 109

imaginary units, 109

income and expense data, 18

independent variables, 11

integers, 28, 78

inverse functions, 4, 25, 103, 109

families of functions, 17–19, 30

Functions Five game, 105

graphs and graphing, 28

inverse operations, 27

inverse variation functions, 8, 45, 85, 105

Investigations

arithmetic and geometric sequences, 32–40

families of functions, 7–19

polynomial expressions, functions, and equations, 85–95

solving quadratic equations algebraically, 63–75

transforming graphs, equations, and functions, 49–57

linear equations, 44

linear functions, 8

arithmetic and geometric sequences, 33, 45, 47

domains, 26

Functions Five game, 105

multiplicative transformations, 53

polynomial expressions, functions, and equations, 85

vertical translations, 51

linear polynomials, 89

lines of symmetry

completing the square, 67

polynomial expressions, functions, and equations, 87, 88, 89

transforming graphs, equations, and functions, 60

transforming $y = x^2$, 56, 57

local maximum, 87, 96, 109

local minimum, 87, 96, 109. *See also* maximum and minimum points

Looking Ahead, 2–3

Looking Back, 103–105

Mathematical Highlights, 4

Mathematical Practices, 5–6, 31, 48, 62, 84, 102

Mathematical Reflections

arithmetic and geometric sequences, 47–48

families of functions, 30–31

polynomial expressions, functions, and equations, 101–102

solving quadratic equations algebraically, 83–84

transforming graphs, equations, and functions, 61–62

maximum and minimum points

polynomial expressions, functions, and equations, 87, 88, 89, 92, 96, 101

solving quadratic equations algebraically, 70, 77, 78

transforming graphs, equations, and functions, 58, 60

transforming $y = x^2$, 56, 57

maximum value of quadratic functions, 69

measurement, families of functions and, 7

multiplication, 83, 92–93, 101, 102

multiplicative transformations, 52–53, 61

negative numbers, 73

nth term, 33, 35, 39, 43

number patterns, 39, 40, 42–43, 44, 48

odd functions, 89, 92

operations

complex numbers, 74

with polynomials, 90–93, 102

order of operations, 71

parabolas, 58, 76

partial sums, 46

patterns, 2. *See also* number patterns
  arithmetic and geometric sequences, 35, 47
  piecewise-defined functions, 31
  polynomial expressions, functions, and equations, 102
  step functions, 26, 31
  transforming $y = x^2$, 56, 57

perfect squares, 67, 68, 77

perfect square trinomials, 105

piecewise-defined functions, 4, 24–25, 103, 110
  families of functions, 14–16, 30, 31
  Functions Five game, 105
  horizontal translations, 55

points, 52, 62, 79

polygons, 44

polynomial expressions, functions, and equations, 4, 103, 110
  ACE, 96–100
  defined, 86
  Factor Game II, 94–95
  graphs and graphing, 85
  Mathematical Reflections, 101–102
  operations with polynomials, 90–93
  properties of, 86–89

polynomials, 86, 107, 110

positive and negative signs, 57

positive integers, 45

positive numbers, 56, 57

prime numbers, 44

products, 77, 93, 95, 97

profits, 18, 90–92

properties of equality, 65

quadratic equations, 4, 99, 100, 111

quadratic equations, solving algebraically
  ACE, 76–82
  applying square roots, 64–66
  completing the square, 66–69
  complex numbers, 73–75
  forms of quadratic functions, 63–64
  Mathematical Reflections, 83–84
  quadratic formula, 70–73

quadratic expressions, 56

quadratic formula, 70–73, 75, 77, 81, 83, 103, 110

quadratic functions, 8, 103
  arithmetic sequences, 45
  domains, 26
  forms of, 63–64
  Functions Five game, 105
  graphs and graphing, 49
  multiplicative transformations, 52
  polynomial expressions, functions, and equations, 85
  vertex form, 57

quadratic polynomials, 86, 88, 89, 90

quadratic relationships, 80

quartic polynomials, 86, 89, 98

range, 103, 110
  ceiling rounding function, 28
  families of functions, 4, 10, 11, 22, 30
  inverse functions, 19, 25
  piecewise-defined functions, 16
  taxi fares, 12
  variables and, 31

rational numbers, 78

ratios, geometric sequences and, 45

real numbers, 3
  complex conjugates, 82
  complex numbers, 74
  domain and range, 28
  linear, quadratic, and exponential functions, 26
  polynomial expressions, functions, and equations, 100
  solving quadratic equations algebraically, 78

reasoning, explaining your
  arithmetic and geometric sequences, 48
  complex numbers, 75
  families of functions, 9, 18, 28, 31
  horizontal translations, 54, 55
  polynomial expressions, functions, and equations, 95, 99, 102
  quadratic formula and, 71, 72, 81
  solving quadratic equations algebraically, 68, 76, 78, 81, 84
  square roots and, 65–66
  transforming graphs, equations, and functions, 60, 62

recursive processes, 33

relationships
  among variables, 4, 12
  arithmetic and geometric sequences, 34, 35, 38

rounding numbers, 13

rules, writing, 51, 53. *See also* function rules

sequences, 32–33, 111
  arithmetic sequences, 33–36
  geometric sequences, 37–40

side lengths, 98

slopes, 25

square roots
  complex numbers, 75
  negative numbers and, 73
  solving quadratic equations
    algebraically, 64–66, 70, 84

squares, area of, 105

standard form
  polynomial expressions,
    functions, and equations,
    91, 93, 96
  of quadratic functions, 63,
    68, 69, 77

standard rounding rule, 13, 24

step functions, 4, 103, 111
  families of functions, 14, 30,
    31
  Functions Five game, 105
  patterns and, 26

subtraction, 83, 90, 101, 102

sums, 75, 77, 91–92, 96

**symbolic methods of solving
  equations,** 65, 66, 67

symmetry, 89. *See also* lines of
  symmetry

tables of values
  absolute value function, 15
  arithmetic sequences, 34, 41
  geometric sequences, 37, 38
  multiplicative
    transformations, 52
  quadratic relationships, 80
  ratios and, 45
  rounding numbers and, 27
  solving quadratic equations
    algebraically, 78
  vertical translations, 50

taxi fares, 12

time and distance
  graphs and graphing, 20, 21
  inverse functions, 17, 18
  piecewise-defined functions,
    16, 29

time functions, 8–9, 10, 20

time payments, 12–13, 23, 35

transformations
  horizontal translations,
    54–56
  multiplicative
    transformations, 52–53
  transforming graphs,
    equations, and functions,
    49, 58–60, 61–62
  transforming $y = x^2$, 54–56
  vertical translations, 50–51

transforming $y = x^2$, 54–56

translations, 4

trinomials, 77

unit cubes, 98

units of measurement, 7, 8

Use Your Understanding,
  103–105

variables
  domain and range, 31
  families of functions and, 7,
    8, 30
  function notation $f(x)$, 11
  functions and, 4
  inverse functions, 17–19

vertex forms, 4, 103, 111
  completing the square,
    66–67
  Functions Five game, 105
  of quadratic functions, 63,
    68, 69, 70, 77
  solving quadratic equations
    algebraically, 76, 78, 81, 83
  transforming graphs,
    equations, and functions,
    61
  transforming $y = x^2$, 57

vertical translations, 50–51, 61

whole numbers, 78

x-intercepts
  piecewise-defined functions,
    25
  polynomial expressions,
    functions, and equations,
    87, 88, 89, 93, 96
  solving quadratic equations
    algebraically, 77
  transforming graphs,
    equations, and functions,
    60

$y = x^2$, transforming, 54–56

y-intercepts
  piecewise-defined functions,
    25
  polynomial expressions,
    functions, and equations,
    87, 88, 89, 93, 96
  solving quadratic equations
    algebraically, 77
  transforming graphs,
    equations, and functions,
    60

zeros of a function, 63, 70, 76,
    78, 87, 111

Index

Acknowledgments

Cover Design

Three Communication Design, Chicago

Photographs

Photo locators denoted as follows: Top (T), Center (C), Bottom (B), Left (L), Right (R), Background (Bkgd)

003 iStockphoto/Thinkstock; **042** Christian Delbert/Shutterstock.